The Technique
of Composition

Richard S. Beal
Consulting Editor

THE TECHNIQUE OF COMPOSITION

Fifth Edition

Kendall B. Taft
Roosevelt University

John Francis McDermott
Washington University

Dana O. Jensen
Washington University

Charles Kaplan
San Fernando Valley State College

HOLT, RINEHART AND WINSTON, INC.   NEW YORK

28306-0210

July, 1963

Printed in the United States of America

Library of Congress Catalog Card Number: 60-6492

Preface to the Fifth Edition

Teachers of composition are aware of the changing nature of language, but in practice we often find ourselves, out of habit or inertia, doing the same kinds of things in our classrooms semester after semester. Besides providing another example of the not uncommon gap between precept and practice, this tendency paradoxically makes unconscious defenders of old-fashioned concepts and attitudes out of precisely those persons who know that a living language is a language in flux, but whose classroom behavior does not show this knowledge. The cartoon stereotype of the English teacher as a grim-visaged authoritarian whose main purpose in life is to keep his students from saying "ain't" has a basis, however remote, in actuality.

"Each age," said Emerson, "must write its own books. . . . The books of an older period will not fit this." As generally true as this aphorism is, it is perhaps uncomfortably accurate when applied to textbooks, where "an older period" may be no more than a few years past. A physics textbook published in the pre-Hiroshima era is as hopelessly antique today as the ancient Greek physics which divided the world into four elements. In order to take into account changes in the language itself, therefore, as well as to incorporate recent developments in the study of language, this fifth edition of *The Technique of Composition* has seemed desirable.

The over-all plan and organization remain substantially the same. The discussion of grammar, however, has undergone a considerable revision. The work of linguistic scholars during recent years has taught us to look at a language as it *is;* our

discussion here draws freely and eclectically from their contributions. Throughout, we have placed special emphasis on the
problem of how learning a grammar helps one learn to write—
the problem with which the book as a whole deals. Our discussion
stresses the mechanism of the language, assuming that the
mechanism determines the meaning, and not vice versa. Instruction in grammar is aimed at teaching the forms and structures of
English words and word-groups for the purpose of making exact
and meaningful statements.

Our approach attempts to retain that which is viable in the
"traditional" grammar while utilizing the insights of the "new"
grammar. For better or worse, some of the traditional grammatical
terminology has become part of the intellectual baggage of
educated persons, and rather than abandon these terms completely
we have attempted to define them structurally and functionally.
In any case, the debate between the grammarians is a matter
of only the remotest interest to undergraduate students; what
is vital is not the knowledge of the names that are given to the
things, but the manipulation of the things themselves. A rifleman
who can name all the parts of his weapon but who can't hit a
barn door at fifteen paces isn't a very effective marksman, and
the student who can rattle off definitions but who can't write a
coherent paragraph is his twin. In no other field of study is the
confusion between ends and means so marked, as witness the
freshman's conception of his composition course as "a course in
grammar" or (worse yet) the final examination which tests
the student not on his ability to write clearly and accurately but
on his ability to identify the "parts of speech."

The treatment of usage in this edition also stresses the state of
things, noting the variety of choice possible in the selection of
words in American English. Grammar is structure, which determines meaning; but the only thing that usage determines is
the social and intellectual status of the writer or speaker. "I
ain't done it" is as meaningful as "I have not done it." Instruction in usage is aimed at teaching the word choices characteristic
of educated adults engaged in the business of the mid-twentieth-
century world; it is a study of "verbal etiquette" (to borrow

Professor Robert Pooley's term) based on an observation of the systems of etiquette. Choice is recommended, in order to differentiate the language of the student writer from that of five-year-old children or of uneducated persons.

Emerson's remark that "colleges and textbooks only copy the language which the field and work-yard made" is as true today as it was in 1837, and will be as true tomorrow. It does not follow from this, however, that there are no principles governing standard written usage, and that a relaxed, unbuttoned attitude toward language is necessarily the one to adopt. Our position is described in the Preface to the Fourth Edition:

> . . . most good writers of English today tend toward standard and moderately conservative practice in formal and semiformal writing such as most college students will be asked to do in classes after their freshman year and in what writing they will do in their post-college life. This is not to say that we believe such writing, in or out of college, need be stiffly formal or imitate customs of previous centuries. It should, to the contrary, be based on twentieth-century, preferably mid-twentieth-century, practice, but it should be the best standard practice of the time, not merely the whim of the moment. We have therefore attempted to embody in our recommendations to the student the standard practice of the educated writing of our own day.

We find equally untenable the traditionalism which places talismanic value on, for example, the "shall-will" distinction, and the laissez-faire radicalism which permits any usage as long as it is used by great numbers of people (an attitude which is not "democratic" but its very opposite, bowing as it does to another kind of authoritarianism). We believe that it is possible to maintain a moderate position, advocating neither a language strait-jacketed by outworn dogma nor one given over to anarchy; we recognize the changes taking place in a living language but do not feel compelled to welcome and applaud each change as an improvement (for, in language as in life, not all change is growth); and, finally, insisting that the purpose of writing is communication, we maintain that any kind of language which gets in the way of this purpose is faulty language.

To be confronted by meaningful statements expressed in the language of educated persons would bring about an unprecedented state of bliss for teachers of English composition, but also to find these statements organized into effective and artistic patterns would create the Earthly Paradise itself. The study of rhetoric, like the study of painting, shows the student what has been done in the past, but it can never predict what may yet be done in the future. The miracle of style is the miracle of any artistic creation: given a relatively limited number of basic elements—so many primary colors, so many tones—what the craftsman does with his materials is primarily determined by his technique but ultimately limited only by his imagination and, at the highest level, his genius. To use language effectively at any level approaches the quality of art. The examples of prose style and patterns of organization are designed only to show what has been done; for the beginning writer, exposure to good writing is an influence on his own development that cannot be overestimated. A study of how writers have written will suggest to the student the limitless possibilities and richness of the language.

The relationship between rhetoric and grammar is close, if not overlapping. What the grammarian calls morphology, lexicology, and syntax, the rhetorician calls diction and structure. Relevant discussion of the style of the sentence can be made only on the basis of clearly understood and consistent grammatical concepts. It is at this point that a descriptive grammar and a realistic, practical attitude toward usage can be used in the teaching—and learning—of the technique of composition.

Talk about language, while it is certainly relevant and may even be interesting, is never a substitute for the actual writing. The exercises throughout, therefore, have been designed to elicit a minimum of theoretical discussion and a maximum of practical application. They are designed to get writing done, not to get students to identify or classify grammatical elements. The instructor certainly need not feel himself bound to use these exercises in the manner suggested, or even at all. But if he does use them he should not lose sight of the end which they try to reach. And, of course, the exercises in themselves are by no means a substitute for regular, sustained practice in the writing of longer pieces of expository prose.

In preparing this edition, as in preparing the previous ones, we find ourselves heavily indebted to the many suggestions and criticisms from our colleagues in universities and colleges in all parts of the United States. We wish we had space here to name all of those who have helped us as we prepared each edition, from the first through this, the fifth. We must limit ourselves, however, to those whose assistance and suggestions have played an important part in the shaping of this edition. We record with gratitude the specific help of Professor Richard Abcarian, Professor Richard S. Beal, Professor Byron Guyer, Professor Charles S. Mudd, Professor Malcolm O. Sillars, and Professor James Steel Smith, as well as the editorial help of the College Department of Holt, Rinehart and Winston, Inc.

Specific acknowledgments of our indebtedness to authors and publishers for the use of extracts from works still in copyright appear in the text of this book.

K. B. T.
J. F. McD.
D. O. J.
January, 1960 C. K.

Contents

ONE | The Mechanics of Writing

The Sentence: Structure Determines Meaning

1

INTRODUCTION TO AN INTRODUCTION

This chapter provides an overview of the sentence—its structure, its parts, its logic. It introduces, in a generalized way, certain topics which are dealt with in greater detail in later chapters. For example, although grammatical concepts are introduced here, grammar is given a closer look in the second chapter. Punctuation, likewise referred to briefly, makes up the content of the third chapter. Going over the route more than once is a useful way of familiarizing ourselves with the terrain. As we begin our examination of the sentence, it will be profitable to conceive of it as a bundle of signal systems operating simultaneously in order to transmit an unambiguous message.

A. The Signal Systems. There is obviously an important difference between stepping on somebody's toe and then apologizing, and apologizing first and then stepping on that same toe. One action would probably bring you a polite dismissal of the incident, but the other could quite conceivably bring you a punch in the jaw.

What we have here is a clear-cut example of the importance of order in any sequence of elements. The elements remain the same, but because of a switch in the order, the intention and, of course, the outcome are quite different. In English, *word order* is one of the most important signals affecting meaning. Consider, for example, the differences in meaning between *A fisherman ate the shark* and *The shark ate a fisherman*. Nothing is changed but the order; but the meaning (not to mention the fisherman) is radically altered. Word order, then, is obviously an important element in meaning, more important even than the individual words themselves. (See section C, below.)

A sentence which communicates its idea clearly and accurately, so that the reader understands exactly what the writer intended, is a grouping of words and symbols arranged in such a way as to facilitate transmission of that idea. (Incidentally, the sentence has not been defined to anyone's complete satisfaction in three hundred years, but we will make another stab at it toward the end of this chapter.) Since the concept of simultaneously operating signals is the controlling principle governing our discussion of sentence structure and grammar, we will here briefly review some of the basic signals.

As we have seen, the meaning of a sentence may be changed by an alternation in word order. With other changes in the order and the forms of the given elements, different meanings come through:

The fisherman ate sharks.
The fishermen ate sharks.
The fishermen ate a shark.
A fisherman eats sharks.
Sharks eat fishermen.
The shark a fisherman ate.

The first five sentences send slightly different meanings which we understand immediately in each case. But we pause when we read the last sentence, for it seems to be sending two possible meanings. It could be interpreted as saying (1) the shark ate the fisherman, or (2) the shark was eaten by a fisherman. The conventional or normal word order has been inverted, creating an ambiguity. We accept the sentence, finally, but with reservations; which meaning is intended can be discovered only by inspection of the larger passage in which the sentence occurs.

But even ambiguity is to be preferred to total obscurity, which is what we find in

The fisherman sharks a ate.
Fisherman sharks ate a the.

In other words, some inversion of normal word order is permissible, while other sequences of words result in chaos. What the permissible sequences are (as well as what is meant by "normal word order") will be discussed in fuller detail later.

To be clear, furthermore, a sentence must include all the necessary components. For example, although the following sentences are not as informative as the clear messages given earlier, we do understand

The shark ate.
The fisherman ate.

We may not know what they ate, but we do know what they did. On the other hand, we know little from

The shark fisherman.

and absolutely nothing from

The ate a.

We may at first suspect that too much has been eliminated here for any message to come through; however, since *The shark ate* and *The ate a* both contain three words, it becomes apparent that it is not how much but what is eliminated from a sentence that drains it of meaning.

Even when the word order is normal and all the necessary parts are included, the message may still be obscured if certain other faulty signals are sent. These include (1) wrong word endings, (2) lack of punctuation or wrong punctuation, and (3) wrong word choices. Note the blurs in meaning that result from these errors:

1. A fisherman ate a sharks.
2. A shark ate the fisherman the ship sailed on.
3. A goldfish ate the fisherman.

In the first, the plural ending on *shark,* used together with the singular *a,* is the source of the confusion. In the second, the trouble lies in the lack of punctuation. As we will see later, there are several ways of eliminating this particular kind of trouble, but the simplest is simply to insert a semicolon after *fisherman*. The sentence now makes sense. We reject, however, the addition of other punctuation marks:

A shark? ate the fisherman the, ship sailed on!

And in the third sentence above, the unlikelihood of such an event taking place makes us suspect that the message has been garbled in the sending, that neither order nor punctuation but one of the words in the message is the trouble spot.

As users of the language, our sensitivity to the operating signal systems in English is so strong that we know when a message is ambiguous, incomplete, or garbled. Because of this sensitivity, we can even detect faint glimmers of meaning in these sentences:

The wiglet bleefully ofters the smurgeon to a gloober.

Did the gloober portle the smurgeon with braction?

Or consider the familiar lines from Lewis Carroll's "Jabber-wocky":

'Twas brillig and the slithy toves
Did gyre and gimble in the wabe:
All mimsy were the borogroves
And the mome raths outgrabe.

If we find those passages even dimly recognizable, why are we totally lost in this sentence?

The to bleefully a ofters the smurgeon gloober wiglet.

It is because the signals are faulty—the signals which we know and respond to. When the signals are faulty, the message gets garbled beyond hope. We will look into this matter of the arrangement of the parts more fully in the next chapter, where we will also try to explain the "sense" in nonsense sentences.

B. An Aside on "Grammar." You may have noticed a forbidding word in the preceding section: it is the word "grammar." To clear up any possible misunderstandings, let us state immediately that the study of grammar is the study of the arrangements of words into more or less meaningful groups. To study grammar is to study the ways in which words are related to each other; or, using the terms introduced earlier, to learn how to construct signal systems which will make for effective and efficient communication.

Grammar study does not and should not consist of memorizing a set of inflexible rules. A knowledge of rules will not make you an educated or "cultured" person; it may, on the contrary, make you self-conscious about the way you speak and write and may even inhibit your expression. A knowledge of grammar, as defined in this book, will enable you to analyze the basic unit of written discourse—the sentence—and to see how different kinds of sentences are put together for different purposes and with different results. A clear understanding of these different kinds of relationships will help you analyze your own sentences and practice eliminating from them what communications technicians call "noise"—anything that gets in the way of the clear reception of the intended signals. The study of grammar, in other words, is merely one means to the end of more accurate and effective writing; it is not an end in itself.

Everybody uses some kind of grammar; the objective is to use a better grammar. The beginner sending his first message in Morse code may go slowly and make mistakes, but with time and practice he raises his level of proficiency to the point where his sending is automatic and relatively free from mistakes. Mastery of the resources of English grammar can be attained by careful study of how the signal systems operate and by practice in manipulating the elements of those systems.

C. English Word Order—Compared with Other Languages. We are talking about the English sentence, not the Latin or the German or the Chinook. Each language develops its own set of signals, which are usually not interchangeable from one language to another. Whereas English, as we have seen, relies heavily on word order to communicate meaning, both Latin and Chinook rely instead on certain endings attached to words (called "inflections") and make word order relatively unimportant. Thus, in Latin, *Puella amat matrem* and *Matrem amat puella* and *Amat puella matrem* all mean *The girl loves her mother,* although only the first is in what we could call the word order of English.

One of the most common patterns of word order in English is seen in the nonsense phrase *the bleeful thrum.* Whatever this means, we understand that a *thrum* is something that can be described as being *bleeful,* or having the quality of *bleefulness.* But in French the order would be *the thrum bleeful.* In German, word order is also of fundamental importance, but it is a system of order quite different from that of English. One of Mark Twain's funniest essays, "The Awful German Language," describes his difficulties in mastering this system. He illustrates by a dead-pan translation of a newspaper item:

In the daybeforeyesterdayshortlyaftereleveno'clock Night, the inthistownstandingtavern called 'The Wagoner' was downburnt. When the fire to the onthedownburninghouseresting Stork's Nest reached, flew the parent Storks away. But when the bytheraging, firesurrounded Nest itself caught Fire, straightway plunged the quickreturning Motherstork into the Flames and died, her Wings over her young ones outspread.[1]

Twain uses the same trick in "The Private History of the 'Jumping Frog' Story," allegedly retranslating his famous tale from a French translation, where it is called "The Frog Jumping of the County of Calaveras." In both cases, the humor derives principally from distortions of normal English word order.

The inflectional system that is so important in Latin is also found in French, German, Russian, and Spanish. But the historical changes in English have been in the direction of simplification, in eliminating a complex set of inflections. As a result, although changes in the forms of words, as we shall see, are still important signals of changes in meaning and relationships, the greater share of signaling the meaning in an English sentence falls upon word order. Even when mistakes in inflections occur, they do not necessarily impair meaning.

I *gived* him a shove in the ribs.
He *slud* into third base.
The farmer was feeding his *oxes.*

---

[1] From *A Tramp Abroad* (1880).

In these examples, the strong signal of word order overrides the static induced by the wrongly inflected forms, which turn out to be of minor importance.

FORM AND FUNCTION

D. Classifying Sentences. A classification of any sort is imposed on groups of items for purposes of convenience or study only. The names are assigned to the things after the fact, and different labels may be assigned to the same things depending upon the purpose of the classifier.

Sentences, for example, may be classified either by the purpose behind the expression or by their formal structure. Classification by purpose gives us four kinds of sentences:

1. A SENTENCE PRIMARILY CONVEYING INFORMATION: I like peanuts.
2. A SENTENCE CALLING FOR A VERBAL RESPONSE: Do you know him?
3. A SENTENCE CALLING FOR AN ACTION RESPONSE: Please shut the window.
4. A SENTENCE EXPRESSING STRONG FEELING: It's a shame!

These sentences are referred to, respectively, as declarative, interrogative, imperative, and exclamatory.

Classification by formal structure also gives us four types. All the four sentences above, regardless of their differences in word order and punctuation, are *simple* sentences. Here are other variations of the declarative sentence:

1. SIMPLE: I like peanuts.
2. COMPLEX: I like peanuts that have been roasted.
3. COMPOUND: I like peanuts, but they don't agree with me.
4. COMPOUND-COMPLEX: I like peanuts that have been roasted, but they don't agree with me.

You will note that the different kinds of structure carry different kinds of meaning, and that, at least in these examples, the most expanded structure carries the largest number of ideas. The single word *peanuts* is merely a verbal term for a group of things; it indicates no relationship between these things and other things, as each of our other sentences does. We will see later how sentences grow in levels of complexity by the addition of words or word-groups arranged in certain sequence patterns.

E. Punctuation and Intonation.   A writer puts an undue strain on his readers when he commits sentences like these to paper:

> You said the judge are clearly not telling the truth.
> Without warning the soldiers suddenly began to fire.
> He said that, "He would go when he was ready?"

Unpunctuated or unconventionally punctuated sentences hinder the communication of an idea, for the meaning in a written sentence is partially shaped and controlled by the addition of some otherwise meaningless symbols known as punctuation marks. Written language, unlike speech, cannot show stress (degree of loudness), pitch (voice level), pauses, and those other vocal markings which help us understand a speaker by means other than his words. The written language, therefore, has to resort to punctuation, another system of signals, to achieve some of those ends.

Despite the importance of word order in signaling meaning, in some sentences the order is overridden by the punctuation system:

> Do I like peanuts?
> Do I like peanuts!

The word order of these sentences is identical, but the difference in end punctuation establishes a different intonation for each, and hence a different meaning. Despite the interrogative word order, the second version is really an exclamation. The differences in meaning between the following sentences are likewise signaled only by end punctuation:

> Marilyn has the leading role in the play.
> Marilyn has the leading role in the play?

The Spanish convention of placing an inverted question mark at the start of an interrogative sentence is a useful signal, putting the reader on notice that his voice should go up at the end. In a sentence like the last one above, where the structure does not reveal the intonation, it would also be of value in English.

Although the chief function of punctuation is to signal the intonation in a sentence, it should be added that there are certain symbols which have little to do with translating the spoken language onto the printed page. These include the period that is used to indicate an abbreviation (*Dr.* is pronounced *Doctor*); the apostrophe, wherever it is used (*it's* and *its* sound exactly alike); quotation marks (as in *I like Frost's reading of "Mending Wall"*); and the hyphen (as in *free-lance,* but not in *freehand*).

Furthermore, as the following sentences show, the same intonation may be punctuated in a variety of ways:

All graduating seniors—particularly those on the Dean's List—must have their photographs taken this week.

All graduating seniors, particularly those on the Dean's List, must have their photographs taken this week.

All graduating seniors (particularly those on the Dean's List) must have their photographs taken this week.

Despite the differences in punctuation, these three sentences sound exactly alike.

Some marks of punctuation, then, are "significant" in that they affect meaning, while others like the apostrophe and the hyphen are "nonsignificant." In Chapter III, we shall discuss in greater detail the grammatical and conventional functions of the individual punctuation symbols.

We need not be like Albert the Alligator, in this panel reproduced from Walt Kelly's literate comic strip, "Pogo."[2] Presumably Albert will continue to be as vocal and articulate as he has always been, despite his feeling that his "vocabulary" has been impoverished; but, deprived of punctuation marks, our ability to write comprehensible sentences would truly be "cut to the bone." When we read a properly constructed and punctuated sentence, we are decoding a message, and, in effect, hearing the author's voice in our mental ear. In writing a sentence, the writer's intention is to try to make his voice heard and his message understood by every reader, and appropriate punctuation can help him achieve this intention.

Incidentally, the sentences at the start of this section are properly punctuated as follows:

"You," said the judge, "are clearly not telling the truth."
Without warning, the soldiers suddenly began to fire.
He said that he would go when he was ready.

F. Subject and Predicate. Most of our attempts to communicate meaning are expressed in the form of sentences, although (given the appropriate context and circumstances) even an utterance like "Wow!" can express a good deal of meaning and emotion, too. In the words of Edward Sapir, a sentence is "the linguistic expression of a proposition. It combines a subject of discourse with a statement in regard to this subject. . . . each or either may be so qualified as to lead to complex propositions of many sorts."[3] Thus, most sentences have a *subject* and a *predicate,* together with other qualifying words known as *modifiers,* which change or limit our conceptions of either the subject or the predicate (or any of the individual components of the predicate). Modification is discussed more fully in section H of this chapter. Sapir continues: ". . . the sentence does not lose its feeling of unity so long as each and every [qualifying element] falls

---

[2] "Pogo," December 17, 1958. Copyright, Walt Kelly, and reprinted by permission.

[3] Edward Sapir, *Language* (New York: Harcourt, Brace and Company, 1921), p. 35.

in place as contributory to the definition of either the subject of discourse or the core of the predicate."[4]

The subject of discourse tells what is being talked about; it names the person, object, action, idea, place, or quality discussed or addressed. Grammatically, the predicate is everything in the sentence that is not part of the subject. It may, among other things, make an assertion about the subject; finish a question, wish, or command; or complete the description of the subject.

Subject	*Predicate*
Babies	cry.
I	dropped my book.
The president	asked the dean a question.
Tomorrow	will be sunny.
He	is good old George.
Tom Sawyer	painted the fence white.

It is not a rule that every sentence must contain a subject and a predicate. It is simply a fact that most of our statements are likely to fall into that kind of construction. To say that sentences contain subjects and predicates is merely to describe the state of things, not to lay down laws. For example, it is merely a convenient fiction for us to say that the subject of the sentence *Shut the door* is an "understood" *you*. It is literally true that this sentence does not have a subject, but it is convenient to say that psychologically it does. (This is similar to other convenient fictions implicit in such phrases as *the setting sun,* which, of course, are scientifically inaccurate.) Kenneth Burke has pointed out that this conventional subject-predicate pattern is "natural" only as a path worn across a field is natural: if our linguistic experience and habits have created the path, then the path is there—and we use it. But this is not the same as absolutely forbidding anyone to go outside the path.

In the normal English sentence, one of the most important signals is the fact that the subject precedes the predicate:

---

[4] *Ibid.,* p. 36.

Subject	Predicate
The strong MAN	became undisputed ruler of the republic.
Even the old HOUSES on Pond Point, which are ugly and shabby when seen by day, ...	seem beautiful in the twilight.
Hit by three tacklers, HE	fumbled the ball on the five-yard line.
The two-story Victorian MANSION at 221 W. Peak Street, formerly the home of Mayor Elmer Throckmorton, ...	was wrecked last week in order to make room for a parking lot, despite the efforts of the Society for the Preservation of Historical Monuments.
Clinging to the rigging of the tall, three-masted schooner, THEY	surveyed the swarming crowd on the docks below.

The *simple subject* in each of the illustrative sentences has been capitalized; it is the one word that identifies the subject of discourse, without any modification. The grammatical elements most frequently found to be simple subjects are *nouns* (man, houses, mansion) and *pronouns*—a subclass of nouns (he, they). Sometimes, however, other grammatical elements may act as subjects:

Here .... is where we live.	*Adverb*
Handsome .... is as handsome does.	*Adjective*
Over the fence .... is out.	*Prepositional phrase*
Fighting the good fight .... can be as important as winning it.	*Verbal phrase*
To get an appointment to Annapolis .... was his greatest ambition.	*Verbal phrase*

What the distinguished speaker, Dr.
Brown, has said at our convocation
today .... will be remembered for many
years on this campus. *Clause*

At this point, it is not necessary to distinguish among these various kinds of possible subjects, since fuller discussion of grammatical details will be withheld until the next chapter. Here it is enough to note that the subject may be an element other than the noun or pronoun, and that, as in the last example above, the subject may be a rather complicated word-group.

As you can see in both sets of the preceding examples, the complete predicate contains all the words necessary to complete a statement in regard to the subject of discourse. At the heart of every predicate is the *verb,* and associated with it in the predicate may be *objects, complements,* and *modifiers.* How these components of the complete predicate work together in regular and predictable sequences is the subject of the next two sections, which deal with the topics of sentence patterns and modification.

G. High-Frequency Sentence Patterns. Five basic sentence patterns occur with great preponderance in English. These patterns may be altered or expanded almost limitlessly, providing for variety of style. In each, the most important element is the verb, the mainspring in the intricate mechanism of the predicate. Not to be confused with verbs are a class of words known as *verbals* (fighting, to get), which do not complete a statement. The distinction between verbs (referred to as *finite*) and verbals (referred to as *nonfinite*) is discussed at greater length in Chapter II. Our examination in this section of the high-frequency sentence patterns will show how the three classes of finite verbs operate: these three are, respectively, *intransitive, transitive,* and *linking,* this classification depending on their use.

1) SV (Subject-Verb)

Babies .... cry.

In this sentence, the action originates in the subject and finishes in the verb. The statement regarding the action is complete; we may add other words such as *small* or *at night* or *when they are hungry,* but these modifiers do not affect the basic pattern at all. In this sentence, the verb *cry* is called intransitive; that is, it does not go "across" ("trans-") to affect something else. Another illustration of the SV pattern is

He fumbled on the five-yard line.

2) SVO (Subject-Verb-Object)

I . . . . .dropped my book.

The action originates in the subject and ends by affecting something else. This something else is the *direct object,* which may be thought of as answering the question "What?" Since the action does go across to the object *(book)* through the verb, the verb is transitive. It is clear, therefore, that transitive verbs and direct objects are inseparable. Another illustration of the SVO pattern is

He fumbled the ball on the five-yard line.

The verb *fumbled* is transitive in this sentence because the action it refers to ends by affecting the direct object *(ball).*

An important conclusion that we can establish this early, then, is that some verbs are either transitive or intransitive, depending on the particular sentence in which they appear.

He painted the fence.	*SVO*
He painted swiftly, with sweeping brush strokes.	*SV*
Lefty Hallahan pitches a high, sharp-breaking curve ball.	*SVO*
Lefty Hallahan pitches high and inside to the next hitter.	*SV*

3) SVoO (Subject-Verb-Indirect Object-Direct Object)

The president . . . . asked the dean a question.

Another part of the predicate that may occur in sentences containing transitive verbs is the *indirect object.* The indirect object names the thing or person to which or for which the action is done. In the following sentences, the indirect objects are capitalized.

Father brought ME a new bicycle.
(COMPARE: Father bought a new bicycle for me.)
I passed SALLY the milk.
(COMPARE: I passed the milk to Sally.)
They gave their CHILDREN ballet lessons.
(COMPARE: They gave ballet lessons to their children.)

In each case, the transitive verb and the direct object *(bought . . . bicycle, passed . . . milk, gave . . . lessons)* occur in the fixed SVO order. The position of the indirect object is also fixed: it always precedes the direct object. Another of the characteristics of the indirect object is that, without change in idea, it can be rephrased as a word-group known as a *prepositional phrase (for me, to Sally, to their children).* Although the prepositional phrase usually follows the direct object, the order may be inverted for reasons of emphasis: *To their children they gave ballet lessons.* (For a fuller discussion of prepositional phrases, see Chapter II, section G 4.)

4) SVC (Subject-Verb-Complement)

He . . . . is good old George.
Tomorrow . . . . will be sunny.

The third class of verbs establishes not the direction of an action but rather an identity or quality; these verbs may be thought of, roughly, as serving the function of "equal signs" (although not in any mathematical sense). Such verbs are called linking verbs, linking the subject with its *predicate complement.* Most complements, as the two examples above indicate, are of two kinds. In *He is good old George,* the linking verb connects or equates two terms referring to the same entity. In *Tomorrow will be sunny,* the complement is not wholly identical with the subject of discourse. We could also say of tomorrow that it will be Wednesday, or a holiday, or the end of the month. The word *sunny* merely describes one aspect or quality of the subject. The complements illustrated above are, respectively, *predicate noun* and *predicate adjective.*

Other sentences illustrating the SVC pattern are as follows (linking verbs are in capitals):

> The strong man BECAME undisputed ruler of the republic.
> Even the old houses on Pond Point SEEM beautiful in the twilight.
> My coffee TASTES exceptionally good this morning.

A fuller discussion of linking verbs and their characteristics occurs in Chapter II, pp. 52-53.

Although most complements are either predicate nouns or predicate adjectives, there are also other kinds of complements which you will occasionally find:

You're my EVERYTHING.	*Pronoun*
The time to strike is NOW.	*Adverb*
This gift is FOR MY MOTHER.	*Prepositional phrase*
My desire is TO WIN THE SCHOLARSHIP	*Verbal phrase*
His hobby was WHITTLING WOODEN WHISTLES.	*Verbal phrase*
Your trouble is THAT YOU ARE TOO LAZY.	*Noun clause*

5) SVOC (Subject-Verb-Object-Complement)

> Tom Sawyer painted the fence white.
> The committee elected Waldo chairman.
> I consider this choice disastrous.
> We asked him to resign.

In this pattern, we find both object and complement following the transitive verb. There are relatively few verbs which will occur in this pattern: some of them are *make, name, call, appoint, choose,* and *select.* Because the complement in this pattern refers not to the subject but to the direct object, it is sometimes called an *objective complement.* It may be a noun *(chairman)* or an adjective *(white, disastrous).* In the last example, *to resign* is one of the class known as verbals, which, as we shall see later, are extremely flexible in function. Here *to resign* assumes the place of the noun complement in the SVOC pattern.

For illustrative purposes, our preceding discussion of sentence patterns has been confined to declarative sentences, but the same patterns hold true in sentences which ask questions. In analyzing an interrogative sentence, the first thing to do is to rearrange its parts into the declarative (that is, subject-predicate) order. Thus,

Will you take me to Chicago with you?

becomes, for purposes of analysis,

You will take me to Chicago with you.

—and the SVO pattern emerges clearly. One of the signals that most obviously distinguishes declarative from interrogative sentences is the inverted order of the latter:

Will you go?
Are they going to be there?
Have I finished this job?[5]

We have enumerated in this section the five basic patterns in the normal English sentence. To recapitulate: SV is built around the intransitive verb; SVO, SVoO, and SVOC around transitive verbs; and SVC around the linking verb. The fixed word order of these sentences is to the complete sentence as the steel framework is to a skyscraper; on it may be hung a work of strength, efficiency, and—sometimes—art.

STRUCTURAL VARIATIONS

H. The Concept of Modification. For all its alleged newsworthiness, *Man bites dog* is not a very satisfactory sen-

---

[5] The one interrogative pattern which does not demand a verbal response is the so-called *rhetorical* question: "How could he have been so stupid?" or "What have I done now?" Despite the order, these are closer to being declarative or exclamatory than interrogative, the form being less significant than the purpose behind the utterance.

tence. We immediately want to know "Which man?" and "Which dog?" let alone being curious about the circumstances under which the action occurred. The sentence is structurally complete—you will recognize the SVO pattern—but is so lacking in particulars as to be practically devoid of meaning. The following sentence is even less satisfactory, because it may be read in two ways: *Bank deposits slip.* If this is the SVO pattern, then the bank has done something to some piece of paper (since it is unlikely that a bank has somehow become involved in lingerie). The other possibility is that it is the SV pattern:

Bank deposits ... slip.

The ambiguity in these truncated sentences (most frequently found in newspaper headlines) results in part from their omission of the *modifiers,* those words that qualify, describe, limit, or in some manner change our conception of the meaning of another word. A modifier is a means of particularizing the meaning of the word it is tied to.

A stout, red-faced MAN sitting next to me at the football game BITES his fourth hot DOG with great pleasure.

According to the morning papers, BANK DEPOSITS at our town's two major banks SLIP in total volume whenever the local manufacturing plants receive cutbacks in federal defense orders.

Modification is a process of progressive limitation. The effect of adding modifiers is to keep restricting the identity of the thing being modified:

Tree

Oak tree

The oak tree on the corner

The old oak tree on the corner of Spring and Olive Streets

The old, blighted oak tree on the corner of Spring and Olive Streets that has a 75-year history behind it

Each addition cuts out further possibilities of ambiguity or confusion until the precise object or action is identified.

Blows
Blows briskly
Blows briskly and steadily from the Pacific
Blows briskly and steadily from the Pacific when the tides are high

The two most common modifiers in English are the *adjective* and the *adverb,* although these are not the only elements that may modify. In the examples above, the words and word-groups modifying *tree* are *adjectives;* the words and word-groups modifying *blows* are *adverbs.* The formal characteristics of adjectives and adverbs will be treated fully in the next chapter. For our preliminary overview at this point, we will note how they function in sentence patterns.

1) **Word order of adjectives.** Single-word adjectives almost always precede the nouns they modify: *stout* man, *red* ink, *shaggy* dog, *frabjous* day. (A few rare exceptions to this rule are stock phrases such as bar *sinister* and body *politic.*) Most adjective word-groups follow the nouns they modify.

ADJECTIVE:	The man IN THE WHITE COAT will come for you later.
PREPOSITIONAL PHRASES:	The lecture ON AUTOMATION proved to be rather dull.
	Each night I am kept awake by the birds IN THE TREES.
ADJECTIVE CLAUSES:	The boy WHO SCORED THE TOUCHDOWN is an All-American halfback.
	This section, WHICH DEALS WITH THE TOPIC OF MODIFICATION, is important.
	A house THAT I OWN is over 150 years old.

Another kind of phrase, the participial phrase (a form of verbal phrase), is less fixed in its order. It may either follow or precede the noun that it modifies:

WEARING GRECIAN SANDALS AND A ROMAN TOGA, the swami can be seen strolling the streets of Hollywood with his dog.

The swami, WEARING GRECIAN SANDALS AND A ROMAN TOGA, can be seen strolling the streets of Hollywood with his dog.

but not

The swami can be seen strolling the streets of Hollywood with his dog, WEARING GRECIAN SANDALS AND A ROMAN TOGA.

The common and frequently comical error of the so-called **dangling participle (DM)** is illustrated in the last sentence. One safe (but not foolproof) way to avoid the error is to keep the modifying phrase close to the thing it modifies. There are some perfectly legitimate uses of the construction in which the modifying phrase has only an implied subject, but the beginning writer would do well to avoid risking ambiguity by firmly attaching his participial phrase to the noun it modifies.

2) **Word order of adverbs.** In contrast to adjectives, adverbs move freely within the sentence:

QUIETLY, he entered the sickroom.
He QUIETLY entered the sickroom.
He entered the sickroom QUIETLY.

but not

He entered the QUIETLY sickroom.

The position immediately preceding the noun is, of course, reserved for the adjective.

Consider the following sentences:

1. ONLY she was a farmer's daughter.
2. She ONLY was a farmer's daughter.
3. She was ONLY a farmer's daughter.
4. She was a farmer's daughter ONLY.

The movability of the adverb is both its strong point and its weakness. On the one hand, careful placement of adverb modifiers imparts exact and subtle shadings in meaning; on the other, this free-wheeling modifier sometimes results in ambiguities in the *written* version of a sentence. In order to avoid the ambi-

guities of sentence 2, above, it is probably better to write either
sentence 1 (if you mean that the girl was the sole person whose
origins were rural among a number of persons) or sentences 3
or 4 if you don't mean to stress her uniqueness. The spoken
version of sentence 2, of course, would not have created any
ambiguity in the first place, but in print the sentence "squints"—
that is, the modifier may go either way.

In the sentence

She was a farmer's ONLY daughter

note that *only* is no longer an adverb but is an adjective; and
note also that the placement of a single word in a sentence may
be the difference between communicating and confusing.

The wind blew FROM THE OCEAN.
FROM THE OCEAN blew the wind.

The difference in effect gained from altering the structure is
worth observing here. Placing the adverbial phrase at the start
of the sentence has the effect of emphasizing the source of the
wind, at the same time creating the inverted pattern VS. This is
not an unusual pattern, being often used for variety and emphasis. It is bad writing, of an affected and pseudopoetical style,
only when overused.

Notice the movability of the adverbial clauses in the following
sentences:

UNTIL THE STORM ENDS, you must stay indoors.
Jack, WHEN HE HAD FINISHED HIS WORK, fell wearily on his
bed.
A good writer will attempt, WHENEVER HE CAN, to vary his sen-
tence length and structure.
Roland persisted in fighting to the end, ALTHOUGH HIS CAUSE
WAS HOPELESS.

3) **Levels of modification.** As we have seen, a word
may be particularized by three kinds of modifiers: a single word,
a phrase, or a clause. We will examine the structure of phrases
and clauses in the next chapter. although you should have formed

a rather good idea of what they are by studying the examples on the preceding pages. It is enough at this point to repeat that the three kinds of modifying elements form a series of expanding structures; that is, a limiting concept can be expressed in several ways:

The FURIOUS, RED-FACED man	*Single-word modifiers*
The FURIOUS man WITH THE RED FACE	*Single-word modifier and prepositional phrase*
The man WHO WAS SO FURIOUS THAT HIS FACE TURNED RED	*Clause modifiers*

The man remains the same, in the world of experience, but the words used to describe him are arranged in different ways. In the hands of a careful writer, this change in the grammatical packaging produces subtle differences of emphasis. Conscious choice in arranging modifying elements is one way for a writer to give his sentence the exact shade of meaning that he has in mind. If he sorts out and distributes his ideas properly, the major idea will be clearly revealed as major, with the supporting or qualifying ideas being distributed in grammatical elements of relatively lesser importance. Modification is thus part of a larger problem in sentence structure that we call co-ordination and subordination.

I. Co-ordination and Subordination. We have already classified sentences in section D (using one principle of classification) as simple, compound, complex, and compound-complex. Let us see how their differences in formal structure develop different emphases.

> The old, blighted oak tree stood on the corner of Spring and Olive Streets. *Simple*
> The old, blighted oak tree stood on the corner of Spring and Olive Streets, and it was blown down last night by a gale. *Compound*

The simple sentence, consisting of one independent clause, makes a statement about the location of the tree. The compound sentence joins two ideas, each one expressed in an independent clause. The *and* implies that the two ideas are equal; however, the fact of location is probably not as important as the fact of the accident. Since the *and* here co-ordinates ideas of unequal value, let us subordinate the lesser idea.

> The old, blighted oak tree THAT STOOD ON THE CORNER OF SPRING AND OLIVE STREETS was blown down last night by a gale.   *Complex*

By reducing one independent clause to the status of a dependent clause (in capital letters), which now serves as a modifier, we have redistributed the ideas and sharpened the point of the sentence.

> The old, blighted oak tree on the corner of Spring and Olive Streets has a history behind it; however, that history was ended last night when the tree was blown down by a gale.   *Compound-complex*

In this sentence, the writer expresses two equal ideas in the co-ordinate independent clauses. He also puts his modifiers into two packages: *on the corner of Spring and Olive Streets* (prepositional phrase); and *when the tree was blown down by a gale* (dependent clause). His structure now reflects his conception of levels of importance among the various ideas. Compare the loose and unemphatic product of a careless writer:

> There was an oak tree that stood on the corner of Spring and Olive Streets that was old and blighted, and that had a history behind it. There was a gale last night, and the tree was blown down, and that ended its history.

J. Parallelism.   The basic principle underlying the structural device of parallelism is that similar ideas are cast into similar grammatical forms.

> CUTTING THE LAWN and CLEANING THE SIDEWALKS took Jack all of Saturday afternoon.

> His reading for the research paper included not only ARTICLES and BOOKS on witchcraft, but also contemporary DIARIES and JOURNALS.

A good student WILL READ THE ASSIGNED MATERIALS RECOMMENDED BY HIS INSTRUCTORS, WILL TAKE COMPLETE NOTES, and WILL ASK QUESTIONS ABOUT THE THINGS HE DOES NOT UNDERSTAND.

The Oxford Companion to English Literature is useful TO LAYMEN and TO UNDERGRADUATES, but not TO SCHOLARS who want a detailed knowledge of literary allusions.

There was not one candidate who told us WHAT HE WOULD ATTEMPT TO DO ABOUT THE INTERNATIONAL SITUATION and HOW HE WOULD BEGIN TO IMPROVE THE CONFUSED DOMESTIC ECONOMY.

Parallelism is a device which enables the writer to signal to his readers that he is attaching an equal amount of emphasis to two or more ideas; it also permits him to incorporate economically a good deal of related material into a single sentence pattern and to achieve unity within variety.

As the examples show, parallel structure is, basically, one kind of subordination. To be able to sort out one's ideas into appropriate grammatical packages and to relate ideas to each other within the sentence structure by means of modification, co-ordination, and subordination—these are among the first skills required of an effective writer.

DON'T AND DO

K. The Complete Sentence: "Frags" and "Run-ons." The sentences discussed in the preceding pages have all been complete sentences. We have assumed, for purposes of illustration, that grammatically complete sentences are the rule; but, as any teacher of composition will testify, the concept of completeness is one of the major problems he has to struggle with each semester. In this section, we will describe the two most common errors of sentence structure affecting grammatical completeness: (1) the "fragmentary sentence," in which the writer commits the error of letting what should be a part stand for the whole; and (2) the "run-on" or "comma splice" sentence, in which the writer fails to separate two grammatical elements that should properly be independent. These are, respectively, the errors of too little and too much.[6]

1) **The fragmentary sentence.**   The writer commits the error of the fragmentary sentence by doing one of three things:

a) **By omitting either subject or verb:**

An old-fashioned percolator, copper on the outside and pewter on the inside, using alcohol for heat, and complete in every respect, in a dilapidated junk shop.

POSSIBLE REVISIONS: HE FOUND an old-fashioned percolator. . . . An old-fashioned percolator, etc. . . . WAS FOUND in a dilapidated junk shop.

b) **By using verbals instead of verbs:**

Driving the truck grimly through the snowstorm, and gripping the wheel so hard that his knuckles stood out white and his arms ached.

POSSIBLE REVISIONS: HE DROVE the truck grimly. . . . Driving the truck, etc. . . . CASSIDY FINALLY REACHED HIS DESTINATION.

She wants to see the Russian Ballet. Having read the biography of Nijinsky.

POSSIBLE REVISIONS: She wants to see the Russian Ballet, having read . . . .

Having read the biography of Nijinsky, she wants to see the Russian Ballet.

c) **By prefixing to the sentence a word that signals dependency or subordination** (known as a *subordinator*—see Chapter II, section G 2F). This converts the word-group into a dependent clause.

He never had any real friends. Because he could not resist quarreling with people.

---

[6] Errors involving idiomatic incompleteness, as opposed to the structural incompleteness discussed here, are treated under "The Exact Idiom" in Chapter V, section D 5.

POSSIBLE REVISIONS: He never had any real friends because he could not. . . .

He never had any real friends. He could not resist quarreling with people.

In the word-group *because he could not resist quarreling with people* there are, true enough, a subject and a verb, but because the word-group is preceded by the subordinator, it assumes a subordinate, or included, function within the sentence.

2) **The run-on sentence and the comma splice.** The writer commits the error of the run-on sentence by bringing two independent clauses together and failing to co-ordinate them by any punctuation or conjunction signals. He commits a comma splice (or comma fault) if he separates the two clauses only by a comma.

The debate is almost over we may expect a vote soon.   *Run-on*
The debate is almost over, we may expect a vote soon. *Comma splice*

There are four ways to improve a run-on sentence:
a) **By separating the clauses into two separate sentences:**

The debate is almost over. We may expect a vote soon.

b) **By using a semicolon between the clauses:**

The debate is almost over; we may expect a vote soon.

c) **By inserting a co-ordinating conjunction and, usually, a comma between the two clauses.** (For a fuller discussion of co-ordinating conjunctions, see Chapter II, section G 2E.)

The debate is almost over, and we may expect a vote soon.

d) **By subordinating one of the clauses:**

Since the debate is almost over, we may expect a vote soon.

The method used will necessarily depend on the exact shade of emphasis the writer wishes to give each clause and on the style of the preceding and succeeding sentences.

The four methods of revising a run-on sentence may also be used in improving a sentence containing a comma splice.

He refused to approve the budget until March, the policemen were therefore unpaid for three months.

1. He refused to approve the budget until March. The policemen were therefore unpaid for three months.

2. He refused to approve the budget until March; the policemen were therefore unpaid for three months.

3. He refused to approve the budget until March, and the policemen were therefore unpaid for three months.

4. Because he refused to approve the budget until March, the police-men were therefore unpaid for three months.

The comma, as we shall see in Chapter III, section P 4, is the lightest of all marks of punctuation; furthermore, its principal function is to separate, not to connect. The comma splice is the result of using the wrong signal between two major grammatical units.

3) **Permissible exceptions.** It should be added, as an obvious fact of life, that in the hands of experienced writers, both of these "errors" of sentence incompleteness can be turned to stylistic advantage. This is how one author makes effective use of fragmentary sentences:

In 1698 the ninth edition of the *Bay Psalm Book* presented New England with the first music printed in the colonies. Ugly little book, showing in every page the sad fall of Puritan song! Psalm translations made in rugged defiance of all poetic or musical cadence, and a miserable thirteen tunes, clumsily printed, with the names of the notes indicated by initial below the staffs, for the use of the illiterate.[7]

And this is the famous opening sentence of Charles Dickens' *A Tale of Two Cities,* with its series of comma splices:

It was the best of times, it was the worst of times, it was the age of wisdom, it was the age of foolishness, it was the epoch of belief, it was

---

[7] Beatrice H. Flexner, "The Music of the Puritans," *American Heritage,* December, 1956. Reprinted by permission.

the epoch of incredulity, it was the season of Light, it was the season of Darkness, it was the spring of hope, it was the winter of despair.

But the beginning writer should lean over backward to avoid writing either "frags" or "run-ons," at least until he is familiar enough with the principles of sentence structure and punctuation to know when he can occasionally safely depart from conventional practice in the interests of developing a more personally effective style.

L. What Is a Sentence?   Let us attempt a definition of the sentence.

A sentence is a word-group containing a subject and a finite verb (not a verbal like *being* or *to be*). This word-group begins with a capital letter and ends with a mark of terminal punctuation. As for its logical content, it may or may not express a complete thought.

A sentence may express either a complete thought or a small part of a larger one. *These sidewalks are full of holes* is a self-sufficient statement, but *However, he did not* is clearly not a "complete thought." What is required to make it meaningful is a knowledge of the total context in which it appears.

On the opening day of the semester, we expected Professor Stafford to give a short introductory talk and then dismiss us. *However, he did not.* He lectured for the entire hour and concluded by assigning two hundred pages of reading for the next day.

The complete thought of any writer is rarely, if ever, expressed in a single sentence. Benjamin Franklin's fictional creation, Poor Richard Saunders, who expresses himself epigrammatically, lets a single sentence stand as a compressed version of an extended idea: "Fish and visitors smell in three days." But most of us do not, as a usual practice, write epigrams. We write reports, essays, examination papers, research papers, and other pieces of exposition. The complete thought we have to express is found only in the complete piece of writing. While each sentence may be logically complete, each is still merely a small functioning part of the large idea. To make our task of examination and analysis easier in this book, however, we shall generally treat each sentence as if it contained a thought complete and independent in itself.

In this introductory chapter, we have presented the major patterns of the English sentence. In the next chapter, we shall take a closer look at the kinds of grammatical packages available to the writer which allow him to make his statements with the greatest precision and accuracy. Following the bird's-eye view presented here, we are about to undertake a more detailed study of the grammar and structure of the English sentence.

In later chapters, we shall pay attention to the sentence in its larger context—to the relationship of a particular sentence to the sentences which precede and follow it. Again, as we shall see, it is structure that determines meaning. Through the arrangement of sentences in an order determined by the situation (the subject matter, the audience, and the writer's purpose), the writer follows certain principles of rhetoric to make his total communication meaningful and effective.

A knowledge of grammar is not a substitute for the practice of composition, but it is an important kind of knowledge for a prospective writer to have. Likewise, a knowledge of rhetorical principles is not the same as putting these principles into operation so that the written product emerges with all its statements in logical and coherent order. The tools of grammar and rhetoric are just that—not ends in themselves but means to the end of better writing.

EXERCISES

A. Subject and Predicate

I. Copy the following sentences and draw a vertical line between the complete subject and the complete predicate of each sentence.

1. The solution to our problem was fantastically difficult.
2. We knew our own limitations in regard to staff, money, and equipment.

3. The laboratory facilities were inadequate.

4. Mr. Lodge, our chief researcher, was unsympathetic to our task.

5. We persisted in our work despite all of the discouraging factors.

6. Jones's experiment gave me the first clue.

7. Watkins then made the brilliant discovery which has since made him famous.

8. The entire staff of dedicated scientists went without sleep for forty-eight hours.

9. We walked home elated.

10. Neoplox had at last been successfully refined.

11. The newspapers called the discovery sensational.

12. The company gave Watkins his first promotion.

13. All of the other people in the laboratory, from the lowliest bottle-washer to the president of the foundation himself, came to the office to congratulate us.

14. Neoplox is a universal solvent.

15. Our only remaining problem is to find something to carry it in.

II. Underline the simple subject and the verb in each sentence.

III. Encircle all the direct objects. (You will then have the SVO patterns.)

IV. Encircle all the predicate complements. (You will then have the SVC patterns.)

V. Encircle the indirect objects. (You will then have the SVoO patterns.) Rewrite the SVoO sentences, making phrases out of the indirect objects.

VI. Which sentence illustrates the SVOC pattern?

VII. In the preceding group of sentences, you should have found five direct objects, two indirect objects, and six predicate complements.

VIII. Of the SVC patterns, which one does not have a single-word noun or adjective serving as predicate complement?

B. Transitive and Intransitive Verbs

Using ten verbs, write twenty sentences showing how each verb may fit either the SV or the SVO pattern.

C. Expanding Sentence Patterns

I. Come to class prepared to provide, as rapidly as possible, *oral* examples of each of the basic sentence patterns. The intention of this oral exercise is to let you fix the patterns firmly in mind. (Your first illustrations need be no more complicated than—for the SV pattern—"He died." As the exercise proceeds, you should try to amplify the basic sentence without losing the pattern: "When the cruel princess refused to marry the prince who had come to woo her, he immediately died of a broken heart," or "Although the first batter up in the ninth inning tripled to right field, he died on third base because the next three men struck out, victims of Drabowsky's blazing fast ball.")

II. Write sentences using each of the following word-groups in the sentence pattern as directed.

1. Use "the faded and tattered brocade robe which he had found in the attic" (a) as subject in SVC; (b) as object in SVO.

2. Use "what he thought of his instructor at the time" (a) as subject in SV; (b) as complement in SVC.

3. Use "a rather elderly but nevertheless still vigorous-looking gentleman with an erect military posture" (a) as subject in SVO; (b) as complement in SVC.

4. Use "the cheerful little girl next door" (a) as indirect object in SVoO; (b) as object in SVO.

5. Use "every word of wisdom that fell from his lips" (a) as subject in SV; (b) as subject in SVO; (c) as object in SVO; (d) as direct object in SVoO; (e) as complement in SVC.

6. Use "an unhappy choice which could only lead to the saddest consequences" (a) as complement in SVOC; (b) as object in SVO; (c) as subject in SV.

D. Co-ordination and Subordination

Combine each of the following groups of items into a single sentence, making whatever changes in order, wording, and form are necessary. Select the idea which you consider most important, placing it in the independent clause. Subordinate the other ideas by reducing them to one-word modifiers, phrases, or dependent clauses. If you consider two ideas to be of equal importance, co-ordinate their clauses into a compound sentence. After writing your sentence one way, try doing it again; this time select a different idea to receive the emphasis. Note the structural differences between the two versions.

I. 1. The state oratorical contest was held at Springfield.
   2. It was won by Jim Smith.
   3. He is my second cousin.
   4. Over two hundred participants spoke in the contest.
   5. Jim is only eighteen years old.
   6. It was held last week.

II. 1. He drove through the night.
   2. It was freezing cold.
   3. The roads were icy.
   4. He was tired from lack of sleep.
   5. He had to reach Syracuse by 8 A.M.
   6. He was determined that he would not be late for his appointment.
   7. The other man slept in the back seat.

III. 1. Herman Melville died in almost total obscurity.
   2. His first books were *Typee* and *Omoo*.
   3. They are hardly read today.
   4. His readers did not care for *Moby Dick*.
   5. Melville is thought of today as one of America's greatest novelists.
   6. This reputation rests largely on *Moby Dick*.
   7. *Typee* and *Omoo* are adventure tales of the South Seas.

IV. 1. The volume of trading was over six million shares.
   2. The gong closing the day's trading rings at 3 P.M. on the N. Y. Stock Exchange.
   3. The tape was 104 minutes late when trading ended.
   4. The averages for 50 leading stocks lost 18.24 points.
   5. This was the biggest stock market break of the year so far.
   6. This all took place on Wednesday, October 23, 1929.

V. 1. Smog is a feature of the climate in Los Angeles.
   2. It is particularly bad in summertime.
   3. It makes Los Angelenos sneeze, cry, and cough.
   4. It is always at its worst in the downtown section.
   5. It is a feature which the Chamber of Commerce does not publicize.
   6. A local joke is that the birds cough instead of sing.

VI. 1. Montreal fell in 1760.
   2. Robert Rogers was a well-known guerrilla leader.
   3. His men were known as Rogers' Rangers.
   4. After the fall of Montreal, they were sent to Detroit.
   5. He received the surrender of the Western forts in Detroit.
   6. It was the British who surrendered these forts.

VII. 1. The Abbé Jean-Pierre David was a world-famous scientist.
   2. He died in 1900, aged seventy-four.
   3. He had been on numerous expeditions into the interior of East Africa.
   4. The French government had subsidized these expeditions.
   5. He had worked almost alone.
   6. He had brought back large collections of all kinds of species and plants.
   7. His most famous discovery is the giant panda.

E. Parallelism

Rewrite the following sentences to give them parallel structure.

1. He was handsome and also brave, in addition to being rich.

2. Working his way through college, he learned industry, determination, fortitude, anthropology, and French.

3. The man who knows how to dress well, dance gracefully, and who can converse fluently will have an active social life in college.

4. He spoke first of the principles of cybernetics, then going on to discuss some of their applications.

5. In our literature course we read Sophocles, Dante, Milton, Tolstoy, and also had to write a short paper each week.

6. We hope you will visit our lodge. Not only do we have ample facilities for our guests but also plenty of recreation is available.

7. The effective writer will learn how to express his ideas effectively, economically, and using correct grammatical principles.

8. To operate the machine properly, first oil the frommets and attach the widgets. Then the greevers should be slowly rotated.

9. When building a terrace, leveling the surface and making sure that the bricks are laid in a straight line are the two most important tasks.

10. And so, as the golden sun sinks in the west, we say farewell to Hawaii, the land of tropical beauty, enchantment, and where freedom from worldly care is everybody's way of life.

F. Fragmentary and Run-on Sentences

I. Rewrite the fragmentary and run-on sentences in the following passages so as to make them structurally complete and independent. Try to vary your method of correction, but for each sentence use the particular method that the logic and the style seem to call for. NOTE: Not all the sentences are incorrect.

1. The halfback leaping over the line of scrimmage, evading the tacklers, and racing sixty yards to the goal line in a thrilling demonstration of broken-field running.

2. This was what he had long dreamed about. Going to college at last!

3. I hope you will forgive me, my memory is not what it once was.

4. Fourteen cents being all I had at the time, because of a hole in my pants pocket which I discovered when I reached for my money to pay for lunch.

5. There we were, lost on the desert. Three inexperienced, city-bred vacationers, without a knife, without water, without even a compass.

6. You need not be angry, it was only an accident.

7. April may be the cruelest month, but in California the hottest one is September.

8. The Auditorium in Chicago is one of the world's finest theaters for acoustical values, it is not now in use.

9. To sleep, perchance to dream! That was Hamlet's dread.

10. A curious incident, which, although insignificant in itself, never-

theless eventually led to the dismissal of two Prime Ministers and to tremblings in four European capitals.

11. We are temporarily out of sprockets, therefore we are returning your check.

12. Each year, the automobiles from Detroit sprouting bigger and more knifelike tail fins, flashing more strips of dazzling chrome, and blossoming out in a variety of two-tone and three-tone color combinations that make the gaudiest surrealist painting look positively pallid in comparison.

13. The Sunday edition of *The New York Times* providing me with enough reading matter to carry me through to the next Sunday, I finish one week's news just in time to be swamped by another ocean of newsprint.

14. I like the little foreign cars myself, they seem neat and compact.

15. Of course he came in first. We all thought he would.

16. Fables, myths, and epics are quite different from each other. In spite of the fact that they are sometimes taken to be the same.

17. Study the voting record of my opponent, then consider if you want to see him returned to Congress.

18. He becomes very angry each time they mention the incident that embarrassed him and made him a laughingstock at the fraternity house for an entire year.

19. The more money he made the more money he wanted.

20. The Virginia colonial planter was an eighteenth-century English gentleman living in the wilderness instead of London he had Lubberland.

21. Being one of this community's most respected citizens, a man who gives unselfishly of his time, his money, and his labors in order to aid the needy and improve the social and economic well-being of his fellow men.

22. It was ominously quiet in the cavern. I could hear the slow gurgle of some remote underground stream, the only sound in an otherwise deathlike stillness.

23. How could she ever forget her debut at the Met? The backstage excitement, the frantic last-minute whisperings, the stirring strains of the overture, and, finally, the moment when the great golden curtains swept open.

24. Although he was only a mediocre student in college, he was the first man in his class to be worth a million dollars. Which simply shows that success cannot always be predicted on the basis of a man's scholastic record.

25. The fact that he became president of the International Widget Company within a few short years after graduation because he married the daughter of the board chairman.

II. From a quality magazine (e.g., *Harper's, Atlantic, The Reporter, Scientific American, National Geographic, The New Yorker*), select an article at random and bring to class any examples you find of fragmentary and run-on sentences. Are they justifiable departures from the conventional practice?

II | Words in Sentences: "The Consort Dancing Together"

INTRODUCTION: GRAMMATICAL FORM AND FUNCTION

Writers of books on English grammar have been disagreeing with each other for several hundred years about the classifications and definitions of the words we use. "New" grammarians disagree with "traditional" grammarians, and frequently with each other. This state of affairs does not indicate anarchy, as you might suppose, but merely a laudable desire to describe the English language system in the most complete and scientific way. Although different grammarians may use the same term to refer to two quite different things, or different terms to refer to the same thing, all are attempting to classify the objects in a quite complicated system for the benefit of the people using that system.

If we were to classify automobiles as (1) eight-cylinder cars, (2) Plymouths, (3) station wagons, and (4) luxuries, our illogical classification would be plain to all. But a somewhat similar system of classifying words is present in the traditional approach to English grammar through the "parts of speech." That is, four of these parts of speech are defined in terms of how they work, three in terms of what they mean, and one in terms of both how it works and what it looks like.[1]

---

[1] For the curious: in the first group, adjective, adverb, pronoun, and conjunction; in the second group, noun, verb, and interjection; and the last one, the preposition.

Recently, grammarians who have found illogical a system which confuses function, form, and meaning have attempted to describe English on the more scientific bases of form and function. A scientific description of a flower, or of a part of a flower, treats only of its form or its function; as for its meaning, the botanist leaves that to the poet, because meaning, the most subjective attribute of all, is the least reliable as a basis of classification. For example, the traditional meaning-based definition of a verb is "a word that shows action or state of being." Now, "explosion" certainly shows action, but it is just as certainly no verb; likewise, "happiness" is clearly a state of being, but it isn't a verb either.

In this chapter, we intend to describe the main aspects of English grammar, primarily employing formal and functional definitions. Our intention is not to teach you how to classify every word in every possible sentence, but only to show you how the mechanism of the language works and what its parts look like, so that you can make it work for you without feeling that you might get your fingers cut off whenever you want to manipulate any of its parts. In any event, the final aim is that of mastering the whole, and not the "parts" of speech.

I. FORM CLASSES AND FUNCTION GROUPS

Because transatlantic cable costs are high, overseas telegrams are apt to be condensed and cryptic:

Important send data pictures French U. N. delegation issue June 15.

Expanded and translated, this message, presumably addressed to a foreign correspondent, might mean: "It is important that you send the information about and pictures of the members of the French delegation to the United Nations for the issue of June 15."

On the other hand, consider this sequence of words, even more cryptic than the telegram:

It _____ _____ that _____ _____ the _____ about and _____ of the _____ of the _____ _____ to the _____ _____ for the _____ of _____.

These, you will recognize, are the words added in amplifying the original cablegram. By themselves, they transmit no message, but form a framework only, into which various kinds of messages can be poured:

It became clear that newspapers printing the rumors about and discussions of the identity of the congressional delegation to the candidate acted for the sake of politics.

It is there that natives whisper the stories about and legends of the quarrels of the family leading to the famous battle for the ownership of Castlecrest.

What the preceding examples show is that the language is composed of two major word-groups. One group consists of the *form classes*—of which there are four—and the other consists of the *function groups*—of which there are an indefinite number comprised of fewer than 300 words. You will get some idea of the difference between these two large divisions if we consider some other terms that have been used to describe them. They have been referred to as "open" classes and "closed" classes; "full" words and "empty" words; "content" words and "connector" words; words with meaning and words with function; and "significant" words standing for actions, things, ideas, and qualities, as against "relational" words standing for relatively little but needed to show connections among words in the four form classes. In the illustration above, the cablegram consists of form class words, while the framework consists of function words.

Many form class words are characterized by their formal elements, such as changes in word endings—*depart* to *departure; grace* to *gracious; honest* to *honesty; boy* to *boys* and *boy's*. Some words move through all four classes with changes in their endings: for example, we have *glory* (noun), *glorify* (verb), *glorious* (adjective), and *gloriously* (adverb). Others, however, may not change, even while belonging to more than one class: for example, *iron* is a noun in *The bar was made of iron* and a verb in *She will iron my shirt*. Recognition of the form class words, then, in some cases depends upon function as well as form.

Words in the function groups, on the other hand, serving

merely as "frame" words, are fixed and steady, never changing their forms: for example, *the, an, each, all, and, but, too, after, some, since, then.* Such words are defined functionally, in terms of their relationship either to the form class words or to the entire sentence. Later in this chapter, function words will be classified into some of the most important groups, but without an attempt to make exhaustive lists.

G1   THE FORM CLASSES

A. Nouns: Form Class I.   The words in capitals in the following passage are nouns:

A typical MAMMAL is four-footed and small, like a MOLE or a WOODCHUCK. The PLAN of the SKELETON displays certain general and significant ALTERATIONS in that of its reptilian PARENT. These CHANGES are really worthy of close ATTENTION, because in them are established many FEATURES of human ANATOMY. The FRAMEWORK as a WHOLE has achieved still more SOLIDITY, combined with FLEXIBILITY, by MEANS of a better developed ARTICULATION of the JOINTS and in the spinal COLUMN, and through the FACT that OSSIFICATION is very complete, with little CARTILAGE serving in the ADULT. The MAMMALS are very active and this FIRMNESS of CONSTRUCTION allows a strong as well as a refined DEVELOPMENT of their muscular SYSTEMS. Even during GROWTH this PURPOSE is served.—WILLIAM HOWELLS[2]

We identify many of the words in the preceding passage as nouns because they show some of the formal signals that are characteristic of words in this form class. (See page 45.) Others are to be recognized only in terms of both form and function. Nouns of the first kind are *alterations, attention, solidity, flexibility, articulation, joints, ossification, mammals, firmness, construction, development, systems,* and *growth.* But *plan, changes, features, whole, means,* and *purpose* have to be looked at in terms of their

---

[2] *Mankind Thus Far.* Copyright, 1947, by Doubleday & Company, Inc.

particular functions in the sentence, clause, or phrase. (Recall how *iron* belongs to two form classes.)

The PLAN was enthusiastically endorsed by the group.	*Noun*
We PLAN to visit Mexico this coming summer.	*Verb*
On my last visit home, I was struck by the many CHANGES that had taken place.	*Noun*
The chameleon CHANGES color almost instantaneously.	*Verb*
He has a very pleasant set of FEATURES.	*Noun*
The theater this week FEATURES a Japanese art film.	*Verb*
It is necessary to consider the sentence as a WHOLE.	*Noun*
It is necessary to consider the WHOLE sentence.	*Adjective*
We must think of MEANS whereby our end can be reached.	*Noun*
I wonder what that remark MEANS?	*Verb*
His PURPOSE was to create confusion among the enemy.	*Noun*
I PURPOSE to make an "A" in this course.	*Verb*

1) **Noun functions.** Nouns commonly function in the following ten ways. (See Chapter I to refresh your memory about sentence, clause, and phrase patterns.)

a) **As the subject of a verb:**

His CONSCIENCE hurt him.
Often GORDON[3] was unhappy.
SPRING is here at last.
The MAID spilled the soup.

---

[3] *Common nouns and proper nouns.* A conventional formal distinction between nouns is to be made on the basis of capitalization. Nouns like *story, parade, resistance, hatchet, scissors,* referring to any of a class of things, are called common nouns, and are not capitalized. Nouns like *Omaha, Mark Twain, Thanksgiving Day,* the *Gobi Desert,* the *Los Angeles Dodgers,* the *Chicago River,* referring to a particular place, person, or institution, are called proper nouns, and are capitalized.

b) As the object of a transitive verb:

He sang the ARIAS beautifully.
The comedian hit his STOOGE with a pie.
We were given three DOLLARS each.

c) As the indirect object of a transitive verb:

Give the MAN twelve silver dollars.
He sent his SECRETARY a birthday gift.

d) As the objective complement:

We elected him CHAIRMAN.
They made Frank SERGEANT.

e) As predicate complement of a linking verb:

Beethoven was a GENIUS.
Monaco is a tiny COUNTRY.

f) As the object of the preposition, to form a prepositional phrase:

The first line of the POEM escapes me.
The reason for his ANGER was not apparent.

g) As an appositive (an appositive is a noun that renames another noun and that is structurally identical with the first one):

Walter, my FATHER, is a reasonable man.
Dr. Jones, the history PROFESSOR, gave me this biography to read.

h) As a word of direct address, which designates the person named and spoken to by another:

WALTER, my father is a reasonable man.
DR. JONES, the history professor gave me this biography to read.

i) In an absolute construction, which consists of the noun and a modifying participle:

The PARADE having finished, we went home.
His WISDOM having been demonstrated, he was crowned king.

j) **As a modifier of another noun:**

The president discussed the ORGANIZATION chart of the company.
We were impressed by the FOOTBALL stadium.

Many of the functions performed by nouns in these patterns may also be performed by other kinds of words; for example, an adjective may replace the noun in

We were impressed by the MAGNIFICENT stadium.

And pronouns may be used in the following sentences:

HE (in place of "Gordon") was unhappy.
He sang THEM (in place of "arias") beautifully.
IT (in place of "spring") is here.
Give HIM (in place of "the man") twelve silver dollars.

Pronouns will be discussed below as constituting a special subclass of nouns.

2) **Formal features of nouns.** Having seen the *functions* that a noun may perform, let us now examine the characteristics of *form* that identify nouns. These are three: noun plural endings, noun possessive endings, and noun suffixes.

a) **Noun plural endings.** Nouns usually change their forms to show whether they are singular or plural. A singular noun names one of a class:

mammal, tree, paper, notebook, class, mass

A plural noun names two or more of a class and is regularly formed from the singular by the addition of "s" or "es":

mammals, trees, papers, notebooks, classes, masses

For the approximately one hundred nouns with irregular plurals, most of which are familiar to you, other form changes are made:

(1) **By changing the spelling:** louse, lice; child, children; foot, feet; woman, women.

(2) **By using the form of the plural in the original language if the word is a foreign one:** alumnus, alumni; analysis, analyses;

datum, data; criterion, criteria. The tendency in present-day English is to standardize the "s" plural, the large regular group absorbing the exceptional instances. Many words that once belonged in class (2)—for example, "stadium"—are now regularly used with the "s" plural. The irregular words most likely to stay irregular are common words like "man," the plural of which gets drilled into us at about the age of four. But because "stadium" is a fairly uncommon word, enough people, when talking about several of them, add the regular ending so that eventually the *ia* ending disappears, except from the formal writing of some English professors.

Words like *deer, sheep,* and *quail* do not change in the plural; the number of the noun is shown by modifiers, or by its agreement with either the verb or a pronoun. A good sentence builds in enough signals to eliminate ambiguity: *He was shearing the sheep* can mean either one sheep or a whole flock. Add *when it ran away* and the singular number is made plain.

b) **Noun possessive endings.** Another formal feature of nouns is the ending that shows either actual or figurative possession ("The *man's* suit was his only property" or "*New York's* loss is *San Francisco's* gain").

(1) **Singular nouns add** *'s*: *bandit's* hideout, *horse's* hoof, *hero's* reward.

(2) **Regular plural nouns add an apostrophe after the final** *s*: *bandits'* hideout, *horses'* hooves, *heroes'* reward; the *Norrises'* novels, the *bosses'* attitude.

(3) **Singular nouns ending in** *s* **may add only the apostrophe:** *Charles'* desk (or *Charles's* desk), *Norris'* novels (or *Norris's* novels).

(4) **Irregular plural endings add** *'s*: *children's* toys, *women's* club, *men's* lounge.

The apostrophe is a punctuation signal used, among other things, to differentiate plural from possessive endings. For a fuller discussion of the apostrophe, see Chapter III, section P 8.

Nouns with possessive endings usually modify other nouns, but may also be subjects, complements, or objects.

The FARMER'S is a hard lot.   *Subject*
The slipper was CINDERELLA'S.   *Complement*
My turn at bat comes after JOE'S.   *Object of preposition*

c) **Noun suffixes.** The flexibility of the English language is beautifully demonstrated by the ease with which words flow from one form class to another. (Recall *glory, glorify, glorious, gloriously.*) Nouns, for example, may be created from adjectives, verbs, or other nouns with great facility through the addition of various other kinds of endings, known as *suffixes.* These noun-markers, about twenty in number, serve as a third formal feature to distinguish nouns from other form classes. The process of noun formation and some of the more common suffixes are both shown below.

(1) *Adjective*   plus   *Noun suffix*   equals   *Noun*

dull	ness	dullness
hard	ship	hardship
maiden	hood	maidenhood
merry	ment	merriment
electric	ity	electricity

(2) *Verb*   plus   *Noun suffix*   equals   *Noun*

break	age	breakage
contrive	ance (ence ense)	contrivance
draft	ee	draftee
employ	er	employer

(3) *Noun*   plus   *Noun suffix*   equals   *Noun*

mathematics	ian	mathematician
violin	ist	violinist
gangster	ism	gangsterism
road	ster	roadster

Some suffixes, like *ess*, occur in only a few words (*hostess, actress*), while others, like *tion* and its spelling variant of *sion*, make up a sizable number of nouns (*deprivation, destitution, dessication, evacuation, abstention, fusion, fission, precision*).

Another important signal which marks nouns from all other words is the function word known as a *noun-determiner* (words like *a, an, the,* and so forth). A fuller discussion of noun-determiners occurs in the next section and also later in this chapter, in section G 2A.

To summarize: Nouns may be recognized either by their formal changes or by their form in combination with their function. The functions of nouns, in turn, may be recognized by their roles in word-group patterns.

  B. Pronouns: A Noun Subclass. The words in capitals in the following passage are pronouns:

A lady went into an uptown bookstore the other day and, after looking around by HERSELF for a while, approached a clerk and asked about books on art; SHE wanted SOMETHING, SHE explained, THAT would be suitable for a nephew of HERS WHO at the moment was studying painting at Pennsylvania Academy. The clerk's eye lighted on a new book of Cézanne reproductions, and HE laid THAT out for the lady's inspection. SHE turned a few pages, staring at the French master's elegantly simplified, carefully distorted compositions, and then, rather regretfully, rejected IT. "No," SHE said. "I'm afraid IT won't do, really. HE'S been studying for quite some time, YOU know, and I'm afraid HE'S a little beyond THIS."—THE NEW YORKER[4]

Because many words referred to as pronouns function like nouns, we may consider the entire group to be a subclass of nouns. But there are also many pronouns which never function like nouns, and there are still others which do so only in certain cases. Before considering these various groups, however, since the most familiar (and troublesome) of the whole pronoun group are the *personal pronouns,* let us see what they look like in their various forms:

---

[4] From "Advanced." Reprinted, by permission, from *The New Yorker*. Copyright, 1947, The New Yorker Magazine, Inc.

Singular	*Nominative*	*Objective*	*Possessive*
1st person (doing the speaking)	I	me	my, mine
2nd person (being spoken to)	you	you	your, yours
3rd person (being spoken about)	he, she, it	him, her, it	his; her, hers; its

Plural			
1st person	we	us	our, ours
2nd person	you	you	your, yours
3rd person	they	them	their, theirs

It can be seen at a glance that the words in this very important group have a much greater variety of form than have the nouns we looked at previously. These various forms make for problems of "Agreement and Selection," which will be discussed at the end of this chapter.

1) **Pronouns always functioning like nouns.**   Three groups of pronouns always function like nouns. The largest of these groups consists of the nominative and objective forms of the personal pronoun: *I, me, you, he, him, she, her, it, we, us,* and so on. Some of the possessive forms are also in this category: *mine, yours, ours, theirs, hers, its.*

NOMINATIVE CASE: SHE turned a few pages of the magazine.
HE has been taking medicine for six weeks.
OURS is a heavy burden.

OBJECTIVE CASE: He scolded THEM for an hour.
Give HIM the book.
Between YOU and ME, that's the whole story.

The second group of pronouns always functioning like nouns includes *none, others,* and words ending in *body* and *thing.*

NONE went to the four o'clock meeting.
Professor Graves gave his lecture notes to SOMEBODY.
She couldn't tell him ANYTHING about the play.

The last group consists of words ending in *self* (plural, *selves*):[5]
I'll hate MYSELF in the morning.
She HERSELF will be there.
They always make fun of THEMSELVES at their parties.

2) **Pronouns never functioning like nouns.** In this second category are words like *my, your, its, our, their.* Although obviously related to *mine, yours,* and so forth, they function quite differently:

That is MY book.
That book is MINE.

YOUR youngest brother won the race.
YOURS won the race.

THEIR home is on the side of a hill.
THEIRS is on the side of a hill.

Pronouns of this category are really *noun-determiners,* or function words which mark the presence of nouns instead of serving as nouns themselves.

3) **Pronouns sometimes functioning like nouns.** The largest category of pronouns is that group of words which, depending on the sentence, may function either like nouns or like noun-determiners:

his, her, other, another, that, those, this, these, each, few, many, some, several, such, both, either, neither, all, any, less, enough, more, most, much, one, two, three . . . ninety-nine, and so on.

The area of overlap between pronouns and determiners is so large, in fact, that grammarians disagree as to whether pronouns are a subclass of nouns (as they are called here) or a function group. The argument, however, is not important. When the word functions like a noun, it is a pronoun; when it precedes a

---

[5] The inconsistency of Standard American English is revealed in this last group of pronouns. Although we have *herself* and *itself,* we don't have *hisself;* we have *ourselves* and *yourselves,* but not *theirselves.* The exceptional forms are found only in some regional dialects conventionally considered "ungrammatical."

noun, it is a determiner. (Incidentally, by the time you finish studying the paired sentences below, you will know a good deal about determiners—even before officially studying them.)

Which is HIS?	*Pronoun*
Which is HIS typewriter?	*Determiner*
I gave it to HER.	*Pronoun*
She traded in HER old model.	*Determiner*
THESE are the days when birds come back.	*Pronoun*
THESE birds are lovely.	*Determiner*
WHOSE is that?	*Pronoun*
WHOSE woodpile is that?	*Determiner*
THREE make up a team.	*Pronoun*
THREE players make up a team.	*Determiner*
MANY are cold but FEW are frozen.	*Pronouns*
MANY students went to the rally, but FEW freshmen were admitted.	*Determiners*

Pronouns like *who, whose, whom, that, what,* and *which* are discussed below in describing the function group known as *subordinators* (section G 2F). Their function as *relative pronouns* in the following sentences is to signal the presence of a subordinate clause within the sentence:

She wanted something for her nephew, WHO was studying painting.
The man WHOSE hand I hold is the new president of this organization.
The class WHICH I look forward to most meets daily at 10 o'clock.

In other sentences, these words signal questions:

WHO is studying painting?
WHOSE hand do I hold?
WHICH is your classroom?

C. Verbs: Form Class II. The words in capitals in the following passage are finite verbs:

Now BEGAN a laborious progress up the long street. Pushing the drum ahead of him like a huge rolling pin, Cobb PACKED down a path sufficiently firm to bear his weight. Street lamps CAST murky gleams over the senseless spectacle of a lone man pushing an oil drum through the snow. Tenement dwellers peeping out of top-story windows WONDERED what the man WAS DOING out there. They DID not KNOW that he WAS PUTTING to primitive use the greatest of inventions, the wheel. A window WAS FLUNG up and a voice SHOUTED, "Hey, mister, GOT a match?" Cobb HAD no breath for drolleries. Gasping, rolling his barrel, he STRUGGLED on.—HENRY MORTON ROBINSON.[6]

1) **Kinds of finite verbs.** In an earlier discussion of sentence patterns (Chapter I) we classified finite verbs as intransitive, transitive, and linking. To review:

a) **Sentences with intransitive verbs:**

The dog BARKED.
It was RAINING steadily.
Now BEGAN a laborious progress up the long street.

b) **Sentences with transitive verbs:**

The gypsy WHISTLED a plaintive tune.
I BOUGHT tickets for all of us.
The dancer was EXCITING the audience.

c) **Sentences with linking verbs:**

The dancer WAS exciting.
The light SEEMED dim.
Sandy Chase IS our new secretary.

2) **Problems in finite verbs**

a) **Linking verbs.** Since linking verbs differ from either intransitive or transitive verbs in being normally followed by adjectives rather than adverbs, it is important to be able to recognize them.

Forms of the verbs *to be* and *to seem* are the most commonly used linking verbs, but there are many other linking verbs and

---

[6] *The Great Snow.* Copyright, 1947, by Henry Morton Robinson. Simon and Schuster, Inc., publishers.

many other verbs that may be used as linking verbs. George O. Curme has estimated that there are about sixty,[7] a few of which are used in sentences below:

become:	We soon BECAME good friends.
come:	Wishes never COME true.
fall:	He FELL ill on Friday.
feel:	He FELT very anxious about the result.
grow:	The boy WAS obviously GROWING uneasy.
look:	The player LOOKED hot and tired.
remain:	She REMAINED an old maid.
run:	The brook RUNS dry every summer.
smell:	The bread SMELLS appetizing.
ring:	Every one of his replies RANG false.
sound:	Your plan SOUNDS extravagant.
stand:	He always STANDS aloof from quarrels.
taste:	Her cooking always TASTES good.
turn:	His hair TURNED white overnight.
wear:	The suit WORE thin at the elbows.

Notice that in every sentence the present verb may be crossed out, a form of *to be* or *to seem* substituted, and the basic meaning of the sentence will remain:

    WAS
He ~~FELL~~ ill on Friday.

     SEEMED
The player ~~LOOKED~~ hot and tired.

    SEEMS
Your plan ~~SOUNDS~~ extravagant.

      IS
Her cooking always ~~TASTES~~ good.

b) **Classification of verbs.** As has been mentioned before, the same verb may shift its classification depending on the pattern of the sentence in which it is used.

---

[7] *Parts of Speech and Accidence* (Boston: D. C. Heath & Company, 1935), p. 60.

Frank LOOKED exhausted.	*SVC-linking*
Frank LOOKED at me suspiciously.	*SV-intransitive*

The surface FELT rough.	*SVC-linking*
He FELT the rough surface.	*SVO-transitive*

She READ Emily Dickinson's poetry with great interest.	*SVO-transitive*
Last night, she READ until almost midnight.	*SV-intransitive*

c) **Similar verbs.** Some sets of similar verbs are particular sources of trouble even for native speakers. The more common practice, and a wise one for students to follow, is to regard *set, lay,* and *raise* as transitive, and *sit, lie,* and *rise* as intransitive.

He SET the statuette carefully on the table.	*SVO-transitive*
I SAT down on the sofa.	*SV-intransitive*

He RAISED his hand in farewell.	*SVO-transitive*
The moon RISES late this week.	*SV-intransitive*

She LAID the sleeping child down tenderly.	*SVO-transitive*
I shall LIE among the daisies.	*SV-intransitive*

However, as always, usage operates to add a few idiomatic exceptions and to break down the "rule" (see section D 5 for discussion of idiom):

The sun SETS in the west at 5:33 P.M.
The fruit has SET early this year.
SIT the baby up.

3) **Formal features of verbs.** Which are the verbs in the following sentences? Are they intransitive, transitive, or linking?

A prohock fleebles calbushes.
Because the noosh swurgled, we flabbed.
The gooby gadger is greeming grullions.
The smiggles had olliped in the zee.
Don't jennebize that dilly shawn.

The value of "double-talk" sentences is that they show us how we unconsciously respond to structural signals in grasping meaning—through word order, word endings, and function words. Sometimes it is possible for us to "understand" a sentence without knowing the meaning of each word, because enough other signals come through to carry the message, despite the temporary break in the circuit; sometimes we understand a sentence even when the speaker or writer has used a word incorrectly, because, as John Locke said: "Misnaming disturbs not the certainty of knowledge." The writer or speaker has supplied enough other signals for us to grasp the import of his communication, enabling us to correct, quickly and silently, what he has omitted or misused.

> What this laboratory needs is a new pycnometer.
> He never lost his marmoreal attitude.
> Anaphora is a characteristic of his later verse dramas.
> He is a virtual progeny of learning.

Of course it helps if you know what *pycnometer, marmoreal,* and *anaphora* mean; but the sentences at least establish an opportunity for a meaningful response. Almost simultaneously, we smile at—and correct—malapropisms like *progeny* for *prodigy.*

Without knowing what the first nonsense sentence means, we know that one of a class known as *prohocks,* the subject of discourse, is performing an action, probably known as *fleebling,* upon more than one of a class known as *calbushes.* Several *prohocks* would probably *fleeble.* Furthermore, as used here, *fleeble* is a transitive verb. How do we know this? First of all, the pattern is the familiar one of SVO. Second, we recognize the noun-determiner *a* preceding *prohock.* Third, we recognize the signal for the plural noun in the *es* ending of *calbushes.*

a) The first formal feature that helps identify the verb is the *s* ending on *fleeble.* This is the third person singular inflection, as in the following: (He . . .) *hops, wipes, thinks, blows, swims, stops, loves.* The only significant exception to this is the third person singular of the verb *be;* but this verb is a complicated and rather special case which will be treated separately below (see page 62). The fact that this ending is identical with the plural ending of singular nouns is a source of ambiguity in condensed statements like telegrams and headlines. A recent newspaper headline read: "City Maps Wage Fight." The body of the story made it clear that *Maps* was meant as a transitive verb, not as a plural noun:

City———→ Maps Wage Fight

rather than

City Maps ————→Wage Fight

In speech, this ambiguity is avoided by means of intonation. Try reading the headline aloud both ways and note the differences in pitch, stress and internal pause. In Chapter III, we will see that punctuation is one means of specifying intonation in the written utterance, but no punctuation marks can help in utterances which, like the one above, lack too many other signals. What missing signals have to be restored in order to make different meanings emerge from the following?

Niagara Falls Behind; Guard Arms Center; Local Plans Shift; Infant Needs Change

b) A second feature of verb forms is seen in "Because the noosh swurgled, we flabbed." This is the *d* or *ed* ending, known as the regular *past tense ending,* as in the following: *stopped, wiped, hoped, loved, ended, baited, saved.*

Irregular past tense endings are found on about two hundred very common verbs. When a child says, *The bird flied away,* he is perfectly consistent in using the regular *ed* ending that he uses in the majority of his verbs; but eventually he learns that consistency does not apply here, any more than it does in making *men,* not *mans,* the plural of *man. I knowed it* and *I bited it* are logical, but they are not acceptable outside the nursery school set.

In "The smiggles had olliped in the zee," we apparently find the same *ed* ending; but the auxiliary word *had* which precedes it is a signal denoting a change in the form of the verb, called the *past participial form.* For some verbs, the past tense and past participle are identical (*bid, climbed*); for others they are different (*flew, flown; ate, eaten; shook, shaken*). A table of the principal parts of some common verbs, giving the infinitive (or base form), the past tense, and the past participle, is printed for your convenience, starting on page 59. Note that all regular verbs (like *drown*) and some irregular verbs (like *flee*) have identical forms for past tense and past participle. The often troublesome variations in the forms of other irregular verbs must be learned individually.

c) In "The gooby gadger is greeming grullions," we find a recognizable, consistent, and absolutely regular form feature— the *ing* ending associated with the *present participle form.* The only verbs without the *ing* inflection are those functioning as auxiliaries. Note that this sentence would be ambiguous without the word *grullions.* We might think that the sentence said something about a *gooby, greeming gadger.* But with the direct object present, we read *is greeming* as the transitive verb phrase.

d) "Don't jennebize that dilly shawn." Some verbs are identified by a few familiar suffixes, listed below:

(1) *ate,* as in *operate, orchestrate, duplicate*
(2) *ize,* as in *organize, criticize, militarize*
(3) *fy,* as in *horrify, liquefy, beautify*
(4) *en,* as in *tighten, loosen, blacken*

4) **Separable verbs.** "Get in!" is obviously different from "Get out!" and "Get up" and "Get over." The variations illustrated here are typical of a small but important group of two-part verbs, known as *separable verbs.* "Get" may function in its own right as a transitive verb, but it also functions with other words to carry quite different meanings. These words also appear on the list of function words called prepositions, but when used in the position immediately following a verb, they do not function as prepositions do (i.e., they do not have objects), but as adverbs. Note the importance of knowing whether the word is an adverb or a preposition in the following sentence:

The lights were blinking out in the bay.

If *out* is a preposition, the meaning of the sentence is that the action of the lights was continuous and sustained; if *blinking out* is a separable verb, the sentence describes the gradual extinction of the lights. Whether the lights are on or are going off makes a considerable difference! To determine the classification of the word as either a preposition or an adverb, try the substitution test, replacing the word with another adverb:

The lights were blinking (softly, quickly, romantically) in the bay.

The term *separable verb* indicates that the parts may be separated from each other. Some of the many possibilities for combining the parts are shown below. These separable verbs are often the more colloquial versions of a formal term: "get in" for "enter"; "give off" for "exude"; "throw over" for "spurn"; and so on.

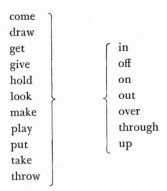

come	
draw	
get	in
give	off
hold	on
look	out
make	over
play	through
put	up
take	
throw	

5) **Principal parts of verbs.** The principal parts are the forms of the verb: (1) in the present infinitive; (2) in the first person, singular number, past tense, indicative mood; and (3) in the past participle. For convenience of reference there follows a selected list of principal parts that are sometimes troublesome. Whenever there is a choice of forms, that preferred in modern usage, as indicated in *Webster's New Collegiate Dictionary,* is given first. Colloquial, technical, and slang usages are not considered, and obsolete and archaic forms are omitted.

Infinitive	*Past tense*	*Past participle*
to abide	abode	abided
to awake	awoke, awaked	awaked, awoke
to awaken	awakened	awakened
to be	was	been
to bear (bring forth)	bore	born
to bear (carry)	bore	borne
to beat	beat	beaten
to begin	began	begun
to bend	bent	bent
to beseech	besought, beseeched	besought
to bet	bet	bet, betted
to bid (command)	bade, bid	bidden, bid
to bid (offer)	bid	bid
to bite	bit	bitten
to blow	blew	blown
to break	broke	broken
to broadcast	broadcast	broadcast
to burn	burned, burnt	burned, burnt
to burst	burst	burst
to catch	caught	caught
to chide	chid, chided	chid, chidden, chided
to cleave (adhere)	cleaved	cleaved
to cleave (split)	cleft, cleaved, clove	cleft, cleaved, cloven
to climb	climbed	climbed
to clothe	clothed, clad	clothed, clad
to come	came	come
to deal	dealt	dealt
to dig	dug, digged	dug, digged
to dive	dived[8]	dived
to do	did	done
to drag	dragged	dragged
to draw	drew	drawn
to dream	dreamed, dreamt	dreamed, dreamt

---

[8] The colloquial form of the past tense, *dove,* is appearing more and more in print. *The American College Dictionary* labels this form *U. S. Colloq.*

Infinitive	*Past tense*	*Past participle*
to drink	drank	drunk, drunken
to drive	drove	driven
to drown	drowned	drowned
to dwell	dwelt, dwelled	dwelt, dwelled
to eat	ate	eaten
to fall	fell	fallen
to fight	fought	fought
to fit	fitted	fitted
to flee	fled	fled
to flow	flowed	flowed
to fly	flew	flown
to forget	forgot	forgotten, forgot
to freeze	froze	frozen
to get	got	got, gotten
to go	went	gone
to grow	grew	grown
to hang (put to death)	hanged	hanged, hung
to hang (suspend)	hung	hung
to have	had	had
to hold	held	held
to kneel	knelt, kneeled	knelt, kneeled
to know	knew	known
to lay	laid	laid
to lead	led	led
to lend	lent	lent
to lie (recline)	lay	lain
to lie (tell an untruth)	lied	lied
to light	lighted, lit	lighted, lit
to loose	loosed	loosed
to lose	lost	lost
to mean	meant	meant
to mow	mowed	mowed, mown
to overflow	overflowed	overflowed
to pass	passed	passed, past

Infinitive	Past tense	Past participle
to pay	paid	paid
to plead	pleaded	pleaded
to prove	proved	proved, proven
to raise	raised	raised
to read	read	read
to rear	reared	reared
to rid	rid, ridded	rid, ridded
to ride	rode	ridden
to ring	rang, rung	rung
to rise	rose	risen
to run	ran	run
to saw	sawed	sawed, sawn
to say	said	said
to see	saw	seen
to set	set	set
to shake	shook	shaken
to shine (to give light)	shone	shone
to shine (to polish)	shined	shined
to show	showed	shown, showed
to shrink	shrank, shrunk	shrunk, shrunken
to sing	sang, sung	sung
to sit	sat	sat
to slink	slunk	slunk
to speak	spoke	spoken
to spend	spent	spent
to spit	spat, spit	spat, spit
to spring	sprang, sprung	sprung
to steal	stole	stolen
to swear	swore	sworn
to sweep	swept	swept
to swim	swam	swum
to swing	swung	swung
to take	took	taken
to tear	tore	torn
to throw	threw	thrown

Infinitive	*Past tense*	*Past participle*
to thrust	thrust	thrust
to tread	trod	trodden, trod
to wake	waked, woke	waked, woken
to wear	wore	worn
to weave	wove, weaved	woven, wove
to weep	wept	wept
to work	worked, wrought	worked, wrought
to write	wrote	written

Whenever in doubt about the principal part of any verb not found in this list, consult a reliable dictionary.

6) ***To be*** (*or **not** to be*). The verb *to be* is a special case because of its numerous form changes. Although every native speaker handles the intricate inflectional patterns unconsciously and, for the most part, accurately, the forms look and sound different from each other.

Subject	*Present*	*Past*	*Past participle*	*Present participle*
I	am	was	have been	am being
he, she, it	is	was	has been	is being
we, you, they	are	were	have been	are being

7) **Tense.** Except for a few auxiliaries like *ought* and *must,* all verbs have two tenses marked by form changes. The *present tense* forms (with the exception of those for *to be*) are as follows:

I, you, we, they	walk, travel, hunt, and so on
he, she, it	walks, travels, hunts, and so on

The *past tense* form is the infinitive form with the *d* or *ed* ending: *walked, traveled, hunted.*

Actually, the term "present tense" is not quite accurate. "I travel to Chicago next month" is a statement not about a present action but about one that is anticipated in the future. Likewise,

"Swift is the father of modern English prose" does not describe a present condition but refers to actions concluded many years ago. "I dream of Jeanie with the light-brown hair" is (note the tense!) Stephen Foster's way of describing a series of recurrent events occurring at a previous time and continuing into the present. Finally, "Light travels at a rate of 186,000 miles per second" is a sentence about a present action which will undoubtedly continue into future times. This looseness in the concept of "present tense" has led some grammarians to refer to the "non-past," but we can continue calling it the present tense as long as we recognize the built-in vagueness of the term.

These are the only tenses marked by formal features. *Formally speaking,* there is no such thing as a future tense. The concept of an action taking place at a time following the statement is expressed in two ways: (1) by the use of the present tense form, as in "Dr. Smith leaves for the convention tomorrow" (or ". . . is leaving for . . ." or ". . . plans to leave for . . ."), where the idea of futurity is located in the modifier "tomorrow" and not in the verb; and (2) by the use of the present tense form plus the auxiliary word "will," as in "Dr. Smith will leave for the convention."

With the addition of other auxiliary words, particular shades of meaning dealing with ideas of starting, continuing, repeating, and concluding, either in past or present, can be imparted to the sentence:

I hunt in these woods.	*Present, but could be a continuing or habitual action*
I hunted in these woods yesterday.	*Past, time specified*
I will hunt in these woods tomorrow.	*Future, time specified*
I have hunted in these woods before.	*Action concluded in the unspecified past*
I had hunted in these woods last November.	*Action concluded at a specific past time*
I will have hunted in these woods by tomorrow night.	*Action to be concluded before a specified future time*

I am hunting in these woods now.

Action continuing in the present

I am hunting in these woods to-morrow.

Action to begin at a specified future time

The last two sentences illustrate a form that is sometimes referred to as the progressive tense; however, that form does not indicate that the action is progressing at the time referred to. "He is leaving school next week" is as clear a reference to future action as "He will leave...."

8) **Active and passive voice.** Verbs have two voices, known as *active* and *passive*. The active voice occurs in the normal SVO pattern: "The shortstop hit a triple." The passive voice form consists of the past participle and a form of the auxiliary "be": "A triple was hit by the shortstop." Here the pattern becomes SV ("by the shortstop" is a prepositional phrase).

If the writer wants to stress the person doing the acting, he uses the active voice (it was the shortstop, not the third baseman, who tripled). He uses the passive voice when he wants to stress the thing or person that receives the action (a triple, not a double) or when the thing or person that does the acting is not definitely known.

A crucial error in judgment WAS MADE by the captain.

This book WAS READ by almost the whole class.

The gas tank WAS BLOWN to pieces.

The sheep ARE HERDED toward the valleys when winter approaches.

The object of a transitive verb in the passive voice is sometimes called a *retained object:*

ACTIVE: The judge gave Wilbur thirty days.

PASSIVE: Wilbur was given *thirty days* by the judge.

The structural signals which mark the active and passive voices are useful for the writer to be able to handle. He can achieve variety and flexibility in sentence structure and at the same time put his emphasis on what he considers important, departing from the SVO pattern when necessary. Excessive use of the passive voice results in a flabby style, but, properly used, it can help the writer attain precision of thought and statement.

D. Verbals: A Verb Subclass.   In the preceding section, we have been dealing only with *finite* verbs. The *nonfinite* verb forms are called verbals; although very useful and very important, they are not to be confused with the finite forms.

The definition of a sentence given at the end of Chapter I read: "A sentence is a word-group containing a subject and a finite verb (not a verbal like *being* or *to be*)." It is clear that when a verbal is used in place of a verb, no predication—no assertion—results. To illustrate, if we rewrite this same sentence, using nonfinite for finite forms, we get: "It to be clear that when a verbal being used in place of a verb, no predication—no assertion—resulting." This is a sentence with the signals flying upside down. Verbals, then, although they resemble verbs, as children resemble their parents, do not function as verbs but as *nouns, adjectives,* and *adverbs.*

1) **The verbal forms.**   The formal marks of the verbals are as follows:

INFINITIVE:	*to* work	*to* fall	*to* defeat
PRESENT PARTICIPLE:	work*ing*	fall*ing*	defeat*ing*
PAST PARTICIPLE:	work*ed*	fall*en*	defeat*ed*

Note that the only irregularities are in the past participial form.

2) **The verbal functions.**   All three verbals may function like **nouns.**

a) **As subject:**

TO ERR is human.
The CHIRPING of the birds awoke me.
The FORGOTTEN shall be remembered.

b) **As direct object:**

The children love TO PLAY.
I did not like his PRETENDING.
The minister tried to uplift the FALLEN.

c) **As complement:**

What is left for her is TO DIE.
It's only the BEGINNING, folks.
All that the novelist can start with is the GIVEN.

d) **As object of preposition:**

Off TO SWIM is my intention.
I don't understand the reason for his FIGHTING.
Dante spoke to the DAMNED.

All three verbal forms may function like **adjectives.**

His desire TO SUCCEED became stronger each year.
I was squelched by the CUTTING remark.
The BURNT child dreads the fire.

All three verbal forms may function like **adverbs.**

They do not go to college TO LEARN.
EXCLUDING the mosquitoes, we had a fine time on our trip.
I could solve this puzzle, GRANTED enough time.

3) **Versatile verbals.**   The verbals further illustrate
the flexibility of the language. They show qualities deriving from
both their present functions and their inheritance.

a) **When a verbal functions like a noun, it is modified by an
adjective.**

The wild CHEERING of the crowd deafened him.

When it functions like an adjective, it is modified by an adverb.

Wildly CHEERING crowds met them at the station.

When it functions like an adverb, it is modified by an adverb.

They went TO CHEER wildly.

b) **But verbals also retain some of the characteristics of the
verbs from which they derive.**   A verbal may take an object or a
complement, together with modifiers, to form a *verbal phrase.*

The entire unit then functions in the sentence exactly as the one-word verbal does.

(1) **As noun** (subject):

TO PLAY GOLF WELL demands practice.
HITTING THE SHUTTLECOCK is difficult at first.

As noun (direct object):

Some day I hope TO WRITE A BEST-SELLER.
The noise prevented OUR HEARING YOUR VOICE.

As noun (object of preposition):

I don't understand the reason for HIS CREATING SCENES IN THE CLASSROOM EVERY DAY.
Cowboys develop bowlegs from RIDING HORSES.

(2) **As adjective:**

His desire TO SWIM THE HELLESPONT became an obsession.
PUSHING THE CART AHEAD OF HIM, Cobb marched down the path.

(3) **As adverb:**

TO OPEN THE BOX, press along the perforated line.
The export trade in widgets declined, CAUSING A DEPRESSION IN THE AREA.

4) **Verbals back into verbs.** The forms which mark the verbals are in themselves not enough to differentiate them from verbs. Indeed, it doesn't take much to turn the verbals back into verbs.

VERBAL: TO GO HOME was their dream.
VERB: They OUGHT TO GO home.

VERBAL: SWIMMING is his hobby.
VERB: He IS SWIMMING.

VERBAL: DEFEATED, the team went sadly home.
VERB: The team WAS DEFEATED.

What has been added in each case is an *auxiliary,* a word that functions with verbs (just as determiners function with nouns).

To go home is a *verbal* phrase functioning as subject in the first sentence. But *ought to go* is an intransitive *verb* phrase. Other auxiliaries shown above are *is* and *was.* In a sentence like *The dancer was exciting* (or *revealing, interesting,* or *charming*), there are two possible meanings. Again, structure will determine meaning. If the pattern intended is SVC, then the intensifier *very* may be used before the *ing* word (*The dancer was very exciting*). If the pattern intended is SV, then the verb phrase may be followed by an object (*The dancer was exciting the audience, revealing her charms, interesting the police*).

E. Adjectives: Form Class III. The words in capitals in the following passage are adjectives:

. . . The sources tapped by Barlow and his contemporaries in their search for a knowledge of what would be **GOOD** for mankind were **VARIOUS** and often **INCONSISTENT** with one another. Barlow himself drew upon three: a belief in an **INTERNAL** sense, **COMMON** to all men, by which they perceived the most **IMPORTANT ABSTRACT** truths; a trust in **IMPULSIVE HUMANITARIAN** sentiment; and, finally, an acceptance of **DETERMINISTIC** materialism which denied everything except the perceptions of the **EXTERNAL** senses and the **FUNDAMENTAL** law of motion. . . . All of these supported his **DEMOCRATIC POLITICAL** philosophy, but **LONG** and **EXTENSIVE** observation convinced him that if men possessed an **INTERNAL COMMON** sense it was frequently **UNDEVELOPED** and **USELESS** and that **HUMANITARIAN** sentiment was by no means **UNIVERSAL.** His materialism was the offspring of his **DEMOCRATIC** optimism.— LEON HOWARD[9]

In Chapter I, it was noted that the single-word modifiers known as adjectives normally appear before the nouns they limit or modify: the *lavish* house, the *angry* woman, the *purple* range. The SVC sentence pattern may find an adjective following a link-

---

[9] *The Connecticut Wits.* The University of Chicago Press, 1943. Reprinted by permission.

ing verb: She was *furious*. He is *handsome*. This peach is *ripe*. Although the position that words occupy is one of the important signals by which we recognize them, it is important to realize that position alone is not a sufficient criterion for identifying adjectives, since other words may also appear in normal adjective positions: the *stucco* house, the *beggar* woman, the *kitchen* range. As for the other pattern, consider: She was *eating*. He is *ahead*. This peach is *Betsy Brown*. Furthermore, single-word adjectives may also appear in a pattern like the following, from the illustrative paragraph:

... a belief in an internal sense, *common* to all men . . . .

and in still another pattern like

Tired and *weary*, we continued our explorations.

Adjectives, however, can be identified very quickly by the use of test patterns, or frames: "That _____ one did it," and "It is very _____." That is to say, only adjectives can fit between determiners and nouns, and also immediately after function words like *very, quite,* and *rather.* (See section G 2C for discussion of *intensifiers.*) Using these test frames, you will think of adjectives almost as fast as you can say them: *green, little, Italian, famous, near, good,* and so on.

1) Formal features of adjectives
a) Endings of comparison. Most adjectives can be compared; that is, by adding the suffixes *er* and *est,* it is possible to show their three *degrees.* Most one-syllable adjectives and many two-syllable adjectives are compared, as the following table shows.

Normal degree	Comparative	Superlative
lovely	lovelier	loveliest
hard	harder	hardest
ugly	uglier	ugliest
white	whiter	whitest

Some two-syllable adjectives and all adjectives of more than two syllables are compared in the following manner:

healthful   more (or less) health-   most (or least)
                  ful   healthful
intricate
alcoholic
extravagant

Some adjectives are compared irregularly:

Normal degree	Comparative	Superlative
bad	worse	worst
far	farther	farthest (distance)
	further	furthest (additionally)
good	better	best
little	less	least
much	more	most
old	elder	eldest (age of person in a family)
	older	oldest (age of a person or thing)

The "good-better-best" triad is frequently not observed in idiomatic usage. We say "best foot forward," although "best" implies a comparison involving more than two objects. (In Hollywood, it is said, the degrees are "good-fabulous-fantastic.")

According to some authorities, certain adjectives name qualities that should not be compared. These authorities support their contention not only by written usage but by reasoning that an absolute quality is either true or not true. If a ball is *round,* for example, they say that the quality of roundness cannot be compared because round means "like a circle or sphere" and that every point is either equally distant from the center or the object named is not round at all. If an object is *perfect* its quality of perfection cannot be compared because *perfect* means "without blemish or defect." Similar adjectives are *dead, unique, square, entire,* and *equal.*

Other authorities, however, point out that often in good colloquial usage, and at times in good written usage, comparisons of these adjectives are found. George O. Curme,[10] for example, is among those who present illustrations from both good colloquial and good written usage of comparisons of adjectives naming absolute qualities. He also feels that when such forms as *more perfect* and *most perfect* are used, a writer is attempting to express something that is approaching perfection although not quite perfect.

On the whole, the use of the comparative and superlative degrees of absolute adjectives should be the exception rather than the rule in most writing. The writer is best advised, however, to base his own practice on what he observes in his own community and his own reading and on the degree of formality of any given piece of his own writing.

b) **Suffixes of adjectives.** As we have seen earlier in discussing noun suffixes, many nouns are made from adjectives (*strangeness* from *strange, hardship* from *hard,* and so on). The process also works the other way. Many adjectives are made by adding suffixes to nouns and verbs. A few familiar examples follow:

Noun	plus	*Suffix*	equals	*Adjective*
nature		al		natural
remark		able		remarkable
Europe		an		European
care		ful		careful
poet		ic, ical		poetic, poetical
book		ish		bookish
wood		en		wooden
mercy		less		merciless
home		like		homelike
game		some		gamesome
fame		ous		famous
health		y		healthy

Verb	plus	*Suffix*	equals	*Adjective*
measure		able		measurable
defy		ant		defiant

[10] *Syntax* (Boston: D. C. Heath & Company, 1931), pp. 500, 504.

Verb	plus	*Suffix*	equals	*Adjective*
learn		ed		learned
abhor		ent		abhorrent
use		ful		useful
love		ing		loving
marvel		ous		marvelous
act		ive		active
please		ing		pleasing

2) **Noun adjuncts.** When is an adjective not an adjective? In *the beautiful plate, beautiful* is an adjective; in *the book plate, book* is not an adjective but a *noun adjunct.* That is to say, *beautiful* may be preceded by the intensifier *very,* but *book* may not. In addition, *beautiful* becomes *more beautiful* and *most beautiful,* but we do not speak of *booker* and *bookest* (or *more book* or *less book*). On the other hand, *book* does show all the formal features of a noun: it takes the plural ending, *books,* the possessive ending, *book's,* and it can become an adjective through the addition of the noun suffix *ish.* Other examples of noun adjuncts (and you will be able to supply many others) are as follows:

magazine article, typewriter table, kitchen sink, highway patrol, football stadium, railroad engineer, Sunday driver, ice cream

This very common pattern is one way in which the English language increases its potential for flexibility. It is not, ultimately, of great importance whether we choose to say that the noun adjunct is a "substitute adjective," or that nouns may modify nouns. In any case, there are two things to remember: (1) this is the way the mechanism operates, regardless of how we label it; and (2) the noun preceding another noun is not a member of that class of words which can be clearly grouped and referred to as "adjectives." Finally, to say that "an adjective is any word that modifies a noun" is as good as giving up any attempt to deal objectively with the forms of the language. You may drive a nail with your shoe, but that does not make a hammer out of your shoe.

The stylistic value that results from using nouns as adjectives is, of course, terseness. For instance, it has been convenient in this book to use the phrases *word order* and *sentence structure* rather than *the order of the words* and *the structure of the sentence*. Newspaper headlines frequently carry this terseness to the point of bafflement, however, when they run a series of nouns together in the adjective position in order to save space:

Plan County Election Board Ballot Theft Inquiry

When the structural convenience results in ambiguity it is no longer an aid to expression. A different signal order (or, if you will, order of the signals) is needed.

As we have observed earlier, many words can be either nouns or adjectives. When a word can belong to either class, ambiguity may result in the sentence unless enough signals are present to control the meaning. In speech, intonation gives the principal signal, but in its written form, the following sentence is ambiguous:

He came in carrying a light fixture.

If the fixture is not heavy, the speaker's stress will fall on the *fix;* if the fixture is designed for an electric light, the stress will fall on the noun adjunct. The writer must compensate for the inadequacy of the written version by sending another combination of signals: *a fixture for the light, an electric light fixture, a very light fixture, a fixture weighing eight ounces,* and so on. The reader's grasp of the meaning depends on how well he can tell the difference between a noun and an adjective; the writer likewise must know how to manipulate the signals available to him.

F. Adverbs: Form Class IV.   The words in capitals in the following passage are adverbs:

The plane teetered FORWARD SLIGHTLY as the derrick started to hoist us. Several men hung ON to the pontoons to steady us as we swung FREE. NOW we were above their heads; and NOW gliding over the rail to the water BELOW. It seemed rather abnormal and a LITTLE perilous to be sailing QUIETLY through the air, NOT propelled by our own power. I felt relieved when FINALLY, after a slow descent, we touched the water. Headed UPSTREAM, the idling motor NOW quickened to a roar, we seemed SAFELY launched.—ANNE MORROW LINDBERGH[11]

The most remarkable thing about the adverb as a modifier, as was pointed out in Chapter I, is its movability. Furthermore, adverbs make up a rather complicated class of words not always recognizable by form. However, one test frame that will identify most adverbs is "That one did it _____." The following words are typical adverbs (and note their miscellaneous quality): *sadly, eagerly, usually, stealthily, happily, later, sometimes, seldom, well, here, there, out, in, home, yesterday, alone, ahead, fast, backwards, sideways, hard.*

Some of these words occur in other word classes: *fast* and *hard* may be adjectives; *home* and *yesterday* may be nouns; *in* and *out* may be function words in the prepositional group. And despite the fact that many adverbs end in *ly,* so do some adjectives (*kindly, goodly, lovely*).

Like adjectives, also, some adverbs can be compared in three degrees:

Normal degree	Comparative	Superlative
slowly	more slowly	most slowly
hard	harder	hardest

1) **Where, how, when?** One way of classifying adverbs would be to note the precise formal markers which serve to differentiate them into eight subgroups; but for our purposes it will be better to generalize somewhat and to say that there are three main subgroups of adverbs, each imparting a specific kind of direction to the utterance to which it is attached. These subgroups are frequently referred to as the "there, thus, and then" groups.

a) **The first subgroup, referred to as the "there" group, answers**

---

[11] *North to the Orient.* Copyright, 1935, by Anne Morrow Lindbergh. Harcourt, Brace and Company, publishers.

the question "where?" Some adverbs of this group have endings in *where (nowhere, everywhere, somewhere)*; in *ward(s) (westward, backward)*; and in *ways* or *wise (sideways, lengthwise)*. Other adverbs of this group have been noted earlier, in discussing the separable verbs—words like *in, out, off, over, around*. Adverbs of the "there" group are found most often in positions immediately following the verb:

> Let us go THERE, you and I.
> Crabs scuttled EVERYWHERE along the beach.

b) **The second subgroup, referred to as the "thus" group, answers the question "how?"** A "thus" adverb is formed by adding *ly* to the adjective form: *horrible, horribly; regular, regularly; expensive, expensively*. Adverbs in this group may be placed either before or after adverbs of the "there" subgroup.

> We walked QUICKLY HOME.
> We walked HOME QUICKLY.

c) **The third and smallest subgroup is the "then" group, answering the question "when?"** These adverbs are a mixed lot, and are indistinguishable by any formal criterion. They include words like *seldom, often, daily, sometimes, afterward, later*.

In any sentence where all three kinds of adverbs are found, the following variations in pattern may occur:

> USUALLY, soldiers return HOME HAPPILY
> Soldiers USUALLY return HOME HAPPILY.
> Soldiers return HOME HAPPILY USUALLY.

> But NOT: Soldiers return USUALLY HOME HAPPILY.

Adverbs are thus not completely freewheeling. Furthermore, some adverbs can fit certain positions which others cannot.

> She RELUCTANTLY threw her old toys AWAY.
> She RELUCTANTLY threw AWAY her old toys.

> But NOT: She threw RELUCTANTLY her old toys AWAY.

The movability of adverbs makes for subtle differences in pattern-ing which a skillful writer learns to take advantage of, in order to achieve his intended shade of meaning and emphasis.[12]

2) **Adjective or adverb?** The patterns of the language are not haphazard; the parts work together to help us select the appropriate forms.

He sings Mozart WELL.	*Adverb*
He sings Mozart GOOD.	*Adjective*

It is the adverb that appears after the transitive or intransitive verb and modifies it; therefore, *well* is the appropriate choice. This is not to be confused with the SVOC pattern, "He painted the fence white" where *white* is an adjective.

The boys looked EAGER.	*Adjective*
The boys looked EAGERLY.	*Adverb*

In the first sentence, *looked* is a linking verb, which is followed by the predicate adjective; in the second, carrying a different meaning, it is intransitive and is modified by the adverb. (The boys looked *at something.*) Only the writer can tell what message he wants to send, and then he must use the appropriate signals.

When an adverb has two forms, one identical with the adjective form and the other ending in *ly*, the conventional practice is to use the latter in formal writing. Today, most authorities on usage

---

[12] The "split infinitive," long a bugbear in grammar texts, results when an adverb is used between the *to* (the infinitive signal) and the infinitive form itself:

I asked the contractor when he expected to finally finish the work.

Despite mythical rules about never splitting the infinitive, this construction is natural and proper. A split infinitive is to be avoided only when the construction is awkward:

The speaker tried to humorously describe his travels through Europe.

Avoid splitting the infinitive with long adverbial elements:

You had better decide to, if you want to have any luck, fish with worms.

But don't fret about juggling your sentence around merely to avoid splitting an infinitive. There are more important things to remember.

accept the shorter forms in colloquial or informal style, in brief
sentences, and in imperatives: Drive SLOW; Come QUICK. But
slowly and *quickly* are more common in relatively long sentences,
or when the adverb comes before the verb, or when the sentences
contain verbs in the past tense:

He always comes QUICKLY whenever I call him. (NOT: He always
comes quick. . . .)
He QUICKLY measured the site of the camp. (NOT: He quick measured. . . .)
He drove SLOWLY along the ridge of the mountain. (NOT: He drove
slow. . . .)

The form you select at any given time should be appropriate to
the tone and context of your entire communication.

G. The Versatility of the Form Classes

I attended a party SUNDAY, where a WORLD famous author sat a
FOOT away from me. He lives FAR away, but has been visiting here a
MONTH. Among other things, he said that the way UP is the same as
the way DOWN, and that the MEEK are the STRONG. Others at the
party turned LIGHT green with envy because of his attention to me, but
my questions were DEAD serious and his replies COLD sober. The
dinner LATER was excellent; I especially liked the CHICKEN liver.

This perhaps pointless paragraph is designed to illustrate an
essential fact about the language: namely, that a free exchange
of words within the four classes is normal and habitual. Let us
note the italicized words:

1. *Sunday:* a proper noun modifying a verb.
2. *World:* a noun modifying an adjective.
3. *Foot:* a noun modifying a verb.
4. *Far:* an adverb modifying an adverb.
5. *Month:* a noun modifying a verb.
6. *Up, down:* adverbs modifying nouns.
7. *Meek, strong:* adjectives functioning as nouns.
8. *Light, dead, cold:* adjectives modifying adjectives.

9. *Later:* an adverb modifying a noun.
10. *Chicken:* a noun modifying a noun.

None of these sentences is ambiguous, and all are grammatical, despite the fact that the four parts of speech are apparently able to replace each other at will. But the substitutions are not random or disordered. The English language in the course of its development has established certain orderly patterns marked by specific signals. We unconsciously "get" these signals as we receive the message. A *world famous* author is different from a *worldly famous* author; noun-determiners alert us to words like *foot, month, meek,* and *strong,* however they are used; *dinner later* is different from a *later dinner;* a *chicken liver* is different from *chicken-livered* or a *living chicken.* Previously, we saw how verbals, formed from verbs, may serve as nouns, adjectives, and adverbs; it should not surprise us, therefore, to see members of the other form classes be equally versatile in assuming other roles—but only in certain patterns—within the sentence.

The word classes are real and distinguishable, and in any given sentence there will be enough signaling to keep them from being confused with each other, but they are not always mutually exclusive. As we have already learned, some words belong to two or more form classes:

Everybody got a RAISE in salary.	*Noun*
We expect to RAISE the money at a bazaar.	*Verb*
The big FISH got away.	*Noun*
Let's FISH in this river.	*Verb*
The judge gave us a $10 FINE.	*Noun*
It was a FINE day.	*Adjective*
He played the HEAVY in the school play.	*Noun*
The desk was too HEAVY to move.	*Adjective*
He was sawing the HARD wood.	*Adjective*
He was sawing the wood HARD.	*Adverb*
For a guard, he's a pretty FAST runner.	*Adjective*
He runs FAST.	*Adverb*

The tribe will FAST on its ritual days.   *Verb*
The FAST began at sundown.   *Noun*

The signals of order and pattern in the preceding sentences are strong enough to sort out the words. The next sentence, however, is ambiguous precisely because we can't tell which class one of the words (*fast*) belongs to.

The door was shut FAST.

Unless the context makes the meaning of the sentence clear, other signals must be applied.

The door was QUICKLY shut.   *Adverb*
The door was shut TIGHT.   *Adjective*
The door was shut FAST, so we had to force it open.   *Adjective*

H. A Last Word on Form Classes.   What has been said in the last few pages regarding the ability of words to move freely from one form class to another may have left you with the impression that the criteria for determining the parts of speech are too shifty and unsteady to be useful. It is wise to remember, however, that a part of speech is an active and functioning element; it cannot be put in formaldehyde and pinned down permanently on a board. Charles C. Fries uses an illuminating analogy to make this point clear.[13] To define a part of speech accurately and completely, he says, is like defining a "strike" in baseball. All strikes resemble each other in function; that is, if three of them are accumulated by the batter, he is out. But there are many different formal features of the things which we classify as strikes—a swung strike, any kind of foul ball (except when the batter already has two strikes, but not excepting a foul bunt), a called strike (which is different for one batter who is five feet ten and for another who is six feet three), and a foul tip which the catcher manages to hang on to, but only after the hitter already has two strikes. However, if the foul tip rises a certain distance in the air, it is not a strike-out but a foul-out. And if the catcher

---

[13] *The Structure of English* (New York: Harcourt, Brace and Company, 1952).

drops the ball on the third swung strike, it is not a strike-out but a play which requires him to throw out the batter—who is now suddenly converted into a runner!—at first base. These astonishing variations would seem to defy classification, but even nine-year-old boys discuss the intricate conventions of baseball with a good deal of knowledge and subtlety. What matters in the ball game is not the definition of a strike; likewise, what matters in an understanding of grammar is not what a noun or a verb *is* but how it functions as a vital element in the sentence.

G2   THE FUNCTION GROUPS

The structural job that the function words perform has already been briefly described in Chapter I. You may want to review that discussion now, before proceeding with the following pages, in which we will examine the function groups in greater detail. There are seven main groups of function words, together with some smaller groups having a fairly limited number of words. In our discussion of the four form classes, we have anticipated some part of this analysis; you have learned of, and probably are already able to recognize, a few of the main groups. The following lists are not exhaustive (or mutually exclusive):

Noun-determiners, which function with nouns: *the, a, an, every, my, our, your, their, all, any, enough, less, no, both, more, some, one, two . . . ninety-nine . . . ,* and so on

Auxiliaries, which function with verbs: *do, does, did, have, has, had, can, could, may, might, will, would, shall, should, used to, ought to, must, be* (in all forms)

Intensifiers, which function with adjectives and adverbs: *very, somewhat, quite, rather, too, pretty, so, much, more, less, a lot, a little, still, even, some, no,* and so on

Prepositions:

1) **Single-word prepositions:** *about, above, across, against, along, among, around, at, behind, below, beneath, beside, between, beyond, by, despite, down, except, for, from, in, inside,*

into, like, near, of, off, on, onto, out, outside, over, past, through, throughout, to, toward, under, underneath, up, upon, with, within, without

2) **Compound prepositions:** *by means of, on account of, in front of, in accordance with, according to, in addition to, in case of, as for,* and so on

Co-ordinators:

1) **Single-word co-ordinators:** *and, but, or, nor, so, yet, for*

2) **Correlative conjunctions:** *both . . . and . . . , either . . . or . . . , neither . . . nor . . . , not only . . . but also . . .*

Subordinators:

1) **Adverbial clause-markers:** *because, since, if, although, as, when, while, unless, for*

2) **Relative pronouns:** *who, which, that, what, whose*

Transitional conjunctions (or "sentence-connectors"):

1) **Single-word transitions:** *therefore, furthermore, however, consequently, moreover, nevertheless, otherwise, yet, hence,* and so on

2) *Phrase transitions:* on *the other hand, from now on, in the same manner, in addition to this, to continue, in conclusion,* and so on

Expletives (or "fillers"): *it, there*

Some words may fall into either of two function groups, according to their use in particular sentences, just as some other words may fall into either of two form classes, and still others into either one form class or one function group. *Before* is either a subordinator or a preposition; *that* is either a subordinator or a pronoun; *fairly* is either an adverb or an intensifier; *any* is either a pronoun or a determiner. Again, however, a grasp of the total structure will clarify the specific function of the single word in any specific case.

I put out some dog biscuits BEFORE Jack could.	*Subordinator*
I put out some dog biscuits BEFORE Jack.	*Preposition*
Who told you THAT I went to the movies?	*Subordinator*
Who told you THAT?	*Pronoun*

Grandfather made his difficult decisions FAIRLY.   *Adverb*
Grandfather made some FAIRLY difficult decisions.   *Intensifier*

When I looked for his work, there wasn't ANY.   *Pronoun*
When I want him to do ANY work, he disappears.   *Determiner*

A. Noun-determiners. A determiner is a signal to indicate that, within a few words, a noun will appear in the utterance. (Before going on, reread this first sentence. How many determiners do you find? Which nouns do they announce?) A determiner may help signal an otherwise ambiguous term and consequently help us to see the pattern in a sentence. Compare:

He stole home.
He stole a home (OR: . . . the home.)

Whereas *home* is an adverb in the first sentence, the presence of the determiner *a* in the second clearly marks it as a noun—and, of course, changes the structure and the meaning of the sentence completely. (Traditionally, *a* and *an* are called indefinite articles, and *the,* the definite article. The authors of this text prefer to classify them in the larger group of determiners rather than set them off by themselves.)

Other determiners have been previously referred to in the discussion of pronouns (see page 50). You will recall from that earlier discussion that many words which function like pronouns also function like determiners: *her, his, each, all, some,* and so forth.

We were speaking of HER.   *Pronoun*
This is HER life.   *Determiner*

And other pronouns never function as anything but determiners:

YOUR brother is a nuisance.
THEIR lawn is the greenest one on the block.
Carpentry is MY hobby.

It should be pointed out that determiners are not adjectives, despite the fact that in normal word order they both precede nouns. For one thing, determiners do not show the formal features of adjectives. Furthermore, the order of determiner-adjective-noun is fixed and not interchangeable: we say *the yellow book,* not *yellow the book.* And, finally, determiners are never found in the adjective position following a linking verb:

He seemed THE.

B. Auxiliaries.   An auxiliary is a signal to indicate that a verb will appear soon in the utterance. It is a "helping" word that functions with a verb to indicate changes in person, number, time, possibility, probability, duration, conclusion, and so on. A verb and its auxiliary or auxiliaries make a *verb phrase.*

1) For the most part, ***auxiliaries are used with the infinitive, or base, form of the verb*** (*read, walk*):

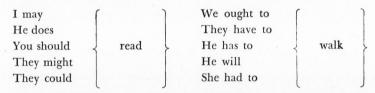

I may		We ought to	
He does		They have to	
You should	read	He has to	walk
They might		He will	
They could		She had to	

2) ***Be,*** with its five variations in form, **is not only a verb but also a very important auxiliary.** It is used with the present participle form of the verb it supports (the *ing* ending):

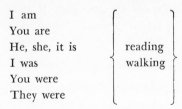

I am	
You are	
He, she, it is	reading
I was	walking
You were	
They were	

3) **Like *be,* several other verbs also act as auxiliaries.** These are *have, has, had; do, does, did; can,* and *will* (the corresponding forms *could* and *would* are auxiliaries only).
Have is unique in that it is used with the past tense form of the verb it supports (the regular *ed* ending):

I have				I do		
You had	{	walked	} but	You did	{	walk }
He has				He does		

Some auxiliaries may function as full verbs: I *have* my ticket; She *did* an imitation of her father; and so on. Whether the word is an auxiliary or a verb in any particular sentence can be determined from the structure. If the word appears before another verb, it is an auxiliary; if it appears before any of the other form class words, it is a verb.

I WILL eat my dinner.	*Auxiliary*
I WILL my estate to my family.	*Verb*
She HAD decided to return home.	*.Auxiliary*
She HAD a headache.	*Verb*
He WAS fishing.	*Auxiliary*
He WAS angry.	*Verb*
He DID paint the house after all.	*Auxiliary*
Under pressure, he DID beautifully.	*Verb*

For discussion of more complex auxiliary structures, see page 63.

C. Intensifiers.   An intensifier is a word that signals the appearance of an adjective or an adverb, and defines the intensity of the quality in the modifier it precedes, as in these sentences:

He was *very* unhappy.
The party went off *rather* well.

Intensifiers are not adverbs. For one thing, intensifiers never modify verbs, while adverbs do. We say, "He behaved very courteously," but not "He behaved very." We say, "She sang prettily" (using the adverb form), or "She sang a pretty song" (where the adjective form modifies the noun *song*); but we do not say, "She sang pretty." If we do, we also immediately add an adverb like *well*. In this case, we are using *pretty* correctly as an intensifier and not incorrectly as an adjective. In other words, the typical intensifier functions only with modifiers. Intensifiers, furthermore, do not have the movability of adverbs. In the sentence, "I was reading my book," the adverb *quietly* can appear in several places:

> Quietly, I was reading my book.
> I was quietly reading my book.
> I was reading my book quietly.

But if we add an intensifier (like *rather*) there is only one place for it to go: before the word *quietly,* wherever it appears.

Adjectives and adverbs in the comparative degree (the *er* ending) take intensifiers like *still, even, no, much, some.*

> He is a very happy fellow.
> I am an even happier fellow.

Some words used as intensifiers may, in other sentences, function in other ways:

> He was MORE furious than I had ever seen him before.   *Intensifier*
> He asked for MORE water.   *Determiner*
> He asked for MORE.   *Pronoun*

> I was TOO tired to continue up the trail.   *Intensifier*
> I was hungry and cold; I was tired, TOO.   *Conjunction*

D. Prepositions. A preposition is a word that signals the appearance, within a few words, of a noun or pronoun (then referred to as the object of the preposition). The preposition also signals us that the entire prepositional phrase, from first to last, functions in the sentence as a single unit, usually as an adverbial or an adjective phrase. Sometimes the object follows the preposition directly: *after lunch.* Sometimes a determiner may intervene: *after the lunch.* Sometimes an adjective may also appear: *after the excellent lunch.* Sometimes an intensifier may precede the adjective: *after the very excellent lunch.*

In order to see how prepositional phrases function in a sentence, let us analyze this fairly normal sentence: "She looked with delight at the unusually delicate teakwood carving which her brother, recently discharged from the Navy, had brought home with him from his last tour of duty in the Orient."

The basic sentence pattern is SV:

She ⟶ looked.

Now, from the preposition signal "with" to the end, we have a complicated but not at all unusual pattern of successive step-down modifications:

1. "with delight" is an adverbial phrase modifying the verb "looked";
2. So is "at the unusually delicate teakwood carving";
3. "which her brother . . . had brought home" is an adjective clause modifying the verbal noun "carving," which in turn is the object of the preposition "at" in the preceding adverbial phrase;
4. "discharged" is a verbal adjective (past participle form) modifying "brother"; the adverb "recently" modifies the verbal;
5. "from the Navy" is an adverbial phrase also modifying the verbal "discharged";
6. "with him" and "from his last tour" are adverbial phrases modifying the verb phrase "had brought";
7. "of duty" is an adjective phrase modifying the noun "tour" (itself the object of the preposition "from");
8. "in the Orient" is an adjective phrase modifying the noun "duty" (itself the object of the preposition "of").

Compound prepositions function exactly like single-word prepositions:

He lost his position BECAUSE OF an industry-wide cutback.
I enclose the check, IN ACCORDANCE WITH your request.
BY MEANS OF hard work, he became the superintendent.

E. Co-ordinators. A co-ordinator is a signal indicating that the grammatical elements being added are of equal rank and form.[14] The typical co-ordinator *and* may join any pair of similar elements:

1) **Nouns:** *The cat and the dog had a fight.*
2) **Verbs:** *They snarled and quarreled.*
3) **Adjectives:** *It was noisy and nerve-racking.*
4) **Adverbs:** *They fought fiercely and bravely.*
5) **Prepositional phrases:** *They could be heard in the streets and over the rooftops.*
6) **Verbal nouns:** *Running and fighting seem to be their main pleasures.*
7) **Infinitives:** *They also love to eat and to sleep.*
8) **Dependent clauses:** *After they had fought for a while and after they had awakened the neighbors, they went quietly home.*
9) **Independent clauses:** *They seem to be bitter enemies, and they are really the best of friends.*

The correlative conjunctions act together to emphasize the compounded relationship:

BOTH the house AND the barn were destroyed by the fire.
They were NEITHER loved NOR hated.
It was NOT ONLY insulting BUT ALSO degrading.
EITHER I dictate the terms OR I take back the ball.

F. Subordinators. Subordinators are signals indicating differences in rank and importance between two clauses which are being joined. Subordinators are of two kinds: (1) *adverbial clause-markers,* signaling the appearance of a dependent adverbial clause; and (2) *relative pronouns,* signaling the appearance of a dependent adjective or noun clause. Either kind of subordinator warns us that the clause, from the first word to the end, is to be regarded as a single functioning unit within the larger unit of the sentence. A detailed structural analysis of a fairly com-

---

[14] But strict formal equivalence is not always present: "This is the story of Five Little Peppers and how they grew." Here the *and* connects a noun and a dependent clause; both, however, are objects of the preposition *of.*

plicated sentence will show how clauses actually function. (See below, section G3.)

Subordinators may appear either between the clauses or at the start of the sentence, if it is desired to have the dependent clause precede the principal idea. This construction is called a *periodic* sentence.

He studied his homework WHILE he waited for his train.
WHILE he waited for his train, he studied his homework.

1) Adverbial clause-markers:

WHEN HE WAS IN SAN DIEGO, he visited the zoo.
Drive carefully *WHERE* THE ROAD IS NOT MARKED.
UNLESS YOU RETURN BEFORE FIVE P.M., we will miss the plane.
I enjoyed meeting him, *ALTHOUGH* I DON'T CARE FOR HIS POETRY.

2) Relative pronouns:
a) As adjective clause-markers:

The boy *WHO* IS WEARING THE HUNTER'S CAP is Bill Jinks.
This novel, *WHICH* I READ AS A YOUTH, now seems superficial.
Our strawberry patch grew from a seed *THAT* A BIRD HAD ACCIDENTALLY DROPPED.

b) As noun clause-markers:

WHATEVER YOU DO will be all right with me.	*Subject*
I don't know *WHO* IS RIGHT.	*Direct object*
The result was *THAT* WE WON BY SIX POINTS.	*Complement*
Give it to *WHOEVER* ASKS FOR IT FIRST.	*Object of preposition*

c) Some overlapping between the two kinds of markers occurs in certain constructions (noun clause as direct object); *where* and *when,* normally adverbial clause-markers, here mark noun clauses:

I know WHERE I'M GOING.
I know WHEN I'LL GET THERE.

G. Transitional Conjunctions. A transitional con-junction is a word that signals the presence of a second independent clause within a sentence. It may be thought of as a sentence-linker. It differs from the co-ordinator, which may also connect independent clauses (*I like the girls, AND the girls like me*), in that it is much freer in placement than the co-ordinator. Transitional conjunctions may appear in several places in the sentence:

I gave him my key; HOWEVER, he was not destined to use it.
I gave him my key; he, HOWEVER, was not destined to use it.
I gave him my key; he was not destined to use it, HOWEVER.
I gave him my key; he was, HOWEVER, not destined to use it.

On the other hand, co-ordinators always appear *between* the clauses:

I like the girls, AND the girls like me.

One would never write

I like the girls, the girls like me, AND.
I like the girls, the girls AND like me.

Another point of difference is that the transitional conjunction links only independent clauses, whereas the co-ordinator can link any equal grammatical structures.

Finally, the transitional conjunction need not appear in the compound sentence at all; the sentence you are now reading contains two independent clauses which are not linked by any kind of transitional conjunction. We could have used "for example" just after the semicolon to show more clearly the relationship between the second clause and the first.

That a transitional conjunction can often steer the meaning of a sentence is clear by examining the following sentences:

The fish were not biting that day; $\left\{\begin{array}{l}\text{nevertheless,}\\\text{therefore,}\end{array}\right\}$ we stayed there until dark.

He is an old-style, cliché-spouting orator; $\left\{\begin{array}{l}\text{consequently,}\\\text{however,}\end{array}\right\}$ he was nominated on the first ballot.

To review the differences among these last three function groups:

1. Co-ordinators join any two equal grammatical structures.
2. Subordinators connect dependent clauses to independent clauses.
3. Transitional conjunctions connect only independent clauses.

These distinctions must be clearly understood in order to punctuate meaningfully. If *however* in the following sentence is a transitional conjunction, it is punctuated like this:

I will not kiss you; however, you urge me.

If it is a subordinator, it is punctuated like this:

I will not kiss you, however you urge me.

And, of course, the signaled meaning is different in each sentence. In Chapter III, we will examine the eleven signals of punctuation and see how this signal system is related to sentence structure; but the preceding example illustrates how structure, grammar, and punctuation are inextricably linked in the communication of ideas.

H. Expletives (*it* and *there*). The words *it* and *there* constitute a small and special function group, sometimes called "anticipatory subjects" or "pattern-fillers." They serve to start the sentence whenever the usual SV pattern is inverted. Compare:

A tavern is in the town.
There is a tavern in the town.

A time comes when a man just wants to relax.
There comes a time when a man just wants to relax.

The road to Tipperary is long.
It's a long road to Tipperary.

That he said it is true.
It is true that he said it.

Although this VS pattern is a common one in English, there are three potential trouble spots:

> 1) **The filler *there* is not the same as the adverb *there*.**

There was a tornado in Kansas last week.	*Filler*
I know because I was there.	*Adverb*

> 2) **The filler *it* is not the same as the third person singular *it*.**

It's a beautiful day in Chicago.	*Filler*
He picked up the ball and threw it away.	*Pronoun*

> 3) **The inverted pattern does not affect the relationship between subject and verb.** This relationship, referred to as *agreement* or *concord,* is seen easily enough in

The sisters were sitting on the porch.

Here the plural subject takes the plural form of the auxiliary verb. However, that agreement may be obscured when the writer begins an inverted pattern:

There was the sisters, sitting on the porch.

(For a fuller discussion, see "Agreement and Selection," Section G 7.)

> **I. Other Function Groups.**   In addition to the function groups described above, there are other quite small groups: *interjections* (oh, ouch, hey, alas); *hesitators* (indeed, to be sure, well, see here); *starters* (let's); *proposers* (please). Although the function words in total form an extremely small proportion of our vocabularies, they constitute an overwhelming proportion of our actual speech and witing. As an operating signal system, therefore, they are of prime importance. Neither form class words nor function words, operating alone, make fully meaningful utterances. Working together, they provide us with a literally unlimited means of expression and communication.

II. WORD-GROUPS: CLAUSES AND PHRASES

A clause has been defined as a word-group containing a subject and a finite verb. If it "stands by itself," we have an independent clause, or a sentence (review the definition of a sentence at the end of Chapter I). If it is included within the sentence, this group of words is a dependent (or a subordinate) clause. A dependent clause, regardless of its length or internal complexity, is a single functioning unit—a noun, an adjective, or an adverb. When it is a noun clause, it does everything that a single word functioning as noun can do; when it is an adjective or adverbial clause, it does everything that adjectives and adverbs (or adjective phrases and adverbial phrases) can do. As a modifier, the dependent clause is the most expanded of the three levels of modification discussed in Chapter I.

Adjective and adverbial clauses, since they are modifiers, may be removed from a sentence without destroying the structure of that sentence. To illustrate, removing the adverbial clause in the preceding sentence leaves it essentially intact. But a noun clause is firmly embedded in the structure, and to amputate it is to destroy the sentence:

WHATEVER HE SAYS makes me laugh. *Subject*
He never did see THAT HE HAD BEEN SWINDLED. *Direct object*
His arrogance was WHAT INFURIATED THE JUDGE. *Complement*
I will give the trophy to WHICHEVER TEAM WINS.
Object of preposition

What complicates the recognition of some dependent clauses is the fact that they are not always preceded by subordinators. But we are so familiar with the signals which sort out the larger units from the smaller ones that, in these structures, we can get along even without some of the signals.

This was the game THE BOYS WANTED TO WIN.

The message comes through although a subordinator (*that* or *which*) is missing. The more powerful signal of word order operates here to tell us that *the boys wanted to win* is an adjective clause in the normal adjective clause position following the noun it modifies. The subordinator, of course, may be omitted only when it is not the subject of the dependent clause:

This is the book (THAT) HE RECOMMENDED.   *Optional use*
This is the book THAT WAS RECOMMENDED.   *Required use*

A sample analysis. Our illustrative sentences in this textbook have, for the most part, been designed to show easily the structure of fairly elementary sentences. But outside of textbooks and first-grade readers, simple-minded sentences like *The grass is green* and *The cat chases the rat* are the exception rather than the rule. More often than not, in adult exposition, you will find a sentence like this:

To allow the continued existence in the United States of an organization like the Communist party, which operates outside the democratic process and which would destroy that process if it ever achieved power, displays a degree of tolerance that seems almost like blindness; however, the correlation between a country's professed ideals and its actual practice can best be measured under conditions of this most extreme kind, when the theory has to meet the severest strain.

This is a fairly complicated sentence, but it contains nothing that has not previously been discussed. Watching for some of the many operating signals, let us examine the way in which the various word-groups are put together, starting with the independent and dependent clauses, and then turning to the verbal, prepositional, and verb phrases.

G3   CLAUSES

We can begin with the first words in the sentence, looking for the subject and the verb if the independent clause is first; or we can begin by noting the presence of the transitional conjunction *however* in the middle of the sentence, which tells us that this sentence has at least two independent clauses. The second way is preferable. To get a bird's-eye view of the sentence at the start of the analysis is useful, for it provides a sense of the relationship between any particular word-group and the complete sentence.

A. **Independent Clauses.** *To allow the continued existence in the United States of an organization like the Communist party*—the complete word-group up to the subordinator *which*—is the subject of the first clause. Noting that the *which* signals a dependent adjective clause, we file this information away for future reference, and proceed to determine the predication in the independent clause. The predicate begins with the verb *displays,* and continues to the semicolon: *displays a degree of tolerance that seems almost like blindness.* What is the pattern of this statement? We begin by looking at the verb. *Displays* is followed immediately by the determiner, *a,* and the noun, *degree.* The pattern of noun following verb is that of the direct object following a transitive verb. The pattern, thus, is SVO.

To allow . . .	displays	a degree . . .
S	V	O

We will return to this first clause, examining its subordinate elements, after we study the structure of the second independent clause.

After the transitional conjunction comes a determiner, *the,* followed by the noun, *correlation* (note the *tion* ending). As we search for the verb, we rapidly note the various signals in consecutive order: *between* (preposition), *a* (determiner), *country's* (possessive form of the noun, patterning before another noun and signaling the arrival of another noun), *professed* (the past participle *ed* ending on the verbal, here in the adjective position before the noun), *ideals* (the noun, with a plural ending), *and* (co-ordinator; co-ordinating what?), *its* (determiner), *actual* (adjective), *practice* (can't be a verb here, since it follows the "determiner-adjective" pattern and thus must be a noun), *can* (verb? auxiliary?), *best* (adjective? adverb?), *be* (verb? auxiliary?), *measured*—and the last four words suddenly fall into place as a verb phrase with the mediate adverb *best*. Looking ahead, we note that a new word-group is about to form, starting with the preposition *under*. But we can stop now, having located subject and verb: *correlation* (subject) *can . . . be measured* (verb phrase).

Obviously we never consciously go through this process except for purposes of analysis; we respond as quickly as we read, and we pull up short to ask questions of the writing only when the signals are missing or are ambiguous, just as we slow up on the highway when we approach an intersection where we cannot see or do not understand the traffic signals. The process we have detailed above is a slow-motion version of the way we fit words together into word-groups, and word-groups together into sentences.

The pattern for the second independent clause, then, is SV:

correlation . . .   can . . . be measured
     S   V

B. Dependent Clauses. Returning to the first part of the sentence, we now begin to sort out the various word-groups which flesh out this SVO pattern. The subordinator *which* is given twice:

which operates outside the democratic process
S   V
which would destroy that process if it ever achieved power
S   V   O

The parallelism of the clauses is reinforced by the presence of the co-ordinator *and*. They occur after the proper noun *Communist party,* in the normal position of adjective clause modifiers. Within the second clause we find another subordinator, the adverbial clause-marker *if*.

if it ever achieved power
S   V   O

The box-within-a-box relationship, in which we find clauses within clauses, phrases within phrases, clauses within phrases, and phrases within clauses, is a way for our language to achieve greater precision and variety of statement: any word in any of the four form classes can be expanded into a phrase or a clause, the larger unit positioning and functioning like the single part of speech: *WHICH would destroy that process*

tomorrow ⎫
immediately ⎪
brutally ⎬ adverbial
slowly ⎪ modifiers
if it ever achieved power ⎭

Following the noun *tolerance* we find a subordinator, *that,* announcing another adjective clause:

that seems almost like blindness

There are thus three adjective clauses hooked into the first independent clause.

In the second part of the sentence, the adverbial clause-marker *when* announces the only dependent clause:

when the theory ⎯⎯⎯⎯→ has to meet the severest strain

G4   PHRASES

The subject of the first independent clause, as has been noted, is an infinitive phrase, consisting of the infinitive, *to allow,* and its object, *the continued existence,* followed by a rapid-fire series of three prepositional phrases: (1) *in the United States,* (2) *of an organization,* and (3) *like the Communist party.* These phrases are not co-ordinate, however. The first is a movable adverbial phrase (try moving it around). The second is an adjective phrase modifying the noun *existence,* and the third is an adjective phrase modifying the noun *organization.* The latter two are fixed in position.

To allow . . .   the existence
     in the United States   of an organization
                                like the Communist party

Despite the fact that it can be thus analyzed into its five parts, we must again emphasize that the entire infinitive phrase functions as a single noun unit, the subject of the clause.

Within the first adjective clause, cited earlier, we now find an adverbial prepositional phrase:

which operates
S   V
      outside the democratic process

Following the direct object, *degree,* we find another adjective phrase, *of tolerance:*

a degree
    of tolerance
       that seems almost like blindness

And, as the step-down modification indicates, within the adjective clause that modifies *tolerance,* we pick out another adjective phrase, *like blindness,* acting here as predicate complement following the linking verb *seems.*

The first part of the sentence has only one verb phrase: *destroy* and its auxiliary *would,* in the dependent clause, *which would destroy.* . . . For the second part of the sentence, an adjective prepositional phrase modifies the subject of the independent clause:

correlation   can . . . be measured
                         under conditions
     between . . . ideals and . . . practice   of this most extreme kind

This not unusual construction shows how objects of the preposition can be compounded. The adverbial phrase modifying the verb, *under conditions,* itself includes another word-group, the adjective phrase *of this most extreme kind,* modifying *conditions.* Parenthetically, note the characteristic order in *of this most ex-*

treme kind: preposition, determiner, intensifier, adjective, noun.

This part of the sentence has two verb phrases: (1) *measured* and its auxiliaries, *can* and *be,* in the independent clause; and (2) *meet* and its auxiliary, *has to,* in the dependent clause.

T. S. Eliot has aptly characterized a good sentence as one "where every word is at home, taking its place to support the others . . . the complete consort dancing together." In the sentence just analyzed, we have seen how all the parts of the sentence, large and small, intricately mesh and interweave. We have seen how they support each other without getting in each other's way, and how they take their places according to ordered and familiar patterns of conventional signals.

G5   AMBIGUOUS CONSTRUCTIONS:
TROUBLE SPOTS

When parts of a sentence do get in each other's way, however, the signal gets blurred. What is wrong with each of the following sentences?

1. I saw the dog that had been bobtailed on the roof.
2. There was the girl in the green dress that he had fallen in love with.
3. He corresponded with the girl he had met on his vacation in the Empire State Building.
4. She read a book about a teacher that inspired her.
5. The mailman gave me a big package sitting on my porch.

The answer is easy. Each is ambiguous because in each the arrangement of the modifying phrases and clauses sends out two meanings instead of a single one. Although these sentences do not illustrate the only kinds of potential ambiguities, an examination of how to remove the errors should help you avoid other trouble spots.

1. Moving the adverbial phrase around merely creates other ambiguities.

On the roof, I saw the dog that had been bobtailed.
I saw the dog on the roof that had been bobtailed.

Perhaps the best, and most economical, revision is to cut the adjective clause down to a one-word modifier:

I saw the bobtailed dog on the roof.

2. Reshuffling the adjective phrase and adjective clause doesn't help in this sentence, either.

There was the girl that he had fallen in love with in the green dress.

Depending on the intended meaning, the sentence could read:

There in the green dress was the girl that he had fallen in love with.

or

The girl was wearing the green dress that he had fallen in love with.

3. As this sentence stands, it contains a second adverbial phrase modifying the first. You will recall from our discussion of adverbs that when several adverbial modifiers appear in a single sentence they usually fall into a "where-how-when" sequence: *I ran there quickly today.* The ambiguous sentence can be corrected by shifting the adverbial phrases into this sequence:

He corresponded with the girl he had met in the Empire State Building on his vacation.

4. There are several ways of clearing up this ambiguity:

She read a book about a teacher who inspired her.
She read a book about a teacher, which inspired her.

The relative pronouns *who* and *that* refer to both persons and objects, but *which* refers only to objects. Choosing the appropriate subordinator is thus one way to make the intended meaning clear. There are other ways, too:

She read an inspiring book about a teacher.

The book she read was about the teacher that had inspired her.

5. Maybe the mailman had stopped to rest, in which case the sentence could read:

While sitting on my porch, the mailman handed me a big package.

Or maybe it was the package itself that he had temporarily placed on the porch:

The mailman handed me a big package which was sitting on my porch.

But if it was the speaker who was sitting, the sentence could read:

Sitting on my porch, I was handed a big package by the mailman.

This is the passive voice construction. In the active voice, it would be:

The mailman handed me a big package while I was sitting on my porch.

To sum up: there is no single way in which to eliminate ambiguous constructions. There are many operating signals which the writer must learn how to control. Sometimes the word order has to be changed, sometimes the form of a word has to be changed, sometimes a new word has to be chosen, and sometimes it is best to throw the whole sentence out and begin all over again. The important thing is that the writer know the signals, and not merely stumble around, revising aimlessly. Not knowing the signals in the language can lead to the same results as not knowing the signals in a football game: you're likely to be thrown for a loss.

The next section of this chapter deals with one of the most important signals of all—the "tied" relationship of certain words to one another within the sentence.

III. AGREEMENT AND SELECTION

G6   AGREEMENT OF PRONOUNS
AND ANTECEDENTS

What is the source of the ambiguity in this sentence?

When the steamer approached the pier, it was crowded with people.

Because the pronoun *it* can refer to either the steamer or the pier, the sentence must be clarified by relating the pronoun to its antecedent, the word to which it refers.

The steamer was crowded with people when it approached the pier.
The pier was crowded with people when the steamer approached.

The principle expressing the relationship between pronoun and antecedent is that every pronoun should have a clear and definite antecedent. In the actual practice of many experienced writers, however, this principle is frequently ignored. But, as in the case of "frags" and "run-ons," the beginning writer should follow the rule until he can confidently take a few liberties with the language. In the following passage, Robert Maynard Hutchins starts his second sentence with an unattached pronoun, but the flow of thought makes his meaning clear:

After I graduated from college and ended my first year of law I took a year off and taught English and History in a preparatory school. THIS continued my education in the liberal arts.—ROBERT MAYNARD HUTCHINS[15]

Hutchins' example is to be compared in precision of meaning with this passage from a student theme:

[15] *Education for Freedom.* Copyright, 1943, by Louisiana State University Press.

I was graduated from high school last June in a memorable ceremony. At that time I was given a scholarship to the University of Southern California, a scroll by the members of the Letterman's Club, and a trophy by the Aeolian Society. I treasure THIS above all else.

Only in the next paragraph was the confusion eliminated, when the writer went on to say that what he treasured was the memory of the graduation ceremonies.

The general principle of agreement, then, may be formulated as follows: A pronoun should have an appropriate antecedent whenever the lack of one results in ambiguity. Some special applications of the general principle follow:

A. Definite Antecedent. A pronoun should not be made to refer to several possible antecedents.

John had an apple in one hand and his knife in the other. He ate the APPLE before I could stop him. (NOT: . . . He ate it. . . .)

B. Indefinite *they*. Avoid the indefinite *they* in formal writing, not because it is inelegant but because it is ambiguous. (For discussion of *you* as opposed to the more formal *one,* see section G 8E.)

All my relatives say that the winters nowadays are not as severe as they once were. (NOT: They say that. . . .)

C. *Each, any, every, none.* Words like *each, any, every,* and *none* are usually considered as being in the third person, masculine gender, even though their group antecedent may be composed of masculine and feminine objects or persons:

EACH member of the committee wore HIS badge—the men red ones, the women blue ones.
In coeducational classes EVERYONE is expected to do HIS lesson in spite of the distracting influence of the opposite sex.

D. Antecedents Which Are Both Masculine and Feminine. When a noun has both a masculine and a feminine sense, a personal pronoun which refers to it is normally considered masculine:

Every student must have completed HIS registration by five o'clock. (NOT: . . . HIS or HER registration. . . .)

E. *Everybody, everyone, none.* It has generally been held that pronouns like *everybody, everyone,* or *none* must always be singular, and hence, when used as an antecedent, that the pronoun should always be referred to by a singular personal pronoun. Current usage, however, does not justify a rigorous application of this rule. The difficulty can be illustrated by sentences like these:

When the President left, EVERYBODY cheered; he lifted his hat in acknowledgment to HIM.

The lake was crowded and EVERYONE seemed to be having a good time; I watched HIM in envy as we marched along.

In these sentences *everybody* and *everyone* are obviously used in a plural sense; the personal pronouns for which they are antecedents should in both instances have been *them.*

The solution to this difficulty requires only the exercise of sound judgment. Such pronouns should normally be considered singular. If, however, logic and meaning clearly demand that they be considered plural, personal pronouns referring to them should be plural.

F. Collective Nouns as Antecedents. The number of a pronoun that refers to a collective noun is determined by the number of the collective noun in the particular sentence. If the class of things within the collective noun is described as behaving like a single unit, the collective noun is singular and so is its pronoun; if the members of the class are doing different things, then logically, psychologically, and grammatically, the noun and the pronoun should both be plural.

The CROWD is stopping and ITS leader is now coming forward.

The CROWD were scattering down the side streets, smashing windows and carrying away everything THEY could lay THEIR hands on.

G7   AGREEMENT OF SUBJECTS AND VERBS

In our previous discussion of nouns and verbs, we noted that both have singular and plural forms: *book, books; man, men; swims, swim; writes, write.* The obvious fact to point out now is that the singular verb is tied to the singular noun, and the plural verb to the plural noun, when they occur as SV in any clause. That is, subject and verb are in "agreement" (or they show "concord," or they are "tied forms").

Since the noun occurs first in normal word order, we say that the noun form "selects" the verb form:

The DOGS BARK loudly.
The DOG BARKS loudly.

CHILDREN LOVE to play in the sand.
My CHILD LOVES to play in the sand.

YOU SEE the sunset.
SHE SEES the sunset.

HE HAS gone.
THEY HAVE gone.

Selection rarely affects meaning: *Children love to play* carries the same meaning as *Children loves to play,* but the latter choice of forms marks the user as an uneducated, perhaps illiterate, person. Thus, agreement between subject and verb is a matter of convention more than of meaning.

In the last set of paired sentences above, note that when the verb takes an auxiliary, it is the auxiliary that changes its form.

I was
You were
He, she, nobody, the journal-
ism class was   } reading the newspaper.
We, you, they, the boys,
my mother and my father were

The general principle of agreement is that a verb agrees in number and person with its subject. Some specific applications of this principle follow:

A. Compound Subject with *and*. Usually, when elements of a compound subject are co-ordinated by *and*, the subject is considered plural:

> The BOY, the GIRL, and the DOG ARE going down the street.
> The BOOK and the PENCILS belonging to Nita HAVE been found.

However, when the parts of the subject are intended to be thought of as a unit, they take a singular verb despite the plural form:

> My best FRIEND and severest CRITIC IS my wife.
> STRAWBERRIES and CREAM IS my favorite dessert.
> The TUMULT and the SHOUTING DIES.—KIPLING
> I should know what GOD and MAN IS.—TENNYSON

B. Compound Subject with *or*. When the elements of a compound subject are joined by *or, either . . . or,* or *neither . . . nor,* the subject is considered singular if all the elements are singular, and plural if all the elements are plural:

> Neither JULES nor JOSEPHINE READS English fluently.
> Either the WILSONS or the SMITHS HAVE it.

However, when one of the elements is plural and the other is singular, the number of the verb is selected by the element that occurs last.

> Neither the PONY nor the SADDLES BELONG to Jim.
> Neither the SADDLES nor the PONY BELONGS to Jim.

C. Word Intervening between Subject and Verb. A word, phrase, or clause intervening between the subject and its verb does not affect the agreement of subject and verb:

> The LEAVES on the maple tree in our front yard HAVE LOST their color.

The AUTOMOBILE, as well as our luggage and our hats and coats, WAS STOLEN.

D. Number of a Relative Pronoun.   The number of a pronoun and its verb in the relative clause is determined by the number of the antecedent of the pronoun:

John is the only one who, in spite of everything, still BELIEVES in me.

He is the one, of all these boys, WHO works hardest.

He is one of those persons WHO ARE never satisfied. (NOT: . . . who is. . . .)

In writing a sentence like the last, one is sometimes momentarily confused about the antecedent of *who,* hesitating between *one* and *persons.* The antecedent is the latter, for the meaning of the sentence seems to be "He is one of the dissatisfied PERSONS," not "He is a dissatisfied ONE."

E. *All, some, none, half.*   The number of pronouns like *all, some, none,* or *half* is determined by the number of the object of the preposition, expressed or implied, which follows the pronoun. The pronouns and their verbs are, according to this rule, singular in the following sentences:

ALL of the CROWD WAS shouting its indignation.

SOME of the APPLE on the table WAS spoiled because it had lain in the same position for several days.

HALF of the one SIDEWALK in the town IS disintegrating because it was carelessly laid by the contractor.

NONE of Joe's LETTER to me WAS intelligible.

The pronouns and their verbs in the next group of sentences, however, are correctly plural:

ALL of the CROWDS which formed throughout the week WERE indignant.

SOME of the APPLES in the barrel ARE spoiled because they have lain in the same position for several weeks.

HALF of the SIDEWALKS in the town ARE disintegrating because they were carelessly laid by the contractor.

NONE of Joe's LETTERS to me WERE intelligible.

F. *Any, each, everybody, everyone.* Pronouns like *any, each, everybody,* and *everyone* usually take a singular verb. If they are used in a plural sense, the number of the verb should be plural to accommodate the shift in meaning. (See the discussion of the number of these pronouns above, section G 6C.)

EACH of the boys WAS swinging from a limb.

EVERYBODY in the room WAS singing.

Although the next sentence might very well be "They were all enjoying themselves," the meaning is clear despite the lack of consistency.

G. Nouns Plural in Form but Singular in Meaning. A noun that is plural in form but singular in meaning or use usually takes a singular verb:

The NEWS is never very good these days.

Ten MINUTES seems like an hour at one of her parties.

A man's POLITICS is his own business.

But note these exceptions:

His MORALS leave much to be desired.

The old couple's SAVINGS were invested in government bonds.

H. Contractions. Contractions should agree with the subject in number and person:

The BELL in the tower of Monterey Hall DOESN'T sound cracked. (NOT: . . . don't sound cracked.)

Unless she wants to, SHE DOESN'T have to smile. (NOT: . . . don't have to smile.)

G8   SELECTION OF PRONOUN FORMS

	Nominative			*Objective*	
Singular		*Plural*	*Singular*		*Plural*
I		we	me		us
	you			you	
he, she, it		they	him, her, it		them
who (all persons, singular and plural)			whom (all persons, singular and plural)		

The nominative form is used whenever the pronoun is used as a subject.

$$\left.\begin{array}{l} \text{I} \\ \text{You} \\ \text{We} \\ \text{He, she, it} \\ \text{They} \end{array}\right\} \text{ate the steak hungrily.}$$

The objective form is used whenever the pronoun is used as an object.

The car hit HIM hard, but it missed US.   *Direct objects*
I gave HER my notes.   *Indirect object*

The foregoing sentences are not likely to cause much difficulty, but a few other constructions may do so.

        A. Pronoun as Subject.   A pronoun used as the subject of a clause is expected to be in the nominative form, even though the clause itself may be an object:

I know WHO will break the record. (NOT: . . . whom will. . . .)
Give the package to WHOEVER comes first. (NOT: . . . to whomever comes. . . .)

B. Pronoun and Verb with Intervening Word-Group. A word-group coming between the subject and its verb does not affect the form of the subject, if the subject is a pronoun:

I see the boy WHO, they think, took the bread. (NOT: . . . whom they think took . . . .)

We wanted to see only people WHO we knew were honest. (NOT: . . . whom we knew were . . . .)

Especially in the last sentence there may be a temptation to consider *who* as the object of *we knew.* But the fact that *who* is actually the subject of *were* may be discovered in two ways. First, strike out *we knew;* the meaning and structure of the clause will be evident. Second, search for some other word that may possibly be the subject of *were.* None can be found, and *who* remains the only possible subject.

C. Pronoun as Predicate Complement. In strictly formal writing, a pronoun used as predicate complement in the SVC pattern takes the nominative form: *It is I.* In colloquial usage, the use of *me* is widespread and standard. The use of *him, us,* and *them* in such circumstances is also common, but not the use of *her.* Formal usage:

It is HE who must free his people. (NOT: It is him . . . .)

It was SHE who determined the policy of the committee, not THEY, the members selected by popular vote. (NOT: . . . was her . . . not them . . . .)

D. Pronoun as Subject of Elliptical Clause. The subject of an elliptical clause (one in which a part has been omitted) is expected to take the nominative form:

John is as short as HE. (NOT: . . . as him.)

He likes parsnips better than I. (NOT: . . . than me.)

In the first sentence *he* is the subject of the verb in the clause "he is short," although *is short* is "understood," not expressed. In the second sentence *I* is the subject of the verb in the clause "I like them." If the second sentence were intended to mean "He likes parsnips better than he likes me," then, of course, *me* would be the correct form of the pronoun to use.

E. *Who* and *whom; one* and *you.* Historically, the written language has always followed the spoken language. *Whom* has long since passed out of good colloquial speech, according to the *Oxford English Dictionary,* and today it exists only in writing of a formal nature. As far back as 1921, Edward Sapir referred to the grammarians' insistence on maintaining the *whom* form as an interesting example of a convincing theory which goes unheeded in practice. He also gave four rather detailed reasons for the gradual drift away from *whom.*[16] Compare the degree of formality in following sentences:

> To whom was the question referred?
> Who was the question referred to?
> She did not know to whom she could turn.
> She did not know who she could turn to.

Generations of students have been brought up on the virtues of distinguishing between *who* and *whom.* For some people, the ability to differentiate between the forms is the touchstone for "good English." Frequently, however, in their desire to maintain propriety, they lean over backward and commit the error referred to by *The New Yorker* as "the ubiquitous whom."

> I spoke to the candidate whom I imagine will be our next mayor.

Among contemporary authorities, it is rather generally agreed that the distinction is disappearing even from formal prose. Standard American English today finds *Who did you see?* less affected than *Whom did you see?* General usage is always preferable to one that may strike the reader or listener as pretentious or stuffy. When in doubt, use *who.* The one position where *whom* is required is that following a preposition:

> Send not to know for whom the bell tolls.

---

[16] *Language* (New York: Harcourt, Brace and Company, 1921), pp. 156–161.

The formal tone of John Donne's sentence has its modern equivalent in

> This is the man of whom I was speaking.

But only the most vigorous defenders of formality would frown on

> This is the man (that) I was speaking about.

The *who-whom* situation has a counterpart in the pronouns *you* and *one*, when used in the impersonal sense.

> One should always be prepared to do his best.
> You should always be prepared to do your best.

Because English has no impersonal pronoun (equivalent to the German *man* or the French *on*), and because the use of *one* sometimes results in an excessively formal tone, the growing tendency has been to use *you* in the impersonal form. This practice has its dangers, however; careless use may result in accidental insult:

> When you are released from jail, you are given a suit and $20.

The best advice on questions of usage is for the student to know the possibilities and the alternatives, and to choose the appropriate tone and level of usage for any particular piece of writing. (See Chapter V, section D 4, for a fuller discussion of usage.) We unconsciously practice linguistic adaptation to audience in all our utterances, written and spoken. Figuratively speaking, we are always shifting our verbal gears as we move through the day and find ourselves communicating with different kinds of people for different kinds of reasons in different kinds of situations; but this shifting is so unconscious that it may be compared to an automatic transmission. To tell you, then, that you should choose appropriately among the levels of discourse is to give advice that applies equally well to every other topic dealt with in this chapter. It is another way of saying that you should raise to the conscious level that easy mastery of your language which you have possessed since the age of six. A conscious, but not self-conscious, mastery of the intricate system of interlocking parts that is the English sentence will enable you to express yourself confidently, accurately, and in "good English."

EXERCISES

A. The Form Classes

I. Write ten sentences illustrating the ten noun positions. Try to use the same noun in as many sentences as you can.

II. By supplying appropriate suffixes, change the words in list 1 to nouns. By supplying appropriate suffixes, change the words in list 2 to adjectives.

1	2
engage	analysis
detract	temper
fanatic	continue
consistent	marvel
false	angel
long	consul
fluent	truth
leak	fiend
comply	bleed
young	honor
sober	create
clear	despise
sane	mercy
separate	fury
drape	brass

III. Using each of the suffixes which you have had to employ in Exercise II, find other examples in which verbs and adjectives become nouns.

IV. Write sentences showing most of the following words being used both as pronouns and as determiners. *One word on the list cannot be used in two ways.*

enough, this, her, seven, few, several, none, such, another, one, whose

V. Verbals

1. Write sentences showing verbal phrases in the following functions: (a) subject, (b) direct object, (c) object of preposition, (d) adverb, (e) adjective.

2. Use the same *ing* word in the following constructions: (a) subject, (b) direct object, (c) object of preposition, (d) modifier of direct object, (e) part of a verb phrase.

3. Use the same infinitive (to ———) in the following constructions: (a) subject, (b) direct object, (c) predicate complement, (d) adverb, (e) adjective.

VI. For each of the following sentences, supply the appropriate form of the verbs for which the infinitive is given in parentheses.

1. The news was (to broadcast) at every hour of the day.

2. My suit was (to fit) by a tailor I had never seen before.

3. The burglar (to slink) quickly into the shadows as I came around the corner.

4. By the time the plumber gets here the sink will have (to overflow).

5. As I (to sit) in the chair I counted the triangular panes in the window.

6. The large tree trunk had been (to saw) in two within a few minutes.

7. When I passed him he (to thrust) the ticket into my hand.

8. You will find that most of their clothes have been (to weave) by hand.

9. The duck (to dive) into the water when he heard the noise.

10. He stopped a moment and (to light) the lantern again.

VII. Rewrite the following sentences so that the verbs are in the active voice.

1. The idea was held by us that perhaps our car had been stolen by the suspicious-looking character who had been seen earlier.

2. The professor was asked by his students whether the examination had been marked yet.

3. He is regarded with distrust.

4. At our house, Sunday brunch is eaten with great pleasure by all, including the small children.

5. Mitchell broke down the gate, strode vigorously through the hallway, and then the last door was approached quickly.

VIII. Choose either the adjective or the adverb from within the parentheses in each of the following sentences. Justify your choice. Where is either choice justifiable?

1. Whenever the door slammed, Father frowned (fierce, fiercely).

2. Whenever the door slammed, Father looked (fierce, fiercely).

3. He does not feel as (bad, badly) as he looks.

4. (Slow, slowly) and deliberately Sam Jones strapped on his gun belt.

5. (Slow, slowly) Sam Jones is noted for his deliberation.

6. Helen looked (exquisite, exquisitely) in her evening dress.

7. Though her grade depended on it, Martha could not speak (distinct, distinctly).

8. It is a (distinct, distinctly) pleasure to introduce Dr. Kemp tonight.

9. It is (distinct, distinctly) a pleasure to introduce Dr. Kemp tonight.

10. It is a (distinct, distinctly) great pleasure to introduce Dr. Kemp tonight.

11. The (usual, usually) practice is for us to go to the Coffee Shop after class.

12. The practice is for us to (usual, usually) go to the Coffee Shop after class.

13. Judging from his comments, this man must be (stark, starkly) mad.

14. (Obedient, obediently), we returned home.

15. All food tastes (good, well) out-of-doors.

IX. Use each of the following words in two sentences, showing how it belongs to two form classes on the basis of its position in the structure:

iron, guard, bow, smell, bridge, stomach, mount, snarl, mop, intellectual, stone, mouth, shelter, expert, gross, book, liberal, weed, pet, kick

X. Make your own list of twenty words which belong to more than one form class. Specify the classes to which each belongs, and illustrate by using the words in sentences.

XI. Write sentences in which the following constructions occur:

1. A noun modifying a noun
2. A noun modifying a verb
3. An adverb modifying a noun
4. An adverb modifying a verb
5. An adverb modifying an adjective
6. An adverb modifying an adverb
7. An adjective modifying a noun
8. An adjective modifying an adjective

XII. Complete each of the following skeleton sentences, which contain nothing but function words, by adding whatever *form class* words are called for by the structure. Note the signals.

EXAMPLE: "All the _____ly _____ _____ and the very _____ _____ were _____ing about the _____ at _____."

POSSIBLE VERSIONS: All the gaily colored birds and the very little animals were dancing about the sands at midnight.

All the thoroughly trained troops and the very colorful banners were visible about the field at reveille.

All the somberly clad Puritans and the very devout travelers were thinking about the sermon at Boston.

1. Although _____ by (a/an) _____, the _____ _____ (is/was) _____.

2. When _____ _____ the _____, his _____ _____ _____ ed the _____.

3. There _____ the very _____ _____ that _____ _____ _____ly.

4. The _____ and rather _____ _____ were _____ in the _____ of the _____ _____.

5. My _____ _____ (a/an) _____, (and/but) _____ does not _____ _____ in the _____.

6. After the _____, the _____, the _____ _____, and the _____ and _____ _____ were _____.

7. A _____ with (a/an) _____ _____ _____, _____ ing in (a/the) _____, was _____ the _____.

8. It _____ a _____ the _____ to which _____ had _____.

9. Some of _____ (may/might) _____ the _____, (but/and) _____ must _____ the _____; however, it _____ a _____ _____.

10. Because the _____ _____ and his _____ _____ were _____ in (a/an) _____, _____ was _____.

XIII. Write one nonsense sentence for each of the high-frequency sentence patterns—SV, SVO, SVoO, SVC, SVOC. Be sure that you are able to specify the signals in each sentence which carry the structural meaning.

B. Word-Groups: Clauses and Phrases

I. Write sentences according to the specifications given below.

1. Use a noun clause as subject of a sentence.
2. Use a noun clause as direct object.
3. Use an adjective clause to modify a direct object.
4. Use a noun clause as object of a preposition.
5. Start a simple sentence with a participial phrase used as subject.
6. Start a complex sentence with a participial phrase.
7. Start a complex sentence with an adverbial clause.
8. Use compound subjects and compound transitive verbs in a simple sentence.
9. In a compound sentence, use one intransitive and one linking verb; use an infinitive phrase.
10. In a compound-complex sentence, use compound subjects in one independent clause and compound verbs in the other; use a transitional conjunction.
11. Rewrite and expand the sentence "He lost his hat" in six different ways, making whatever changes are necessary in order to *begin* each version with a different grammatical element: (a) prepositional phrase;

(b) participial phrase used as adjective; (c) participial phrase used as noun; (d) infinitive phrase used as noun; (e) adverbial clause; (f) noun clause.

12. Write a simple sentence containing the following four elements: (a) a participial phrase used as subject; (b) an infinitive phrase; (c) a prepositional adjective phrase; (d) a prepositional adverbial phrase.

II. Write a short sentence for each of the high-frequency patterns below. Then play with each sentence, revising it through the specified sequence of steps.

1. SV
    a. Add one-word adjective and adverbial modifiers.
    b. Add two prepositional phrases.
    c. Change the verb to a verb phrase.
    d. Convert the clause into a dependent clause and hook it into an independent clause, using a subordinator.
    e. Replace the prepositional phrases with dependent clauses.
    f. Invert the emphasis; that is, make the present independent clause the dependent clause and raise one of the dependent clauses to the status of main clause.

2. SVO
    a. Add one-word adjective and adverbial modifiers.
    b. Add two prepositional phrases.
    c. Change the verb to a verb phrase.
    d. Add one adjective and one adverbial clause; start the sentence with the adverbial clause.
    e. Add appositives to both subject and direct object.

3. SVC
    a. Change the verb to a verb phrase denoting futurity.
    b. Add two prepositional phrases.
    c. Start the sentence with a new participial phrase.
    d. Change prepositional phrases to dependent clauses.
    e. Add an independent clause, using a co-ordinating conjunction.

4. SVoO
    a. Change the direct object into a noun clause.
    b. Change the indirect object into a prepositional phrase.
    c. Start the sentence with an adverbial clause.

    d. Add a participial phrase to precede the adverbial clause.

    e. Make whatever changes are necessary in order to turn your sentence "inside out"; that is, the object of the preposition is now to be the subject of the sentence.

III. Identify the basic pattern in each of the following sentences. Then, for each sentence, show the relationship of the various word-groups to the basic sentence pattern. Sort out the dependent clauses, sort out the phrases, and then indicate how both kinds of word-groups help to amplify the pattern. (Illustrative procedure above, pages 93-98.)

1. In the friendly household of Hans, the unlettered woodchopper who had rescued him from the pack of wolves, Caspar grew to maturity knowing the meaning of togetherness.

2. With their cruel-looking knives clutched in their brawny fists, the two giant keelboatmen bared their teeth at each other across the space that had been cleared for them by a hushed and expectant crowd.

3. If you ever return to New Orleans, you might get me the name of that superb little French restaurant that is tucked away in an alley off Bourbon Street, the place where we ate the best shrimp gumbo on earth.

4. I don't know what this modern generation expects to make of itself.

5. After a trip in which we had lost our luggage in London, paid plenty for pleasure in Paris, and run through our ready cash in Rome, home seemed good to us.

6. The absent-minded professor, with a faraway look in his eye and tugging at his ear as was his habit, was walking slowly across campus that morning, when I stepped in his path and tried to get his attention.

7. Regardless of the pleas of urgency and necessity which have been advanced, I call your behavior disgraceful in permitting this scandalous situation to continue.

8. He remained an active member of the organization long after the rest of his colleagues who had founded it in a burst of enthusiasm were concerning themselves with other matters.

9. The poor man used to say, with an ironical smile, that he was giving his children the best education that he could not afford.

10. People like you and me gather in a darkened hall to watch other people feign passions that none of us have the right to have.

11. What I heard him say on those memorable occasions when we walked together in the woods beyond his pond was simply inspiring.

12. During those walks, he taught me the simple but universal truths that I have lived by ever since.

13. In giving voice to the longing of every man for a decent and just society, he struck profoundly human chords, without descending to the commonplaces of political slogan-makers.

14. Despite the opposition of the professionals to a relative new-comer, and the fear of the conservative representatives that they were backing a wild-eyed radical, the delegates, by an overwhelming majority, today chose Judge Woods their standard-bearer in the forth-coming election.

15. For the execution of this delicate mission, I have chosen among the various brave volunteers who offered to sacrifice their lives so that the rest of us might return safely home.

IV. The sentences below illustrate various kinds of ambiguities. Explain the reason for the confusion in each instance, and re-write the sentences.

1. The party was held up in the mountains.

2. The mob in the streets was revolting.

3. The girl was playing with the doll that she had received at her birthday party in the back yard.

4. I read my history assignment about the outbreak of the Civil War in my bath.

5. Frozen solid, she could not get the tray of ice cubes out of the refrigerator.

6. The enemy will you defeat.

7. "He's trying, all right."
   "Yes—very."

8. Creeping silently around the campfire, the wagon train was soon surrounded by Indians.

9. The amount of money which I can borrow is hardly enough to make all the repairs on the automobile that I need.

10. Her salon was visited by many famous artists, cool and refreshing.

11. "Tattooing in the rear." (A sign at 516 S. Main St., Los Angeles.)

12. The professor spoke sharply to a student in the class that was half asleep.

13. Being a later Puritan, Jonathan Edwards' God was a God of mercy as well as of wrath.

14. After swimming in the river all afternoon, Jack came up with a girl that he brought to the party.

15. This is a movie about Japan, which we have wanted to see for a long time.

16. We watched them crown the King from the remote gallery where we were sitting.

17. Casey Stengel is warming up a pitcher who was knocked out yesterday in the bullpen.

18. Just returned from two years in Iceland, the Statue of Liberty was a welcome sight to him.

19. They're striking out in Detroit this afternoon.

20. What practicing physicians do on their charity cases is a measure of their sensibilities.

C. Agreement and Selection

I. Rewrite the following sentences to eliminate vague or faulty reference of pronouns.

1. They say it will be cooler tomorrow.

2. Every worker at Oak Ridge must show his or her pass before being admitted.

3. The magician pulled the rabbit out of his silk hat, waved his hand twice, and suddenly it disappeared.

4. When one is trying to write, it will help if you concentrate on it.

5. It is said that every dog will have their day.

6. Sometimes the lights flickered unsteadily, and sometimes they flashed a regular pattern of alternating longs and shorts. This was a signal I could not understand.

7. People in Florida boast of their sunshine, which gets quite monotonous after a while.

8. The jury were silent as its foreman stood up to deliver the verdict.

9. It is true that each of us has his weakness, but we cannot therefore refuse our help to others on the ground that they are not perfect, for this is a denial of what it means to be human.

10. This is the time of year when outdoor cooking is at its peak. While usually done with prepared charcoal, sharp sticks to cook hot dogs are frequently used. This is where oleander comes in. Death of cattle is not uncommon in California where they occasionally eat dry oleander leaves when they become mixed with hay or other dry feed.

II. From within the parentheses, select the verb form which agrees with its subject.

1. My favorite fruit (is, are) cherries.

2. On the hill behind the trees (stands, stand) a curious stone tower.

3. Most of the people in the neighboring town (is, are) simple and pious.

4. The flock of crows (was, were) settling in the cornfield.

5. The sum and substance of their deliberations (is, are) that you may not go.

6. Each of the candidates (has, have) some merits.

7. For candidates for the B.S., either chemistry or physics (is, are) required.

8. *Tales of a Traveller* (is, are) a collection of some of Washington Irving's short stories.

9. Irving's legends of the Alhambra (is, are) also interesting short stories.

10. I, the Grand High Mogul and Chief Potentate, (speaks, speak).

11. To me, five dollars still (seems, seem) like a great sum of money.

12. After the stillness and the dark (comes, come) the dawn.

13. The cow or one of the horses (has, have) run into the fence.

14. The estate, including 250 acres of pasture, a stable, and a mansion of sixty rooms, (was, were) sold at auction.

15. The House of Representatives (has, have) passed legislation vitally affecting your pocketbook.

III. In some of the following sentences, the nominative and objective pronoun forms are properly used, according to strict conventional usage; in others they are not. If the form in any sentence is not the conventional one as employed in formal written discourse, rewrite that sentence.

1. When you have finished reading this magazine, please give it to him and me.

2. It was he who spoke first.

3. Whom do you think should have it first?

4. Bill, who gave me my first job, and for whom, consequently, I have the highest regard, will be in town this weekend.

5. Just between you and I, this information is secret.

6. If you practice your backhand, you will soon play better tennis than me.

7. Who shall I say is calling?

8. Fred is the boy who, they agree, will make his way in the world.

9. I am heartbroken because she loves him more than me.

10. I have always felt that it was them who should have been penalized.

11. I have always felt that it was people like them who should have been penalized.

12. The society column reported that mother and me had gone to Florida.

13. The scoundrel implied that I was no better than he.

14. Mr. Harris is a man of whom I have heard the most glowing remarks.

15. As we trudged wearily home, the rain began to fall upon her and I.

III | Punctuation: Pointing up Meaning

Read the following sentences aloud:

What is this thing called Love?
What is this thing called? Love?

Are you ever late to class?
Are you ever late to class!

My aunt who lives in Boston never reads a modern novel.
My aunt, who lives in Boston, never reads a modern novel.

Would you like an orange, little boy?
Would you like an orange little boy?

It is clear that similar arrangements of words may differ quite radically in meaning, depending on the way in which these arrangements are read. The stress, pitch, and pauses we impart to a word-group thus constitute another system of signals by which we help shape the meaning of a given utterance. This system is apart from and yet important to sentence structure.

In speech, which is man's primary medium of communication, our intonation patterns and signals take care of themselves. We drop the voice at the close of a declarative sentence; we usually hold it up or raise it at the end of a question. With either we make a distinct pause to inform the hearer that we have completed a sentence and are ready to begin a new one. We make slighter, less noticeable pauses at the end of introductory word-groups before proceeding with the main word-group. So with the other

123

elements of expression—by tone of voice, facial movement, and gesture we punctuate our speech.

But when we set down our thoughts in writing, when we strive to communicate with someone who cannot see and hear us, we must find an equally effective method of marking off the sections of an idea, of showing how one portion is related to another, and which part is the more important. Although it is not true of all marks, most punctuation is the written version of this vocal marking by means of which the logical and grammatical structure of our sentence is quickly made clear to a reader.

The importance of the intonation patterns in speech can hardly be overemphasized, although we take them for granted. It is a failure to grasp these signals that accounts for the difficulty many people have when traveling abroad. Although they may have extensive vocabularies and an excellent reading knowledge of the foreign language, they find that they cannot "hear" the language. It is not that the native speaks exceptionally rapidly; it is simply that the visitor has not yet habituated his ear to the pattern of the speech flow. That is why the laborious memorization of long lists of words or of the conjugations of verbs is not the best way to learn a foreign language.

The eleven symbols which constitute the punctuation system of English are attempts to transfer the intonation patterns onto the printed page. As a matter of strict historical fact, the space between words is also a punctuation symbol, but for practical as well as metaphysical reasons it is not normally so considered. It is hard for us to think of a blank space as being a something; furthermore, except when we are trying to decide whether to write *inkwell, ink well,* or *ink-well,* we are not much troubled about the space between words. Yet, at one time in our linguistic history, writtenwordswerestrungtogetherlikethis. Trying to decipher that last clause should make you appreciate the importance of the blank space and offer up silent thanks to the scribe who first thought of separating individual words.

Most of our so-called rules of punctuation came into being as a result of the development of printing in the sixteenth and seventeenth centuries. After rather eccentric and individualized punctuation had been the rule for some time, with each printer blithely following his own whims and impulses, a more or less standardized system of practices grew up among the printing houses. These conventions, with some changes in the direction of simplifying and reducing the amount of punctuation, are what we today refer to as the rules of punctuation.

Some marks of punctuation are "significant"; that is, they vitally affect meaning. Note the difference between these sentences (previously cited in another connection):

> I will not kiss you; however, you urge me.
> I will not kiss you, however you urge me.

But whether the salutation in a letter ("Dear John") is followed by a comma (,), a dash (—), or a colon (:) in no way affects the meaning. The question of which mark to use here is one merely of language etiquette. Such marks are "nonsignificant." Significant or nonsignificant, however, all the uses of punctuation marks are conventional. Writers, editors, and publishers have agreed to follow, more or less closely, certain usages which they hope will make for easier comprehension by readers. The Chicago *Tribune* has one set of conventions and *The New York Times* has another; both of these differ from the conventions printed in the Modern Language Association *Style Sheet*. But the differences are minor as compared to the general agreement about which marks to use in certain situations.

The fact that even these generally agreed upon conventions are sometimes disregarded is not sufficient reason for you to forget them. When a writer like John Dos Passos, for example, seems to abandon conventional practices entirely (in certain sections of his novel *U.S.A.*), he is aiming at certain carefully calculated effects—he is not simply forgetting to punctuate. The one basic principle to be kept in mind is that significant punctuation is a system of signals to promote clarity. Therefore, you should use only those marks that are necessary to make clear your meaning. You know how you want your words to sound in your reader's inner ear; you are the one who should decide what punctuation marks will best reproduce the intonation pattern. Reading your written work aloud will, in many cases, help you decide questions of punctuation, for the intonation pattern will select the punctuation for you—and for your reader.

We should think of punctuation, therefore, not as a set of rigid rules but as a set of conventions upon which writers and readers more or less agree, and which we should know about and observe if we want our writing to be understood. Most of the major conventions of our day are summarized in the sections below.

P1 THE PERIOD, THE QUESTION MARK, THE EXCLAMATION MARK

The period (.), the question mark (?), and the exclamation mark (!) are most commonly used to show that a sentence (whether completely expressed or elliptical) is ended. The use of each mark depends upon the kind of sentence it concludes and upon the emphasis the writer wishes to give. Each of the three marks also has certain other conventional uses that will be explained.

A. A period is used after a declarative or an imperative sentence unless it is excited or very emphatic in tone (see section G below):

The national income for 1958 was larger—and the cost of living higher—than ever before.

Cheers. More cheers. The crowd seemed unable to stop.

Please get that typed as soon as possible.

Notice that the period is used after fragmentary sentences used as complete sentences. For a discussion of the fragmentary sentence see Chapter I, section K 1.

B. A period is generally used after an abbreviation:

In a pompous manner he announced that he was Thomas Smith, M.D., our new instructor in anatomy.

The show will not be over until 9 P.M.

When an abbreviation followed by a period comes at the end of a sentence, only one period is necessary to punctuate both the abbreviation and the sentence. For a discussion of the use of abbreviations, see section M 6.

After letters standing for agencies or institutions with long titles familiar to everyone, the periods are omitted: AFL–CIO, UCLA, TV, AEC.

        C. Three periods, also called ellipsis dots or points, are used to show the omission, from quoted matter, of a word or group of words. If the omission occurs at the end of a sentence, the ellipsis dots *precede* the end punctuation of that sentence.

Dr. Thompson wrote, ". . . he will not recover for a long time . . . ." (*Originally:* "In spite of your care, he will not recover for a long time, for reasons which I cannot reveal now.")

He asked, "Where . . . were you on the night of the big fire . . . ?" (*Originally:* "Where in the world were you on the night of the big fire that burned down the barn?")

For the omission of entire sentences or paragraphs, see section M 2A.

Ellipsis dots are also used—chiefly in dialogue or soliloquy—to indicate broken or uncompleted statements. This is a practice to be used sparingly by the inexperienced writer.

"No," Henry mused, "I don't think that she will want . . . ." His mother waited. "Want what?"

"Oh, nothing. I was just thinking out loud. But what if . . . no, that's impossible," he concluded.

        D. A question mark is used at the end of an interrogative sentence:

Who gave you that watch? Are you coming to the game?

But notice that in an indirect quotation cast in the form of a declarative sentence no question mark is used:

He then asked when we would be ready.

E. A question mark in parentheses may be used to indicate doubt:

Chaucer was born in 1340 (?) and died in 1400.

F. A question mark in parentheses, used to indicate irony or sarcasm, is usually weak and ineffective:

We had such a pleasant time that everyone left two hours before the party was supposed to be over. (NOT: We had such a pleasant (?) time that everyone left two hours before the party was supposed to be over.)

G. The exclamation mark is used after an exclamatory sentence, an excited command, or an expression of strong emotion:

The British are coming!
Look! That tree is falling.
Get in the car, quick!

The exclamation mark, like the question mark, should not be used in a weak attempt to indicate sarcasm or satire.

P2   THE SEMICOLON

The semicolon (;) is used primarily between two grammatically independent clauses that are so closely related in thought that a period would cause too definite a break for the meaning intended. In other words, the semicolon is a mark showing a definite separation of thought but not as sharp a one as the period. To show this separation is its principal function today; it does, however, have certain other conventional uses. Both the principal use and some of the minor uses are explained and illustrated below.

A. The semicolon is used between two closely related independent clauses not joined by a co-ordinating conjunction:

He will not bring the picture to me; therefore I shall have to go to his studio for it.

Douglas had had three accidents within three weeks' time; his mother was nervous as he backed out of the driveway onto the street.

1) Notice that (a) if a comma instead of a semicolon is used between clauses such as those described above, a comma splice is the result, and that (b) if no punctuation is used, a run-on sentence is the result.

a) I deliberately avoid such bores; they have already spoiled many a pleasant evening for me. (NOT: I deliberately avoid such bores, they have already spoiled many a pleasant evening for me.)

b) You may believe what he says; I cannot. (NOT: You may believe what he says I cannot.)

2) Notice that a transitional conjunction does not perform the function of a co-ordinating conjunction.

Of course I like you; however, my sentiment does not influence my decision regarding your grade. (NOT: Of course I like you, however, my sentiment does not influence my decision regarding your grade.)

She missed her bus; therefore she was late in arriving. (NOT: She missed her bus, therefore she was late in arriving.)

(See Chapter I, section K 2.)

B. A semicolon may be used between two independent clauses in addition to a co-ordinating conjunction if the writer wants to show separation less sharp than that implied by a period but sharper than that implied by a comma:

A cynic would have hoarsely laughed; but there were no cynics left.—
ERIC LINKLATER

The boy started to obey him mechanically; but his uncle checked
him.—FRANCIS BRETT YOUNG

In other compound sentences the same authors, wishing to give
an impression of a less definite separation, use commas:

She sang another song, but her audience would not be satisfied.—
ERIC LINKLATER

Even the cramped berth irked him less, for two of its occupants had
removed themselves.—FRANCIS BRETT YOUNG

Only the writer himself can decide whether a semicolon or a
comma should be used between two independent clauses connected by a co-ordinating conjunction. The decision, as we have
said, must depend upon the degree of separation desired. In
making it, the author must know exactly what he wants to say
and exactly the emphasis he wants the reader to get.

**C. Although a co-ordinating conjunction may be
present, a semicolon should be used to separate two or more independent clauses if one of the clauses contains commas within it:**

In the midst of the garden, just below the fountain, grew the lilac
bush; and it sent its fragrance into the window of our house.

This added meaning is what I am accustomed to term an overtone
in words; and it is manifest that, in view of the necessity for economy
in poetic art, those words which are the richest and deepest in overtones will be preferred . . . .—GEORGE E. WOODBERRY

**D. A semicolon may be used for clarity between
members of a series of parallel sentence elements which, although
not necessarily complete, are in themselves long and involved and
have internal punctuation:**

The captain, with a worried look on his face, explained that he had
had to retire from the bridge for a moment, to go down to the engine
room; that while he was in the hold of the ship he felt a slight jar,
hardly more than a brief tremble of the boat; and that he had not

realized that there had been an accident until the mate told him
about it.

I chose to go by the longest route because, although the road was
rough, the scenery was very fine; because I wanted to see my old friend,
Herbert Jost, who lived in the southern part of the country; and because, not knowing that you were waiting for me, I thought that I had
no need to hurry home.

Please send me the following order as soon as you possibly can:
2000 sheets of white typewriter paper, your best quality; 1500 en-
velopes, size no. 11; and 4 silk typewriter ribbons.

Notice that if even only one element of the series contains internal punctuation the semicolon should be used between all
elements.

P3   THE COLON

**The colon (:) is a punctuation mark used principally to introduce
or to emphasize the material that follows it.** Its appearance
causes the reader to anticipate the information that follows it.
Perhaps its effectiveness depends partly upon the fact that today
it is not used as often as are most other marks of punctuation;
when a reader sees a colon, consequently, he feels that something
important, possibly something more important than usual, is
coming; and he is in an interested, and thus a receptive, mood.
Overuse of the colon, of course, soon destroys its effectiveness.

**A. A colon is used to introduce formal or lengthy
statements, questions, or quotations:**

Mr. Chairman, I should like to make the following suggestion: Mr.
Smith should be informed of our proposal as soon as possible, so that
he may prepare to leave the city at once.

Senator Hopkins rose slowly to his feet and said, in a deliberate
manner: "Before this question is put to the vote . . . ."

To all who believe that this plan cannot succeed I want to ask this question: Do you know of anyone who has proposed a better scheme?

In the introduction to his *Collected Poems,* Vachel Lindsay has written:

> I was stuffed with family history in my helpless infancy. The last of my tribe to reach this land arrived in Baltimore in 1800. An aunt of mine once told me that there was one red Indian among the ancestors . . . .

B. A colon is generally used to introduce a series to be emphasized, whether the series consists of words, phrases, clauses, or sentences:

The following list gives you some idea of what you should take on a camping trip: a complete change of clothing, two blankets, a skillet, . . .

As the dog looked up at me, he seemed to be asking these questions: Where, in the name of heaven, have you been? Why didn't you take me with you? And when am I going to get something to eat?

It seems to me that we have before us three possibilities of action: We can accept his proposal and pretend to like it. We can reject it completely and fight to the bitter end. Or we can compromise, if we do not antagonize him too much first.

C. Most modern writers use a colon before introductory and explanatory expressions like *namely, i.e.,* and *that is,* especially if the expressions are followed by clauses:

Few teachers have decided how best to solve the last problem I am going to discuss: namely, what subjects do students like to write about?

Another type of story is frequently found in these magazines: that is, it is found in the copies of the magazines which I have seen.

D. A colon may be used for rhetorical effect to introduce an explanation, a consequence, a contrast, or an elaboration:

Martin never went near the quarry: two of his brothers had been killed there in the explosion in the dynamite shed.

She had worked hard for many years: now she was the head of her department.

He had intended to be an engineer: today he is teaching school.

He was a man of few words: he never even owned a dictionary.

In all of these examples, other marks of punctuation could be used without loss in either clarity or precision, but with different effects.

E. A colon is conventionally used after the salutation of a business letter:

Dear Madam: My dear Sir: Dear Dr. Oviatt:

F. A colon is conventionally used between Biblical chapter numbers and verse numbers, when they are cited; between numerical expressions of an hour plus a certain number of minutes; and between title and subtitle of a written work.

He then quoted I Samuel 25:7.

The announcer said that the train would arrive at 6:27.

The name of the article is "Holden and Huck: The Odysseys of Youth."

P4   THE COMMA

The comma (,) is a mark of punctuation used entirely within sentences.   It helps make clear the grammatical structure of similar parts of the same sentence and shows the rank and function of relatively nonessential introductory, explanatory, or identifying parts of the sentence. The comma sets off units of writing in somewhat the same way that a short pause or a slightly emphatic tone of voice may emphasize certain words or sentence elements in speech; it is frequently described as being a "slight stop," in contrast to the period, described as a "full stop."

The comma is the most frequently used mark of punctuation, and at the same time it is one of the most valuable, especially if handled with common sense. The common-sense rule for the use of the comma is to use it where you want your reader to hear it.

Two general principles govern the use of the comma: A single

comma is used to separate sentence elements; a pair of commas is used to set off an element from the rest of the sentence. These principles are embodied in the adage, "Between subject and predicate use two commas or none." Subject and predicate, that is to say, should never be separated, although certain intervening elements may (as in this sentence) be logically set off.

A. A comma is generally used before the co-ordinating conjunction that joins two independent clauses:

Ralph looked at the sailboat, but George was more interested in the motor launch.

I wish you would do it, for Mother will be pleased.

Clyde would not go near the insane-looking character without me, and my presence did not give him any too much courage.

The sentences given above demonstrate the reason why a comma is needed before the co-ordinating conjunction when it is used to connect clauses. *But* and *for* may be prepositions as well as conjunctions. The comma before either one tells the reader instantaneously that it is a co-ordinating conjunction; the lack of punctuation indicates that in most instances it is a preposition. In the third sentence the comma before *and* prevents misunderstanding; without it one might first read the sentence as "Clyde would not go near the insane-looking character without me and my presence . . . ."

The comma is not necessary before *and* when it joins co-ordinate clauses if the clauses are short and if the meaning of the sentence is clear without the punctuation:

At Mary's party John played the piano and I sang.

The flame died down and Martha rose silently to add more fuel.

B. Transitional conjunctions, words of direct address, and interjections, which introduce or guide thought and establish mood, are usually set off from the rest of the sentence by commas:

After lunch, HOWEVER, we were permitted to go to the show.

We must not, CONSEQUENTLY, expect very much from his effort.

PORTER, please shine my shoes.

I told you, MARY, that you should read that book.

WELL, I did not expect to see you here.

NO, I shall not be in town for long.

OH, stop doing that!

Although the word "oh" is always set off by commas, the word "O," when used in direct address, is not separated from the word which follows it:

O King, grant me thy favor.

C. All modifiers that are clearly nonrestrictive are usually set off by commas. A restrictive modifier limits the scope of the noun or pronoun; it modifies or adds a specific and necessary qualification to the meaning of the verb. In the sentence "Only men *who have red hair* are eligible," the adjective clause is restrictive because it limits the scope of the noun *men.* In the sentence "He left *because he had to,*" the adverb clause is restrictive because it specifically qualifies the action. A nonrestrictive modifier, conversely, is one that, although helpful, is not absolutely necessary for identification or understanding of quality or action. The nonrestrictive element can be dropped from the sentence without seriously altering its meaning; the restrictive is an essential part of the sentence idea. The commas around, or before or after, nonrestrictive modifiers therefore indicate to the reader that the writer considers those modifiers to be less important than the modifiers that he shows, by position or by nonpunctuation, to be restrictive.

1) **Almost all verbal phrases and many prepositional phrases are nonrestrictive:**

Singing loudly and cheerfully, the soldiers marched by.

The wind, now blowing harder than ever, filled the sails.

Eugene O'Neill's plays, bound in blue cloth, stand upon the table.

Having exhausted himself the day before, he was unable to keep up.

After hearing about the offer from Dayton, Martin would not listen to me.

2) **A writer may often consider simple adjectives and adverbs to be nonrestrictive:**

The hunted man, desperate, fought with all possible fury.
The wall, high and impregnable, failed to stop him.
He replied, quietly but firmly, that he would return soon.

Notice that usually adjectives and adverbs, when considered nonrestrictive, follow the words they modify. But not all modifiers that follow the modified word are nonrestrictive, as can be seen in the following sentences:

He walked quickly away.
He replied quietly but firmly that he would return soon.

Notice that the last sentence has previously been punctuated as if it contained nonrestrictive adverbs, and that either the use or the omission of the commas is correct, depending upon what the author intends: with commas, the action of replying and the reply itself is stressed; without commas, the manner of the replying is stressed. To repeat, you will know how you want to punctuate the sentence if you read it aloud. Restriction and nonrestriction are as much a matter of ear as of logic.

D. A comma is generally used after a long adverbial element at the beginning of a sentence.

Because the performance was so dull that it seemed interminable, we left after the second act.

By means of his great physical strength and almost unbelievable energy, Joel was able to accomplish far more than any of us.

If, however, the adverbial elements at the beginning of a sentence are short, and if the omission will cause no confusion, the comma after them is not necessary:

By tomorrow morning you will have forgotten most of the story.
When I get back from the store I will write that letter for you.

E. An absolute phrase (a noun with its participle grammatically independent of the rest of the sentence) should be set off by commas.

The wind having died down, we started out again.

F. Words, phrases, and clauses in series should be separated by commas:

The colors chosen for the flag were RED, WHITE, and BLUE.

Tom's action seemed HASTY, UNNECESSARY, and RUDE.

He pledged the allegiance OF HIS HANDS, OF HIS HEAD, and OF HIS HEART.

FROM CONVERSATIONS WITH HIS FRIENDS, FROM PROTESTS VOICED IN MASS MEETINGS, and FROM ANGRY EDITORIALS IN THE TWO NEWSPAPERS, the mayor soon discovered that the citizens were opposed to his highhanded action.

BECAUSE THE STUDENTS WHISPERED CONTINUALLY, BECAUSE THE WIND RATTLED THE PANES IN THE WINDOWS, and BECAUSE THE SPEAKER TALKED IN A TIMID VOICE, the exercises were a failure.

Notice that a comma is usually placed before the co-ordinating conjunction that joins the last two elements of a series of three or more co-ordinate elements:

She is alert, interesting, AND beautiful.

The book did not have interesting information, valuable diagrams, OR vivid pictures.

There is a growing tendency in contemporary writing to omit the comma before the conjunction in a series. Most writers, however, still prefer the comma. The comma *must* be used before the conjunction when omission would confuse the reader:

She was very handsome, slim and straight.—THOMAS BEER. (Does *slim and straight* merely explain what Beer meant by *handsome,* or are all three adjectives intended to modify *she?*)

G. A comma is generally used between modifiers of the same word if the modifiers are co-ordinate; if they are not co-ordinate, the comma is omitted. There are two ways to test co-ordination. One way is to use the co-ordinator *and* between the modifiers; the other is to try reversing the order of the modifiers. If the modifiers are co-ordinate, the meaning will remain the same despite the alterations.

He was wearing his ragged, comfortable Levis.
He preferred them to his blue flannel slacks.

Ragged and comfortable is the same as *comfortable and ragged.* But *blue flannel* cannot become either *blue and flannel* or *flannel blue.* The original word-group says that the flannel slacks are blue; the adjectives, not being co-ordinate modifiers, are left unpunctuated.

H. For the sake of emphasis and clarity a comma may be used to set off contrasting elements:

Not for your sake, but for my own, will I do it.
Do it, not because I ask you to, but because you want to.

I. A comma should be used wherever it is needed to avoid ambiguity. You are your own first critic:

Long before, Marion had heard it said that college was easier than high school. (NOT: Long before Marion had heard it said that college was easier than high school.)
The claim agent paid the money to Burt, and Jess received nothing. (NOT: The claim agent paid the money to Burt and Jess received nothing.)
When the tide is in, the boats come right up to the dock. (NOT: When the tide is in the boats come right up to the dock.)

J. When *such as* is used to introduce an example, it is preceded but not followed by a comma:

She was interested in many odd subjects, such as magic, astrology, and mind reading.

K. A comma is used to separate introductory or explanatory elements like *he said* from the direct quotations they introduce or explain:

She screamed, "There he goes!"
"I am certain you won't do," I assured him.

"Is it true," she asked, "that you and Anne are engaged?"

If conversation is reported in indirect quotation the comma must not be used before the *that* which introduces the indirect quotation:

Paul said that the snow would not delay us more than an hour. (NOT: Paul said, that the snow . . . .)

We asked whether we would be allowed to vote without our registration cards. (NOT: We asked, whether we . . . .)

A quoted word or phrase used as a single part of speech is not separated from the rest of the sentence:

His use of the term "consumer interest" is very unorthodox.

If the quotation is long or formal, a colon instead of a comma is generally used (see section P 3).

       L. Explanatory elements are usually set off by commas. These include elements in dates, addresses, and names of geographical places; some appositives; and titles and abbreviations of degrees coming after proper names:

He was born on May 2, 1903, and he died on May 3, 1929.

The magazine was founded in February, 1924.

Send a telegram to him at 1505 Halter Street, Portland, Oregon.

It seemed strange to me to be in Springfield, Missouri, just after I had been in Springfield, Illinois.

In the second example above, the comma between month and year would be omitted as unnecessary by many writers today. In the first sentence, however, the comma is needed to avoid confusion between the separate figures.

Harry Bennett, the leading man of the musical comedy, was forced to resign.

The next ship, the "City of Seattle," arrived that afternoon.

His two sons, Ernest and Jules, were not interested in his factory.

At times a substantive and its appositive are so closely related in meaning that they should not logically be separated. In other words, appositives, like modifiers, may be restrictive or nonrestrictive; those in the sentences above are nonrestrictive. Those in the following sentences, however, are probably restrictive, if we can judge from the meanings of the sentences, and so the commas are properly omitted:

Her son Harry was much less important to her than her daughter Margaret.

The actor George Talmadge soon submerged the individuality of the man George Talmadge.

The watchdog Rover sniffed disdainfully at the lap dog Fritzi.

M. Because of its informality, a comma is generally used after the salutation of a personal letter:

Dear Fred,

Although it has been two months since I received your letter, I have been able to do little about your request . . . .

A colon is preferred to a comma after the salutation of a business letter, but the colon is now considered too formal a mark to be used in a personal letter (see section P 3).

P5   THE DASH

The dash (—) is a mark of punctuation used primarily to indicate abruptness or emphasis. When properly and sparingly used, it is very helpful to the writer, who must gain his emphasis partly through the arrangement of the written word on his page rather than through the tone or volume of his voice. When improperly used, however, or when too often used, the dash loses its effectiveness and becomes merely an indication of hasty punctuation, lax thought, and undirected emotion.

A. A dash may be used to show an abrupt change of thought within a clause or sentence:

When the captain called to me—but you know what happened after that.

I started to cross the street—I did not intend to tell you all this—when I saw Mrs. Howard approaching.

Notice that, in the last sentence given above, parentheses might have been used instead of dashes, but that the dashes give more emphasis to the structurally independent clause than would parentheses.

B. A dash may be used to show that a speech has been interrupted, or that part of a thought has been abruptly suppressed by the speaker or by the writer who is using an informal style:

"I do not think that you should go, Louise, but if you insist—"
"Why don't you—" He stopped abruptly and began to blush.

C. Dashes may be used to indicate hurried thought or action:

The infuriated fellow sprang into the crowd; he struck out with his fists—kicked at shins—pulled hair—twisted arms—adopted any tactics that would serve to disrupt the meeting.

D. A dash may be used to emphasize repetition of a word or phrase within a sentence:

Let me tell you a story—a story that you may have heard before—the story of my life.
When I read the book—the book about which everyone seemed enthusiastic—I was disappointed.

E. A dash may be used to emphasize a word, phrase, or dependent clause at the end of a sentence:

It is true that what the mind does easily, it does happily—if it is worth doing.—M. H. BUCKHAM
After our long journey through the north woods, after being completely out of touch with civilization for almost a week, the trading center looked like a metropolis; we walked into the general store and each of us, with a fiendish light in his eye, ordered—an ice-cream cone.

F. Dashes may be used to enclose nonrestrictive elements that would ordinarily be set off by commas, but that contain internal punctuation likely to make the addition of more commas confusing:

His fate—which, as you may expect, was important to all of us, his friends and his enemies—did not seem to interest him in the least.

The seeming inconsistency between his speech—in which, according to the newspaper reports, he had advocated municipal ownership—and his action—by which he prevented our town from having its own power plant—will be made less glaring if we consider his background.

G. A dash may be used after a long compound subject and before a word or expression that summarizes that subject:

The manner in which his hair was combed, the precise knot of his necktie, the careful way in which his coat was buttoned—all this told me what manner of man I could expect him to be.

P6   PARENTHESES AND BRACKETS

Parentheses (. . .) and brackets [. . .] are marks of punctuation used to enclose explanatory material. Brackets are the more specialized of the two marks and should be used to enclose only certain kinds of parenthetical material, as illustrated below. Parentheses may be used to set off explanatory material only indirectly related to the rest of the sentence or paragraph in which it appears. A discussion of the specific uses of these marks follows:

A. Parentheses should be used to enclose explanatory material that is structurally independent of a sentence or paragraph, and that is not intended to be emphatic:

Last night I went to see a dramatization of *Tom Jones* (adapted from the novel of that name by Henry Fielding) at the Little Theater.

When the embezzler, Henry Blanke, reached the small town of Royal, he sent a telegram to his partner, Charles Lark (who was described in yesterday's issue of this paper), and asked whether the theft had been discovered.

The panic-stricken crowd listened in terror to the trumpeting of the angry elephant (they did not know that five minutes after the accident the animal had been safely chained to a post by his keeper), and watched the entrance, momentarily expecting him to appear and toss someone high into the air.

If the explanatory material is to be emphasized, it may be enclosed by dashes rather than by parentheses (see section P 5D).

If the material within the parentheses is a complete sentence, and if that parenthetical material is within the body of another sentence, the enclosed statement is not begun with a capital letter and is not concluded by a period. If, however, the material within parentheses is an exclamatory sentence or a question, an exclamation mark or a question mark should be used and enclosed in the following manner:

After a short introduction descriptive of a storm (we had hardly reached our seats when it began!) the curtain rose on the first act of *Die Walküre.*

I drove across the drawbridge (do you remember the day we almost got caught in the middle of it?) before the traffic policeman could stop me.

The material within parentheses, however, is begun with a capital letter and concluded by proper end punctuation, including the period, if the parenthetical material is not in the body of a sentence:

By five o'clock I had cut almost all of the front lawn. (Tom had still not arrived.) By five-thirty I had finished the side lawn and was ready to stop.

When an end parenthesis and another mark of punctuation occur together, the other mark, if it applies to the sentence as a whole and not to the material within the parentheses, follows the second parenthesis.

B. Parentheses should be used to enclose material which confirms in another manner something which has been written immediately before it:

The contract will specify that the manager is to receive one hundred dollars ($100) a week.

This use of parenthetical material for purposes of confirmation is restricted to legal, business, and technical documents in which all possibilities of mistake must be eliminated. In other formal and informal writing the writer should use either words or numerals according to the rules given in section M 7.

C. Parentheses may be used to enclose numerals or symbols which introduce separate parts of a series:

He violated the rule in three ways: (1) he granted an interview, against our instruction, to a newspaper reporter; (2) he expressed his own personal opinion as if it were the opinion of the committee; and (3) he made public some proceedings of the committee which were intended to be strictly private.

Please read the following chapters in Havelock Ellis' *The Dance of Life:* (a) "The Art of Thinking," (b) "The Art of Writing," (c) "Conclusion."

D. Brackets should be used to enclose material that an editor inserts in a passage he did not write:

"It [the Grand Canyon]," Jerry had written to his sister, "is not nearly so remarkable as I had expected it to be."

Thomas Beer says, "He [Roscoe Conkling] created excitement out of nothing and made simpletons believe that his causes were real issues."

E. Brackets are used to enclose material that the editor, because he could not interpret it, is conjecturing about:

"The [love?] was one that had come unwanted."

Because his handwriting was poor, I can only guess that he intended to say, "Be sure to have a large [brave?] steak ready for me when I get there."

F. Brackets are used to enclose a parenthetical element within material already enclosed in parentheses:

This word (which is sometimes [1] a noun and sometimes [2] an adverb) has an interesting history.

G. Brackets are used to enclose *sic* when an editor wishes to indicate that an error occurs in the original text:

"The mezzanine of the hotel was a joyful madhouse [*sic*]."
"Surprisingly Hardy achieved after his death an immorality [*sic*] that no one who knew him would have expected."

Neither parentheses nor brackets should be used to indicate deletion of words that the writer intends to cross out. (See section M 1H.)

P7   QUOTATION MARKS AND ITALICS

By the conventional use of quotation marks ("..." or '...') and of italics (*italic type* or underlining) a writer is enabled to be sure that in certain situations the reader will understand clearly what is being written. The use of quotation marks to enclose conversation or quoted material, for instance, is one way in which punctuation helps the reader's comprehension. Another instance in which the lack of punctuation hinders comprehension, although perhaps only momentarily, is seen in a sentence like "The legendary figure of William Tell was, as might be supposed, the inspiration for Rossini's William Tell." The use of quotation marks or italics would have done away with any danger of misunderstanding: "The legendary figure of William Tell was, as might be supposed, the inspiration for Rossini's *William Tell*." (Admittedly, of course, the writer might have inserted some phrase like "Rossini's opera" before the second "William Tell" and the meaning would have been clarified; but let the student try using such an explanatory phrase instead of italics or quotation marks every time clarity calls for them, and he will soon see how bulky and awkward his style becomes.)

Although there exists today some overlapping of conventions in the uses of quotation marks and italics, each type of punctuation has certain preferred uses which are given below.

A. All conversation should be enclosed within quotation marks:

The mechanic said, "This car is in such bad condition that I can't do anything with it."

"I am going to eat this sandwich," he said, "and then I'll be ready to play ball."

A few modern writers have omitted the quotation marks around conversation, but their practice is not generally followed; most authors prefer to sacrifice any possible advantage which the omission may give them and gain the clarity and emphasis resulting from the conventional practice.[1]

Notice that when indirect conversation is reported, it is not enclosed by quotation marks:

The mechanic said that the car was in such bad condition that he could not do anything about it.

He said that he was going to eat his sandwich and that he would then be ready to play ball.

B. Direct quotations, whether of prose or poetry, that are used in the body of the text are enclosed in quotation marks:

His favorite line of poetry was "Let me not to the marriage of true minds admit impediments."

After some hesitation he took up his pen and wrote, "As I told you at first, you have nothing to fear."

In his preface to *The Road to Rome,* Robert Sherwood says, "In the year 195, Hannibal solved the difficulty by going into voluntary exile. The Romans, however, were still unsatisfied."

---

[1] See section ¶ 2C for discussion and illustration of the way in which conversation should be paragraphed.

If the passage of quoted material, whether prose or poetry, is long, the student should use indention (and single spacing in typed manuscripts) rather than quotation marks. The criterion of "long" is generally said to be two or more consecutive lines of poetry and three or more sentences of prose. Such passages should be indented about five spaces from each margin of the text if they are prose, and they should be centered upon the page if poetry:

In *Twenty Thousand Years in Sing Sing*, Warden Lawes gives us the picture of the typical prison school. He begins by writing:

Toward the far end of the same floor we find the prison school. Five classes are in session; they change every hour. Eighteen inmate teachers conduct these classes under the supervision of two civilian instructors. They average about thirty pupils for each hour of instruction.

The Head School Teacher tells us something about his work. A total of 1,111 men attended his school during the last year . . . .

I like especially the lyric of Heinrich Heine which begins:

> High up on yonder mountain
> A castle stands, and three
> Fair maidens live within it;
> They love me generously.

Notice that the words introducing the long quotations in this section are followed by colons (see section P 3A).

     C. Cited titles of subdivisions of writing, or subdivisions of any creative work, are enclosed in quotation marks. These subdivisions include titles of magazine articles, chapters of books, short poems or other brief creative works, and plays which are not published in a separate volume:

Margaret Culkin Banning's article, "What a Young Girl Should Know," appeared in *Harper's Magazine*, December, 1933.

The condition of the United States before 1860 is described in Chapter XVII, "The Approach of the Irrepressible Conflict," in Charles and Mary Beard's *The Rise of American Civilization*.

I read Lewis Carroll's "Four Riddles," but I shall have to confess that that kind of poetry means little to me.

Rimski-Korsakov's "Flight of the Bumble Bee" is played at almost all concerts for school children.

Titles of books, magazines, newspapers, and long poems or major creative works are italicized (see section F, below) to distinguish them from shorter or dependent works.

      D. Single quotation marks are used to enclose material quoted within a quotation:

"I am reminded," John said, "of President Roosevelt's remark, 'We have nothing to fear but fear itself.'"

He smiled and said, "Don't forget the old saying, 'All that glitters is not gold.'"

If the quotation contains still other quoted material, double and single quotation marks continue to alternate.

      E. When quotation marks and other marks of punctuation occur together at the end of phrases or sentences, these practices are followed by most publishers and writers:

      1) **Commas and periods** are *always* placed before the end quotation marks:

"Bring me the pencil," said Howard.

"If you finish reading 'Intimations of Immortality,' as I expect you to do, go on to 'The Ode to Duty.'"

You will not pass the course if you insist upon writing "don't" when you mean "does not."

      2) **Question marks and exclamation marks** may, as the occasion demands, be placed either before or after the end quotation marks; they should be placed before if they apply to the quoted material or to both the sentence as a whole and the quoted material, but they should be placed after if they apply only to the sentence as a whole:

Did he say, "I must go"?

Did he say, "Must I go?"

How pleased we were to hear him say, "Hurrah!"

How pleased we were when he said slowly, "I think I'll go"!

We were much pleased when he exclaimed, "Hurrah!"

3) **Colons and semicolons** are always placed after the end quotation mark:

He laughed and said, "He walks just like a cat"; then he picked up his book again.

This is what I want you to do before you fill in the blank spaces under "Options": turn the first page upside down, take out your spelling books . . . .

F. **Titles of books, newspapers, magazines, and other large or important works are usually written in italics:**

I was reading Thomas Beer's *Hanna* and did not notice that the *Post-Courier* had arrived.

Emerson's *Representative Men* contains the essay "Montaigne," which I like better than anything else the American philosopher has written.

He was idly turning over the pages of *The Man without a Country* when he heard the mail arrive. He wondered if his copy of *Harper's Magazine* had come, for he was anxious to see if his essay "On Manners" had been published in that issue.

The titles of chapters of books, of articles in magazines, or of short poems are usually enclosed in quotation marks.

When the title of a book or subdivision of a book is preceded by the article *a, an,* or *the,* the article is considered part of the title, and is either italicized and capitalized, or quoted and capitalized, as the case may be. But when an article is used with the title of a magazine or newspaper, it is not considered part of the title when the magazine or newspaper is quoted unless it appears as such on the title page. Thus, *The,* in *The Man without a Country,* must be italicized, but *the* before *Post-Courier* need not be.

G. **Words from foreign languages are generally italicized when they are used in English:**

We certainly need, in English, an equivalent for the German *man*.

Note that foreign words which have been absorbed into the language are not italicized.

It seemed to Johnson that the questions were very naïve. (NOT: It seemed to Johnson that the questions were very *naïve*.)

When he returned home from Congress, his townsmen prepared a fete in his honor. (NOT: When he returned home from Congress, his townsmen prepared a *fête* in his honor.)

A good dictionary will show whether or not a word has been absorbed.

H. A word or expression that the writer wants to emphasize may be written in italics. A constant use of italics for this purpose, however, is self-defeating. Any device for gaining emphasis must be used sparingly if it is to remain effective. The following sentences illustrate the effective use of italics for emphasis:

I was amused, interested, instructed by what he said. To ask myself if I also liked what he *was*—this was, no doubt, beside the point.— ALDOUS HUXLEY

If the recognized and the usual . . . have so far failed us, it is time to turn, in the matter of our method, to the *un*recognized and the *un*usual.—J. B. RHINE

I. A letter, word, or phrase taken out of its context and used as a unit may be italicized or enclosed in quotation marks, as the writer desires:

You must learn to make an *e* so that it will not look like an *i*.

Every time I come to what looks like *of* in one of his manuscripts, I have to stop, to see whether it is *of*, or perhaps *if*.

The word "time" seems to mean nothing to him.

I have never been able to discover exactly what he means by "the good of the few."

J. Names of ships may be italicized or enclosed in quotation marks:

Morris barely escaped with his life when the *Preceptor* sank after striking a derelict hull.

I remember seeing the *Olympic* from the deck of a tug called the *Betsy Anne*.

He sailed for Europe aboard the "America."

P8 THE APOSTROPHE

The apostrophe (') is used to form the possessive case, to indicate omission of letters or figures, and to form the plural of letters, figures, and symbols. One of the reasons why many people do not use the apostrophe according to conventional practice is that it does not correspond to anything in the spoken language.

A. The apostrophe is used before the *s* to form the possessive case of singular nouns:

child's, brother's, mother's, God's, man's, woman's, lady's, Charles's

The common practice today in forming the possessive case of nouns ending in *s* is to add the second *s*, as in *Charles's*, and *James's*. If, however, the possessive noun is found in a phrase in which there are already several sibilants (hissing sounds), and in which the addition of another sibilant would be disagreeable, the second *s* should be omitted:

CHARLES' security of position seemed uncertain.
The SMITHS' style is uneven as a result of their collaboration.

B. The apostrophe is used before the *s* to form the plural possessive of nouns not ending in *s:*

children's, men's, women's

C. The apostrophe is used after the *s* to form the plural possessive of nouns ending in *s:*

brothers', mothers', gods', ladies'

D. Notice the following special uses of the apostrophe in forming the possessive case of nouns:

1) **In a compound word, the '*s* is used after the last word of the compound:**

brother-in-law's, brothers-in-law's, somebody else's

2) **If two nouns both possess the same thing, the apostrophe need be used only after the last noun:**

JACK AND MARY'S party was not a success.
SMITH AND JONES'S truck ran into a lamp post.

Notice, however, that both nouns must be in the possessive case if the word they modify is possessed by each individually:

I went to many parties last winter; only JACK'S and MARY'S parties were not successful.
SMITH'S and JONES'S trucks ran into each other.

3) **In forming the possessive of nouns used in business or group titles the writer should omit or use the apostrophe, according to the practice of the particular organization:**

The Harvard TEACHERS Record
HARPER'S Magazine
The CITIZEN'S (or CITIZENS or CITIZENS') National Bank

4) **The apostrophe is used to form the possessive case of only a few pronouns:**

ONE'S duty, each OTHER'S theme, NEITHER'S desire

Notice that the possessive case of most personal or relative pronouns is shown by a special form of the word and not by the use of the apostrophe:

I	my, mine
you	your, yours
he	his
she	her, hers
it	its
we	our, ours
they	their, theirs
who	whose

The use of the apostrophe with a personal or relative pronoun indicates the contraction of a pronoun plus a verb: *who's,* for example, means *who is; you're* means *you are; it's* means *it is;* and *they're* means *they are.*

E. An apostrophe should be used to show the omission of letters in contractions of two or more words, the omission of a letter from one word, or the partial expression of a numerical combination:

I DON'T believe in superstitions.
The class of '50 published a poor yearbook.

F. An apostrophe is used to form the plural of a letter, a word used as a unit, and of a sign or symbol:

He forms his *s*'s like *f*'s.
I cannot tell his *or*'s from his *of*'s.
There were too many #'s in his paper.
In making the list you may omit the %'s.
Put *6*'s on every note card containing information from this book.

EXERCISES

A.

Rewrite the following sentences, correcting whatever marks of end punctuation are inappropriately used.

1. She asked the students if they would like to be dismissed early?
2. How it did rain that night.
3. This is a very funny (?) book.
4. "Ouch," he bellowed!
5. He asked me who the lady was?
6. The sergeant said, with ominous softness, "Come here!"
7. Who do you think you are? Anyhow?
8. Sir John Grierson is the man who edited the book, but who wrote the introduction.

9. Will you please send me the catalogue for the next academic year.

10. Should you ever be in Alaska, look up my friend Klondike Cal.

B.

Rewrite the following sentences. Insert semicolons wherever necessary, and replace other marks of punctuation by semicolons when semicolons seem called for.

1. These people are well acquainted with the forms of good breeding, and furthermore observe them, for the rest, however, they have gone far beyond the forms themselves.

2. The atmosphere is cozy and comfortable, even a trifle dull, it affords the good women who breathe it the advantage of foregoing the labor of thought.

3. That is why I treasure this curious acquaintance, that is why I follow his career with the greatest interest and, I must admit, a trace of envy.

4. The waves come up almost to the edge of the landing, sometimes they threaten to engulf the stairs.

5. After the wasp clips off the tip of one of the beetle grub's legs and drinks some blood, she leaves, she has more eggs to deposit elsewhere.

6. The way to get along in the world is to let others lie and to believe them as much as possible, then you, too, will be given a chance to lie whenever you are tempted to do so.

7. The Bay of Monterey has been compared by no less a person than General Sherman to a bent fishing-hook, and the comparison, if less important than the march through Georgia, still shows the eye of a soldier for topography.—ROBERT LOUIS STEVENSON.

8. During the expedition, Coronado's perfumed Mexico City gallants became seasoned veterans, getting by on short rations, the mountain slopes and waterless marches turned them into sunken-eyed, perpetually starving foragers by the time they reached what is now Arizona.

9. In the early stages of its development, the Knickerbocker literature was especially indebted to such eighteenth-century writers as Pope, Addison, Goldsmith, and Johnson, in its middle years it was profoundly affected by the writings of Scott, Byron, Moore, Campbell, and Lamb,

and its decline was coincident with the increasing influence of Dickens, Bulwer, Disraeli, and a number of lesser writers.

10. Staid, conventional, conservative, blood-proud, they could ignore the rapidly shifting winds of political and economic doctrine, they could look with disdain upon the bearers of outlandish Yankee and other "foreign" names who jostled them in the market place and clamored for social recognition, but laughter they could not withstand.

C.

Rewrite the following sentences. Insert colons wherever necessary or effective, and replace other marks of punctuation by colons when colons seem called for. Remove colons inappropriately used.

1. A final point, perhaps the most important to be made in our discussion, Aristotle can best be described as a pluralistic philosopher.

2. The very first day at dancing class changed her life completely, she fell in love with the ballet master.

3. Please be sure to buy: a Coleman stove, a Dacron sleeping bag, a pair of stout hiking shoes, and a reliable compass.

4. In the last chapter, Burke summarizes his position as follows; he is neither a Jungian nor a Freudian but an eclectic psychologist who has been most strongly influenced by the work of Sullivan.

5. Toward the end of FDR's life, many foreign governments issued sets of postage stamps with his name and portrait, twenty-three countries honored him with a total of eighty-five issues.

6. After all these years, I still know Pope's lines by heart, "What dire offense from am'rous causes springs, What mighty contests rise from trivial things."

7. Harshly but honestly he told her the truth, she had no talent as an actress.

8. They hope to accomplish for sociology what other inquirers have done for the natural sciences namely collect a multitude of facts and derive from them general laws about human behavior.

9. All vital and crucial human activities are connected with the dance as ritual birth, puberty, marriage, death, planting and harvesting, battle and victory.

10. Suzanne Langer states that poetry is not genuine discourse at all, it is the creating of an illusion by means of discursive language.

D.

Rewrite the following sentences. Insert commas wherever you think necessary and correct those misused. Some sentences need no further punctuation. Some sentences may be punctuated in more than one way, depending on the meaning intended.

1. As William knew the true facts of the case were quite different from the rumor which had spread all over town.

2. No Aunt Helen is not a schoolteacher.

3. The newspaper I read is completely unreliable as a source of information.

4. To Mary Jane revealed the reason for her success as a rising young star.

5. On my study table now are books by Henry James Joyce Cary Upton Sinclair Lewis Mumford etc.

6. I spent all day Sunday ridding my front lawn of weedy Bermuda grass.

7. The witness further testified, that he had seen the accident at close range.

8. For dinner I had a steak and Rita had lobster.

9. I don't understand his use of the term, "ecological symbiosis."

10. Having finished their chores by noon they went off to the swimming pool.

11. Students who wish to become good writers, should practice writing and rewriting.

12. You must show me your latest water colors, and also your etchings.

13. The president finally entered the limousine, carrying his chief of staff.

14. After all we did what we could do was not enough.

15. Warren my cousin writes that he is enlisting in the marines.

16. The magazine article that he sold to *Harper's,* and the book review that appeared in the *Times,* were his only published pieces of writing all year.

17. We had better start walking immediately for camp is about six miles away.

18. To be effective writing must first of all be interesting.

19. He is kindly gentle and patient.

20. The proud, happy mother sat in the audience beaming at her three, freshly scrubbed, little children.

21. When they arrived at Reno Nevada Margery discarded her old shoes and her husband threw away his battered fedora hat.

22. The essence of moral judgment is, that it endeavors to divide men into the good and the bad by determining whether or not their purposes and their behavior accord with certain fixed principles and rules not established by themselves.

23. The rich aroma reminding him of the days long past when his mother used to bake her own bread drifted across the fire to him.

24. Starting out as a soldier in 1570 he fell into slavery to the Turks from whom it took him eight years to escape.

25. The talented conscientious and ambitious students of the violin virtuoso Auer are the leading concert performers of our time.

26. A notable contrast to John Lyly is that Thomas Kyd who wrote *The Spanish Tragedy.*

27. As I walked on the water seeming to assume a special quality of lightness sparkled and glittered as though from a hidden source of radiance.

28. Sternly he mounted to the pulpit and sternly he began to deliver his sermon.

29. His work consists of a series of brilliant and inconsistent intuitions witty generalizations couched in memorable prose and verse and a handful of acutely penetrating instructive and painfully accurate evaluations of his fellow men.

30. Abner Kneeland created a famous political scandal in 1833 by writing "Universalists believe in a god which I do not"—a declaration that could be interpreted in two different ways depending on whether or not Kneeland meant the comma to have been omitted.

E.

Rewrite the following sentences. Replace the present marks of punctuation by one or two dashes wherever dashes will improve effectiveness.

1. Our major problem is how to reconcile the dissident irregulars, the so-called Young Turks, with the conservative members.

2. The lightning gleamed, and the loud claps of thunder rattled

through the lofty, narrow streets, but I should first tell you something about our hero.

3. "American thought" is the product of a vast pattern of forces, economic, ethnic, geographic, cultural, political, religious,

4. The telephone, the telegraph, and the television, these are things which the average man does not really understand but nevertheless cannot see how his ancestors got along without them.

5. I had a very unhappy childhood and was beaten by my wicked stepfather, but why should I trouble you with my problems?

F.

Insert parentheses or brackets wherever needed in the following sentences.

1. The faces on the snapshot were out of focus, but one of them, it was that of Mary Ward, who was later to become his wife, had a special attraction for him.

2. When the noise had ceased, he, Patrick Henry, calmly continued to talk.

3. Work on the *Linguistic Atlas of the Pacific Coast*—see Map 4—has led to one important study dealing with regional dialects.

4. The manuscript, at this point, refers to "an upstart poet named Whittman—sic—and his nauseous effusions."

5. There is a vital difference between the goodness that has survived temptation and what Milton calls "a fugitive and cloister'd virtue," Mark Twain's story, "The Man That Corrupted Hadleyburg," tells us exactly how worth while that kind of virtue is, in that the first is a real, the second only an apparent goodness.

G.

In the following sentences insert single or double quotation marks wherever necessary and italicize words wherever italics seem called for. Correct quotation marks that are incorrectly used.

1. He always says infer when he really means imply.

2. According to Schlesinger's The Age of Jackson, the name locofoco, at first confined to a small group in New York, was soon applied to the whole Jacksonian party.

3. One of the most depressing aspects of our political life is the extent to which cliches and stereotypes, like creeping socialism, the American way of life, and bureaucratic payrollers, are accepted in lieu of intelligent discussion.

4. In Shakespeare's Sonnet 87, which is a love poem, we find him surprisingly using such words as charter, bonds, patent, estimate, and grant.

5. But when, I asked, are you going to tell us what the phrase the intense inane means?

6. It occurs in Arnold's essay, Shelley, which you will find in his Selected Criticism, Volume I, Professor Thurlby replied.

7. She contends that her success as a hostess is the result of her laissez-faire policy.

8. The vagrant said "that he had wandered over the countryside since Tuesday."

9. One of the funniest parodies I have ever read is A Garland of Ibids, by Frank Sullivan, in E. B. White's A Sub-Treasury of American Humor.

10. "My first published work, he said, was a story entitled The Bicycle, which appeared in the St. Nicholas Magazine. This was eventually the title piece in my earliest collection of short stories, The Bicycle and Other Tales. However, I like best the story entitled Sunset Spooks.

H.

I. Form the possessive case, singular and plural, of the following words:

baby	deer	kangaroo
postman	Adams	osprey
mongoose	aide-de-camp	Sioux
	Cyclops	

II. Rewrite the following sentences so that in each sentence the apostrophes are used correctly. Add or delete apostrophes as necessary:

1. Back in the 20s life seemed easier than it does today.

2. He seemed ashamed because he didnt know what apothecaries measure was.

3. Who's voice is that I hear in the next room?

4. That book is yours; this one is our's.

5. Its going to rain today for certain.

6. The Talcott's are coming to dinner tonight.

7. He had been brought up on Moody's and Lovett's *History of English Literature*.

8. I wish she would learn to dot her *i*s properly.

9. Odysseus's story is told in the *Odyssey*.

10. *Aint* is a word that can be grammatically correct, but it's social standing generally prevents it's use even when correct.

I.

Supply all needed punctuation in the following sentences, and eliminate inappropriate or incorrect punctuation.

1. J. P. Morgan once said, that if you have to ask how much a thing costs you can't afford it

2. The seasons repertory was conventional enough Aida Rigoletto La Boheme and the other old chestnuts

3. One of the requirements for eligibility is that applicants have completed one-quarter of German during their freshman year

4. James Shirleys comedy, The Bird in a Cage, 1633, satirizes Prynne who was then in prison

5. The grocers helper who was a young awkward boy was unable to find anything I asked him for the salt the biscuits or the coffee

6. No I have not been studying on the contrary I have been reading this hair raising blood chilling ghost story

7. The Good said these philosophers is like everything else an Idea and the various virtues Benevolence Justice Purity and the rest can exist only as Ideas entertained by the mind

8. I propose to take a fresh look at the American tradition under three aspects first by searching American political thought for its liberal and conservative elements second by trying to determine the relationship between political precept and political practice and third by examining American history to see how progressive this allegedly progressive nation has really been

9. Adults accompanied by children are admitted free to the amusement park

10. It is difficult to believe that the Shakespeare who wrote The Comedy of Errors is the same as the Shakespeare who wrote King Lear?

11. Lucy said Bob is the type of person well worth watching furthermore she expects to be watched

12. In the 1820s and 1830s the great historical collections such as the Feldenheimer Festschriften the Mommzeren Monumenta and the Katzenjammer Kinderstudien were begun often with official government sponsorship and subsidies

13. The terrible winters on the great plains the life of the trappers and the Indians the sense of living on the edge of a tidal movement westward all these are in Mr Mudds first novel by any criterion an impressive feat of the historical imagination

14. Edgar Allan Poe 1809 1849 who has been the subject of many fanciful, biographical interpretations is the real father of the detective story when all is said and done perhaps his most significant contribution to literature

15. A comma and a co-ordinating conjunction may be used to connect two independent clauses a semicolon may also be used but a comma standing by itself in the between clause position is to be avoided

16. The subjects I am studying are English history engineering drawing and Russian

17. Malcolm began on my first date with the campus queen I took her skating we were gliding along holding hands when suddenly my feet flew out from under me and I fell on my oh excuse me theres the doorbell

18. The pressure of public demand for entertainment caused brisk dramatic activity of a rather low order during much of this period farce comedy burlesque opera and melodrama were readily thrown together by the practiced theater hacks

19. For even the normal child distinctions like those between s sun and sh shun and between th thin and f fin may be hard to hear

20. Born at Clinton New York on February 15 1845 Elihu Root studied at Hamilton College in Clinton and at New York University after a notable legal and political career in which he became a reform leader in New York Republican politics he was appointed Secretary of War by President McKinley in 1899

21. In spite of all that man does gradually progress

22. Swifts Gullivers Travels written in the early part of the eighteenth century is a satire on the vices and follies of mankind and not as most people think a mere fairy tale for young children the professor declared

23. Hamlet gave the following advice to the players Speak the speech I pray you as I pronounced it to you trippingly on the tongue but if you mouth it as many of your players do I had as lief the town crier spoke my lines.

24. Our English instructor thinks hes so smart he growled every time I get back a theme its all marked up with red ink and theres some comment usually at the bottom of the page which reads Why not try using your textbook for something besides a paperweight

25. Dr Christopher told the many faithful friends who had traveled to his remote island home from distant lands in order to hear his last words that he looked forward confidently and optimistically to the successful continuation of the humanitarian project which they were engaged in furthering in every civilized nation throughout the world.

Mechanics:
The Etiquette of Composition

In the preceding chapter we have referred to punctuation as a system of symbols used conventionally to aid in the transmission of meaning. In this chapter we shall consider other conventions, some of which help in transmitting meaning and some of which are merely agreed-upon ways of doing certain things—"the manners of written discourse." A mannerly way of doing things—for example, like not picking one's teeth in public or wearing a hat in the classroom—is important in writing, as well as in social intercourse. In the next chapter, dealing with language, usage, and diction, we shall have further occasion to discuss the verbal etiquette implicit in the choice of words the writer makes.

M1   APPEARANCE

Although the ideas in an essay, and the way in which those ideas are expressed, may seem to a writer more important than anything else, he should remember that the reader will be impressed by the general appearance of the manuscript long before he will be impressed by the contents. No matter how sprightly or original the material may be, pages that are out of order, illegible writing, or blurred erasures will most certainly give the reader an unfavorable impression of the composition as a whole. Any writer, then, and especially a beginning writer, should adopt some accepted form for his manuscript, and should take pains to make that manuscript, through its physical qualities at least, as readable as possible. Although rules may vary in different places, the suggestions which follow are generally accepted guides to the appearance of literary compositions and are designed expressly for the student who is writing the usual type of expository, narrative, or descriptive theme. For the form of the research paper and the forms of letters, the student should refer to the chapters dealing specifically with those types.

A. Use ruled white paper if the manuscript is to be handwritten, and unruled white paper 8½ by 11 inches in size if the manuscript is to be typewritten. A standard theme paper is always to be found in the college bookstore. Buy a good grade and not an inferior one.

B. Use a smooth-flowing pen and either black or dark blue ink—never pencil—if the manuscript is to be handwritten, or black or blue ribbon if the manuscript is to be typewritten.

C. Use only one side of the paper.

D. Center the title between the side margins of the page.

1) **Place it on the top line of ruled paper, or at least two inches from the top of the first page of unruled paper.**

2) **Do not place a period after it, but use a question or exclamation mark if the nature of the title calls for one.**

3) **Do not mark the title for italics** by underscoring it and **do not place quotation marks around it** unless it is a quotation. In print, titles usually appear in solid capitals; the indication for this in a manuscript being prepared for the press is triple underscoring.

E. Make all indentions and spacings liberal and clear.

1) **Leave one line or, in a typed manuscript, the space of an inch between the title and the first word of the body of the manuscript.**

2) **Leave a margin of at least one inch at the top of all pages except the first** (on which the margin should be at least two inches), **and one of at least a half inch at the bottom of all pages.**

3) **Leave a margin of at least one inch at the left-hand side of all pages, and one of at least a half inch at the right-hand side.**

4) **Leave a line between the body of the manuscript and the beginning and end of prose quotations over three sentences long.**

5) **Center a quotation of poetry** so that it is indented at least a half inch from each side of the body of the manuscript; begin such a quotation on a line separate from the introductory prose phrase, and arrange it so that the continuation of the first line, if the lines are long, does not extend as far to the left as the beginning of the second line.

F. Be sure the handwriting is clear and legible.

G. Make all typewriting follow the accepted conventions.

1) **Leave four spaces between the title and the first line of the body of the manuscript.**

2) **Always double-space lines except footnotes and long quotations, which should be single-spaced.**

3) **Underline** (underlining in manuscript of typescript represents italics in print) **by using the sublinear mark found, on most keyboards, above the figure 6.**

H. Make all corrections, such as insertions and deletions, neatly.

1) **Rewrite the entire page if there are many corrections.**

2) **Do not attempt to erase a wrong or misspelled word,** but cross it out with a single horizontal line, never with scratches or blots. Do not use parentheses as a mark of deletion.

3) **If a word or phrase is to be added, place a caret**

($_\wedge$) at the point where the addition should occur, and write the added material above the line.

4) **If a new paragraph is desired** where none occurs in the manuscript, place the symbol ¶ before the word which is to begin the new paragraph.

5) **If a paragraph division already made is to be done away with**, write "no ¶" in the left-hand margin of the manuscript, on the same line as the beginning line of the wrong paragraph.

I. Be certain that the heading or endorsement (your name, class, date, or whatever else is required) **is correct.** Observe exactly the form prescribed by your instructor.

J. Be certain that the pages are numbered and are in their proper order.

K. Do not, under any circumstances, fold the manu-script more than once.

L. Before submitting the manuscript, proofread it carefully, making certain that all instructions have been followed, and that in appearance, at least, it leaves nothing to be desired.

M2   DOCUMENTATION

The source of borrowed material should always be acknowledged. Some ideas are, of course, so widespread that they are common property; if a writer uses them their source does not have to be indicated. But to use phrases and sentences from an editorial, for example, without enclosing those phrases and sentences in quotation marks, is obviously dishonest. To use the central idea of the same editorial in a theme supposedly composed around an idea of the writer's own, without acknowledging the source of that idea, is just as dishonest as to use someone else's actual phrases. The following suggestions on documentation in ordinary writing will help the writer avoid even the appearance of plagiarism. For a full discussion and explanation of documentation in particular types of writing, see Chapter XII, "The Research Paper."

A. If the exact words of another person are used, whether those words compose a phrase or one or more sentences, the borrowed material should be enclosed in quotation marks (see section P 7B). In the following examples the borrowed ideas are stated in the exact words of the teacher, Hawthorne, and Boswell:

I had a teacher in high school who used to say that I had an "enviable knack of getting out of trouble."

The critics objected to Hawthorne's statement, in *The Blithedale Romance,* that "we seldom meet with women now-a-days, and in this country, who impress us as being women at all."

Boswell was not the only one to say that Goldsmith had a "singular character."

We saw in the previous chapter the accepted way to treat an omission from a quotation of a part of a sentence (see section P 1C). The omission of a whole sentence, or of a number of sentences, also is shown by the use of three ellipsis dots. If the omitted sentence follows an uncompleted sentence, no additional dots are needed. We can illustrate this principle by using the opening paragraph of this chapter:

In the preceding chapter we have referred to punctuation as a system of symbols used conventionally to aid in the transmission of meaning. In this chapter we shall consider other conventions, some of which help in transmitting meaning and some of which are merely agreed-upon ways of doing certain things . . . . In the next chapter, dealing with language, usage, and diction, we shall have further occasion to discuss the verbal etiquette implicit in the choice of words the writer makes.

If, however, the omitted sentence follows a completed sentence, the ellipsis dots should follow the end punctuation of that sentence:

In the preceding chapter we have referred to punctuation as a system of symbols used conventionally to aid in the transmission of meaning. In this chapter we shall consider other conventions, some of which help in transmitting meaning and some of which are merely agreed-upon

ways of doing certain things—"the manners of written discourse." . . .
In the next chapter, dealing with language, usage, and diction, we shall
have further occasion to discuss the verbal etiquette implicit in the
choice of words the writer makes.

If the omission is of an entire paragraph, or of a number of paragraphs, the modern convention is to use a row of spaced dots
equal in width to the entire quotation. The same convention
applies to the omission of even a single line of verse:

> For oft, when on my couch I lie,
>
> . . . .
>
> They flash upon that inward eye
> Which is the bliss of solitude.

**B. In quoting, the borrower must use the exact
wording, spelling, and punctuation of the original author.**
Hawthorne, in the example above, used hyphens in spelling *now-
a-days,* whereas today the word is spelled *ṇowadays.* Yet, since the
quotation is directly from *The Blithedale Romance,* the old-fashioned spelling of that word must be kept.

**C. If another person's idea, but not his exact word-
ing, is used, the source should be acknowledged without enclosing the idea in quotation marks:**

I agree with Hawthorne's views, expressed in *The Blithedale
Romance,* that we Americans rarely meet with women who have really
feminine qualities.

**D. In quoting directly or indirectly in more or less
informal writing, acknowledgments may be made by**

1) Explanatory statements:

I agree with Hawthorne in *The Blithedale Romance,* when he says,
"We seldom meet with women now-a-days, and in this country, who
impress us as being women at all."

or

As Hawthorne says, "We seldom meet with women now-a-days, and
in this country, who impress us as being women at all."

2) A note at the end of the manuscript:

If the indebtedness is slight:

The idea for this paper was suggested by Bacon's essay, "Of Truth."

If the indebtedness is heavy, the writer should give a bibliography as illustrated on page 589.

3) A note in the body of the manuscript:

One philosopher has dared to assert that although the truth may be as valuable as a pearl, it is never as valuable as a diamond. (See Francis Bacon, "Of Truth," in *Essays . . . and Other Pieces,* edited by Richard Foster Jones, p. 4.) We must remember, however, that the assertion was made by one whom we today would call a "practical politician," and that his ideas can hardly be expected to agree with those of the usual layman.

4) A footnote:

One philosopher has dared to assert that although the truth may be as valuable as a pearl, it is never as valuable as a diamond.[1] We must remember, however, that the assertion was made by one whom we today would call a "practical politician," and that his ideas can hardly be expected to agree with those of the usual layman.

---

[1] Francis Bacon, "Of Truth," *Francis Bacon: Essays, Advancement of Learning, New Atlantis, and Other Pieces,* ed. Richard Foster Jones (New York, 1937), p. 4.

M3   SPELLING

For most people, faulty spelling is the clearest symptom of illiteracy. Although English words are often spelled illogically and inconsistently, the blame is always placed on the writer and not on the system. For this reason, the writer given to misspelling should note the words he consistently misses and should try to determine what principle (if any) he is violating. No principle will account for the spelling of some words, which simply have to be memorized. Fortunately, there are relatively few of these.

A few important principles of spelling are given below. Don't memorize them. There is no reason to learn all the rules when the chances are that the words you misspell fall under only one or two. By noting the kinds of spelling errors you make, you will be able to generalize out to a particular principle. Grasp the principle, and the specific errors will disappear. An invaluable aid in improving spelling is a standard reference work, such as *Webster's New Collegiate Dictionary, The American College Dictionary,* or *Webster's New World Dictionary.* (See Chapter V, section D 1, for a discussion of the use of the dictionary.)

A. To spell words containing *ei* or *ie,* pronounced like *ee:* use *ie* after any letter but *c:*

believe, handkerchief

use *ei* after *c:*

deceive, receipt

These suggestions have been combined in the familiar jingle *"i* before *e* except after *c."* The rule, however, has some exceptions, like *weird, either, neither, seize,* and *leisure,* the spelling of which must be memorized.

B. When a suffix beginning with a vowel is added to most words of one syllable, ending in a single consonant, or to a word of more than one syllable, ending in a single consonant preceded by a vowel and accented on the last syllable, double the final consonant:

bid, bidden; hit, hitting; plan, planned; repel, repellent

When in doubt, before the student doubles the final consonant, he must apply the above rule to the word, considering the number of syllables, the accent, the letter before the final consonant, and the first letter of the suffix. He will then realize that

1) He will not double the final consonant of a word of more than one syllable if the word is not accented on the last

syllable: *develop, developed; worship, worshiped; travel, traveling; kidnap, kidnaped.*

    2) **He will not double the final consonant of a word if more than one vowel precedes the final consonant:** *defeat, defeated; proceed, proceeding.*

    3) **He will not double the final consonant of a word if the first letter of the suffix is not a vowel:** *fit, fitness; allot, allotment.*

Note that when the final consonant is doubled, the preceding vowel sound is short: *dine, dinner.*

    C. When a suffix beginning with a vowel is added to a word ending in silent *e*, drop the final *e*, unless so doing would change the pronunciation or meaning of the word:

bride, bridal; force, forcible; college, collegiate; judge, judging; love, lovable; dye, dyeing; shoe, shoeing

Note that when the silent *e* is necessary to indicate the pronunciation of long vowels like *o*, and of soft *c* and *g*, the *e* is usually retained:

hoe, hoeing; courage, courageous; change, changeable; singe, singeing

    D. When any suffix except *ing* is added to a word ending in a *y* preceded by a consonant, change the final *y* to *i*:

happy, happiness; bounty, bountiful; study, studying, studious

    E. When a suffix beginning with *e, i,* or *y* is added to a word ending in *c*, add *k* before the suffix:

picnic, picnicking; panic, panicky

    F. Add *s* to the singular forms of most nouns ending in a consonant or a silent *e*, but add *es* if the singular form of the noun ends in a sibilant (hissing sound) without the silent *e*:

cab, cabs; plume, plumes; dress, dresses; topaz, topazes; church, churches

G. Add *s* to most nouns ending in *o* preceded by a vowel, but add *es* to most nouns ending in *o* preceded by a consonant:

cameo, cameos; folio, folios; hero, heroes; mosquito, mosquitoes

Almost all musical terms ending in *o,* and almost all words of foreign derivation simply add *s* to form the plural, regardless of the letter preceding the final *o: alto, altos; crescendo, crescendos; fiasco, fiascos.*

H. Add *s* to nouns ending in *ey,* but when a noun ends in *y* preceded by a consonant, change the *y* to *i* and add *es:*

monkey, monkeys; turkey, turkeys; lady, ladies; country, countries

I. Change the final *f* of some of the singular forms of nouns ending in *f* to *v,* and add *es:*

sheaf, sheaves; thief, thieves; loaf, loaves

The exceptions to this rule are many, and seemingly without reason: *belief, beliefs; chief, chiefs;* and so forth.

J. Add *'s* to numerical symbols, letters of the alphabet, and words used as a unit:

4, 4's; a, a's; the, the's

K. Add *s* to infinitive forms ending in consonants like *k, p, t,* but add *es* to infinitive forms ending in sibilants:

keep, keeps; protect, protects; hiss, hisses; watch, watches

L. Change the final *ie* of the infinitive form to *y* before adding *ing* to form the present participle:

lie, lying; die, dying

M. Change the final *y* of the infinitive form to *i,* and add *es* to form the third person singular:

cry, cries; rely, relies

N. For the use of the hyphen in forming compound words see section M 4E.

O. The following list contains the words most commonly misspelled by student writers:

abbreviate	altogether	bachelor
abridgment	amateur	balance
absence	ambidextrous	baptize
absurd	analogous	barbarous
accept	analysis	bare
acceptance	analyze	barren
access	angel	battalion
accessible	angle	bear
accessory	annihilate	beggar
accidentally	annual	believe
accommodate	antecedent	benefit
accumulate	anxiety	benign
accustom	apology	beseech
acknowledgment	apparatus	biscuit
acquainted	apparent	blamable
across	appearance	boarder
addressed	appreciate	border
advertise	appropriate	born
advice	arctic	borne
advise	arguing	boundary
adviser	arithmetic	bridal
affect	arouse	bridle
aggravate	arrival	Britain
aghast	article	Briton
aisle	ascend	buoyant
allege	asinine	bureau
alley	assassin	burglar
all right	assay	
allusion	athletic	calendar
ally	attacked	candidate
almanac	attendance	candor
altar	audience	canvas
alter	avoirdupois	canyon
alternative	awkward	capital

capitol
carburetor
carcass
career
caricature
cemetery
centennial
chamois
changeable
chaperon
characteristic
chauffeur
chautauqua
chloroform
chord
clothes
colonel
colossal
commission
committee
comparative
compel
competent
complacent
complement
compliment
concede
conceit
conceivable
conferred
confidant
confident
Connecticut
connoisseur
conquer
conqueror
conscience

conscientious
conscientiousness
consensus
consonant
contemptible
continuous
control
convenience
co-operate
cord
corroborate
council
councilor
counselor
countenance
courteous
courtesy
cylinder

dealt
deceit
decision
defamatory
defendant
deferred
definite
delusion
demur
dependence
depth
derisive
descend
descendant
describing
desert
desiccate
desperate

despicable
dessert
device
devise
dictionary
difference
dilemma
dining
diphtheria
dirigible
disappear
disappoint
disastrous
disciplinary
disease
disparate
dispatch
dissimulate
dissipate
distribute
divine
doctor
dormitories
dutiful

ecstasy
edifice
effect
eighth
elevator
eliminate
elucidate
embarrass
emergency
emigration
eminent
encouraging

enforce
enhance
enterprise
entity
envelop
envelope
epidemic
epoch
equipment
equipped
errand
especially
European
evasion
exaggerate
exasperate
exceed
excellence
except
excusable
exhaust
exhilarate
existence
expense
experience
explicit
extemporaneous
extraordinary

facetious
facility
facsimile
falsify
familiar
fascinate
fatal
feasible

February
feminine
fiery
Filipino
financier
flamboyant
forbode
forceful
forcible
forehead
foreign
foremost
forfeit
formally
formerly
forth
fourth
fragile
fragmentary
frantically
fraternity
friend
fumigate
fundamental
funnel
furniture

gallant
gambling
gamboling
garage
gasoline
generally
genius
gesture
ghastly
ghost

glossary
gnat
goddess
governor
grammar
grandeur
grief
grievous
grippe
guarantee
guard
guerrilla
guidance
gymnasium

handicapped
handkerchief
hangar
harass
hearth
height
heinous
heir
hemorrhage
heredity
heroes
hesitancy
hindrance
hoping
hopping
hospitable
human
humane
humorous
hypnotize
hypocrisy

hypothetical	ingenuous	leisure
hysterical	initiate	liable
	innate	library
illegible	innocence	lieutenant
illiterate	innuendo	lightning
illuminate	inoculate	literature
illusion	instance	livelihood
imaginary	instant	loneliness
imitative	insufficient	loose
immediately	intellectual	lose
immigration	intelligence	ludicrous
immortal	intercede	luncheon
immovable	intermediary	luxurious
implement	interpretative	lying
implicit	intrigue	
impromptu	inveigle	mackerel
improvise	irrefutable	maelstrom
inadequate	irrelevant	magnificent
inadvisable	irreligious	maintain
inaugurate	irresistible	maintenance
incessantly	isle	malign
incidentally	isthmus	maneuver
incompatible		manipulate
incompetence	judgment	manual
inconsolable	juvenile	manufacturer
incredible		marriage
incredulous	kerosene	Massachusetts
indecorous	knowledge	massage
independence		mathematics
indescribable	laboratory	mattress
indict	lacerate	meander
indispensable	lacquer	medicine
induce	lagoon	menagerie
inevitable	laid	metal
infinite	laudable	metaphysics
influence	legislate	mettle
ingenious	legitimate	mezzanine

millennium
miniature
mischievous
missile
Mississippi
misspelled
mobilize
moccasin
molecule
momentous
mortgage
mosquito
mucilage
mulatto
murmur
muscle
mysterious

naïve
naphtha
napkin
narrate
necessary
negligible
Negroes
nonchalant
noticeable
notoriety

obedient
obeisance
obligatory
obliterate
oblivious
observance
obstacle
occasion

occur
occurred
octopus
ominous
omit
omitted
operate
opportunity
optimistic
oratorical
originate
ornament
ostracize
outrageous
overrun

pageant
palatable
palisade
pamphlet
pantomime
parable
parallel
paralyze
parenthesis
parliament
participate
participle
partisan
partner
pastime
pedagogical
pendulum
peninsula
perceive
perception
percolate

peremptory
perform
permanence
permissible
perpetrate
perseverance
persistence
perspiration
persuade
pertain
pertinent
phenomenal
Philippines
phlegm
physical
physician
physiology
picnic
picnicking
pillory
piquant
piteous
plagiarize
plaguy
plateau
playwright
pneumonia
poignant
politician
porcelain
porridge
possession
possibility
practically
prairie
precedent
precipitate

preference
preferred
prejudice
preliminary
preparatory
prescription
presence
prestige
primeval
primitive
principal
principle
privilege
proceed
prodigy
professor
program
prologue
promissory
pronunciation
propaganda
prophecy
prophesy
proportion
protestant
psychology
ptomaine
pumpkin
pursue
pyramid

quandary
quantity
quarrel
querulous
quiet

quite
quizzes

raccoon
radiance
rationalize
recapitulate
recede
receipt
receive
reciprocal
recognize
recommend
recompense
reconcile
recuperate
reference
referendum
referred
refrigerate
regiment
region
rehearse
reign
reiterate
relevance
religion
Renaissance
renegade
repellent
repetition
representative
reprimand
repugnant
reservoir
residue
resource

respectfully
respectively
restaurant
reverberate
rhapsody
rhetoric
rheumatism
rhinoceros
rhyme
rhythm
ridiculous
righteous
rite

sacrifice
sacrilegious
salary
sandal
sandwich
sanguine
sarcasm
scene
schedule
scientific
scream
screech
scrupulous
secretary
segregate
seize
sensible
sensitive
sensuous
separate
sergeant
severely
shriek

siege	superintendent	ultimatum
sieve	supersede	undoubtedly
signify	suppress	unique
silhouette	surgeon	universally
similar	surmise	unprecedented
simplicity	surprise	until
simultaneous	susceptible	usage
sincerely	syllable	usually
soliloquy	symbol	
sophisticated	symmetrical	vacancy
sophomore	synthesis	vaccinate
sovereign		vacuum
specifically	tableau	valance
specimen	tailor	valence
spontaneity	tantalize	valise
stadium	temperament	vandal
stampede	temperature	variant
stationary	tendency	vehement
stationery	thorough	veil
statue	thousandths	vengeance
stature	till	veritable
statute	toboggan	vernacular
sterilize	tornado	versatile
stevedore	tortoise	victual
stomach	tragedy	village
strategic	tranquillity	villain
strictly	transferred	vindicative
stubborn	translate	vindictive
submissible	transpire	visibility
subservience	treacherous	vocabulary
substantiate	treasurer	volcano
subtle	tries	voluntary
succeed	Tuesday	
successful	tumultuous	wanton
suffrage	turquoise	warrant
suite	typical	warring
summarize	tyranny	weather

Wednesday	whether	writing
weird	wintry	wrought
welfare	wiry	
wherever	women	yacht

M4   HYPHENATION

The hyphen (-) is a mark of punctuation used for dividing words into syllables and for combining two or more words into a single grammatical unit. Whenever a writer is uncertain about hyphenation he should consult a good dictionary. The tendency in modern writing is to hyphenate sparingly. For example, many words which were once generally hyphenated, such as *today,* are now normally written solid, that is, without the hyphen.

Although many modern writers combine words which the dictionary lists separately, the student should follow the dictionary's practice unless he has a clear reason for disregarding it. Syllabication is indicated, by various means, in every good dictionary.

    A. If it is necessary to divide a word at the end of a line, the division should be made only between syllables, and the hyphen should be placed at the end of the line in which the division occurs, not at the beginning of the next line. Although it will be wise for the student to consult a dictionary when in doubt, the following suggestions may be helpful for syllabication:

    1) As a rule, syllables are determined by pronunciation. If a group of letters cannot be pronounced as in normal speech, it should not be taken from a word and put at the beginning of a new line:

laughed	(NOT: laugh-
	ed
friend	frie-
	nd
through	throu-
	gh)

Closely related to this principle is a corollary: Although in speech a single letter often forms a syllable (try pronouncing *enough* or *above*), a syllable of a single letter should not be allowed to stand either at the beginning or at the end of a line if the syllable is part of a longer word.

2) **Usually a consonant at the junction of two syllables should go with the second of the syllables:**

repre-
    sent
hesi-
    tate
	(NOT: repres-
	    ent
	hesit-
	    ate)

As a corollary of this principle, when two or more consonants occur together at the junction of syllables and when both consonants are pronounced, the consonants usually divide, one staying with the first syllable, one going with the second:

rep-
    resent
com-
    posed
	(NOT: re-
	    present
	comp-
	    osed)

This division usually occurs although the two consonants may be the same, and are pronounced as one:

com-
    mutation
run-
    ner
	(NOT: comm-
	    utation
	runn-
	    er)

3) **Two or more consonants which, like *gh, gn, ng, ph, tch,* and *th,* are pronounced as one letter, or are silent, should never be divided at the end or the beginning of a line:**

perish-
    able
catch-
    ing
	(NOT: peris-
	    hable
	cat-
	    ching)

4) **A prefix or a suffix may usually be set off from the word to which it is attached:**

non-
operative

help-
less

In forming compound words a writer will sometimes hyphenate or not, depending on how close a relationship he wishes to indicate. Or, for the same reason, he may either combine words or leave them separate. Whenever he is uncertain, he should consult a dictionary. The following are standard practices for hyphenation:

B. When the writer uses as a single word one noun followed by an adverb or a prepositional phrase, the hyphen is used unless the dictionary omits it:

runner-up, son-in-law, *but* kickoff, editor in chief

C. When numerals or fractions to ninety-nine and consisting of more than one word are used as adjectives, a hyphen is usually advisable for clarity of meaning:

a TWO-THIRDS majority, TWENTY-SIX tires, ONE HUNDRED AND THIRTY-FOUR dollars

D. When expressions of time are written out, a hyphen is generally used:

at ONE-THIRTY in the morning

E. When two or more words are used as a single part of speech, it is usual, although not obligatory, to hyphenate them:

The milk left a white-blue ring around her lips.—BRADFORD SMITH
He was a notably hard-working, hard-fighting, liberal-minded officer.
—VINCENT SHEEAN

but

The dictionary makers are more likely to err on the side of including words . . . .—GEORGE PHILIP KRAPP

Mr. Salter went to work at midday.—EVELYN WAUGH

My father was a merry playfellow.—HARRIET MONROE

In sentences like those from which the hyphen has been omitted other authors might well write *dictionary-makers, mid-day,* or perhaps *play fellow* or *play-fellow.* As usual, if the student wishes to write conventionally, he will look up the compound word in a reliable dictionary and follow its recommendation.

F. Although prefixes are usually not set off from the word to which they belong (unless at the end of a line), they should be followed by a hyphen (a) if the word they precede is capitalized or (b) if, when joined to the word without a hyphen, that word would be confused with another word:

a) pro-British; anti-British; *but* antiseptic, etc.

b) The RE-FORMATION of the army corps was difficult because of the geography of the country.

The REFORMATION of the drunkard was soon accomplished.

G. A hyphen is generally used between elements of an imitative expression and between the elements of an expression in which the words are only temporarily combined for effect:

The tick-tick, tick-tick, tick-tick of the watch drove him nearly mad.

His hurry-up-with-the-bad-news attitude exasperated me.

H. A hyphen may be used when the final vowel of a prefix is repeated in the initial vowel of the following word:

pre-eminent, co-operate, anti-imperialism

This practice is followed by *Webster's New Collegiate Dictionary. The American College Dictionary,* on the other hand, prints as one word with the diaeresis over the second vowel to show that each is pronounced separately: *coöperate,* but lists *co-operate* and *cooperate* as alternate spellings. There is an increasing tendency to write such words solid without any mark of punctuation: *cooperate.*

M5   CAPITALIZATION

In general, capitalize the first word of a sentence or a line of poetry, a proper name or a term used as a proper name, an adjective derived from a proper name or from a race or nationality, all important words in titles of all sorts, and the pronoun *I*. The rules for the uses of capital letters are so varied that these suggestions are enlarged in detail below.

A. Capitalize the first word of every complete sentence or group of words used as a sentence, whether the sentence stands as an independent unit or as a quotation:

The farmer indignantly answered, "You still have not told me how to raise more corn."

B. In quoting poetry, follow carefully the capitalization of the original writer. Herrick may write

> Gather ye rosebuds while ye may,
> Old Time is still a-flying,
> And this same flower that smiles to-day,
> To-morrow will be dying.

But H. D. in "Pear Tree" prefers

> Silver dust
> lifted from the earth
> higher than my arms reach,
> you have mounted.
> O silver,
> higher than my arms reach
> you front us with great mass . . . .[1]

C. In a title of a literary composition, a musical composition, a magazine, a newspaper, a chapter or other divi-

---

[1] Reprinted by permission, from *H. D.—Selected Poems,* published by Grove Press, Inc., 1957.

sion of a book, or of a person, capitalize all words but determiners, prepositions, and conjunctions, and capitalize these when they are initial or final words.

> The essay which took the prize was called "A New and Startling Theory of Poetry."
>
> Do you still read *Harper's Magazine?*
>
> He was on that steamboat, *The Belle of the Bends,* which made the record run between St. Louis and Memphis.

D. Capitalize the first and last word of the salutation of a letter, but only the first word of the complimentary close.

> Dear Sir: (NOT: Dear sir:).
>
> My dear Sir: (NOT: My Dear Sir:).
>
> Sincerely yours, (NOT: Sincerely Yours,).

E. Capitalize the proper names of persons, personified abstractions, organizations, days, months, special events, and places.

> Jarvis liked the masque his class was producing because he was given the role of Courage.
>
> As he looked across the valley, he admired the remarkable combinations of color which the artist Autumn had devised.
>
> In August she finally got a position with the Board of Education.
>
> He refused to vote for the candidates who had been nominated by either the Citizens' party or the People's party.
>
> The race was held on the Illinois River.
>
> The San Francisco Peaks rise abruptly from the surrounding plateau.
>
> Henry was to meet his wife at Track 4.
>
> For the exact figures see Table 1.
>
> In Figure 7 the proportionate strength of the navies of the world is indicated.

It should be noted that unless the generic terms, as well as the actual names in some of the examples above are capitalized, the questions arise: It is really *the* Illinois River that is meant, or merely some river in the state of Illinois? Are the peaks near San

Francisco? The first question cannot be answered except by the writer; the second question might be answered by a person who knows that they are near Flagstaff, Arizona, and not in California. In other words, if we insist upon writing *Arkansas river* for *Arkansas River, Michigan boulevard* for *Michigan Boulevard, New York university* for *New York University,* we may expect to be misunderstood.

F. Capitalize the titles of officials of high government rank when the titles are used instead of the names of the officials:

The President returned to the White House today.

The Secretary of State delivered an ultimatum.

G. Capitalize the titles of other officials, or of professional men, only when they accompany proper names, or when they are used in place of a definite person.

I saw many dukes and counts when I was on the Continent.

The Duke of Bedford died the other day.

I heard that Professor Mallory was there.

I heard that my old professor had retired.

"Have you seen a doctor about the pain in your arm?" "Yes, I saw the Doctor [meaning a particular doctor] yesterday." (NOT: "Have you seen a Doctor about the pain in your arm?" "Yes, I saw the doctor [meaning a particular doctor] yesterday.")

H. Capitalize the names of the deities of any race, nationality, or age.

The amazed traveler saw the crowd of people fall to their knees and call upon Allah.

Very few Americans know much about Attis or Osiris.

I. Capitalize the pronoun *I* and the interjection *O* (not *oh,* except at the beginning of a sentence).

Mother did not think I would ever get home.

"Come back, O Day," he prayed.

J. Capitalize nouns and adjectives derived from proper nouns, or from races and nationalities.

Among the people described by Melville are Indians and South Sea Islanders.

K. Do not capitalize a word merely to emphasize it.

He is certainly a great man. (NOT: He is certainly a Great Man.)

L. Do not capitalize a word of designation like *company, college, river, street, university, freshman, liberal arts, economics, engineering* unless it is a necessary part of a proper noun.

The irate woman pushed him into the street. (NOT: The irate woman pushed him into the Street.)

I am not going to the university today because my history professor is out of town. (NOT: I am not going to the University today because my History Professor is out of town.)

Many children go through high school without hearing anything said about their going to college. (NOT: Many children go through High School without hearing anything said about their going to College.)

My father founded a manufacturing company. (NOT: My father founded a manufacturing Company.)

However, when such a word is obviously intended to stand for the complete title, and when not to capitalize it would be ambiguous, it should be capitalized.

The League's last home was in Princeton, New Jersey. (The League of Nations.)

The Society has had an influence out of proportion to its size. (The Fabian Society.)

M. Do not capitalize the names of seasons.

This fall I want to do some hunting. (NOT: This Fall I want to do some hunting.)

But in midwinter I intend to stay in town to attend basketball games. (NOT: But in Midwinter I intend to stay in town to attend basketball games.)

N. Do not capitalize the directions *north, south, east, west,* and derivatives from them, unless they are used to designate divisions of the country or geographical regions.

They saw a large flock of ducks flying north. (NOT: They saw a large flock of ducks flying North.)

The Middle West produces a great deal of corn. (NOT: The middle west produces a great deal of corn.)

In the war between the North and the South, moral sentiment played a large part. (NOT: In the war between the north and the south, moral sentiment played a large part.)

If I remember correctly, we turned south when we came to the cross-roads. (NOT: If I remember correctly, we turned South when we came to the crossroads.)

M6   ABBREVIATIONS

It is incorrect to use most abbreviations in formal writing. A few abbreviations, however, have become customary, and some, not otherwise permissible, may be used in special types of writing mentioned below.

A. The following abbreviations may be used in all types of writing:

Mr.	Messrs.
Mrs.	Dr.

(used with proper names)

B.C. (used only after a date)   A.M. (used only with a number)
A.D. (used only before a date)   P.M. (used only with a number)
St. (Saint, as part of a proper name)

B. The following kinds of terms must always be spelled out in formal writing:

1) **All titles** (except those given above):

Professor Smith, Lieutenant Jackson, the Reverend Mr. Lloyd (NOT. Prof. Smith, Lt. Jackson, Rev. Mr. Lloyd)

2) **All names of months, states, and countries:**

August 2, Massachusetts, United States (NOT: Aug. 2, Mass., U.S.)

3) **All given names:**

William Jones, Joseph Howe (NOT: Wm. Jones, Jos. Howe)

4) **All names of weights and measures, except in statistics, technical writing, and tabulations:**

pound, quart, foot (NOT: lb., qt., ft.)

5) **All terms of designation, like** *street, park, company, mountain, manufacturing:*

Halton Manufacturing Company, Pritchard Brothers, Forest Park, Bell Railroad (NOT: Halton Mfg. Co., Pritchard Bros., Forest Pk., Bell R.R.)

C. Abbreviations like those below, if they follow the name, are always permissible:

Ph.D.	D.D.	Jr.
LL.D.	Esq.	Sr.

D. In business correspondence, technical writing, tabulations, bibliographies, and footnotes, and wherever brevity is necessary, abbreviations may be used if their meaning is perfectly clear to the reader:

vol.	volume
ch.	chapter
p.	page
pp.	pages
Co.	company
ed.	edition, editor
St.	street
U.S.	United States

M7   NUMBERS

In ordinary writing, numerical figures are generally used only for dates, street numbers, page numbers, chapters or parts of books, and sums of money which cannot be expressed in less than three words. On all other occasions numbers should be spelled out, except, of course, in special kinds of writing like legal and commercial documents and communications, statistics, and tabulations.

A. Dates

It was on June 4, 1912, that Hallam met the Colonel. (NOT: It was on June fourth, nineteen hundred and twelve, that Hallam met the Colonel.)

The date 1066 should be familiar to every Englishman and to every American. (NOT: The date ten hundred and sixty-six should be familiar to every Englishman and to every American.)

Notice, however, that in formal letters and notes, whether of invitations, acceptance, regret, or condolence, all dates are spelled out.

Mrs. Alfred Hendricks requests the company of Mrs. Henry L. Truslow at dinner on Wednesday, May the seventh, nineteen hundred and fifty-one, at eight o'clock. (NOT: Mrs. Alfred Hendricks requests the company of Mrs. Henry L. Truslow at dinner on Wednesday, May 7, 1951, at 8 p.m.)

B. Sums of Money

The salesman offered to reduce the price of the whistle to five cents. The youngster thought that his seventeen cents was a large fortune. I bought the machine for $621.

The eloquent promoter told me that if I would give him $225 on January first, he would give me $300 on the fifteenth of the following month—and I believed him.

Notice that when two or more sums of money are expressed in the same sentence, or in close proximity to each other, they should both be expressed in the same form, that is, either in letters or in figures. When one of two sums might be written out, because, like *three hundred*, it may be expressed in only two words, and when the other sum must be expressed in figures, because, like *$225*, it would take more than two words to express if spelled out, both numbers should be written in figures. Notice also that when a sum of money does not include cents, the decimal point and the two zeros (.00) are omitted.

C. Miscellaneous Uses

It took the ship five days to reach port. (NOT: It took the ship 5 days to reach port.)

The tract that he intended to subdivide contained 12,762 acres. (NOT: The tract that he intended to subdivide contained twelve thousand, seven hundred and sixty-two acres.)

The native proudly told me that the last census showed that Hawk City had increased its population by more than twelve thousand. (NOT: The native proudly told me that the last census showed that Hawk City had increased its population by more than 12,000.)

Numbers are expressed in words or in figures according to the same rules which apply to sums of money. The figure 5 may be expressed in one word, the figure 12,000 in two; both, consequently, should be spelled out. But the figure 12,762 requires seven words if spelled out; it should therefore be expressed in numerical symbols.

He lives at 1005 Ninety-first Street. (NOT: He lives at 1005 91st Street.)

If you can visit me this winter, I should like you to stay for at least ten days. (NOT: If you can visit me this winter, I should like you to stay for at least 10 days.)

The practice of using both words and figures, one or the other being in parentheses, should always be avoided except in commercial or legal documents and letters in which all chances for a possible misunderstanding must be prepared for. Even in such writing, however, the figures, and not the spelled-out words, should be put in parentheses.

As I wrote you last month, I shall be very glad to pay you twenty-five (25) dollars a month for the use of the truck.

or

As I wrote you last month, I shall be very glad to pay you twenty-five dollars ($25) a month for the use of the truck. (NOT: As I wrote you last month, I shall be very glad to pay you $25 [twenty-five dollars] a month for the use of the truck.)

In a sentence or paragraph when several round numbers are used for comparison, they are generally given in figures.

At this conference 2,500 Cherokee warriors, 1,500 Osage, and 600 Creek were present.

Unless it occurs in mathematical or statistical writing, in footnotes, or in tables, the word "per cent" is always spelled out; figures are used with the word and with the symbol (%) unless they begin a sentence.

At least 15 per cent of the crop was spoiled.

Figures beginning a sentence should be spelled out.

Three hundred and forty warriors threatened us from the riverbank.

EXERCISES

A. Documentation

I. What are the ways in which the author of the Sample Research Paper (Chapter XII) has made acknowledgment of the use of borrowed material?

II. Using any of the examples given in St 8, rewrite the passage in your own words. Incorporate at least four excerpts in direct quotations.

B. Spelling

Keep an up-to-date record of the words you have misspelled on your compositions. Group them according to the principles of spelling which they violate.

C. Hyphenation

I. How would you divide the following words if they came at the end of a line of manuscript and you wanted your division to be correct? Do not put a hyphen between every two syllables of a word, but only where the actual division would occur. If there are several possibilities in any one word, write the entire word each time you demonstrate each possibility. We suggest that you consult a dictionary while doing this exercise:

bustard	suture	exercise
feldspar	atonement	execution
harlequinade	portfolio	executor
Spaniard	portend	lesion
printery	digamy	leopard

II. Should the items in the following list be written as separate words, as hyphenated words, or as solid words? In preparing this exercise consult a good dictionary:

day by day	knuckle duster	oyster man
mill wheel	non professional	oyster farm
warm blooded	armor bearer	day coach
washed out	British French Ameri-	co tangent
wash goods	can co-operation	ball and socket joint
neo Platonism	ad lib.	sixty year old man
draw string	Adam's needle	China berry tree

D. Capitalization

Supply all necessary capitalization in the following paragraph:

the date of american authority in the lake country may be placed in 1796. it was, however, but feebly felt in its influence on the northwest fur trade for several years. congress first legislated on the subject in

1802, but four years afterwards lieut. pike, on reaching the upper mississippi, found it the exclusive possession of the north west company. the
indians were then as much attached to the english, as they had been to
the french in 1759. it cost the british crown the expenses of a war to gain
this ascendancy, and the americans were not permitted to succeed them,
as the sovereign power over indian territory, at a less hazard. the war
of 1812 found all the northern tribes confederated with the english.
tecumseh had risen to re-act the part which pontiac had failed to accomplish, fifty-two years before, namely, driving back the infringing
power. this happened, in 1759, to be great britain; but in 1812 it was
the united states. with less sterling capacity to organize and command,
however, than his great predecessor had, and with the powerful resources
of england to back him, he utterly failed. it was not until after this
failure, and the re-establishment of american garrisons at detroit
michilimackinac, that the jeffersonian indian code of 1802 began to be
put into effect in the northwest. in 1816, a law was passed by congress to
exclude foreigners from the trade. in 1819 st. peter's was established.
in 1820 gov. cass personally visited the tribes; and in 1822, a military
post was advanced to st. mary's falls, the most northern point occupied
by the united states army.—HENRY ROWE SCHOOLCRAFT[2]

E. Abbreviations

In your book of readings note all the examples of abbreviations
in one formal essay and in one informal. Do likewise on the first
page, the women's feature page, and the sports page of your newspaper. Make a written report on the current tendencies of the
use of abbreviations in writing.

F. Numbers

Rewrite the following paragraph according to the conventions
for the use of numbers laid down in section M 7:

The first regiment of Missouri mounted volunteers was composed
of eight companies . . . numbering eight hundred and fifty-six men. The
battalion of light artillery consisted of two companies from St. Louis
under Capts. Weightman and Fischer, numbering near two hundred

---

[2] *Narrative of an Expedition to Itasca Lake* (1834).

and fifty men, with Major Clark as its field officer. The battalion of
infantry from the counties of Cole and Platte . . . numbered one hundred
and forty-five. The Laclede Rangers from St. Louis, under the command of Capt. Hudson, one hundred seven in number, attached to
the First Dragoons, whose strength was three hundred,—composed the
entire force of Col. Kearney. Thus it will appear that the advance of the
Western Army under the immediate command of Col. Kearney, consisted
of one thousand six hundred and fifty-eight men, and sixteen pieces
of ordnance, twelve six pounders and four twelve pound howitzers.—
JOHN T. HUGHES[3]

---

[3] *Doniphan's Expedition* (1848).

V | Language and Usage: Words, Words, Words

> If language is not correct, then what is said is not what is meant; if what is said is not what is meant, then what ought to be done remains undone; if this remains undone, morals and art will deteriorate; if morals and art deteriorate, justice will go astray; if justice goes astray, the people will stand about in helpless confusion.—CONFUCIUS

> O, be some other name!
> What's in a name? that which we call a rose
> By any other name would smell as sweet. . . .
> *Romeo and Juliet*

Confucius stresses the acquisition of "correct" language as the basis upon which an organized society rests, thus testifying to the power of words in our everyday existence. But Juliet, to judge from her familiar question, knows more about language than does the Chinese philosopher. In this chapter, we shall explore the implications of both of these quotations. Using words to talk about words may seem about as circular a process as a dog chasing his own tail; however, we shall try to relate this discussion to something outside itself. An examination of some of the problems of *meaning* and *usage* will help us break out of the apparently futile circle. By considering the question of what a word "means" (if anything), we will be led to the problem of the relationship between words and things—between the sounds we utter or the scratches we make on paper and the things in the nonverbal world that we are thus designating. By considering the question of the choice of a particular word for any given communication

196

situation, we will be led to the problem of language and society. In considering both meaning and usage, our discussion of words leads outward.

I. THE PROBLEM OF MEANING

A word "means" just what we want it to mean, whether that word is *grass, paper, stick, truth, goodness, evil, romanticism,* or *whatchamacallit.* When reading Lewis Carroll's *Through the Looking-Glass,* we smile at Humpty-Dumpty:

> Humpty-Dumpty said: "There's glory for you." "I don't know what you mean by 'glory,'" Alice said. Humpty-Dumpty smiled contemptuously. "Of course you don't—till I tell you. I meant, 'There's a nice knock-down argument for you.'" "But 'glory' doesn't mean 'a nice knock-down argument,'" Alice objected. "When I use a word," Humpty-Dumpty said in a rather scornful tone, "it means just what I choose it to mean, neither more nor less."

But communication would literally be impossible if we were not, to a certain degree, like Humpty-Dumpty. To facilitate understanding, we agree that certain words "mean" or "stand for" certain things—objects, ideas, emotions, situations, and so on.

There are clearly not enough words to go around, so we often may use the same word to refer to different things; very few words have only one fixed meaning. When the context is ambiguous, we are frequently forced to puzzle out which meaning is intended, as in the case of the news item reporting a meeting of a Women's Garden Club at which "an exchange of slips and bloomers was conducted."

On the other hand, we may also have several different words to refer to the same thing. Although each has a slightly different shade of meaning and emphasis, *join, unite, combine, connect, associate, link,* and *couple* all point to essentially the same idea.

Finally, as a matter of historical fact, the meanings assigned to words change through the years. T. S. Eliot writes: ". . . words strain, crack and sometimes break . . . slip, slide, perish, decay with imprecision, will not stay in place." For instance, *opinion* originally meant *reputation, curious* meant *careful, cunning* meant *skillful*, and *pompous* referred to *a procession.*

Communication is possible only when the sender and the receiver—writer and reader, speaker and listener—understand and agree on the "referent," or the thing behind the word being transmitted. Consequently, Humpty-Dumpty and Alice find communication difficult—almost as difficult, in fact, as the U.S. and the U.S.S.R. when each uses the term "democracy" with a different referent. We should not leap to the conclusion that one definition is "right" and the other "wrong." A more proper conclusion is that, in order to have better communication, both sender and receiver should agree on a common meaning for "glory."

Failure to agree can result in a situation similar to that which existed in 1958, in East and West Germany, where a single ethnic people was being divided into two groups by means of the different "languages" spoken on the two sides of the border. The "Duden" Dictionary, the traditional dictionary for the pronunciation and meaning of German words, has two versions, one for East Germans and one for West Germans. The variations in definitions are revealing and tragic. Here are some contrasting definitions. *Cosmopolitanism:* West Duden—"world citizenship"; East Duden—"today primarily a concept of imperialistic ideology which seeks to destroy the cultural heritage of nations and undermine the national independence of peoples by using the idea of 'world citizenship' as a subterfuge." *Objectivism:* West Duden—"the tendency to deal with existing facts and truths rather than subjective thoughts and feelings"; East Duden—"a doctrine by which, under the pretext of scientific objectivity, essential aspects are ignored, while events and opinions are merely registered in an unselective and passive manner." *Atheism:* West Duden—"denial of the existence of God"; East Duden—"scientifically founded denial of the existence of God." Other examples from the East Duden follow: *idealism*—"a philosophical belief which has been surpassed by materialism"; *individualism*—"self-interest without any consideration for society"; *humanism*—"today limited

to the struggle against suppression and exploitation of human
beings in class society."[1]

D1   USE OF THE DICTIONARY

One way in which we can learn what a word means (which is
simply a convenient shorthand way of saying "what, through
precedent, custom, habit, and usage, we have agreed a word refers
to") is by looking the word up in a good dictionary. It is therefore
important that we understand clearly the function of a dictionary.

A dictionary is not a compilation of laws or regulations, like the
Articles of War or the Municipal Code of New York City, although it is commonly regarded and treated as such. In fact, a
dictionary is more like a telephone book than a statute book. It
gives information about what is; it does not lay down rules about
what should be. The most complete dictionary of the English
language, *The Oxford English Dictionary,* in this respect may be
compared to a compendious telephone book which lists all the
people who have ever had a listing in a particular city. As its subtitle ("Compiled on Historical Principles") indicates, the *OED* is
a record of eight hundred years of the English vocabulary, a
series of biographies of individual words. Look up a familiar word
in the *OED* and notice how it has changed since its first recorded
usage. Although less elaborate than the *OED,* all modern dictionaries are similarly reports of the agreed-upon way or ways
in which words have been used and are being used. Understood
as such, and properly used, the dictionary can become your most
valuable reference book.

The intelligent and efficient use of a dictionary requires that
you know something about the various dictionaries available and
also that you know something about the variety of information
available in them. Whenever possible, consult an unabridged dictionary in looking for answers to the problems concerning the

---

[1] Quoted in *PMLA,* June, 1958.

choice of words. Its size and cost usually make it prohibitive for students to own; however, a desk dictionary will serve you well enough for most purposes. Good modern dictionaries include *The American College Dictionary (ACD), Webster's New Collegiate Dictionary,* and *Webster's New World Dictionary.* See the next three pages for sample pages from these books, which illustrate their respective treatment of definitions and other details.

Knowing something about the most important kinds of information your dictionary contains other than definitions will increase its value for you. The following brief summary will indicate the variety of these materials.

1) **The dictionary is authority for spelling, pronunciation, syllabication, and hyphenation.** If the writer is uncertain of the past participle of *refer,* he will find that *referred* is correct (not *refered*). In case of doubt he can reassure himself that the adjective made from *desire* by the addition of *able* drops the final *e* of the original word, whereas that made similarly from *notice* retains the *e (desirable, noticeable).* When he looks up the word "research," he finds the commonly preferred form to be accented on the second syllable. He discovers that the word "literary" is pronounced as a four-syllable word with the accent on the first syllable (not *lit'-ry*). Of two spellings or pronunciations, that which is given first is the preferred (American) form: *judgment, judgement; ramekin, ramequin; el'-e-gi'-ac, e-le'-gi-ac.* In *Webster's New Collegiate Dictionary,* pronunciation is generally shown by respelling following the entry: **cay** (kē; kā); explanation of the symbol used is given in the "Guide to Pronunciation." When in doubt the writer can make sure that *hypocrisy* is divided *hy-poc-ri-sy;* and *hypocrite, hyp-o-crite;* or that *runaway* is written as one word, whereas *run-on* must be written with the hyphen.

2) **The dictionary gives the grammatical classification and the derivation of each word.** The part of speech is indicated by the customary abbreviations; the principal parts of verbs, the plurals of nouns, and other inflectional forms are given

hi·run·dine (hĭ'rŭn'dīn, -dĭn), *adj.* of, pertaining to, or resembling the swallow. [t. LL: s. *hirundineus*]

his (hĭz), *pron.* **1.** the possessive form of *he: this book is his.* **2.** the person(s) or thing(s) belonging to him: *himself and his, a friend of his.* —*adj.* **3.** belonging to; pertaining to, or owned by him; made, done, experienced, etc., by him. [ME and OE; gen. of masc. *hē* HE, also of neut. *hit* IT]

His·pa·ni·a (hĭs pā'nĭə, -nyə), *n. Poetic.* Spain. [t. L the Spanish peninsula (with Portugal)]

His·pan·ic (hĭs păn'ĭk), *adj.* Spanish.

His·pan·i·cism (hĭs păn'ə sĭz'əm), *n.* a Spanish idiom.

His·pan·io·la (hĭs'pan yō'lə; *Sp.* ēs'pēln yō'lä), *n.* an island in the West Indies, including the republic of Haiti and the Dominican Republic. 5,796,805 pop. (est. 1953); 29,843 sq. mi. Formerly, **Haiti.**

his·pid (hĭs'pĭd), *adj. Bot., Zool.* rough with stiff hairs, bristles, or minute spines. [t. L: s. *hispidus*] —**his·pid′i·ty,** *n.*

hiss (hĭs), *v.i.* **1.** to make or emit a sharp sound like that of the letter *s* prolonged, as a goose or a serpent does, or as steam does rushing through a small opening. **2.** to express disapproval or contempt by making this sound. —*v.t.* **3.** to express disapproval of by hissing. **4.** to force or drive by hissing (ful. by *away, down,* etc.). **5.** to utter with a hiss. —*n.* **6.** a hissing sound, esp. in disapproval. [unexplained var. of d. E *hish,* ME *hisshe*(*n*) hiss, OE *hyscan* jeer at, rail] —**hiss′er,** *n.*

hiss·ing (hĭs'ĭng), *n.* **1.** act of hissing. **2.** the sound of a hiss. **3.** *Archaic.* an object or object of scorn.

hist (hĭst), *interj.* **1.** a sibilant exclamation used to attract attention, command silence, etc. —*v.i.* **2.** to use the exclamation "hist" to.

hist., **1.** histology. **2.** historical. **3.** history.

his·tam·i·nase (hĭs'tăm'ə nās'), *n.* an enzyme capable of making histamine inactive, used in treating allergies.

his·ta·mine (hĭs'tə mēn', -mĭn), *n.* an amine, $C_5H_9N_3$, obtained from histidine and found in ergot. It is released by the tissues in allergic reactions, is a powerful uterine stimulant, and lowers the blood pressure. —**his·ta·min·ic** (hĭs'tə mĭn'ĭk), *adj.*

his·ti·dine (hĭs'tə dēn', -dĭn), *n.* an amino acid, $C_6H_9N_3O_2$, derived from fish protamines or from ptomaines when acted upon by sulfuric acid, converted by putrefactive organisms into histamine. [f. HIST- + -ID² + -INE². Cf. G *histidin*]

histo-, a word element meaning "tissue," as in *histogen.* Also, before vowels, **hist-.** [t. Gk., comb form of *histós* web, tissue; also used as comb. form of Gk. *histán* check]

his·to·gen (hĭs'tə jĕn), *n. Bot.* the regions in a plant in which tissues undergo differentiation.

his·to·gen·e·sis (hĭs'tə jĕn'ə sĭs), *n. Biol.* the formation and differentiation of a tissue.

his·to·gram (hĭs'tə grăm'), *n. Statistics.* a graph of a frequency distribution in which equal intervals of values are marked on a horizontal axis and the frequency corresponding to each interval is indicated by the height of a rectangle having the interval as its base.

his·toid (hĭs'toid), *adj. Pathol.* denoting a tumor composed of connective tissue or its equivalent.

his·tol·o·gy (hĭs tŏl'ə jĭ), *n.* **1.** the science that treats of organic tissues. **2.** the study of the structure, esp. the microscopic structure, of organic tissues. —**his·to·log·i·cal** (hĭs'tə lŏj'ə kəl), **his·to·log′ic,** *adj.* —**his·tol′o·gist,** *n.*

his·tol·y·sis (hĭs tŏl'ə sĭs), *n.* ˙ *Biol.* disintegration or dissolution of organic tissues.

his·tone (hĭs'tōn), *n. Biochem.* any of a class of protein substances, as globin, having marked basic properties. Also, **his·ton** (hĭs'tŏn). [f. HIST- + -ONE. Cf. G *histon*]

his·to·ri·an (hĭs tōr'ĭən), *n.* **1.** a writer of history. **2.** an expert in history; an authority on history.

his·tor·ic (hĭs tôr'ĭk, -tōr'-), *adj.* **1.** well-known or important in history: *historic scenes.* **2.** historical.

his·tor·i·cal (hĭs tôr'ə kəl, -tōr'-), *adj.* **1.** relating to or concerned with history or historical events. **2.** dealing with or treating of history or historical events. **3.** pertaining to or of the nature of history or historical events. **4.** pertaining to or of the nature of history as opposed to legend or fiction: *the historical King Arthur.* **5.** narrated or mentioned in history; belonging to the past. **6.** historic. **7.** *Gram.* used in the statement of past facts or the narration of past events. [f. s. L *historicus* (t. Gk.: m. *historikós*) + -AL¹] —**his·tor′i·cal·ly,** *adv.* —**his·tor′i·cal·ness,** *n.*

historical geography, 1. the study of the geography of a past period or periods. **2.** geographic history.

historical method, the development of general principles by the study of the historical facts.

historical present, *Gram.* the present tense used in narrating a past event as if it were happening at the time of narration. Also, **historic present.**

historical school, 1. a group of economists who adhere to the so-called historical method, as compared with the method of theoretical analysis. **2.** *Law.* the school of jurists who maintain that law is not to be regarded as made by commands of the sovereign, but is the result of its historical and social circumstances.

his·to·ric·i·ty (hĭs'tə rĭs'ətĭ), *n.* historical authenticity.

his·to·ri·og·ra·pher (hĭs tōr'ĭ ŏg'rə fər), *n.* **1.** a historian. **2.** an official historian, as of a court, an institution, etc. [f. s. LL *historiographus* (t. Gk.: m. *historiográphos*) + -ER¹] —**his·to′ri·og·ra·phy,** *n.*

his·to·ry (hĭs'tərĭ), *n., pl. -ries.* **1.** the branch of knowledge dealing with past events. **2.** the record of past events, esp. in connection with the human race. **3.** a continuous, systematic written narrative, in order of time, of past events as relating to a particular people, country, period, person, etc. **4.** the aggregate of past events. **5.** a past worthy of record or out of the ordinary: *a ship with a history.* **6.** a systematic account of any set of natural phenomena, without reference to time. **7.** a drama representing historical events. [ME, t. L: m.s. *historia,* t. Gk.: a learning or knowing by inquiry, information, narrative, history] —**Syn. 2.** account, record, chronicle; annals. See **narrative.**

his·tri·on·ic (hĭs'trĭ ŏn'ĭk), *adj.* **1.** of or pertaining to actors or acting. **2.** artificial; affected. Also, **his·tri·on′i·cal.** [t. LL: s. *histriōnicus*] —**his′tri·on′i·cal·ly,** *adv.*

his·tri·on·ics (hĭs'trĭ ŏn'ĭks), *n.pl.* **1.** dramatic representation; theatricals; acting. **2.** artificial behavior. See **speech,** etc., for effect.

hit¹ (hĭt), *v., hit, hit·ting, n.* —*v.t.* **1.** to deal a blow or stroke; bring forcibly into collision: *to hit a child.* **2.** to come against with an impact or collision, as a missile, a flying fragment, a falling body, or the like does. **3.** to reach with a missile, a weapon, a blow, or the like (intentionally or otherwise), as one throwing, shooting, or striking. **4.** to succeed in striking: *to hit the mark.* **5.** to drive or propel by a stroke. **6.** to touch effectively; affect severely. **7.** to assail effectively and sharply: *to be hit by satire.* —*v.i.* **8.** to strike with a missile, a weapon, or the like; deal a blow or blows. **9.** to drive the piston in the cylinder of an internal-combustion engine by the combustion of fuel. **10.** hit or miss, whether one hits or misses; at haphazard. —*n.* **11.** an impact or collision, as of one thing against another. **12.** a stroke that reaches an object; a blow. **13.** a stroke of satire, censure, etc. **14.** *Baseball.* a ball so hit that even when fielded without error it enables the batter to reach base safely and without forcing out another baserunner. **15.** *Backgammon.* **a.** a game won by a player after his opponent has thrown off one or more men from the board. **b.** any winning game. [ME *hitte, hutte, hete,* of unknown orig.] —**hit′ter,** *n.* —**Syn. 1.** See **strike, beat.**

hit² (hĭt), *v., hit, hit·ting, n.* —*v.t.* **1.** to come or light upon; meet with; find: *to hit the right road.* **2.** to agree with; suit exactly: *this hits my fancy.* **3.** to guess correctly. **4.** to succeed in representing or producing exactly: *to hit a likeness in a portrait.* **5.** *U.S. Colloq.* to arrive at: *to hit town.* **6.** *U.S. Colloq.* to go to or upon: *to hit the trail.* **7.** hit off, *Colloq.* to agree; get on: as with a person, or with each other. **8. hit off, a.** to represent, reproduce, or describe aptly. **b.** to produce readily or offhand. —*v.i.* **9.** to come into collision (often fol. by *against, on,* or *upon*). **10.** to come or light (fol. by *upon* or *on*): *to hit on a new way.* —*n.* **11.** a successful stroke, performance, or production; success: *the play is a hit.* **12.** an effective or telling expression or saying. [ME *hitte*(*n*), OE *hittan,* t. Scand.; cf. Icel. *hitta* come upon (by chance), meet]

hitch (hĭch), *v.t.* **1.** to make fast, esp. temporarily, by means of a hook, rope, strap, etc.; tether. **2.** to harness (an animal) to a vehicle (often fol. by *up*). **3.** to raise with jerks (usually fol. by *up*): *to hitch up one's trousers.* **4.** to move or draw (something) with a jerk. —*v.i.* **5.** to harness an animal to a vehicle (fol. by *up*). **6.** to become fastened or caught, as on something. **7.** to stick, as when caught. **8.** to fasten oneself or itself to something (often fol. by *on*). **9.** to move jerkily: *to hitch along.* **10.** *Colloq.* to get on together; agree. **11.** to hobble or limp. —*n.* **12.** a making fast, as to something, esp. temporarily. **13.** *Naut., etc.* any of various forms of knot or fastening made with rope or the like. **14.** a halt; an obstruction: *a hitch in the proceedings.* **15.** a hitching movement; a jerk or pull. **16.** a hitching gait; a hobble or limp. **17.** a fastening that joins a movable tool to the mechanism that pulls it. **18.** *U.S. Colloq.* period of military service or the like. [ME *hytche*(*n*); orig. uncert.] —**hitch′er,** *n.* —**Syn. 1.** fasten, attach, tie, tether. **2.** yoke. —**Ant. 1.** loosen.

hitch·hike (hĭch'hīk'), *v.i.* —**hiked, -hiking.** *Colloq.* to travel by walking, with occasional rides in passing automobiles. —**hitch′hik′er,** *n.*

hitching post, a post to which horses, etc., are tied.

hith·er (hĭth'ər), *adv.* **1.** to or toward this place: *to come hither.* —*adj.* **2.** on or toward this side; nearer: *the hither side of the hill.* **3.** earlier; more remote. [ME and OE *hider,* c. Icel. *hethra; der.* demonstrative stem represented by HE]

hith·er·most (hĭth'ər mōst'), *adj.* nearest in this direction.

hith·er·to (hĭth'ər tōō'), *adv.* **1.** up to this time; until now: *a fact hitherto unknown.* **2.** *Archaic.* to here.

hith·er·ward (hĭth'ər wərd), *adv.* hither. Also, **hith′er·wards.**

Hit·ler (hĭt'lər), *n.* **Adolf** (ăd'ŏlf, ä'dōlf; *Ger.* ä'dōlf), ("*der Führer*") 1889–1945, N-zi dictator of Germany, born in Austria: Chancellor, 1933–45; Führer, 1934–45.

Hit·tite (hĭt'īt), *n.* **1.** one of a powerful, civilized ancient people who flourished in Asia Minor and adjoining

b., blend of, blended; c., cognate with; d., dialect, dialectal; der., derived from; f., formed from; g., going back to m., modification of; r., replacing; s., stem of; t., taken from; ?, perhaps. See the full key on inside co▸

Reduced in size by permission. From *The American College Dictionary,* copyright 1947 by Random House, Inc.

hip'po·pot'a·mus (hĭp'ō·pŏt'ȧ·mŭs), *n.; pl.* HIPPOPOTAMUSES (-ĕz; -ĭz), HIPPOPOTAMI (-mī), sometimes HIPPOPOTAMUS. [L., fr. Gr. *hippopotamos*, fr. *hippos* horse + *potamos* river.] Any of a family (Hippopotamidae) or of its typical genus (*Hippopotamus*) of herbivorous mammals allied to the hogs, and largely aquatic in habits; esp., one (*Hippopotamus amphibius*) found in African rivers, and, next to the elephant, the largest existing quadruped.

-hip'pus (-hĭp'ŭs). [Gr. *hippos*.] *Zool.* A combining form meaning *horse*, used in generic names, esp. in paleontology, as eo*hippus*.

hip roof. A roof with sloping ends and sides; hipped roof.

hip'shot' (hĭp'shŏt'), *adj.* [*hip* + *shot*.] Having the hip dislocated; hence, having one hip lower than the other.

hir'cine (hûr'sīn; -sĭn), *adj.* [L. *hircinus*, fr. *hircus* he-goat.] Goatlike, esp. in smell; also, goatish; lecherous.

hire (hīr), *n.* [AS. *hȳr*.] **1.** The price paid for the use of a thing or a place, for personal service, or for labor; pay. **2.** Act of hiring something. — **Syn.** See WAGE. — *v. t.* **1.** To engage the labor or services of, for hire. **2.** To procure for temporary use, for a compensation. **3.** To grant temporary use of, for compensation; let; lease. — *v. i.* *Colloq.* To give one's services for hire. — **hir'a·ble** (hīr'ȧ·b'l), **hire'a·ble**, *adj.* — **hir'er** (hīr'ẽr), *n.*

Syn. (1) See EMPLOY.

(2) **Hire, let, lease, rent, charter** mean to engage or grant for use at a price or rate. **Hire** and **let** are usually complementary terms, *hire* implying the act of engaging and *let*, the act of granting for use; **lease**, in precise use, implies a letting, but in current and not always approved use it implies hiring on a lease; **rent** strictly implies the payment of money for use and, so long as this idea is stressed, it may connote either hiring or letting; **charter** strictly implies hiring a ship on a lease, but is now used of any vehicle, especially a public one.

hire'ling (-lĭng), *n.* One who is hired; hence, a mercenary. — **hire'ling**, *adj.*

hir'ple (hûr'p'l; hĭr'-), *v. i. & n.* *Scot.* Hobble; limp.

hir'sle (hûr's'l; hĭr'-), *v. i. & t.* *Scot.* To hitch along.

hir'sute (hûr'sūt; hûr·sūt'), *adj.* [L. *hirsutus*.] Rough with hair or bristles; shaggy. — **hir'sute·ness**, *n.*

hir·tel'lous (hûr·tĕl'ŭs), *adj.* [From L. *hirtus* hairy.] Finely hirsute.

hi·ru'di·noid (hĭ·rōō'dĭ·noid), *adj.* [L. *hirudo*, *-inis*, leech + *-oid*.] *Zool.* Resembling a leech.

hi·run'dine (hĭ·rŭn'dĭn; -dīn), *adj.* [L. *hirundo* swallow.] *Zool.* Like or pertaining to the swallows.

his (hĭz; 4), *pron.* [AS. *his* of him, his, gen. masc. & neut. of *hē*, neut. *hit*. See HE.] Of him; — the possessive case of *he* used as an objective genitive (as, *his* memory will live long) or absolutely (as, the book is *his*). — *adj.* Belonging or pert. to him; made, done, etc., by him.

His·pa'ni·a (hĭs·pā'nĭ·ȧ; -pān'yȧ), *n.* [L.] An ancient country comprising modern Spain and Portugal; now, *Poetic*, Spain.

His·pan'ic (hĭs·păn'ĭk), *adj.* Spanish. — **His·pan'i·cism** (-ĭ·sĭz'm), *n.*

his'pa·ni·dad' (ēs'pä·nē·thäth'), *n.* [Sp. See HISPANIA.] A movement based on assertion of the spiritual unity of Latin culture in Europe and America and the doctrine that Spain is destined to control Latin America.

his'pid (hĭs'pĭd), *adj.* [L. *hispidus*.] Rough with bristles, stiff hairs, or minute spines. — **his·pid'i·ty** (hĭs·pĭd'ĭ·tĭ), *n.*

his·pid'u·lous (hĭs·pĭd'ū·lŭs), *adj.* [Dim. of *hispid*.] *Bot. & Zool.* Minutely hispid.

hiss (hĭs), *v. i.* [ME. *hissen*, of imitative origin.] To make a sharp sibilant sound like the prolonged sound of the letter *s* or the sound emitted by an angered goose or snake; esp., to make such a sound as an expression of hatred or disapproval. — *v. t.* **1.** To condemn by hissing. **2.** To utter with a hiss. — *n.* The sound made in hissing or one like it, esp. as an expression of hatred or disapproval. — **hiss'er**, *n.*

hiss'ing, *n.* **1.** Act of emitting a hiss or hisses. **2.** *Archaic.* An object of scorn or contempt.

hist (hĭst), *interj.* Hush! Be silent! Listen! — *v. t.* To say "Hist" to, or urge by or as if by that sound.

his'ta·mine (hĭs'tȧ·mēn; -mĭn), *n.* [*hist*idine + *amine*.] *Biochem.* A compound, $C_5H_9N_3$, occurring in ergot and many animal tissues, also made synthetically. It is thought to be responsible for the dilatation and increased permeability of blood vessels which play a major role in allergic reactions, as in hives and asthma, and in certain respiratory affections. — **his'ta·min'ic** (-mĭn'ĭk), *adj.*

his'ti·dine (hĭs'tĭ·dēn; -dĭn), *n.* Also **his'ti·din**. [Gr. *histion* tissue.] *Biochem.* A crystalline basic amino acid, $C_6H_9N_3O_2$, formed in the splitting of proteins.

his'tie (hĭs'tĭ), *adj.* *Scot.* Bare; barren.

his'to- (hĭs'tō-), **hist-**. [Gr. *histos* loom, warp, web.] *Chiefly Biol.* A combining form, meaning *tissue;* as in:

histoblast	**histography**	**histopathology**
histochemistry	**histolysis**	**histophysiology**
histogenesis	**histomorphology**	**histotome**

his'to·gram (hĭs'tō·grăm), *n.* [*histo-* + *-gram*.] *Statistics.* A graphical representation of a frequency distribution by a series of rectangles which have for one dimension a distance proportional to a definite range of frequencies and for the other dimension a distance proportional to the number of frequencies appearing within the range.

his'toid (hĭs'toid), *adj.* [*hist-* + *-oid*.] *Med.* Resembling the normal tissues; as, *histoid* tumors.

his·tol'o·gy (hĭs·tŏl'ō·jĭ), *n.* [*histo-* + *-logy*.] **1.** That branch of science which treats of the minute structure of animal and vegetable tissues. **2.** The tissue structure or organization, as of an organism. — **his'to·log'i·cal** (hĭs'tō·lŏj'ĭ·kăl), *adj.* — **his·tol'o·gist** (hĭs·tŏl'ō·jĭst), *n.*

his'tone (hĭs'tōn), *n.* Also **his'ton** (-tŏn). [Gr. *histos* tissue.] *Biochem.* Any of a class of basic proteins, soluble in water and dilute acids, yielding amino acids on hydrolysis. Injected into an animal, they show a toxic action and prevent coagulation of the blood.

his·to'ri·an (hĭs·tō'rĭ·ăn; 70), *n.* **1.** A writer of history; chronicler; annalist. **2.** One versed in history.

his·tor'ic (-tŏr'ĭk), *adj.* Historical; esp., famous in history.

his·tor'i·cal (-ĭ·kăl), *adj.* [L. *historicus*, fr. Gr. *historikos*. See HISTORY.] **1.** Of, pertaining to, or of the nature of history; narrating, dealing with, or based upon history; true to history; as, *historical* evidence, fidelity, or novels; few details were *historical*. **2.** Not now used except in historical accounts; — of words. **3.** Famous in history; associated with history. — **his·tor'i·cal·ly**, *adv.* — **-cal·ness**, *n.*

historical, *or* **historic, present.** See PRESENT, *adj.*, 5.

historical school. A number of economists who have been variously classed together as pursuing the **historical method**, that is, basing their teaching upon the facts revealed by historical research and the inductions to be drawn from them.

his'to·ric'i·ty (hĭs'tō·rĭs'ĭ·tĭ), *n.* Actual occurrence or existence; historical genuineness.

his'to·ried (hĭs'tō·rĭd), *adj.* Having a history; storied.

his·to'ri·og'ra·pher (hĭs·tō'rĭ·ŏg'rȧ·fẽr), *n.* [F. *historiographe*, fr. L., fr. Gr. *historiographos*, fr. *historia* history + *graphein* to write.] A historian; esp., one designated to write a history. — **his·to'ri·og'ra·phy** (-fĭ), *n.*

his'to·ry (hĭs'tō·rĭ; -trĭ), *n.; pl.* -RIES (-rĭz; -trĭz). [L. *historia*, fr. Gr. *historia* history, information, fr. *histōr* knowing.] **1. a** A narrative of events; a tale; story. **b** A record of facts about a person, as a ***case history***, which lists details relating to ancestry, environment, experiences, and the like, for use in analyzing a case as for treatment or discipline. **2.** A systematic written account of events, particularly of those affecting a nation, institution, science, or art, usually connected with a philosophical explanation of their causes. **3.** The branch of knowledge that records and explains past events. **4.** Events which form the subject matter of a history; as, to survey the *history* of a movement. **5.** Something that belongs to the past; as, that is all *history*.

his'tri·on'ic (hĭs'trĭ·ŏn'ĭk), *adj.* [LL. *histrionicus*, fr. L. *histrio* an actor.] Of or pertaining to the stage or actors; theatrical. — **Syn.** See DRAMATIC. — *n.* An actor; also, *pl.*, dramatic representation; theatricals. — **his'tri·on'i·cal** (-ĭ·kăl), *adj.* — **his'tri·on'i·cal·ly**, *adv.* — **his'tri·on'i·cism** (-ĭ·sĭz'm) *or* **his'tri·o·nism** (hĭs'trĭ·ō·nĭz'm), *n.*

hit (hĭt), *v. t.;* HIT; HIT'TING. [ON. *hitta*.] **1.** To reach with or as if with a stroke; to strike or touch, usually with force and often as a result of an aim. **2.** Hence: **a** To bring into violent contact; knock; as, to *hit* one's head in falling. **b** To deliver; as, to *hit* a blow. **3.** To affect to one's detriment, discomfort, or discomfiture, as, the taunt *hit* him hard. **4.** To come upon or meet with as after search or by chance; arrive at; as, to *hit* the answer to a riddle. **5.** To accord precisely with; suit. **6.** To represent, mimic, or reproduce; as, to *hit* the right note. **7.** To set in operation as by striking or touching. — *v. i.* **1.** To deliver a blow; make thrusts; strike; — often with *out*. **2.** To come in contact forcibly; collide. **3.** To come, happen, or light (*upon*); as, to *hit* upon a solution. **4.** To accord; suit; agree. **5.** Of an internal-combustion engine, to fire the charge in its cylinders. — **Syn.** See STRIKE. — ***hit off.*** To improvise, imitate, etc., neatly and easily.

hit, *n.* **1.** A blow striking the object aimed at. **2.** A collision. **3. a** A stroke of success. **b** A conspicuously successful play, book, etc. **4.** An effectively turned or directed phrase; esp., a stinging remark. **5.** *Backgammon.* A game won after the adversary has removed some of his men, counting less than a gammon; sometimes, any game won. **6.** *Ball Games.* A stroke by which the ball is hit so as to result in a score, or some other advantage; specif., *Baseball*, a base hit. — **hit'ter**, *n.*

hit'-and-miss', *adj.* Sometimes hitting, or corresponding in position, and sometimes not.

hit'-and-run', *adj.* **1.** *Baseball.* Designating or pert. to a play in which a base runner starts for the next base as the pitcher starts to pitch, and the batsman attempts to hit the ball. **2.** That hits and runs away; — orig. and esp. used of motor-vehicle drivers who flee after being involved in an accident.

hitch (hĭch), *v. t.* **1.** To move with jerks. **2.** To catch or fasten as by a hook or knot; to make fast, unite, or yoke. — *v. i.* **1.** To move haltingly, jerkily, or discontinuously; hobble; hop. **2.** To become entangled, caught, or yoked; to catch or cling to something. **3.** *Colloq.* To agree; harmonize. — *n.* **1.** A sudden movement or pull; a jerk. **2.** A hobble; a hop. **3.** A stop or sudden halt; impediment; obstacle. **4.** Act of catching hold of or on something. **5.** A connection between a portable implement, as a plow, and the source of draft, as a tractor. **6.** *Naut.* A knot or noose that can be easily untied; — used for temporary fastening. See KNOT, *n.*, *Illust.* — **hitch'er**, *n.*

hitch'hike' (hĭch'hīk'), *v. i.* *Slang.* To make one's way, esp. when hiking, by getting rides in automobiles.

hith'er (hĭth'ẽr), *adv.* [AS. *hider*.] To this place. — *adj.* Being on the side next or toward the person speaking; nearer; also, of time, earlier.

hith'er·most (hĭth'ẽr·mōst), *adj.* Nearest on this side.

hith'er·to' (hĭth'ẽr·tōō'; 2), *adv.* **1.** To this place. **2.** Up to this time; as yet; until now.

hith'er·ward (hĭth'ẽr·wẽrd), *adv.* Also **hith'er·wards** (-wẽrdz). Toward this place; hither.

Hit'ler·ism (hĭt'lẽr·ĭz'm), *n.* *Ger. Hist.* The extreme nationalistic doctrines of the National Socialist party under the leadership of Adolf Hitler, from about 1930; German fascism. — **Hit'ler·ite** (-īt), *n. & adj.*

hit or miss. Haphazardly. — **hit'-or-miss'**, *adj.*

Hit'tite (hĭt'īt), *n.* [Heb. *Ḥittīm* Hittites.] **1.** One of an ancient people (or group of peoples), of undetermined origin, who invaded and conquered Asia Minor and Syria in the 2d millennium B.C. **2.** The official language of the Hittite empire. — **Hit'tite**, *adj.*

hive (hīv), *n.* [AS. *hȳf*.] **1.** A beehive. **2.** The bees of one hive; a swarm of bees. **3.** Something suggestive of a beehive as in a place swarming with busy occupants. — *v. t.* **1.** To collect into, or cause to enter, a hive. **2.** To store up in a hive, as honey; hence, to lay up a store of. — *v. i.* To enter a hive together, as bees; to reside in a body. — **hiv'er** (hīv'ẽr), *n.*

Hives, 1. 1 Old-fashioned; 2 Modern; *A* Cover; *B* Super; *C* Brood Chamber; *D* Bottom.

hives (hīvz), *n.* [Scot.] Urticaria; any eruptive skin disease.

ho (hō), *interj.* [OF.] Stop! Stand still! Whoa!

ho (hō), *interj.* Also **hoa.** **1.** A cry of surprise, delight, etc., or when repeated, of derisive laughter. **2.** Halloo! Attend! **3.** Expressing a (specified) direction or destination; as, westward *ho*.

ho·ac'tzin (hō·ăk'tsĭn). Var. of HOATZIN.

hoar (hōr; 70), *adj.* [AS. *hār* gray, old.] **1.** White or light gray. **2.** Gray or white with age; hoary; venerable. **3.** *Now Dial.* Moldy; musty; stale. — *n.* **1.** Hoariness. **2.** Hoarfrost.

Hi·ro·shi·ma (hēr'ō-shē'mä), *n.* a city on the southwestern coast of Honshu, Japan: pop., c. 200,000 (1947), 344,000 (1940): on August 6, 1945 it was largely destroyed by an American atomic bomb, the first ever used in warfare.

hir·sute (hŭr'sōōt, hẽr-sūt'), *adj.* [L. *hirsutus*], hairy; shaggy; bristly.

hi·ru·di·noid (hi-rōō'də-noid'), *adj.* [< L. *hirudo, hirudinis*, a leech; + *-oid*], of or like a leech.

hi·run·dine (hi-run'din, hi-run'din), *adj.* [< L. *hirundo, hirundinis*, a swallow], of or like a swallow (bird).

his (hiz), *pron.* [AS. *his*, of him, his, genit. masc. & neut. of *he*], that or those belonging to him: used without a following noun, often after *of*, as, a friend of *his*, that book is *his*, *his* are better. *possessive pronominal adj.* of, belonging to, or done by him.

His·pa·ni·a (his-pā'ni-ə, his-pā'nyə), *n.* [L.], 1. a division of the ancient Roman Empire, including what is now Spain and Portugal. 2. [Poetic], Spain.

His·pan·ic (his-pan'ik), *adj.* [L. *Hispanicus*], Spanish.

His·pan·io·la (his'pan-yō'lə), *n.* an island in the West Indies, between Cuba and Puerto Rico: area, 28,242 sq. mi.; pop., 4,656,000: divided between Haiti and the Dominican Republic: formerly called *Haiti*.

his·pid (his'pid), *adj.* [L. *hispidus*], covered with rough bristles, stiff hairs, or small spines.

his·pid·i·ty (his-pid'ə-ti), *n.* the state of being hispid.

hiss (his), *v.i.* [ME. *hissen*; of echoic origin], 1. to make a sound like that of a prolonged *s*, as of a goose or snake, or of escaping steam, air, etc. 2. to show hatred or disapproval by hissing. *v.t.* 1. to say or indicate by hissing. 2. to show hatred or disapproval of by hissing. 3. to force or drive by hissing. *n.* a sound like that of a prolonged *s*.

hist (st, hist *is a sp. pronun.*), *interj.* an exclamation to attract attention, call for silence, etc., equivalent to "be quiet! listen!"

hist., 1. historian. 2. historical. 3. history.

his·ta·mine (his'tə-mēn', his'tə-min), *n.* [< *histidine* + *amine*], an amine, $C_5H_9N_3·CH_2·CH_2·NH_2$, produced by the decomposition of histidine and found in all organic matter: it is released by the tissues in allergic reactions, lowers the blood pressure by dilating blood vessels, stimulates gastric secretion, etc.

his·ti·din (his'tə-din), *n.* histidine.

his·ti·dine (his'tə-dēn', his'tə-din), *n.* [< Gr. *histion*, dim. of *histos* (see HISTO-); + *-ine*], an amino acid, $C_6H_9N_3O_2$, formed by the hydrolysis of proteins.

his·to- (his'tō, his'tə), [< Gr. *histos*, a loom, warp, web, tissue], a combining form meaning *tissue*, as in *histology*: also, before a vowel, hist-.

his·toid (his'toid), *adj.* [*hist-* + *-oid*], like the surrounding or normal tissue: as, a *histoid* tumor.

his·to·log·i·cal (his'tə-loj'i-k'l), *adj.* of histology.

his·tol·o·gy (his-tol'ə-ji), *n.* [*histo-* + *-logy*], 1. the branch of biology concerned with the microscopic study of the structure of tissues. 2. the tissue structure of an organism or part.

his·tol·y·sis (his-tol'ə-sis), *n.* [Mod. L.; see HISTO- & -LYSIS], in *biology*, the breaking down and dissolution of organic tissues.

his·ton (his'ton), *n.* histone.

his·tone (his'tōn), *n.* [< Gr. *histos* (see HISTO-); + *-one*], any of a group of simple proteins that yield amino acids on hydrolysis, as the globin of hemoglobin: they are often poisonous when injected into an animal, and prevent the clotting of blood.

his·to·ri·an (his-tôr'i-ən, his-tō'ri-ən), *n.* [Fr. *historien*], 1. a writer of history; chronicler. 2. an authority on or specialist in history. Abbreviated hist.

his·tor·ic (his-tôr'ik, his-tor'ik), *adj.* [L. *historicus*; Gr. *historikos*], historical; especially, famous in history.

his·tor·i·cal (his-tôr'i-k'l, his-tor'i-k'l), *adj.* [< L. *historicus*; + *-al*], 1. of or concerned with history as a science; as, the *historical* method. 2. providing evidence for a fact of history; serving as a source of history: as, a *historical* document. 3. based on or suggested by people or events of the past: as, a *historical* novel. 4. established by history; not legendary or fictional; authentic; real; factual. 5. showing the development or evolution in proper chronological order: as, a *historical* account. 6. famous in history: now usually *historic*. Abbreviated hist. (in senses 1, 2, 3).

historical linguistics, the branch of linguistics which describes the evolution of language structures.

his·tor·i·cal·ly (his-tôr'i-k'l-i, his-tor'ik-li), *adv.* 1. so as to show the development or evolution in chronological order. 2. according to the facts or principles of history; as history.

historical present, the present tense used in telling about past events: also **historic present.**

his·to·ric·i·ty (his'tə-ris'ə-ti), *n.* historical nature or authenticity.

his·to·ried (his'tə-rid), *adj.* having a history or told about in history.

his·to·ri·og·ra·pher (his-tôr'i-og'rə-fẽr, his-tō'ri-og'rə-fẽr), *n.* [LL. *historiographus*; Gr. *historiographos* < *historia* (see HISTORY) + *graphein*, to write; + *-er*], a historian; especially, one appointed to write the history of some institution, country, etc.

his·to·ri·og·ra·phy (his-tôr'i-og'rə-fi, his-tō'ri-og'rə-fi), *n.* the work of a historiographer; the writing of history.

his·to·ry (his'tə-ri, his'tri), *n.* [*pl.* HISTORIES (-riz, -triz)], [L. *historia*; Gr. *historia*, a learning by inquiry, knowledge, narrative < *histōr*, knowing, learned, wise man < base of *eidenai*, to know], 1. an account of what has happened; narrative; story; tale. 2. *a*) what has happened in the life or development of a people, country, institution, etc. *b*) a systematic account of this, usually with an analysis and explanation. 3. all recorded events of the past. 4. the branch of knowledge that deals systematically with the past; a recording, analyzing, co-ordinating, and explaining of past events: abbreviated hist. 5. a known or recorded past: as, this coat has a strange *history*. 6. something that belongs to the past: as, that argument is *history* now. 7. something important enough to be recorded. **make history,** to be or do something important enough to be recorded.

his·tri·on·ic (his'tri-on'ik), *adj.* [LL. *histrionicus* < L. *histrio*, actor], 1. of, or having the nature of, acting or actors. 2. overacted or overacting; theatrical; melodramatic; artificial; affected. *n.* [Rare], an actor: see also **histrionics.**

his·tri·on·i·cal·ly (his'tri-on'i-k'l-i, his'tri-on'ik-li), *adv.* in a histrionic manner.

his·tri·on·ics (his'tri-on'iks), *n.pl.* 1. [construed as sing.], theatricals; dramatics. 2. an artificial or affected manner, display of emotion, etc.; theatricality.

hit (hit), *v.t.* [HIT, HITTING], [ME. *hitten*; AS. *hittan*; ON. *hitta*, to hit upon, meet with; IE. base **keid-*, to fall, as also in W. *cwydd*, a fall], 1. to come against, usually with force; strike: as, the car *hit* the tree. 2. to give a blow to; strike; knock. 3. to give (a blow): as, she *hit* him a blow. 4. to strike by throwing, shooting, or otherwise sending a missile: as, he fired and *hit* the deer. 5. to cause (something) to knock, bump, or strike, as in falling, moving, etc. (often with *on* or *against*): as, he *hit* his head on the stairs. 6. to affect strongly; distress; injure: as, the Irish were hard *hit* by the potato famine. 7. to come upon by accident or after search; reach; find; light upon: as, he *hit* the right answer. 8. to fall into exact accord with; appeal to; suit: as, the hat *hit* her fancy. 9. in *baseball*, to get (a specified base hit): as, he *hit* a double. *v.i.* 1. to give a blow or blows; strike. 2. to knock, bump, or strike (usually with *against*). 3. to come by accident or after search (usually with *upon*). 4. to ignite the combustible mixture in its cylinders: said of an internal-combustion engine. 5. in *baseball*, to get a base hit. *n.pl.* 1. a blow that strikes its mark. 2. a collision of one thing with another. 3. an effectively witty or sarcastic remark. 4. a stroke of good fortune. 5. a successful and popular song, book, play, etc. 6. in *backgammon*, a game won by a player after one or more of his opponent's men have been removed from the board. 7. in *baseball*, a base hit. —*SYN.* see **strike.** **hit it off,** to get along well together; be congenial.

hit off, 1. to mimic; imitate. 2. to portray or describe briefly and well.

hit or miss, without regard to success or failure; in a haphazard or aimless way.

hit (out) at, 1. to aim a blow at; try to hit. 2. to attack in words; criticize severely.

hit-and-run (hit'n-run'), *adj.* hitting and then escaping: usually of an automobile driver who flees from the scene of an accident in which he is involved: also **hit-skip.**

hitch (hich), *v.i.* [ME. *hicchen*, to move jerkily; prob. echoic var. (? via LG. *hicken*) of OFr. *hocier* (Fr. *hocher*), to move jerkily], 1. to move jerkily; walk haltingly; limp; hobble. 2. to become fastened or caught, as by becoming entangled or hooking on to something. 3. to strike the feet together in moving: said of a horse. 4. [Colloq.], to be in harmony; agree. 5. [Slang], to hitchhike. *v.t.* 1. to move, pull, or shift with jerks. 2. to fasten with a hook, knot, etc.; unite; tie. 3. [Colloq.], to marry: usually in the passive. *n.* 1. a short, sudden movement or pull; tug; jerk. 2. a hobble; limp. 3. a hindrance; obstacle; entanglement. 4. a catching or fastening; thing or part used to connect or join together; catch. 5. [Slang], a ride in hitchhiking. 6. [Military Slang], a period of enlistment. 7. in *nautical usage*, a kind of knot that can be easily undone: see **knot**, pl1us. **without a hitch,** smoothly, easily, and successfully.

hitch·hike (hich'hīk'), *v.i.* [HITCHHIKED (-hīkt'), HITCH-HIKING], [*hitch* + *hike*], to travel by asking for rides from motorists along the way.

fat, āpe, bāre, cär; ten, ēven, hêre, ovēr; is, bīte; lot, gō, hôrn, tōōl, look; oil, out; up, ūse, fũr; get; joy; yet; chin; she; thin, *then*; zh, leisure; ŋ, ring; ə for *a* in *ago*, *e* in *agent*, *i* in *sanity*, *o* in *comply*, *u* in *focus*; ' as in *able* (ā'b'l); Fr. bàl; ě, Fr. coeur; ö, Fr. feu; Fr. mon; ö, Fr. duc; H, G. ich; kh, G. doch. See pp. x-xii. ‡ foreign; * hypothetical; < derived from.

where they vary from normal expectation. With the first entry of
a word in the dictionary the derivation is generally noted:

> **es · pouse′** (ĕs-pouz′), *v.t.* [O.F. *espouser,* fr. L. *sponsare* to betroth, fr.
> *sponsus* betrothed, past part. of *spondere* to promise solemnly.]
>
> **lil′y** (lĭl′ĭ), *n.; pl.* -IES (ĭz). [A.S. *lilie,* fr. L. *lilium,* prob. fr. Gr. *leirion*].

A knowledge of derivations enlarges and strengthens a writer's
vocabulary; it will help him to avoid tautological constructions
and will assist him in attaining the precision and flavor characteristic of good writing. If he knows that *initiate* is derived from
Latin *initiatus,* past participle of *initiare (to begin),* he will not
use such an expression as *first initiated. Supercilious* will take on
new and special meaning when he discovers that the word is derived from the Latin for *eyebrow* and therefore suggests the
scornful and haughty raising of the eyebrow. The knowledge that
martyr is derived from a Greek word meaning *witness* considerably enriches one's understanding of the English word: in the
early Christian days a person who gave up his life in witness of
his faith was a martyr. The student particularly interested in the
origin and history of words will wish to consult the *Oxford English Dictionary* and the *Dictionary of American English.*

    3) **The dictionary gives a list of synonyms—other**
words with the same or nearly similar meanings—and, sometimes,
of antonyms—words opposed in meaning. For instance, following the definition of "hinder" (in *Webster's New Collegiate Dictionary*) is this entry:

> **Syn. Hinder, impede, obstruct, block** mean to put obstacles in the way
> of one in action. **Hinder** stresses harmful or annoying interference with
> progress; **impede** implies a slowing up, as by clogging, hampering, or
> fettering; **obstruct** implies interference with something in motion or in
> progress or the placing of obstacles in a path or channel; **block** implies
> more effective, but not necessarily insurmountable, obstruction.—**Ant.**
> **Further.**[2]

The final portion of the entry for "polish" in the *ACD* is devoted to synonyms:

---

[2] Copyright, 1949, by G. & C. Merriam Co.

—Syn. 10. Polish, Gloss, Luster, Sheen, refer to a smooth, shining or bright surface from which light is reflected. Polish suggests the smooth and shining quality given to a surface by friction: *a high polish on a varnished surface.* Gloss suggests a superficial, hard smoothness such as characterizes a lacquered surface: *a gloss on oilcloth.* Luster denotes the characteristic quality of the light reflected from the surfaces of certain materials (pearls, silk, wax, freshly cut metals, etc.): *an opaline luster.* Sheen, sometimes poetical, is a glistening brightness such as that reflected from the surface of silk or velvet, or from furniture oiled and hand polished: *a rich velvety sheen.*[3]

There is always a noun, or a verb, or a modifier which will express your meaning more precisely than any other. A frequent and careful study of synonyms, and especially of the shades of difference between them, will repay any writer, professional or amateur; from that study he will learn how to express himself with good taste, exactness, and forcefulness.

4) **The dictionary contains much miscellaneous information.** Other useful matter is to be found within the pages of a good desk dictionary. Among other things, dictionaries provide abbreviations used in writing and printing, a gazetteer, biographical names, a list of colleges and universities in the United States and Canada, a vocabulary of rhymes, a letter-writing guide, directions for the preparation of manuscript and the handling of proof, and arbitrary signs and symbols.

5) **The dictionary gives usage labels.** Many words have special or limited uses in various sections of the country, or among various groups of people; many are no longer in common use or occur only as slang. Such special or limited uses are indicated in the dictionary by notations indicating their level of usage. If a particular word is a scientific or technical term, an abbreviation (such as *Med., Chem., Bib.*) makes clear its particular significance. If it is English or American usage, colloquial or dialectal, archaic or slang, or in any other way of specialized quality, the dictionary will indicate this. *Webster's New Collegiate* reports *provisionary* (for *provisional*) as *Now Rare; assoil* as

[3] Copyright, 1947, by Random House, Inc.

Archaic; peg as *Colloq.* in the United States for foot, leg, or tooth, but as *Brit.* for a small drink of spirits; a *pillbox* is a box for pills, but it is *Mil.* for a low round concrete-and-steel machine-gun shelter; *peaked,* meaning thin, emaciated, is *Chiefly Colloq.; piano* means soft when marked *Music; pica (Print.)* is a printing term for 12-point type.

Any word not labeled in such fashion belongs to the "general vocabulary" of **Standard English.** It is from this common vocabulary, of course, that the writer will draw most of his words. This does not mean that words from the specialized vocabularies are "wrong" or forbidden but that they should be used only when necessary and appropriate. **Omissions** from the dictionary are especially significant; if a word cannot be found in an unabridged dictionary, it ought to be used with caution, for it may have no common meaning or acceptance. Since the living language is constantly changing, however, it is obvious that many words which have come into use since the publication of a dictionary may be effective and appropriate additions to one's vocabulary. Some of the linguistic and social problems raised by questions of usage, which are questions of verbal etiquette, will be discussed later in this chapter (see "The Problem of Usage"). For another discussion, see the brief but excellent article on "Usage Levels and Dialect Distribution" by Charles C. Fries in *The American College Dictionary.*

The major difference among the three desk dictionaries mentioned above occurs in their classifications of levels of usage. (Incidentally, if ever proof was needed of the fact that dictionaries are made by men, a study of how the dictionaries differ from one another will supply that proof.) The oldest of the three is *Webster's Collegiate Dictionary,* first published in 1898. Its fifth edition—the first one to be based on the unabridged *New International Dictionary*—appeared in 1936, and in 1949 became known as *Webster's New Collegiate.* It reflects a somewhat formal approach to the question of usage. The *ACD,* first appearing in 1947, simplified the pronunciation symbols and also laid a greater stress on American English. In addition, the *ACD* tended to label some words "colloquial" which the more conservative *New Col-*

Amer College Dict.

legiate had labeled "slang." The newest of the three, *Webster's New World* (1953), is even more liberal in its labeling of contemporary American usages. The editors of the *New World* pride themselves on the abundance of their entries of idiomatic expressions, which outnumber those of their competitors.

D2   THE LANGUAGES OF FACT AND OPINION

A. Denotation and Connotation. Structurally and grammatically, there is no difference between these statements:

> That animal prowling around the forest is a wolf.
> That senior driving around the campus is a wolf.

There is, however, a *semantic* difference: the first is a statement of fact, the second a statement of opinion. We can check the first, and presumably we can get a number of informed people to agree that the large animal in question is really a wolf and not Uncle Henry's hound. That is, the statement is factual and literal, intended to convey information. The second statement, however, is a figurative, suggestive designation intended to evoke an emotional response or to create a particular attitude on the part of the reader. No person in his right mind would read that second sentence as a factual statement about a student suffering from lycanthropy. The difference between the two uses of the word "wolf" is that the first sentence stresses its *denotation*, the second its *connotation*.

Since dictionaries must record the various uses of a word, they sometimes must supply connotative as well as denotative definitions. "Propaganda," for instance, is defined by *Webster's New World* as "any systematic, widespread, deliberate indoctrination or plan for such indoctrination," followed by the phrase, "now often used in a derogatory sense, connoting deception or distortion." Connotations are legitimate and normal extensions of meaning, frequently imaginative and poetic.

An interesting example of how a connotative meaning can overpower the denotation is provided by the word "controversy,"

defined by the *ACD* as a "dispute, debate, or contention; dispu-
tation concerning a matter of opinion." During the politically
nervous early 1950's, the word "controversial" (meaning "de-
batable") acquired, in some circles, the overtones of "dangerous,"
if not "subversive." This led the manager of a radio station to
ask a college debate squad about to broadcast one of their
debates "not to talk about anything controversial"!

           B. Extensional and Intensional.   "The facts, ma'am
—just the facts" would seem to be a simple request. But how
much fact and how much opinion are present in this passage?

> Struggling against the virtually unbeatable jinx which has plagued
> them all season, the Mudville Monarchs last night fell victim again to
> Lady Luck. Because Sandy Twiggs, ace Monarch pitcher, hurt his ankle
> sliding into second base in the 7th inning, he lost his control in the 8th
> and quickly surrendered six runs to the Cayuga Coyotes, enough to hand
> them the game, 7–6.

There is more opinion and interpretation in this "news" report
than fact. Where the reader seeks interpretation and knows that
he is getting it, no harm is done; but when he reads an account
that purports to be factual but that is loaded with judgment and
inference, and remains innocently unaware of that fact, then he
is his own victim. When the writer, pretending to give facts,
actually supplies interpretation, he misleads his audience; when
he himself is unable to discriminate between the language of
report and the language of judgment, *he* is his own victim.

    Statements expressed in the language of fact are sometimes
referred to as "extensional" statements; that is, they point to
referents "outside" the sender.

> The average mean temperature in Mudville in August is 72°.
>
> Our football team has won twenty games and lost ten in the past three
> years.
>
> The textbook in my course in educational psychology, edited by
> Duffy and Perkins, consists of twelve different research studies written
> by nine different men. The articles originally appeared in professional
> and scholarly journals.

At 4:15 P.M. yesterday, driving east, I stopped for a red light at Melrose and Vermont Avenues. A gray Ford convertible (license XYZ123), driven by Mrs. Olive Lannon, hit my car from the rear, the collision throwing me against the steering wheel. The trunk on my car was sprung open, the left rear fender and bumper were torn off, and the gas tank was punctured.

Statements expressed in the language of opinion are sometimes refered to as "intensional" statements; that is, they are "inside" reports, telling us more about how the writer feels or what he thinks than about the subject he is allegedly dealing with.

The weather in Mudville is very pleasant in August.

In the past three years our football team has been fairly successful.

The textbook in my course in educational psychology, edited by Duffy and Perkins, is very interesting and is organized in a novel way.

I was in a pretty bad auto accident yesterday afternoon. While waiting for the light to change, I was hit in the back by one of those woman drivers, who must have been going about 45 miles an hour, probably dreaming about something else while she was driving. The rear end of my car was smashed up and I got hurt in the chest.

C. Names and Things: "Word-Magic." Throughout history, man has held his verbal symbols in great esteem or in great dread. The Greek Goddesses of revenge, the Furies, or the "Erinyes" (the furious ones), were referred to as the "Eumenides" (the gracious ones). Today, an announcer broadcasting the play-by-play account of a baseball game is, by popular superstition, not supposed to tell his listeners that a pitcher is pitching a no-hit game; to utter the words aloud is somehow to break the spell. This is a modern relic of a belief enshrined in fairy tales: the spell, the curse, or the charm which is laid on by the uttering of magical words.

In the middle of the twentieth century, belief in magical incantation is not widespread, but examples of "word-magic," or confusion of the thing with the name for the thing, are not particularly difficult to find. In government, in politics, in education, in advertising, we find words being used in ways which obscure, rather than promote, meaning. That words are powerful is a fact universally recognized, but it is less generally realized that they can be misdirected in ways that vary from the ludicrous to the catastrophic. According to Sir Norman Angell, "The power of words is such that they have prevented us from learning some of the most important events in the world's history." *statement of facts*

In the world of experience—the extensional world—the thing exists regardless of the names that attach to it, or even if it has no name. Likewise, if a thing does not exist in the extensional world, creating a name for it will not bring it into being. A surgeon recently wrote to the editor of one of the major dictionaries asking him to include in the next edition a word that he had coined describing a new surgical technique that he had devised; the doctor hoped that publication of the word would help gain acceptance for the technique. It is to be hoped that he was a better surgeon than a linguist. A business recession is a measurable phenomenon, even when referred to as "a retrogradation of economic ebullience," and "consumer hesitancy" is used to explain the reason for fewer retail sales. A standard phrase used in dismissing government workers is the impersonal "reduction in force." Government personnel officers don't speak of "firing" a man; they "terminate his services." These euphemistic expressions are examples of word-magic designed to lessen the feelings of fear and insecurity which blunter words might arouse. The American Medical Association has endorsed the use of a new and "neutral" name, "Hansen's disease," for the ancient "leprosy." And, similarly alert to connotations, the Los Angeles City Council approved a resolution urging that the word "cop" be dropped from common usage, to be replaced by the "more respectful" phrase, "law enforcement officer." When the winner of a beauty contest was disqualified on the grounds that she was twice married and the mother of two children, she declared: "I know in my heart I'm not a liar. I'm just a prevaricator." And when a state-aid patient was treated at Maine General Hospital for what was diagnosed as "a pain in the neck," the State Department of Health requested that a more professional diagnosis be entered on the official record. So the record was changed to show that the patient suffered from torticollis—or pain in the neck.

Example of euphemisms (or terms designed to make things in the extensional world more palatable or acceptable or "respectable") may be multiplied almost endlessly. A curious language is used in the world of education to take the edge off some harsh facts about substandard students. When a teacher reports to a parent that Johnny "needs guidance in developing habits of punctuality and needs further supervision in order to work at optimum capacity," the parent must read this as "Johnny is often late and lazy." Wartime communiqués illustrate language the principal purpose of which is *not* to deliver information. Depending on which side is doing the reporting, the same event can be described as "a disastrous retreat in which enemy troops were forced to flee" or "a strategic withdrawal to a previously prepared system of fortification."

Other familiar euphemisms include the following:

to retire	**to go to bed**
to pass away to cash in one's chips to breathe one's last to go on the Great Adventure to be called to Jesus to be gathered to one's fathers to be called to one's reward	to die
unmentionables silks lingerie	ladies' underwear
cuspidor	spittoon
casket	coffin
mortician	undertaker
realtor	real-estate salesman
cosmetician, beautician	girl working in a beauty shop
shoe rebuilder	man repairing old shoes, cobbler
abdomen, midriff solar plexus	belly

The art of using words to create emotional responses reaches its peak in the language of advertising copy, where facts are scarce and connotation reigns supreme; this language is, in Dean Acheson's phrase, "the gilding without the lily." The various kinds of appeals which advertisers make constitute a subject too complex to explore here, but some of the leading devices are familiar:

1. The testimonial: Linda Luscious says, "I like Smith's Soap because it keeps my skin satin smooth."

2. The appeal to prestige (or snob appeal): Of course our cigarettes cost more, but to those who must have only the best, quality comes first. This is a smoke for the discriminating few.

3. The bandwagon appeal: Anybody who is anybody drinks Old Horse Blanket—it's *everbody's* drink!

4. The "scientific" appeal: Our product has been clinically tested in many of the nation's leading institutions.

For the most part irrelevant and nonsensical, such uses of language are nevertheless powerfully effective. In his short story, "The Door," E. B. White portrays a twentieth-century reaction to what Jacques Barzun calls "the echo of science" in trade names:

Maybe (he kept thinking) it was the names of the things. The names were tex and frequently koid. Or they were flex and oid or they were duriod (sani) or flexsan (duro), but everything was glass (but not quite glass) and the thing that you touched (the surface, washable, crease-resistant) was rubber, only it wasn't quite rubber and you didn't quite touch it but almost.[4]

In the face of the constantly increasing amount of language which pours out through the mass media, the average person sometimes has to fight hard to remember that, as Alfred Korzybski put it, the map is not the same as the terrain. "Slanting" a report can be achieved by attaching either "honorific" (positively charged) labels or derogatory (negatively charged) labels. Newspaper accounts during a political campaign, in cases where two

---

[4] E. B. White, "The Door," in *The Second Tree from the Corner.* Copyright 1954. Reprinted by permission of Harper & Brothers.

newspapers have opposing political preferences, provide interesting studies in slanting. In extreme cases, it becomes difficult to recognize that the stories may be dealing with the same event.

Here is an example of a "neutral" denotative report, followed by two slanted versions:

Jack Gridley and his wife, Jan, live in Chicago near the Institute of Design, where he attends classes. His wife makes $400 a month as a stenographer; they have no other income. They live in a one-room apartment in an eighty-year-old building. Jack takes classes in design, photographic techniques, and drawing. He made the furniture in their apartment. The sofa consists of a slab door mounted on pipe legs and covered with a sheet of foam rubber. He made their two chairs out of barrels. There is no rug on the floor. Jack cooks the dinners.

1) "Honorific" interpretation:

Jack and Jan Gridley, a happy young couple, live a carefree but not careless existence while Jack studies at the Institute of Design in Chicago. Jan, confident of her husband's talents and of his eventual success, cheerfully supports them by working as a stenographer. Jack has carefully chosen his courses to prepare him for his career in photography. In the meantime, they are enjoying living in a cozy apartment in a remodeled building, a historic old mansion near Chicago's Gold Coast. Jack, who is a versatile and skillful craftsman, designed and built the attractive, original-looking furniture, and keeps the uncarpeted parquet floor shining in order to best display his handiwork. In addition to his other talents, he is also an expert chef, specializing in gourmet cookery. Because he gets home before Jan, he prepares their tasty and unusual dinners.

2) Derogatory interpretation:

Jack Gridley attends a few classes at the Institute of Design in Chicago while his hard-working but uncomplaining wife supports him. An unapologetic sponger, he makes no effort to supplement her inadequate income. They are forced to live in one small room in an old building near the edge of the slum district. Because they cannot afford to buy any decent furniture, Jack knocked together an uncomfortable-looking object which he calls a sofa. Instead of chairs, they sit on partially demolished barrels. There is, of course, no carpeting on the bare wooden floors. Despite their lack of money, this irresponsible Bohemian, in his pseudoartistic way, insists on buying expensive foods, experimenting with exotic recipes, and playing around in the kitchen instead of going out and finding a decent job to help support his loyal little wife.

D. **"The Pinnacle and the Trench."** From what has been presented in the preceding pages, the writer should not assume that the language of report is "better" than the language of opinion (or vice versa). Again, the issue is not one of better or worse, right or wrong, but merely one of appropriateness to the given communication situation.

However, very little writing is done exclusively in the language of report. A strictly factual account, stripped of connotation and without inferential statements, creates a rather deadening effect, somewhat like hearing a piano played with one finger.

The chassis of the Spitfire 8 is an arc-welded frame with double-channel box-section side rails and five cross-members; the convertible has an X-member design. The car also has torsion-bar springs and heavy-duty shock absorbers at both front and rear, with 6-leaf rear springs. Its braking mechanism consists of eleven-inch hydraulic brakes over a lining area of 184 square inches; the brake shoes are of the internal expansion type, with self-centering action. Each front wheel has two brake cylinders, and the rear wheels have one. Models with standard transmission have a separate, externally contracting parking brake; models with automatic transmission come equipped with a heavy-duty expanding parking brake.

On the other hand, writing that remains aloft in the realm of generalizations, without ever mooring itself to facts, tends to be easily removed from reality and to become empty, fuzzy, or simply meaningless, as in this example.

Our American people, today, are being deluged with a cleverly planned and skillfully executed barrage of propaganda, designed to promote the adoption of so-called mental health legislation by national, state and local government, under the broad and disarmingly innocent title of the "mental health program."

For the past three years these programs have been rapidly "mushrooming" in most parts of the country under the guidance of unknown and untrained alien psychiatrists who have been quick to seize upon the innate kindliness, hospitality, and altruism of our Christian American people, and to offer a variety of programs for "mental health" and "collectivist" schemes.

Most of the suave, high-pressure speakers who present these programs are saturated with a heavy alien accent and it doesn't require too much analysis of the beautifully packaged, deceptively named "mental health" programs, already become law, or now pending before our national and state lawmaking bodies, to understand that the ultimate, intended goal of these proposed legislative acts is a vicious attempt to destroy the self-reliance of the American citizen—and that it is an ominous threat to deprive him of his freedom and liberty.

In good writing, the languages of fact and opinion mutually support each other. The inferences and conclusions derive from the given data, and statements of opinion are not confused with statements of fact. The writer moves freely and deliberately from his evidence to his interpretations, instead of accidentally or crudely mingling the two. He knows when he is describing objective reality and does not confuse factual report with the feelings that go on inside himself.

My former instructor, Dr. John William Byron, associate professor of history at Blank University, is an expert in the field of American civilization, but he is also well known for his ability to write for a popular audience as well as for a specialized one. He has published many articles in professional journals like the *Journal of the History of Ideas, American Quarterly, Journal of American Folklore,* and the *American Historical Review;* in addition, his book, *The Force of American Politics,* is found in many bibliographies and reading lists, besides being used as a textbook at Blank. However, Professor Byron has also written articles for periodicals like *The Saturday Review, Esquire, The New York Times Magazine,* and *The Reporter.* In class, he combines his extensive knowledge with a human, down-to-earth approach. Last semester, when I took his course in "Puritan Thought," he was informative and interesting without ever playing down to please the crowd. I received the impression that he was not simplifying his lectures merely in order to be popular, but he was popular nevertheless. It was probably his ability to make even a remote and complex subject seem alive and interesting to us, the same ability he shows in being able to write for mass publications and for scholarly publications, that was the reason for his success.

The writer must be able to recognize and distinguish between factual and general statements, just as he must distinguish between denotation and connotation. Then what he writes will resemble neither the dead-level monotony of the statistical table nor the windy generalizations of campaign oratory; in the words of Ralph Waldo Emerson, "one design unites and animates the farthest pinnacle and the lowest trench."

D3   GOOD DICTION

From what has been said in the preceding pages, certain conclusions can be drawn regarding an effective and accurate choice of words. Some other positive qualities (as well as some to be avoided) are discussed below.

A. Naturalness. Express yourself naturally; simplicity in diction adds to clearness and emphasis. An idea does not become more impressive because it is expressed in big words; seriousness, interest, importance, humor are achieved by selection and arrangement of thoughts rather than by display of vocabulary. Unless exactness of meaning demands large words, use simple, everyday expressions. Natural, unpretentious language is more pleasing than a forced, self-conscious jargon. Avoid pomposity, affectation, false elegance, and false delicacy. It is almost always better to say

buy	*than*	purchase
drunk		inebriated
eat, drink		indulge in
father		progenitor
fire		conflagration

funeral	obsequies
gathering	concourse
healthful	salubrious
hobby	avocation
home	domicile
lie	untruth
light meal	collation
live	dwell, reside
name	cognomen
read	peruse
repay	reimburse
rider	equestrian

Always make the phrasing of sentences as simple and as natural as possible:

He asked everyone he met, but no one could tell him where he could buy such an object. (RATHER THAN: He interrogated everyone he met, but no one could instruct him where he could purchase such an object.)

Mrs. Meyer insisted on having a sunroom in her new house. (RATHER THAN: Mrs. Meyer insisted on having a solarium in her new residence.)

The pay, he found, was out of proportion to the job. (RATHER THAN: The emoluments, he discovered, were out of proportion to the employment.)

(See also Chapter VI, sections St 7 and St 8.)

B. Concreteness. To be effective, express ideas in terms which are specific and concrete. Each word in the sentence should be the exact one needed; it should be specific rather than general and should be chosen carefully to bring out the particular shade of meaning desired. But although the study of precise meanings is of great importance, good writing—interesting and convincing expression—is in large part dependent on the use of concrete terms. When precision demands it, the general or the abstract must be used, but whenever possible a writer should use a concrete word in preference to an abstract one. It is generally better to name a member of a class than the class itself: *tree* will do in many contexts but *elm* or *oak* or *maple* is individual and alive and vivid. It is better to choose a verb which describes a particular action rather than a general one: *burn* may be sufficiently accurate, but *blaze* is frequently more effective; *fall* names an action, but *crash* describes a special kind of falling. If an adjective or an adverb is called for, it should be one vividly describing or sharply limiting the word it modifies. Appeals to the sense are more effective for most purposes than appeals to the mind. A writer chooses, therefore, words that have definite visual or aural or olfactory or spatial values like *rush, black, silver, chirping, ripple, crunch, spicy, pungent,* or *triangular.* It is hardly necessary to add that a writer must not overwork this principle. He must determine carefully whether the general or the specific, the abstract or the concrete, is the word he needs at the moment.

The audience rushed for the doors because the theater was on fire. (RATHER THAN: The audience got up because the theater was on fire.)

The Natural Bridge and Florissant Roads form a Y here. (RATHER THAN: The Natural Bridge and Florissant Roads meet here.)

He dropped the pencil abruptly.

or

He laid the pencil carefully on the table. (RATHER THAN: He put the pencil down.)

The boy liked to watch his grandfather trimming the hedge or cultivating the tomatoes. (RATHER THAN: The boy liked to watch his grandfather working in the yard.)

She stared intently at him. (RATHER THAN: She looked at him.)

He was delighted with the pale apple-green walls of the house. (RATHER THAN: The attractive color of the house pleased him.)

In the evening the crows, sitting in the treetops, cawed incessantly. (RATHER THAN: The birds were too noisy in the evening.)

Cheating in examinations is reckless, for the cheater is in great danger of being thrown out of school. Once caught, of course, he has joined the class of the sneak, the thief, the sly pilferer. What is even worse to some people, he is held up to light as a clumsy person. Many who are not inherently honest forbear to cheat simply because they fear the consequences of being caught. (RATHER THAN: Cheating is bad because

it is dishonest and dangerous. The possible results are serious and unpleasant. Consequently, there is not much cheating going on.)

C. Exactness. For each idea or fact to be expressed,
choose the word or phrase which conveys the intended meaning
better than all others. Precision in choice of words is essential
to clearness and effectiveness in writing; careless diction obscures
thought and prevents effectiveness. A study of synonyms is particularly useful to the writer. No two words have exactly the
same significance; the writer must search with care among those
similar in meaning for that word whose slightly different meaning expresses most forcefully and precisely the exact shade of
meaning he desires. He must guard both against words that are
similar in appearance but different in meaning and against the
tendency to use words so loosely and vaguely that they fail to
express any definite idea. For all these reasons writers must consult the dictionary freely and frequently.

1) **The specific term is commonly more effective
than the general.** To be clear, to be forceful, the writer must be
specific and direct. Particularly he must avoid the effect of
jargon which too often results from dependence on such general
nouns as *case, character, asset, factor, nature, element, condition,
instance.*

Action dominates the book. (NOT: The element of action dominates
the book.)
The theme [*or,* the dialogue, *or,* the subject] of the play disgusted
him. (NOT: The character of the play disgusted him.)
The subject matter of Hazlitt's essays I find dull. (NOT: In the matter
of the subject matter and general content I find Hazlitt dull.)
The romantic essayists wrote interestingly. (NOT: The romantic essay-
ists put out some very readable prose.)
His answer was no. (NOT: His answer was of a negative character.)
The party was tiresome. (NOT: The party was of a tiresome nature.)
Jane is fat. (NOT: Jane is rather overweight.)

2) **To find the specific term, study synonyms. Choose the word which expresses the exact shade of meaning, the precise degree of force, the particular tone desired.** Some words have little or no connotative meaning; others have a high degree of connotation. In choosing the exact word, the writer must be certain that the word he selects has the right connotation as well as denotation. For example, *kill, execute,* and *murder* share a common denotation, *to deprive of life. Kill* is the basic word, and has no further connotations. *Execute,* however, connotes putting to death in accordance with a legal sentence, and *murder* connotes killing a human being unlawfully, especially after premeditation. The dictionary is helpful to the writer in differentiating among synonyms. Synonyms are grouped and explained at the end of the entry for the basic word, and cross references are provided from the other entries. (For example, the explanations of *murder* and *execute* are taken from *The American College Dictionary.*) The actual choice the writer makes, of course, is dependent on the context, not merely on the sentence in which the word appears but on the paragraph and complete composition as well.

Despite the fact that, as previously noted, the dictionary may supply a word's connotation, the *full* range of connotative meanings will not be found there. Connotations include the subtlest overtones of meaning that our use of a word suggests; the most elusive ones vary from time to time and from situation to situation, and are undefinable except in context. For example, in the America of the 1880's, the word "anarchist" commonly carried a connotation of immediate danger and violence which, with the change of times and politics, has since been considerably reduced. The same thing has happened to "Jacobite," which had highly inflammatory connotations in eighteenth-century England.

3) **Distinguish carefully between words which are not closely synonymous.** The paired words in the following list are often confused in meaning. Explanation of some of them will be found in the Glossary of Faulty Expressions; for others consult the dictionary.

abbreviated–abridged
ability–capacity
admit–confess
advise–inform
aggravate–provoke
allude–refer
alternative–choice
amateur–novice
among–between
anxious–eager
apparently–evidently
balance–rest
chiefly–largely
claim–assert
condone–repay
custom–habit
discover–invent
evidence–testimony
excuse–pardon
fewer–less

generally–usually
homicide–murder
imply–infer
inaugurate–begin
indorse–sanction
juvenile–puerile
likely–apt
maintain–support
majority–plurality
more than–over
oblivious–unconscious
practically–virtually
premature–early
protagonist–champion
raise–rear
talent–genius
transpire–occur
verbal–oral
whole–entire

4) **Distinguish between words similar in appearance or in sound, but which often differ widely in meaning.** The paired words in the following list are often confused in meaning. Explanations of some of these will be found in the Glossary of Faulty Expressions; for others consult the dictionary.

accede–cede
accept–except
advance–advancement
adverse–averse
affect–effect
allusion–illusion
alternate–alternative
carton–cartoon
ceremonial–ceremonious
cession–cessation
complacent–complaisant ✓

complementary–complimentary
compose–comprise
conscious–conscience–
    consciousness
consequent–consequential
contemptible–contemptuous
contend–contest
continual–continuous
continuance–continuation
convince–convict
council–counsel

disposed to please, courteous, obliging

credible–creditable–credulous
decided–decisive
definite–definitive
deprecate–depreciate
derisive–derisory
disinterested–uninterested
distinct–distinctive
dominant–dominate
enormity–enormousness
equable–equitable
exceptional–exceptionable
expect–suspect
expiate–expatiate
falsity–falseness
fatal–fateful
forceful–forcible
glimpse–glance
human–humane
imaginary–imaginative
immigrant–emigrant
immovable–irremovable
judicial–judicious
last–latest
latter–later
laudable–laudatory
let–leave
lose–loose
luxuriant–luxurious
masterful–masterly
missile–missive

moral–morale
most–almost
neglect–negligence
noted–notorious
observance–observation
official–officious
perspicacity–perspicuity
policy–polity
practical–practicable
precipitate–precipitous
predict–predicate
principal–principle
proportion–portion
proscribe–prescribe
prosecute–persecute
purport–purpose
quiet–quite
recourse–resource
regretful–regrettable
relative–relation
respectfully–respectively
sensible–sensitive
sensual–sensuous
signification–significance
specie–species
stationary–stationery
stimulant–stimulus
their–there
to–too–two
triumphal–triumphant

D. Freshness. Express yourself in fresh language. Do not resort to worn-out phrases to carry your ideas. Many expressions once vivid have lost much of their force because they have been worked too many times. Figurative and imaginative words, epithets, and allusions increase effectiveness when they express exactly the suggestion or shade of meaning the writer wants in a specific instance; but they should not be used as stock phrases.

or counter words. Writing which depends on worn-out expressions will be weak, flat, tiresome, boring. **To attain freshness, replace trite, hackneyed expressions either by simple, unpretentious words or phrases that clearly mean what you want to say, or by apt, fresh, and appropriate allusions and descriptive phrases which have the connotations proper to the particular context.** Avoid, however, straining after picturesque patter for its own sake.

1) **Avoid such trite and hackneyed phrases as the following,** for whatever individuality or life they may once have had is now gone completely from them:

aching void	dull, sickening thud
acid test	each and every
agree to disagree	eagle eye
all in all	enjoyable occasion
among those present	fair sex
arms of Morpheus	fast and furious
as luck would have it	fills a long-felt want
at one fell swoop	filthy lucre
beat a hasty retreat	gave the finishing touch
blushing bride	glassy stare
brave as a lion	goes without saying
brawny arms	good as gold
breathless silence	goodly number
breathless suspense	green with envy
briny deep	gripping story
brown as a berry	had the privilege
carpet of grass	happy pair
checkered career	hard as a rock
clear as crystal	herculean efforts
clinging vine	her nether limbs
completed the scene	hungry as wolves
conspicuous by its absence	in all its glory
devouring element	in evidence
doomed to disappointment	in my humble opinion
downy couch	inner man

innocent as a lamb
in our midst
in the last analysis
in this day and age
in touch with
irony of fate
justice to the occasion
last but not least
last sad rites
lonely sentinel
making night hideous
mantle of snow
masculine brawn and feminine
   beauty
meets the eye
mental picture
more forceful than polite
Mother Earth
motley crowd
nestles below the hill
never in the history of
nipped in the bud
no sooner said than done
not a sound broke the stillness
order out of chaos
partake of refreshments
pedal extremities
plot thickens
proud possessor
psychological moment
put in an appearance
red as a rose
rendered a selection
replete with interest
rosebud mouth
royal reception
severely simple

sigh of relief
silence reigned supreme
single blessedness
slow as molasses
slow but sure
specimen of humanity
staff of life
stands like a sentinel
sumptuous repast
sun-kissed meadows
sweat of his brow
table groaned
thrown on the tender
   mercies of
tired but happy
too full for utterance
took his departure
toothsome viands
to the bitter end
tumultuous applause
undercurrent of excitement
untiring efforts
vast multitude
was the recipient of
watery grave
wee, small hours
we have with us today
wended our way
white as snow
with bated breath
with feverish haste
words cannot describe
words fail me
work like a Trojan
worse for wear
young hopeful

2) **Avoid time-worn quotations, literary allusions, and proverbs.** The use of quotation and allusion enriches expression but the continual repetition of such aged phrases as the following will bore the reader and therefore destroy effectiveness:

all that glitters is not gold	look upon the wine when it is red
best-laid plans	
better late than never	love's young dream
but that is another story	method in his madness
cups that cheer but not inebriate	monarch of all I survey
	money is the root of all evil
easier said than done	more sinned against than sinning
exception proves the rule	
far from the madding crowd	music hath charms
feast of reason and the flow of soul	not wisely, but too well
	of purest ray serene
fools rush in where angels fear to tread	sadder but wiser
	suffer a sea-change
give hostages to fortune	there's the rub
holy bonds of wedlock	'twas ever thus
last rose of summer	variety is the spice of life
leave the world to darkness	where ignorance is bliss
light, fantastic toe	where there's a will, there's a way

3) **Do not use exhausted modifiers.** Careless and excessive use of the following terms has made them vague and ineffective. Use them in their precise meanings:

awful	lovely
fierce	nice
fine	perfect
glorious	splendid
gorgeous	terrible
grand	unique
hectic	weird
horrid	wonderful

4) **Avoid the trite epithets and hackneyed straining after novelty found in much journalistic writing.** Phrases like the following do not fit the tone of most standard expositions:

ax slayer	officialdom
beer baron	officiating clergyman
double triumph	scantily attired
favorite dumping ground	slab duel
heart balm	southpaw hurling
hops off	stellar role
mystery death	taken for a ride
	torch murder

II. THE PROBLEM OF USAGE

The meaning of a word, as we have seen, is determined by its use. But uses change, and handbooks of usage go out of date even faster than dictionaries. It is obvious that a complete and final dictionary of English usage cannot be made—that is, not until English is no longer spoken and becomes another dead language. The fact that it lives and grows and changes makes finality of description impossible.

Whenever people feel disturbed about change, they want to stabilize the *status quo.* In England during the eighteenth century, there were proposals to "fix" the language permanently by means of an Academy for the regulation of English usage. And in 1958 a bill was introduced into the House of Representatives to establish a National Grammar Commission for the same purpose. To try to freeze the present moment into an unalterable fixity is, however, like asking for a suspension of the laws of growth and decay.

D4   LEVELS OF USAGE

Good usage is not some hypothetical, "correct" usage. Good usage is merely the usage appropriate to the particular situation. It is not *correctness* that counts in usage—it is *appropriateness.* There are many levels of English at our command, each of which is correct and good when it is consistent with the attitude we have taken, the tone we have established, in the piece of writing at hand. Briefly, formal expression makes use of the Standard English vocabulary;[5] informal expression calls for the admixture of the colloquial; familiar expression permits the use of slang and other terms inappropriate on the first two levels. There is, of course, no rigid division between these kinds of expression. Formal expression is suitable for the communication of facts and serious ideas from an impersonal point of view; the informal is the proper vehicle for most polite conversation, informal speeches, and writing which has any reason to include the personal element; the familiar is the diction of casual and hasty talk and will, of course, be found in narrative but is most of the time unsuitable for expository communication. Of the three levels, the informal style and diction is now more widely used than the formal, literary expression commonly found in writing and speech in the last century.

It is the writer's business to determine what sort of reader he is reaching for and to choose that language which will best aid him to make the reader understand him. A paper on historical geography, quantum physics, or technical aspects of modern poetry, presented to a learned society, will be a formal piece of writing; that is, it will be expressed in a formal rather than informal style and language but in addition it will use freely a specialized or technical vocabulary with which the writer expects the members of his audience to be familiar because they are geographers or physicists or poets and critics. If, however, the writer wishes to present the same ideas to literate and intelligent readers who are *not* specialists, he will retain the formal tone but will eliminate as much as possible the specialized diction which on the other occasion had been appropriate. This change in style merely means that different subjects and different audiences call for different choice and use of words.

The writing that the student of freshman composition is gen-

---

[5] See "The Dictionary Contains Usage Labels," in section D 1 (5).

erally called upon to do will vary from the formal (but seldom the technically specialized) to the informal. Most of the writing that the student will do outside this course, and in later life, will probably be informal rather than formal—examinations, letters, and the like. However, there will be many occasions, both now and in later life, when he will be called upon to express himself effectively at the formal level—in formal or technical reports or in business letters, for example. It therefore behooves the student to learn to write effective formal and informal English. No general rule can be established, however, for what level of usage should be employed at one time or another; each time the student undertakes a paper he must determine whether the nature of his subject and his audience demands a formal, an informal, a familiar treatment, or some judicious mixture of these levels. In this, as in every other problem of composition, he should feel free to seek advice from his instructor. What the student must learn is to make words do what he wants them to do; he must learn to use them effectively and appropriately.

If usage is the "verbal etiquette" that it has been called, it follows that a user of substandard English will find himself regarded by an important portion of the community as a person without language manners. For instance, an employee who writes a business letter containing a sentence like

We will not send you these kind of widgets again which was because of a mistake.

might very shortly thereafter be looking for a new job. Even those linguists with the most liberal views regarding usage point out that the standard forms are those that should be used (despite the prevalence of some substandard forms), on the very realistic basis that this is the way to get along in the world.

Though it sometimes happens, substandard language does not necessarily fail to communicate. "I ain't never comin' nohow" communicates a meaning with real force; it is, however *socially* not acceptable. Thus we are concerned here not with matters of language but with manners, which are, strictly speaking, extralinguistic considerations.

The following definitions and illustrations will help to guide the student in some of the problems of usage.

A. Colloquialisms. Colloquialisms are words or phrases acceptable in informal speech and dialogue, in familiar letters, and in other informal communication, but not in formal expository writing. As Fries says, "The word *colloquial* . . . is used to mark those words and constructions whose range of use is primarily that of the polite conversation of cultivated people, of their familiar letters and informal speeches, as distinct from those words and constructions which are common also in formal writing. The usage of our better magazines and of public addresses generally has, during the past generation, moved away from the formal and literary toward the colloquial."[6] The following brief list illustrates the difference in usage between the colloquial and the Standard English vocabulary; in most instances the difference in tone is obvious:

Colloquial		*Standard English*
alibi	*for*	excuse
angel		financial backer
around		approximately, somewhere about, here and there
cute		pretty
date		appointment, engagement
deal		business transaction
doctor		repair or mend, to adulterate
fix *(v.)*		tamper with, get even with
fix *(n.)*		predicament, dilemma
fizzle		failure
funny		odd, queer, strange
go back on		repudiate, abandon
have it in for		bear a grudge against
heap		many
inside of		within the space of

---

[6] *The American College Dictionary.* Copyright, 1947, by Random House, Inc.

Colloquial		*Standard English*
lots of	*for*	much, many
mighty		very
most		almost, nearly
outsmart		outwit, prove too clever for
plumb		completely
quite a few		many
show		chance, undertaking
slicker		swindler, cheat
snooty		snobbish
take off		imitate, mimic; start
tote		carry
two bits		twenty-five cents
weed		cigarette, cigar
wire		a telegram

Contractions (*can't, don't, won't, wouldn't*) are classed as colloquialisms; they are used freely in both familiar and informal expression but do not normally appear in formal expository writing.

B. Slang. Slang is a term used to describe several related but not entirely similar kinds of words which are not a part of the Standard English vocabulary. The most comprehensive as well as the most generally applied definition of slang is "language of a markedly colloquial character, regarded as below the standard of cultivated speech."—*ACD*. In this sense, slang includes all those subcolloquial words which, however widely used, are not generally considered appropriate to cultivated, though informal, speech (colloquialisms, it will be remembered, were defined as being used in "the polite conversation of cultivated people"). A characteristic of slang is that it is closely related to a particular time and generally to a particular group.

One of the values of slang is its freshness and originality—although today's originality easily becomes tomorrow's cliché. As with usages of a less transitory sort, slang phrases should be used carefully, with an eye to possible ambiguous or ludicrous meanings. A magazine article reviewing a new record album concluded:

"If you really want to get back down to earth try *Juanita Hall Sings the Blues*. It's out of this world."

1) **Coinages** are a distinctive feature of the slang vocabulary. Some coinages have added welcome variety to the language, but many are often awkward, pedantic, or simply unnecessary.

Boost, from *boom* and *hoist* (according to the *ACD*), is an example of successful coinage. Gelett Burgess made up *blurb,* and Lewis Carroll, *chortle.* World War II added many words, such as *jeep* and *snafu.* Words like the following, however, do not make for effective writing:

to make America two-car-conscious	selectionized
	ridability
photographable	weight-o-meter
fictionize	luncheteria
accessorize	lubritorium
prosperize	decorateria

Unnecessary coinage can be illustrated by *analyzation,* which is simply an awkward way of saying *analysis,* or *channelize,* which is merely a longer substitute for the existing verb *to channel.*

2) **Clipping** is another characteristic of the slang vocabulary. *Mob* (short for *mobile vulgus*), *spats* (short for *spatterdashes*), and *bus* (short for *omnibus*) are examples of one-time slang clippings which have become completely acceptable in formal English. The history of *bus,* incidentally, is an interesting illustration of the way words develop new meanings which, by virtue of becoming generally accepted, pass from one level of usage to another. Originally slang itself, *bus* acquired, after becoming Standard English, a new slang meaning (a passenger automobile) which has already become sufficiently accepted to be listed in the dictionary as colloquial. *Ad* and *phone* are examples of clipping which are now considered colloquial and which may eventually become generally used in formal English.

The dictionary provides a convenient check on the general

acceptability of particular clippings. Well-established words may, of course, be used: *piano, cello, bus,* and *plane* are part of the Standard English vocabulary. Other clippings, such as *ad, bike, dorm, exam, gas, phone,* are listed as colloquial. Still others (*champ* and *frat,* for instance) are listed as slang. Slang abbreviations like *doc, grad, chem,* and *prof* may be used on the familiar level but should not be used in formal or informal writing.

Objections to the use of slang in standard informal or formal writing are based on the hard practical fact that, unless the writer is addressing a very specialized audience, slang is not likely to be effective. Levels of usage are not levels of moral judgments; as codified in dictionaries, they represent the best available assessment of our general habits of literate usage. If a word is considered subcolloquial, there is a reason why it has not become widely used in cultivated speech and writing. Perhaps its use is confined to a relatively narrow group and its meaning will therefore be unfamiliar to many readers. Perhaps its meaning is too ephemeral or too generalized to have induced writers in general to accept it. Because slang is created by a particular group at a particular time, its proper use quite naturally becomes the mark of the initiate; any student will remember how certain slang words became so popular at particular times that they had little meaning except to show that the one who used them was one of the gang. It is this tendency of slang words to become vague to the point of meaninglessness that makes the use of a word like "swell" (as an adjective) objectionable. "Swell" means so many things, from "wonderful" to "stylish," that it means little or nothing.

    C. Special Languages. The special languages of classes or groups, known as "speech communities," may be either colloquial or slang. In extreme cases, a speech community may have a vocabulary which is unintelligible to those outside the community.

    1) **"Localisms"** are usages current in a particular section of the country. Although their use in formal writing may be of doubtful propriety, in less formal and more personal ex-

position, as well as in narrative, occasional localisms may give color and life to one's writing. However, one must always be sure that their meaning will be clear to readers from other areas. A few illustrations will show the individuality of such terms and the gradual shift of useful words into wider currency. A *sawyer* in the great days on the Mississippi or the Missouri was a tree floating and bobbing in the water. *Disremember (forget)* and *reckon (think, suppose)*, once localisms, are now fully accepted colloquialisms. *Chaps* and *dogie,* both still classified *Western U.S.,* are words which cowboy songs have helped make readily understood anywhere in the United States. *Canyon (cañon)* is an example of a word which was once regional but has now, through general acceptance, passed into the standard vocabulary. The student interested in the relationship between the written standard language and his own regional language might find it a fascinating exercise to look into such works as the *Linguistic Atlas of New England, Word Geography of the Eastern United States, Survey of Verb Forms in the Eastern United States,* or the linguistic atlas for his particular section of the country (if work on this project has been completed).

2) **"Shoptalk," or occupational diction,** is used by lawyers, doctors, psychologists, printers, farmers, soldiers, sports writers—every group of people working together develops a kind of talk which is meaningful to its members but not always to outsiders. "When the soup is ready, pour it . . ." is a construction that may be found in the writing or speech of various occupations: a cook has one concept of soup, but for the steelworker it will mean molten lead, and for the worker in explosives it will be nitroglycerin. The bulls and bears of the stock exchange are not quite the same as those seen in the city zoo; "long" and "short" in the stockbroker's language have nothing to do with linear relationships. An angel on Broadway will seldom be confused with one in heaven; in Air Force talk during World War II, however, "angel" was a term signifying a thousand feet of elevation. In the kitchen an egg beater is a well-known instrument; for the airman it is a helicopter. Some of this occupation-talk may pass

into general slang use or become acceptable colloquialisms; some of it may become part of the standard vocabulary (for instance, *flash back* or *close-up*). The use of shoptalk may often add life to one's informal writing; however, the context should make clear the meaning of the expression. In formal writing, shoptalk will almost invariably be inappropriate.

D. Jargon is a term referring to generally meaningless writing or speech. One man's shoptalk, of course, is another man's jargon; to the professor of poetry, terms like *anacrusis, anaphora, caesura,* and *oxymoron* are precise technical terms conveying exact meanings, but they are likely to be gibberish to the nonspecialist. Technical terms become jargon when they are used merely to impress one's audience or when they are used in a context where perfectly acceptable Standard English is called for. When a student uses the phrase *sibling rivalry* in a term paper for his sociology course, he is not writing jargon; when he tells a friend that his brother and sister are constantly fighting and he uses that same phrase, he is speaking jargon. A former congressman once labeled pretentious official language "gobbledygook," an expressive coinage that has passed into common use to refer to any kind of jargon.

E. Archaic and Obsolete Words. Archaic and obsolete words are terms that were once in good usage but are no longer current. The dictionary must include them, for we meet them when we read books written in the past, but since they are no longer part of the living language they ought not to be used in writing or in speech. Avoid such words as the following:

aroint thee	perchance
assoil	prithee
bedight	quoth
deal (portion, share)	sooth to say
eftsoon	spake
eke (also)	whilom
kine	wight
mayhap	withal

F. **Foreign Words or Phrases.** Foreign words or phrases may be misunderstood by the reader; they are not to be used, therefore, if there exists an adequate equivalent in English. Foreign words should never be used for the purpose of showing one's familiarity with the language. (Naturalized words are entered in the dictionary without comment.) In ordinary English prose a writer has no need of such expressions as the following:

affaire de coeur	*for*	love affair
artiste		artist
bas bleu		bluestocking
beau monde		high society
bêtise		stupidity
bien entendu		well understood
chef-d'oeuvre		masterpiece
con amore		with love *or* devotion
Deo volente		God willing
dernier ressort		last resort
distingué		distinguished
gaucherie		awkwardness
genus homo		mankind
mal de mer		seasickness
par exemple		for example
quantité négligeable		negligible quantity
robe-de-chambre		dressing gown, bathrobe
sans doute		no doubt
tempus fugit		time flies
tout de suite		immediately
ut infra		as below

G. **Improprieties.** An impropriety is the use of a word in a function contrary to good linguistic usage. Words do move from one grammatical category to another: many words, as we have seen, are acceptably used as several parts of speech. Others, however, are generally used in only one function. The following examples illustrate expressions which are not acceptable above the familiar level at the present time:

ADJECTIVE USED AS ADVERB: A REAL handsome man.

NOUN USED AS VERB: This street DEAD-ENDS here.

NOUN USED AS VERB: She CARPET-SWEEPERED the rug hastily.

PREPOSITION USED AS CONJUNCTION: He would not do LIKE I wanted him to.

H. Barbarisms. Barbarisms are words or phrases heard almost exclusively in the speech of uneducated people. Such expressions as the following ought not to be used (except when, in narrative, they appear in the speech of a character):

ain't	*for*	are not, am not, is not, has not, have not
being as I was		since I was
between you and I		between you and me
could of		could have
drownded		drowned
had ought		ought, should have
hain't		has not, have not
hisself		himself
irregardless		regardless
should of went		should have gone
theirself		themselves
unbeknownst		unbeknown, unknown
would of		would have

(See "Glossary of Faulty Expressions," section D 6).

D5   THE EXACT IDIOM

Correct idiom, in any language, is determined by usage, and may or may not conform to the rules of grammar. In the course of time certain peculiarities in the combination of words become characteristic of a language. Such peculiarities, which may defy logical or grammatical explanation, are looked upon as correct, and any deviation from the accepted usage is called "unidiomatic." Idiomatic usage can be assured only by one's becoming ac-

quainted with the established combinations of words. An unabridged dictionary is the best guide for one who is not certain
that he is using accepted English idioms.

1) **Note the extensive lists of idioms to be found in
an unabridged dictionary and the level of expression on which
they are being used.** With the word "back," for instance, *Webster's New International Dictionary*, Second Edition, gives the
following idiomatic uses: at one's back, behind one's back, behind
the back of, (to) give or make a back, in back of, on one's back, (to)
put or get one's back up, the back of beyond, the back of one's
mind, with one's back to the wall, (to) back an anchor, (to) back
and fill, (to) back a sail, (to) back off, (to) back out or back down,
(to) back the field. (to) back the worming, (to) back the wrong
horse, (to) back up, (to) back water. Some of these phrases are
marked colloquial, some slang, some technical; others not labeled
in such fashion are acceptable in formal writing.

2) **Even in familiar speech and writing, do not violate idiomatic usage:**

Unidiomatic	*Idiomatic*
all the farther	as far as
among one another	among themselves, *or* with one another
as regards to	as regards, *or* with regard to
couldn't scarcely hear	couldn't hear, *or* could scarcely hear, *or* could hardly hear
equally as good as	equally good, *or* as good as
in the state Iowa	in the state of Iowa
in the year of 1940	in the year 1940
kind of a	kind of
remember of	remember
there is no doubt but that	there is no doubt that
to home	at home
with regards to	with regard to

3) **In your writing, use the preposition that is called for, either by idiom or meaning, following any given word.** For convenience of reference a selected list of terms with the prepositions called for by idiom or meaning is given and illustrated below:

abhorrence *of:* His abhorrence *of* (not *to*) violence was widely known.

abide *at, for, in:* We abided *for* three months *at* the Ronson House *in* Seattle.

abide *by:* The company did not abide *by* the court's decision.

abound *in, with:* The room abounded *in* (or *with*) curios.

absorbed *by:* The child was absorbed *by* (not *in*) the show.
absorbed *in:* The child was deeply absorbed *in* thought.

accede *to:* The teacher acceded *to* my request.

accommodate *to:* I accommodated myself *to* the circumstances.
accommodate *with:* The bank will not accommodate me *with* (not *by*) a loan.

accountable *for, to:* You will be accountable *to* me *for* your actions.
accused *by, of:* The thief was accused *of* theft *by* the woman.
acquiesce *in:* They would not acquiesce *in* (not *to*) the will of the majority.
adept *in:* He is adept *in* (not *at*) swimming.

admit *of:* Many grammatical problems admit *of* several solutions.
admit *into:* He was admitted *into* the house.
admit *to:* Your ticket will not admit you *to* this game.

agree *in:* The officials agreed *in* their desire to continue the game.
agree *on:* The officials were agreed *on* (or *upon*) their desire to continue the game.
agree *to:* The officials agreed *to* continue the game.
agree *with:* The officials did not agree *with* the coach.

aim *at:* He aimed the gun *at* the target.

All his actions were aimed *at* the presidency of the company.

aim *to:* His every action was aimed *to* please (not *at* pleasing).

analogy *between:* He drew an analogy *between* electricity and water.

analogy *of . . . to, with:* The analogy *of* electricity *to* (or *with*) water is apt.

anger *at, with:* Father was angry *at* my carelessness but not *with* me.

apprehensive *for:* We were apprehensive *for* our safety.

apprehensive *of:* We were apprehensive *of* the overhanging ledge.

attitude *toward:* His attitude *toward* us is exasperating.

averse *from, to:* John is not averse *to* (or *from*) work.

burden *with:* The donkey was burdened *with* (not *by*) a large trunk.

capable *of:* They were capable *of* causing much hardship in the town.

center *in, on:* His attention was centered *in* (or *on*) (not *about* or *around*) the scene before him.

compare *to:* We cannot compare an orange *to* a billiard ball, because they are not similar.

compare *with:* But we can compare one orange *with* another orange, because they are similar.

concerned *about:* He seemed concerned *about* the outcome of the trial.

concerned *for:* He seemed concerned *for* his freedom.

concerned *in, with:* He acted as if he had never been concerned *in* (or *with*) the theft.

conducive *to:* This climate is not conducive *to* (not *for*) good health.

confide *in:* The child would not confide *in* me.

confide *to:* The child would not confide his secret *to* me.

confidence *in:* I had no confidence *in* (not *about*) his ability.

conform *to, with:* They tried to make the freshmen conform *to* (or *with*) (not *in*) the traditions of the school.

connect *by, with:* Central Junction is connected *with* Central City *by* a bus line.

connive *at, with:* Although he secretly connived *with* the criminals he could not openly connive *at* their crimes.

consist *in:* The essential quality of school spirit consists not *in* football teams but *in* the attitude of the students toward the school as a whole.

consist *of:* The speech consisted *of* nothing but platitudes.

correspond *to:* The human eyelid corresponds *to* a window shade.

correspond *with:* Your laughter does not correspond *with* the solemnity of the occasion.

She corresponded *with* Joe for over two years.

craving *for:* Every child has a craving *for* (not *of*) candy.

die *by:* In those days almost all the men died *by* violence.

die *from:* Very few people lived to die *from* starvation.

die *in:* Now many people die *in* poverty, neglected by everyone.

die *of:* Many more, too, live to die *of* old age.

differ *from:* The atmosphere in his office differs *from* that in his home.

differ *in:* We differ *in* the way we walk.

differ *on:* We differ *on* every theory you have mentioned.

differ *with:* I must differ *with* (or *from*) you about that matter.

different *from:* Harry's bicycle was different *from* (rather than *to*) mine.

different *than:* (occasionally, when followed by a clause): Harry's bicycle is much different *than* I expected it to be. ✓

distaste *for:* I cannot overcome my distaste *for* (not *of*) that kind of music.

enamored *of:* The hero, of course, was enamored *of* (not *with*) the heroine.

entertain *at:* Mother entertained six guests *at* (not *to*) dinner.

envious *of:* My sister is very envious *of* (not *toward*) me.

fearful *of:* The diplomats were fearful *of* (not *for* or *about*) his safety.

filled *with, by:* We filled the jug *with* water *by* using the garden hose.

free *of:* At last he was free *of* (not *from*) the mortgage.

good *at:* Bill is good *at* drawing figures.

good *for:* But more training will be good *for* him.

hatred *of:* Our hatred *of* (not *for*) cheating is well known.

heedless *of:* You seem heedless *of* (not *for*) the harm you may do.

hint *at:* She kept hinting *at* (not *toward*) the secret.

identical *with:* Your hat is identical *with* (not *to*) mine.

independent *of:* I am now completely independent *of* (not *from*) my parents.

in search *of:* He went in search *of* (not *for*) an honest man. —

insensible *from:* His face was insensible *from* the intense cold.

insensible *of:* As they walked along casually, they were insensible *of* their danger.

insensible *to:* The intense cold made his face insensible *to* further pain.

interest *in:* He had no interest *in* (not *for* or *toward*) what I did.

jealous *of:* She was very jealous *of* (not *for*) her privileges.

liable *for:* I will not be liable *for* his debts.

liable *to:* The child who plays with matches is liable *to* injury.

live *by:* He continued to live *by* his wits.

live *in:* He was not accustomed to living *in* poverty.

live *on:* For two months they lived *on* nothing but fish.

live *to:* She lived *to* the age of ninety-two.

live *upon:* They lived *upon* the open prairie, far from a town.

mania *for:* My little brother seems to have a mania *for* fires.

necessity *for, of:* I see no necessity *of* (or *for*) your going.

negligent *of:* He has always been negligent *of* (not *for* or *about*) his health.

object *to:* She did not object *to* (not *at*) waiting for me.

oblivious *of:* Joel was oblivious *of* (not *to*) all insults.

overrun *by:* The old man was overrun *by* the speeding automobile.

overrun *with:* The farm house was overrun *with* rats.

prevail *against, over:* I determined that my opponents should not prevail *against* (or *over*) me.

prevail *on, upon, with:* He finally prevailed *on* (or *upon* or *with*) me to wait.

privilege *of:* He had the privilege *of* being (not *to* be) absent from his classes.

proficient *in:* Mary is very proficient *in* (not *at*) painting.

resemblance *between:* There was no resemblance *between* Harold and his mother.

resemblance *to:* In Harold I could see no resemblance *to* his mother.

responsible *for, to:* Melvin must be responsible *to* George *for* finishing the scenery on time.

suspected *by, of:* The soldier was suspected *by* his officers *of* leaving his post.

treat *for:* The new ambassador continued hopelessly to treat *for* an accord.

treat *of:* This agreement treats *of* the commercial relations between the two countries.

treat *with:* The ambassador treated *with* the head of the new government.

wait *for:* We waited *for* (not *on*) them to arrive.

wait *on, upon:* The new maid waited *on* (or *upon*) the table.

4) **Don't worry about ending a sentence with a preposition.** There is no reason to get yourself entangled in an unnatural and awkward construction merely to avoid violating this mythical "rule." The following sentences are good idiomatic English:

Which book did you want me to read FROM?
He was inspired by the musicians he played WITH.

5) **Do not use the parts of a verb phrase in a false double capacity:**

The summer was unusually hot last year, and many crops WERE lost. (NOT: The summer was unusually hot last year, and many crops lost.)

I always have BEEN and always will BE pessimistic about his success. (NOT: I always have and always will be pessimistic about his success.)

6) **Do not use one preposition to complete two or more idiomatic expressions unless the preposition is correct for both:**

He was interested IN and excited ABOUT his experiments. (NOT: He was interested and excited about his experiments.)

He agrees WITH Arthur and also UPON Arthur's plan. (NOT: He agrees with Arthur and also Arthur's plan.)

7) **If the superlative degree of the same adjective is to modify both the plural and the singular forms of the same noun, express both forms of the noun or express the plural form;** do not express the singular form alone:

That was one of the most exhausting games that Stephen had ever played; perhaps it was his most exhausting game.

or

That was one of the most exhausting games, if not the most exhausting, that Stephen had ever played. (NOT: That was one of the most exhausting, if not the most exhausting game, that Stephen had ever played.)

8) **It is generally wise to express the full comparison when the comparative or superlative degrees of adjectives are used:**

Some doctors say that cold weather is much more healthful THAN WARM WEATHER. (NOT: Some doctors say that cold weather is much more healthful.)

Tom seems to have the quickest wit THAT I KNOW OF. (NOT: Tom seems to have the quickest wit!)

The context of any particular passage may remove the chances of confusion. In passages such as the following, the sentences given above in parentheses would be quite satisfactory:

He cannot decide whether to move where the weather is generally cool or generally warm. Some doctors say that cool weather is much more healthful.

Each of the three boys has very distinctive traits that should make them good toastmasters. Tom, however, seems to have the quickest wit.

9) **Whenever there is danger of confusion, express all parts of comparisons.** It is of course unnecessary to express sentences like the following in other than elliptical form:

That tree is taller than this.
Ray has grown faster than Susan.

In these two sentences there is no possible chance for confusion. In sentences like the following, however, the omission of the full comparison, or of a part of it, results in confusion and sometimes in illogical statement:

Sally likes her better than Helen.
The man went down the street in the opposite direction of the dog.

In the first sentence the reader has no way of knowing whether Sally likes "her" better than Sally likes Helen, or whether Sally likes "her" better than Helen likes her. In the second sentence the omission of the phrase introduced by *to that* has led to an illogical statement, for although a dog may *go* in a certain direction, it cannot *have* direction. The sentences and others like them should be clear in meaning:

Sally likes her better than Helen DOES.

or

Sally likes her better than SHE LIKES Helen.
The man went down the street in the direction opposite TO THAT TAKEN BY the dog.

10) **Complete the comparisons suggested by *different* and *differently* in the same sentences in which the words are used.** Although *unusual* is an accepted meaning for *different* in both *Webster's New Collegiate Dictionary* and *The American College Dictionary,* the loose use of *different* in this sense when a more exact comparison is intended should be avoided:

His accent is certainly different from most of those you hear; it's more Southern than Midwestern. (NOT: His accent is certainly different.)

The arrangement of the rooms in his house is different FROM ANY THAT I HAVE EVER SEEN IN SPRINGFIELD.

The younger generation of today does not act differently FROM WHAT IT DID A CENTURY AGO.

or

The younger generation of today does not act differently THAN IT DID A CENTURY AGO.

Notice that *different* is usually completed by an expression introduced by *from,* but that when the sentence is to be completed by a clause in which the introductory preposition would be awkward, *than* may be used, as it is in the last sentence given just above (see section 3, above).

11) **Words like *too, so,* and *such* imply comparison. Complete them, according to meaning, by a phrase introduced by *to* or *for,* or by a clause usually introduced by *that* unless the completing element has been previously expressed.** These intensives, when used without comparisons, are likely to be as meaningless as they frequently become in polite patter:

We have had such a pleasant time THAT WE WOULD LIKE TO COME AGAIN.

or

We have had A VERY PLEASANT TIME. (NOT: We have had *such* a pleasant time.)

She is so beautiful THAT EVERYONE TURNS TO LOOK AT HER. (NOT: She is so beautiful.)

D6 GLOSSARY OF FAULTY EXPRESSIONS

Words must be used carefully and intelligently. Imperfect knowledge of meanings, failure to make necessary distinctions, and a readiness to use the vague approximation rather than the precise word are responsible for practically all elementary faults in diction. In the following list will be found many common faulty expressions. Such a list is necessarily incomplete, and should be supplemented by the study and use of a good modern dictionary or a reference work like *A Dictionary of Contemporary American Usage,* by Evans and Evans.

A, an. The determiner *a* is used before all words beginning with a consonant or a vowel sounded like a consonant. *An* is used before all words beginning with a vowel sound. With words beginning with *h, an* is used when the *h* is silent, *a* when the *h* is sounded.

> A cylinder, a muskrat, a union, a use, a honeybee, a pretty picture, a historical fact
> An alley, an idiom, an upheaval, an honor, an attractive girl

Ability, capacity. Do not confuse these words. *Ability* means the *power to perform; capacity* means the *power of receiving.*

> Jim shows great ability in chemistry.
> Bob has great capacity for punishment.

Accept, except. Do not confuse these words. *Accept* means *to receive; except* means *to omit* or *leave out.*

> The captain said, "I will accept your requests before five o'clock; I can except no one from this regulation."

Accidently. The correct form is *accidentally.*

Affect, effect. Do not confuse these words. *Affect* means to *influence; effect* means to *bring about* or *accomplish. Effect,* as a noun, means *result; affect* (almost never a noun) has the special meanings *to pretend* and *to be fond of.*

> Her tears affected him no more than had her pleading.
> If every man votes, we hope to effect a change.

(The noun *affect*—a term of psychology, accented on the first syllable, and signifying "feeling, emotion, and desire as factors in determining thought and conduct"—should be used only as a technical term.)

Aggravate, annoy. In the Standard English vocabulary *aggravate* means *to make worse, to make more severe, to intensify; annoy* means *to disturb, to irritate*. On the colloquial level *aggravate* may be used as a synonym for *annoy*.

The shock of his mother's death aggravated his condition.
He annoyed her with his attentions.

Ain't. Dialect in first person, singular, present tense. Illiterate in all other uses.

All over. Colloquial for *everywhere, finished*.

All ready, already. Each is correct, if used properly. *Ready,* in the first instance, is an adjective modified by the adverb *all; already* is an adverb, meaning previous to some specified time.

The soldiers were now all ready to stand inspection.
"I have already spent three hours on the problems," said Dolores.

All the farther, all the faster. Colloquial or dialect for *as far as, as fast as*.

That is as fast as he can run. (NOT: That is all the faster he can run.)

All together, altogether. Each is correct, if used properly. *Together* is an adjective modified by the adverb *all; altogether* is an adverb meaning *entirely*.

The members of the family were all together for the first time in fifteen years.
Your statement is altogether false.

Allude, refer. Do not confuse these words. *Allude* means *to suggest indirectly; refer* means *to mention directly* or *specifically*.

The student thought that the lecturer had alluded to *As You Like It*.
For illustration, he referred to Daniel Boone.

Allusion, illusion, delusion. Do not confuse these words. An *allusion* is an indirect reference; an *illusion* is a deceptive or false appearance; a *delusion* is a false belief, a fixed misconception.

His allusion to the *Dunciad* was readily understood.

No illusions could survive such a logical analysis of the facts.

He suffers from the delusion that he is Julius Caesar.

Alright. The correct form is *all right.*

Alternative. One of two possible choices. Strictly speaking there is no *third alternative,* though this latter phrase is sometimes used colloquially. *Alternative* should be used only where there is a compulsion to choose.

And etc. *Etc.* is the abbreviation for *et cetera,* meaning *and others,* or *and so forth.* The combination of *and* with *etc.* is illiterate. Both *etc.* and *et cetera* should be avoided in formal writing.

Annoy. See **Aggravate.**

Anyplace. Colloquialism for *anywhere, in* (or *to*) *any place.*

Anywheres, nowheres, somewheres. Barbarisms for *anywhere, nowhere, somewhere.*

Apt. See **Liable.**

Around. Colloquial for *about* or *nearly.*

The program starts about three o'clock. (NOT: The program starts around three o'clock.)

Joe Simms weighs nearly three hundred pounds. (NOT: Joe Simms weighs around three hundred pounds.)

As. An impropriety when used for *that* or *whether.*

I am not sure that I can tell you. (NOT: I am not sure as I can tell you.)

He did not know whether he could go with us. (NOT: He did not know as he could go with us.)

At about. Usually redundant.

I will be there about eight o'clock.

or

I will be there at eight o'clock. (NOT: I will be there at about eight o'clock.)

Aught. Means *anything.* Not to be confused with the symbol 0 *(naught).*

Awful, awfully. Although colloquial for *very,* not to be used vaguely. *Awful* means *awe inspiring.*

Bad, badly. Should not be confused. *Bad* is an adjective; *badly,* an adverb.

Balance. Colloquial when used in the sense of *the rest, the others,* or *the remainder.* Correct in the sense of *remainder* only when referring to the difference between two amounts.

> The rest of the evening was given to dancing. (NOT: The balance of the evening was given to dancing.)

Being as. Localism for *since* or *because.*

Beside, besides. Each is correct, if used properly. *Beside* refers to position; *besides* means *in addition to.*

> The dog crouched beside his kennel.
> Besides the members, many guests were present.

Between each. *Between* should be followed by a plural, or by two expressions joined by *and;* following it with *each* or *every* is illogical.

> Between games, the team rested.
>> *or*
> Between one game and the next, the team rested. (NOT: Between each game, the team rested.)

Between . . . or. Should not be used for *between . . . and.*

> Larkin had his choice between paying a fine and going to jail. (NOT: Larkin had his choice between paying a fine or going to jail.)
>> *or*
> Larkin had his choice of paying or going to jail.

Blame . . . on. Colloquial for *blame.*

> The newspapers blamed the engineer for the wreck. (NOT: The newspapers blamed the wreck on the engineer.)

Both. Should not be used carelessly in place of *the two* or *they.*

> The two novels have much in common. (NOT: Both novels have much in common.)

Bust, busted. *Bust,* meaning *burst,* is colloquial; *busted* is an undesirable corruption of *burst.*

But, hardly, only, scarcely. These words, used as adverbs, are all negative in implication and should not be used with a negative form of the verb.

> There were but three students present. (NOT: There weren't but three students present.)
> I could hardly hold the dog. (NOT: I couldn't hardly hold the dog.)
> The captain permitted his men to advance only in small groups. (NOT: The captain wouldn't permit his men to advance only in small groups.)
> I could scarcely believe what I heard. (NOT: I couldn't scarcely believe what I had heard.)

But that, but what. *But that,* used as a preposition, means *other than.* As a conjunction used to introduce a subordinate clause following verbs of saying, thinking, and the like with a negative sense, use *but* or *but that* in formal writing; *but what* is colloquial in effect and should be used only in informal expression. In many instances *that* will be correct and sufficient as the conjunction.

> Nothing would stop her weeping but that he promise to abandon the expedition.
> I do not doubt but that he will go.
> There is little doubt that Luigi is guilty.

Calculate. Localism for *expect, intend, suppose, think.*

Can, may. *Can* denotes power or ability to act; *may* denotes permission, probability, possibility.

> Can you write a good theme in class?
> May I help you across the street?
> He may be asked to read a paper at the next meeting.

Can't help but. A confusion between two idioms: *cannot help* and *can but.*

> I can but feel that the doctor is wrong in his diagnosis.
>
> *or*
>
> I cannot help feeling that the doctor is wrong in his diagnosis. (NOT: I can't help but feel that the doctor is wrong in his diagnosis.)

Can't seem to. See **Seem.**

Capacity. See **Ability.**

Case. Jargon when used loosely as a substitute for a more exact word, or merely to pad a construction.

His predicament was very much like that of a dethroned king. (NOT: His case was very much like that of a dethroned king.)

He has used the same material before in a short story, "The Night Flyer." (NOT: He has used the same material before, in the case of a short story, "The Night Flyer.")

Censure. See **Criticize.**

Character, reputation. Do not confuse these words. *Character* is the sum of all the qualities of an individual: what he really is. *Reputation* is what people think about him: the qualities he is supposed to have.

Common, mutual. Should not be confused. *Common* denotes *sharing; mutual,* an *interchange.*

The two men discovered that Radley was their common enemy.

The young couple exhibited many signs of mutual affection.

Complected. U.S. dialect form of *complexioned.*

Comprise, compose. Do not confuse these words. *Comprise* means to *include; compose* means to *form.*

Detective stories compose his library.

The nation now comprises fifty states.

Considerable. In formal writing to be used as an adjective before a partitive; colloquial when used as a noun; an impropriety when used as an adverb.

He gave considerable sums of money to charity. (NOT: He gave considerable to charity.)

He was very angry. (NOT: He was considerable angry.)

Contact. Colloquial when used as a verb to mean *to make a business or social connection.*

Continual, continuous. Not to be confused. *Continual* implies that an action takes place at closely *recurrent intervals; con-*

tinuous implies that the action takes place *without pause* or *break*.

As far as we could see, there was a continuous expanse of forest.

Could of.   A corruption of *could have;* a barbarism.

Couple.   Not to be used indiscriminately for *two*. Should be used of persons or things only when they are considered together, or when they are connected.

I had dinner with Lester two nights last week. (NOT: I had dinner with Lester a couple of nights last week.)

Credible, creditable, credulous.   Not to be confused. *Credible* means *believable; creditable* means *deserving honor or credit; credulous* means *ready to believe anything.*

Criticize, censure.   Do not confuse these words. *To criticize* means *to judge; to censure* means *to reprimand or condemn.* Note that one may criticize (i.e., judge) favorably.

Crowd.   Colloquial when used for *company* or *group.*

Cute.   Colloquial and trite. Avoid its use.

Date.   Colloquial for *appointment* or *engagement.*

Delusion.   See **Allusion.**

Detract.   See **Distract.**

Different than.   *Webster's* permits *different than* and *different to* (colloquial in England) but prefers *different from. Different than* is generally used only to introduce a clause.

Disinterested, uninterested.   Do not confuse these words. *Disinterested* means *impartial* or *not influenced by self-interest; uninterested* means *without interest.*

The uninterested student cannot learn much.

We must have a disinterested person to settle this controversy.

He was not interested in schoolwork. (NOT: He was disinterested in schoolwork.)

Disremember.   Colloquial. A negative form of *remember.*

Distract, detract. Do not confuse these words. *Distract* means *to divert; detract* means to *defame* or *disparage.*

Done. Should never be used as the past tense of *do.*

Don't. Should not be used in formal writing, nor as the contraction for *does not.*

Drownded. A barbarism. The correct form is *drowned.*

Due to. An adjective construction. An impropriety when used in formal writing to modify a verb or adverb. In informal expression *due to* is now becoming an acceptable preposition.

> My absence was due to illness.
>
> *or*
>
> I was absent because of illness. (*Rather than:* I was absent due to illness.)

Each, every. Both singular. *Each* is applied to individual members of a group considered separately; *every* to the group treated as collective singular.

> Every boy was required to attend the game and each was told to bring a banner with him.

Effect. See **Affect.**

Else. Not to be used redundantly. As an adjective, *else* means *other.*

> There was no one but Helen in the house. (NOT: There was no one else but Helen in the house.)

Emigrate, immigrate. Not to be confused. *Emigrate* means *to go out; immigrate* means *to go in* or *to come into.*

Endorse on the back. Tautological. *Endorse* in this sense (also, *indorse*) means to *write on the back.*

Enthuse. A colloquialism for *to be* or *make enthusiastic.* Not to be used in formal writing.

> Tranton was enthusiastic about the new play he had seen. (NOT: Tranton enthused about the new play he had seen.)

Etc. See **And etc.**

Every so often.   A colloquialism. Not to be used in formal writing for *occasionally,* or *at regular intervals.*

Except (v.).   See **Accept.**

Except (conj.).   Archaic when used for *unless.*

Expect.   Means *to look forward to, as likely to happen.* Colloquial when used for *suppose* or *think.*

Extra.   Should not be used in formal writing for *unusually.*

Factor.   *Factor means any one of the circumstances or elements which produce a result.* Not to be used loosely as a synonym for *phase, quality,* or *characteristic.*

Fellow.   Means *associate, comrade, mate, peer.* Colloquial when used for *person.*

Fewer.   See **Less.**

Fine.   Not to be used vaguely as a substitute for a more exact word. Colloquial when used as adverb.

Former, latter.   Should not be used when more than two persons or objects have been named.

> Of the three men, Lewis, Talberg, and Stein, only the first-named is now living. (NOT: Of the three men, Lewis, Talberg, and Stein, only the former is now living.)

Gent.   *Gent* is a barbarism for *gentleman* and should never be used.

> No gentleman beats a lady. (NOT: No gent beats a lady.)

Gentleman, lady.   Not to be used indiscriminately in place of *man* and *woman.*

> Eighty men have entered the Valley golf tournament. (NOT: Eighty gentlemen have entered the Valley golf tournament.)
> Nowadays women go to barber shops. (NOT: Nowadays ladies go to barber shops.)

Get up.   Often used colloquially to mean *organize, incite, instigate, direct, dress, prepare,* and the like. Should be avoided in formal writing.

Go.   Almost all uses of *go* as a noun are colloquial. Consult the dictionary for them.

Got. Often used carelessly, colloquially, and redundantly with *have*. Correct in the sense of *obtained*.

> Have you an extra sheet of paper? (NOT: Have you got an extra sheet of paper?)
>
> Must you leave? (NOT: Have you got to leave?)

Graceful, gracious. *Graceful* means *displaying grace in form or action;* gracious means *kindly, benignant.*

Guess. Means *to conjecture.* Should not be used loosely as a blanket word for *think, suppose, expect,* or *intend.*

Had of. A corruption of *had have.* Both expressions are barbarisms for *had.*

> If Cooley had known that he was to be called upon, he might not have gone. (NOT: If Cooley had of known that he was to be called upon, he might not have gone.)

Hanged. See **Hung.**

Hardly. See **But.**

Have got. See **Got.**

Honorable. See **Reverend.**

However, whatever, whoever. Colloquial when used as interrogatives.

Hung, hanged. Should not be confused. *Hanged* is the preferred form when the sense is *put to death* by hanging. *Hung* is correct if the meaning is merely *suspended.*

> The convicted man was hanged last Thursday.
>
> At the end of a rope, the boys hung a heavy rock.

If, whether. Either may be used to introduce an indirect question. *Whether* should be used with alternatives expressing doubt or hesitancy.

> I asked him if he was ready to go.
>
> Whether we succeed or not, we must not cease to fight.

Illusion. See **Allusion.**

Immigrate. See **Emigrate.**

Imply, infer. Should not be confused. *Imply* means *to express* *a meaning indirectly but designedly; infer means to derive a conclusion from known facts or from what has been said.*

I do not wish to imply that Jenkins is dishonest; although, of course, some of you may have inferred that he is from what you know of the man.

In.   Do not misuse for *into. In* should be used for place or position, with respect to enclosure; *into* should be used for direction, commonly after verbs of motion, change, and the like.

Gerald was in the boat when I spoke to him.
Gerald stepped into the boat. (NOT: Gerald stepped in the boat.)

In back of.   Colloquial for *behind* or *beyond.*
Incident, instance, instant.   An *incident* is an *event* or *occurrence;* an *instance* is an *example;* an *instant* is *a moment of time.*
Incidently.   Not to be used for *incidentally.*
Incredible, incredulous.   Should not be confused. See **Credible.**
Infer.   See **Imply.**
Ingenious, ingenuous.   Should not be confused. *Ingenious* means *clever* or *resourceful; ingenuous* means *frank* or *innocent.*
Inside of.   The *of* is unnecessary; say *inside.* In formal writing do not use *inside of* for *within.*

He placed the kitten within the box. (NOT: He placed the kitten inside of the box.)

Mrs. Garland sat primly erect inside her automobile. (NOT: Mrs. Garland sat primly erect inside of her automobile.)

Instance, instant.   See **Incident.**
Is because.   See **Reason.**
It's.   The contraction for *it is.* The possessive form of the pronoun *it* is *its.* The contracted form should not be used in formal writing.
Just exactly.   Tautological. Use either one word or the other; not both.

Uncle John has been dead just thirty-six years. (NOT: Uncle John has been dead just exactly thirty-six years.)

Kind of, sort of. Colloquial when used as intensifier meaning *rather, somehow,* or *somewhat.*

Kind of a, sort of a. Omit the *a* (or *an*).

> The scientist believed that he had found a new kind of plant. (NOT: The scientist believed that he had found a new kind of a plant.)

Lady. See **Gentleman.**

Latter. See **Former.**

Lay, lie. Should not be confused. *Lay* is transitive and means *to place* or *cause to lie; lie* is intransitive.

Learn. Should not be used for *teach.*

Leave go of. Barbarism for *leave hold of* or *let go.*

> I was tempted to let go the oars. (NOT: I was tempted to leave go of the oars.)

Less, fewer. Should not be confused. *Less* is used as a comparative of *little; fewer* is the comparative of *few. Less* therefore refers to amount or degree and *fewer* to number.

> Hortense eats less butter than Jane does.
>
> There have been fewer snowstorms this winter than there were last year.

Liable, likely, apt. Should not be confused. *Apt* means *appropriate, suitable, quick in understanding;* followed by *to* with an infinitive, *apt* means *having a tendency. Liable* means *legally responsible,* or merely *responsible;* followed by *to* with an infinitive, *liable* means *exposed to a risk or an evil consequence. Likely* means *believable, favorable, well adapted;* followed by *to* with an infinitive, and ordinarily modified by *very, more,* or *most, likely* means *probable.*

> He made an apt remark.
>
> Delicate porcelain is apt to break easily.
>
> Every man is liable for his actions.
>
> One who handles nitroglycerin carelessly is liable to be injured.
>
> The weather is very likely to be uncertain for several days.

Lie. See **Lay.**

Like, as. Should not be confused. *Like* may be used as a preposition, but not as a subordinator. If the construction requires a subordinator, use *as* or *as if*.

Tony fought as he had never fought before.
The little boy cried as if his heart would break.
Calvin said that his order was like the rest.
In many ways, Henry is like his brother.

Liked. Colloquial when used as a verb form immediately following *would* or *should*.

I should have liked to see the parade. (NOT: I should liked to have seen the parade.)

Likely. See **Liable.**

Locate. Means *to establish in a particular spot, to designate a site, to assign a place to, to find, to place*. It is used colloquially, but not in formal writing, to mean *settle*.

Johnson located his house near the river.
Our family settled in Virginia in 1760. (NOT: Our family located in Virginia in 1760.)

Lose out, win out. Colloquial for *lose, win*.

Governor Blythe lost in the last election. (NOT: Governor Blythe lost out in the last election.)

Mad. Means *insane*. Should not be used for *angry*, except colloquially.

Many. See **Much.**

May. See **Can.**

Mean. Colloquial (U.S.) for *cruel, unkind,* or *vicious*. The formal significance of *mean* is *humble, contemptible, base*.

Might of. A corruption of *might have;* a barbarism.

Most. Used as an adverb (except in forming superlatives), *most* is colloquial for *almost* and should not be used in formal writing.

It is almost three years since I last saw him. (NOT: It is most three years since I last saw him.)

Much, many.   Although compared alike (*more, most*), should not be confused. When used as determiners, *much* indicates a great quantity of, while *many* indicates a great number of.

The troops had much equipment of the best kind.
The army consisted of many platoons of foot soldiers.

Must of.   A corruption of *must have.*
Mutual.   See **Common.**
Myself.   Should not be used as a substitute for *I* or *me.*

My sister and I will be glad to take the trip. (NOT: My sister and myself will be glad to take the trip.)
I told myself the storm would not last.

Nice.   Not to be used vaguely as a substitute for a more exact word.
No account.   Colloquial for *worthless.*
Noted, notorious.   Should not be confused. *Noted* means *well known, remarkable, eminent; notorious* means *widely but unfavorably known.*

Dr. Gray is a noted scholar.
That man is a notorious gambler.

Nowhere near.   A barbarism for *not nearly.*

I'm afraid I have not nearly enough money to pay the bill. (NOT: I'm afraid I have nowhere near enough money to pay the bill.)

Nowheres.   See **Anywheres.**
Off of.   Should not be used for *off.*

Stay off those freshly painted floors. (NOT: Stay off of those freshly painted floors.)

O.K.   Should not be used in formal writing.
Only.   See **But.**
Ought.   A barbarism when combined with *had.*

We ought to be there at eight o'clock. (NOT: We had ought to be there at eight o'clock.)

We ought not to have done that, ought we? (NOT: We hadn't ought to have done that, had we?)

Ought to of. A corruption of *ought to have;* a barbarism.

Out loud. Colloquial for *aloud.*

Over with. Tautological; use *over.*

When the game is over, we shall go home. (NOT: When the game is over with, we shall go home.)

Party. Colloquial when used for *person.*

Who was the fat man (*or* person) with you yesterday? (NOT: Who was the fat party with you yesterday?)

Per. May be used with Latin words, such as *diem, annum, cent* (*centum*), and *se,* but should never be used with English words in formal writing.

His salary is two hundred dollars a month. (NOT: His salary is two hundred dollars per month.)

Phase. Not to be used vaguely as a substitute for a more exact word. *Phase* means *stage in development, aspect,* or *appearance.*

The course deals with many kinds (*or* types, *or* qualities) of poetry. (NOT: The course deals with many phases of poetry.)

Plan on. Colloquial for *plan.*

FORMAL: The committee plans to have a tournament next year.
COLLOQUIAL: The committee plans on having a tournament next year.

Practicable, practical. Should not be confused. *Practicable* means *capable of being accomplished; practical* means *related* or *adapted to actual conditions, not theoretical.*

Goldman's plan was a practical one, but a lack of money made it impracticable.

Prefer . . . more than. Violation of idiom for *prefer to.*

I prefer Bach's compositions to Beethoven's. (NOT: I prefer Bach's compositions more than Beethoven's.)

Principal, principle. Should not be confused. *Principle* is always a noun, and means *a general truth, a rule, a law of action or conduct; principal* may be either noun or adjective and has several meanings, among them *chief, first, most important. Principal* also means *a sum of money which draws interest.*

Harland was asked to state his principal objection.

His speech was limited to a discussion of economic principles.

Robertson invested all his principal in government bounds.

He was one of the principals in the controvesy.

Proportion. Should not be used carelessly for *part. Proportion* means *the quantitative relation or ratio of a part to the whole.*

His mother gave him a larger proportion of the cake than she gave his sisters.

Proposition. Not to be used vaguely as a substitute for a more exact word. A *proposition* is *something offered for consideration or discussion, a proposal.*

Here is one of the most convenient articles that can be bought. (NOT: Here is one of the neatest propositions on the market.)

The opposing team is powerful and dangerous. (NOT: The opposing team is a tough proposition.)

Put in. Colloquial for *spend.*

I wish I could spend more time on my Latin. (NOT: I wish I could put in more time on my Latin.)

Quality. Not to be used vaguely as a substitute for a more exact word. *Quality* means *characteristic, trait,* or *essential nature.*

Quite. Means *completely* or *wholly.* It is used colloquially to mean *to a great extent.* It should not be used carelessly as a blanket word for *very, slightly, rather.*

Those paintings are rather (*or* very) valuable. (NOT: Those paintings are quite valuable.)

Raise, rise. Should not be confused. *Raise* is transitive and means *to lift* or *cause to rise; rise* is intransitive. See Table of Principal Parts, Chapter II, page 58.

Real. An impropriety when used for *very*.

> He is very good-natured. (NOT: He is real good-natured.)

Reason. In formal writing, constructions beginning *the reason is* (*the reason was,* and the like) should always be completed with a *that* clause, in order that the copulative verb may have its necessary complement.

> The reason I am late is that I was talking to the dean. (NOT: The reason I am late is because I was talking to the dean.)
>
> The reason he could not be present is that there was sickness in the family. (NOT: The reason he could not be present is on account of sickness in the family.)

There is, however, an increasing tendency toward the colloquial use of *because.*

Refer. See **Allude.**

Remember of. Barbarism for *remember.*

> Hamilton does not remember seeing the officer. (NOT: Hamilton does not remember of seeing the officer.)

Replace, substitute. Should not be confused. *Replace* means *to take the place of,* or *to restore to a former place; substitute* means *to put in the place of.* The correct preposition following *replace* is *by* or *with;* following *substitute, for.*

> Many archaic words have been replaced by new ones.
>
>   *or*
>
> New words have been substituted for many archaic ones. (NOT: Many archaic words have been substituted by new ones.)

Reputation. See **Character.**

Respectful, respective. Should not be confused. *Respectful* means *showing or having respect; respective* means *relating or belonging to each of several persons or things.* The adverbs *respectfully* and *respectively* are likewise distinct in meaning.

> He maintained a respectful attitude throughout the speech.
>
> Blake summarized their respective faults in a few terse sentences.

Reverend, Honorable. Good taste requires that these titles should be preceded by *the* and should be followed by a given name or by another title.

> The Reverend Wellington Jones; the Reverend Mr. Jones; the Reverend Dr. Jones; the Honorable James A. Newton; the Honorable Mr. Newton. (NOT: Rev. Jones; the Reverend Jones; Hon. Newton; the Honorable Newton.)

Rise. See **Raise.**

Same. Should not be used as a pronoun, except in legal writing.

> We have filled your order, and will ship the goods today. (NOT: We have filled your order and will ship same today.)

Scarcely. See **But.**

Seldom ever. Should not be used for *seldom* or *hardly ever.*

> I seldom see you since you moved. (NOT: I seldom ever see you since you moved.)

Set, sit. Do not confuse these words. *Set* is transitive and means *to place* or *cause to sit; sit* is intransitive.

Shan't. Contractions are not to be used in formal writing. Write: *shall not.*

So. 1) Do not use *so* for *so that.* So, meaning *with the result that, in order that,* is colloquial.

> Bill rushed home so that he might cut the lawn. (NOT: Bill rushed home so he might cut the lawn.)

   2) Do not use *so* loosely as the equivalent of *exceedingly* or *very.*

> Bill said he was very glad to help. (NOT: Bill said he was so glad to help.)

   3) Do not overwork *so* as a conjunction.

> Because I forgot my books, I had to go back to the university for them; consequently I missed my car. (NOT: I forgot my books; so I went back to the university for them and so I missed my car.)

Some. An impropriety when used as an adverb.

While on my vacation, I did some fishing. (NOT: While on my vacation, I fished some.)

Father is feeling somewhat better this morning. (NOT: Father is feeling some better this morning.)

Somewheres. See **Anywheres.**
Sort of. See **Kind of.**
Sort of a. See **Kind of a.**
Substitute. See **Replace.**
Sure and, try and. Colloquial when used for *sure to, try to.*

Be sure to be prompt. (NOT: Be sure and be prompt.)

I shall try to get the motor started. (NOT: I shall try and get the motor started.)

Suspicion. A noun; colloquial when used as a verb.

I suspected that he was dishonest. (NOT: I suspicioned that he was dishonest.)

Swell. Slang. Not in reputable use as an adjective.

This is a fascinating (*or* interesting, *or* well-written) novel. (NOT: This is a swell novel.)

Take. Colloquial when used for *study.*

I am studying Latin and French. (NOT: I am taking Latin and French.)

Take and. Should not be used unless the sense requires it.

You now place the pattern on the material. (NOT: You now take and place the pattern on the material.)

Take in. Colloquial when used for *attend, go to, see.*

We saw a baseball game that night. (NOT: We took in a baseball game that night.)

Take it. An awkward localism when used for *for example, for instance,* and the like.

During the World War, for example, spies were often betrayed by their accents. (NOT: Take it during the World War, spies were often betrayed by their accents.)

This here, these here, that there, those there. Redundant substitutes for *this, these, that, those*.

Till, until. Should not be used for *when* or *before*.

Francis had hardly started to speak when it began to rain. (NOT: Francis had hardly started to speak until it began to rain.)

Too, very. Should not be used immediately before a past participle in place of *too much, very much*.

He was too much occupied with his driving to notice the scenery. (NOT: He was too occupied with his driving to notice the scenery.)
Everyone was very much pleased with Hoyt's recitation. (NOT: Everyone was very pleased with Hoyt's recitation.)

Transpire. *Transpire* means *to become known*. Of the use of *transpire* to mean *occur, Webster's New Collegiate* says: "A sense disapproved by most authorities but found in writings of authors of good standing."

Soon after the game, a fight occurred. (NOT: Soon after the game, a fight transpired.)
It transpired that Will was the person who spread the rumor.

Try and. See **Sure and.**

Two first, two last. Should not be used for *first two, last two*.

The first two chapters of the novel are very interesting. (NOT: The two first chapters of the novel are very interesting.)

Type. A common colloquialism, unacceptable in formal English, is the use of *type* before a noun.

He organized the Society for the Elimination of Redundant Phrases. (NOT: . . . for the Elimination of Redundant Type Phrases.)

Uninterested. See **Disinterested.**

United States. As a proper noun, *United States* should be preceded by *the*. It should not be abbreviated to U.S. in formal writing.

Until. See **Till.**

Up. Used colloquially with words which do not require it to complete their meaning. Such colloquial usage, however, is not desirable in formal writing.

> He opened the gate. (NOT: He opened up the gate.)
>
> The surface was badly scratched. (NOT: The surface was badly scratched up.)
>
> After the team had rested, the game was resumed. (NOT: After the team had rested up, the game was resumed.)
>
> Let us divide the profits. (NOT: Let us divide up the profits.)
>
> Uncle Leonard has been crippled for many years. (NOT: Uncle Leonard has been crippled up for many years.)

Use. Sometimes erroneously used for the past tense, *used.*

> I used to do what I was told. (NOT: I use to do what I was told.)

Used to could. A barbarism for *once could, used to be able,* or *was once able.*

Very. See **Too.**

Way. Should not be used for *away.*

Ways. Should not be used for *way.*

> It is a long way to Tibet. (NOT: It is a long ways to Tibet.)

Whatever. See **However.**

Where. Should not be used carelessly for *that.*

> I read that Joe had been arrested for speeding. (NOT: I read where Joe had been arrested for speeding.)

Where at, where . . . at. Crude substitutes for *where.*

> Where will I find this man? (NOT: Where at will I find this man? *or* Where will I find this man at?)

Which. In referring to persons, *which* should not be used for *who* or *that.*

> The players who were injured were O'Brien, Fisk, and Hoban. (NOT: The players which were injured were O'Brien, Fisk, and Hoban.)

While. Means *during the time that.* It should not be substituted for *although, but, and,* or *whereas.*

Whoever. See **However.**

Win out. See **Lose out.**

Wise. The overuse of this normal adverbial suffix, as in *money-wise, athletics-wise, meaning-wise,* and so on, is not only monotonous but reveals an impoverished vocabulary.

Without. A colloquialism when used for *unless,* according to the *ACD.*

> We cannot give him the place unless we have first seen him. (NOT: We cannot give him the place without we have first seen him.)

Would have. Should not be used for *had* in *if* clauses.

> If you had been prompt, we might not be here now. (NOT: If you would have been prompt, we might not be here now.)

Would of. A corruption of *would have;* a barbarism.

Yourself. Should not be used as a substitute for *you.* See **Myself.**

EXERCISES

A. Use of the Dictionary

I. The editor of one of the most popular dictionaries says that people frequently write him, submitting words which they have coined (some of which are quite useful and ingenious) and urging their adoption in the dictionary. Does this practice make sense? What does it reveal of the concept of the dictionary these people hold?

II. Look up some common words in the oldest dictionary your library possesses. Compare these definitions with their counterparts in a modern dictionary. (If your library has a copy of Dr. Samuel Johnson's *Dictionary* [1755], don't miss the chance to become familiar with it.) What does this comparison tell you about the advantages of keeping your dictionary up-to-date?

III. Look up the following words in the *O.E.D.* to note how their present meanings differ from their original ones:

gossip, wench, hussy, fanatic, villain, superb, quaint, communicate, expect, atone, humorous, marshal, silly, sly, nice

IV. Find in your dictionary the correct or preferred spelling of the past participles of:

alloy	gulp	pine
aver	kidnap	rebel
billet	lead	rely
broadcast	marvel	travel
cancel	mop	vex
commit	panic	
gallop	pin	

V. Find in your dictionary the correct or preferred spelling of the plural of:

addendum	formula	pastry
attorney general	freshman	peccadillo
basis	half	stratum
bus	hero	talisman
criterion	larynx	veto
cupful	looker-on	wharf
dormouse	mesa	
focus	Negro	

VI. What is the correct or preferred pronunciation of the following words?

adult	exquisite	philately
banal	harass	pianist
blackguard	gesticulate	prelude
Boise	gnostic	Sault Ste Marie
Cairo (Illinois)	lamentable	schism
chagrin	Mackinac	schizophrenia
chantey	municipal	sciatica
Charon	often	sleazy
comparable	parliament	status
demesne	parquet	vagary

VII. Find in your dictionary the correct division of syllables for the following words:

disputatious	macroscopic	preferential
exegesis	mellifluous	pyramidal
exogamy	monolatry	spirometer
geomancy	perspiratory	superfluous
hierocracy	pestle	Thersites
hydropathy	Petrarch	zoography
litigate	plasmolysis	

VIII. Find in your dictionary whether the following words should be written as one word or as two words or should be linked by a hyphen:

anticommunist	latchstring	plainsong
clubcar	livestock	quarterhour
clubhouse	moonstone	rightminded
drugstore	nightgown	selfcontained
firstrate	nightrobe	slapstick
flashback	onesided	welldressed
greatuncle	pilotfish	

IX. What does your dictionary tell you about the level of usage of the following words?

blockhead	fizzle	movies
bogus	gaol	mutt
bouse	girn	natty
carrel	guerdon	noddle
confabulate	harken	rhinoscopy
counterjumper	hebetude	rubato
debunk	johnnycake	rubricate
dimwit	largess	snob
dustman	larrikin	sourdough
enthuse	mike	swain

If possible, compare two dictionaries for this exercise.

X. How many meanings does your dictionary have for the following words?

acute (*adj.*)	ill (*adv.*)	lead (*v.*)
brass (*n.*)	intelligent (*adj.*)	mark (*n.*)
dress (*v.*)	knock (*v.*)	romance (*n.*)
fine (*adj.*)		

XI. What is the meaning of the following foreign expressions?

ad hominem	hic jacet	petit-maître
aubade	hoi polloi	¿quién sabe?
bona fides	in saecula	ranz des vaches
carpe diem	saeculorum	sic
delineavit	inter vivos	sirvente
de profundis	mot juste	vogue la galère
genius loci	passim	Wanderjahr

XII. Who were the following persons and when did they live?

Apuleius	Hakluyt	Osceola
Barnum	Iturbide	Palladio
Canova	Juvenal	Rossini
Daguerre	Kossuth	Saint-Gaudens
Empedocles	Lermontov	Torquemada
Frémont	Mencius	Zwingli
Gogol	Nobel	

XIII. With the aid of your dictionary locate the following places:

Aruba	Great Bear Lake	Otterburn
Bernese Alps	Hyrcania	Pharos
Carcassonne	Irrawaddy	Scapa Flow
Chautauqua	Kunming	Timbuctoo
Devon	Lambeth	Uganda
Edessa	Montenegro	Wagram
Fortaleza	Naxos	

XIV. From what languages were the following names derived and what was the original meaning of each name?

Aurelius	Herbert	Nicholas
Barbara	Hortense	Phoebe
Camilla	Irene	Rosalind
Cora	Leila	Sophia
David	Leo	Theodore
Eugenia	Margaret	Ursula
Felix	Morgan	

XV. What glimpses of man's activities and behavior are to be found in the following words?

bacchanalian	gerrymander	peripatetic
bedlam	hazard	poinsettia
bloomer	labyrinth	pompadour
cardigan	laconic	sapphics
colossal	meander	sarcophagus
corduroy	mugwump	sedan
cravenette	omnibus	sherry
demiurge	ottoman	stoic
forsythia	pagan	titan
galvanize	pantaloon	tontine

B. The Languages of Fact and Opinion

I. Discuss the following observation: "People don't object to what one *does* but to what one *says*." In your own experience, is this true?

II. What is the difference in connotation between Travelers' *Checks* and Travelers' *Cheques?* Between the product of Barrel No. 133 of the Montane Perfume Company and *Parfum de Nuit Ravissant (Montane Perfumery, Paris)?* Between *bit player* and *starlet?* Between *Perkins Brothers Co.'s Tweed Coats* and *Regency Square Tweeds?*

III. Define the appeals in these two advertisements. What is the factual content of each?

Jim's Junkies!
Come an' get 'em!
Bigger an' better than ever!

Casa de Cadillac
Announces Enlargement
Of Its
Resale Facilities

IV. A radio commercial for a brand of oleomargarine never refers to butter but instead uses the phrase "the high-priced spread." Why?

V. What are the connotations in these excerpts from advertisements? In each case, what is the factual content?

1. Get the best for Father—he appreciates fine craftsmanship.

2. Aquapure Spring Water comes from mile-high springs.

3. Imperial Majesty Cologne—favored by Men and Women for 100 Years.

4. Barky Dogfood is "climatized"!

5. France's Finest Champagne since 1760. There's only one question: can you afford it?

6. A significant break-through in cigarette engineering places Puffoes among the leading filter cigarettes in mild smoke delivery.

7. "I never carry more than $50 in cash," says Clark Gable.

8. Gibby's Baked Beans—every bean is individually baked!

9. The new four-lane highway is of sound-conditioned concrete with 20% greater flexural strength.

10. The Man in Leather. You know him. He's the one who lives a little harder than the rest . . . plays to win, hates to lose—and admits it. He's the one whose constant companion is virile, versatile leather. He wears it. He rides on it. It goes with him when he plays, when he works, when he travels. He likes its feel and the way it smells. He likes its toughness. Its supple comfort. He likes the things the leather industry has been doing to it. Things that have been possible because of new tanning methods and processes and the contributions of Octagon Alkali, a leading supplier of chemicals to the leather industry.

VI. Fill in the blanks below by supplying the missing term or terms.

Honorific term	Neutral term	Derogatory term
elder statesman	Senator X, aged 72	old politician
brilliant conversationalist		gossipy bore
juvenile delinquents		
	member of the police force	
		alien scum
original, creative genius		
		decadent, reactionary imperialists
	Kentuckian working in Detroit or Chicago	
the free-enterprise system		
	banker	
		egghead

VII. Make up another chart resembling the one above, with ten sets of terms.

VIII. Write three paragraphs, the first a factual report, the second an honorific interpretation of these same facts, and the third a derogatory interpretation.

IX. Read the following statements carefully. Which are statements of fact?

1. This is the coldest day we've had all year.

2. Since I had the carburetor adjusted, I'm getting better mileage than I used to.

3. The State College catalogue for this year lists 26 departments, of which 13 offer programs leading to the M.A. or M.S. degree.

4. With men who know tobacco best, it's Whammos two to one.

5. On the exciting, modern Pegasus 800 model, with the 8-cylinder, overhead-valve, V-type engine, the horsepower is 225 at 440 revolutions per minute, and the compression ratio is 9 to 1. This makes for dramatically powerful engine performance.

6. Russian scientific developments within the past few years show that at least in the fields of science and technology their educational system is as good as that of the United States.

7. At 3:47 P.M. on Tuesday, May 12, 1953, an exciting and significant event occurred at the Lying-in Hospital in Chicago, Illinois.

8. The new interoffice memo system which was instituted last month has greatly speeded up the process of disseminating routine information throughout the entire organization.

9. I came, I saw, I conquered.

10. As a ten-year player with the Yankees, he had a lifetime batting average of .278. His best year was 1956, when he batted .323 and hit 31 home runs.

X. Discuss the following advertisement in terms of the copywriter's use of the word "fact" and his distinction between "judgment" and "opinion."

The Man Who Thinks for Himself Knows

Only Puffo has a thinking man's filter . . . a smoking man's taste! This man thinks for himself. Knows the difference between fact and fancy. Trusts judgment, not opinion. Such a man usually smokes Puffo. His reason? Best in the world. He knows for a fact that only Puffo has a thinking man's filter and a smoking man's taste.

XI. Discuss the use of the word "facts" in the following letter:

Dear Dr. Brown:

I would like to make a complaint regarding one of the teachers on your staff. As principal, you should know about her unfair and prejudiced behavior. Miss Driscoll, the fifth-grade teacher, has had a grudge against my son Alfred ever since he entered her room, and as a result he has not done as well this year as he did in the fourth grade. She picks on him and makes fun of him in front of the whole class. Consequently he is very nervous and hates to go to school nowadays. Because of these facts I believe you should do something either about having her dismissed or seeing to it that she does a better job of teaching.

Yours truly,

I. M. CROTCHET

XII. Rewrite the following passages so that all inferential statements are excluded. Retain the original ideas.

1. Prof. David C. Jones, Asst. Professor of Biology (B.S., University of Michigan, 1948; M.S., Scripps Institute of Oceanography, 1950; Ph.D., University of California, 1953), one of the leading authorities in the field of marine biology, will address the Graduate Science Council next Tuesday, April 25, in a highlight of the organization's lecture season.

2. In the roaring, madcap world of Grand Prix auto racing, the power axis is shifting. For years, daring, lead-footed Italians bestrode the field until fiery death picked them off one by one, from Ascari to Musso. Spain's dashing Alfonso de Portago was killed in 1957, and Argentine's five-time world champion, aging (47) Juan Manuel Fangio, announced this summer that he is retiring. Today, dominance in racing belongs to the British, especially to flaxen-haired, temperamental Mike Hawthorn, 29, and balding, easygoing Stirling Moss, 28. The two are battling head-to-head for the world driving championship.

3. Last week, full in the buzzing hot Ohio July, the Butler Institute of American Art was crammed with a new show of U.S. paintings and jammed with people to see them. It was no leader yet of world art, but a happy model of the small-city U.S. museum in summer bloom.

4. Congress wreaked a lot of costly mischief when, out of solicitude for the individual armed services, it flawed 1947's defense unification act with service-independence safeguards that fostered disunity and snarled Defense Department lines of authority. Last week, with rumblings over-

seas sharply reminding the lawmakers of the nation's need for military efficiency, the Senate took a long step toward undoing the mischief. Texas' Majority Leader Lyndon B. Johnson called to the floor the President's defense reorganization bill and the Senate unanimously passed it, heavily rephrased but scarcely damaged in substance. By imposing more command unity on the sprawling defense establishment, the measure will do more than save money: it will put the Defense Department in better organizational trim to function swiftly and effectively in case of big or little war.

5. The hearing room in Washington reeked with the ugly smell of shakedown, of labor hoodlums sweating behind the Fifth Amendment, of sordid fear, as testimony on the Chicago restaurant protection racket went into its second week. To the members of the Senate's labor-management investigating committee, it was quite clear that they had caught the scent of one of the dirtier trails in labor history.

6. Foreign-car boom will boost Volkswagen production in West Germany from 470,000 cars last year to 630,000 in 1959. Waiting list for new VW's is five to six months long in Germany, four to 14 months in U.S.

7. U.S. osteopathy last week underwent the most drastic spinal manipulation in its history, designed to give it a straight-backed stance, let it hold its head higher among the nation's healing professions. In the process, the long-revered founding father of osteopathy was gently but firmly shouldered out of the picture.

8. Two years ago a brilliant Brazilian architect took on one of the world's most exciting assignments in art: to design the palaces, public buildings, courthouses, churches—even the yacht club—of a whole new city that will house 500,000 people. Now Brasilia, the great new inland national capital, is bustling toward completion, much to the pride and satisfaction of Architect Oscar Niemeyer.

In a county alive with spectacular and imaginative new architecture, the work of Oscar Niemeyer ranks at the top.

9. Despite their air-conditioned offices and silk suits, the executives of the nation's three television networks have good reason to sweat this summer. Never before have program sales for the fall and winter season fallen so far behind schedule. At the end of last week the three networks moodily reported that a total of $16\frac{1}{4}$ hours of their prime evening

time—the equivalent of five full evenings' programming for one network —was still up for sale. Value: some $65 million.

10. The world's biggest sugar daddy is a stocky, Venezuela-born Cuban who in light moments proclaims that "sugar is my mistress," and in serious moments insists that "the degree of a people's civilization is related to their sugar consumption—less civilized people use less sugar." The man: Julio Lobo (meaning wolf), 59, who bears the scars of his lifelong love affair with sugar.

XIII. Make your own collection of examples of "word-magic." Bring them to class for discussion.

C. Good Diction

I. Rewrite each of the following sentences, which are guilty of being unnatural, abstract, inexact, or trite.

1. Individuals who are habitually domiciled in vitreous structures of patent frangibility should perforce refrain from employing petrous formations as projectiles. (This is an old proverb.)

2. He transmitted the message to the corporal verbally.

3. The character of this case is of such a nature that it is difficult to ascertain the elements which comprise the whole.

4. He performed the Brahms Violin Concerto with great credibility.

5. Illumination is required to be extinguished upon departing the premises.

6. I fail to see what these footnotes infer to in the text.

7. After the play, tired but happy, he was the recipient of tumultuous applause.

8. Reimbursement will be forthcoming at the earliest possible opportunity.

9. When he visited Rome, the enormity of St. Peter's Cathedral surprised him.

10. Are you inferring that you don't believe what he says?

11. We left for our trip at the incredulous hour of 5 A.M.

12. I propose to take my ablutions upon completion of this task.

13. Contract bridge is a game I am completely disinterested in.

14. She had her first formal affair when she was seventeen.

15. I thought that Mr. Williams' talk was interesting.

II. Examine one of your recent compositions for errors of the kind illustrated in the sentences above. Rewrite each faulty sentence.

D. Levels of Usage

I. Write a paragraph in the language of a particular speech community with which you are familiar (geographical, occupational, avocational, and the like). Then rewrite the paragraph, discussing the same topic but addressing it to a more general audience.

II. From a newspaper or magazine, take an article in which the diction is colloquial or slangy—a sports column, a feature article, a review of the latest jazz recordings, and so on. Rewrite the article in language appropriate to formal exposition.

III. Rewrite a paragraph from one of your textbooks in the colloquial diction appropriate in a letter to your family.

IV. Rewrite one of your recent compositions in slang.

V. For the ambitious: Try rewriting a short scene from Shakespeare in good, colloquial, idiomatic English.

E. The Exact Idiom

I. List, with their meanings, the idiomatic uses the dictionary gives for the following words. Note the level of usage for each of the idiomatic phrases.

bear	cast	out
book	get	run
by	keep	stock
call	line	

II. Idiom can be very confusing to a foreign-born student of English.

TOMMY: Daddy, is it correct to say "water the horse" when he is thirsty?

FATHER: Yes, certainly.

TOMMY: Well, then, I'm going to milk the cat.

Can you supply other examples of the same kind of illogical but idiomatic constructions?

VI | Style: Proper Words in Proper Order

"The style is the man" is an old maxim which implies that others know us through what we say and how we write. A writer's style is the result of many things, including his background, his education, his experience, his personality, his intelligence, and his temperament. We infer the man from his style. "Do your work and I shall know you," wrote Emerson.

More specifically, style is the way in which a writer orders his thoughts in words. In the preceding chapters we have had occasion to look at language as grammatical structure and at language as words. Properly speaking, style is the individual treatment of these basic elements. We can describe the grammatical aspects of a language scientifically, but we can never predict what a writer will do with these elements within the boundaries of the language. The great writers frequently extend the boundaries, invading and exploring new territories of language possibility. There are only so many notes in music, too, but the miracle of musical composition is what the artist can create out of these notes. It is at this point that composition becomes art.

The opportunity for individual style is almost limitless. In 1957 the Data Processing Laboratory of the National Bureau of Standards conducted an electronic computer study of sentence structures. Out of 550 sentences, 335 unique structures emerged, with the most common structure representing only 2.2 per cent of the whole sample—and this variation in sentences taken from scientific sources, with "a maximum of straightforward, factual

statements and a minimum of ambiguity and emotional or at-
titudinal factors."[1]

Given the considerable freedom which the English language
allows, no textbook can hope to treat all the elements of style. It
can deal only with the more obvious and more mechanical elements which make for clarity, smoothness, and at least a moderate
effectiveness. Ease and simplicity of expression, brevity and directness, congruity of subject matter and language, variety in
form, euphony, and the assistance of special devices of style—all
these things depend upon the skill with which the writer chooses
and blends his sentences and words into a pleasing and effective
whole. How personality and mannerism affect style may be seen
in section St 8, a section given over to specimens of style to which
the student may turn for further illustrations of the principles
discussed in the first seven sections.

St 1   SIMPLICITY

As suggested in the preceding chapter, naturalness is to be preferred to "fine writing," or the expression of ideas in an inflated
and pretentious manner. This statement does not mean that a
writer should not use descriptive or connotative language, or that
he should make his writing so bare as to appear childlike. It
implies, rather, that his style should be easy and natural, free
from feeble elegance, euphemism, and unnecessary formality.

**A. Expression should be as simple as the subject
and the occasion permit.**   In the Age of Science, the layman may
find himself perplexed by shoptalk, as illustrated by the following
true story:

A New York plumber wrote to the U.S. Bureau of Standards his discovery that a dose of hydrochloric acid would quickly open a clogged
drainage pipe and asked if it was a good thing to do. A Bureau scientist

---

[1] The experiment is described in the *Technical News Bulletin* of the NBS,
June, 1957.

replied, "The efficacy of hydrochloric acid is indisputable, but the corrosive residue is incompatible with metallic permanence."

The plumber wrote back thanking the Bureau for telling him the method was fine. The scientist, a little disturbed about the misunderstanding, showed the correspondence to his boss (another scientist). The latter wrote the plumber, "We cannot assume responsibility for the production of toxic and noxious residue with hydrochloric acid and suggest you use an alternative procedure."

The plumber answered again. He agreed with the Bureau—hydrochloric acid worked fine. The two scientists, upset over the future of New York's drainage, called in a distinguished colleague to break the impasse. In a final letter to the plumber the third scientist reluctantly lapsed into the layman's language: "Don't use hydrochloric acid. It eats hell out of the pipes."[2]

Don't write: *The vertical extent of the edifice is astounding* when you mean: *The building is very high.*

Don't write: *He assimilated his evening meal in a dilatory manner* when you mean: *He ate his dinner slowly.*

Don't write: *The encomium is not excessive when one considers the magnitude of the accomplishment* when you mean: *The praise is not too great for the deed.*

Finally, to borrow Professor Lionel Trilling's example of academic double talk, don't write: *Their libidinal impulses being reciprocal, they activated their individual erotic drives and integrated them within the same social frame of reference* when you mean: *They fell in love and got married.*

Notice that the preceding examples emphasize saying what you mean. What you mean, however, may call for language that is not simple in the everyday sense. In the first example, for instance, if the Bureau of Standards had been writing an engineer, its letter might have said: "Although hydrochloric acid is efficacious in opening pipes that are clogged with organic material, the acid also accelerates metallic corrosion and produces a toxic and noxious residue. The Bureau therefore cannot recommend the

---

[2] "Age of Science," *The New Republic*, February 24. 1947. Reprinted by permission.

use of hydrochloric acid for opening metal drainage pipes." Simplicity of expression, moreover, does not necessarily mean choosing prosaic language, since that may be too flat for the subject or occasion. Lincoln did not mean "Eighty-seven years ago our ancestors founded a new government" when he said: "Four score and seven years ago our fathers brought forth, on this continent, a new nation . . . ."

B. Expression should be natural. Avoid poetical flourishes unless you have some reason to think you can bring them off.

Don't write: *In all the days of my life, never have I had the good fortune to perceive, never have my orbs been blessed by such a vision of beauty as yonder sunset* when you mean: *I have never seen a more beautiful sunset.*

Don't write: *Our clan emulated the pioneers of '49 in making a hegira to the Golden State just a century later* when you mean: *Our family moved to California in 1949.*

Likewise, avoid formality or pompousness through excessive use of the "editorial *we*."

Don't write: *The facts that we have presented in this paper have led us to this conclusion* when you mean: *The facts that I have presented in this paper have led me to this conclusion.* Although Mark Twain once remarked that the only people properly entitled to use "we" were editors and people with tapeworm, this use is an accepted convention where the individual is speaking or writing as a member of a group—a debating team, a law firm, or a corporation, to name a few instances. A lawyer might very well write: *We are sorry to say that we cannot reply to the charge made against us.* A debater might very well say: *We shall now refute the arguments presented by the affirmative side.* Another conventional use of *we* is frequently found in textbooks, when the author means "you and I, the reader and the writer," as in a sentence like *We shall discover this fact to be important when we return to some of the implications in a later chapter.*

St 2   ECONOMY

Effective writing is economical; that is, it uses no more words than are appropriate to the subject and the occasion. Despite the rich and ornate prose of writers like John Donne, John Milton, Sir Thomas Browne, Henry James, Herman Melville, and William Faulkner, the student writer is best advised to avoid imitating their examples. Compactness and directness are positive qualities making for clarity; wordiness may bore the reader or obscure the meaning. Ethel Merman, the musical comedy star, recounts the following anecdote in her autobiography:

> Following the first night of "Anything Goes" the New York Herald Tribune printed a thing I couldn't understand. It went like this: "Miss Merman's part of the song goes along bars, so to say, while the orchestra indulges in contrapuntal ripples and waves which have nothing to do with tune, and meanwhile also the rhymes themselves fall on first and middle syllables, in a delightfully tricky sort of syncopation which calls for the most delicately accurate timing on the part of all concerned. The dash and precision with which Miss Merman lands each syllable where it belongs is enchanting."
>
> What I finally figured the man must have meant is this: it was a very tricked-up orchestration and the band was playing against me, but I came out ahead. Period.[3]

A. Avoid verbosity.   Do not use many words where a few will do; do not use several word-groups or sentences where one is enough:

> Four of us went to town Saturday. (NOT: There were four of us who went to town Saturday.)
>
> A man will often spend more money than he makes. (NOT: It is often the case that a man will spend more money than he makes.)

---

[3] From *Who Could Ask for Anything More* by Ethel Merman as told to Pete Martin. Copyright © 1955 by Ethel Merman Six. Copyright 1955 by The Curtis Publishing Company. Reprinted by permission of Doubleday & Co., Inc.

Mr. Griggs lectured this morning on character education. (NOT: Mr. Griggs gave a lecture this morning along the lines of character education.)

Few college students are indifferent to grades. (NOT: There are not many young men and women in our colleges who are indifferent to the grades which are given them for their work.)

The art museum is noted for its many beautiful paintings by famous French, Belgian, and German artists. (NOT: The art museum is noted for its many beautiful paintings. These paintings are by famous artists, who are natives of the three countries of France, Belgium, and Germany.)

B. Avoid introducing unnecessary details. A unified and coherent sentence will consist of only relevant information.

When my father as a little boy came to Kansas, living conditions were very primitive. (NOT: When my father, who was then a little boy—he was just eight years old—first came to the country west of the Mississippi, in fact to Kansas, where we have lived ever since, the living conditions, which were different from what they are now in these modern times, were very primitive.)

C. Avoid useless repetitions of the same idea in different words. Such expressions (called "tautologies") merely waste the reader's time. Here are a few familiar ones:

combined together	repeat again
divide up	return back
fellow classmates	small in size
few in number	sum and substance
first initiated into	throughout the entire
important essentials	try an experiment
join together	volunteered of their own
perfectly all right	free will
quite round	where . . . at
refer back	

St 3   CONGRUITY

Style must harmonize with subject matter. Even though correct grammatically, any phrase not in tone must be omitted. A single incongruity can ruin the effect that the writer has carefully built up. In a light or whimsical article, the style must not become heavily serious. In a serious piece of work, there must be no feeble attempts at humor, no flippancy. There must be no *straining* after effects. There must be no ludicrous association of ideas or incongruous use of figurative language.

A. Humorous effects should not be introduced unless the writer's material or purpose requires them. A deliberately pedantic array of "big words" may produce a humorous effect, but only if very artfully controlled (as, for example, in the sketches of S. J. Perelman):

The howling of the wolf at the door did not disturb him. (NOT: The gentle ululations of the lupine visitor at his door did not disturb his equanimity.)

The poor old man wandered unhappily down the street. (NOT: The poor old biped peregrinated unhappily down the street.)

His nose was as long as an elephant's, and his eyes were as small as a pig's. (NOT: His proboscis was as lengthy as that of a pachyderm, and his eyes were as small as those of the porcine tribe.)

B. Descriptive effects should be natural, not forced. A straining after such effects often overreaches itself and distracts the reader from more important ideas, or makes a ludicrous picture:

There were a great many books in that room.

or

He had never seen so many books before. (NOT: There seemed to be as many books in that room as there are bees in a hive.)

The book ended abruptly. (NOT: The book ended with the abruptness of an explosion.)

He bumped his head against the sideboard when he bent over. (NOT: As a ship crashes against a rocky shore, so his head struck the sideboard when he bent over.)

C. In serious writing only ideas or expressions that are congruous should be brought together:

His smile was abject and pitiful. (NOT: His smile, like a dog limping along on three legs, was abject and pitiful.)

You will always be pleased with this washing powder. (NOT: This washing powder will be a delight to your soul forever.)

He gazed meditatively on the scene before him. (NOT: He gazed before him with eyes as meditative as those of a cow.)

D. Subject matter should be presented in congruous language. A mixture of figurative and technical or of figurative and prosaic language should be avoided:

There were very many dishes in the sink, all of them waiting to be washed. (NOT: The dishes in the sink waiting to be washed were as many as the stars in the heavens.)

The dazzling snow fell most of the time. (NOT: The dazzling snow fell a great per cent of the time.)

E. Unless anticlimax is desired for humorous effect appropriate to the subject, the words used at the end of a climactic series should be strong enough to carry out the effect of climax. (For a brief consideration of anticlimax as a legitimate rhetorical device see section St 7.)

The fire spread from the house to the barn; everything he had was burning. Walsh was sunk in despair. (NOT: The fire spread from the house to the barn; everything he had was burning. Walsh was despondent.)

He had worked hard to supply them with luxuries. He had struggled, he had drudged, he had slaved. (NOT: He had struggled, he had drudged, he had slaved; he had certainly worked hard to supply them with luxuries.)

Warning had reached the village but a moment before. Now the terrified people heard the roar of the waters and almost immediately a gigantic wall of water rushed upon them. (NOT: Warning had reached the villagers but a moment before. Now the terrified people heard the roar of the waters and almost immediately a gigantic wall of waters came in sight.)

F. Figures of speech must be used carefully. An abrupt shifting from one image to another causes confusion and often absurdity. Like the concrete word, figures of speech give variety, vividness, and emphasis to writing, but too frequent figurative language is likely to develop into an objectionable mannerism and to weaken effectiveness. When a writer does use a figure of speech he should complete logically the image with which he begins and he should be careful to see that there is no incongruity between the image in a concrete noun or verb and that of the figure introduced. (For the correct use of the most common figures of speech see section St 7.)

His voice shook with the emotion that racked his body.

or

His voice shook with the emotion that cut through him like a knife. (NOT: His voice shook with the emotion that racked his body like a knife.)

His rage grew while she was speaking and he flung a sharp answer back at her. (NOT: He flew to pieces while she was speaking and he flung a sharp answer back at her.)

If our country is to prosper, it must be progressive, industrious, and democratic. (NOT: If our country is to prosper, she must take vast strides upon the wheel of progress, sowing with one hand, reaping with the other, ever holding high above her the torch of liberty for all.)

He imagined himself reaching out and plucking an apple from the old tree in the farmyard. (NOT: With his mind's eye he reached out and plucked an apple from the old tree in the farmyard.)

G. The same tone of expression should be maintained. A paper or a paragraph that begins seriously should be serious throughout; one that is ironic should be sustained as irony. A writer should not slip carelessly in and out of the ironic tone, nor should he mix the formal and the extremely colloquial:

A college education is a fine thing to have. Greek, for instance, is a great consolation to the graduate looking for a job. Surely he will find innumerable uses for it every day. Higher mathematics, too, is important when one is down to his last dime. And what a fascinating geologic study he can make of the pavements he tramps! (NOT: A college education is a fine thing to have. Greek, for instance, is a great consolation to the graduate looking for a job. It is, I truly believe, the most useless subject in the curriculum. Higher mathematics too is important when one is down to his last dime. And what a fascinating geologic study one can make of the pavements he tramps.)

Professor Roberts had long been known as an authority on Shakespearean texts, but the publication of the newly found manuscripts would force him to alter his long-defended theory concerning Hamlet. His position was a difficult one. (NOT: Professor Roberts had long been known as an authority on Shakespearean texts, but the publication of the newly found manuscripts would make him go back on the theory concerning Hamlet that he had stuck with for so long. He was surely in a fix.)

H. The intensity of expression should be appropriate to the matter presented. Hyperbole (see section St 7) must not be used carelessly or excessively. Superlatives should be used only when the writer wishes to convey very strong feeling:

Johnson shouted his answer in his angriest voice. (NOT: Johnson shouted his answer in his most violently angry voice.)

Willard had never seen such a beautiful woman before. (NOT: Willard had never seen such a perfectly beautiful woman before.)

This was the greatest day in his life, for he had won high praise from the leading man in the profession. (NOT: This was the greatest day in his life, for he had won the highest praise from the man who was recognized as the most outstanding in the profession.)

St 4 EMPHASIS

The beginning and the end of a sentence are the most emphatic positions, and of the two positions the end is the more emphatic.

Important ideas or details should be expressed at the beginning or at the end, according to the stress the writer wishes to place upon them, and less important elements should be "tucked in." Some special applications of this principle follow.

A. In order to gain suspense or to achieve emphasis by a variation in sentence structure, use the periodic sentence. A periodic sentence is a sentence in which the grammatical structure is so arranged that the complete meaning is not apparent until the last word or almost the last word of the sentence has been read. The following sentences illustrate the form:

Of all the early savants to interest themselves in the language of the country, the one destined to be the most influential was Webster.—H. L. MENCKEN[4]

As we shrieked ourselves hoarse and pounded one another on the back, Klotz raced across the goal line with the winning touchdown.

Like the parallel sentence (see Chapter I, section J), the periodic sentence is very useful, but, like the parallel sentence, it should be used skillfully so that one's style will not seem overly self-conscious. "Loose" sentences—that is, sentences in which the basic meaning is stated before the actual end of the sentence—are far more common than periodic sentences; the following are examples of loose sentences:

Two brothers named White had introduced Mah Jong to the English-speaking clubs of Shanghai, where it became popular.—FREDERICK LEWIS ALLEN[5]

The pantomime flourished throughout the eighteenth century and, along with other theatrical forms, also throughout most of the nineteenth century, its widespread popularity frequently diverting the activities of actors like David Garrick from more serious drama.

Because loose sentences are common, of course, they do not have the value of either the periodic or the parallel sentence when a

---

[4] *The American Language: Supplement One.* Copyright, 1945, by Alfred A. Knopf, Inc.

[5] *Only Yesterday.* Copyright, 1931, by Harper & Brothers.

writer is especially anxious to emphasize a point. The periodic sentence is especially valuable when a writer wants his style to reflect the measured and deliberate thought he has put into the formulation of an idea or concept.

B. Arrange details in separate sentences to emphasize an action, detail, or thought:

Every college spends more on each student than it receives in tuition and fees, whether from the student, his parents, or the government. Every college student in the United States is on a scholarship in the sense that none pays the full cost of his education—JAMES PHINNEY BAXTER[6] (RATHER THAN: Every college spends more on each student than it receives in tuition and fees, whether from the student, his parents, or the government, and thus every college student in the United States . . . .)

C. Arrange elements in a series in the order of their climax.   That is, place the least important element first and the most important one last, so that the reader's interest may be stimulated as he reads. There are times when an arrangement which will lead to an anticlimax may prove effective. For a discussion of this method of arrangement, see section St 7.

D. Modifying clauses or phrases at the end of a sentence will detract from the emphasis which should normally be upon the verb or upon the word which completes the verb:

WHEN A FRESHMAN IS ONCE ESTABLISHED IN OXFORD, his life falls into a pleasantly varied routine.—JOHN CORBIN (RATHER THAN: His life falls into a pleasantly varied routine, when a freshman is once established in Oxford.)

IF MY ESTIMATION OF HIS CHARACTER IS CORRECT, Allen is the type of boy who needs encouragement.

or

Allen is the type of boy who, IF MY ESTIMATE OF HIS CHARACTER IS CORRECT, needs encouragement. (RATHER THAN: Allen is the type of boy who needs encouragement, if my estimate of his character is correct.)

---

[6] "Inflation Hits the Colleges," *The Atlantic Monthly*, March, 1948.

E. As a general rule, place transitional words and phrases like *moreover, therefore, however, in the first place,* and *for this reason* within a sentence, just after the word to be emphasized; unless the sentence is very short they should never be placed at the beginning or at the end:

A civilization takes seven or eight centuries to reach its highest point. American civilization, THEREFORE, will not reach its peak for several centuries. (NOT: . . . American civilization will not reach its peak for several centuries, therefore.)

What would we do, IN THE FIRST PLACE, if this press stopped?
           or possibly
IN THE FIRST PLACE, what would we do if this press stopped? (NOT: What would we do if this press stopped, in the first place?)

St 5   VARIETY

Variety is necessary for a readable style.   Monotony results from a succession of short sentences, from a series of compound sentences, or from any extended repetition of the same structure. It frequently arises from a persistent overuse of participles, adjectives, or adverbs. Needless to say, the mixing of long and short sentences with those of medium length, the varied use of simple, compound, and complex sentences, and the mixing of sentences that begin with modifying phrases with those that do not, will all help the writer to avoid monotony. (Special devices for achieving variety in style are suggested in section St 7.)

Note, however, that in the first two examples below, the versions in parentheses—those lacking variety in sentence structure —are of a kind often found in the fiction of an author like Ernest Hemingway, who uses such devices of syntax to achieve carefully calculated effects. In his writing, if not in that of most students, the sequence of simple declarative sentences is not the result of accident or inability to write otherwise but a product of the art that conceals art.

Standing at the window, I watched the rain pour down. I wished that it would stop, for I wanted to go walking. (NOT: I stood at the window. The rain poured down. I wished that it would stop. I wanted to go for a walk.)

He went fishing, but failed to catch any fish because he fell asleep. When he finally awoke, to discover that the sun was going down and that it was too late even to try to fish, he started home. (NOT: He went fishing and fell asleep. Later he awoke and the sun was going down. It was too late to fish and so he went home.)

Everybody should turn out to vote in this election, for the triumph of the Reform party means the end of corruption in office. If the voters will only come to the polls in large enough numbers, they can surely elect the men they wish to see in power. (NOT: Now is the time for everyone to come out to vote, for everything depends upon this election. All are against corruption, and so they should vote the Reform ticket. This is not a foolish thing, for the voters can elect anyone they want. But the people must turn out heavily, for if they do there is little doubt that they will elect the men they want.)

Glowering upon his enemy, Johnson swore and struck out. He choked with rage when he saw the man turn and run away before he could stop him. (NOT: Glowering upon his enemy, Johnson, swearing and raging, struck at him. Choking with rage, he saw the man turning and running away before he could stop him.)

The moon shone down upon the wood. The water flowing in the bush-fringed creek made a music that touched the cold heart of Simon Malvern. (NOT: The pale, silvery, distant moon shone down upon the quiet, shadowy wood. The gently stirring waters of the little bush-fringed creek gave the lonely, empty night a lovely, alluring sound of music that touched the cold, bitter heart of Simon Malvern.)

St 6 EUPHONY

Euphony, the succession of pleasing sounds, is desirable in writing. On special occasions when a writer wishes to create an unpleasant effect, he will make use of unpleasant or irritating sounds and combinations of sound. Commonly his intention is to present his ideas as smoothly and agreeably as possible; he will therefore write nothing that by its sound will annoy the reader or distract him from the idea presented.

A. Clumsy repetition of sound is irritating:

Because he whistled in violation of the rules, he was put out. (NOT: Whistling being the violating of the rule, he was put out.)

Rather unpleasantly, Jackson gave his opinion and departed. (NOT: Mildly unpleasantly giving his opinion, Jackson departed.)

Accused by Sneeders, the man admitted he had laughed. (NOT: The man who Sneeders declared laughed admitted he laughed.)

B. The introduction into prose of such devices of poetry as rhyme and meter and the excessive use of alliteration are generally distracting:

The friendly senator walked rapidly away. (NOT: The sociable senator strode swiftly away.)

The thunder rolled threateningly about us. (NOT: Threateningly the thunder hurled its horrid sound about us.)

After breaking a rule which he knew was dear to sophomores' hearts, the freshman ran away. (NOT: The simple freshman broke a rule dear to the hearts of sophomores, but when he found what he had done, he ran away in sudden fear.)

St 7   SPECIAL DEVICES OF STYLE

The effectiveness of style is greatly increased by the occasional and varied use of many special stylistic devices, some of them structural, some of them figurative. These devices, of course, are not equally adapted to all kinds of writing; it should always be understood that care and discretion must be observed in employing them. Even when the subject matter or the spirit of the composition calls for and justifies the use of similes, antitheses, and balanced sentences, for example, the writer must not overwork any particular device. Examples of some of the commonly used stylistic devices are listed alphabetically below.

Anticlimax is the arrangement of a series of words or phrases in order of climax, except that the last of the series is quite out of keeping with the others; that is, the last of the series is deliberately incongruous. The entire effect created by the climactic order is made ludicrous by the sudden relaxing of tension which comes at the end of the series. Anticlimax is most often found in humorous writing and should, of course, be handled circumspectly and be used infrequently.

The lights on the stage grew brighter, the orchestra burst into a triumphal strain of mighty overture, the vast audience roared with applause, and then, full into the glare of spotlight waddled Nunia, the Trained Seal.

On the one hand . . . . & on the other . . . .

Antithesis is the opposing of ideas; it is often made more emphatic by the arrangement of the contrasting terms in parallel form. *Contrasting one things another. Good way to end paragraph but not entire paper.*

He prostrated himself in the dust before his Maker, but he set his foot on the neck of his king.—THOMAS BABINGTON MACAULAY

The wicked flee when no man pursueth: but the righteous are bold as a lion.—PROVERBS

The **balanced sentence** is one in which the weight of idea is proportionately distributed. In its simplest form it is the ordinary compound sentence. Symmetry and evenness of flow are the characteristics of such sentences.

So David reigned over all Israel and executed judgment and justice among his people.—FIRST CHRONICLES

Crafty men contemn studies, simple men admire them, and wise men use them: for they teach not their own use; but that is a wisdom without them and above them, won by observation.—FRANCIS BACON

There were better teachers, no doubt, than Christopher Jones, but there were few with his variety of knowledge; there were better writers, but none with his strange experience to draw upon.

Instead of parallel structure an antithical one

Chiasmus is the expression of two parallel ideas in such form that the construction of the second part is the reverse of that used in the first.

[handwritten: Old King Cole was a merry old soul / a merry old soul was he.]

He could not flee any further; to stop he did not dare.

He had no love for his sister; of his brother he was ashamed.

His hand flew up; off came his hat.

Climax is the arrangement of a series of words, phrases, clauses, or sentences in the order of their increasing strength or importance. (See also sections St 4B and ¶ 6B.)

Chambers was handsome, good-natured, and intelligent.

Wyatt protested against the accusation, he asserted his innocence, and he denounced the instigator of the movement.

An **epithet** is an adjective expressing some relation or quality that vividly describes a person or an object. It is one of the most effective stylistic devices, for the selection of the most exact modifier gives sharpness and emphasis to writing. The student cannot make too great an effort to find the epithet suited to the occasion.

The silver, *snarling* trumpets 'gan to chide.—JOHN KEATS

I know that entertainments of this nature are apt to raise *dark* and *dismal* thoughts in *timorous* minds, and *gloomy* imaginations.—JOSEPH ADDISON

Many people would have called her a fat woman, but Mr. Polly's innate sense of epithet told him from the outset that *plump* was the word.—H. G. WELLS

The **historical present tense** is a sudden dropping into the present tense in narrative for the sake of vividness or of greater intensity. Since, however, all effectiveness will quickly be lost if the writer overworks this device, he is warned to use it sparingly. He must also be sure that he does not shift carelessly from past tense to present and back again.

. . . Hark! a rap again! A musical woman's voice, refusing to be rejected: it is the citoyenne who would do France a service. Marat, recognizing from within, cries, Admit her. Charlotte Corday is admitted.—THOMAS CARLYLE

Hyperbole, or **overstatement,** is deliberate exaggeration, not for deception, but for increased emphasis.

A thousand pardons!
The delighted boy sat with a mountain of ice cream before him.
His knowledge was boundless.

Invective is the use of uncomplimentary and violent language. It should not be used too often or the effect of it will wear off.

Some have called Chester a scoundrel; but he is only a half-wit.

How should he, a serving man both by nature and function, an idiot by breeding, and a solicitor by presumption, ever come to know or feel within himself what the meaning is of gentle?—JOHN MILTON

> If inspiration should her aid refuse
> To him who takes a pixy for a muse,
> Yet none in lofty numbers can surpass
> The bard who soars to elegize an ass.
> So well the subject suits his noble mind,
> He brays, the laureate of the long-eared kind.
>
> LORD BYRON

Inversion is the reverse of a normal sentence construction. It is used for the securing of greater emphasis than is possible with the ordinary construction.

Happy is the man who can make such a speech.
To him I would give the papers and to no other man.
What a piece of work is man!—WILLIAM SHAKESPEARE
Never, never more shall we behold that generous loyalty to rank and sex.—EDMUND BURKE

Irony is a form of expression in which the intended meaning is the opposite of the literal interpretation.

I have computed the charge of nursing a beggar's child . . . to be about two shillings per annum, rags included; and I believe no gentleman would repine to give ten shillings for the carcass of a good fat child, which, as I have said, will make four dishes of excellent nutritive meat, when he hath only some particular friend or his own family to dine with him. Thus the squire will learn to be a good landlord, and grow popular among his tenants; the mother will have eight shillings net profit, and be fit for work until she produces another child.

—JONATHAN SWIFT

Litotes. See **Understatement.**

Metaphor is a figure of speech which implies, but does not state, a comparison. Instead of making an actual comparison between two objects or ideas (see **Simile**), metaphor directly applies to one object a term which is ordinarily associated with another object, but which has some quality or aspect appropriate to the first.

The whirlwind of war is upon us. (As a simile, the statement would be: "War, like a whirlwind, is upon us.")

Life is a flame and we live by an invisible sun within us.—SIR THOMAS BROWNE

He plowed his hands through his hair.

Metonymy and **synecdoche** are both figures of substitution or association. **Metonymy** is the term employed when one word is used for another which it suggests. **Synecdoche** is the term applied to those figures in which the part is substituted for the whole, an attribute or quality for an object, and so forth. The academic distinction between the terms is finely drawn, however, and the two figures are commonly treated together. Many of the forms which these figures take are illustrated in the examples which follow.

AUTHOR SUBSTITUTED FOR HIS WORKS: Thornton has read all of Shakespeare.

MATERIAL SUBSTITUTED FOR THE THING MADE OF IT: Whenas in silks my Julia goes . . . .—ROBERT HERRICK

SYMBOL SUBSTITUTED FOR THE THING SYMBOLIZED: The struggle between the Cross and the Crescent dragged on for centuries.

CONTAINER SUBSTITUTED FOR THE CONTENT: Since he forgot to replenish the water supply, the radiator of his car soon boiled.

PART SUBSTITUTED FOR THE WHOLE: At the inn door he left the wheel upon which he had been riding.

WHOLE SUBSTITUTED FOR A PART: America won the international tennis matches.

PLACE SUBSTITUTED FOR ITS INHABITANTS: St. Louis felt the effect of the sudden cold wave.

ABSTRACT SUBSTITUTED FOR THE CONCRETE: Manly rose to address the chair.

CONCRETE SUBSTITUTED FOR THE ABSTRACT: Tompkins had little respect for Hawley's gray hairs.

ATTRIBUTE OR QUALITY SUBSTITUTED FOR OBJECT: The nation assembled its strength on the field of battle.

PARTICULAR SUBSTITUTED FOR A CLASS: He was a very Galahad.

INSTRUMENT SUBSTITUTED FOR ITS AGENT: Diccon led his troop of sabres at a mad gallop upon the enemy's rifles.

SPECIES SUBSTITUTED FOR GENUS: Down with rum!

Onomatopœia is the use of words in which the sound is imitative or suggestive of the sense.

The frogs croaked, the horses whinnied, and the cows mooed.

> Dry clashed his harness in the icy caves
> And barren chasms, and all to left and right
> The bare black cliff clang'd round him, as he based
> His feet on juts of slippery crag that rang
> Sharp-smitten with the dint of arméd heels.
>
> ALFRED TENNYSON

Oxymoron is an expression in which are combined terms ordinarily contradictory.

> . . . O loving hate!
> O any thing, of nothing first create!
> O heavy lightness! serious vanity!
> Misshapen chaos of well-seeming forms!
> Feather of lead, bright smoke, cold fire, sick health!
>
> WILLIAM SHAKESPEARE

Parallelism is the maintenance of uniform construction for ideas of equal value within a sentence or a series of sentences. (See also Chapter I, section J.)

Reading maketh a full man, conference a ready man, and writing an exact man.—FRANCIS BACON

If you can love me for what I am, we shall be the happier. If you cannot, I will seek to deserve that you should.—RALPH WALDO EMERSON

The **periodic sentence** is one in which the completion of the main idea is delayed until the end or almost the end of the sentence. (See section St 4.)

Through the darkness, through mud and rain, through the tempest, Arthur struggled on.

Somber, imperishable, majestic, stands the mighty mountain.

Like the dwelling-place of our infancy revisited in manhood, like the song of our country heard in a strange land, they produce upon us an effect wholly independent of their intrinsic value.—THOMAS BABINGTON MACAULAY

Personification is the endowing of inanimate objects or abstract ideas with human qualities or attributes.

See what a ready tongue suspicion hath!—WILLIAM SHAKESPEARE

> Night's candles are burnt out, and jocund day
> Stands tiptoe on the misty mountain tops.
>   WILLIAM SHAKESPEARE

Oxford, by her ineffable charm, keeps ever calling us nearer to the true goal of all of us, to the ideal, to perfection . . . .—MATTHEW ARNOLD

The **rhetorical question** is a question introduced solely to give emphasis to the idea presented in the answer, which is generally obvious to the reader. It is sometimes used as a transitional device. If it is to be effective, it must not be overused.

A man may send you six sheets of letter-paper covered with the most entertaining gossip, or you may pass half an hour pleasantly, even profitably, over an article of his; do you think the service would be greater if he had made the manuscript in his heart's blood, like a compact with the devil? Do you really fancy you should be more beholden to your correspondent if he had been damning you all the while for your importunity? Pleasures are more beneficial than duties because, like the quality of mercy, they are not strained, and they are twice blest.—ROBERT LOUIS STEVENSON

With such qualifications as arise out of the last-mentioned fact, it may be truly said that the acts of all living things are fundamentally one. Is any such unity predictable of their forms? Let us seek in easily verified facts for a reply to this question.—T. H. HUXLEY

Rhythm is the regular recurrence of an accent or an emphasis. In prose writing, a uniform movement of words and word-groups can often be stylistically effective. (See, for example, the selections from Ecclesiastes, Macaulay, and Rachel L. Carson in section St 8.) Although difficult to describe, rhythm is an important and individualizing aspect of an author's style: the rhythm of John Milton's prose is different from that of Ernest Hemingway, yet each has his distinct rhythm. The best advice for the beginning writer is to avoid writing "prose poems" in the mistaken belief that rhythm is more important than content, organization, or logic.

Simile is a figure of speech in which two different objects are compared; that is, a likeness between the two objects is suggested. The comparison is generally indicated by such words as *like, as,* and *seem.*

> Life, like a dome of many-coloured glass,
> Stains the white radiance of eternity.
>
> PERCY BYSSHE SHELLEY

People buzzed around him as thick as flies at a picnic.
Unconsciousness swept over him like a wave.
A magnificent death had come like a grace, like a gift, like a reward to that old ship at the end of her laborious days.—JOSEPH CONRAD

Understatement (the opposite of **hyperbole**) is the deliberate saying of less than one means in order to heighten the effect. It is common in colloquial writing and speech but it is also a favorite device in more formal expression. **Litotes** is a special form of understatement which substitutes a negative contrast for the positive statement expected.

It is possible that I shall be at the party. (SUBSTITUTED FOR: I shall certainly be at the party. HYPERBOLE: Nothing in the world could keep me from that party.)

He is not a bad sort at all. (SUBSTITUTED FOR: He is a very good sort.)

It is not impossible that I may go. (SUBSTITUTED FOR: It is possible that I may go.)

There was no lack of stags at the dance. (SUBSTITUTED FOR: There were many stags at the dance.)

I am not filled with admiration for Senator Blank.

During that spring I saw not a little of both of them.—THEODORE DREISER

I hear his majesty is returned with some discomfort from the wars.— WILLIAM SHAKESPEARE

St 8   SPECIMENS OF STYLE

Style, as we have seen, is essentially a writer's manner of expressing himself. His choice of words and images and his arrangement of them in sentences are characteristic of him. Since each person has individual peculiarities which cause his style to be at least slightly different from the style of anyone else, the following selections are offered to the student as evidence of various ways in which one may express his personality in writing. It is not suggested that the student model his style upon any of the extracts represented in this section. **He should, however, analyze them to see how the different styles suit different subject matters, and how figures of speech, varying kinds of diction, and artfully varied sentence structures aid each writer in setting forth his ideas.** With the knowledge gained from the analyses of these and other pieces of writing, and with diligent effort to express himself in a clear, natural, and emphatic manner at all times, the beginning writer will find that sooner or later his style will shape itself into a mode of expression that is essentially his own.

> This is an evil among all things that are done under the sun, that there is one event unto all: yea, also the heart of the sons of men is full of evil, and madness is in their heart while they live, and after that they go to the dead. For to him that is joined to all the living there is hope: for a living dog is better than a dead lion. For the living know that they shall die: but the dead know not any thing, neither have they any more a reward; for the memory of them is forgotten. Also their love, and their hatred, and their envy, is now perished; neither have they any more a portion for ever in any thing that is done under the sun.—ECCLESIASTES 9:3–6

The effect of simplicity which a reader gets from this selection is the result of the straightforward sentence structure and the unadorned diction, both structure and diction being peculiarly suited to the starkly elemental subject of life and death. It would be hard to find, anywhere in the English language, a statement so full of inevitability as: "For the living know that they shall die: but the dead know not any thing, neither have they any more a reward; for the memory of them is forgotten." Three of the four clauses have sentence elements arranged in the normal order —that is, subject, predicate; monotony is avoided by having one, the third, inverted. The dearth of modifiers is also notable; each adjective and adverb is used only because it is necessary to give the full meaning desired. But the most significant characteristic of this passage is the pronounced rhythm; above all else the King James Version is noted for the grandeur of style which has resulted from the carefully balanced prose of the translators. The combination, then, of simplicity in sentence structure, ornamentation, diction—in the whole passage there are only two words over two syllables long—and rhythm has made the book of Ecclesiastes powerful and moving.

> In this journey my dog surprised a young kid, and seized upon it, and I, running in to take hold of it, caught it, and saved it alive from the dog. I had a great mind to bring it home if I could, for I had

often been musing whether it might not be possible to get a kid or two, and so raise a breed of tame goats, which might supply me when my powder and shot should be all spent. I made a collar for this little creature, and with a string, which I made of some rope-yarn, which I always carried about me, I led him along, though with some difficulty, till I came to my bower, and there I enclosed him and left him, for I was very impatient to be at home, from whence I had been absent above a month.—DANIEL DEFOE[7]

The simplicity and directness (frequently associated with the journalistic style) of this passage differs from the poetic simplicity of the selection from Ecclesiastes, since here the subject matter is not sublime but comparatively trivial. Seeing an ordinary event through the eyes of an ordinary person, Defoe has wisely used a homely, matter-of-fact diction and a sentence structure that tells of actions in the order in which they have occurred, directing the entire attention of the reader to the unexciting but decidedly practical details of Crusoe's life.

Some persons of a desponding spirit are in great concern about that vast number of poor people, who are aged, diseased, or maimed, and I have been desired to employ my thoughts what course may be taken to ease the nation of so grievous an encumbrance. But I am not in the least pain upon that matter, because it is very well known that they are every day dying and rotting by cold and famine, and filth and vermin, as fast as can reasonably be expected. And as to the young laborers, they are now in as hopeful a condition; they cannot get work, and consequently pine away for want of nourishment, to a degree that if at any time they are accidentally hired to common labor, they have not strength to perform it; and thus the country and themselves are happily delivered from the evils to come.—JONATHAN SWIFT[8]

Swift's power as an ironist is due largely to his skillful choice of words, aided, of course, by exaggeration. He says "persons of a *desponding* spirit" when he obviously means "all *humane* persons." He insists that he "is not *in the least* pain" because the poor

---

[7] *Robinson Crusoe* (1719).
[8] "A Modest Proposal" (1729).

people are dying "as fast as can *reasonably* be expected." Intermingled with this suavity, he has introduced words of stark bitterness: *dying, rotting, cold, famine, filth, vermin.* He speaks offhandedly about the equally *"hopeful* condition" of the young laborers, and emphasizes his irony by mitigating the description of their condition. By use of epithet, hyperbole, and understatement, Swift made himself such a master of irony that he has seldom, if ever, been surpassed.

A foolish consistency is the hobgoblin of little minds, adored by little statesmen and philosophers and divines. With consistency a great soul has simply nothing to do. He may as well concern himself with his shadow on the wall. Speak what you think now in hard words, and tomorrow speak what tomorrow thinks in hard words again, though it contradict everything you said today. "Ah, so you shall be sure to be misunderstood." Is it so bad, then, to be misunderstood? Pythagoras was misunderstood, and Socrates, and Jesus, and Luther, and Copernicus, and Galileo, and Newton, and every pure and wise spirit that ever took flesh. To be great is to be misunderstood.—RALPH WALDO EMERSON[9]

Emerson's style is here strong and dispassionate. His calm and balanced aphorisms and his moderate quietness of words give the effect of deliberate thought, an effect which lends weight to the idea he sets forth.

Thus the Puritan was made up of two different men, the one all self-abasement, penitence, gratitude, passion; the other proud, calm, inflexible, sagacious. He prostrated himself in the dust before his Maker, but he set his foot on the neck of his king. In his devotional retirement, he prayed with convulsions, and groans, and tears. He was half-maddened by glorious or terrible illusions. He heard the lyres of angels or the tempting whispers of fiends. He caught a gleam of the Beatific Vision, or woke screaming from dreams of everlasting fire. Like Vane, he thought himself intrusted with the sceptre of the millennial year. Like Fleetwood, he cried in the bitterness of his soul that God had hid his face from him. But when he took his seat in the council, or girt on his sword for war, these tempestuous workings of the soul had left

---

[9] "Self-Reliance" (1841).

no perceptible trace behind them. People who saw nothing of the godly but their uncouth visages, and heard nothing from them but their groans and their whining hymns, might laugh at them. But those had little reason to laugh who encountered them in the hall of debate or in the field of battle . . . .—THOMAS BABINGTON MACAULAY[10]

Macaulay's sentences are distinguished for their powerful, deliberate rhythm. The effect is gained, of course, by the careful and elaborate sentence structure, in which balance, parallelism, antithesis, and other stylistic devices play an important part.

"Plain Folks" is a [propaganda] device used by politicians, labor leaders, business men, and even by ministers and educators to win our confidence by appearing to be people like ourselves—"just plain folks among the neighbors." In election years especially do candidates show their devotion to little children and the common, homey things of life. They have front porch campaigns. For the newspaper men they raid the kitchen cupboard, finding there some of the good wife's apple pie. They go to country picnics; they attend services at the old frame church; they pitch hay and go fishing; they show their belief in home and mother. In short, they would win our votes by showing that they're just as common as the rest of us—"just plain folks,"—and, therefore, wise and good. Business men often are "plain folks" with the factory hands. Even distillers use the device: "It's our family's whiskey, neighbor; and neighbor, it's your price."—ANONYMOUS[11]

During World War II the rejection and discharge of soldiers for psychiatric reasons made the nation realize its stake in mental health, and in 1946 Congress passed the National Mental Health Act. This Act established the National Institute of Mental Health at Bethesda, Maryland, one of seven Institutes concerned with various diseases. The Institute conducts research of its own at Bethesda. It also grants money to researchers elsewhere, to medical schools for training more psychiatrists, and to states for community mental health services.

After the passage of the Act of 1946 the states bestirred themselves. They started to build buildings. They hired more doctors, nurses, and

---

[10] "Milton" (1825).
[11] "How to Detect Propaganda." *Propaganda Analysis,* December, 1937.

attendants and raised their salaries. They matched federal grants. They reorganized their mental-health departments. They established preventive programs—community clinics, child-guidance clinics, out-patient clinics. By 1953 the states were spending three times what they had spent on their state hospitals nine years before—half a billion dollars a year. Some states had multiplied their expenditures fantastically during that same period—Kansas by 610 per cent. Capital outlays became enormous—New York alone spent $350 million building hospitals. New research and training centers were set up. Salaries were increased until in some states mental health officials were earning more than governors. State spending far outran federal.

Why all the sudden interest? Citizens' groups, such as the National Association for Mental Health and the National Committee Against Mental Illness, helped arouse it. So did journalists. As the stigma of insanity began to diminish, it became possible to discuss insanity publicly. Governors discovered that mental health had become the third biggest item in their budgets, exceeded only by schools and roads. About the same time the new psychiatric drugs came along, encouraging citizens to believe that psychotics can be cured—that pouring money into state hospitals isn't pouring money down a rathole. Finally, during the prosperous postwar years, the country could afford to attend to the sick.
—JOHN BARTLOW MARTIN[12]

In these last two passages we see the plain, straightforward expression typical of much American prose in recent years. Both writers use a matter-of-fact style; each has an idea important to him and each seeks a choice and arrangement of words that will convey that idea briefly, directly, and graphically to the reader. The first of these selections, in explaining one of the common devices of propaganda, illustrates by choosing both typical objects mentioned by propagandists and the typical phrases used by them; the result is an easy, colloquial style that allows the reader no opportunity to misunderstand the point of the paragraph. The second selection not only provides a good deal of factual information concerning spending for mental health programs but also interprets that information in the light of

---

[12] *The Pane of Glass.* Copyright, 1959, Harper & Brothers, publishers.

recent social and scientific developments, achieving an orderly and economical statement about a very large subject. Like the passage which follows, it is a good example of the best American journalistic style today.

The hired farm work force in the United States is composed of three main groups: regular workers, seasonally employed workers, and the foreign farmhands, mostly Mexicans brought in under a special program approved by Congress. The seven hundred thousand regular hired workers, those employed for more than 150 days a year by one employer, are almost all male; they take care of livestock, repair buildings, maintain equipment, drive tractors, and generally work without supervision. Frequently they live on or near the farm where they are employed. About half of this group are hired by the largest farms; forty-eight per cent of them are working for farms of more than 1,900 acres.

The million seasonal farm workers normally work less than 150 days in a year, and they work for more than one employer. They do work that can be completed in a short time and are usually paid by the day, hour, or piece. They clear land, lay fertilizer, chop, weed, and do the harvest work—cutting, picking, packing, and toting. Forty-eight per cent of all hired seasonal workers were employed on the two largest groups of cotton and fruit-and-nut farms in Texas, California, Arkansas, Mississippi, Louisiana, Tennessee, and North Carolina.

The seasonal farm workers split into two main groups: the larger group of local day-haul employees who may go out with a different farmer each day and are picked up by truck from a central employment point; and the much smaller number of migrants, mostly employed by labor contractors in the South and West and by crew leaders in the East. The contractors or crew leaders take the migrants from farm to farm along the migrant stream. They set a flat price with the farmer for the harvesting work, then paying the workers from their own pockets, or else they get a commission from the farmer for each worker supplied. The lush financial rewards open to an unscrupulous labor contractor are obviously tempting, and there has been a sharp increase in the number of people with criminal records who have applied for contractors' licenses in California.—PAUL JACOBS[13]

---

[13] "The Forgotten People," *The Reporter*, January 22, 1959. Reprinted by permission of the publisher and the author.

The author of this article presses into three paragraphs many facts about the seasonal farm workers in America, and most of these statements are specific and concrete. The style is plain and neutral in tone. Although the language is that of formal English, there is no attempt to be literary or impressive. Indeed, the most obvious quality of Mr. Jacobs' style is its impersonality; the emphasis is not on what the writer thinks but on the subject itself. (Elsewhere in the article he clearly indicates his opinions on the subject.) Only in the last sentence above does he allow himself the liberty of drawing an inference from the facts presented—an inference which is immediately supported by another statement of fact.

Nowhere in all the sea does life exist in such bewildering abundance as in the surface waters. From the deck of a vessel you may look down, hour after hour, on the shimmering discs of jellyfish, their gently pulsating bells dotting the surface as far as you can see. Or one day you may notice early in the morning that you are passing through a sea that has taken on a brick-red color from billions upon billions of microscopic creatures, each of which contains an orange pigment granule. At noon you are still moving through red seas, and when darkness falls the waters shine with an eerie glow from the phosphorescent fires of yet more billions and trillions of these same creatures.

And again you may glimpse not only the abundance but something of the fierce uncompromisingness of sea life when, as you look over the rail and down, down into water of a clear, deep green, suddenly there passes a silver shower of finger-long fishlets. The sun strikes a metallic gleam from their flanks as they streak by, driving deeper into the green depths with the desperate speed of the hunted. Perhaps you never see the hunters, but you sense their presence as you see the gulls hovering, with eager, mewing cries, waiting for the little fish to be driven to the surface.

Or again, perhaps, you may sail for days on end without seeing anything you could recognize as life or the indications of life, day after day of empty water and empty sky, and so you may reasonably conclude that there is no spot on earth so barren of life as the open ocean. But if you had the opportunity to tow a fine-meshed net through the seemingly lifeless water and then to examine the washings of the net, you would find that life is scattered almost everywhere through the surface waters like a fine dust. A cupful of water may contain millions upon millions of diatoms, tiny plant cells, each of them far too small to be seen by the human eye; or it may swarm with an infinitude of animal creatures, none larger than a dust mote, which live on plant cells still smaller than themselves.—RACHEL L. CARSON[14]

Rachel L. Carson's account of subsurface marine life is scientifically accurate, but, more importantly, her style reflects an emotional, almost poetic, response to the sea. The syntax is rhythmical but not monotonously so, like the sea itself; and the diction is full of vivid and pictorial images. This is modern scientific prose of an unusually imaginative kind.

Even before I knew that the redwood forest of Jasper Ridge is to all intents and purposes a surviving Miocene forest, I had occasionally toyed with the idea that it would be nice if some zoological or botanical garden were to make up a few paleobiological exhibits. The customary and time-honored method of arranging exhibits is "systematic"; it has found its expression in terms like monkey house, reptile house, and so on. A more modern version is the geographic exhibit: one can and does have exhibits which are condensed versions of, say, the African plains, showing the animals occurring there with the plants that grow there. To carry out my idea, one could start with the natural Miocene forest of Jasper Ridge. By putting animals from the same era into it (tapir and rhinoceros come to mind first, but the list can be lengthened), one could reconstruct a Miocene landscape. Not necessarily American Miocene, but alive. Of course the further back one goes in geological history the less material there is to work with. One would, of necessity, have to be content with very narrow segments of the older periods. Still, a saltwater tank with sharks in the water, horseshoe crabs on the bottom, certain clams in the sand, and a few living crinoids on the rocks would be a piece of pretty ancient sea, say, early Triassic.

For a lack of living ichthyosaurs we could not reconstruct a piece of the European Lias Sea. But we could produce a very reasonable replica of the forest that grew on the islands in the Lias Sea. China has pre-

---

[14] *The Sea Around Us.* Copyright, 1950, by Oxford University Press.

served both the ginkgos and the metasequoias that grew them. We have tree ferns from Australia and Tasmania. We have araucarias from Norfolk Island, popularly miscalled Norfolk pine. We have the smaller ferns for underbrush. And we could gather cycads from all over the earth—I mean that a scientific institution could; personally I have been singularly unsuccessful in my private attempts to buy a small cycad tree. —WILLY LEY[15]

In this passage, Willy Ley discusses scientific "exhibits," but he does so in an informal and personal manner, imparting to his subject the tone of the familiar essay. The diction is colloquial ("it would be nice . . ."); the artful casualness of the last sentence carries out the idea of "toying with an idea" that is mentioned at the start. But note that informality of tone does not necessarily mean triviality of subject matter.

Well, we are where we are politically. The Gentleman no longer governs. The Masses do not govern either; they have not been taught how to govern or even to look upon government as more than a dispenser of lollipops and toy ballons. But there must always be government and governors. Therefore, to fill the vacuum created by the demise of the Gentleman ruler, along has come the demagogue with slogans, sophistical rhetoric, parades, pseudopatriotic bombast, ridiculous promises of much for nothing, skilled and unprincipled propaganda. We have had Hitler's hullabaloo and Mussolini's and Stalin's, all applauded by the credulous common people. Nearer home, we have had the Atlantic Charter and the United Nations cum veto. Neither of these devices, designed to quiet the idealistic crowds while their authors went in for power politics, would have fooled the ruling classes of former days for a moment. They would not have fooled the Common Man of today if we had bothered to educate him instead of merely train him technically. They and their European equivalents have been clamorously approved by the mistaught multitudes, who, having tossed their dry-cleaned, mass-produced nightcaps in the air to the political profit of the shrewd, now sit sorrowing as they await the advent of new Caesars for whom to cheer and die.—BERNARD IDDINGS BELL[16]

---

[15] *Dragons in Amber.* Copyright, 1951, The Viking Press.
[16] *Crisis in Education.* Copyright, 1949, McGraw-Hill Book Company.

A sardonic and skeptical viewer of contemporary values in education, Canon Bell employs a pungent style, using some striking figures of speech to drive his points home (government as "a dispenser of lollipops and toy balloons"; the "dry-cleaned, mass-produced nightcaps"). Each paragraph begins with fairly short and simple grammatical units, reaching its climax in the last sentence, which is more complex and more detailed than the preceding ones, and marked by such devices as syntactical inversions, alliteration, and parallelism.

The Post Office Department may not be so good at delivering the mail these days, but it has worked to deliver us from temptation and evil, a chore that we used to ask Somebody Else to handle. Several years back, under a different Administration, the department was going to save us from the pictures of pretty girls in *Esquire*. But the Supreme Court ruled against that high-minded and higher-handed effort, with the result that today we are all presumably in danger of becoming sex-mad fiends while leafing through the magazines in the dentist's waiting room.

In 1955 this same department acted to save us from being demoralized by Aristophanes' comedy *Lysistrata*, a play which the world has somehow managed to survive, despite repeated performances since 411 B.C. The ban on *Lysistrata* was lifted when somebody whispered into the cauliflower ears of the authorities that it was a classic.

Official and unofficial censorship boards have spared no effort to save us from seeing movies that they regard as fit only for their own eyes. However, those devilish fellows on the U.S. Supreme Court, debauched by dipping into racy books on Constitutional law, have more than once stepped in to interfere with the censors' noble aims. It is only recently that newsreels have become exempt from censorship in all 48 states. Whither are we drifting? If this keeps up, people may have to decide for themselves what to see. It's almost enough to make the senses reel or make the reels sensible.—HERBERT BLOCK[17]

The witty quality of Herbert Block's (Herblock's) cartoons is matched by his prose, as this excerpt demonstrates. The humorous effect is achieved partly by playing on words ("deliver" in

---

[17] *Herblock's Here and Now*. Copyright, 1955, Simon and Schuster, Inc.

the first sentence, for example; "high-minded and higher-handed"; and the pun in the last sentence). Herblock also uses the carica-turist's device of exaggeration and unexpected juxtapositions, as in the ironical reference to "those devilish fellows on the U.S. Supreme Court . . . dipping into racy books on Constitutional law." Despite the humor, the intention is a serious criticism of official censorship; the wit is acid.

There's a trade word for what happens to Americans living overseas. It's "cultural shock," and to a certain extent, it hits them all.

First of all, different philosophic, moral, and living standards rock many of them back on their heels. Wives especially find it hard to adjust to an environment where supermarkets, super service, and super entertainment often don't exist. The second-class status of women in many countries irks them, too. They are thrown for company upon a narrow circle of friends. After one tour, many want to come home.

It isn't quite so difficult for the men. Business, though maybe con-ducted differently, is still business. Also, because of the demands of nationalism and because it's expensive to get U.S. personnel overseas, companies turn over the direction of foreign operations to a relatively small number of men. This in turn means they get top responsibility early—with high pay. But they also have to play by a different set of rules.

In many countries, for example, "gifts" to government officials and awarders of contracts are standard procedure. Whether they admit it or not, many companies abide by this practice. Those that do need a man who can carry through the deal smoothly, without putting the company on a hook—and without succumbing to the temptation to deal himself in.[18]

An anonymous discussion of some importance to American business firms, this article appearing in *Business Week* is informal and colloquial. Note the contractions throughout, as well as the slangy phrases in the concluding sentence ("putting the company on a hook," and "to deal himself in").

---

[18] "Who's the Man to Send Abroad?" *Business Week,* August 9, 1958. By special permission of the publishers.

Seventy-five years ago the great railroad moguls were a law unto themselves, with an empire, as Beard points out, equal in size to all of New England and New York, plus a large slice of Pennsylvania, most of it in public lands given out by a remarkably open-handed government. Today they can't abandon a spur from Overshoe to East Overshoe unless a state commision agrees; they can't beat a lower freight rate set by a competing barge line unless the ICC lets them, which it won't; and the Railway Brotherhoods still refuse to let them drop a fireman from a Diesel locomotive, where he is no more needed than a Pullman porter on a cattle car.

As late as the turn of the century, J. P. Morgan had the arrogance to propose to President Theodore Roosevelt that the Attorney General and a Morgan lawyer settle a railroad anti-trust suit without bothering the sovereign principals—"If we have done anything wrong, send your man to my man and they can fix it up." A few weeks ago, by way of contrast, twenty-two railroad presidents gathered in New York's Grand Central Terminal, like a delegation from a teachers' union local, to demonstrate for legislative relief. Hats in hands, they posed before a huge bulletin board on which were pasted 1,071 newspaper editorials pleading for "Action to Modernize Railroad Regulation!" To imagine such old-time moguls as Edward Harriman and James J. Hill, not to mention cutthroats like Jim Fisk and Jay Gould, in such a position is to envision Blackbeard, Lafitte, and Long John Silver on a picket line.
—ROBERT BENDINER[19]

The same kind of breezy informality noted in the excerpt preceding this one is found in Robert Bendiner's magazine article on the decline of railroad power in America, a subject which might not at first appear to lend itself to such treatment. But Bendiner makes his points more effective by using a number of vivid comparisons ("no more needed than a Pullman porter on a cattle car"; "like a delegation from a teachers' union local"; and the ludicrous picture of the pirates on a picket line).

---

[19] "The Railroads: From Overlord to Underdog," *The Reporter,* August 7, 1958.

EXERCISES

A.

The following sentences illustrate, among other errors, faults in style common in the writing of beginners. Point out the faults in each sentence; then revise it.

1. He pounces upon an idea only to find that it has been lost in the foliage of wordage.

2. The city was suddenly caught in the arms of national aggrandizement.

3. I shall present in this chapter a review of St. Louis's life during the forties because I believe that its spirit of boundless energy, broad vision, and varied interests was vividly expressed in that versatile personality, Joseph M. Field, the subject of this dissertation.

4. That the young ladies were not drowned in this deluge of mental acceleration is a credit to their rugged American heredity.

5. At that time a scarcity of jobs was prevalent.

6. He was caught in the toils of the spoils system.

7. Among the gentlemen of the plays we find that individuality which was lacking among their servants.

8. She is opposed to any suggestion proposed by her aunt, Mrs. Malaprop.

9. Every pebble, rock, and fish which occupies the bottom of the stream is seen while passing over it with the most perfect accuracy.

10. I had a horrible feeling of being overwhelmed by miasmal mists of confusion.

11. Events were occurring that finally culminated in the Protestant Reformation in the field of religion and the rise of the middle class with regard to social position.

12. Marie's mother was a very bright woman—a writer in a small way because she had a large family and married a Methodist minister.

13. In the estimation of my opinion of the two poems I believe that "The Solitary Reaper" is by far the superior poem.

14. I looked up and saw a bayonet and its point was tickling my throat.

15. I actually despised Marie Antoinette when I read about her actions in grammar school.

16. We have lived in four different neighborhoods and are on the verge of adding the fifth.

17. I frequently attend symphony concerts where I can obtain a greater appreciation of fine music.

18. The smooth-running surroundings made it possible for him to accomplish a great deal.

19. To pick a subject that even the most experienced men know so little about shows a certain amount of foolishness on the part of the writer of this paper.

20. He had come so near the end of his rope that he was about ready to jump off the cliff.

B.

Analyze the following passages for variety in sentence structure.

I. Is there a variety of simple, complex, compound, and compound-complex sentences? Do you find any nonsentences?

II. Is there a variety of structure in the beginnings of the sentences? What kinds of grammatical units are used to start the sentences?

III. Is there variety in sentence lengths?

1. In anything fit to be called by the name of reading, the process itself should be absorbing and voluptuous; we should gloat over a book, be rapt clean out of ourselves, and rise from the perusal, our mind filled with the busiest kaleidoscopic dance of images, incapable of sleep or of continuous thought. The words, if the book be eloquent, should run thenceforward in our ears like the noise of breakers, and the story, if it be a story, repeat itself in a thousand colored pictures to the eye. It was for this last pleasure that we read so closely, and loved our books so dearly, in the bright, untroubled period of boyhood. Eloquence and thought, character and conversation, were both obstacles to brush aside as we dug blithely after a certain sort of inci-

dent, like a pig for truffles. For my part, I liked a story to begin with an old wayside inn where, "towards the close of the year 17—," several gentlemen in three-cocked hats were playing bowls. A friend of mine preferred the Malabar coast in a storm, with a ship beating westward, and a scowling fellow of Herculean proportions striding along the beach; he, to be sure, was a pirate. This was further afield than my home-keeping fancy loved to travel, and designed altogether for a larger canvas than the tales that I affected. Give me a highwayman and I was full to the brim; a Jacobite would do, but the highwayman was my favorite dish. I can still hear that merry clatter of the hoofs along the moonlit lane; night and the coming of day are still related in my mind with the doings of John Rann or Jerry Abershaw; and the words "post-chaise," the "great North road," "ostler," and "nag," still sound in my ears like poetry. One and all, at least, and each with his particular fancy, we read story-books in childhood, not for eloquence or character or thought, but for some quality of the brute incident. That quality was not mere bloodshed or wonder. Although each of these was welcome in its place, the charm for the sake of which we read depended on something different from either . . . .—ROBERT LOUIS STEVENSON[20]

2. Why was it that the Indian trader passed so rapidly across the continent? What effects followed from the trader's frontier? The trade was coeval with American discovery. The Norsemen, Vespucius, Verrazani, Hudson, John Smith, all trafficked for furs. The Plymouth pilgrims settled in Indian cornfields, and their first return cargo was of beaver and lumber. The records of the various New England colonies show how steadily exploration was carried into the wilderness by this trade. What is true for New England is, as would be expected, even plainer for the rest of the colonies. All along the coast of Maine to Georgia the Indian trade opened up the river courses. Steadily the trader passed westward, utilizing the older lines of French trade. The Ohio, the Great Lakes, the Mississippi, the Missouri, and the Platte, the lines of western advance, were ascended by traders. They found the passes in the Rocky Mountains and guided Lewis and Clark, Frémont, and Bidwell. The explanation of the rapidity of this advance is connected with the effects of the trader on the Indian. The trading post left the unarmed tribes at the mercy of

---

[20] "A Gossip on Romance" (1882).

those that had purchased firearms—a truth which the Iroquois Indians wrote in blood, and so the remote and unvisited tribes gave eager welcome to the trader. "The savages," wrote La Salle, "take better care of us French than of their own children; from us only can they get guns and goods." This accounts for the trader's power and the rapidity of his advance. Thus the disintegrating forces of civilization entered the wilderness. Every river valley and Indian trail became a fissure in Indian society, and so that society became honeycombed. Long before the pioneer farmer appeared on the scene, primitive Indian life had passed away. The farmers met Indians armed with guns. The trading frontier, while steadily undermining Indian power by making the tribes ultimately dependent on the whites, yet, through its sale of guns, gave to the Indian increased power of resistance to the farming frontier. French colonization was dominated by its trading frontier; English colonization by its farming frontier. There was an antagonism between the two frontiers as between the two nations. Said Duquesne to the Iroquois, "Are you ignorant of the difference between the king of England and the king of France? Go see the forts that our king has established and you will see that you can still hunt under their very walls. They have been placed for your advantage in places which you frequent. The English, on the contrary, are no sooner in possession of a place than the game is driven away. The forest falls before them as they advance, and the soil is laid bare so that you can scarce find the wherewithal to erect a shelter for the night."—FREDERICK JACKSON TURNER[21]

3. A great deal has been said about the duty of the artist to society. It is argued that the poet, the novelist, the painter, the musician, has a duty to the community; he is a citizen like everyone else; he must pull his weight, he must not give himself airs, or ask for special terms, he must pay his taxes honorably, and keep the laws which have been made for the general good. That is the argument and it is a reasonable one. But there is another side: what is the duty of society to the artist? Society certainly has a duty to its members; it has a duty to the engineer who serves it loyally and competently: it must provide him with the

---

[21] "The Significance of the Frontier in American History," from *The Frontier in American History.* Copyright, 1920, Henry Holt and Company, publishers.

necessary tools and must not allow him to starve; it has a duty to the stockbroker who is a competent dealer in stocks: since he is part of a financial system which it has accepted, it must support him and ensure him his due percentage. This is obvious enough. So what is its duty to the artist? If he contributes loyally and competently, ought not society 'o reward him like any other professional man?—E. M. FORSTER[22]

4. It is a vision which fascinates and appalls us, which strikes us with a kind of awe, this evolution of mechanical production and of the magnetic accumulation of capital, rising out of the feudal world, with its more primitive but more human handicrafts; wrecking it and over-spreading it; accelerating, reorganizing, reassembling, in ever more in-genious complexity, ever more formidable proportions; breaking out of the boundaries of nations; sending out the tracks and cranes of its commerce across countries and oceans and continents and bringing the people of distant cultures, at diverse stages of civilization, into its system, as it lays hold on the destinies of races, knocks new shapes out of their bodies and their minds, their personalities and their aspirations, without their really grasping what has happened to them and independently of any individual's will. Yet all this development is not merely techno-logical; it is not actually the result of the operation on humanity of a remorseless non-human force. There is also a human principle at work— "those passions which are," as Marx says, "at once the most violent, the basest and the most abominable of which the human breast is capable: the furies of personal interest." For another element of Marx's genius is a peculiar psychological insight: no one has ever had so deadly a sense of the infinite capacity of human nature for remaining oblivious or indifferent to the pains we inflict on others when we have a chance to get something out of them for ourselves.—EDMUND WILSON[23]

5. The biggest challenge to any translator is of course one of the best poems in the world: the *Iliad* of Homer. It is a huge work, many thou-sands of lines long. It is written in a splendid meter, far stronger and more varied than English blank verse. Its language is both clear and

[22] From *Two Cheers for Democracy*. Copyright 1951, by E. M. Forster. Re-printed by permission of Harcourt, Brace and Company, Inc.

[23] *To the Finland Station*. Copyright, 1953. Reprinted by permission of Doubleday & Company, Inc., publishers.

complicated, like a Beethoven symphony or a great cathedral; and it is trenchantly expressive, full of brief phrases which, once heard, can never be forgotten, but which therefore are the despair of the translator. Its range is wide, moving all the way from a crying baby to a god roaring with fury, from a wily diplomatic speech to a savage hand-to-hand battle. It is full of action and passion, myth and history, psychology and rhetoric; it is full of music. It is a world.—GILBERT HIGHET[24]

C.

Identify the figures of speech (defined in section St 7) used in the following paragraphs; comment also on other uses of figurative language to be found there:

1. Let us spend one day as deliberately as Nature, and not be thrown off the track by every nutshell and mosquito's wing that falls on the rails. Let us rise early and fast, or break fast, gently and without perturbation; let company come and let company go, let the bells ring and the children cry,—determined to make a day of it. Why should we knock under and go with the stream? Let us not be upset and overwhelmed in that terrible rapid and whirlpool called a dinner, situated in the meridian shallows. Weather this danger and you are safe, for the rest of the way is down hill. With unrelaxed nerves, with morning vigor, sail by it, looking another way, tied to the mast like Ulysses. If the engine whistles, let it whistle till it is hoarse for its pains. If the bell rings, why should we run? We will consider what kind of music they are like. Let us settle ourselves, and work and wedge our feet downward through the mud and slush of opinion, and prejudice, and tradition, and delusion, and appearance, that alluvion which covers the globe, through Paris and London, through New York and Boston and Concord, through Church and State, through poetry and philosophy and religion, till we come to a hard bottom and rocks in place, which we can call *reality,* and say, This is, and no mistake; and then begin, having a *point d'appui,* below freshet and frost and fire, a place where you might found a wall or a state, or set a lamp-post safely, or perhaps a gauge, not a Nilometer, but a Realometer, that future ages might

---

[24] "The Art of Translation," in *People, Places, and Books.* Copyright, 1953. Reprinted by permission of Oxford University Press.

know how deep a freshet of shams and appearances had gathered from time to time. If you stand right fronting and face to face to a fact, you will see the sun glimmer on both its surfaces, as if it were a cimeter, and feel its sweet edge dividing you through the heart and marrow, and so you will happily conclude your mortal career. Be it life or death, we crave only reality. If we are really dying, let us hear the rattle in our throats and feel cold in the extremities; if we are alive, let us go about our business.—HENRY DAVID THOREAU[25]

2. That the end of life is death may be called a truism, since the various kinds of immortality that might perhaps supervene would none of them abolish death, but at best would weave life and death together into the texture of a more comprehensive destiny. The end of one life might be the beginning of another, if the Creator had composed his great work like the dramatic poet, assigning successive lines to different characters. Death would then be merely the cue at the end of each speech, summoning the next personage to break in and keep the ball rolling. Or perhaps, as some suppose, all the characters are assumed in turn by a single supernatural Spirit, who amid his endless improvisations is imagining himself living for the moment in this particular solar and social system. Death in such a universal monologue would be but a change of scene or of metre, while in the scramble of a real comedy it would be a change of actors. In either case every voice would be silenced sooner or later, and death would end each particular life, in spite of all possible sequels.—GEORGE SANTAYANA[26]

3. Publication of *Ulysses* in 1922 was a thunderclap in the world of letters more resounding in its time than the thunderclap of *Madame Bovary* three-quarters of a century before. Like Gustave Flaubert, James Joyce had produced a calculated work of art to which he had dedicated himself for years, with a versatility of craftsmanship far surpassing this one among his several masters. Like its predecessor, *Ulysses* was intended to astonish the world—and there is little doubt of the effect it has had upon a whole generation of writers. If Flaubert wrote into his novel his inner rage against the bourgeoisie, Joyce's work was an act of vengeance

---

[25] *Walden* (1854).
[26] From *Some Turns of Thought in Modern Philosophy*. Copyright, 1933. Reprinted by permission of Charles Scribner's Sons, publishers.

against an Ireland which (as Joyce insisted in one of his broadsides) sent its writers into banishment. In truth Joyce-Dedalus, the writer who had soared on literary wings over Europe, had banished himself, and using his own selected tools—silence, exile, cunning—had forged a complex labyrinth: forged it by the light of aesthetic theories hammered out in the days of his youth. It was Joyce who, possessing an incomparable mastery of words, succeeded above all writers in capturing the atmosphere of the mind. The cunning artificer who could construct a labyrinth could also dare the labyrinth of consciousness. With him the inward turning penetrated to the deepest recesses of mental experience. He is the fountain-head of the modern psychological novel.—LEON EDEL[27]

D.

Examine the following passages for the application of the principles discussed in this chapter.

1. The gate is strait, and therefore a man must sweat and strive to enter; both the entrance is difficult and the progress of salvation too. Jesus Christ is not got with a wet finger. It is not wishing and desiring to be saved will bring men to Heaven; Hell's mouth is full of good wishes. It is not shedding a tear at a sermon, or blubbering now and then in a corner, and saying over thy prayers, and crying God's mercy for thy sins, will save thee. It is not a "Lord, have mercy upon us," will do thee good. It is not coming constantly to church; these are easy matters. But it is a tough work, a wonderful hard matter to be saved.—THOMAS SHEPARD[28]

2. [Let us] direct our flying footsteps along the valley which spreads its verdant bosom as if to welcome our escape. A sea of gold surrounds us undulating as far as vision can extend, with a regular and successive motion. Innumerable flowers of the brightest yellow, intermingled with others of a "thousand dyes," lift their fragrant cups towards the heavens, and offer the incense of their perfume to the Lord of universal nature. To diversify this beautiful meadow, a number of *tumuli* are to be seen forming a chain across the prairie, interrupting by their

---

[27] *The Modern Psychological Novel.* Copyright 1955. Reprinted by permission of Grove Press, Inc.

[28] "Nine Easy Ways to Hell" (1641).

soft swells the monotony of the plain. Their shapes are various; circular, oblong, and quadrangular. In these mounds are said to repose the remains of an Indian battle field; here they threw their dead promiscuously together, and covered them with a rude barbaric monument. Oft have I ascended the loftiest of these eminences, and in the lightest moment of existence felt the ebullition of my youthful spirits checked by a reverential awe, which the profound stillness of the scene, accompanied by a sentiment of what might once have been achieved upon this very spot, assisted to promote. How many hearts that once swelled high with passion and with glory, have forever united with the dust beneath my feet! . . . Let us now descend a few miles lower down the valley, and we shall suddenly be arrested in our progress by one of the most venerable ruins human eye hath ever rested upon. Lifting its deserted head amid a scene of desolation, the remains of Fort Chartres are still to be found on the eastern shore of the Mississippi, resisting, with the importance of age, the assaults of that dark and impetuous flood. The western tower, and the principal part of the fortress on that side, have already yielded to the reiterated assaults of its inexorable foe, and the probability is, that, after a few revolving years, the traveler who directs his footsteps to Fort Chartres, to ponder over that venerable memorial of past ages, will find it a yawning gulf, over which the rapid stream of the Mississippi is hurrying its turbid and agitated flight.— ANONYMOUS[29]

3. One of these signs is the fact that the same movement which effected the elevation of what was called the lowest class in the state, assumed in literature a very marked and as benign an aspect. Instead of the sublime and beautiful, the near, the low, the common, was explored and poetized. That which had been negligently trodden under foot by those who were harnessing and provisioning themselves for long journeys into far countries, is suddenly found to be richer than all foreign parts. The literature of the poor, the feelings of the child, the philosophy of the street, the meaning of household life, are the topics of the time. It is a great stride—is it not?—of new vigor when the extremities are made active, when currents of warm life run into the

---

[29] "A Description of . . . the American Bottom in 1807, by a Lady." (St. Louis) *Missouri Republican,* January 5, 1826.

hands and feet. I ask not for the great, the remote, the romantic; what is doing in Italy or Arabia; what is Greek art, or Provençal minstrelsy; I embrace the common, I explore and sit at the feet of the familiar, the low. Give me insight into today, and you may have the antique and future worlds. What would we really know the meaning of? The meal in the firkin; the milk in the pan; the ballad in the street; the news of the boat; the glance of the eye; the form and gait of the body;—show me the ultimate reason of these matters; show me the sublime presence of the highest spiritual cause lurking, as always it does lurk, in these suburbs and extremities of nature; let me see every trifle bristling with the polarity that ranges instantly on an eternal law; and the shop, the plough, and the ledger referred to the like cause by which light undulates and poets sing;—and the world lies no longer a dull miscellany and lumber-room, but has form and order; there is no trifle, there is no puzzle, but one design unites and animates the farthest pinnacle and the lowest trench.—RALPH WALDO EMERSON[30]

4. I crept away and courted solitude for the rest of the day. I did not go to dinner; I stayed away from supper until everybody else had finished. I did not feel so much like a member of the boat's family now as before. However, my spirits returned, in installments, as we pursued our way down the river. I was sorry I hated the mate so, because it was not in (young) human nature not to admire him. He was huge and muscular, his face was bearded and whiskered all over; he had a red woman and a blue woman tattooed on his right arm—one on each side of a blue anchor with a red rope to it; and in the matter of profanity he was sublime. When he was getting out cargo at a landing, I was always where I could see and hear. He felt all the majesty of his great position, and made the world feel it, too. When he gave even the simplest order, he discharged it like a blast of lightning, and sent a long, reverberating peal of profanity thundering after it. I could not help contrasting the way in which the average landsman would give an order with the mate's way of doing it. If the landsman should wish the gangplank moved a foot farther forward, he would probably say: "James, or William, one of you push that plank forward, please"; but put the mate in his place, and he would roar out: "Here,

---

[30] "The American Scholar" (1837).

now, start that gangplank for'ard! Lively, now! *What*'re you about!
Snatch it! *snatch* it! There! there! Aft again! aft again! Don't you
hear me? Dash it to dash! are you going to *sleep* over it! 'Vast heaving,
I tell you! Going to heave it clear astern? WHERE're you going with
that barrel! *for*'ard with it 'fore I make you swallow it, you dash-dash-
dash-*dashed* split between a tired mud-turtle and a crippled hearse-
horse!"

I wished I could talk like that.—SAMUEL L. CLEMENS[31]

5. One proof that there was a new nation in the making would be
the appearance of a new and characteristic literature. No sooner was
political independence from the Old World assured than the hue and
cry for an independent literature set in. The problem was a simple
one; the answer not easy. Here, far from the sophistication and corruption of Europe, were unspoiled nature waiting to be described and
regenerated man eager to express his ideas. The materials of a new
civilization and a new literature were at hand; but art is form, and new
form does not suddenly appear. The colonists from long habit looked to
British poetry, fiction, drama, and essay for their standards of literary
expression. The eighteenth century had been a time of formal art. Somehow the new wine must be put into old bottles. Somehow American
literature must equal or surpass its British models in perfection of expression and at the same time be faithful to its native ideas and experience. Caught between the urge of youth to break all ties with the past
and the need of art for a tradition and a model by which to bend the
raw materials of life to formal expression, our earliest men of letters
were at once naïve, experimental, conformist, self-conscious, and imitative.—ROBERT E. SPILLER[32]

6. When Shelley was writing his poem "Hellas," his ironic friend
Trelawney took him aboard a Greek caique at Leghorn, so that he
might meet some Greeks in the flesh. Trelawney reports how he found
a dirty little ship infested by a gypsy crew, "shrieking, gesticulating,
smoking, eating, and gambling like savages," and captained by a trader
who was upset by the Greek war of independence, because it was bad

---

[31] *Life on the Mississippi* (1875).

[32] *The Cycle of American Literature*. Copyright, 1955. Reprinted by permission of The Macmillan Company, publishers.

for business. He was appalled to find not the faintest trace of the "lofty and sublime" spirit of Hellas—he was reminded only of Hell. If Shelley could visit Athens today, when the Greeks have enjoyed independence for more than a hundred years, he would no doubt remain disenchanted. He would find a gay, gregarious people, charming in their friendliness and vivacity, but volatile, restless, noisy, disorderly, garish, and generally unplatonic. They are shrewd businessmen, with a special talent for trade. They have a quick, sharp, practical intelligence but seem little concerned with fundamentals or universals. They are passionately interested in politics but more as a game, or struggle for power, than as a conflict of principles and ideals. Their national life has usually been a Balkan melodrama, a tragic farce of intrigue and brawl, animated by a spirit of liberty that has precluded law and order but permitted rule by oligarchs and dictators.—HERBERT J. MULLER[33]

7. Since the end of the war there has been a revival of Dostoevsky's vogue. Witness the flood of new translations, biographies, critical works. It is noteworthy that the emphasis of the commentators has been less on the novelist's art, than on his thinking, on the ideas to which his fictions give body and pressure. Re-examination of the values of liberal democracy has brought some of his writings into focus, and much of his work has acquired new relevance by virtue of the intensified concern with religion. More than one author has been at pains to harmonize Dostoevsky's views with the teachings of Catholicism—not an easy task, considering his hostility toward the Church of Rome and his infirmities as a theologian. On the other hand, his vehement anti-intellectualism, which leads him to cast reason in the role of the villain of the human drama, his reliance on faith as a means of apprehending reality, his tendency to place his characters in extreme situations, his emphasis on the individual's self-determination through free choice, his sense of tragedy— all this has enabled the existentialists to recruit him for their camp, at least for its Christian sector.—AVRAHM YARMOLINSKY[34]

8. There are many types of poetical obscurity. There is the obscurity which results from the poet's being mad. This is rare. Madness in poets

---

[33] *The Uses of the Past.* Copyright, 1952. Reprinted by permission of Oxford University Press.
[34] Reprinted from *Dostoevsky, His Life and Art,* by Avrahm Yarmolinsky, by permission of the publisher. Copyright © 1957 by Criterion Books, Inc.

is as uncommon as madness in dogs. A discouraging number of reputable poets are sane beyond recall. There is also the obscurity which is the result of the poet's wishing to appear mad, even if only a little mad. This is rather common and rather dreadful. I know of nothing more distasteful than the work of a poet who has taken leave of his reason deliberately, as a commuter might of his wife.

Then there is the unintentional obscurity, or muddiness, which comes from the inability of some writers to express even a simple idea without stirring up the bottom. And there is the obscurity which results when a fairly large thought is crammed into a three- or four-foot line. The function of poetry is to concentrate; but sometimes over-concentration occurs, and there is no more comfort in such a poem than there is in the subway at the peak hour.—E. B. WHITE[35]

E.

Select in your book of readings, or in one of the quality magazines (such as *Harper's, The Atlantic Monthly, The Yale Review, The Virginia Quarterly Review*), one essay formal in tone and one informal. Examine the style of the essays in the light of the principles discussed in this chapter.

F.

Select in your newspaper, and clip from it, an editorial, a news story, a feature column, and a sports story. Examine the style in each in the light of the principles discussed in this chapter.

G.

Analyze a piece of your own writing in accordance with the instructions in exercises E and F.

---

[35] From "Poetry," in *One Man's Meat*. Copyright, 1944. Reprinted by permission of Harper & Brothers.

VII | The Paragraph: Organization and Development

Paragraphing, or the arrangement of sentences in groups, is one more aid to written communication. On page 30 we pointed out that a writer, wanting to communicate with a reader, generally uses many sentences instead of one. He expresses his thought one portion at a time, so that a reader can grasp the idea bit by bit instead of having to absorb the whole at once. The paragraph serves exactly the same purpose as the sentence does, the only difference being that in the paragraph the writer presents larger units of thought than he does in the sentence. In other words, in a sentence he places together small bits of related information (their relationship is made clear by the subject and the predicate), and in the paragraph he gathers together the sentences that are concerned with a single larger part of his information and presents them as a unit.

Thus a paragraph is a group of sentences related to one another by the fact that each sentence in the group is concerned with the same idea or the same part of an idea. It is a device that the writer uses to explain, clarify, and emphasize his meaning. Let us say that a student writes a theme on politics. In the first paragraph he presents in one sentence his belief that there are certain necessary evils in both rural and urban politics, and in three more sentences he adds that he is going to consider the political situation as found only in large cities and small towns, not in agricultural areas. In the second paragraph he announces in a sentence that he knows there is a certain amount of cor-

327

ruption in the politics in the city in which he lives, and takes five sentences to give an incident that illustrates his opening statement. In the third paragraph he uses five sentences to say that he believes that village politics are similar and to give several instances to prove his point. And so on. If he were describing Yellowstone Park he would probably present each of his impressions in a separate paragraph; if he were telling a story he would present each of a series of actions in a separate paragraph. He would use his paragraph to explain the parts of the whole idea—whether expository, argumentative, descriptive, or narrative—so that any reader could comprehend his meaning.

¶1   THE LOGIC OF DIVISION

A. A paragraph should bring together all the sentences that develop any particular idea in the larger composition. A reader's previous experience has trained him to expect that a writer has said all he is going to say about any one portion of an idea when the end of a paragraph is indicated, and that the succeeding paragraph will present a new portion. The mental readjustment the reader must make when he finds that the succeeding paragraph is also on the same subject as the previous one, as brief a time as that readjustment may take, diverts his attention from what is being said and hence adds to his difficulty in comprehending what the writer has to say.

In the passage which follows, we have divided a paragraph—one correctly *undivided* in the original—to show how faulty indention interrupts assimilation of a single paragraph subject.

As might be expected, *Life's* critical articles generally have a racy, journalistic tone, created mainly by the inclusion of all sorts of miscellaneous facts—an author's marriages, his favorite foods and drinks, his daily routine, what he got paid, his cronies, and so forth. But these articles are generally more than journalistic reporting. They contain critical analysis and evaluation, often serious in tone and relatively complex in method. Charles Wertenbaker, in an article on Malraux, does not dodge the intricate intellectual problems that Malraux has concerned himself with, and he relates Malraux's writing to the central crises of modern European thought.

Roger Butterfield, writing on Marquand, is urbanely and intelligently interested in the purposes behind Marquand's characterizations and in the special qualities of Marquand's satire. True, *Life's* critical articles are not so fully and intensely concerned with matters of literary craftsmanship and intellectual content as are most articles in the literary or scholarly quarterlies, but they are not in this respect as far as might be expected from the critical writing to be found in the *Atlantic, Harper's,* the *Nation* or *New Republic.*—JAMES STEEL SMITH[1]

The next passage is even more difficult to comprehend easily, for in it two consecutive topics are shredded into choppy paragraphs:

Recently I received a bundle of books for review. They all dealt with conditions in the United States, and most of them were extremely pessimistic. One author believes that the horde of immigrants who poured into the country in the years just preceding the World War have brought us to the verge of ruin.

Unrestricted immigration, he says, has filled our cities with morons, criminals, and the physically unfit, has lowered wages, imperiled our institutions, and impaired the racial stock.

We have now closed the doors, it is true, and we are trying to keep them closed, but it will be centuries before we can assimilate the conglomerate mass of humanity which we have admitted. It is a permanent disaster, perhaps an irretrievable disaster. With a troubled mind I turn to the next volume. But it, too, sounds the alarm bell. This time it is our tendency toward undirected reproduction which appears as a great peril.

The best classes, leaders in every walk of life, we are told, are restricting the size of their families, while the unfit . . . are reproducing with great rapidity. It is the survival of the unfittest. The race ascends the ladder by centuries of laborious striving, only in the end to cut off its own head. Seeing in this volume only the blackest future for the United States, I lay it aside more troubled than ever.

---

[1] *"Life* Looks at Literature," *The American Scholar,* Winter, 1957–1958.

Analysis of the first, brief introductory paragraph shows that the author is discussing the subject matter of two books he has read; in other words, there are two main topics. What is now the second paragraph and part of the third deals with the contents of the first book. The last part of the third paragraph begins the discussion of the contents of the second book, a discussion that is continued in the fourth. Common sense suggests that the material be redivided so that it is in two groups, the first paragraph containing the comment on the book first mentioned, the second paragraph containing the comment on the second book. As a matter of fact, the material was so divided in Thomas Jefferson Wertenbaker's article, "What's Wrong with the United States?"[2]

It should be evident, from glancing at the passage quoted from Wertenbaker, that consecutive short paragraphs give a page a choppy, disconnected appearance. If the student finds himself falling into the habit of writing choppy paragraphs, he should make an effort to combine into one paragraph several of his shorter paragraphs that are related in subject matter, as was suggested above. If the parts of thought cannot be combined, then two courses of action remain: (1) some of the material must be omitted, or (2) the short paragraphs must be developed into longer ones (see section ¶ 4).

       B. A paragraph should develop one—and only one—major idea. One advantage of paragraphing is that it enables the writer to present one thing at a time, or, to express it another way, it enables the reader to absorb one part of the writer's idea at a time. The writer who overloads his paragraph also overloads the reader's mind; the reader is forced to absorb several things at a time instead of one. For example, the second paragraph of the following passage is needlessly hard to comprehend because three distinct units of a larger idea have been placed in the same paragraph:

First, then, what is science? Surely there can be no difficulty in answering this, and yet I fear that, if I should pass through this or any other audience with the question, I should get many different answers.

---

[2] *Scribner's Magazine,* October, 1928.

A certain lady, whom I know better than any other, has told me that, should she ever be permitted to marry a second time, she would not marry a scientific man, because scientific men are so terribly accurate. I often hear the same general idea expressed, and it is clear that accuracy is one attribute of science according to prevailing opinions. *But accuracy alone is not science.* When we hear a game of baseball or of whist spoken of as thoroughly scientific, I suppose the idea here, too, is that the games are played accurately; that is, to use the technical expression, without errors. *Again, there are those who seem to think that science is something that has been devised by the Evil One for the purpose of undermining religion.* The idea is not so common as it was a few years ago, when the professors of scientific subjects in our colleges were generally objects of suspicion. The change which has come over the world in this respect within my own memory is simply astounding. In general terms, an agreement has been reached between those who represent religion and those who represent science. This agreement is certainly not final, but it gives us a *modus vivendi;* and the clash of arms is now rarely heard. Religion now takes into consideration the claims of science, and science recognizes the great fundamental truths of religion. Each should strengthen the other, and in time, no doubt, each will strengthen the other. *Probably the idea most commonly held in regard to science is that it is something that gives us a great many useful inventions.* The steam engine, the telegraph, the telephone, the trolley car, dyestuffs, medicines, explosives— these are the fruits of science, and without these science is of no avail. I propose farther on to discuss this subject more fully than I can at this stage of my remarks, so that I may pass over it lightly here. I need only say now that useful inventions are not a necessary consequence of scientific work, and that scientific work does not depend upon useful applications for its value. These propositions, which are familiar enough to scientific men, are apt to surprise those who are outside of scientific circles. I hope before I get through to show you that the propositions are true.

Even if we had not italicized some of the sentences to show where the thought divisions occur, those divisions should be obvious. The introduction announces that the author is going to consider the answers he might get when he asks for a definition of science. We may thus consider each answer a unit and correctly divide the long paragraph into three shorter ones, as Ira Remsen, the author, did.[3] Such a division would not only emphasize more correctly the thought division, but would also make the appearance of the passage more attractive and inviting, for any work which contains an overbundance of long paragraphs seems heavy and dull, whether it is or not.

¶2   THE MECHANICS OF DIVISION

By following modern conventions of length and indention, the writer provides the reader with visual evidence of the logical division of his material. Two or three hundred years ago the student developing an idea in fifteen or twenty sentences would probably have written his essay without any paragraph division, for the fashion then was to use longer paragraphs than we expect today, and the readers of those days were accustomed to long paragraphs. A modern reader, however, expects paragraphs much shorter than those customary in the seventeenth or eighteenth century, and hence convention as well as thought must determine the student's paragraphing.

A. The first line of every paragraph is usually indented. If the writing is in longhand, the indention from the lefthand margin is usually about half an inch; if the paper is typed, the indention is usually about five spaces.

Besides indenting, authors of textbooks and handbooks sometimes also use boldface type and numerals and letters in order to indicate divisions of thought. (Look at the opening paragraphs of this section.) Such typographical practices, however, are exceptional; in normal composition, only indention should be used.

B. The length of a paragraph is determined by its purpose and by the emphasis the writer wishes to place on an idea. Even the most unobserving writer will have noticed, of course, that in any piece of writing there are rarely two para-

---

[3] "The Age of Science." An address delivered at the Worcester Polytechnic Institute, June, 1904.

graphs of the same length. This variation is only natural, since no two thoughts and no two parts of a thought are of exactly equal importance, nor are they likely to need exactly the same number of words to explain them. This variation in length, purpose, and subject can be seen in the following two passages, both of which contain three paragraphs. The first has paragraphs of 45, 76, and 55 words and was written to deliver interesting but relatively unimportant information that would entertain readers effortlessly:

In the spring of 1890 a liner from Europe steamed into New York harbor to discharge its passengers in lower Manhattan. Sixty of these passengers rode ashore in cages. They were dark, chunky birds with yellow bills. The vessel was the *Mayflower* of the starling.

Every one of the untold millions of these birds in America today has descended from 100 immigrants—the 60 that arrived in 1890 to be set free in Central Park and 40 more that reached New York the following year. Their coming was the result of one man's fancy. He was Eugene Schieffelin, a wealthy New York manufacturer whose curious hobby was the introduction into America of all the birds mentioned in the works of Shakespeare.

Skylarks, chaffinches, nightingales, as well as English sparrows and starlings, rode across the Atlantic in cages consigned to Schieffelin. He even incorporated a society for the importation of foreign birds. Today, partly because of lessons learned from his activity, no foreign bird or animal may be imported without permission from the U.S. Department of Agriculture.—EDWIN WAY TEALE[4]

The next passage is written on a serious subject, to present information that is important. Its paragraphs of 99, 55, and 71 words are among the shortest in the complete article from which it was taken; the passage quoted below was preceded by a paragraph of 212 words:

It would be a mistake, of course, to assume that money alone will assure a quick solution to the cancer problem. You occasionally hear

---

[4] "In Defense of the Pesky Starling." Reprinted from November, 1947, *Coronet*. Copyright, 1947, by Esquire, Inc.

someone say, "We shelled out two billion and got an atom bomb in four years; we can spend a similar amount on cancer and lick it in the same length of time." The analogy is fallacious. The basic principle of atomic fission had been discovered in Germany before we laid out a nickel for the Manhattan Project. The basic principles of the insidious biologic fission we call cancer, however, are still among the scientific unknowns.

Search for these fundamental formulas must be continued, even though it may be many years before they are found. "But in the meantime," as one New York surgeon put it, "the patient with cancer can't afford to wait for the absolute answer. We may have to do everything we possibly can for him here and now."

One of the most logical setups to hasten the transition from laboratory to bedside is the cancer institute. Here research scientists and physicians tackle the job as a team. A pioneer example is Memorial Hospital in New York, founded in 1884, given a large new building by the Rockefellers in the late 30's, and recently broadened by the addition of the Sloan-Kettering Institute for Cancer Research, which was dedicated in April.—STEVEN M. SPENCER[5]

A glance at the passage by Wertenbaker on page 329 and the one by Remsen on page 330 will show that both of them contain introductory paragraphs much shorter than the paragraphs (when correctly divided) that follow the introduction.

But the reader who notices the variations should also notice that in most essays the appearance of the paragraphs on the pages makes a visual pattern that is rather well balanced. The balance or lack of balance is particularly noticeable in a comparatively short paper having only from four hundred to a thousand words. We do not intend to imply that in order to secure this balance, when writing a theme, the student should self-consciously make his first paragraph have 100 words, his second 80, and his third 120. We do, however, intend to suggest that if, after writing his theme, he finds that he has six paragraphs of 50 words each and one of 200 words, there is probably something wrong. It may be that one

[5] "Where Are We Now on Cancer?" *The Saturday Evening Post,* June 5, 1948.

part of his topic has been overexplained in his long paragraph; it may be that the parts in the short paragraph have been under-explained; it may be that some of his paragraphs could have been combined, as suggested in section ¶ 1. No mechanical rule can ever be followed entirely if one is to write paragraphs that are just as long as they should be, and no longer. But some attention to the visual balance of a series of paragraphs will frequently reveal errors in logic in the construction of at least some of the paragraphs.

C. In dialogue each speech is usually placed in a separate paragraph; the introductory or explanatory material accompanies the speech to which it belongs.   The following passage illustrates this rule:

. . . I went out and found the major sitting at a table in the bare room with maps and typed sheets of paper on the wall.

"Hello," he said. "How are you?" He looked older and wiser.

"I'm good," I said. "How is everything?"

"It's all over," he said. "Take off your kit and sit down." I put my pack and the two musettes on the floor and my cap on the pack. I brought the other chair over from the wall and sat down by the desk.

"It's been a bad summer," the major said. "Are you stronger now?"

"Yes."

"Did you ever get the decorations?"

"Yes. I got them finally. Thank you very much."

"Let's see them."

I opened my cape so he could see the two ribbons.—ERNEST HEMING-WAY[6]

When, however, passages of dialogue are brief and are inserted into a work to give a single impression rather than to stress the individual speeches, all the dialogue may be placed within one paragraph, as is done in the following selection:

The two men sat quietly, almost apathetically, in the deck chairs placed under the awnings near the bow of the steamer. The water

---

[6] *A Farewell to Arms.* Copyright, 1929, by Charles Scribner's Sons.

shimmered, reflecting the stars and the phosphorescent trail of the ship. Stars and phosphorescence both seemed pressed into the liquid blackness by the overpowering heat, heat that weighed so heavily upon the men that the mere act of speaking took physical effort. "Like this in town?" asked the trader, not caring whether his question was answered or not. "Worse . . . much worse," was all Jules could find strength to reply.

When each speech is placed in a separate paragraph, the speech and its introductory material are emphasized. But when all the dialogue is placed in the same paragraph the dialogue is used either to give a single impression or to emphasize the topic sentence.

¶3 THE TOPIC SENTENCE

An effective paragraph will almost always have a topic sentence, that is, a sentence that states or clearly indicates the subject to be discussed in the paragraph. Such a statement is helpful because it informs the reader what the paragraph is going to be about and directs his attention to the significance and relationship of the rest of the sentences in the paragraph. The topic sentence is usually found at or near the beginning of the paragraph, but it may be at the end.

A few of the many ways in which topic sentences guide and direct the reader may be seen in the following paragraphs, in which the topic sentences have been italicized:

A. Sometimes the topic sentence generalizes about the contents of the paragraph:

It was an extraordinary situation. A more brilliant group of scientists, scholars, and creative writers had never congregated about a university —yet Harvard clung to her ancient rules, doing all she could, apparently, to prevent these professors from functioning fully. Teaching was the same old system of grammar-school recitation. You got through college

by memorizing the textbooks. Even philosophy was committed to memory. A student was not expected to question either textbook or lecturer. He learned a principle, a definition; from it he made certain deductions. If they agreed with the deductions in the book, he got a good mark; if they differed he got a bad one. Term after term, professors gave the same lectures; the story goes that one professor's notes dropped apart before he wrote a new lecture. Dr. Holmes himself, although a brilliant lecturer, used, in one of his anatomy classes, the same identical notes for thirty-five years. Why not, when man's anatomy did not change?
—CATHERINE DRINKER BOWEN[7]

The author has made a general statement in the opening sentence of the paragraph. She has presented her conclusion before the facts that led to the conclusion, so that the reader will be certain to see the relationship of the details given by the rest of the sentences.

B. The topic sentence may forecast, or tell more precisely than a generalization would, exactly what the paragraph is to be about:

Prosperity was assisted, too, by two new stimulants to purchasing, each of which mortgaged the future but kept the factories roaring while it was being injected. The first was the increase in installment buying. People were getting to consider it old-fashioned to limit their purchases to the amount of their cash balance; the thing to do was to "exercise their credit." By the latter part of the decade, economists figured that 15 per cent of all retail sales were on an installment basis, and that there were some six billions of "easy payment" paper outstanding. The other stimulant was stock-market speculation. When stocks were skyrocketing in 1928 and 1929 it is probable that hundreds of thousands of people were buying goods with money which represented, essentially, a gamble on the business profits of the nineteen-thirties. It was fun while it lasted.
—FREDERICK LEWIS ALLEN[8]

[7] *Yankee from Olympus.* Copyright, 1945, Little, Brown and Company and Atlantic Monthly Press.
[8] *Only Yesterday.* Copyright, 1931, by Frederick Lewis Allen and reprinted by permission of Harper & Brothers, publishers.

We say that the opening sentence of this paragraph forecasts because it tells exactly how many subtopics will be discussed: "two new stimulants to purchasing." The topic sentence might have been made to read, "Prosperity was assisted, too, by stimulants which mortgaged the future but kept the factories roaring while they were being injected." It would have then resembled the first sentence of the paragraph by Catherine Drinker Bowen.

C. The topic sentence may be phrased as a rhetorical question:

Who was General Andrew Jackson, the new popular favorite? To the nation he was known primarily as a military hero. In the Revolution, an English officer had slashed him with a saber for refusing to clean a pair of boots. In the War of 1812 he had shown great energy and resource in putting down some Indian uprisings, and in 1815, after the treaty of peace had been signed, he won at New Orleans the greatest American victory of the war. His nominal profession was the law, and he had served in the House of Representatives and Senate of the United States, as well as on the Tennessee Supreme Court. For the decade past, his life had been mainly that of a Tennessee gentleman, living on a fine plantation near Nashville, entertaining his friends, racing his horses and heatedly talking politics. In 1828 he was sixty-one years old.—ARTHUR M. SCHLESINGER, JR.[9]

It is thought that the rhetorical question stimulates the reader's attention at the same time that it arouses his curiosity, causing him to read more closely than he otherwise would. Yet although the question as a topic sentence may be a useful device to stimulate interest, it must be used sparingly and with caution. Questions, whether "rhetorical" or not, are always dangerous. They have been used so often in florid speeches that their novelty has worn off. In all but a few circumstances the writer will be much more successful if he states his topic sentence affirmatively, that is, as Schlesinger might have said, "General Andrew Jackson was the new popular favorite." We do not intend to imply that ques-

[9] *The Age of Jackson.* Copyright, 1945, by Arthur M. Schlesinger, Jr., and used by permission of Little, Brown and Company, publishers.

tions should never be used. One in a theme, for example, will not bore the reader, especially if it is used to create suspense or dramatic effect, but if the student finds himself getting into the habit of using questions he will do well to give them up altogether for a time.

D. The topic sentence may come at the end of a paragraph and serve as a summarizing statement:

In addition to the "tongues," as the classics were called, the course of study at Yale embraced a few other subjects. English composition had just barely infiltrated the curriculum. Mathematics and natural science held a secure place, though neither subject went much beyond the rudiments, and if a student managed to master algebra and geometry, he probably learned more than the average. By the time Barlow entered, the scientific side of the program had been greatly strengthened by the appointment of Nehemiah Strong, first professor of mathematics and natural philosophy. Theological instruction, of course, figured prominently in any Yale undergraduate's life. All students studied the Westminster Confession of Faith and recited their catechism. Freshmen and sophomores digested William Ames' "Medulla Theologiae" and juniors fed on Johannes Wollebius' "Compendium Theologiae Christianae." *The Yale faculty and corporation tried mightily to water their garden from the pure springs of Puritanism unpolluted by heresy.*—JAMES L. WOODRESS[10]

Like the question, the summarizing topic sentence is effective if used sparingly. It is especially useful when the writer wishes to attain a climactic effect. Its use, however, has one danger: unless the preceding paragraph makes clear the details, the lack of a topic sentence at the beginning of the following paragraph may confuse rather than guide the reader. Seeing a number of details, but not understanding how they are related, he may conceivably become lost.

E. Occasionally, paragraphs may lack topic sentences. The following paragraph, for example, contains no sentence that may be definitely labeled as topic.

---

[10] *A Yankee's Odyssey.* Copyright, 1958, J. B. Lippincott Company.

Total advertising budgets in the United States recently approached the $10 billion mark, with newspaper advertisements accounting for about $3 billion, TV $1 billion, magazines $757 million, and radio about $500 million. Advertising expenditures have grown faster than the total productivity of the economy as a whole since 1952, something that might be expected during a period when the buyer's market seemed to be reappearing. There has been more advertising indoors than outdoors: national TV in 1955 took in about 48 per cent of all the new money for advertising that entered the market during the year, while outdoor advertising showed the lowest percentage growth of all major media.— REUEL DENNEY[11]

The significance of the facts in this paragraph, the first one in a chapter, is made clear only by the first sentence in the *next* paragraph: "None of this means that advertising men can always prove a direct relationship between sales and advertising." From this point, the author goes on to discuss the general influence of advertising on society.

For the beginning writer, however, the topic sentence is an extremely useful device for achieving clarity. He can afford to dispense with it only if he is absolutely certain that the logic and the structure of his paragraph are clear.

¶4   DEVELOPING THE TOPIC SENTENCE

The body of the paragraph should fully and clearly explain what the writer means by the idea stated in the topic sentence. When someone with whom we are talking makes a statement expressing an idea that is new or with which we are not familiar, we usually ask, "What do you mean?" He usually answers by giving us examples, by explaining in different words, or perhaps merely by enlarging upon the various parts of his original statement. He "develops" his idea for us. The informal speaker has an opportunity to explain if he sees that his listener does not understand,

---

[11] *The Astonished Muse.* The University of Chicago Press. Copyright, 1957, by the University of Chicago.

but the writer, whether his work is formal or informal, seldom has that opportunity. He must, in fact, guard against the possibility of such misunderstanding from the very beginning. He, too, must develop his idea, always remembering that his reader may be miles away from him, always elaborating so that there will be no need for the reader to ask, "What does he mean?"

Most such development will be clear and effective only when the writer knows enough about his subject to develop it spontaneously and from varying points of view. There are times, however, when spontaneous development seems impossible. Even accomplished writers have been known to fumble for ways of explaining their ideas, and almost any student will testify that sometimes, when he has composed a topic sentence, he seems to have nothing more to say about his subject. In such circumstances it sometimes helps to know how others have enlarged on their topic sentences and to be able to do likewise. It is with this thought in mind, not because we believe that writers consciously develop paragraphs by any one method, that we offer the following paragraphs to show a few of the ways by which some professional writers have developed their topic sentences. The student must realize, of course, that the following paragraphs illustrate only a few of the many ways by which topic sentences may be elaborated: almost every paragraph will call for its own method.

A. A paragraph may be developed by giving several examples of the idea stated in the topic sentence:

Clothes, budgetary bane of women of lesser mettle, have never proved so to the Boston woman. A familiar legend is the story of the lady who, asked by an amazed visitor to Boston where Boston women get their hats, replied: "Our hats? Why, we have our hats." Like most Boston legends, however, there is something behind the story. For a woman to dress too smartly in Boston is to open herself to the charge that she is a social climber. First Family ladies view with alarm such evidence of the parvenue. A typical expression of contempt is the phrase, "She has everything she owns on her back." One Society editor, long inured to the habit of Boston women indulging in parsimony by ignoring all fashion trends and "making things do," claims she saw a First Family lady emerge from the Chilton Club dressed in a mandarin coat dating from the days of the Boston clippers and the China trade. Other editors have also struggled with the problem of reporting the party-going clothes of Boston's best. The custom has usually been to describe the lady's costume once or twice only and then if the costume continues to appear —as so often it does—to ignore the lady herself. One lately deceased grande dame, however, was such a Society standout she could not be ignored. Year after year on every formal occasion she appeared in the same white satin evening gown in which she had been presented at the Court of St. James's. One year the gown would be described as white, next as "off-white," then "oyster-white," and once more as "pearl-gray." Finally, exhausting their repertoire, the Society reporters would again go back to white and start all over again.—CLEVELAND AMORY[12]

Development by examples is one of the most effective ways of enlarging on a topic sentence. Examples tell the reader that the writer is drawing conclusions based upon more than one instance and thus help to validate the logic of the paragraph.

B. A paragraph may be developed by defining one or more of the terms used in the topic sentence:

The last stage of business size is the *very large business*. It is characterized first by the fact that both the action and the over-all objective-setting part of the chief-executive job must be organized on a team basis. And each job requires the full-time services of several people. Secondly, it can only be organized on the federal principle of management structure. The business is too big and too complex to be organized any other way. Finally, the organization of the chief executive and its relationship to operating management tend to become major problems which engage the attention and energy of top-management people before everything else. It is in the very large business that systematic organization of the chief-executive job is both most difficult and most needed.—PETER F. DRUCKER[13]

---

[12] *The Proper Bostonians.* Copyright, 1947, E. P. Dutton & Co., Inc.
[13] *The Practice of Management.* Copyright, 1954, by Peter F. Drucker. Reprinted by permission of the publishers, Harper & Brothers, Inc.

Another method of developing a paragraph by definition is illustrated in the next example. Here the author uses a negative definition in the opening sentence, continues by eliminating other possibilities, and concludes with his topic sentence, which is phrased in positive terms.

The present collection is not an orthodox one. It does not focus on the history or the development or the "form" of the essay and does not concentrate on the professional essayists at all—and by "professional" I refer to those writers, such as Lamb and de Quincey and, in modern times, Mencken and E. B. White, who find their best and fullest expression in the essay medium. What it does instead is show how the large creative minds, those which produced the novels, plays, and poems of the past century and a half, put the essay to their use.—CHARLES NEIDER[14]

C. A paragraph may be developed by analysis; that is, by breaking down a large topic into its component parts:

The defense of American capitalism runs largely in broad abstractions like "the American system" or "the free-enterprise economy," or in epithets like "serfdom" or "totalitarian" applied to noncapitalist systems. Underlying these catchwords are some basic arguments. One is the argument from incentive: that men's brains and energy work best when they have no hampering restrictions, and when they see an immediacy of relation between effort and reward. The second is the argument from a free market: that an economy runs best as the result of millions of individual decisions made through the operations of a free production, wage and price system; that when it goes off kilter, it can generally set itself right again by individual adjustments within a frame of government spurs and checks; and that even government regulation is best accomplished by the indirect methods of inducements and pressures on the free market, rather than the direct method of planning and control. The third is the argument from managerial efficiency: that the corporate managerial group is recruited from the men with the best skills, who deal with the problems of industrial production more flexibly than a governmental bureaucracy could.—MAX LERNER[15]

---

[14] Introduction to *Essays of the Masters*. Copyright, 1956, Rinehart & Company, Inc.
[15] *America as a Civilization*. Copyright, 1957, by Simon and Schuster, Inc.

D. A paragraph may be developed by comparison and contrast:

The ideal band pianists were Fats Waller, at his best, and Jelly Roll Morton. Different in individual styles, both had the same concept of the piano in the band. They kept it subordinate in the ensemble; in their hands it became a sort of liaison agent between the rhythm section and the polyphonic melody section. They both produced a steady, firm, and continuous beat but did not indiscriminately add treble melodies to confuse the polyphony and to be lost in it. In this respect they were adroit and highly imaginative, placing their melodic comments on, and in addition to, the polyphony, much as the clarinet does in the caesuras of the progressing counterpoint. At other times, by a wise selection of register and melodic line, they would fit a melody into a complete band polyphony. The piano would emerge in solo, as Fats and Jelly Roll played it, not in a fatuous exhibition unrelated to the context but in real variation on the basic theme that carried the musical development onward. Such is the ensemble and solo work of Morton as we find it in "The Chant," for example, and of Waller in "You're Not the Only Oyster in the Stew." In the jazz period of 1925–1928, the much lauded Earl Hines provided no such intelligent piano part in the band. Rhythmically he tended to be a disrupting influence and in solo he said the little he had to say in a sensational, exhibitionistic manner.— RUDI BLESH[16]

E. A paragraph may be developed by illustrative narrative:

As town-site promotion gave way to carefully planned subdivisions, new methods of selling real estate were rapidly perfected. Before any lots were sold in Hollywood, streets and highways were plotted and trees planted along the walks. The Hollywood Hotel was built on one corner of Hollywood Boulevard and Highland and an imposing bank structure on the opposite corner. Loads of brick, sand, and lumber were hauled to the tract and dumped on vacant lots so as to give the impression that hundreds of lot-purchasers had actually started to construct homes. Al-

---

[16] *Shining Trumpets: A History of Jazz.* Copyright, 1946, by Alfred A. Knopf, Inc.

most every other lot in the tract carried a sign marked SOLD, although not a single lot had actually been disposed of. The stage being set, the new subdivision was opened with a "grand excursion" on May 3, 1903. Two special Pacific Electric cars, the Mermaid and No. 400, decorated with flags, bunting and flowers, carried the first excursionists to the tract where they were greeted by a brass band. In a speech at the tract headquarters, General M. H. Sherman, who with Harry Chandler and E. P. Clark had organized this fancy promotion, waving his arms at the sold signs and the scattered piles of building material, sobbed: "Behold What God Hath Wrought!" On this subdivision, the promoters made a net profit of 60% on their investment. The technician who outlined this new-style subdivision was H. J. Whitley, a professional town-site promoter for the Rock Island and Northern Pacific Railroads. Using much the same techniques, Chandler, Sherman, and their associates later subdivided and sold more than 47,000 acres of land adjoining Los Angeles.—CAREY MCWILLIAMS[17]

F. A paragraph may be (and usually is) developed by more than one means:

It is a paradox, but the truth nevertheless, that our absence of ideas, the exclusion of ideas from American political life, gives us a superior kind of public morality. In New York some years ago a German refugee, who was just beginning to breathe freely our sooty but impartial air, was attacked and robbed in broad daylight on First Avenue. The young muggers looked to him like the stuff storm troopers are made of, and he said to himself, "There it goes again!" But there was a vast difference, a difference, as he told the court, that on reflection he was able to appreciate. In the first place, the attack had no idea wrapped around it, it was just plain greed. In the second place, the police had no ideology either. They were for the victim whoever he was.—JACQUES BARZUN[18]

How many means does Barzun use to develop his idea?

[17] *Southern California Country.* Copyright, 1946, by Duell, Sloan & Pearce, Inc.

[18] *God's Country and Mine.* Copyright, 1954, by Little, Brown and Company and Atlantic Monthly Press.

¶5   UNITY AND COHERENCE

Since the main purpose of division into paragraphs is to separate and emphasize the phases of an idea, that purpose must not be thwarted by a lack of unity or by incoherence. A paragraph can be considered unified only when all the details in the paragraph belong together. Once the reader's mind is prepared to accept details about topic A, he will be confused if details belonging to topic B or C are inserted without warning. But this unity is not enough. The details must also be coherent; that is, the reason for the presence of the details in the paragraph must be quickly and obviously evident to the reader so that his reception of them will be unimpeded by needless questioning. By study and concentration the reader can, of course, eventually discover what a disunified and incoherent paragraph is about. But he can easily discover the significance of a unified and coherent paragraph, and hence the writing will be more successful. The writer will have succeeded in his aim, which is effective communication of his idea. Some ways by which unity and coherence may be gained are illustrated in the rest of this section.

        A. A clear topic sentence (see section ¶ 3) **is one of the best ways of showing how a series of seemingly unrelated details are in reality unified.** In the following paragraph, although the five individual sentences are not without interest, their full significance and the relationships between them become clear only when the topic sentence is supplied:

Critical improvements in steam capacity were achieved by the increase in heating surface secured by the U-shaped flues introduced by Oliver Evans and Timothy Hackworth, but the final boiler design was based on the use of tubes. The work of Booth was not without precedent, but the boiler constructed for the famous "Rocket" was the first effective development of this concept. Hackworth's improved design and location of the jet for the introduction of exhaust steam into the stack was also essential to the achievement of satisfactory working capacities for the production of steam. In the "Rocket," these new elements of design were carried to a point which ensured the success of steam locomotion, and led to further improvements in the capacity and effectiveness of the condensing engines. The Rainhill test (1830) thus marks the end of the early history of steam engineering.—ABBOTT PAYSON USHER[19]

Notice how this information assumes a unity if the topic sentence (with which the author originally began his paragraph) is read first:

The development of an effective locomotive required primary modifications in the design of boilers and in the production of the necessary draft in the stack.

B. Unity may be attained by excluding extraneous material from a paragraph (see section ¶ 1). The following selection, for example, lacks unity because details which have nothing to do with the topic sentence, "Hyder was everywhere triumphant," are present:

Hyder was everywhere triumphant. The sepoys in many British garrisons flung down their arms. Some forts were surrendered by treachery and some by despair. In a few days the whole open country north of Coleroon had submitted. The English inhabitants of Madras could already see by night, from the top of Mount St. Thomas, the western sky reddened by a vast semicircle of blazing villages. The white villas, to which our countrymen retire after the daily labors of government and trade, when the cool evening breeze springs up from the bay, were not left without inhabitants; for bands of fierce horsemen of Mysore had already been seen prowling among the tulip-trees and near the gay verandas. Even the town was not thought secure, and the British merchants and public functionaries made haste to crowd themselves behind the cannon of Fort St. George. There were the means, indeed, of assembling an army which might have defended the presidency, and even driven the invader back to his mountains. Sir Hector Munroe was at the head of one considerable force; Baillie was advancing with another.

[19] *A History of Mechanical Inventions.* Revised edition, 1954. Copyright © The President and Fellows of Harvard College. Reprinted by permission of the Harvard University Press.

United, they might have presented a formidable front even to such an enemy as Hyder.—THOMAS BABINGTON MACAULAY[20]

The first six sentences elaborate upon the topic sentence and show the extent of Hyder's victory. The seventh sentence, however, begins a new idea; it is a new topic sentence, a fact which is evident if we read the details which follow it. They all have to do, not with Hyder's triumphs, but with another phase of the Indian rebellion, the means used to oppose him. To improve the unity of the paragraph the information about the English army should be dropped from the paragraph. It may then be put into a paragraph of its own or, if it is unimportant, omitted altogether. Macaulay chose the first method and began a new paragraph with "The white villas . . . "

C. Coherence may be gained by the logical arrangement of material. All the details present may belong in a paragraph, but if they are not put in the proper order the reader cannot see their relationship. In the following paragraph everything obviously explains the topic sentence, which is the first sentence, but the rest of the sentences are illogically arranged:

Gone, too, or fast going, is the old authority of the home. The flapper feels that her mother and all her ideas are antiquated, and she is inaugurating a new type of emancipated womanhood. We must believe, too, that on the whole her revolt is beneficent. The school eclipses the influence of the home, and, as it becomes more and more paternal, of the parents. The boy, almost in his infancy, Freudians tell us, or at least long before he knows it, begins to hate and even to feel jealousy toward his father. The homes of the poor, especially in the cities, are less and less attractive to the young. Especially do the children of foreign families which land upon our shores—all the more if they speak another language —soon learn to become ashamed of their parents and their ways. In modern society parents have less and less to do with their children, and thus discipline and respect have declined.

This selection begins with the statement about the loss of the authority of the home and it concludes with one which reinforces

[20] *Lord Clive* (1836).

the opening. One would expect, then, the details to be arranged in one of the following ways: (1) from the specific to the general, (2) from the loss of influence in one place to the loss of influence in another, (3) from the familiar to the unfamiliar. As a matter of fact, no such plan can be found; the material jumps from the modern girl to the influence of the school, to the modern boy, to the children of foreign families. Furthermore, the first example of loss of authority is the modern girl, and common sense suggests that the example of the modern boy be used next. Instead, however, two sentences intervene between the details which obviously belong together. Other details are arranged as badly, and it is obviously impossible to gain a definite idea of what the writer is trying to say. That the details do belong together may be seen from reading the original version:

Gone, too, or fast going, is the old authority of the home. The flapper feels that her mother and all her ideas are antiquated, and she is inaugurating a new type of emancipated womanhood. We must believe, too, that on the whole her revolt is beneficent. The boy, almost in his infancy, Freudians tell us, or at least long before he knows it, begins to hate and even to feel jealousy toward his father. Especially do the children of foreign families which land upon our shores—all the more if they speak another language—soon learn to become ashamed of their parents and their ways. The school eclipses the influence of the home, and, as it becomes more and more paternal, of the parents. The homes of the poor, especially in the cities, are less and less attractive to the young. In modern society parents have less and less to do with their children, and thus discipline and respect have declined.—G. STANLEY HALL[21]

D. Coherence may be gained by a judicious use of transitional words and phrases, expressions that connect the thought of one sentence with that of another sentence. Their use is illustrated in the following selection:

The social hierarchy of the nation is basically a division of society into economic and occupational classes. The groups at the very top

[21] "Can the Masses Rule the World?" *The Scientific Monthly,* May, 1924.

(Imperial Family and nobility) and at the very bottom (*Suiheisha* and Koreans) are more in the nature of castes, being largely hereditary so that it is difficult for one not born into the top group to enter it and for one born into the bottom group to get out of it. The custom of adoption, *however,* provides a special channel whereby individuals may rise in social rank—even into the nobility. *Similarly* girls may climb the ladder through marriage even into the Imperial Family. A sister of Prince Tokugawa, *for instance,* is the wife of the Emperor's younger brother, Nobuhito. Such changes of status by marriage or adoption are rarely of more than one rung in the ladder in one generation. An exception to this rule was the marriage of Setsuko, a daughter of Tsuneo Matsudaira of an upper-middle-class family, to Prince Chichibu, younger brother of the Emperor. Despite advice to the contrary, the Prince insisted on marrying Miss Matsudaira; *hence* the situation was saved by her being adopted into another branch of the Matsudaira family which is of the nobility. *In this way* the marriage was the traditional one of an imperial prince with a daughter of the nobility. The fact that this stratagem, while legitimate, was stretching a point is reflected in the critical attitude many people took toward Prince Chichibu's bride, remarking that she should not have let the prince marry her.—JOHN F. EMBREE[22]

Note the words that we have italicized in the selection above. Each of these transitional expressions refers the reader to what has gone before or foretells what is coming; he is never allowed to forget the matter in hand. As we will see in section ¶ 7, the practice of leading the reader through a series of statements is also a common one—and a useful one—in units of prose longer than one paragraph.

E. Coherence may be gained by the use of "linking" words and expressions. These are words and phrases that refer to some idea which has been expressed earlier in the paragraph or in the essay. In the following example, C. Wright Mills repeats the key phrase ("the conception rests"):

The conception of the power elite and of its unity rests upon the corresponding developments and the coincidence of interests among

---

[22] *The Japanese Nation.* Copyright, 1945, by Rinehart & Co., Inc.

economic, political, and military organizations. It also rests upon the similarity of origin and outlook, and the social and personal inter-mingling of the top circles from each of these dominant hierarchies. This conjunction of institutional and psychological forces, in turn, is revealed by the heavy personnel traffic within and between the big three institutional orders, as well as by the rise of go-betweens as in the high-level lobbying. The conception of the power elite, accordingly, does *not* rest upon the assumption that American history since the origins of World War II must be understood as a secret plot, or as a great and co-ordinated conspiracy of the members of this elite. The conception rests upon quite impersonal grounds.—C. WRIGHT MILLS[23]

At other times the linking words may be **synonyms, pronouns,** or expressions which merely "echo" words or ideas previously ex-pressed, as may be seen in the following passage:

Fifty-seven years ago Mr. James Russell Lowell published in the *Atlantic Monthly* an urbanely caustic essay, "On a Certain Condescen-sion in Foreigners." Despite discursiveness (it was a leisurely age), this *apologia pro patria sua* is a model of good temper, good taste, and good feeling. *Its author* regretted England's dislike of *our* food, and Germany's contempt for *our* music; but *he* did not suffer *himself* to be cast down. With modesty past all praise, *he* even admitted, what no good American will admit today, that popular government "is no better than any other form except as virtue and wisdom of the people make it so," and that self-made men "may not be divinely commissioned to fabricate the higher qualities of opinion on all possible topics of human interests." Nevertheless, *he* found both purpose and principle in the *young nation,* hammered into shape by four years of civil war. "One might be worse off than even in America," mused *this son of Massa-chusetts;* and *we* are instantly reminded of William James's softly breathed assurance: "A *Yankee* is also, in the last analysis, one of God's creatures."—AGNES REPPLIER[24]

James Russell Lowell is referred to by *its author, he,* and *this son of Massachusetts;* the essay is referred to by *apologia pro*

---

[23] *The Power Elite.* Copyright, 1956, by the Oxford University Press.
[24] "On a Certain Condescension in Americans," *Harper's Magazine*, May, 1926.

patria sua; America, by *young nation;* and Americans, by *our, we,* and *Yankee.* If lines are drawn between the sets of words that refer to Lowell, his essay, America, and Americans, respectively, each word will be seen as a link in an imaginary chain which holds the paragraph together just as a metal chain holds together a group of logs. Notice that even with the liberal use of linking words Miss Repplier has seen fit to include several transitional expressions; *but* in the third sentence and *nevertheless* in the fifth are the most obvious. John Embree's paragraph, cited above for its use of transitional expressions, also uses a number of linking terms to reinforce the structure of the statement: *such changes, an exception to this rule, this stratagem.*

¶6   EMPHASIS

Besides being unified and coherent, the material within a paragraph should be arranged so that the most important details will be properly emphasized. As in the sentence, the most important positions in the paragraph are the beginning and ending, because information placed at the introduction or at the conclusion will usually be remembered longer by the reader than material placed within the body. This and other means of securing emphasis are illustrated in the following selections.

A. For emphasis, important material is placed at the beginning or at the end:

The artist is likely to be looked upon with some uneasiness by the more conservative members of society. He seems a little unpredictable. Who knows but that he may arrive for dinner in a red shirt, appear unexpectedly bearded, offer—freely—unsolicited advice, or even ship off one of his ears to some unwilling recipient? However glorious the history of art may be, the history of artists is quite another matter. And in any well-ordered household the very thought that one of the young may turn out to be an artist can be a cause for general alarm. It may be a point of great pride to have a Van Gogh on the living-room wall, but the prospect of having Van Gogh himself in the living room would put a good many devoted art lovers to rout.—BEN SHAHN[25]

The first sentence in this paragraph propounds a general thesis which is developed in the succeeding sentences. Shahn gradually develops a distinction between attitudes toward "art" and attitudes toward "artists." In the third sentence, the allusion to an artist's shipping off one of his ears subtly forecasts the climactic last sentence, where Van Gogh (who did just that) is used as a vivid and concrete illustration of the author's thesis.

In the example given above, "emphasis by position" requires, as it does in almost all such examples, that the significant statement be placed at or near the beginning of the paragraph, and that the most forceful statement be the concluding sentence. This principle is also caried out in the following selection, with the introductory sentence stating the thought which the rest of the paragraph is to enlarge upon, and with the concluding sentence summarizing, in a new and forceful manner, what has already been stated:

This eclipse of the national is almost complete in the realm of the great Shakespeare's works, translated, are read in German schools side by side with Goethe's and Schiller's; Palestrina's masses are sung in St. Patrick's in New York and in the cathedral of Cologne as they are in St. Peter's in Rome; Michelangelo's *Pieta* is fully at home in Brugge in Flanders, and Rodin's "Thinker" could easily stand on a Florentine piazza, on the Red Square in Moscow, or in front of the White House. Nobody would exclaim: How English is Shakespeare! How French is Rodin! How Italian is Michelangelo! Just as nobody would emphasize how German Mozart was, or as no Protestant or Catholic who sings a psalm of David would think of its Jewish creator. The inner size of these men has outgrown the limits of nationhood; they have entered the lofty realm of supranational humanity; they are landmarks.—CURT SACHS[26]

---

[25] *The Shape of Content.* Copyright, 1957, by the Harvard University Press.
[26] *The Commonwealth of Art.* Copyright, 1946, by W. W. Norton & Company, Inc.

Notice, too, how the concluding sentence in the paragraph by Frederick Lewis Allen, quoted on page 337, suddenly clarifies Allen's point of view toward his subject.

B. Emphasis may be gained by ranking material in order of climax, that is, by saving the most dramatic material until the end. The following selection illustrates this arrangement:

I was sitting on the edge of the bed, loosening the heel of one of my rubber boots with the toe of the other, when suddenly, through the stillness of the sleeping town, from the power-house half a mile away, came a low and rising note, the great siren whistle in the power-house. Almost fascinated, I listened as the great note rose higher and more shrill and died away again. One blast meant a fire in the town; two blasts, fire in the buildings at the mine; and three blasts, the most terrible of all, a disaster or trouble in the mine. Once more, after an interminable pause, the sound came again; and once more rose and died away. I did not move, but there was a sudden coldness that came over me once more, as, for the third time, the deep note broke out on the quiet air. Almost simultaneously the loud jingle of my telephone brought me to my feet. I took down the receiver: *"The mine's blown up,"* said a woman's voice.—JOSEPH HUSBAND[27]

After describing the first blast of the whistle, the author stops to explain what the signals of the whistles mean so that he will not have to explain the fact when the third blast sounds. He manages, too, to get in all the necessary explanatory details before telling of the all-important third blast. The intensity of the climax is further heightened by the jingling of the telephone and by the final climactic statement confirming his worst fears and suspicions.

C. Emphasis may be gained by repetition of words or structure. Especially valuable is parallel structure, which is emphatic because of the obvious grammatical similarity it gives to similar ideas.

---

[27] *A Year in a Coal Mine.* Copyright, 1911, by Joseph Husband and reprinted by permission of Houghton Mifflin Company, publishers.

Putting intellectual matters aside, I submit that the motto of our present prevailing system of interchangeable parts is "adjustment." The freshman "adjusts" to his college. The sophomore "adjusts" to his professors, and by and by the senior is supposed to "adjust" to the outside world, nobody asks why. I doubt that "adjustment" would have made much sense to Emerson or Thorstein Veblen or Edgar Allan Poe or John Sloan or Jonathan Edwards or Frank Lloyd Wright or Carlson of Chicago or Einstein of Princeton. In my observation the world adjusts to the genius, not the genius to the world; and if Woodrow Wilson was right in saying that the principal purpose of a liberal education is to enable you to know a good man when you see him, I doubt that psychological testing is a proper telescope. Of course it can be argued that the thousands who annually pass through the American college are not geniuses, and this is true. But what about the genius who would like to be trained in his calling? Are we keeping paths open for the lonely talents who really shape culture and who are not content to imitate culture in others? Or are we so universally bent on "adjustment," all in the interests of a smoothly running society, we propose to break or smother the John Reeds and the Thorstein Veblens before they develop into dangerous reds?—HOWARD MUMFORD JONES[28]

The best way to write emphatic paragraphs is to present one's material according to some definite order. Exactly what that order should be cannot be predicted, for it will differ with every paragraph, the topic of every paragraph being different from that of its neighbors. It must, however, be a means of progression that will fit the subject matter at the same time that it presents the writer's idea, step by step, to the reader in such a way that both the idea and the steps are unobtrusive yet seemingly inevitable. In good writing, form and content are inseparable. The structure of the paragraph shapes the thought, providing it with form and meaning—or leaving it formless and confused. Again, as in the case of the individual sentence, it is the structure which determines the meaning.

---

[28] "Undergraduates on Apron Strings," *The Atlantic Monthly*, October, 1955. Reprinted by permission of the author.

¶7   LINKING PARAGRAPH TO PARAGRAPH

In the preceding sections, for purposes of discussion and analysis, we have treated the paragraph as a self-sufficient unit of expression. Normally, however, the paragraph is merely one in a series of paragraphs making up a report, an essay, or an article. A paragraph like the one following cannot be discussed in the terms employed in the preceding sections of this chapter, for it has a quite special function:

> The reconstruction foretold by Dewey in 1920 is now well on its way. It was launched when modern philosophy became rooted in scientific practice. The resulting intellectual revolution, reflected in the rise of operational philosophy, is now with us. It is this revolution and the postulated urgent necessity for pursuing it further that we intend to examine.—ANATOL RAPAPORT[29]

This paragraph is designed to serve only as a transitional paragraph between discussion of two major ideas—John Dewey's "reconstruction in philosophy" and the "intellectual revolution" of today.

A paragraph which begins with a sentence like "Take New England as an example" clearly looks backward to a preceding paragraph, immediately establishing its relationship to that paragraph, and is fully understandable only when read in the context of the whole:

> Any careful consideration of the urban regions and how they grow should make it quite plain that old concepts of regional planning just don't apply to them. As life in America becomes more and more urbanized, the sectional and historical boundaries which we have long taken for granted have less and less meaning.
>
> Take New England as an example. Southern New England has a great deal more in common with the New York–New Jersey area than with

---

[29] *Operational Philosophy.* Copyright, 1953, by Harper & Brothers, publishers.

any part of New Hampshire, Vermont, or Maine. In a part of the country whose resources consist largely of the skills of urban workers, it doesn't make much sense to apply the old concept of "regional resources" to planning. You can't foster the idea of an agrarian culture in Connecticut, for example, when the base of the culture has become urban. You are wasting your time when you hold onto the ideal of the small town (as television soap opera does and as politicians and popular novelists do) as the place where rural virtue persists, when the typical small town is merely part of a fringe area that sends its inhabitants as commuters to many different business and industrial centers. These are not people who live on the land; they live on the highway.—CHRISTOPHER TUNNARD[30]

Unity, coherence, and emphasis are as desirable qualities in a longer piece of writing as they are in a single paragraph—and perhaps are even more necessary. To achieve these qualities, writers employ various devices to link their paragraphs together: transitional paragraphs, repetition of words and phrases, parallel construction, summary sentences which point to the preceding paragraph, and forecasting sentences which anticipate forthcoming paragraphs. In the extended selection below, note the means by which Erich Fromm keeps his ideas flowing smoothly from paragraph to paragraph.

If it is true that the ability to be puzzled is the beginning of wisdom, then this truth is a sad commentary on the wisdom of modern man. Whatever the merits of our high degree of literary and universal education, we have lost the gift for being puzzled. Everything is supposed to be known—if not to ourselves then to some specialist whose business it is to know what we do not know. In fact, to be puzzled is embarrassing, a sign of intellectual inferiority. Even children are rarely surprised, or at least they try not to show that they are; and as we grow older we gradually lose the ability to be surprised. To have the right answers seems all-important; to ask the right questions is considered insignificant by comparison.

This attitude is perhaps one reason why one of the most puzzling

---

[30] "America's Super-Cities," *Harper's Magazine,* August, 1958. Reprinted by permission of the author.

phenomena in our lives, our dreams, gives so little cause for wonder and for raising questions. We all dream; we do not understand our dreams, yet we act as if nothing strange goes on in our sleep minds, strange at least by comparison with the logical, purposeful doings of our minds when *we are awake.*

When we are awake, we are active, rational beings, eager to make an effort, to get what we want and prepared to defend ourselves against attack. We act and we observe; we see things outside, perhaps not as they are, but at least in such a manner that we can use and manipulate them. But we are also rather unimaginative, and rarely—except as children or if we are poets—does our imagination go beyond duplicating the stories and plots that are part of our actual experience. We are effective but somewhat dull. We call the field of our daytime observation "reality" and are proud of our "realism" and our cleverness in manipulating it.

When we are asleep, we awake to another form of existence. We dream. We invent stories which never happened and sometimes for which there is not even any precedent in reality. Sometimes we are the hero, sometimes the villain; sometimes we see the most beautiful scenes and are happy; often we are thrown into extreme terror. But whatever the role we play in the dream *we* are the author, it is *our* dream, *we* have invented the plot.

Most of our dreams have one characteristic in common: they do not follow the laws of logic that govern our waking thought. The categories of space and time are neglected. People who are dead, we see alive; events which we watch in the present, occurred many years ago. We dream of two events as occurring simultaneously when in reality they could not possibly occur at the same time. We pay just as little attention to the laws of space. It is simple for us to move to a distant place in an instant, to be in two places at once, to fuse two persons into one, or to have one person suddenly be changed into another. Indeed, in our dreams we are the creators of a world where time and space, which limit all the activities of our body, have no power.

Another odd thing about our dreams is that we think of events and persons we have not thought of for years, and whom, in the waking state, we would never have remembered. Suddenly they appear in the dream as acquaintances whom we had thought of many times. In our sleeping life, we seem to tap the vast store of experience and memory which in the daytime we do not know exists.

Yet, *despite all these strange qualities,* our dreams are real to us while we are dreaming; as real as any experience we have in our waking life. There is no "as if" in the dream. The dream is present, real experience, so much so, indeed, that it suggests two questions: What is reality? How do we know that what we dream is unreal and what we experience in our walking life is real? A Chinese poet has expressed this aptly: "I dreamt last night that I was a butterfly and now I don't know whether I am a man who dreamt he was a butterfly, or perhaps a butterfly who dreams now that he is a man."

All these exciting, vivid experiences of the night not only disappear when we wake up; but we have the greatest difficulty trying to remember them.—ERICH FROMM[31]

EXERCISES

A.

The following passage is the beginning of an article explaining how certain experiments have led scientists to believe that vitamin K may help abolish tooth decay. Divide the passage into seven paragraphs, keeping in mind the principles of paragraph division as explained in sections ¶ 1 and ¶ 2:

If you had walked into some of the classes of Northwestern University Dental School back in 1942, you would have seen more than 100 pairs of jaws churning furiously on wads of chewing gum. The students were not flaunting rules; they were staging an unusual experiment, one of many that may improve the dental health of millions through the development of powerful weapons against tooth decay. As a result of the Northwestern chewing-gum orgy, scientists have uncovered the trail of an unusually promising—and pleasant—method of preventing cavities. They found that when a small amount of vitamin K is added to chewing gum, there is a significant decrease in decayed teeth. It is

---

[31] *The Forgotten Language.* Copyright, 1951, Rinehart & Company, Inc. Italics added.

believed that vitamin K cuts down on cavities by neutralizing enamel-dissolving acid in the mouth. Ever since man was first plagued by toothache, hundreds of explanatory theories have been put forward by authorities all over the world. The idea behind the action of vitamin K is the carbohydrate theory, which says that tooth decay is caused by particles of food, particularly starch and sugar, left in the crevices between the teeth. When these particles decompose, an acid is formed which dissolves the hard enamel, and decay sets in. Many studies were made to determine the destructive effect of carbohydrates, but proof was still needed. Subjects who had never eaten carbohydrates had to be found. Finally, a remote district in Alaska was decided upon as a promising starting point. Investigators flew to this lonely area and selected a large group of children who showed no evidence of cavities. To these youngsters the investigators offered the "blessings" of civilization in the form of candy bars and lollypops. The children were examined periodically and after six weeks 75 per cent had developed cavities. The high sugar diet was obviously the culprit. Another unusual case served to confirm dentists' suspicions about carbohydrates. The people of Korea, most of whom live on a limited diet, have few cavities. But investigators found one group of Koreans had a higher rate of dental decay than the others. These people, it was discovered, were working as servants in American and British homes. They had access to sugar, candy, and pastry, and the resulting acid brought on cavities. By this time, research laboratories were trying to discover something that would neutralize the acid. Out of these experiments are emerging a series of possible tooth preservers, led by the versatile vitamin K, basis of the tests at Northwestern University.—MARK L. WESTON[32]

B.

Each of the following paragraphs contains one sentence that violates the principle of paragraph unity. In each case, identify the irrelevant sentence.

1. There was a salt marsh that bounded part of the mill pond, on the edge of which, at high water, we used to stand to fish for minnows.

---

[32] Correctly divided, "Chew Your Toothaches Away." Reprinted from October, 1947, *Coronet*. Copyright, 1947, by Esquire, Inc.

By much trampling, we had made it a mere quagmire. My proposal was to build a wharf there fit for us to stand upon, and I showed my comrades a large heap of stones which were intended for a new house near the marsh and which would very well suit our purpose. The house was that of one of Boston's most eminent citizens, the merchant Peter Mason, whose philanthrophy was well known throughout New England. Accordingly, in the evening, when the workmen were gone, I assembled a number of my playfellows, and, working with them diligently like so many emmets, sometimes two or three to a stone, we brought them all away and built our little wharf. The next morning the workmen were surprised at missing the stones, which were found in our wharf. Inquiry was made after the removers; we were discovered and complained of; several of us were corrected by our fathers; and, though I pleaded the usefulness of the work, mine convinced me that nothing was useful which was not honest.

2. When Frank Norris came to Chicago in 1901 in order to gather background material for his novel dealing with grain speculation, he picked up more than the jargon of brokerage and the atmosphere of La Salle Street which were to give the required accurate, realistic finish to his tale: he found the basic action for *The Pit*. Norris and his young wife moved into the social and literary life of Chicago with great ease, forming many acquaintanceships during this period because of their amiability and good looks. Three years earlier, a bold attempt to corner the world's wheat market had come close to succeeding, and stories about the coup, executed by young Joseph Leiter, were still current in Chicago financial circles. For Norris's purposes, here was an almost perfect incident. What could better illustrate the concept of Wheat as Force than the story of one man battling the very earth, only to be eventually overcome by "that gigantic world-force, that colossal billow, Nourisher of the Nations"?

3. Some day an enterprising scientist will undertake a study of the problem which has baffled parents for many years. This problem is the mysterious chemical affinity between a pile of mud on the ground and the clothing of a young boy who has been sent out to play with the strict warning to keep himself clean. I offer my young brother as a good laboratory specimen, whenever such a scientist wants to get to work. There may be only one muddy place on our entire block, but

within ten minutes of his going out to play, it has somehow discovered him and crept up over his knees, his shirt, and even his chin. I must admit, in all honesty, that he is an attractive little ragamuffin when he is bespattered. But solving this minor puzzle, while not as important as discovering the polio vaccine, would certainly help frustrated mothers.

4. Shakespeare is, above all writers—at least above all modern writers —the poet of nature, the poet that holds up to his readers a faithful mirror of manners and of life. His characters are not modified by the customs of particular places, unpracticed by the rest of the world; by the peculiarities of studies or professions, which can operate but upon small numbers; or by the accidents of transient fashions or temporary opinions: they are the genuine progeny of common humanity, such as the world will always supply, and observation will always find. His persons act and speak by the influence of those general passions and principles by which all minds are agitated, and the whole system of life is continued in motion. This motion, this agitation and passion, gives to his plays that feeling of rapidity and excitement which distinguishes them from more slow-moving productions. In the writings of other poets a character is too often an individual; in those of Shakespeare it is commonly a species.

5. Those who have handled sciences have been either men of experiment or men of dogma. The men of experiment are like the ant; they only collect and use: the reasoners resemble spiders, who make cobwebs out of their own substance. But the bee takes a middle course, it gathers its material from the flowers of the garden and of the field, but transforms and digests it by a power of its own. Scientists have been unable to explain fully the biochemical processes by which this transformation is achieved. Not unlike this is the true business of philosophy: for it neither relies solely or chiefly on the powers of the mind, nor does it take the matter which it gathers from natural history and mechanical experiments and lay it up in the memory whole, as it finds it; but lays it up in the understanding altered and digested. Therefore from a closer and purer league between these two faculties, the experimental and the rational (such as has never yet been made), much may be hoped.

6. Many readers have grown timorous in their judgments since the all-pervading currency of criticism. They fear to express a revised, frank opinion about any new work, and to relish it honestly and heartily, lest it should be condemned in the next review, and they stand con-

victed of bad taste. Hence they hedge their opinions, like a gambler his bets, and leave an opening to retract, and retreat, and qualify, and neutralize every unguarded expression of delight, until their very praise declines into a faintness that is damning. This is indeed damning with faint praise.

7. How can a man be satisfied to entertain an opinion merely, and enjoy *it*? Is there any enjoyment in it, if his opinion is that he is aggrieved? If you are cheated out of a single dollar by your neighbor, you do not rest satisfied with knowing that you are cheated, or with saying that you are cheated, or even with petitioning him to pay you your due; but you take effectual steps at once to obtain the full amount, and see that you are never cheated again. There is nothing that is more disturbing to friendly neighborhood relationships than an argument over money. Action from principle, the perception and the performance of right, changes things and relations; it is essentially revolutionary, and does not consist wholly with anything which was. It not only divides States and churches, it divides families; and, it divides the *individual,* separating the diabolical in him from the divine.

8. No truer American existed than Thoreau. His preference for his country and condition was genuine, and his aversion to English and European manners and tastes almost reached contempt. He listened impatiently to news or *bon mots* gleaned from London circles; and though he tried to be civil, these anecdotes fatigued him. The men were all imitating each other, and on a small mold. Why can they not live as far apart as possible, and each be a man by himself? What he sought was the most energetic nature; and he wished to go to Oregon, not to London. Unfortunately, his travels did not take him west of the Mississippi River. "In every part of Great Britain," he wrote in his diary, "are discovered traces of the Romans, their funeral urns, their camps, their roads, their dwellings. But New England, at least, is not based on any Roman ruins. We have not to lay the foundations of our houses on the ashes of a former civilization."

C.

Analyze the organization and means of development in each of the following paragraphs. Point out what seem to you to be faults of organization if you find any paragraphs lacking in unity, emphasis, or coherence. Rewrite the faulty paragraphs.

1. It was a very narrow street—a ravine of tall, leprous houses, lurching towards one another in queer attitudes, as though they had all been frozen in the act of collapse. All the houses were hotels and packed to the tiles with lodgers, mostly Poles, Arabs and Italians. At the foot of the hotels were tiny *bistros*, where you could be drunk for the equivalent of a shilling. On Saturday nights about a third of the male population of the quarter was drunk. There was fighting over women, and the Arab navvies who lived in the cheapest hotels used to conduct mysterious feuds, and fight them out with chairs and occasionally revolvers. At night the policemen would only come through the street two together. It was a fairly rackety place. And yet amid the noise and dirt lived the usual respectable French shopkeepers, bakers and laundresses and the like, keeping themselves to themselves and quietly piling up small fortunes. It was quite a representative Paris slum.—GEORGE ORWELL[33]

2. After Adler and Jung withdrew from the "psychoanalytic movement," there followed several years in which Freud and his remaining followers continued to think along the lines of the earlier theories. Freud's contributions during this time were for the most part of a highly academic nature. To his theoretical speculations about the unconscious, instincts, narcissism, etc., he gave the name metapsychology. His other writings were in the field of applied psychoanalysis. There were numerous such attempts during this time to apply psychoanalytic principles in a theoretical way to literature, art and various other subjects. World War I for several years required the services of many analysts, thus temporarily turning their attention from their specialty. It was a period of growing pessimism about the therapeutic effectiveness of psychoanalysis. The methods of treatment then in use, chiefly the recall of childhood experience through free association, were seen to be often without therapeutic value. Freud himself had become most pessimistic by 1920. He still felt that analysis had much to contribute in theoretical understanding of human personality, but human nature had proved more unchangeable and intractable than he had supposed.
—CLARA THOMPSON[34]

[33] From *Down and Out in Paris and London*. Harcourt, Brace and Company, Inc. Copyright 1933 by George Orwell.

[34] *Psychoanalysis: Evolution and Development*. Copyrighted, Clara Thompson. Published by Thomas Nelson & Sons, New York.

3. Foreign actors, even when they are not better than native ones, by their proficiency in another style make us acutely conscious of our limitations, a state of mind which is the beginning of all improvement. To see the actors of the Comédie Française, now playing at the Broadway Theatre in Manhattan, is to become conscious of limitation in that tradition of acting which we may call naturalistic. Our actors chiefly sit, and when they sit, they lounge. These actors chiefly stand, though, when they sit, they sit well. When our actors do stand, they look for a raised surface to place one foot on; then they lean sagely forward and place an elbow on the raised knee. The French actors stand erect. There is a similar story to tell about arms. To our actors, an arm is an instrument to lean on things with, and the things leaned on are not always inanimate: some of our actors find it hard to keep their hands off their colleagues or even off themselves, for one arm can keep the other busy, and of course our modern costume is provided with an escape from the whole problem—the trouser pocket, the naturalistic actor's first and last refuge. The French actors never seem to lean on anything, and as for clinging to each other's bodies, they hardly ever even touch hands. They have taught their arms to cope with the circumambient air. One of our leading actors, faced with a classic script, once asked me: "But what is there for an actor to do?" He had noted the absence of cigarettes, drinks, food, spittoons . . . for of such is the kingdom of naturalism. The implicit answer in the work of the Comédie Française is: when there is nothing to do, do nothing. For example, there is a "meal" in *Le Bourgeois Gentilhomme* in which the actors neither eat nor pretend to. They just sit. For the focus of the action is elsewhere. Again, the American actor will say: "I can't stand there propping up the wall, give me something to do," while these fine French actors, when the focus is not on them, will contentedly stand to one side doing nothing, and their doing so would never raise a question in any spectator's mind; it is part of the game.—ERIC BENTLEY[35]

4. Man is a rational animal—so at least I have been told. Throughout a long life, I have looked diligently for evidence in favor of this statement, but so far I have not had the good fortune to come across it, though I have searched in many countries spread over three continents.

---

[35] *What Is Theatre?* Copyright, 1956, The Horizon Press, Inc.

On the contrary, I have seen the world plunging continually further into madness. I have seen great nations, formerly leaders of civilization, led astray by preachers of bombastic nonsense. I have seen cruelty, persecution, and superstition increasing by leaps and bounds, until we have almost reached the point where praise of rationality is held to mark a man as an old fogey regrettably surviving from a bygone age. All this is depressing, but gloom is a useless emotion. In order to escape from it, I have been driven to study the past with more attention than I had formerly given to it, and have found, as Erasmus found, that folly is perennial and yet the human race has survived. The follies of our times are easier to bear when they are seen against the background of past follies. In what follows I shall mix the silliness of our day with those of former centuries. Perhaps the result may help in seeing our own times in perspective, and as not much worse than other ages that our ancestors lived through without ultimate disaster.

—BERTRAND RUSSELL[36]

5. Most scholars are the product of that harsh but presumably necessary weeding-out process by which nature, or society, reduces the number of creative writers in every generation. The famous remark—was it Sainte-Beuve's?—to the effect that every man over forty carries a dead poet in his breast might have been made specifically of scholars. When a boy who likes to read books is in high school and college, he is going to be a writer—a journalist if he isn't aiming his sights too high, otherwise a critic like Edmund Wilson, a poet like T. S. Eliot, or a novelist like Thomas Wolfe. He probably gets some of his early efforts into print, in his school magazines and even in commercial publications. (An enterprising blackmailer, by the way, could do worse than dig up the novels and books of verse which today's eminent scholars published before they were thirty.) But somewhere along the line the aspiring artist realizes that the belly's crass demands take precedence over the fine frenzy of the spirit, and he must find some way of making a steady living. The obvious answer, since he can't live away from books, is to teach literature in what are somewhat dreamily called institutions of higher learning. To do so with any prospect of security and advancement he must have his Ph.D. So he goes to graduate school; and there

---

[36] "An Outline of Intellectual Rubbish," *Unpopular Essays.* Copyright, 1950, by Bertrand Russell. By permission of Simon and Schuster, Inc.

he hears about scholarship, rubs elbows with practicing scholars, is even encouraged to take a trial flight himself. Despite the agonies he suffers when he is writing his doctoral dissertation, scholarship gets into his blood. Slowly, and in most cases painlessly (as the new fascination of historical inquiry fastens itself upon him) the dream of becoming a litterateur fades away. What had been, at least to this point, a third-rate writer dies, and what may possibly become a first-rate scholar is born. In very rare cases—two that immediately come to mind are those of Douglas Bush and the late John Livingston Lowes—the writer does not die, but is gloriously assimilated in the scholar, the result being books of scholarly weight and precision which are also joys to read. In some cases, the writer lives on under an alias. It is a curious coincidence that both England and America today have well known specialists in the Elizabethan drama who turn out successful detective novels in their spare time.—RICHARD D. ALTICK[37]

6. During the fifty years between Salamis and the beginning of the Peloponnesian War, the supremacy of Athens increased considerably and seemed to be established for ever. Athens was the head of the Ionian league, which was gradually transformed into her own maritime empire. The Athenian and Attic festivals were the most famous and the most popular of Greece. In spite of its national eminence and its cosmopolitanism, the Athenian culture remained original and spontaneous. It was animated by pride in the present and faith in the future, naïve patriotism, and a good deal of self-conceit, mitigated by the love of discussion, such as is possible in times of peace and prosperity. Those fifty years were the golden age of Athens; we might compare them with the Elizabethan age of England, a period of about equal length (45 years, 1558–1603), and of equal enthusiasm. The last thirty years of that period were dominated by the personality of a great statesman, Pericles (499–429), and therefore it is sometimes called the Periclean age. It is better not to do so, however, for the Periclean age was not the whole of the golden age; it was the most fastuous part and perhaps the most creative, yet the original gold was already beginning to tarnish; spontaneity was being replaced by sophistication,

naïve conceit by skepticism, and dark clouds were gathering in the offing.—GEORGE SARTON[38]

7. The differences between the two types define themselves in every sphere. Thus while the redskin glories in his Americanism, to the pale-face it is a source of endless ambiguities. Sociologically they can be distinguished as patrician vs. plebeian, and in their aesthetic ideals one is drawn to allegory and the distillations of symbolism, whereas the other inclines to gross, riotous naturalism. The paleface is a "highbrow," though his mentality—as in the case of Hawthorne and James—is often of the kind that excludes and repels general ideas; he is at the same time both something more and something less than an intellectual in the European sense. And the redskin deserves the epithet "lowbrow," not because he is badly educated—which he might or might not be—but because his reactions are primarily emotional, spontaneous, and lacking in personal culture. The paleface continually hankers after religious norms, tending toward a refined estrangement from reality. The redskin, on the other hand, accepts his environment, at times to the degree of fusion with it, even when rebelling against one or another of its manifestations. At his highest level the paleface moves in an exquisite moral atmosphere; at his lowest he is genteel, snobbish, and pedantic. In giving expression to the vitality and to the aspirations of the people, the redskin is at his best; but at his worst he is a vulgar anti-intellectual, combining aggression with conformity and reverting to the crudest forms of frontier psychology.—PHILIP RAHV[39]

8. The Indian's personal canoe, ten to twelve feet long, could not be used for freight; the trade canoe was modeled on the larger war canoes of the Far Nations but had undergone a beautiful specialization and refinement. As far as Grand Portage, whether by the route up the St. Lawrence or the more laborious but faster one up the Ottawa River and down the Fench River to Lake Huron—as far as Grand Portage the carriage was by big *canots du maître*. These were up to six feet broad and up to thirty-five or even forty feet long. They could carry four tons of lading and a crew of fourteen, though eight or ten were more usual. After the packs had been taken across the nine-mile Grand Portage—a ten-day carry—they were loaded in *canots du nord,* which

---

[38] *A History of Science*. Copyright, 1952, Harvard University Press.

[39] "Paleface and Redskin," *Image and Idea*. Copyright 1949, 1952, by Philip Rahv. Reprinted by permission of New Directions.

averaged twenty-five feet long, had a crew of five to eight, and carried a ton and a half of lading. An intermediate size, not feasible in the far country, was the *canot bâtard* with a crew of up to ten; a "half canoe" was smaller than the *canot du nord,* say twenty feet. Canoes were usually painted and nearly always had designs in bright color at the bow.—BERNARD DE VOTO[40]

9. What does Jouvet stand for in the history of the French theatre? One is inclined to believe that he stands for experiment and an unremitting search for the basic values of the plays he produced and the methods needed to do them justice. Unlike Stanislavsky, Appia, Craig, Reinhardt, and Antoine, Jouvet recoiled from drawing up fixed sets of rules to which actors must adhere. He felt such rules could only hamper the creative expression of the actor. He therefore approached a script with all his sensibilities and, as far as humanly possible, with a mind devoid of personal, literary, or historical preconceptions. He relied on his experience to assess for him the rhythms of the dialogue and the structure of the play. He did not hesitate to follow the dictates of his intuition, if need be, for he realized that the truths of the theatre are not rational truths.—BETTINA L. KNAPP[41]

D.

Select one of your best recent themes for an intensive study of paragraphing. Follow these instructions, performing all except the last step upon the original draft of the theme:

I. Underline every topic sentence in it; if there is no topic sentence in any paragraph, supply one.

II. Analyze carefully each paragraph in the light of its topic sentence and cross out every detail and sentence which does not obviously belong in the paragraph.

III. See if the coherence within any paragraph is poor because of improperly arranged material. If so, mark the paragraph for revision.

IV. Go through the theme and draw a line *around* every transitional expression. If necessary, add transitional expressions.

---

[40] *The Course of Empire.* Copyright, 1951, by Houghton Mifflin Company.
[41] *Louis Jouvet, Man of the Theatre.* Copyright 1957, Columbia University Press.

V. Then draw two lines *under* every linking expression and, if necessary, revise any sentence that may need to be linked to another sentence.

VI. See especially that each paragraph is connected to the one preceding and to the one following by transition or by obvious linking. If it is not, revise the proper sentences.

VIII. Rewrite the whole theme, incorporating in the revision all corrections of paragraph structure you have made upon the first draft.

E.

Below are ten topic sentences. Select one and write three paragraphs, each having the same topic sentence, but each developed in a different manner. We realize, as you should, that this exercise is basically an artificial way of teaching you to write paragraphs; this exercise, however, is intended purely and simply as a drill, to make you conscious of the fact that there frequently is more than one way of saying the same thing:

1. Almost all my instructors teach their subjects only, without reference to the other courses I am taking.

2. I may have freedom of thought, but I had better keep the thought to myself.

3. Human beings generally think of the future as being like the present.

4. All colleges should offer a course entitled "How to Catch a Husband."

5. ——— is a highly overrated sport.

6. The automobile is mankind's worst enemy.

7. A greater threat to America than Communism is ———.

8. These are the times that try men's souls.

9. I read fiction to be entertained, not instructed.

10. We have no great humorists today.

F.

I. Select one chapter, or a portion of a chapter, from one of your textbooks for a study of paragraphing. Go through the following steps for each paragraph:

1. Underline the topic sentence; if there is no topic sentence, supply one. (Why was it omitted?)

2. Does the topic sentence always occur in the same place in each paragraph? Is the topic sentence always of the same kind? Note the variations, if any, in position and kind.

3. What means of development does the author use to amplify the topic sentence?

4. Is there any irrelevant material in the paragraph?

5. Encircle all transitional and linking devices *within* the paragraph.

6. Draw two lines under all devices which link the paragraphs *to each other.*

II. From a "quality" magazine select an article that is mainly expository. Perform the same paragraph analysis on this article as that described above in question I.

III. What significant differences in paragraph *length,* if any, do you find between the textbook and the magazine article?

IV. What significant differences in paragraph *technique,* if any, do you find between the textbook and the magazine article?

VIII | Organization: The Whole Theme

A student writer—or any other writer, for that matter—should try to remember that writing is an act of communication, of imparting to someone else the writer's own thoughts, experience, and sense impressions. His statements, consequently, must be arranged in such a manner and expressed in such a way that they will be clear to the reader. Any means the writer uses to aid this directness of communication is likely to make his writing better; anything that impedes directness of communication is almost certain to have the opposite effect.

At least part of the effectiveness of a piece of writing depends upon the unity and coherence of the work as a whole. These qualities of unity and coherence—as well as emphasis—depend, in turn, upon careful, intelligent organization. Unity is secured by adopting a definite plan of arrangement to avoid shifting points of view or illogical sequence of material, and by excluding all irrelevant subject matter and unnecessary statements. Coherence is secured by a logical arrangement of material, by the use of forecasting sentences and paragraphs, by the use of transitional expressions, and, in longer compositions, by the use of numerical and topical section headings. These rather broad generalizations are discussed, illustrated, and made more specific in the sections that follow.

01   CHOOSING A SUBJECT

In choosing a subject for essay or theme, the writer should keep in mind his own knowledge of and interest in the subject, the proposed length of the composition, and the probable knowledge and interest of his readers in the same subject. He will find it helpful to ask himself some direct questions: First, is the subject one the writer knows something about and in which he is interested? Second, is the subject one that can be handled within the assigned—or tentatively proposed—number of words? (Experience teaches a writer that he usually needs more words than he thinks he will.) Third, is the subject one in which the intended reader will be—or can be made to be—interested?

    A. The writer should choose subjects that can be developed fully within the assigned or proposed word limits. Even if no maximum word limit is set in the assignment, the student will find that by strictly limiting his subject, and then developing it fully, he can produce a better-organized, clearer piece of communication than he can when he chooses a large, vague, or broadly general subject. Many entire books have been written on such subjects as "International Relations," "Electricity," and "The Development of Television." It is of course foolhardy to expect to deal adequately with subjects like these in a paper of five or six hundred words, or even in one of three thousand words. If a student attempts to do so, he soon discovers, first, that he "doesn't know where to begin," and, second, that there is so much to say about the subject that he is unable to develop or explain the necessary divisions of the topic properly. He should be content to deal with a single (and, ordinarily, a very small) phase of any of the subjects mentioned above. "Early Experiments with Television," "Government Control of Television," "Educational Television at Our College," are parts of a general discussion that might be developed into separate essays; the first two of these topics would probably call for still further particularization.

What has just been said suggests the necessity of a writer's having a *thesis*—a central idea about which his essay or article is built. The selection of a definite topic for one's composition, rather than a broad or a vague topic, is a step in the right direction. But the unity of a piece of writing is made even more certain if the writer develops a specific point of view, or a particular idea or contention *about* the topic. If, for example, a writer on "Educational Television at Our College" formulates (either mentally or in writing) some such thesis as "Although certain departments at our college have already made a limited use of television, there are numerous other ways in which it can be used as an aid to instruction," and keeps this thesis clearly in view as he plans and develops his essay, he will be much more likely to "stick to his subject" and to develop it fully than he would be otherwise. Almost any composition, especially an expository composition, will be given greater unity by its writer's adherence to an explicitly stated thesis.

B. The writer should ordinarily choose subjects with which he is familiar and in which he has an interest. This does not mean that he should avoid fresh and original topics, or even, occasionally, strange and unusual ones; we are merely suggesting that he should, in general, abstain from writing about subjects that are outside *his* experience and knowledge, and in which he has no particular interest. By the time he reaches college, a student should have had enough experience (and remember that experience includes *all* of life—physical, intellectual, imaginative) to provide himself with many topics that are worth writing about, and that, with a little effort, can be communicated clearly, perhaps even vividly, to others. This is easier said than done, as students often remark. Of course it is. But most students will find that if for their themes they draw upon their own experiences—in the large sense indicated above—and if they make a reasonable effort to communicate these experiences to their readers, the problem of choosing a subject will gradually lose much of its difficulty.

Sometimes a student may be assigned a theme topic or required to do a piece of library research—assignments seemingly, or perhaps actually, outside his previous experience. In such instances, he needs to remind himself that these new areas of knowledge can usually be associated with something he already knows, and that they can be made into parts of his own experience. As he learns more about his subject, and as he thinks about it, he will often find himself becoming actively and vitally interested.

C. The writer should choose subjects that he can present clearly and interestingly to the reader. Writing, we have already said, is an act of communication, a two-way process. The writer must constantly remind himself that he has an obligation to be as clear, as precise, as interesting as possible, so that his readers—whether they are his instructors, his fellow students, or others—will be able to participate fully in *their* part of the act of communication. In choosing subjects, then, the writer will do well to select those that he can make clear, explicit, and meaningful.

02   CHOOSING THE MATERIAL

Only material relevant to a chosen subject, or that helps to clarify and illustrate the subject, should be included in a composition. Having selected a subject, the writer should analyze his material carefully, using only those facts, ideas, details, and examples that he considers pertinent or significant, and casting aside everything unnecessary to the development of the thesis or theme sentence.

A. If a composition is to give the reader an impression of unity, it should contain only relevant material. Every idea presented, each illustration used, should contribute something to the development of the announced topic; the reader should not be expected to perform the task of selection that properly belongs to the writer. Nor should the reader have to grope his way through illustrations that do not illustrate or

through passages that merely "add to the number of words" in
a theme.

WHAT IS WRONG WITH COLLEGE FOOTBALL

I. In the beginning, college football was a genuinely amateur sport.

II. As it has become increasingly commercialized, however, it has become less a game for the student than a professional spectacle designed to produce revenue at the box office.

III. A winning team is therefore a team which has been given the best hired hands; the schools which spend the most money on their teams normally have the best teams.

IV. Last year we had the worst season in our history.

V. Commercialization in college football has become so profitable that colleges playing big-time football cannot afford to have losing teams: on a single Saturday afternoon, the difference between fielding an outstanding or a poor team may mean a difference in gate receipts of more than $100,000.

The irrelevant material in this partial outline for a theme is that of topic IV; what is "wrong" with the student's own college team—why it doesn't win—is quite a different topic from the one he has undertaken to discuss.

WHERE I READ MY BOOKS

The earliest stories I heard and the first books I read are closely associated in my mind with particular pieces of furniture. There was one chair especially that soon became my favorite nook. It was a huge black rocking chair with wide arms and a soft-cushioned seat. I can still faintly remember the times I perched on one of the arms while Dad, sunk deep in the upholstery, told me the story of Peter Rabbit. From the same chair I also became acquainted with Reddy Fox, Big and Little Claus, and similar characters. *I suppose that all children have similar places they remember. Further, certain spots become especially dear to every adult. I have a friend, for example, who returns every year to the farm where he was born, not because he cares greatly for the farm, but because on it there is an old maple tree under which he used to lie and read. I might give ten or twenty instances to bear out the same idea, but that would be digressing, and I must return to the old armchair.*

The chair became a veritable home when I was able to read my own first book, *The Overall Boys*. . . .

The student who wrote "Where I Read My Books" should never have had to "return to the old armchair." The title of the theme is one that naturally emphasizes the personal element. But the writer, apparently thinking that he needed words to fill space, and forgetting about his title and his opening sentences, indulged himself in the reflections about favorite nooks of other children and of adults, and so destroyed the logical unity of the first paragraph and of the whole essay. If the topic chosen had been "Where Books Are Read," then the material would have been relevant.

B. If a composition is to give the reader an impression of unity, it should be written from a definite point of view. When, for any justifiable reason, a writer wishes to modify his point of view, he should always make his reason for the change clear to the reader.

WHY I PREFER A LARGE COLLEGE

I. The great variety of people at a large college makes it more interesting for me.

II. The superior quality of the entertainments a large college provides, whether in student activities or outside activities, has acquainted me with a quality of performance I never knew at home and would never have encountered in a small college.

III. The superiority of faculty and facilities in a large college gives me a chance to get better training for my future profession.

IV. It's true that one often gets lonely at a large college; no one here seems to care whether the average student lives or dies.

The title and the first three topics of this partial outline for a theme lead the reader to expect that the unifying viewpoint will be one of preferring large colleges. The fourth topic, however, strikes a discordant note, for it is quite different in tone from what has been said before. For an author to change his mind is no great sin, but he should do it before he begins to write and not after he is more than halfway through his essay.

On the other hand, some of the material in topic IV, *if properly subordinated*, might be used in a theme entitled "Why I Prefer a Large College" without violating the principle of definite point of view. The writer could begin his essay with: "Although I sometimes get lonely here and feel that no one cares whether I live or die, I am glad I came to a large college because it offers many advantages I could not have gotten at a small one." In such a sentence, the writer justifies his use of the "discordant note" by subordinating it (and letting the reader know that he has subordinated it) to his principal point of view. Let us repeat: every piece of expository writing should have a controlling purpose—a purpose made explicit by the writer, and communicated to the reader, through the formulation and development of a thesis or theme sentence.

03   ARRANGING THE MATERIAL

The material in a piece of writing should be so organized, in the light of the controlling purpose, that the relationship and importance of the various parts are made clear to the reader. Sometimes the subject matter may be arranged chronologically, and events discussed in the order in which they occurred. Sometimes the material may be arranged logically, and events or ideas discussed in some order not chronological—possibly from the familiar to the unfamiliar, from the general to the particular, from cause to effect, or from the less important to the more important. The exact method to be adopted will be determined by the subject, the material used to develop that subject, and the particular purpose of the piece of writing. Regardless of the method, however, the arrangement should be such that the relationship of ideas is apparent to the reader as he moves from one idea to another. In considering the following devices for indicating coherence, the writer must remember that any such guideposts are useless without a basic logical sequence of ideas.

A. The coherence of the theme as a whole may be made obvious by the use of a forecasting paragraph:

WHAT IS THOUGHT?

No words are oftener on our lips than *thinking* and *thoughts*. So profuse and varied, indeed, is our use of these words that it is not easy to define just what we mean by them. The aim of this chapter is to find a simple consistent meaning. Assistance may be had by considering some typical ways in which the terms are employed. In the first place, *thought* is used broadly, not to say loosely. Everything that comes to mind, that "goes through our heads," is called a thought. To think of a thing is just to be conscious of it in any way whatsoever. Second, the term is restricted by excluding whatever is directly presented; we think (or think of) only such things as we do not directly see, hear, smell, or taste. Then, third, the meaning is further limited to beliefs that rest upon some kind of evidence or testimony. Of this third type, two kinds—or, rather, two degrees—must be discriminated. In some cases, a belief is accepted with slight or almost no attempt to state the grounds that support it. In other cases, the ground or basis for a belief is deliberately sought and its inadequacy to support the belief examined. This process is called reflective thought; it alone is truly educative in value, and it forms, accordingly, the principal subject of this volume. We shall now briefly describe each of the four senses.— JOHN DEWEY[1]

This is the opening paragraph of the first chapter of Dewey's book *How We Think*. In the paragraph he sums up briefly the important points that he intends to take up, emphasizing them by *first, second,* and *third*. He then says that reflective thought will be the principal subject of his complete volume, and concludes by telling very definitely what he is going to discuss next. The paragraph is, in reality, a summary of his whole book and of the first chapter—a summary that enables the reader to understand exactly what is to come. Since student compositions are much shorter than book length, the forecasting paragraph will usually be much shorter, even a single sentence.

---

[1] *How We Think*. Copyright, 1910, by D. C. Heath and Company.

B. The coherence of the theme as a whole may be made obvious by the use of transitional and forecasting sentences:

FOUR TYPES OF LIBERALS

I shall first discuss the unthinking liberal who snatches at any idea that may be new . . . .

Having seen to what lengths this stupid liberal may proceed, I shall now attempt to portray a second type—he who emotionally but not intellectually chooses from among the new ideas those to which he can give his support . . . .

And now I must present a third type, the liberal who adopts theories only after he has examined them intellectually, but who keeps his emotions submerged when considering them . . . .

The fourth type is he who, forgetting neither the intellectual nor the emotional implications of all new ideas, considers the liberal theories from the theoretical and from the practical standpoint . . . .

In concluding, then, I wish to say . . . .

Although they make the structure of the theme thoroughly obvious, these examples of transitional and forecasting sentences are perhaps overformal. With experience, a writer learns to keep the reader aware of what has been done and what will be done without the reader's being made so conscious of his devices. If there is a choice between being overobvious and clear, or subtle and unclear, the writer should choose the first.

C. The coherence of the theme as a whole may be made obvious by the use of numerical or topical section headings within the article. Those that follow were used, with slight variations, in an essay by Durant Drake:

SELFISH BUSINESS

1. When May Business Be Called Selfish?

   .   .   .   .   .

2. What Harm Is Being Done to Employees?

   .   .   .   .

3. What Harm Is Being Done to the Public?

   .   .   .   .

4. Conclusions

. . . .

This specific labeling of the various large sections of an essay is somewhat formal, and is not recommended for class themes or other short papers. It is sometimes useful, however, in long articles that present a complex body of material. Section headings such as these merely indicate the broad divisions of a subject.

D. The coherence of the theme as a whole may be made obvious by the use of linking and transitional expressions:

In this process we waste a good deal of effort, first in making our data unrealistically accurate, and second in correcting our imperfectly realistic results. There is, however, another method which is now coming into use, and which finds its spiritual father in *Willard Gibbs*.

Gibbs pointed out that when a dynamical system develops according to its own laws as, for example, when a top spins freely, something occurs very much like *the flow of a fluid*. . . .

This flow may be conceived as a flow of probability, and so it was conceived by Gibbs. The probability that a particle will be at one time in a given region of this peculiar space is the same as that at a later time it will be in the corresponding region into which the first has flowed.

Thus the typical equation of flow is no longer a general system of what is known as ordinary differential equations but a set of integral equations. . . .

The method is quite practicable *computationally* . . . .

In addition to purely *computational* advantages in the more complicated cases, this method is also essentially superior to the Newtonian method of computation from the logical point of view. . . . This cuts down a lot of unnecessary effort, but it also increases the real *precision* of what we are doing.

No scientific measurement can be expected to be completely accurate, nor can the results of any computation with inaccurate data be taken as *precise*. The traditional Newtonian physics takes inaccurate observations, gives them an accuracy which does not exist, computes the results to which they should lead, and then eases off the precision of these results on the basis of the inaccuracy of the original data. The modern attitude in physics departs from that of Newton in that it works with inaccurate data at the exact level of precision with which they will be observed and tries to compute the imperfectly accurate results without going through any stage at which the data are assumed to be perfectly known.

If we follow in these *unprecise* problems . . . .

As I have said earlier in the description of my work on prediction . . . .

If *this recognition* of the statistical nature of all science is already proving to be valuable . . . .

Let us consider meteorology as one example. . . .—NORBERT WIENER[2]

The words italicized in the above selection are transitional expressions carrying the mind of the reader from one paragraph to another. Some of the expressions, it will be noted, carry back to what has already been said, while others carry forward either to a change in topic or to a continuation. But whether they carry backward or forward, they all help to reveal the relationship between ideas.

Some expressions that the writer may find helpful for this purpose are *also, another cause of, an exception, as has already been mentioned, equally important, for example, for this purpose, further, however, in consequence of, in fact, in other words, moreover, nevertheless, next, similarly, then, the foregoing, the result is, too.*

E. Lack of coherence may be caused by a shifting point of view and the lack of necessary transition:

OUR SUMMER COTTAGE

. . . and it is but a brief run from the porch, down across the green and well-kept lawn that is my father's pride, to the lake.

The living room is large, almost twice as large as the average. At one end is a fireplace, at the other, a row of bookcases . . . .

In the first paragraph, the conclusion of which is given above, the writer has been discussing the outside of the cottage. In the second paragraph, just as the reader feels he is about to jump into the lake, he discovers that he has landed in the living room.

---

[2] From *I Am a Mathematician* by Norbert Wiener. Copyright © 1956 by Norbert Wiener. Reprinted by permission of Doubleday & Co., Inc.

The reason for the shift might be made clear by inserting at the beginning of the second paragraph a sentence like "The inside of the cottage is as pleasant as are the outside surroundings." Reading the phrase "the inside of the cottage," the reader would then understand that the author has figuratively moved from the outside to the inside of the house.

F. Transitional expressions should not be overused. Convenient as they may seem, such expressions, when used too freely, give an impression of stiffness, even of awkwardness. A writer should strive first to organize his ideas so logically and to express them so clearly that their relation will be apparent without any obvious aid. Should the ideas become involved, however, or should there seem to be too great a gap between them, then a writer will find that a *judicious* use of transitional words and expressions will clarify his meaning.

04 THE OUTLINE

The unity, coherence, and emphasis of a composition are aided by the use of an outline—an arrangement of the major and minor topics of a subject, planned to show the order of treatment, the relationship of parts, and their relative importance. In its simplest form, an outline is a series of words or phrases, or a series of questions, or a combination of the two, that attempts to show the possible—and logical—divisions of the chosen subject.

Let us suppose that a class has been asked to write a short paper on the general topic "My Reactions to a Recent Experience." One student decides almost immediately that she will write about her last winter's trip to Florida, and asks herself the question: "How *did* I react to the experience?" Her answers, tentatively jotted down, look something like this:

I. At first, very excited
II. Later, rather bored
III. Toward the end, definitely homesick

Expanded into sentences, these ideas or "reactions" supply the writer with a useful framework for her theme:

I. The first two weeks everything was new and exciting.
II. The next three weeks everything became a bit stale.
III. The last week of my stay I was very homesick.

The completed theme, which follows, shows how the writer made use of this outline, which is of the topic sentence variety:

MY SIX WEEKS IN FLORIDA

I spent six weeks in Florida last winter. *The first two weeks everything was new and exciting.* The succession of warm sunny days was a constant source of pleasure. The tropic vegetation was strange and interesting. Picking coconuts, oranges, and bananas from trees in our patio was an adventure. The smell of the ocean, the salt taste of the spray, and the sight of the great waves curling up over the beach were all intoxicating.

The next three weeks everything became a bit stale. I could get up in the morning without having as my first thought, "I'm in Florida!" I could pick a grapefruit from a tree as nonchalantly as out of the icebox. I could eat outside in the pavilion without thinking exultantly, "It's snowing up North!"

The last week of my stay I was very homesick. Everything about Florida bored me. Even an exhibition of alligators aroused only a momentary interest. The warm weather fatigued me. The landscape became monotonous instead of stirring. I longed for my Northern friends and for the brisk, bracing days of a Northern winter. My one wish was to return home.—ELIZABETH HOLMES in a student theme

It will be seen that the process of outlining follows a recognizable pattern: (1) asking a question (or questions) about the subject; (2) answering the question (or questions) with words or phrases that indicate the logical divisions of the subject—its logical "topics"; and (3) expressing these topics in sentences that may be expanded into larger units—frequently paragraphs—of the finished composition. All writers go through this outlining process. The experienced writer who is planning a short piece of writing may do all the work in his head. He did not gain this facility by *not* making outlines in his earlier writing days; such planning has merely become habitual. If his finished product is well organized, he has, in one way or another, gone through the process described above. The less experienced writer will probably find that he can improve the organization of his themes and other papers by conscious attention to the details of the same process.

For longer papers a clearly conceived and definitely stated plan of organization is almost indispensable. An analytical outline—of one of the types illustrated below—will be of great help in organizing the complex material that goes into a research paper or other extended compositions.

In the analytical topic outline, the material is divided and subdivided into topics expressed as single words or as phrases. The topic outline that follows was planned by a student for a paper of approximately two thousand words. Note that, although analytically arranged, it gives relatively little indication of the exact content of the paper itself; compare it, in this respect, with the analytical sentence outline.

THE INSULIN TREATMENT OF DIABETES

I. Early research
   A. By von Mering and Minkowski
   B. By Langerhans

II. Work of Banting and colleagues
   A. Preliminary experiments
   B. Success in isolating insulin
   C. Nobel prize to Banting and colleagues

III. The insulin treatment
   A. Methods
      1. Injection
      2. Dosage
   B. Results
      1. Control of symptoms
      2. Effects in severe cases

IV. Conclusions

In the analytical sentence outline, the topics and subtopics are expressed in sentences. This form gives a clearer indication of the development of thought, in detail, than does the topic out-line. For this reason, it is usually the more valuable type of out-line.

THE INSULIN TREATMENT OF DIABETES

Theme statement: In man's prolonged warfare with disease, the discovery and perfection of the insulin treatment of diabetes constitutes a major victory in one campaign.

I. Several nineteenth-century scientists carried on research that prepared the way for the discovery of insulin.

    A. Among those who developed methods that proved useful were von Mering and Minkowski.

    B. Paul Langerhans discovered the islands, or cell bunches, in the pancreas—a discovery of great importance in further research on diabetes.

II. The principal research that led to the discovery and use of insulin in the treatment of diabetes was done by Frederick G. Banting and his colleagues at the University of Toronto.

    A. In a series of early experiments in 1921, on animals, Banting encountered alternate successes and disappointments.

    B. In 1922, with the help of Charles H. Best, he succeeded in isolating the hormone insulin and used it in the treatment of diabetes in human patients.

    C. For his achievement, he was joint recipient (with J. J. R. Mac-Leod) of the Nobel prize for physiology and medicine.

III. The discovery of insulin has brought about great changes in the treatment of diabetes and in the control of the disease.

    A. Insulin must be administered carefully.

        1. It has to be introduced, by hypodermic injection, into the body; it cannot be taken by mouth.

        2. Dosages must be regulated according to the requirements of the individual patient.

    B. When properly administered, insulin has proved to be very effective in the control of diabetes.

        1. Patients who receive insulin treatment regularly, under medical direction, lose most of the symptoms of the disease.

        2. Insulin treatment has saved many lives, even of patients who had been given up as "hopeless."

IV. Because of the discovery and use of insulin, medical science has made great progress in at least one area, and the extension of its use to other areas is an object of continuing experiments.

In making any type of outline, a writer should follow certain principles of consistency and clearness:

       A. Parallel topics should be expressed in parallel form.

Nonparallel:

A. The unpleasant part of selling newspapers
B. But selling newspapers is often very pleasant work.

Parallel:

A. The unpleasant part of selling newspapers
B. The pleasant part of selling newspapers

or

A. Selling newspapers is frequently very unpleasant work.
B. It may also, sometimes at least, be very pleasant.

       B. Each topic should have at least two subtopics or none; it should not have just one. If the minor topic is so important that it must be mentioned, it may be expressed in the major topic, or it may be accompanied by another minor topic. A writer should not go out of his way to find neat pairs or trios of subtopics for each major topic; only when he discovers that a topic lends itself logically to division should he indicate an act of division.

Illogical:

I. The preparations for painting the automobile are simple.
    A. The body should be washed thoroughly.
II. The first coat of paint should be very thin.

Logical:

I. The preparations for painting the automobile, which include washing the body thoroughly, are simple.

II. The first coat of paint should be very thin.

or

I. The preparations for painting the automobile are simple.
    A. The body should be washed thoroughly.
    B. The old coat of paint should be sandpapered.
II. The first coat of paint should be very thin.

C. Guard against placing subordinate material in the same rank as important material and placing important material in a subordinate position.

Illogical:

I. This kind of cloth is affected by several things.
    A. The sunshine damages it.
    B. It causes the colors to fade.
    C. It causes the white portions to turn yellow.
    D. Water also causes the goods to deteriorate.

The general topic, I, shows that the subject to be discussed will be the things that affect cloth; consequently the major topics should be arranged to show what the damaging agents are. Obviously, A and D indicate these agents. Less important, and applying only to A, the damage done by the sunshine, the subtopics B and C are erroneously placed so that they seem to be as important as A. They should, of course, be indented to show that they are only minor statements explaining the damage done by the sunshine.

Logical:

I. This kind of cloth is affected by several things.
    A. The sunshine damages it.
        1. It causes the colors to fade.
        2. It causes the white portions to turn yellow.
    B. Water causes the goods to deteriorate.

If, in the outline above, topic B were placed as subtopic 3 under A, the result would be *false* subordination.

D. Do not burden an outline with illustrations, examples, or other superfluous details. Remember that the topics of an outline represent ideas that are to be developed in the finished composition; the process of elaborating these ideas—by facts, figures, examples, and other details—should be reserved for the theme itself. An outline—which is, after all, merely a plan showing the relative importance and logical relationships of ideas —should be kept as simple and as clear as possible.

E. Arrange the indention of the topics in the order of their importance by indenting topics of equal importance an equal distance from the left-hand side of the page, and immediately beneath the beginning of the first line begin the second line of a topic that is too long to be contained on one line.

Confusing:

I. I like to live near the seashore because of the pleasant sounds I can hear.
A. In the early morning I sometimes hear the incoming tide slap its way up the beach.
1. Although I am frequently too lazy to get out of bed to see it, I can imagine the progress of the tide by the increasing ease with which I can hear it.
2. When my ears tell me that the tide is completely in, I know that it is time for me to get up.
B. At the same time I can hear the sea breeze blowing through the shrubs outside my window.

Clearer:

I. I like to live near the seashore, because of the pleasant sounds I can hear.
   A. In the early morning I sometimes hear the incoming tide slap its way up the beach.
      1. Although I am frequently too lazy to get out of bed to see it, I can imagine the progress of the tide by the increasing ease with which I can hear it.
      2. When my ears tell me that the tide is completely in, I know that it is time for me to get up.

B. At the same time I can hear the sea breeze blowing through the shrubs outside my window.

       F. The most commonly accepted system of symbols to indicate the rank of topics is, in the order of their importance, the Roman numeral, the capital letter, the Arabic numeral, and the small letter.

Example:

I.
   A.
     1.
       a.
       b.
     2.
     3.
   B.
II.
   A.
     1.
     2.
   B.

05   THE TITLE

A good title should describe a composition by indicating the material contained therein, and, at the same time, should catch the interest of the reader by being relatively brief, attractively phrased, and original. Of several books or articles on the same *subject,* each may and probably will have a different *title.* By dictionary definition, a title is a "distinctive designation of a written or printed production." As a *designation* of the subject, the title of a theme or other article should not be too broad, but should show just what part of a broad subject is dealt with in the paper. As a *distinctive* designation, the title should attempt to distinguish the particular treatment from other treatments of the same subject. And, as a device to attract the reader, the title should not be merely clever or unusual, but should have some direct application to the subject.

A. A title should be definite. If a title is to designate, it should be specific, rather than broad; precise, rather than general. When preparing a paper, a writer will find that the use of a definite "working title"—a title that describes the probable content of the composition, but that may be discarded for a more attractive one later on—is of real assistance in delimiting the aim and the scope of the article. The title eventually chosen, whether the "working title" or another one, should clearly tell the reader what aspect or aspects of a general subject are dealt with in the paper.

THE AIM OF A UNIVERSITY EDUCATION

Cardinal Newman shows the limitations of one of his essays by giving it this title. Consider how much less exact the caption would have been had the writer called his essay "A University Education" or "The Aim of Education."

THE CAUSES OF POLITICAL INDIFFERENCE TODAY

Instead of vaguely labeling his essay "Political Indifference," Walter Lippmann shows by the use of the above title that he has limited his discussion to the causes of political indifference as they appear in our times.

THOMAS WOLFE LECTURES AND TAKES A HOLIDAY

William Braswell so designates an essay that might have been called, far less precisely, "Episode in an Author's Life."

B. A title should be distinctive. As suggested above, the first requirement of a title is that it should be definitive, revealing at a glance something about the content of the particular composition that it heads. But a title may be something more than an informative caption; it may distinguish one writer's theme or essay—or any other form of writing—from compositions on the same topic by other writers. A distinctive title may also attract a reader's attention much more quickly and more certainly than will a merely informative heading.

A word of warning is in order here. A writer should not forget that a title—whatever its other qualities—should be *appropriate*. Among the factors that determine appropriateness are form of the writing (short story, technical article, personal essay, poem, novel); tone of the writing (serious, humorous, hortatory, whimsical); and probable audience (children, adults, "general" readers, specialists). Obviously, it would be inappropriate to give a flippant title to a serious discussion of a serious question. It would be equally inappropriate to give a flat, unimaginative title to a light, humorous personal essay, unless, of course, such a title were itself used as a humorous device. No general "law" can be formulated about the appropriateness or inappropriateness of titles; this is a question that the individual writer will have to answer for himself in the light of the various factors mentioned previously.

PROSPECTING FOR DESERT PICTURES

This title was used by Bernard Freeman for an article in the magazine *Popular Photography*. He might have called his article, tritely, "Helpful Hints for Desert Photography," but the more distinctive title chosen attracts the reader with the word "prospecting," which suggests that a photographer, like a gold hunter, may find adventure and reward in the desert.

RINGSIDE SEATS

Katharine Fullerton Gerould went to a championship prize fight; instead of labeling her account of what she saw there with an explicit but rather uninteresting title like "When I Went to a Prize Fight," she chose to use a phrase that would catch the attention of the reader because of its common usage among followers of boxing.

AMID THE ENCIRCLING GLOOM

When Howard Mumford Jones wrote an essay, some years ago, about the widespread lack of cheerfulness in modern literature, he gave it this title—a phrase from the well-known hymn, "Lead, Kindly Light." Such a title, although it only hints at the probable content of the essay, arouses the curiosity of the reader, who is led to wonder what application the familiar phrase may have to the discussion that follows. The "literary" title—quoted from prose, or, more often, poetry—may be very effective in stimulating reader interest, but it should be used cautiously. A title of this kind should have some clear connection with the writing that it heads; and it should be a moderately familiar phrase, for a reader may be annoyed rather than interested by a title that is merely esoteric. On the other hand, one should avoid phrases that frequent use has made *too* familiar.

ARMS AND THE MEN

The editors of *Fortune,* having prepared an article on the individuals who control the international armaments industry, gave their study the above title—a clever variation on G. B. Shaw's *Arms and the Man,* which, in turn, is based on a phrase from the opening line of Virgil's *Æneid.* This title, it may be pointed out, is not merely clever; it is also terse, euphonious, and sufficiently descriptive.

C. A title should be relatively brief. A short title is much more likely to attract attention and to be remembered than a long, cumbersome one. Although explicitness should not be sacrificed for the sake of brevity alone, it should be remembered that a title is supposed to be a "distinctive designation," and not a detailed description of the essay or other writing that it denominates.

MAKING CAMP

Stewart Edward White chose this brief, simple title, rather than an involved statement like "How to Put Up a Tent, Make a Comfortable Bed, and Get a Fire Started."

THE COMEDY OF LEADERSHIP

This is the title Christian Gauss gave to an article on a subject that might have been described, lengthily and awkwardly, as "The Foolishness of Thinking We Can Educate Every College Boy to Be a Leader."

THE GREAT SPORTS MYTH

John R. Tunis so entitled an essay the general theme of which is "Contrary to General Opinion, Our Modern System of Sports Is Not Beneficial to Either the Athlete or the Spectator." It is obvious that a complete statement of the theme would have made an unwieldy, almost absurd, title.

06   THE INTRODUCTION

The introduction should explain the purpose or point of view of the writer and should attempt to interest the reader in the subject.   By defining the scope and by limiting the idea, the introduction should establish the mood or tone of a composition, so that the reader may be prepared for what is to follow. By quickly securing the interest of the reader in some way, it should induce him to continue beyond the opening paragraph to find out what the author has to say about his chosen subject.

It should not be supposed that all papers, especially brief ones, need formal introductory or concluding paragraphs. An opening sentence or two is frequently all that is needed by way of introduction. When the essay is short—or even, indeed, when it runs to some length—it is usually better for the writer to get to his subject immediately, without any elaborate overture. Note that in most of the specimen introductions that follow, much of the material bears directly on the subject of the essay or chapter that is being introduced.

A. An introduction may briefly summarize material to be more fully developed in the paragraphs which follow:

The English newspaper developed in the late seventeenth century out of the political pamphlet and the newsletter. The English magazine developed out of the newspaper within less than fifty years after the first newspaper was founded.—JAMES P. WOOD[3]

B. An introduction may simply forecast:

THE SOCIAL VALUE OF THE COLLEGE-BRED

Of what use is a college training? We who have had it seldom hear the question raised—we might be a little nonplussed to answer it off-hand. A certain amount of meditation has brought me to this as the pithiest reply which I myself can give: The best claim that a college education can possibly make on your respect, the best thing it can aspire to accomplish for you, is this: that it should help you to know a good man when you see him. This is as true of women's as of men's colleges; but that it is neither a joke nor a one-sided abstraction I shall now endeavor to show.—WILLIAM JAMES[4]

William James spends no time in explaining the purpose of his address, or in explaining just what he is going to discuss. He asks a question, gives his answer to it, and states, succinctly and clearly, that he is going to show why his statement about the value of college training is true.

C. An introduction may limit and forecast:

Biology sets its limits, but within them society forms its human personality. How is this done? What is the psychological cost of making men

---

[3] James Playsted Wood, *Magazines in the United States,* Second Edition. Copyright 1956, The Ronald Press Company.

[4] "The Social Value of the College-Bred." An address delivered at Radcliffe College, 1907.

fit a society? These are questions to which our first four chapters are devoted.—RALPH ROSS AND ERNEST VAN DEN HAAG[5]

D. An introduction may forecast and explain the significance of the discussion to follow:

To the casual reader of newspapers, organized labor tends to be identified with large organizations such as AFL-CIO, United Auto Workers, United Mine Workers, etc., with a few outstanding personalities such as John L. Lewis or Walter Reuther, and with dramatic events such as union mergers and strikes. This is not surprising; these organizations, persons, and events are newsworthy. However, headlines are often misleading both as to the motives for and the consequences of the actions of unions and their leaders. To understand what is happening, it is essential that we know the more prosaic and fundamental characteristics of unions, their members, and their leaders.—MELVIN W. REDER[6]

E. An introduction may arouse interest by the use of an anecdote:

One day in the 1930's Jesse Straus, in a hurry to get to his office on Macy's thirteenth floor, stepped into a customer elevator and stood quietly at the rear of the crowded car.

"Going UP!" announced James Cumberbatch, the operator. "Car going to the NINTH floor . . . This car goes only to the NINNNTH floor!"

At the ninth floor everybody got out except Mr. Jesse.

"Everybody out, sir!" sang James Cumberbatch, who had not recognized him. "Going DOWN . . . Car going DOWNNN!"

"I want to go UP," said Mr. Jesse.

"Sorry, sir, this car goes only to the ninth floor. Going DOWN!"

"I'm Jesse Straus," explained Jesse Straus.

"Going UP! Car going UP!" said James Cumberbatch at once.

It is unlikely that such an instance of one-man authority would occur

---

[5] *The Fabric of Society.* Copyright, 1957, by Harcourt, Brace and Company, Inc.

[6] Reprinted with permission from Melvin W. Reder, *Labor in a Growing Economy.* Copyright 1957, John Wiley & Sons, Inc.

in Macy's today. In industry everywhere the day of the individualist
is over. . . .—MARGARET CASE HARRIMAN[7]

**F. An introduction may establish the tone or mood
of an essay:**

OLD SONGS

I like an old song. It is the freshest piece of antiquity in existence;
and is, moreover, liable to no selfish individual appropriation. It was
born far back in the traditionary times, so that its parentage is somewhat
equivocal; yet its reputation suffers not on that account, and it comes
down to us associated with all kinds of fond and endearing remi-
niscences. It melted or gladdened the hearts of our forefathers, and has
since floated around the green earth, finding a welcome in every place
humanized by a ray of fancy or feeling, from "throne to cottage hearth."
It has trembled on the lips of past and forgotten beauty; and has
served, in countless wooings, as the appropriate medium for the first
fearful breathings of affection. The youthful maiden has broken the
silence with it in many a lovely, lonely dell; and the shepherd has
chaunted it on the still hill side. The rude sailor has filled up the pauses
of his watch by whistling it to the shrill winds and sullen waters; and
it has bowed the head, brought the tear to the eye, and recalled home
and home thoughts to the mind of many a wanderer on a distant shore.
It has been heard in the solitudes of nature, and at the crowded, festive
board. . . . Yet, a true-bred, moth-eaten antiquary would sacrifice it, if
he could, for a copper coin fifty years its senior!—WILLIAM COX[8]

The informal style of the introduction to "Old Songs" immediately suggests that Cox, when he wrote it, more than a century
ago, was in a sentimental, reminiscent mood, and that he intended to convey this mood to the reader. A comparison of this
introduction with that of William James to "The Social Value
of the College-Bred" will show the difference in tone of the two.
Cox's is imaginative, gentle; James's is logical, direct, vigorous.
Both pieces successfully continue the moods established in the
introductions.

---

[7] *And the Price Is Right.* Copyright 1958 by Margaret Case Harriman. Reprinted by permission of The World Publishing Company.
[8] *Crayon Sketches* (1833).

G. Occasionally, an introduction may startle the reader into awareness through the use of a dramatic or shocking first sentence:

Serious music is a dead art.

The vein which for three hundred years offered a seemingly inexhaustible yield of beautiful music has run out. What we know as modern music is the noise made by deluded speculators picking through the slag-pile.

This is not to say that there will not continue to be orchestra concerts, recitals, and opera. But the time has come to recognize that Carnegie Hall, Town Hall and the Metropolitan Opera House, as well as their counterparts in other cities of the Americas and Europe, are just as surely museums as the National Gallery and the Louvre.—HENRY PLEASANTS[9]

H. An introduction may arouse interest by the use of some such method as the following:

WALT WHITMAN'S REALISM

The butcher-boy puts off his killing-clothes, or
    sharpens his knife at the stall in the market.
I loiter enjoying his repartee and his shuffle
    and break-down.
Blacksmiths with grimed and hairy chests environ
    the anvil,
Each has his main-sledge, they are all out, there
    is a great heat in the fire.

These lines illustrate forcibly why their author has sometimes been referred to as a pioneer in poetic realism. From the reading of Whitman's poetry one cannot help feeling that realism is one of his notable qualities. He seeks, not to cover up his true sentiments concerning people and things, but, rather, to present them to his readers just as he sees them, devoid of the artificial ornamentation often used by other poets. It can hardly be said that his poetry is always beautiful in the "poetic" sense of the word, but it can most assuredly be said

---

[9] *The Agony of Modern Music.* Copyright 1955, by Henry Pleasants. Reprinted by permission of Simon and Schuster, Inc.

that it is beautiful in its vitality, its truth, and its adherence to much that is real. It is my purpose in this paper to discuss this peculiar beauty in Whitman's poetry, and to show how he achieves it by his choice of subject matter, by his use of forceful and apt language, by his striking imagery, and by his sometimes unconventional sentence structure.—STUDENT THEME

This writer makes his first bid for the reader's attention by giving a quotation typical of Walt Whitman's poetry; this quotation catches the eye and arouses the reader's curiosity as to why poetry should be at the beginning of an essay. Then, in an attempt to tell the reader why the quotation has been given, the author discusses briefly some of Whitman's main characteristics. Finally, to make certain that his point of view and purpose are understood, the writer bluntly states not only the purpose of the essay, but also the plan of organization by which he intends to develop his theme.

I. The subject of an expository theme is normally mentioned in the introductory paragraph, not simply by a pronoun referring to the title. It will be noted that in none of the introductory paragraphs quoted above is there any direct reference to the title of the whole essay. Each composition begins in such a manner that were the title omitted the reader might still understand what the author's subject is, how he is going to develop it, and what attitude he is going to take.

1) Introductory sentence dependent upon title:

A COMMENT ON LEACOCK'S "HOMER AND HUMBUG"
This is a very persuasive essay. The author presents his point of view so humorously, and, at the same time, so convincingly, that one is almost forced into what Coleridge called "a willing suspension of disbelief". . . .

2) Introductory sentence self-explanatory:

A COMMENT ON LEACOCK'S "HOMER AND HUMBUG"
Stephen Leacock's essay "Homer and Humbug" is very persuasive. The author presents his point of view so humorously, and, at the same

time, so convincingly, that one is almost forced into what Coleridge called "a willing suspension of disbelief". . . .

07   THE CONCLUSION

The conclusion of a piece of writing should round out the thought and bring the central idea to a close in such a way that a definite impression is left in the reader's mind.   Since the last words will probably linger in the reader's mind longer than the others, the conclusion shoud be the climax of all the author has to say, either a summary, in fresh and forceful language, of what has gone before, or the author's as yet unexpressed inferences to be drawn from the facts or ideas previously expressed. *The conclusion should never be long and drawn out, should never contain irrelevant material, and should avoid high-flown and far-fetched moralizing.*

A. A conclusion may contain summary and prediction:

The waste of natural resources and the resistance to technological change are but two instances of the price we have paid for ignoring the long-range values of the intellectual approach to life. Without the essential elements of that approach, the reflection and well-considered planning of which Turner spoke, we can look forward to the prospect of further penalties induced by heedlessness and waste in whatever fields they may appear. Changes for the better can be effected only when the realization becomes general that the virtues and resources of the thinking mind are not confined to vague theorizings and distant abstractions but operate effectively within the world of everyday matter. As that realization occurs, much of the antipathy to culture and men of ideas will disappear.—LEO GURKO[10]

---

[10] From *Heroes, Highbrows and the Popular Mind*, by Leo Gurko, copyright © 1953, used by special permission of the publishers, The Bobbs-Merrill Company, Inc.

B. A conclusion may contain a recapitulation:

WHAT IS A COLLEGE FOR?

It is our present purpose merely to be clear what a college is for. That, perhaps, I have now pointed out with sufficient explicitness. I have shown the incompatability of the present social organization of our colleges with the realization of that purpose only to add emphasis to the statement of what that purpose it. Once get that clearly established in the mind of the country, and the means of realizing it will readily and quickly be found. The object of the college is intellectual discipline and moral enlightenment, and it is the immediate task of those who administer the colleges of the country to find the means and the organization by which that object can be obtained. Education is a process and, like all processes, has its proper means and machinery. It does not consist in courses of study. It consists of the vital assimilation of our knowledge; and the mode of life, for the college as for the individual, is nine parts of the digestion.—WOODROW WILSON[11]

The conclusion of Wilson's essay illustrates admirably the manner in which an article may be summed up in the concluding paragraph by a recapitulation of the points that have been emphasized. The last sentence should be noted, for it is an attempt to close the essay with a comparison between the life of a college and of an individual, and to make that comparison one that may be familiar enough to the reader to be understood, yet striking enough to remain in the mind long after the main body of the essay has been forgotten.

C. A conclusion may contain inferences drawn from facts or ideas already presented:

In later chapters, a great deal will be added to these remarks. For the present, the considerations we have taken up regarding the doubtful validity of the artificial psychosocial tests, and regarding the conditions (*a* to *h*) additionally damaging their adequacy, are sufficient to justify a strongly skeptical attitude towards the scientific nature of these tests. All in all, they are hardly more scientific than the old-fashioned tea-leaf

---

[11] "What Is a College For?" *Scribner's Magazine*, November, 1909. Copyright, Charles Scribner's Sons, publishers.

or coffee-grounds tests. Modern testomania is mainly a new form of the old belief in omens. This verdict is well corroborated by a closer examination of the main modern tests and by an inductive testing of the tests themselves.—PITRIM A. SOROKIN[12]

The conclusion to Professor Sorokin's chapter attacking the validity of psychological tests not only draws the inference from his previous data but also, as is clear, looks ahead to the next chapter.

EXERCISES

A.

Write a one-paragraph comment on the suitability, for a five- or six-hundred-word theme, of each of the following topics. Suggest means of narrowing the subjects that now seem too broad:

1. American Foreign Policy
2. The Revival of Religion
3. Housing Projects
4. Professional Football
5. Symbolism in Modern Poetry
6. Milwaukee
7. The Automobile Industry in America
8. The Challenge of Communism
9. What a Summer's Work in a Factory Meant to Me
10. Liberty and Democracy

B.

Rewrite each of the following units, omitting all irrelevant material:

THE ADVANTAGES OF THE NAVY OVER THE ARMY FOR THE DRAFTEE

I. The food was superior.
II. The Navy expanded greatly during World War II.

---

[12] Reprinted from *Fads and Foibles in Modern Sociology* by Pitrim Sorokin, copyright 1956 by Henry Regnery Company.

III. Even on the smallest ships the sailor had a bed to sleep in and a place to wash.

IV. Everyone knows that the Navy was a superior, if smaller, outfit.

V. The total number of casualties in the Navy was less than in the Army.

VI. Because there were, proportionately, many more ratings in the Navy than in the Army, there was much less chance of having to remain a seaman in the Navy than a private in the Army.

THE POPULARITY OF HISTORICAL FICTION

A type of fiction that has been perennially popular since the days of Scott's Waverley novels is the historical romance. There are many examples of the continuing popularity of the story that re-creates a forgotten era. One immediately thinks of Hervey Allen's *Anthony Adverse,* of Margaret Mitchell's *Gone with the Wind,* and of more recent titles like Steen's *The Sun Is My Undoing,* Costain's *The Black Rose,* Shellabarger's *Captain from Castile,* and Waltari's *The Egyptian.* Not long ago, I read the last-named of these novels, and I must say that it is difficult for me to see why it became a best seller. Presumably, a great many people bought it and liked it, but it certainly did not appeal to me. I found it very dull, and though I managed to finish reading it, I was sorry that I spent so much time on it. The approach to the materials of historical fiction is now likely to be more realistic than it was a generation or two ago, but novels of this class still represent, in one way or another, the romantic escape from the conditions of modern life. By the method of conscious or unconscious contrast, they reflect the uncertainties of the period in which they are written, and provide readers a temporary release from worrying about such uncertainties. Though not the only reason, this is surely an important reason for the great popularity of historical romances.

ECONOMIC BACKGROUNDS OF EARLY AMERICAN NATIONALISM

In the post-Revolutionary era, the commerce and manufacture of the thirteen states were in disastrous shape. The war had brought with it enormous governmental debts that the Continental Congress had endeavored to pay for with paper money. At one time, the amount in circulation reached the figure of a hundred million dollars. Then came inflation to such an extent that the paper dollar became almost worthless. Clearly, there is a lesson for the modern world in what happened after the Revolution.

Because of the lack of a sound medium of exchange, commerce and manufactures dwindled almost to the vanishing point. Crops rotted in the ground for want of an incentive to market them. In addition, the various states erected toll and tax barriers to hamper interstate trade in a way that is almost incomprehensible to us today. We now realize that if such trade is to be encouraged, there must be as few barriers of this sort as are consistent with the well-being of local industries, that there must be economic co-operation among the states, and there must be common understanding of the economic problems that confront all political divisions of the nation.

After the Revolution, there was an increasing demand among the conservative segment of the population—the landed and moneyed gentry—that cut across all sectional interests. The Southern planters and the Northern merchants were as one in their desire for a strong central government to put down disorders and restore the country's economic life to a strong foundation, backed by a stable currency. On the other side were the agrarians and the debtor class who strongly resented any encroachments on home rule and fought for a relaxation of the laws that favored the creditor class. In both cases, however, common interests overshadowed sectional differences; consequently, lines were arrayed on a more or less national front.

C.

I. Rewrite each of the following units, arranging the material in logical order:

HOW TO PREPARE FOR A FINAL EXAMINATION

  I. It is more important to get enough sleep the last night before an examination than to wear oneself out cramming.

 II. Unless the student has kept up with his work throughout the semester, it is very possible that all of his last-minute preparations may be wasted.

III. The three or four days preceding the examination are the time the student should do his most concentrated studying.

IV. At periodic intervals during the semester, the student should review the materials of the course up to that point.

THE SATIRE OF GILBERT AND SULLIVAN

I. William S. Gilbert's poems, ballads, and librettos are full of satirical shafts at Victorian customs, institutions, and individuals.

II. Sir Arthur Sullivan was able to give his music a humorous, and often satirical, quality.

III. In *Pinafore,* they satirized the Royal Navy; in *Iolanthe,* the House of Lords; in *Patience,* the aesthetic movement of the 1890's.

IV. They remain the popular theater's most striking example of perfect artistic collaboration.

FEEDING LIVESTOCK FOR THE MARKET

I. Obviously, if the cost of the feed is greater than the increased value of the fattened stock, the operation will result in a loss.

II. Intelligent feeding practices are something the student farmer should study carefully since the stock farmer's success or failure depends a good deal on intelligent feeding systems.

III. If well-fattened animals are brought to market at a time when market prices are comparatively high and the individual's feeding costs comparatively low, the chances are excellent for a favorable profit return, and the operation will have been a success.

IV. The real crux of the feeding problem is achieving a successful balance between feeding costs and anticipated market prices.

THE AIM OF THE STUDY OF HISTORY

The aim of the study of history is not to make a student a walking almanac or chronicle; indeed, very few teachers stress the remembrance of dates, and if they occasionally make exceptions, they do so because the event has real economic, political, or social significance. To the past we owe language, writing, and the materials for preserving and perpetuating human thought. To the past we owe most of the factors that influence our everyday living, including most of our material comforts. Inventions owe just as much to the history of trial and error behind them as they do to the geniuses who eventually perfect them. The inventions of the Industrial Revolution were not the result of spontaneous flares of genius, it may be said; they owed as much to their yesterdays as to their creators. If Robert Fulton had lived in a time of relatively limited knowledge—such as the Stone Age—he would never have invented the steamboat. His and all other inventions have been made possible by an *accumulation* of knowledge, mechanical and scientific. We need to recognize a continuity of human thought and human accomplishment. Man studies history for the very simple reason that "to understand the present and have some idea of the future, one must know the past."

THE WIT OF DANIEL WEBSTER

That men of some wit and humor have lived before the present age is not, we believe, contested. But the age for true wit is decidedly the present age, and the wittiest man of the time, beyond all question, is Daniel Webster, the gentleman once spoken of as a candidate for the Presidency. There was, of course, wit among the Greeks and Romans; there is wit in Boccaccio, and wit in Ariosto. Witty was Rabelais, and witty was Scarron, and witty, in another way, was Paul Courier. Wit has hitherto been only in the bud—Mr. Webster is the full-blown flower; wit has until now remained in the clumsy chrysalis state—Mr. Webster is the broad-winged butterfly. There are things in Cervantes that will make the reader laugh in spite of himself; Molière has been known to coax a grin from the most splenetic, and some passages in Shakespeare no man can read or hear without acknowledging that they are quite droll. These authors were very well known in their time, and some of their works are passable even now. We must not speak disparagingly of what made our fathers and mothers laugh. It would be irreverent. We have indeed had the promise of wit, but Mr. Webster is its fulfilment and perfection.—In original form, part of an editorial by WILLIAM CULLEN BRYANT, 1837

II. Select an essay from a book of readings or from a magazine recommended by the instructor, and read it carefully. Then follow the directions given below:

1. Copy three consecutive paragraphs of the essay, leaving a double space between each two lines of writing.

2. Underscore twice any forecasting sentences, and underscore once any transitional sentences.

3. Draw a circle around each linking word or expression.

D.

I. Make an analytical sentence outline of the essay selected for use in exercise C II (or for another essay assigned by your instructor).

II. Identify as many errors as you can find in the following topic outline. Suggest ways of reorganizing the material, and then construct a new outline.

KINDS OF MAGAZINES

I. Classification of periodicals
   A. History of the magazine in America
   B. Weekly magazines
      1. Fiction
      2. Nonfiction
      3. Women's magazines
      4. Picture magazines
         (a) *Life*
   C. Monthly magazines
      a. *Atlantic*
      b. *Cosmopolitan*
      c. *National Geographic*
      d. *Esquire*
   D. Political magazines ("journals of opinion")
      1. Certain magazines are written from a liberal point of view
         a. *The Nation*
         b. *New Republic*
         c. *The Reporter*
      2. Conservative journals
         a. *Fortune*
         b. *U.S. News and World Report*
         c. *Business Week*
         d. *Saturday Evening Post*

    E. Pulp magazines

        1. These may be divided into four typical classes, depending upon the subject matter.

            a. Mystery and detective

            b. Weird and supernatural

            c. Love

            d. Western and sports

II. The reading public patronizes all kinds of magazines.

III. Rearrange the sentences below so as to form a logical and coherent four-level outline on the topic "The Patterns in Music." (NOTE: You do not have to understand precisely what such terms as *harmony, melody,* or *polyphonic* mean in order to do this exercise. You do have to understand that an outline groups discussions of similar things at similar levels.)

    1. The two major harmonic structures serve different ends.

    2. Rhythm is a time pattern of stresses marking off the time units, or measures.

    3. The second basic structural pattern is found in larger compositions, such as sonatas and symphonies.

    4. An important element affecting rhythm is the speed, or tempo, at which the measures are produced.

    5. Harmony is a pattern of simultaneous sounds.

    6. Melody may be simple, lacking either accompaniment or development.

    7. Dissonance is a harmonic structure creating a feeling of tension or incompleteness.

    8. Musical structure, or formal pattern, is the means of organizing the other three patterns.

    9. In these larger works, there are three or four different movements, each with its separate form.

    10. Melody is a linear pattern of musical tones.

    11. The two most common patterns of rhythm are two beats to a measure and three beats to a measure.

    12. Several melodies may run concurrently, playing against themselves, in polyphonic style.

13. The first basic structural pattern is the "theme-and-variation" pattern.

14. Structurally, there are two basic musical forms.

15. The individual movements are unified by a common expression or purpose.

16. Harmony may result from the weaving of melodic lines, along a "horizontal" pattern.

17. Consonance is a harmonic structure creating a feeling of completion, or resolving the feeling of tension.

18. In the "theme-and-variation" pattern, a single dominant melody is given a number of variations.

19. The organization of all the musical elements into a formal pattern results in its "expressive content," or the message it conveys to the listener.

20. Harmony may result from the creation of chords along a "vertical" pattern.

21. In the "repetition-with-contrast" pattern, several contrasting melodies are given varying harmonic and rhythmic treatments.

E.

Select five or more essays from a book of readings or from magazines recommended by the instructor. If not familiar with the contents of the essays, read them rapidly. Then follow the directions given below:

1. Criticize, in writing, the title of each essay, from the standpoints of explicitness, appropriateness, attractiveness, and brevity.

2. Keeping in mind the subject matter and point of view of the essay involved, recast each title that, in your opinion, would profit by revision.

F.

I. Notice separately the introduction, body, and conclusion of the essay selected for use in exercise C II, or of another essay assigned by the instructor. Write an analysis of the essay, considering the following points:

1. The manner in which the introduction prepares the reader for what is to follow, the actual information given, the mood or tone estab-

lished, and the method or methods by which the author gains (or perhaps fails to gain) the interest of the reader.

2. The manner in which the author develops the body of the essay, the way in which he fulfills the promise of mood or tone and of information given in the introduction, the way in which he introduces new or illustrative material or ideas, and the way in which he limits his subject matter to the scope of the essay as forecast in the introduction.

3. The manner in which the ending brings the essay to a logical conclusion by summarizing what has been said, by adding some new and conclusive fact or idea, or by rewording or expressing in a new and striking fashion something that has already been said.

II. Select one of the following statements. Construct an outline, in a form assigned by the instructor, for a five- or six-hundred-word essay intended to develop the statement; write an introduction for the proposed essay; and write a conclusion based on the introduction and on the topics included in the outline.

1. It is necessary today for young men and women to have an understanding of economic principles if they are to take an intelligent part in local and national political affairs.

2. The well-read person is one who is familiar with the literature both of the past and of the present, and is able to apply his knowledge of "classical" literature to his criticism of that of the present.

3. In its news columns, a newspaper should always refrain from deliberate distortion or even one-sided interpretation of the facts presented.

4. There are some indications that the intellectual-cultural level of television programs is gradually being raised.

5. College students, in spite of everything that has been said to the contrary, learn more from their participation in extracurricular activities than they do from their classes.

TWO | The Forms of Writing

IX | Exposition

COMMUNICATION:

THE AIM OF COMPOSITION

The primary aim of all speaking and writing is communication. An idea, a mood, a sense impression, an event, a character, information—any or all of these may be at least partially expressed through written or spoken words, but no matter what the subject or form of composition, its purpose is always essentially the same —communication.

Reduced to its simplest terms, then, communication is an activity that requires at least two participants—a speaker and a hearer, or a writer and a reader. It is false to assume that a writer pours out words solely for his own delight, or that a speaker would be happy if allowed to rave ceaselessly in an eternal vacuum. Far too many speakers and writers forget the dual nature of communication, forget the existence of hearers and readers, and in forgetting these things defeat their own effectiveness. The really effective speakers and writers are those who remember that they are engaged in the communication of ideas, moods, and so on, and who try to fashion their compositions so that they will be understood and appreciated.

A writer should never forget that it is only in terms of a reader that a composition can finally be considered effective or ineffective. Consider, for example, the following two paragraphs:

Persistent uniform rotations are not felt, however rapid they are; but the beginning and end of the rotation, acceleration and retardation, are felt. The ampullary apparatus is not affected by angular velocities that persist, but only by positive and negative angular accelerations. These cause a momentary displacement of the endolymph-ring and of the cupola terminalis (which as a consistent mass holds the epithelial hairs together in a constant figure of fixed shape), and, concomitantly, set up a tension of the cell-hairs and an excitement of the terminal apparatus of the nerves on one side of the crista involved.—ERNST MACH[1]

It is sometimes said that the great writer seldom quotes, and that in the main is true, for he finds it difficult to mix an alien music of thought and speech with his own. Montaigne, it is also said, is an exception, but that is scarcely true. What Montaigne quoted he often translated and so moulded to the pattern of his own mind . . . . The significant fact to note, however, is not that the great writer rarely quotes, but that he knows how to quote. Schopenhauer was here a master. He possessed a marvellous flair for fine sayings in remote books, and these he would now and again let fall like jewels on his page, with so happy a skill that they seemed to be created for the spot on which they fell. It is the little writer rather than the great writer who seems never to quote, and the reason is that he is really never doing anything else.— HAVELOCK ELLIS[2]

When these two paragraphs are judged with regard to the intended writer-reader relationships, they must both be considered effective writing; but they are effective for widely differing audiences. To understand the first, the reader must have a thorough knowledge of the technical terminology the writer employs. Without such knowledge this paragraph is simply gibberish, and for the layman it is exactly that. This paragraph illustrates a highly specialized form of communication in which the writer intends to be understood only by those few who are already familiar with

---

[1] *The Analysis of Sensations.* Copyright, 1914, by The Open Court Publishing Company, publishers.

[2] *The Dance of Life.* Copyright, 1923, by Havelock Ellis. Houghton Mifflin Company, publishers.

his terminology and concepts. The writer can justifiably ignore all other readers because this limited audience is the only one with whom—*in this specific instance*—he is interested in communicating. Were he, on the other hand, eager to tell a general audience how the human body reacts to movement, he would have to revise not only his choice of words, but the scope and organization of his material.

The second paragraph treats ideas just as complex as those in the first, but because the audience the writer is addressing is different, the writer's method is different. Where Ernst Mach is writing for the specialist in physiological psychology, Havelock Ellis is addressing the average literate reader. Therefore, although Ellis's conclusion involves psychology and aesthetics—both highly technical subjects—he phrases it in terminology the general reader can understand, because the general reader is the one with whom he wishes to *communicate*.

Directing the composition toward the proper reader is of course only half of the art of effective writing. An effective piece of writing must also fully embody the writer's *own* intentions. Ineffective student writing frequently fails to do justice to both writer *and* reader. Consider the following:

We went up to Pikes Peak and we went to Longs Peak, too. We were in Denver the week before we went there and the week after we went there we went back again. You could see it from the city but not hardly except on clear days like the one was the day we went there. It was a big one, but not as big as a fellow I know was telling about. The difference in size doesn't make any difference though.

The writer of these sentences, with an almost magnificent disregard for coherence, has attempted to express in words an experience that he has had, but, unfortunately, his writing means nothing; it communicates no clear idea to the reader.

Let us now examine a piece of student writing less obviously flawed than the previous paragraph.

THE LOS ANGELES *TIMES*

The leading newspaper in Southern California is the Los Angeles *Times,* published by a pioneer California family, the Chandlers. The

Times, a daily morning paper, has a large and versatile staff of veteran reporters and editors whose combined efforts produce a paper that is unbeatable for completeness of coverage. Because of its dominance in the area, it also regularly covers news of New Mexico and Arizona. For international news, it relies on the major press associations. For sports, it has a staff of about a dozen specialists in the various games. And for entertainment and movies, which are especially important in Southern California, it has about six reporters and columnists who not only write daily reports about the latest in films, television, and radio, but also put out a special Sunday supplement. The Sunday edition of the *Times* includes two comic sections, a magazine section, a section devoted to home and garden, and weekly news summaries on the editorial pages. Reading the Sunday *Times,* which often runs to several pounds in weight, is an all-day task, which many Southern Californians are in the habit of doing.

In contrast to the other Los Angeles newspapers, the *Times* is clearly the leader. It leads in circulation, in advertising linage, in amount of news published, and in extensiveness of coverage. These are only some of the reasons why you should buy the Los Angeles *Times.*

It should be evident, after studying this essay, that there are several things wrong with it. To try to determine some of the possible reasons why its author went wrong, we should start with the title, which is so unspecific as to make us suspect that he had no clear purpose in mind when he sat down to write. Lack of specific intention leads to other faults: irrelevant or insufficient data, lack of a consistent principle of order, and a wholly illogical conclusion.

This writer has confused three very different kinds of writing problems which may be distinguished as questions of *fact,* questions of *value,* and questions of *policy.* These questions may be put in another form: (1) What is the fact? (2) What is the importance or significance of the fact? (3) What, if anything, should be done about it? A writer examining the operation of the *Times's* editorial staff, or analyzing the extensiveness of its news coverage, or enumerating the special sections of the newspaper, has as his purpose the communication of information: namely, the dissemination of some facts about the newspaper. But a writer whose purpose is to show that the leading newspaper in Southern California is the Los Angeles *Times* is attempting to establish relative values. The author of this paper fails to give information regarding any of the other papers; indeed, he seems unaware of the fact that it is necessary to establish criteria before evaluations can be made. And, judging from the spectacularly irrelevant last sentence, he also seems unaware that he has veered off on a new subject, for the conclusion is one which properly belongs in a discussion of policy. He has not really given any "reasons" why you—or anyone—should buy the *Times*.

EXPOSITION AND ARGUMENT

Questions of fact are dealt with primarily in expository prose. Questions of value and policy are dealt with primarily in argumentative prose. To confuse explanation of an idea with either judgments about the importance of that idea or arguments in its behalf or against it is to write with a blurred focus. Although the line between exposition and argument is a thin one, it may yet be established in terms of the author's intention. Are you explaining the organization of the federal government in terms of its division into executive, legislative, and judiciary, or are you arguing that the check-and-balance system is the cornerstone of American democracy? Are you describing the way the **T**-formation works, or are you contending that the **T**-formation is better than the single-wing? Some fuzzy-minded people object to what they call "the teaching of Communism" in college political science courses, failing to distinguish between factual exposition of how the Communist system works and the advocacy of this system, which is quite another matter. For the remainder of this chapter we will examine the essentials and methods of expository writing; in the following chapter, we will examine the principles of argument and sound reasoning.

The traditional "four forms of discourse" are conventionally denoted as exposition, description, narration, and argument. While it is true that each form has certain distinguishing characteristics, this classification is, functionally, not very helpful to the beginning writer, for in actual practice the forms tend to merge into one another: exposition becomes description and often includes narration. The "pure" forms rarely exist, as editors of textbooks discover when they start searching for illustrative examples. What they find more commonly in good writing is the rather free and easy mixture of the various forms. For our purposes and yours, it is less to the point to study the theory of the "forms" than to raise the practical question: "What is your intention in this piece of writing?"

Consequently, we will consider description and narration here as subordinate aspects of exposition, setting argument off by itself because of its primary difference in intention. Exposition has as its goal the explanation, clarification, or definition of a subject; but the goal of argument is the *use* of information, either in making value judgments ("What good is it?") or in establishing policy ("What should our course of action be?"). Aristotle, in his *Rhetoric,* said that the end of all rhetoric is belief; that is, an explanation of how the T-formation works is aimed at making the reader believe that this is actually how it does work. But we can retain the useful distinction between concerning ourselves with a thing as it is, and the use of that information in forming judgments and supporting opinions.

Another important distinction between these two large classes of discourse is that which defines the relationship of their statements. A description of the Grand Canyon, a narrative about a ride in a jet plane, a definition of the term *anacrusis,* an analysis of the structure of *The Scarlet Letter,* an explanation of how an oscilloscope works—these various kinds of expository writing include assertions which do not give reasons or inferences. The separate statements do not logically depend upon each other. In argument, however, some assertions become reasons for future assertions; the logical order is of vital importance if the reader is to arrive at the conclusion which the writer desires. It is for this reason that argumentative prose will be more liberally sprinkled with words like *therefore* and *consequently* than will exposition.

The shadowy no man's land between exposition and argument is reached where form and intention intersect. For example, a straightforward, factual, statistical summary of the number of slave laborers in Soviet labor camps, together with data concerning annual deaths, is presented to the United Nations in a report by an investigating commission. By formal criteria, this report is informative; that is to say, it merely communicates factual data. But by the criterion of intention, the report may very well be argumentative; that is to say, it may be designed (even without the *therefore*'s) to establish value and perhaps also policy. Not surprisingly, the Russian delegate protests. An even more complex example is that of John Hersey's well-known book *Hiroshima,* which gives a neutral, almost dead-pan, factual account of the atomic bombing of that city in 1945. It is narrative, it is expository—and it is also, by implication, an eloquent argument in behalf of world peace.

EXPOSITORY METHODS

Expository writing has many types and is developed by a great variety of methods. In any given composition, more often than not, these methods are used in combination rather than separately. In the sections that follow, we have tried to illustrate exposition by definition, by analysis (partition and classification), by comparison and contrast, by description, and by narration. Even among these selections, chosen for their relative "purity" of method, you will notice that there is a considerable amount of overlapping.

EXPOSITION BY DEFINITION

"Sugar," said little Bobby at breakfast, "is the stuff that makes the oatmeal taste bad when you don't put any on."

The inadequacy of this alleged definition is fairly obvious, but is it any less illuminating than "A debt is an obligation or a liability" or "Disobedience means insubordination and non-compliance" or "Jazz is multilinear collective improvisation poly-rhythmically integrated"?

A definition is an attempt to explain a word, a phrase, or a concept in such a manner as to make its meaning clear and unmistakable. None of the definitions above succeeds in doing so, for reasons we will discuss below. Although, in Chapter V, we referred to the dictionary as giving the "meanings" of words, it would perhaps be more accurate to say that the dictionary really substitutes one set of words (presumably familiar to you) for another (the unfamiliar one you are looking up). The disheartening experience of turning hopefully to a dictionary only to find the definition phrased in even more unfamiliar terms suggests the limitations of the dictionary as a source of meaning. The layman, looking up the word *schist,* is probably not greatly enlightened when he reads that it is a "metamorphic crystalline rock having a foliated structure."

Logicians and semanticists distinguish between two kinds of definitions. One kind, represented by the examples in the dictionary, is the verbal or intensional, which replaces one group of words by another; the second kind is the ostensive or extensional, which "points to" the objects referred to by the word.

The most familiar example of the intensional definition—except for the mere listing of synonyms, as in the thesaurus—is the *formal* definition. The form is vital, for in it one first specifies the class (or *genus*) to which the thing being defined belongs, and then adds the details (or *differentiae*) which serve to distinguish it from all other members of that same class:

A square is a rectangle having four equal sides.

The instep is the arched part of the foot in front of the ankle bone.

Poulter's measure is a metrical pattern consisting of a couplet composed of a first line in iambic hexameter and a second line in iambic heptameter.

Other requirements, logical as well as formal, are (1) that the word be defined by use of the same part of speech and (2) that it not be defined in its own terms. To illustrate:

1. Irony is a form of expression in which one means the opposite of what he says. (RATHER THAN: Irony is where you say one thing and mean another.)

2. Aridity is the state of being without moisture. (RATHER THAN: Aridity is the state of being arid.)

For some terms, the formal definition may suffice—*square* and *instep* probably require no further explanation. But a reader unfamiliar with the terminology of versification would certainly need to be presented with an example of lines from a poem written in *poulter's measure*. Dictionaries frequently supplement their verbal definitions with pictorial illustrations. And especially if an idea or concept is being explained—like *honor, classicism, deficit spending,* or *federalism*—it is necessary to help the formal definition along with other means. For extremely complex ideas, extended definitions are often necessary: Lionel Trilling devotes an essay to "The Meaning of a Literary Idea" and Rebecca West an entire book to *The Meaning of Treason.* Now, it might be possible to boil these extended definitions down into a single sentence (at the certain price of destroying the work), in which case we would probably find that the differentiae have been given careful and elaborate amplification in a variety of methods, all of which the authors thought necessary in order to communicate their definitions of "literary idea" and "treason" fully and clearly.

The following one-paragraph definition of *spot* in radio advertising consists of an expanded formal definition, although the form may not be immediately evident. The first sentence, up to the words *rather than,* specifies the genus; everything after that constitutes the differentiating details, some of which are supported by further examples.

Most correctly, the "spot" in spot radio means selection of localities and stations for delivery of radio advertising messages rather than duration or type of announcements. In other words, the advertiser *spots* his radio advertising where he thinks it will do the most good. He may use every station in the country, or just a few of them; he may use regional networks and outlets of national networks; but it is considered *spot* when the network facilities of the national networks are not used. Like network advertising, spot may be a direct selling effort, or it may be devoted to the long-term objective of building good will and prestige for the sponsor. The sponsor may use a 30-second announcement, a day-long promotion, or a regular program on the network format.—HARRY SIMMONS[3]

The following three passages attempt extended definitions of the terms *comedy, life,* and *conservatism.* Note that in no case has the author felt that a single sentence is adequate to do the job of definition.

Comedy is not just a happy as opposed to an unhappy ending, but a way of surveying life so that happy endings must prevail. But it is not to be confused, on that account, with optimism, any more than a happy ending is to be confused with happiness. Comedy is much more reasonably associated with pessimism—with at any rate a belief in the smallness that survives as against the greatness that is scarred or destroyed. In mortal affairs it is tragedy, like forgiveness, that seems divine; and comedy, like error, that is human.

One might perhaps begin by talking about comedy in its philosophic sense, as an attitude toward life, rather than as a mere technical aspect of the theater. One might begin, in other words, by speaking of the comedy that unites such writers and writings as Lucian and Aristophanes, the *Decameron* and *Candide,* Congreve and Peacock and Sterne, *Pride and Prejudice* and *Le Bourgeois Gentilhomme.* Coarse as Aristophanes can be and genteel as Jane Austen, broadly as Aristophanes can clown and exquisitely as Jane Austen can annihilate, the two have much the same vision of life, much the same eye for its absurdities. They have in full measure the comic point of view, as other writers have the tragic point of view.

Comedy, in brief, is criticism. If through laughing at others we purge ourselves of certain spiteful and ungenerous instincts—as through tragedy we achieve a higher and more publicized catharsis—that is not quite the whole of it. Comedy need not be hostile to idealism; it need only show how far human beings fall short of the ideal. The higher comedy mounts, the airier and more brilliant its forms, the more are we aware

---

[3] Harry Simmons, *Successful Sales Promotion,* copyright 1950 by Prentice-Hall, Inc., Englewood Cliffs, N. J., p. 387.

of man's capacity for being foolish or self-deluded or complacent; in the very highest comedy, such as the finale of Mozart's *Marriage of Figaro,* we are in a very paradise of self-deceptions and misunderstandings and cross-purposes. At the heart of high comedy there is always a strain of melancholy, as round the edges there is all gaiety and ebullience and glitter; and Schiller was perhaps right in regarding high comedy as the greatest of all literary forms.—LOUIS KRONENBERGER[4]

"Comedy is . . . a way of surveying life so that happy endings must prevail." Clearly, this formal definition leaves many questions unanswered, so the definition is advanced by the use of comparisons, contrasts, examples, and quotation. Note the signals that Kronenberger gives at the start of each paragraph to indicate the development of his thought: (1) what comedy is not; (2) comedy as an attitude rather than a theatrical form; (3) conclusion: "Comedy, in brief, is criticism"—a statement which, if it had been used to begin the essay, would have meant considerably less than it does at this point.

Life is usually defined as a condition or state that characterizes animate or living matter (plants and animals). Living bodies have certain definite properties that differentiate them sharply from nonliving materials. These properties can be summarized briefly as follows:

Growth

This is a gradual increase of all the components of living systems, no matter how small and simple or large and complex.

Metabolism

This is the capacity of living systems to assimilate food substances and transform them partly into energy and partly into their own cells and tissues.

Respiration

This includes both respiration in the presence of oxygen (aerobic state), and the ability of certain cells to live in the absence of oxygen (anaerobic state).

---

[4] *The Thread of Laughter.* Copyright, 1952, Alfred A. Knopf, Inc.

Reproduction

This characteristic of life ranges from the simple fission of bacteria and budding of yeasts to the complex sexual reproduction of both lower and higher forms of life. All living creatures have the ability to reproduce their own kind. Occasionally variants or mutants occur which are different in one or more respects from their ancestors.

Adaptation to environment

This may be a result of spontaneous mutation, of interbreeding between strains and varieties, or still other factors. Gradually new forms of life may thus arise that are different from their progenitors. The plant and animal breeder takes full advantage of such properties to create new varieties.

Intelligence

Even single-cell organisms often show a rudimentary type of intelligence (such as reactions to heat and other destructive agents), but man has acquired mental processes that enable him to control or at least understand, actually or potentially, virtually all of the activities in the environment with which he is surrounded.

Thus, simple and complex forms of life are characterized by various properties that enable anyone to recognize their living state.—SELMAN A. WAKSMAN[5]

Although Matthew Arnold once wrote that in order to learn the meaning of "that great and inexhaustible word *life*" we should simply "let our minds rest upon" it, the biological scientist uses a rather more analytical approach. Dr. Waksman begins with a formal definition that necessitates explanation of the properties of the differentiae, and the bulk of the passage—except for the summary last sentence—consists of an analysis of these properties.

The first step toward an alert and responsible conservatism is for several million more "old-fashioned liberals" to wake up some morning and admit that they have been conservative all their lives. Too many men on the Right remain perversely or casually indifferent to the not so awful truth that they are on a conservative team. The American who

---

[5] "Nobel Prize Winner Analyzes Mystery." Associated Press, December 4, 1957. Reprinted by permission of the author.

is more concerned with preservation than reform must be a thoughtful as well as practical and possessive conservative, a conservative of principle as well of habit or sloth or fear. He must understand what conservatism is and why it should exist; he must know something of its part in the proper functioning of a free society. The American conservative must discover conservatism.

While he discovers conservatism, we should discover him. Who is this American, this new conservative? I would answer: any American who is clearly happier with things as they are than with things as they would be if our social reformers had their way, and who, further, is equally determined to steer clear of liberalism to his left and standpattism and reaction to his right. He can live anywhere, have any job, own any amount of property, belong to either or no party and to any or no church, just as long as he thinks and acts conservatively; for conservatism, like the middle class, is a state of mind and a pattern of behavior. The active new conservative is most likely to be a businessman, big or little, but he may also be a politician, lawyer, doctor, teacher, editor, minister, farmer, engineer, or administrator. He may even be a figure in organized labor, though most union officials, like the unions they lead, are properly committed to the forces of modern progressivism. While I agree with Daniel Bell, Frank Tannenbaum, and others who have argued the essential conservatism of the American labor movement, I would hesitate to push this argument too far. American labor is conservative in the way that most Americans are conservative: it is far more intent on building up a stake in our present system than in altering it to a new design. Within the system, however, it remains liberal—that is, reform-minded—in attitude and program. Within the same system, American business remains largely conservative. Because of the structure of American society, most new conservatives will be businessmen or professionals in allied fields. Indeed, a conservative movement that fails to enlist the conservative businessman can have little influence on the future of the Republic.—CLINTON ROSSITER[6]

The only sentence even vaguely resembling a formal definition in Rossiter's statement is found in the middle of the second paragraph: "Conservatism . . . is a state of mind and a pattern of

---

[6] *Conservatism in America.* Copyright, 1956, Alfred A. Knopf, Inc.

behavior." But this sentence in itself is not very useful (paranoia is also "a state of mind and a pattern of behavior"). What Rossiter does is to define both *conservatism* and the *conservative man* in terms of each other by characterizing the man, his ideas and beliefs. Not every definition, then, needs a statement in the formal pattern; Rossiter's is a good example of the informal (or rhetorical) definition.

Despite the thought and skill expended in definitions such as those given above, some people have felt that there is something essentially futile about defining a word by means of other words. If the purpose of defining is to relate verbal symbols to actual experience, then the ostensive or extensional definition, pointing to the thing itself, is to be preferred to the intensional. This preference is satirized in Book III of *Gulliver's Travels,* depicting the cloudland of Laputa, where philosophers use no words but carry around huge packs of objects on their backs and converse by pointing to the actual things—a backbreaking task indeed. But modern science has made extensive use of the *operational* definition, in which the object under discussion is explained not by placing it in a large class and then isolating it by an enumeration of all its unique attributes, but by merely describing how it works. Sir Isaac Newton is reported to have said: "Hypotheses non fingo [I never manufacture hypotheses]," refusing to speculate on the "nature" of gravitation or light but insisting on studying and describing their mode of operation. The passages below, from a TWA Route Map, are brief operational definitions:

Mercator's projection. A projection obtained by placing a cylinder around a globe with the center resting against the Equator. The latitude and longitude lines are projected on the cylinder as straight lines and the land masses are projected proportionately within their area. Popular through the centuries for navigational use because a given line between two points represents true direction. Distortion becomes greater from the Equator to the outer edges.

Conformal conic projection. A projection made by placing a cone over the surface of a globe and projecting the information to the surface of the cone. The cone is then cut from the base to the apex and flattened.

This projection is excellent for showing limited areas because it gives minimum distortion.

Webster's New Collegiate Dictionary, on the other hand, defines the Mercator's projection as follows:

A method of map making [genus] in which the meridians are drawn parallel to each other, and the parallels of latitude are straight lines whose distance from each other increases with their distance from the equator. [differentiae]

The formal definition explains the nature of the projection, but the operational definition explains how the projection is made and why. The latter may be clumsier and longer, but it is often more graphic and more helpful.

Webster's New Collegiate Dictionary defines *tornado* as follows:

1. *Obs.* A tropical thunderstorm. 2. **a** A squall off the west coast of Africa in which a violent wind revolves beneath threatening clouds. **b** A whirling wind accompanied by a funnel-shaped cloud, very violent and destructive in a narrow path often for many miles over the land. 3. Any violent or destructive windstorm; a whirlwind.

An operational definition of the same word is presented in the following passage:

What exactly is a tornado? The general picture is familiar enough. The phenomenon is usually brewed on a hot, sticky day with south winds and an ominous sky. From the base of a thundercloud a funnel-shaped cloud extends a violently twisting spout toward the earth. As it sucks in matter in its path, the twister may turn black, brown or occasionally even white (over snow). The moving cloud shows an almost continuous display of sheet lightning. It lurches along in a meandering path, usually northeastward, at 25 to 40 miles per hour. Sometimes it picks up its finger from the earth for a short distance and then plants it down again. The funnel is very slender: its wake of violence generally averages no more than 400 yards wide. As the tornado approaches, it is heralded by a roar as of hundreds of jet planes or thousands of railroad cars. Its path is a path of total destruction. Buildings literally explode as they are sucked by the tornado's low-pressure vortex (where the pressure drop is as much as 10 per cent) and by its powerful whirling winds (estimated at up to 500 miles per hour). The amount of damage depends mainly on whether the storm happens to hit populated areas. The worst tornado on record in the U.S. was one that ripped across Missouri, lower Illinois and Indiana in three hours on March 18, 1925, and killed 689 people.

The tornado's lifetime is as brief as it is violent. Within a few tens of miles (average: about 16 miles) it spends its force and suddenly disappears.—MORRIS TEPPER[7]

In the following passage, a "voice coil" is defined operationally:

The heart of every magnetic speaker is a magnet and a coil of wire, called a "voice coil." A fluctuating electric current is fed through the coil, and sets up an electromagnetic field around the coil. The interaction of this electrically induced field with the permanent field of the magnet pulls the coil to and fro, just as the stroke of the bow sets the violin to vibrating. A voice coil oscillating in the air, however, would make very little sound—no more, in fact, than a violin string vibrating alone in space. The violin string agitates the air in the violin sound box to set up the full characteristic sound of the instrument. The voice coil, in the most common sort of loudspeaker, drives the narrow end of a paper cone which is held relatively stationary at the wide end. The cone, in critic Edward Tatnall Canby's fine phrase, "grabs the air" to set up strong sound waves.—MARTIN MAYER[8]

EXPOSITION BY ANALYSIS: PARTITION AND CLASSIFICATION

Closely related to definition is the method—or process—of analysis, which entails the breaking down of a subject into its component parts according to a specific principle. If the subject under analysis is a single entity—like a three-layer cake, a carburetor, the sonata form, or the idea of progress—the method is

---

[7] "Tornadoes," *Scientific American,* May, 1958. Reprinted by permission of the publisher.
[8] *Hi-Fi: New Revised Edition.* Copyright, 1958, by Maco Magazine Corporation.

referred to as *partition*. If the subject consists of a number of things—like the works of Mozart, the principles of personnel management, the kinds of books shelved in the college library, or the varieties of architecture on Park Avenue—the analytical process is one of *classification*. The discussion of grammar in Chapter II, grouping words by form classes and function groups and further subdividing them within those categories, and then classifying word-groups as phrases and clauses with further subdivisions within those categories, is a typical exposition by classification. A graphic means of representing the completed analysis, whether by partition or classification, is the outline (see section O4).

In both kinds of analysis, a single and consistent principle of division is used throughout. When, for any reason, the principle is changed, that fact should be noted; otherwise, the reader may lose track of the organization. An analysis of a newspaper, if it begins by discussing the content or the editorial departments, should not suddenly shift to an analysis of editorial policy or typography. Likewise, a writer who is classifying the newest automobiles on the principle of gas economy should not find it necessary to discuss cost, body design, or maneuverability, unless he adopts one of these as a new and second principle of classification.

Another requirement of analytical exposition is that it be complete. To write an analysis of the organization of a baseball team without mentioning the outfield is obviously to leave the exposition unfinished. One of the requisites of scientific classification is that it must be carried to a point beyond which further classification is impossible. The student of biology will detect a clear-cut example of this kind of classification in the division of the forms of animal and vegetable life into *phyla, classes, orders, families, genera,* and so on. A principle of classification which groups all peoples is described in the following passage.

Primitive peoples are most conveniently classified according to their linguistic affiliations. Groups whose speech is so similar that they are able to communicate with each other, notwithstanding minor differences, are said to be speaking *dialects* of the same language; if the differences are too great for mutual intelligibility, we speak of distinct *languages*.

However, in many instances of the latter kind, the languages show many resemblances that can be explained only on the assumption that they have diverged from a common parental tongue, perhaps centuries or even milleniums ago. This holds true for English, Dutch, and Swedish, but even Russian proves to be connected with these languages when their vocabularies and grammars are closely examined. Such ultimately related languages jointly form a *family (stock)*. In a large family it may happen that two or more of the languages are closer to each other than to the rest, in which case the family is for convenience divided into *branches*. Thus, most European languages plus certain Asiatic ones form the Indo-European family, which comprises the Germanic, Romance, Slavic, and other branches, most of them composed of several distinct languages, which in turn may split up into various dialects.—ROBERT H. LOWIE[9]

We have already seen examples of analysis in the preceding section. Waksman's definition of *life* is analytical in method, as he distinguishes the properties that differentiate living bodies from nonliving materials. Kronenberger classes various comic writers according to a single principle, in the interests of defining *comedy*. The passages which follow will provide further illustrations of partition and classification. The first three examples of partition are analyses of a method, a concept, a man's qualities; the fourth and fifth are examples of analyses of a process.

Analysis of method:

An Economy Run driver practices an art form that is subtle, demanding and exceedingly remote from ordinary around-town chauffering. His accelerator is of course *never* opened to that jet-spraying, yawning-barreled point where the engine roars with all its big-displacement majesty. But it's not just that a driver stays on the lean side of part throttle, outguesses every possible red light, and avoids the brake like the plague —though these steps are basic. He is also versed in tiny, cumulatively important tricks:

He keeps the windows up: less air drag. He keeps the radio antenna

---

[9] With permission of McGraw-Hill Book Co., Inc., from *Indians of the Plains* by Robert H. Lowie. Copyright, 1954, by the American Museum of Natural History.

retracted: same reason. He uses matches instead of the electric lighter: the generator would spend a spoonful of power in putting the watts back into the system. He keeps the radio and heater fan off: same reason. He even calculates about the windshield wipers: he uses them as little as possible if they are electric. But if they're vacuum, he runs them as much as his official observer will permit: vacuum wipers lean the mixture very slightly by admitting air to the intake manifold.[10]

Analysis of concept:

The Atlantic frontier was compounded of fisherman, fur-trader, miner, cattle-raiser, and farmer. Excepting the fisherman, each type of industry was on the march toward the West, impelled by an irresistible attraction. Each passed in successive waves across the continent. Stand at Cumberland Gap and watch the procession of civilization, marching single file —the buffalo following the trail to the salt springs, the Indian, the fur-trader and hunter, the cattle-raiser, the pioneer farmer—and the frontier has passed by. Stand at South Pass in the Rockies a century later and see the same procession with wider intervals between. The unequal rate of advance compels us to distinguish the frontier into the trader's frontier, the rancher's frontier, or the miner's frontier, and the farmer's frontier. When the mines and the cow pens were still near the fall line the traders' pack trains were tinkling across the Alleghanies, and the French on the Great Lakes were fortifying their posts, alarmed by the British trader's birch canoe. When the trappers scaled the Rockies, the farmer was still near the mouth of the Missouri.—FREDERICK JACKSON TURNER[11]

Analysis of qualities:

When one begins to make a tally of Richardson's qualities, one discovers that he had uniquely all the elements that make up a great architect. What other architect before or since in America has had such a complete equipment? This armoury of qualities included a strong

---

[10] "Yes, the New Cars *Do* Take More Gas." Reprinted by permission from *Popular Science Monthly* for July 1958.

[11] "The Significance of the Frontier in American History," from *The Frontier in American History.* Copyright, 1920, by Henry Holt and Company, publishers.

sense of colour, which perhaps tempted him too far in his use of contrasting stones; it embraced a hitherto unique sense of place, so that he himself said that architecture "cannot be fully judged except in concrete shape and colour, amid actual lights and shadows and its own particular surroundings," a sense which placed him apart from the designers whose work is always best on the drawing-board; and it even extended to an appreciation of the ancillary arts, so that he had the taste to recognize and use some of the best artists his time offered: Saint Gaudens, La Farge, W. M. Hunt. More than this: Richardson worked equally well with his clients, the municipal officials and industrialists and business men, as difficult a collection of patrons as ever an artist was blessed with. If one look for the secret of Richardson's success here, one will not be too easily satisfied with the explanation that his love of good food and good wine brought them swiftly on a common footing; although one cannot doubt that it helped. The main point was that Richardson had an authentic intuition of his society and his age. Mr. Charles Moore in his biography of Richardson's pupil, Charles McKim, says curiously that Richardson's style was not adapted to American conditions: but what is the mark of adaptation? Contemporary jobs? Richardson had them. Durability? His works have lasted better than his successors'. Power to serve as a foundation for later work? That is Richardson's eminent claim to our attention. Richardson did not grovel before practical conditions: he did not think of himself as a mere handyman of business interests, enclosing rentable space: nor did he view the practical needs of his day with contempt.—LEWIS MUMFORD[12]

Analysis of a process is one of the commonest and most useful forms of expository organization. Whenever a writer attempts to explain how something is done or how something should be done, he is concerned with explaining a process. The tone can therefore be either descriptive or hortatory, or a combination of both; whatever the tone, the organizational logic of the composition follows the logic of the process itself. The writer begins with the first step in the process and ends with the last; unless he does, there is an

[12] From *The Brown Decades* by Lewis Mumford. Reprinted through permission by Dover Publications, Inc., New York 10, New York. ($1.65 paperbound.)

excellent chance that he will not have made clear to his reader exactly the sequence in which this procedure is or should be carried out. If he is explaining how to land deep-sea game fish, the writer does not begin by describing what should be done the second hour the fish is on the line.

The tone of the following example is clearly hortatory: the writer is telling the reader precisely how he *should* read a poem. Observe that the sequence reflects the order the writer believes a reader of poetry should follow. If the writer were describing rather than instructing, the order would be the same, although the tone would differ; even though the writer's intention and his audience would then be different, the process and the resultant logical order would remain the same.

1. Read the poem rapidly, *aloud*. This is to get the beginnings of a sense of the whole. Do not bother about details. At the end, you should be able to write down in summary form, two or three short sentences, the gist of the idea of the poem. And usually this summary ought to be written down. But remember, *the summary is not the poem; not even what the poem means.*

2. Read silently, for detailed understanding. Bring the dictionary and the other volumes of the minimum reference library into play. Make notes; preferably, mark the poem. Read not only line by line, but word by word, and allow nothing of the meaning to escape your scrutiny. It is better to overdo than to underdo looking things up. As a result of this second reading, you should be able to correct and amplify the summary you have already made; you should know what sidetracks you went off on in the first reading. Thus you make a beginning of correcting the first impressions, and subsequent readings ought to mean further corrections and amplification.

3. Read silently, for imagery. This calls for special attention to figures of speech, particularly to metaphors and similes. All words should be considered for their picture-suggesting potentialities. Often a dominant image or figure will centralize an entire poem, as in Milton's "On His Blindness," or Keats' "On First Looking into Chapman's Homer." In the latter, the unity and organization rest on a beautifully refined figure of discovery: Keats' discovery of the magic world of Homer through

Chapman's translation is emphasized by comparison with discovery in a more conventional sense— (a) the astronomer discovering a new planet, and (b) the explorer looking for the first time on a new world. The poem begins and ends in discovery.

4. Read silently, paying particular attention to the way the poet has put his poem together, to the organization and structure. Into what major divisions does the poem fall? How are the parts connected? Are they arranged in effective order? Can you see possible improvement of the arrangement? What connections are there between line and stanzaic patterns and the thought-divisions of the poem? Where and how has the poet heightened his meaning by comparison, contrast, irony, or other device?

5. Read silently and aloud. This time the attention should be centered on technique, on the craftsmanship of the poet. Rime and meter, rightly understood, belong here, with devices like alliteration, and assonance. ... Like the fourth, the fifth is an advanced reading and can be efficiently done only with experience. Both call for some special knowledge and may largely be omitted at the beginning of work with poetry. They had much better, at the start, be omitted than overdone, and under all circumstances approach to them should be gradual.

6. Read aloud, in a final, synthetic reading to put together results of all previous readings, so that details may fall into proper places, contributing their part to the effect of the whole. By this time the reader's poem, so far as it is possible for him to make it so, should be pretty much the same in idea and sound as the poem the poet originally wrote.—EARL B. DANIELS[13]

Most explanations of process—especially when they are designed for technical or purely practical use—are best presented by straight exposition, with the obvious assistance, of course, of narrative time order (the order in which the process takes place). In nontechnical composition, however, a writer may wish to explain a process in terms that will be clear and at the same time particularly interesting. Process narration is a convenient method of accomplishing this end. Narrative and descriptive devices may

---

[13] *The Art of Reading Poetry*. Copyright, 1941, by Earl B. Daniels. Rinehart & Company, Inc., publishers.

then be used—as in the passage that follows. Notice that the
writer's problem here is affected by the material: since a simple,
straightforward process exposition cannot be written, the author
has had to use some less directly relevant material.

The tragedy of the recipe for Mother's watermelon cake is more complete, since more exasperating, than that of the recipe for her almond
cake. I can remotely copy, if not duplicate, the almond cake. The watermelon cake is gone beyond recall. She made it at the tail end of the
Victorian era, when objects were designed to imitate other objects and
aesthetic delight was supposed to ensue. It was the era of pictures made
with sea shells, of toothpick holders in the shape of diminutive pot-pots,
of porcelain knickknacks in the form of unnatural and revolting animals.
There was no point in making a cake to give the illusion of a watermelon. The flavor justified it. And the awed comments, "Why, it looks
just like a watermelon," must have rewarded Mother for the long time
it took for its making. I shall never forget the first time I remember
seeing and eating it. It was my fifth birthday. With the long view toward
starting me early on a successful social career, all the members of my
kindergarten class and certain selected juvenile neighbors, were invited
to the party. The occasion was to depart from the custom of accepting
gifts, and it was announced that every child would receive one. I have
wondered if I was not popular and this was a bribe to assure attendance.
I don't remember being unpopular, but children don't always know.
The time was summer and games were played on the lawn. The moment
came for the dispersing of the gifts. Father, an ardent amateur horticul-
turist, had planted a small very choice imported French pear tree. This
was of a size whose slender limbs could all be reached by children of
kindergarten age. The individual gifts had been wrapped in tissue paper
and tied to the imported pear tree with silk ribbons. At the signal, the
guests, who were supposed to approach demurely, one by one, and pluck
a gift, shrieked like Comanches and rushed pell-mell for the tree. It was
torn literally limb from limb, and the neighborhood fat boy, arriving
last in the race, fell prone on all that was left, the slender trunk, and
flattened it to the ground. Anything but ice-cream and the watermelon
cake would have been an anti-climax. These inspired respect in the
savage eyes, and the only indecorous note over refreshments was the

fat boy, who, not to be outdone this time, made a dive for the water-melon cake after slices had been served, and crammed two handfuls in his maw.

The cake was a deep loaf cake. Its base was white, it was thickly streaked with watermelon-pink, and chocolate blobs were scattered through it to represent seeds. It was iced with pistachio frosting in a delicate green. This is the way the recipe reads in my child's cook book:

WATERMELON CAKE

White part

1 cup sugar

⅓ cup butter

⅓ cup milk

White of 3 eggs

ups flour

easpoons baking-p.

Red Part

½ cup sugar

¼ cup butter

¼ cup mi

1 cup fl

½ teaspoon

Whites of 3 e

Florida cockroaches have eaten away both edges. But even if it was all there, it does not tell how much vegetable coloring is used for the "red part," how to blend both parts so that they do not run together, and of what the chocolate seeds consist. My guess is that a small portion of the "white part" was held out, and one square of melted bitter chocolate added to this. But this mixture would be heavier than the rest. What is to keep the "seeds" from settling ignominiously and unnaturally to the bottom?

My guess as to the missing ingredients is one and one-half cups flour and two and one-half teaspoons of baking powder for the white part, and one-half teaspoon of baking powder (it could not be soda with sweet milk) and the whites, of course, of three eggs for the red part. The white and red parts must have been spread alternately in the deep loaf pan, and a tiny spot of the chocolate batter dropped here and there between layers. It is possible that the red part, and the "seeds," were all in the middle, with the white part as a top and bottom layer, but I remember the cake as "streaky." I have never had the courage to try to make it, fearing adult disappointment. If it is as good as I remember it, it is worth a trial by any curious cook.—MARJORIE KINNAN RAWLINGS[14]

The following four passages illustrate the method of classification: each begins with a group and divides that group into appropriate subgroups or parts. The first two examples are little more than simple enumerations; the last two are fully developed discussions.

A study of American place-names reveals eight general classes, as follows: (a) those embodying personal names, chiefly the surnames of pioneers or of national heroes; (b) those transferred from other and older places, either in the Eastern States or in Europe; (c) Indian names; (d) Dutch, Spanish, French, German and Scandinavian names; (e) Biblical and mythological names; (f) names descriptive of localities; (g) names suggested by local flora, fauna or geology; (h) purely fanciful names.—H. L. MENCKEN[15]

This early New York, as everyone knows, was an extremely social place and clubbable to a degree. There were dinner clubs such as the Sub Rosa and the jolly Krout and Turtle and Blackfriars; political, benevolent, humane associations, art and music societies; professional groups, including the Associated Teachers; library societies; debating clubs; *belles-lettres* circles; societies for the promotion of useful knowledge.—ELEANOR BRYCE SCOTT[16]

. . . Roughly, the early Hindu tradition and literature, that known as the Vedic, falls into four parts. These are termed the Samhitas, the Brahmanas, the Aranyakas, and the earlier Upanishads.

The first of these four, the Samhitas, are, as the literal meaning of

---

[14] Reprinted from *Cross Creek Cookery* by Marjorie Kinnan Rawlings. Copyright, 1942, by Marjorie Kinnan Rawlings; used by permission of the publishers, Charles Scribner's Sons.

[15] *The American Language, 4th Edition.* Copyright 1936, by Alfred A. Knopf, Inc.

[16] "Early Literary Clubs in New York City," *American Literature*, March, 1933.

the word indicates, "collections" of verses. These collections, as Surendranath Dasgupta indicates, are four in number: "namely, Rg-Veda, Sama-Veda, Yajur-Veda and Atharva-Veda." Of these the Rg-Veda is the most important, since the others are either repetitions of parts of it or its spirit, or applications in prayers and rituals. These Samhitas are largely in verse form and were sung, being memorized and transmitted from generation to generation. Note again this presence and importance of the aesthetic.

The Brahmanas were ritualistic and more theological in character and written in prose. They dealt with the diversified symbolism of the rituals and were exceedingly imaginative in character. The result, as Surendranath Dasgupta has written, was the "production of the most fanciful sacramental and symbolic system . . . ."

The Aranyakas, or "forest treatises," were meditative in character; but meditative, as their name indicates, in a naturalistic setting. These forest treatises had the effect of breaking the more intelligent members of the religious tradition away from the Brahmanic emphasis upon ritual. Surendranath Dasgupta notes that forthwith philosophical speculation arose. To a Westerner, however, such a description must inevitably be misleading. One merely has to consider the character of these meditations, which their name indicates, to note that it was a meditation and a "philosophical speculation" arising in connection with an immediate apprehension and contemplation of nature, when one is immersed in an overwhelming Indian tropical forest. Out of these forest meditations which revived the original basic intuition of the Rg-Veda the philosophy and religion of the Upanishads arose.

In these Upanishads the philosophy and religion of Hinduism came to expression. Again, it must be noted that the Upanishads are in verse form, and, as we shall see, these verses are heavily loaded with aesthetic content.—F. S. C. NORTHROP[17]

The English, who take their ailments less sadly than some of their other pleasures, have now passed more than six years of the free National Health Service with their enthusiasm for treating their own colds wholly undiminished. These home cures generally follow one of three

---

[17] *The Meeting of East and West.* Copyright, 1953. By permission of the Macmillan Company.

distinct courses, and as each reflects the psychology of the sufferer, let us examine them in detail. They are: (1) the Fresh-Air Treatment; (2) the Scientific Attack; (3) the Coddle.

The Fresh-Air Treatment is practiced only by those large red-faced men in check suits who look you in the eye, slap their chests, and declare they've never owned an overcoat or been to a doctor in their lives, as if claiming freedom from original sin. They have a simple attitude to illness: it's all "psychological," from smallpox to fractured femurs. But they are only human, and in time claimed by both death and colds. The first sneeze affects them like a starter's pistol: they tear off their ties and waistcoats, stamp around the house throwing open the windows, jump into a cold bath, and upset their wives by doing breathing exercises all night in bed. The discomfort in which they wallow for a fortnight makes no difference to the course of the disease, but by rendering their surroundings unfit for human habitation, they rarely manage to infect anyone else.

The Scientific sufferer takes a much calmer view of his cold. He is generally a precise, clerkish man, who files the medical articles from the *Reader's Digest* and reads the patent-medicine advertisements like a girl looking into a bride-shop window. During the winter he gargles for five minutes with antiseptic night and morning, wears wool next to the skin, and eats sufficient calcium to keep a schoolroom in chalks. As soon as his nose starts to run he calls at the druggist's and arrives home with his brief case clinking gently with small bottles. He announces to his wife: "Think I'm getting a touch of a cold, m'dear," as though he were having a baby. He makes for the bathroom and unpacks his bag, which is filled with cough mixtures, fever pills, throat lozenges, nose drops, eye lotions, gargles, and liniments. He sets the bottles carefully on the shelf and works his way through them thoughtfully and solemnly, like a sailor trying out the drinks in a strange port.

This type of invalid follows the directions on the label with scientific precision: if it orders "An egg-cupful four-hourly," he fetches an eggcup; if it says "Rub on the chest till it stings," he scrapes away until his skin begins to peel. He then has a mustard bath, soaks his feet in salt water, puts on two pairs of flannel pajamas, and goes to bed with *The Household Doctor*. No physician ever watched the recovery of a wealthy patient more sadly than he notices his own returning health. For, once he has caught his cold, he does not lightly let it go. From October to May he richly justifies the famous mistranslation of *voici l'anglais avec son sangfroid habituel*—here comes the Englishman with his usual bloody cold.

The Coddler is usually a woman, with a far more fuzzy idea of her internal organs than the Scientific sufferer. Since girlhood she has been told that she must Take Care of a Cold or it will turn into Something Else; her life passes in a terror of Germs, which she imagines as small green animals, with red eyes and long teeth, that hide under the dustbin. Before she has blown her nose twice, the Coddler has phoned her husband's office and all her friends to explain that she has a cold, in the tone of someone announcing that smallpox has just broken out. She then pours herself a large Scotch, lights a fire in her bedroom, piles extra eiderdowns on the bed, shuts the windows, rubs herself all over with camphorated oil, phones out for grapes, calf's-foot jelly, chicken essence, barley water, Eau de Cologne, and the other prerogatives of illness, shifts the television upstairs, collects all the magazines in the house, and goes to bed. She stays there for a fortnight, her family fetching her egg-and-milk, lightly sprinkled with nutmeg, every other hour.—RICHARD GORDON[18]

EXPOSITION BY COMPARISON AND CONTRAST

A tradition of the sports page before a prize fight is the printing of a chart which itemizes all the bodily measurements, from head to toe, of the contestants. Presumably the purpose of this tabulation is to help the reader form an objective picture of the two fighters, and to see which one has the longer reach, the bigger chest, and the thicker biceps. Such a chart gives the reader data on the basis of which he can see both points of similarity and points of difference. Before he draws conclusions from the statistics, he must compare and contrast the two fighters: "Slugger Simpson and Killer King both weigh 210 pounds, and both are 6'2" tall. But Simpson is four years older than King, which makes him a

---

[18] "The Common Cold," *The Atlantic Monthly,* January, 1955. Reprinted by permission of the publishers.

more experienced fighter, and he also has a reach that is $3\frac{1}{2}''$ longer, which gives him an additional advantage. I think Simpson will win."

Comparison and contrast is a frequently used informal expository device. If we comment that the latest cowboy opus on TV is just like every other one, we make a comparison; if we say that it is somehow different from all the other westerns, we point out a contrast. When we tell the proud father of a baby boy, "He looks just like you!" we are establishing some kind of comparison, although obviously the basis of similarity is a limited one. If we say, however, "I don't know who the baby looks like," we are contrasting the principals.

The process of analysis is closely related to that of comparison and contrast. A family, considering buying one house as against another, first of all has to analyze the necessary qualities desired, in order to see which house meets most of the requirements: price, age, size, accessibility to schools, shopping, and transportation are some of the possible bases of comparison. The Andersons might forgo a large back yard for a smaller mortgage; the Browns, with four small children and three dogs, might consider the back yard more vital than modernity of architecture; the Cohens, asking for both style and space, might not object to a remote location. In each case, however, the comparison and contrast are based on clearly defined qualities which emerge as the end product of analysis. Then, and only then, can a logical comparison and contrast between one house and another take place. Even the expert on the television western has unconsciously analyzed the qualities found in that art form, and when he encounters a new specimen of the genus makes his comparison or his contrast on the basis of that preliminary analysis.

All human beings are alike and yet no two human beings are identical. The same thing might be said of all cats, all automobiles, or all leaves of grass. Gertrude Stein, in her famous circular epigraph, "A rose is a rose is a rose is a rose" (and so forth), says that all roses are alike and no two roses are exactly alike. Essentially, this concept is the basis of all our comparisons and contrasts, in which we first find the common denominator between two or more objects and then determine the points of dissimilarity.

The following passages illustrate comparison and contrast as an expository method. (For another example, see the paragraph by Blesh in section ¶ 4D.)

In every cultivated language there are two great classes of words which, taken together, comprise the whole vocabulary. First, there are those words with which we become acquainted in ordinary conversation— which we learn, that is to say, from the members of our own family and from our familiar associates, and which we should know and use even if we could not read or write. They concern the common things of life, and are the stock in trade of all who speak the language. Such words may be called "popular," since they belong to the people at large and are not the exclusive possession of a limited class.

On the other hand, our language includes a multitude of words which are comparatively seldom used in ordinary conversation. Their meanings are known to every educated person, but there is little occasion to employ them at home or in the market-place. Our first acquaintance with them comes not from our mother's lips or from the talk of our schoolmates, but from books that we read, lectures that we hear, or the more formal conversation of highly educated speakers, who are discussing some particular topic in a style appropriately elevated above the habitual level of everyday life. Such words are called "learned," and the distinction between them and "popular" words is of great importance to a right understanding of linguistic process.

The difference between popular and learned words may be easily seen in a few examples. We may describe a girl as "lively" or as "vivacious." In the first case, we are using a native English formation from the familiar noun *life*. In the latter, we are using a Latin derivative which has precisely the same meaning. Yet the atmosphere of the two words is quite different. No one ever got the adjective *lively* out of a book. It is part of everybody's vocabulary. We cannot remember a time when we did not know it, and we feel sure that we learned it long before we were able to read. On the other hand, we must have passed several years of our lives before learning the word *vivacious*. We may even remember the first time that we saw it in print or heard it from some grown-up friend who was talking over our childish heads. Both *lively* and *vivacious* are good English words, but *lively* is "popular" and *vivacious* is "learned" . . . .

The terms "popular" and "learned," as applied to words, are not absolute definitions. No two persons have the same stock of words, and the same word may be "popular" in one man's vocabulary and "learned" in another's. There are also different grades of "popularity"; indeed there is in reality a continuous gradation from infantile words like *mama* and *papa* to such erudite derivatives as *concatenation* and *cataclysm!* Still, the division into "learned" and "popular" is convenient and sound. Disputes may arise as to the classification of any particular word, but there can be no difference of opinion about the general principle. We must be careful, however, to avoid misconception. When we call a word "popular," we do not mean that it is a favorite word, but simply that it belongs to the people as a whole,— that is, it is everybody's word, not the possession of a limited number. When we call a word "learned," we do not mean that it is used by scholars alone, but simply that its presence in the English vocabulary is due to books and the cultivation of literature rather than to the actual needs of ordinary conversation.

Here is one of the main differences between a cultivated and an uncultivated language. Both possess a large stock of "popular" words; but the cultivated language is also rich in "learned" words, with which the ruder tongue has not provided itself, simply because it has never felt the need of them.—JAMES B. GREENOUGH AND GEORGE LYMAN KITTREDGE[19]

To go from Hardy's "Tess" to James's "The Portrait of a Lady" is to go from Stonehenge to St. Peter's and from a frozen northern turnip field, eyed hungrily by polar birds, to the Cascine gardens where nightingales sing. Though both books concern the "campaign" of a young woman—a campaign that, expressed most simply, is a campaign *to live* —a greater difference of atmosphere could scarcely be imagined nor of articulation of what it means *to live*. The gaunt arctic birds in "Tess" have witnessed, with their "tragical eyes," cataclysms that no human eye might see, but of which they retain no memory. The birds offer a symbol

---

[19] *Words and Their Ways in English Speech.* Copyright, 1928, 1929, by Robert B. Greenough and George L. Kittredge. Reprinted by permission of The Macmillan Company.

of Tess's world: a world inimical to consciousness, where one should have no memory (Tess's fatal error is to remember her own past), where the eye of the mind should remain blank, where aesthetic and moral perceptivity is traumatic. The nightingales that sing to Isabel Archer and her lover in the "grey Italian shade" also offer a symbol of a world: they are the very voice of memory, of an imperishable consciousness at once recreating and transcending its ancient, all-human knowledge. It is to the tutelage of the European memory that Isabel Archer passionately surrenders herself in her campaign *to live,* that is, to become conscious; for, in James' world, the highest affirmation of life is the development of the subtlest and most various consciousness. In doing so, she must— like the girl in the barbarous legend of the nightingale, who, likewise in a foreign land, read an obscene crime in the weaving of a tapestry— come into knowledge of an evil which, in its own civilized kind, is as corrupting and implacable as that in the old tale. But consciousness here, as an activity nourished by knowledge, transcends the knowledge which is its content: and this too is in analogy with the ancient symbolic tale, where knowledge of evil is transcended, in the very doom of its reiteration, by the bird's immortal song.—DOROTHY VAN GHENT[20]

Last week, I attended the New York premieres of three operas, whose juxtaposition struck me as particularly interesting, since each of them represents one of the three main traditions that currently appear to be competing in this field of musical expression. Benjamin Britten's "The Turn of the Screw," which was presented by the New York College of Music at the Ninety-second Street Y.M.H.A., belongs to what I am sure historians will someday describe as the early-twentieth-century period of decadence. Dominick Argento's "The Boor," given at the Brander Matthews Theatre, on the Columbia University campus, is a fairly conventional essay in the great international tradition of operatic writing, which preceded the period of decadence, and which is also being kept alive by such better-known composers as Gian-Carlo Menotti and Vittorio Giannini. Douglas Moore's "Gallantry: A Soap Opera in One Act," which followed "The Boor" on a double bill, is a product of the slowly emerging but very vigorous American operatic style that has already been

---

[20] *The English Novel: Form and Function.* Copyright, 1953, Rinehart & Company, Inc.

reflected in Gershwin's "Porgy and Bess" and Carlisle Floyd's "Susannah" —a style in which native folk idioms and the idiom of the Broadway musical show are made to serve operatic purposes. None of the three operas under consideration can be described as a masterpiece, though I found Mr. Moore's unassuming offering thoroughly enjoyable. Yet each is, in its different way, a respectable work of art, and to me there is something intensely exciting about the conflict of traditions that the three operas reflect, for in this conflict I can, I think, detect the birth pains of a new era of vitality in the operatic theatre. . . .

The main contrast between "The Turn of the Screw" and the operas of Mr. Argento and Mr. Moore lies in the fact that the two latter works are written to be sung. I suppose that a confirmed decadent would consider them somewhat innocent compositions. In my opinion, however, this very innocence gives them freshness and exuberance—qualities that I have long been looking for in contemporary opera. Both Mr. Argento and Mr. Moore use technique merely as a conveyance for genuine musical ideas; both regard the voice with the affectionate respect of the true operatic composer; both have the ability and the courage to create melodies that are not only vocally challenging but expressive; and neither is burdened with the morbid fear of sincere sentiment that reduces so much contemporary music to meaningless artifice.—WINTHROP SARGEANT[21]

Fable, myth, and epic are different from each other in many ways, yet all three are not only a part of the great stream of folk literature but they are also embodiments of moral truths in story form.

The *fable* teaches briefly and frankly. A silly milkmaid starts imagining what she will do with the money for her milk and promptly spills it. "Do not count your chickens before they are hatched," says the fable crisply. These fables furnish the child with his first excursion into the realm of abstract ideas, intellectual speculations about conduct. They are amusing in small doses but oppressive in the mass.

The *myth* teaches through symbols which grow more and more complex. "Aspire too high and you will fall far and hard," say the myths of Bellerophon and Icarus. But they also say, and Phaeton reiterates, "It is

---

[21] "A Glimpse Ahead." Reprinted by permission, © 1958 The New Yorker Magazine, Inc.

nobler to aspire and fall from glorious heights than never to aspire and strive." In short, the symbolism of the myths soon ceases to have the simple, obvious moral of a fable and becomes as complicated as life itself, and it is then proportionately difficult for a child to understand. Fortunately, the myth stories possess a beauty that is satisfying in itself. The children cannot analyze the inner meaning of Bellerophon, Icarus, or Phaeton, but they feel their nobility. Living on Mount Olympus with bright gods who transcend space and time, who can be what they will to be, gives a lift to the imagination and the spirit.

The *epic* embodies national ideals in the person of a human hero, a doer of mighty deeds. A long cycle of stories about such a hero allows time for real characterizations, for a continual reiteration of the moral code. The hero lives up to this code and he succeeds, or he fails with glory. If he violates the code, he is punished. In the epic, as in life, morality becomes practical in such human crises as war or a fight for survival. Trickery may be resorted to when lives must be saved from the giant Polyphemus or from the Sheriff of Nottingham. But the code of keeping your word is sacred and is maintained manfully, even at the cost of your life, as in Volsung's tragic promise to visit the Goth King Siggeir. There is little preaching in the epics, but they give a child something to grow on—ideals of conduct in human form. Here are the great men of the race, the courageous, the resourceful, the gay reckless ones, the cool brainy ones—the men who have triumphed because they looked ahead, planned and calculated the cost, then leapt in and laid about them in good style. . . .—MAY HILL ARBUTHNOT[22]

The four women who form the subject of this book might be described as northern shadows flitting across a southern landscape. All of them belonged to the West, to the fast-graying climate of nineteenth-century Europe, where the twentieth-century disintegration of women, as such, was already foreshadowed. Yet although of widely different natures, backgrounds and origins, my subjects all had this in common—each found, in the East, those glowing horizons of emotion and daring which were, for them, now vanishing from the West, to be replaced by "careers" *tout-court*. Each of them, in her own way, used love as a means of in-

---

[22] From *Children and Books*, Revised Edition by May Hill Arbuthnot. Copyright © 1957 by Scott, Foresman and Company, Chicago.

dividual expression of liberation and fulfillment within that radiant
periphery.—LESLEY BLANCH[23]

EXPOSITION BY DESCRIPTION

There is a certain kind of "literary" writing, mostly about Nature, that Mark Twain once parodied:

It was a crisp and spicy morning in early October. The lilacs and
laburnums, lit with the glory-fires of autumn, hung burning and flashing
in the upper air, a fairy bridge provided by kind Nature for the wing-
less wild things that have their homes in the tree-tops and would visit
together; the larch and the pomegranate flung their purple and yellow
flames in brilliant broad splashes along the slanting sweep of the wood-
land; the sensuous fragrance of innumerable deciduous flowers rose
upon the swooning atmosphere; far in the empty sky a solitary esophagus
slept upon motionless wing; everywhere brooded stillness, serenity, and
the peace of God.[24]   *a joke*

attempt to read too much into nature.

That "solitary esophagus" is, of course, the key to the nonsensical-
ity of the entire paragraph; but, as Twain wrote later, had he
omitted this one phrase, the paragraph would have been swallowed by his readers without suspicion.

Much "descriptive writing" (of the kind that Twain was poking
fun at) is misnamed. As the following poem suggests, the trouble
with most so-called descriptions is that they describe the writer's
feelings rather than the object itself, and do so in trite language:

AFTER SENDING FRESHMEN TO DESCRIBE A TREE
Twenty inglorious Miltons looked at a tree and saw God,
Noted its "clutching fingers groping in the sod,"
Heard "Zephyr's gentle breezes wafting through her hair,"
Saw "a solemn statue," heard "a growing woody prayer,"
Saw "dancing skirts" and "the Lord's design,"
"Green arrows to God" instead of pine,

---

[23] *The Wilder Shores of Love.* Copyright, 1954, by Lesley Blanch. Reprinted by permission of the publishers, Simon and Schuster, Inc.
[24] From "A Double-Barrelled Detective Story" (1902).

Recommending realism that does away with glu

Saw symbols in squirrels, heard musings in bees;
Not one of the Miltons saw any trees.

If you must see a tree, clean, clear, and bright,
For God's sake and mine, look *outside* your heart and write.

Take off on another poet Sydney? ROBERT HOGAN[25]

This poem specifies objectivity and clarity as desirable qualities in descriptive writing, qualities which are, of course, important in exposition generally. Some descriptive passages may aim at communicating the subjective impressions created in the writer by (to take a hackneyed example) a sunset; but even such writing should be based on clearly observed and precisely rendered details. In inferior writing, the descriptive portions are "purple passages," or unassimilated and indigestible chunks of writing which impede the development of idea or action. Good descriptive writing is not mere padding but one of the author's most useful methods of exposition.

Oliver Wendell Holmes, in his role as Autocrat of the Breakfast Table, describes his landlady's daughter about as economically as possible. Note the precision of detail and the sharpness of observation. Paradoxically, the result is a "character" sketch of a certain kind of girl represented by this particular girl.

Aet. 19+. Tender-eyed blonde. Long ringlets. Cameo pin. Gold pencil-case on a chain. Locket. Bracelet. Album. Autograph book. Accordeon. Reads Byron, Tupper, and Sylvanus Cobb, Junior, while her mother makes the puddings. Says "Yes?" when you tell her anything.

Washington Irving's description of Governor Wouter Van Twiller tells us all we have to know about the man, even though the paragraph concentrates only on the externals:

The person of this illustrious old gentleman was formed and proportioned, as though it had been moulded by the hands of some cunning Dutch statuary, as a model of majesty and lordly grandeur. He was exactly five feet six inches in height, and six feet five inches in circum-

---

[25] *The AAUP Bulletin,* Winter, 1957. Reprinted by permission of the author and the American Association of University Professors.

ference. His head was a perfect sphere, and of such stupendous dimensions, that dame Nature, with all her sex's ingenuity, would have been puzzled to construct a neck capable of supporting it; wherefore she wisely declined the attempt, and settled it firmly on the top of his backbone, just between the shoulders. His body was oblong and particularly capacious at bottom; which was wisely ordered by Providence, seeing that he was a man of sedentary habits, and very averse to the idle labor of walking. His legs were short, but sturdy in proportion to the weight they had to sustain, so that when erect he had not a little the appearance of a beer-barrel on skids. His face, that infallible index of the mind, presented a vast expanse, unfurrowed by any of those lines and angles which disfigure the human countenance with what is termed expression. Two small gray eyes twinkled feebly in the midst, like two stars of lesser magnitude in a hazy firmament, and his full-fed cheeks, which seemed to have taken toll of everything that went into his mouth, were curiously mottled and streaked with dusky red, like a spitzenberg apple.—WASH-INGTON IRVING[26]

In the selection that follows, R. B. Robertson is faced with the problem of describing a whale. In passing, it should be noted that this description does not occur until the sixth chapter of his book describing a whaling voyage. Why not earlier? Because the description precedes his first account of how a whaler handles and dismembers one of these huge creatures; the ensuing account of that process means more to us because we have just realized the size of the creature that is being dealt with. Notice the various expository methods that are used in the description, including the vivid imagery of the last paragraph:

In talking or writing of whales, especially that greatest of them all, the blue whale or sulphur-bottom, one quickly runs out of adjectives. *Huge, immense, enormous, titanic, mighty, vast, stupendous, monstrous, gigantic, elephantine, mammoth, giant, colossal, Cyclopean, Gargantuan* —these are all the adjectives that Mr. Roget can find to help us. None of them is adequate to convey the bulk of the blue whale to one who has not seen it; some of them, such as *elephantine,* are pygmy adjectives

---

[26] *Knickerbocker's History of New York* (1809).

which give only an emaciated impression of this greatest of all monsters of all time, for he has the bulk and weight of fifty elephants.

So, when I ran out of words, I went to Mansell seeking figures, and, as usual, he was able to give them to me—figures more accurate (I believe) than any yet published of the size and weight of a fairly large blue whale. The whale was weighed and measured piece by piece at Stromness Whaling Station, South Georgia, on November 8, 1926, the day after it was killed. Mansell was present at the operation. He believes—and, considering his great knowledge of whaling, he is probably right—that it is the only occasion in whaling history when such an operation has been performed. The weights were computed for commercial reasons, for I do not believe that any whaling firm would have held up production long enough to perform such a task for scientific purposes; if the figures contain some commercial secret which scientists should not know, I can but say that Mansell and I are more interested in the whale than we are in the whale owner. Here they are ("The whale is what man call a fat nice whale" was Mansell's heading to the page of figures):

Measurements:

Length:	27.18	meters	(89	feet	approx.)
Height (lying on side):	3.10	"	(10	"	")
Circumference:	13.90	"	(46	"	")
Jawbone length:	6.95	"	(23	"	")
Flukes " :	5.90	"	(18	"	")
Fins " :	3.00	"	(9½	"	")

Weights:

Blubber:	25,651	kilos	(26	tons	approx.)
Meat:	56,444	"	(56	"	")
Bone:	22,280	"	(33	"	")
Tongue:	3,158	"	(3	"	")
Lungs:	1,226	"	(1	"	")
Heart:	631	"	(½	"	")
Kidneys:	547	"	(½	"	")
Stomach:	416	"	(½	"	")
Intestines:	1,600	"	(1½	"	")

Liver:	935	″	(1	″	″	)
Blood:	8,000	″	(8	″	″	)
Jawbone:	2,177	″	(2	″	″	)
Skull:	4,508	″	(4½	″	″	)
Backbone:	10,230	″	(10	″	″	)
Ribs:	3,863	″	(4	″	″	)
Flukes:	1,153	″	(1	″	″	)
Fins:	960	″	(1	″	″	)

The total weight of this "fat nice" (but not extraordinarily large) blue whale was 122,004 kilograms—that is to say, about 120 long tons. Reduced to oil (and perhaps this is where the commercial secret, if any, lurks) she made the following:

Blubber Oil:	13,604 kilos	(13½ tons approx. or 80 barrels)				
Meat Oil:	6,880	″	(6½	″	″	or 40	″	)
Bone Oil:	7,224	″	(7	″	″	or 42	″	)
TOTAL:	27,708	″	(27	″	″	or 162	″	)

In passing, compare with the production of oil from this whale by modern methods a statement in a book concerning a cruise of the famous *Charles W. Morgan,* last of the New Bedford whaleships: "We continued our cruise for some six weeks longer and took whales enough to make us about two hundred and fifty barrels . . ." But they did not hunt the "fat nice" whales in those days.

Now, to make these unique figures I have quoted intelligible to mathematical imbeciles like myself, let us correlate them with better-known things: The length of the beast is that of a railroad car, and its height and girth are about the same. An elephant could walk under its upended jawbone without touching at any point. Its fins are the size and weight of a pretty large dining-table, and its flukes would make an excellent pair of wings for a fighter aircraft. (They are also perfectly streamlined, and, as I am sure their toughness and durability exceed that of Duralumin, I commend them to aircraft designers.) Its blubber, Mansell estimates, would keep all the votive candles burning in St. Peter's, Rome, for a century or more; and its meat would supply a hamburger (and a good one, too!) to every person in Boston, Mass. Its tongue would overload a fair-sized truck, and it would take six very strong men to lift its heart. Its skull is the size and weight of a motor car, but the brain contained therein is not much bigger than the carburetor. Its blood would fill seven thousand milk bottles, and, if we wish to go into physiological astronomy, it contains by my reckoning some eight million million red blood corpuscles.—R. B. ROBERTSON[27]

Brigadier General S. L. A. Marshall, recounting the story of a patrol action during the Korean War, first sets the stage by describing the terrain on which the action took place. Notice the economy of the picture and the few but relevant selected details. This description, the first four paragraphs of his account, is not mere introductory padding; the "game" that is about to be played will be determined by these specific facts of topography.

From the mass of hill 172, which was part of the main line at the extreme left of the division sector, three hogbacks ran roughly parallel toward the river. Hill 172 was generously proportioned and a full infantry battalion could stand guard there.

The hogbacks were called "fingers" because they directly abutted the big hill. But they were in fact transverse subridges set perpendicularly to the American fire front. The banks of the river and the extreme ends of the hogbacks were no-man's country though the outposts from both sides pressed close enough to oversee the river trench in daylight. Deep-scored valleys, each having its small stream and complex of paddy fields, separated the hogbacks.

The graduated descent of the hogbacks, their fairly smooth and reasonably straight-running crests marked by well-beaten paths leading to the disputed ground, invited vigorous patrol action. They were like so many staircases permitting a comfortable approach to the danger zone where the Communist enemy was most likely to be found after dark. The terrain features on his side of the river having an almost identical character, his patrolling was not less vigorous.

With the river serving as a kind of neutral buffer, the game played by both sides was to maneuver down to its embankments, set up a deadfall and then wait hopefully. It was like animal trapping, with man as the trapper, the bait and the prey.—S. L. A. MARSHALL[28]

[27] *Of Men and Whales.* Copyright 1954 by R. B. Robertson. Reprinted by permission of Alfred A. Knopf, Inc.

[28] *Pork Chop Hill.* Copyright © 1956 by S. L. A. Marshall. Reprinted by permission of the publisher, William Morrow & Company, Inc.

In describing the contents of the old-fashioned "general store" of the nineteenth century, Gerald Carson had to present an almost overwhelming number of specific details. His method, you will note, was to use a simple device of organization. Notice that these details are not presented only for their nostalgia value, but that the description as a whole develops the idea of the changes that took place in the institution of the country store.

In the interior arrangement, the dry-goods counter usually ran along the right side, as you faced the store from the front entrance, and was heaped with drills, sheetings, calicoes, button molds, and trimmings. Little touches might be seen which showed how new refinements were reaching the country trade. Napkins and towels came already hemmed. Work shirts were sold already made up. There were satchels for traveling, now that people could move around more. Cotton thread came on spools, "run off" by pretty girls called "spoolers," Wilbur Cross recalled, "who easily found husbands." The thread was displayed in a dispenser cabinet which sat on the counter. One type whirled around, shaped like a great cylinder, to show all the gauges and colors of "Merrick's Six Cord Soft Finish Spool Cotton." Another cabinet was made with drawers, one line of lettering on each drawer:

> Sole Agent O.N.T. Spool Cotton On white spools
> George A. Clark

Large bins or "boot boxes," five or six of them, arranged according to size, from boys' up, stood along the floor, the lids loose for easy access. They overflowed with congress gaiters, factory-made shoes for men, high-button shoes for women. No individual packaging for each pair; that came later, after the introduction of the "shoe box." Some of the new styles were even shaped to the foot, right and left, an exquisite new comfort. A wire contraption hung from the ceiling, among the baskets and lanterns, a lady's bustle, serving no purpose other than to provide the silhouette and rear elevation currently prescribed; it was the fashion, and was advertised as having lots of "shelf."

Even the smells and redolences of the store were different as the nineteenth century entered its third quarter. The wet spot under the kerosene barrel contributed a new characteristic, raw and dominant. Among the good things to be seen and sniffed was a row of aromatic pails filled with fine-cut tobacco—one kind of consolation. Gleaming jars behind the counter offered another. They held a bewildering variety of corn kisses, hearts, Gibraltars, cinnamon red hots, lemon gumdrops, Zanzibars, and conversation candy—little lozenges called "cockles," a small crisp candy made of sugar and flour. Tucked inside each shell-shaped piece were little slips of tinted paper delicately printed with rhymes and sentiments. Often the mottoes were printed right on the candy. Some were the very pink of wit: "Why is love like a canal boat?" "Because it's an internal transport." Some were daring: "Did you wink?" and "O you Kid."

. . . . .

Opposite the dry goods counter, with its row of upholstered cast-iron stools for the comfort of the ladies, there was another counter which ran parallel to it for the entire length of the main store. Showcases rested on it for candy, cigars, cutlery, and here the store cheese was kept under glass. Behind the counter were shelves for light groceries, tobacco, chewing gum, and patent medicines. The sugar and cracker barrels stood at the end of the counter. Nail kegs with their tops knocked in were arranged along the front. In some stores the grocery counter had an iron railing about eight inches high along the front, good for keeping the drummers and loafers from lolling there and getting in the way of the customers. There was always a back room behind the main store where "a great hogshead of Porto Rican molasses lay on a stout frame near a large cask of beef in brine, a small cask of pickled mackerel, and a pile of dried codfish, at a safe distance from a barrel of kerosene oil."

The cubbyhole where the merchant did his paper work also showed the spirit of change. The old stand-up desk, the quill pen, and black blotting sand were gone, and in their place the store had an up-to-the-minute roll top which gave an unbroken view of the store, equipped with steel pens, blotting paper, and wire penholders. The big store lamps overhead, with their dangling smoke bells, which were guaranteed not to explode, made the store seem a "white way" compared with the candle and Betty lamp era.—GERALD CARSON[29]

The descriptive process can be summarized as the ordered arrangement of details, within a definite framework, and from a definite point of view or points of view. Obviously, successful

---

[29] *The Old Country Store.* Copyright 1954 by Oxford University Press, Inc.

description depends on the intelligent arrangement of concrete details. Student writers frequently forget, however, that before details can be made to mean anything, a framework and a point of view must be provided. Consider the following description:

His unusual height and broad, heavy-set shoulders combined with his unkempt, dark hair and peculiarly menacing expression to give him an air that was, to say the least, forbidding.

Were we to ask several students to suggest in more detail exactly what the unpleasant looking male here briefly described looked like, we would get a variety of interesting answers, but it is unlikely that we should get the right one; we had intended to describe a gorilla. The fault, of course, is ours; we neglected to supply any framework that would give the details meaning.

In addition to a framework, point of view is another fundamental element of descriptive technique that beginning writers are particularly likely to neglect. In its most elementary form, the importance of a clearly understood and clearly stated point of view can be illustrated by imagining the differences in appearance of our gorilla were we looking at him from a vantage point on the ceiling directly above him or from an airplane two thousand feet in the air, rather than from a position ten feet in front of him. Every description must establish and maintain throughout a clear physical point of view or sequence of points of view.

Point of view is a more complex matter than mere physical point of view. The selection of details is governed by more than what the observer can see and describe from the points he has established for himself. Equally important is emotional point of view, the attitude the writer feels and wishes to convey about what he is describing. To an observer ten feet in front of him, a gorilla must convey a sense of menace and terror; to an observer in an airplane two thousand feet above him, he may seem no more than a curious bump on the terrain. The physical point of view determines what object and how much of the object shall be described; the mental point of view determines the dominant tone of the description. The whole nature of a description can be changed by a shift in either point of view. Sometimes, of course, a change is desirable; the writer may wish the reader to view the described object from various positions, or with varying attitudes. Generally speaking, however, a consistently held point of view, both physical and mental, is prerequisite to clearness in description.

The careless writer is prone to describe objects or persons haphazardly, without any thought for the total effect. As a result, such a writer is more than likely to produce description that confuses rather than clarifies. If, for example, in describing a building, the writer constantly changes from exterior to interior, from front to back, from a distant point of observation to a near one, the impression gained will be decidedly hazy. If, on the other hand, the writer describes the building as seen from one definite point of view, he is much more certain to create a picture that will have reality and vividness for the reader. Should it be necessary to describe a building—or any other object—from several points of view, *the shift from one point of view to another should always be indicated in such a way that the reader will be aware of the change.* Likewise, if the writer is describing an object or scene as beheld by persons of varying temperaments, or as it affects him in different moods, the change from one attitude to another should be made clear.

EXPOSITION BY NARRATION

A narrative is concerned with the reporting of an event or events. It may range from the most trivial remark—"I saw Jim Brock at the theater last night"—to a monumental work of fiction like *War and Peace*. In the hands of the great novelists, the narrative mode is capable of creating works of art that permanently intensify and illuminate all of human experience for us. In other types of prose, such as history and biography, the narrative mode is primarily expository in purpose. When narration is used to illustrate or exemplify an idea, it is also expository. The passages reprinted below show various ways in which narration may be used as an expository method. (For further examples, see section ¶ 4E and section O 6E.)

Long ago, near the beginning of the world, Gray Eagle was the guardian of the sun and moon and stars, of fresh water, and of fire. Gray Eagle hated people so much that he kept these things hidden. People lived in darkness, without fire, and without fresh water.

Gray Eagle had a beautiful daughter, and Raven fell in love with her. At that time Raven was a handsome young man. He changed himself into a snow-white bird, and as a snow-white bird, he pleased Gray Eagle's daughter. She invited him to her father's lodge.

When Raven saw the sun and the moon and the stars and fresh water hanging on the sides of Eagle's lodge, he knew what he should do. He watched for his chance to seize them when no one was looking. He stole all of them, and a brand of fire also, and flew out of the lodge through the smoke hole.

As soon as Raven got outside, he hung the sun up in the sky. It made so much light that he was able to fly far out to an island in the middle of the ocean. When the sun set, he fastened the moon up in the sky and hung the stars around in different places. By this new light he kept on flying, carrying with him the fresh water and the brand of fire he had stolen.

He flew back over the land. When he had reached the right place, he dropped all the water he had stolen. It fell to the ground and there became the source of all the freshwater streams and lakes in the world.

Then Raven flew on, holding the brand of fire in his bill. The smoke from the fire blew back over his white feathers and made them black. When his bill began to burn, he had to drop the firebrand. It struck rocks and went into the rocks. That is why, if you strike two stones togeher, fire will drop out.

Raven's feathers never became white again after they were blackened by the smoke from the firebrand. That is why Raven is now a black bird.

—ELLA E. CLARK[30]

In primitive societies, the man adept in storytelling was honored for his skill and sometimes given special distinctions and rewards. As this retelling of an Indian legend shows, his tales were not only a source of pleasure in themselves, but also embodied

---

[30] *Indian Legends of the Pacific Northwest.* Copyright 1953, University of California Press.

explanations of the phenomena of the natural world. The directness and simplicity of the legends is admirably illustrated here.

A typical use of narrative to illustrate a generalization ("Don't try to bluff a ranger") occurs in the following passage:

A ranger is a man's man. He likes animals and flowers. He can spend all day on a horse and half the night on a square-dance floor. He comes in two styles, the year-round career man and the "90-day wonder," the seasonal ranger who works only during the tourist rush seasons. No matter what kind he may be, he talks facts and listens well. Don't try to bluff a ranger. I made that mistake once. . . .

We camped by a stream brimming with snow melt. Cold winds whistled through the stunted pines at timber line. I looked around at my companions stretched wearily on the ground after a hard day in the saddle, and I thought I had them sized up.

"Personally," I said, "I could go for a nice bath in that pool down there. But of course you fellows are too tired, and I don't want to go alone, so I guess I'll have to do without."

To my horror, the ranger in our party rose and started peeling off his shirt.

The icy water nearly killed me. As I said, don't try to bluff a ranger.

—CONRAD L. WIRTH[31]

The next passage reveals a somewhat more complex handling of narration in the description of a person (in this case, Professor George Lyman Kittredge—"Kitty"—of Harvard). Instead of developing a single event in detail, the author rapidly recounts a number—not a continuous series—of anecdotes, on the basis of which he makes his judgment in the final sentence.

Some professor of economics had great charts and maps on rollers all over the front of the room, and there were two or three long gracefully sloping pointers at hand. "Kitty" picked up one of these and used it as a staff-like cane as he paced back and forth and commented. He was magnificent. He was an Anglo-Saxon king speaking to his people.

Once in his march as he socked the royal staff down, it came in two

[31] "Heritage of Beauty and History: The National Parks," *The National Geographic Magazine,* © copyright May, 1958. Reprinted by permission.

where there was a knot in the wood, and he made a somewhat unkingly lurch. A few students snickered very cautiously.

He glowered upon them. "You have a fine sense of humor!" Then without taking his eyes off the humbled faces, he drew his arm back as if he were hurling a javelin, and drove the long remnant of the pointer into the corner of the room. "Now laugh!" he dared them.

It was always a double experience. "Kitty" might suddenly step out of the Elizabethan world and pounce upon some man and scare him until he was unable to define the diaphragm—it once happened—and require him to come to the next meeting "prepared to discuss the diaphragm" as a preliminary to an hour of *King Lear*. No man might feel altogether sure that he would escape.

Once "Kitty" read with such a poetic impression of reality that a man who was later to be widely known as a magazine editor sat lost in rapturous enjoyment. Suddenly "Kitty" stopped. "Now what is the commanding word in that passage"—and he picked up the printed class list and let his eye run down over the names—"Mr. . . . . Smith?" "Mr. Smith" had been so rapturously lost that he did not even know where the passage was. A neighbor whispered the number of the line to him and he answered correctly, "Why—'God.'" "Don't you 'Why—God' me!" "Kitty" stormed back at him; and then gave him such a dressing down for using the unnecessary word as he had never known, so that he always had that to carry along with his memory of the perfect reading.

On another occasion "Kitty" picked up the class list, started on the R's, became interested in one man's brilliant answers to his rapid-fire cross-examination, and left the rest of the R's dangling in suspense throughout the three remaining months of the year.

Men knew that he was a miracle man, and thought it worth accepting all hazards in order to possess some part of his basic richness of life.

—ROLLO WALTER BROWN[32]

Richard Neutra, the architect, in the following passage gives a generalized account of the early formation of certain tastes which have influenced his work. As in the preceding passage, no single event receives detailed development; and here the narra-

[32] "'Kitty' of Harvard," *The Atlantic Monthly*, October, 1948. Reprinted by permission.

tion is even less "storylike." Neutra's narrative has less of the anecdotal than any of the preceding illustrations do, but the function is still that of developing an idea.

Early in life we spend much time floored baby-fashion, perplexed, most curious. As a two- and three-year-old, I often sat on the parquet of my parents' apartment, studying the raised, splintery grain of the worn hardwood and the warped boards. The cracks beween the boards were filled with a compact something which I liked to dig out with my fingers. To grown-ups the floor is distant. Had they stooped to examine what I produced from this quiet resting place of open parquetry joints, they would have called it dirt. Magnification could have shown it to be a teeming microbiotic world. I tested it by the toddler's ancient test— put it into the mouth and found it "no good."

Strange as it may seem, my first impressions of architecture were largely gustatory. I licked the blotter-like wallpaper adjoining my bed pillow, and the polished brass hardware of my toy cupboard. It must have been then and there that I developed an unconscious preference for flawlessly smooth surfaces that would stand the tongue test, the most exacting of tactile investigations, and for less open-jointed, and also more resilient flooring. I recall, that scantily dressed or naked as I was, I became uneasily aware of the surface on which I sat and moved.

It was then, also, that I first experienced the sensation of towering height by looking upward to the carved top of a Victorian dresser. I was more awed and impressed then, later, by the gigantic columns that support the vaults of the cathedral of Milan or the roof of the Temple at Luxor.

The idea of shelter is associated in my mind with a feeling that took root in me during those days. Our parlor ceiling was uncomfortably high, and so I used to sit and play under the grand piano. The low headroom under our piano provided me the coziest place I knew. Many likes and dislikes must have taken shape in the child I was, as they do in every child. At night there were dark, inaccessible, mysterious spaces—such as that frightening area back of the olive-green upholstered love seat, placed "catty-corner" into the room. I still shudder at the memory. And I still loathe the waste of space behind furniture.

Those many childhood experiences taught unspoken lessons in appreciation of space, texture, light, and shade, the smell of carpets, the warmth of wood, and the coolness of the stone hearth in front of our kitchen stove.—RICHARD NEUTRA[33]

Clarity is just as important in narration as it is in any other kind of composition. In order to tell a clear and coherent narrative, a writer must keep in mind the importance of selection and proportion. Inclusion of unimportant or irrelevant details clogs the flow of narrative, and may even divert it into a different channel. A character in Mark Twain's *Roughing It* never finishes telling a wonderful story about his grandfather's old ram, because each new detail he mentions reminds him of another story, ad infinitum.

Related to the quality of selection is proportion. Obviously, limitations of time, space, and purpose must be considered in telling a narrative. It is up to the writer to decide how much time is to be covered, how long the narrative is to be, and what its purpose is. Then he can place his emphasis by eliminating or foreshortening certain parts of the story and developing more fully the parts he considers most vital. Failure to observe these two requirements of narration may result in a story that is confused, pointless, or—worst fate of all—simply dull.

EXERCISES

A. Definition

I. Evaluate the following statements as satisfactory formal definitions. Rewrite each, first formally and then in operational terms.

1. "Home is the place where, when you have to go there, They have to take you in."—ROBERT FROST

2. Basic research is something you're doing when you don't know what you're doing.

3. Love is a many-splendored thing.

4. Abstract art is art that is not realistic.

---

[33] *Survival Through Design.* Copyright 1954 by Oxford University Press, Inc.

5. Religion is the opium of the people.—KARL MARX

6. A slide rule is a timesaver for the person who knows how to use it.

7. Freedom is the power to do what you like.

   Freedom is liberty.

   Freedom is freedom to do the will of God.

   Freedom is the recognition of necessity.

   Freedom is what we have in America.

II. Write two extended definitions of any term from the list below—one definition for a general audience and the other for a specialized audience. Assume that all your readers are intelligent adults, but that only those in the second group are trained in the field from which the term comes.

butterfly stroke	mutant
cathode-ray tube	myopia
Chippendale	noun-determiner
clover-leaf intersection	pan dissolve
dissonance	place setting
em	quanta
fuel injection system	referendum
full court press	stratified random sample
Italian sonnet	Texas leaguer
jet propulsion	topic sentence

III. In a textbook or a specialized periodical, find an extended definition of a term similar to those in the list above. Rewrite the definition for an audience of nonspecialists.

B. Analysis

1. Write a paper analyzing your college or university (or your home town, or the place you are now living in). First classify it as part of a larger whole, specifying your principle of classification. Then partition it into its component parts, according to a single and consistent principle of division.

2. Write an analysis based on one of the suggested topics below. A principle of division is also suggested for each topic, but you may want to choose another.

Athletes (academic incompetence)
Automobiles (mechanical deficiencies)
Campus organizations (usefulness)
Coeds (vanity)
Eating places (service)
Jobs (monotony)
Movies (realism)
Teachers (aloofness)
Television commercials (silliness)
Textbooks (dullness)

Before writing your paper, review the section on the outline (O 4), and draw up an outline for your projected theme.

C. Comparison and Contrast

Draw up an outline for a theme to be developed by means of comparison and contrast, based on any one of the following suggested topics. Write a theme developing the outline.

City life and farm life
High school and college
Partnership and corporation
Television drama and legitimate theater
The campus cafeteria and a fine restaurant
The Model T and the Thunderbird
Brother and sister (or father and son, or mother and daughter, and so on)
Canasta and contract bridge
Astronomy and astrology
Two candidates
Two teams
Two political systems
Jet planes and propeller planes
Two movies (or books, magazines, plays, poems, and so on)
Two friends (or presidents, parents, authors, and so on)
Two occupations (or cities, hobbies, processes, and so on)

D. Description and Narration

1. From another source—a book of readings, a novel, a newspaper, a magazine article—bring to class examples of descriptive and narrative writing used for expository purposes. How has the author's purpose determined his point of view, framework, selection, and proportion?

2. Write a description of a person you know, developing it by means of illustrative narrative. Then (for purposes of this exercise) turn the exposition inside out: write a narrative in which the character is described. Compare the two versions. How has your purpose in each affected your selection, order, and emphasis?

X | Argument

"An Argument," wrote a facetious editorialist in 1835, "is a series of positive assertions and denials, ending in a quarrel."[1]

Although some today might still agree with this definition, we can think of argument less cynically and more profitably as a mode of persuasive discourse the object of which is to change someone's ideas or actions *through the use of logical proofs.* Before examining the principles of argument, let us look briefly at the means by which men try to win assent for their beliefs or to cause changes in the thought and behavior of others.

ARGUMENT AND PERSUASION

JIM WHITE FOR SCHOOL BOARD!

Purple Heart Veteran—Businessman—Father of Four—Member of American Legion, VFW, Chamber of Commerce, Rotary, Elks, and PTA

VOTE FOR JIM WHITE!

This not unusual advertisement, of a kind which springs up and flourishes widely around election time, is clearly designed

[1] The New York *Mirror,* March 14, 1835.

to influence action. But the basis of its appeal is very little to the mind. Mr. White gives no reasons why he would make an especially desirable member of the school board; his qualifications are aimed at evoking irrelevant responses—to create warm and sympathetic feelings toward him as a family man, a wounded veteran, a civic-minded member of the community, and so on. A scapegrace character in James Russell Lowell's *Biglow Papers* (1848), returning from the Mexican War minus a leg, defines the best qualification for political office: "Wooden leg!" is his campaign slogan and his answer to the invitation to discuss issues. The formula hasn't changed much in over a hundred years.

Political discussion is only one area—if the most obvious— where persuasive appeals are aimed not at the head but the heart. Despite his title, "Common Sense," and his opening statement that he will "offer nothing more than simple facts, plain arguments, and common sense," Thomas Paine's famous propaganda pamphlet advocating American independence is full of inflammatory emotional appeals: besides the appearance of logical reasoning, he uses the devices of name-calling, ridicule, irony, heavily charged abstractions, and slanted emphasis. In the twentieth century, a dictator like Adolf Hitler relied less on appeals to rationality than on rabble-rousing techniques to gain power. History, in fact, is full of demagogues whose success was due not to their skill in using rational proof but to their ability to sway audiences by the force of their personality or by appealing to greed, prejudice, and fear.

The lawyer who pleads for a verdict of not guilty for his client on the grounds that, although a convicted bank robber, he is a devoted parent, and the advertising man who promotes a certain brand of cigarettes by suggesting that this brand is preferred by virile outdoorsmen, are also trying to persuade. But they are not presenting logical *arguments*. Nonrational appeals are often extremely successful in bringing about changes in thought and behavior; human nature being what it is, one can never overlook the force of sheer emotionalism as a persuasive device. But it is not that kind of persuasion that we are concerned with in this chapter: our subject matter is the form of persuasion known as argument, which is distinguished from the emotive appeal by its use of logical proof.

It should be noted that emotive persuasion in itself is not necessarily dishonest or immoral. The appeal in Winston Churchill's famous Dunkirk speech in 1940 had the effect of reinspiring the British people after a crushing military disaster. Franklin D. Roosevelt's speech on the theme "We have nothing to fear but fear itself" had the same objective during the darkest days of the economic depression. In each case, the obvious confidence and strength of the speaker and his emotion-charged language combined to create a powerful *persuasive* effect. But in neither case was there the pretense that these speeches were discussions of military strategy or economic policy, dealing with the question "What shall we do now?" They were frankly—and successfully— "pep talks."

The extent to which we can be convinced by an argument depends in part on our response to the character and personality of the speaker or writer as well as on the logical proof supplied. But when the logical proof is either shaky or completely absent, we should at least know that we are being persuaded by nonrational means. Sometimes we have a predisposition to accept a writer's statements regardless of the nature of his proof; this may be satisfying, but it is not logical. And since that kind of subjective response gets us over into the field of psychology and away from the methods of argument, let us now return to our subject.

Like good expository writing, good argument demands that the writer focus on a specific purpose, that he consider his audience, that he provide definition, detail, and organization to clarify his ideas, and that he select clear and appropriate language. Argument does not take us into a new world; it tries merely to explore another part of the same world. As was pointed out in Chapter IX, exposition may very well achieve the same result that argument sets out to do: that is, to effect changes in thought and action. For example, a colorful description of the Gaspé Peninsula may make a reader decide to go there on his next vacation. A young boy, reading a biography of Charles Steinmetz, the electrical genius, may very well develop an interest in science that may change his future life. In this chapter, however, we are concerned with the *conscious* attempt of the writer to convince through reasoned discourse—the discourse that is built on the principle that, because one assertion is true, another one should be believed.

THE PROBABLE TRUTH

Whether you argue that the college cafeteria needs a good nickel cup of coffee, that the football team needs a new coach, or that America needs a different foreign policy, argument is the same. Its effectiveness lies in proving the *probability* that something is as you say it is. You cannot be absolutely certain that the coffee is overpriced, but you may, on examining all the evidence you can muster, believe that it is; thus, you believe that the coffee is probably overpriced. Rarely, if ever, are we provided with absolute proof. Even in the sciences, our knowledge is quite tentative and based on "laws" which turn out to be only working hypotheses, always subject to change upon the discovery of contrary evidence. Consequently, when we try to prove something, all we can ordinarily hope to do is to show that we are probably right. The concept of probable truth is crucial to argument. When two absolutists face each other, each convinced that the other belongs in a mental institution because he does not see THE truth, resolution of any issues through argument is impossible.

The concept of probability is important for another reason. What will seem probable to different audiences will vary according to their backgrounds and predispositions. It takes less thoroughly developed reasoned discourse to convince a Democratic reader that his party is "the party of the people" than it would to convince a Republican. Your roommate might agree with your argument in favor of abolishing final examinations, but your instructors might find your argument weak. An American presidential candidate addresses the entire nation, but a candidate for the office of senior class president addresses a smaller group.

In writing for the campus literary magazine or newspaper, or for the *New Republic, Fortune,* or the *American Mercury,* the vast differences among the readers of these journals as to what constitutes proof will greatly affect the scope and shape of your presentation.

But, even though probabilities and not absolutes are the basis of argument, and even though audiences may differ widely in their requirements for satisfactory proof of probable truth, there are some standards we can apply; for argument is based upon certain well-known principles of logic. It is not our purpose to provide a one-chapter course in logic, but logic—which is the attempt to build a science of reasoning apart from considerations of audience—does provide the ground rules for testing our own and others' arguments.

ANALYZING THE ARGUMENT

Since argument arises out of controversy, let us classify the kinds of controversy in which men find themselves. Men ask questions about whether something is true or false (a question of *fact*); whether it is good or bad, and if so, good or bad by what criteria (a question of *value*); and whether some course of action should be adopted (a question of *policy*). Before we can discuss such questions profitably, however, they must be clearly formulated. We phrase these questions as propositions; that is, we phrase them in such a way as to indicate the exact conclusion we wish the reader to draw from them. The proposition of facts asserts that a statement is true: "Professor Reardon is a teacher of biology." The proposition of value asserts the value of something: "Professor Reardon is a good undergraduate teacher of biology." The proposition of policy asserts that a given action should be undertaken: "You should take Professor Reardon's course in biology." Now, it is quite possible that the first two propositions may be untrue, and the third an unwise recommendation. Indeed. to have argument there must be some reason to question the proposition; otherwise the writer is not arguing but merely explaining something already accepted as true by the reader—a waste of time for both.

Once you have phrased the proposition exactly as you mean to prove it, you must analyze it in order to discover the real basis of the controversy: that which must be proved.

The statements at the basis of the controversy are called *issues*. An issue is a controversial statement, of vital importance to the proof of the proposition. It is necessary to determine the real issues, because argument about accepted or trivial points degenerates into either a mutual admiration society or pointless, illogical controversy. Two students are arguing about the comparative advantages of various makes of automobiles.

PAT: The Spitfire is the best car on the market.
MIKE: I agree.

No argument. Now, again:

PAT: The Spitfire is better than the Thunderbolt because more Spitfires are sold than Thunderbolts.
MIKE: The Thunderbolt is better because it rides more smoothly than the Spitfire.

Here there is merely controversy. The issue ("Which is the better car?") has been defined, but the means of resolving the controversy have not been agreed upon: the criteria are not clearly established. Now, once more:

PAT: More Spitfires are sold than Thunderbolts.
MIKE: That's true. I saw the same sales figures you did.
PAT: That proves that the Spitfire is the better car.
MIKE: Now, hold on! Sales figures have nothing to do with determining the better car. Let's consider such other criteria as performance, mileage, styling, and cost of maintenance.

At last we have the argument. The issues have been sorted out, the question of fact has been agreed upon, and the question of value is about to be explored by first deciding on appropriate criteria.

The logical thinker will find the issues and center his writing around them. He will spend little time on the unimportant, secondary matters, the ideas that are commonly accepted, or the facts that are easily available. One of the major weaknesses in argumentative writing is the tendency to develop incidental topics while ignoring the real areas of controversy. This tactic, incidentally, is widely employed for purposes of emotional persuasion: "So you say that Baker is your favorite author? Well, did you know that he's a Communist?" How to handle this kind of argument will be treated below, in discussing methods of refutation.

Issues are found in propositions of fact and value by establishing criteria. In the final dialogue between Pat and Mike, Mike has gotten around to doing just that. When a man is taken to court on the charge that he has committed a crime, the judge or jury requires some criteria for judging him. The laws which society has enacted form those criteria; they are the basis upon which his guilt or innocence is determined. You pay a fine for driving past a stop light, because one criterion for calling you guilty is failure to stop at a stop light. If you wish to prove that capital punishment deters crime, you will need criteria. Now your criteria will be based on how you define your terms: "capital punishment" may be defined easily enough, but what do you mean by "deters crime"? If you say that to deter crime means to prevent crimes from taking place, you have one criterion. You must then search the evidence to see if you can prove that capital punishment prevents crimes that would otherwise take place were such punishment not in effect.

Other questions may require more than one criterion. You are trying to prove the following proposition of value: "Willie Mays is the best outfielder in the major leagues." If you say that there are four criteria for evaluating outfielders—hitting, fielding, running, and team play—you would evaluate Mays against other players to see which best meets all four criteria. The issues will be found and the argument focused when your opponent says that Mickey Mantle is a better hitter and fielder than Mays. If you agree that the most important criteria are those of hitting and fielding, it is then up to you to prove your original contention by summoning valid evidence. Another possibility exists, however, in the definition of criteria. You may deny that hitting and fielding are more important than running and team play, in which case you must decide which criteria of value your argument will employ—just as Pat and Mike must decide which criteria they will have to use in order to decide the question of which is the best car on the market.

Propositions of policy are somewhat more complex, but we do have some help in the so-called stock questions of policy. These are three questions which help us decide whether or not a policy should be adopted: (1) Is there a situation which warrants a change? (2) Will the proposed change work? (3) Will the proposed change be desirable? If these questions can be answered affirmatively, we may conclude that the policy should be adopted. Within each of these stock questions we will find areas of disagreement which will lead to the issues, because, as explained earlier, the answers to the questions will be propositions of fact which can be analyzed.

Let us look at an example. You argue that a "B" average should be required of all student government officials. (1) Everyone involved in student activities on your campus agrees that a real problem exists; many student leaders get low grades because the extra work their offices entail cuts into their study time. (2) To require a "B" average is certainly workable: it is an easy matter to change the constitution, and there are other people on campus with "B" averages who could be officials. But (3) opponents of your measure may disagree on the grounds that it is undemocratic to deny office to a person on the basis of his grades. They argue that your proposal is undesirable because it is undemocratic. You must then argue that the requirement of a "B" average for student government officials is a democratic one. From this proposition of value, you can find the issues by establishing a criterion based on the word "democratic" and applying it to your proposition. The proposition of policy, in the final analysis, is based on propositions of fact and value.

Issues once found will form the basis for the argumentative paper. You will note that this process of analysis must be completed before the paper is written: it is a process of determining *what to write about*. In your paper, taking these issues as a basis, you must supply reasoning to show that your conclusions are (probably) true. The two kinds of reasoning processes—the inductive and the deductive—are discussed in the following sections.

INDUCTIVE REASONING

Logic concerns itself with two major problems: *material truth* and *formal validity*. This means that we are concerned about whether our statements are probably true and whether the conclusions we deduce from these statements have been reached by acceptable methods. The process of examining instances to see if we can find in them generalizations that are acceptable as being materially true is known as *induction*. The process of reasoning from generalizations to find out things about individual cases within the generalizations is known as *deduction*. Induction is grounded in the instances of the real and experiential world, but deduction has no necessary connection with the world of experience (a deductive argument, as we shall see, may have the required formal validity and yet lack material truth).

Just as we need specific details to make exposition clear and interesting, we also need specific evidence to prove arguments. This evidence is of two kinds: evidence of fact and evidence of opinion. Of either kind, evidence must be of sufficient quantity and reliability to prove to the reader that the generalization has material truth. You might try to form a dependable generalization about the intelligence of freshmen. How true are the following statements for you? How much evidence would you demand before accepting them as true?

All college freshmen are intelligent.
Most college freshmen are intelligent.
Some college freshmen are intelligent.
A few college freshmen are intelligent
One college freshmen is intelligent.

Note how the change of a single strategic word changes the believability of the statements. In the first sentence is a generalization about every case, in the last a statement about a single case. At the lower end of the scale a few examples—or even one—will provide proof; at the upper end, more proof is necessary.

For the first statement we would soon give up trying to provide examples of Sam, Alice, Jack, Patricia, Peter, Mary, and so forth, and would have to turn to more impersonal forms of evidence, such as statistics in a study made by the National Education Association or the Department of Health, Education, and Welfare, or a statement from the chancellor of the University of Chicago. Such evidence does not itemize all the examples upon which the generalizations were formed, but we are asked to accept the generalizations because the agency or the person making them has, we assume, examined a sufficient number of instances to make a valid generalization. We tend to accept the generalization because we may have the opportunity to know the actual cases that the writer has observed, or because the generalization comes from a source we consider reliable. The personal evidence is both more immediate and more interesting, but the impersonal is more believable when a greater number of instances is involved. In either case, we are merely asking the writer, "How many examples do you have to support your generalization?"

Three major pitfalls in inductive argument may be identified: the fallacies of abstract language, false use of authority, and hasty generalization.

Fallacy of abstract language. Problems of meaning have been discussed earlier (see Chapter V). The same word, you will recall, may have one connotation for you and quite another for your reader. Therefore, before accepting another's generalization or before making one yourself, be sure that both you and your reader understand the terms in the same way. "All college freshmen are intelligent." "Most men are handy with tools." "All women are bad drivers." "Most rich people are Republicans." "Most Democrats come from the middle class." "Most preachers are good public speakers." Do you and your reader agree on what you mean by intelligence, being handy with tools, bad drivers, rich people, middle class, good public speakers? If you cannot be sure that the terms of your generalization are clear to all concerned, then you must define your terms before you reason from this generalization. Your position may be materially true, but the reader will never accept your proposition if he does not understand your generalization as you do.

False use of authority. Because our limitations of experience force us to use other people as sources of evidence, we must be certain that we use only qualified authorities. Your neighbor may be a competent automobile mechanic, but is he a competent authority on ballistic missiles? Is the president of the local Rotary Club an expert on juvenile delinquency? Is your state senator competent to evaluate your state's educational system? In our democratic society, where everyone may speak and write as he chooses, too many of us accept as true anything that appears in print. "I read it in a book," is often regarded as signifying "It must be true." The real question to ask is: "Who wrote the book—and when?" The *Reader's Digest* is not the last word on science and medicine; nor is *Time* an outstandingly objective authority on international politics. Furthermore, even granted authority of source, recency must also be weighed. Ancient geographers, who maintained that the earth was flat, are obviously not reliable sources today on matters geographical; likewise, a statement on atomic physics that may have been up-to-date in 1941 is probably reliable no longer.

In presenting your evidence, you are under another obligation: if you have satisfactorily ascertained the competence of your source, who may, however, be unknown to your audience, you must authenticate his reliability. Otherwise, when you write, "As Aloysius McGonigle says . . ." your reader may very well respond with "Who's he?"

Besides being authoritative, a reliable source should also be as objective as possible. Some authoritative sources are quite biased. That is why the CIO–AFL and the National Association of Manufacturers often find themselves on opposite sides of the fence. Both are authorities on labor-management relations, but both speak from special positions. On the other hand, we have come to accept as unbiased such sources as the Brookings Institution, the Weather Bureau, and the Bureau of Labor Statistics.

Finally, in building your argument, you cannot afford to overlook or dismiss negative evidence. If you select only the authorities who tend to support your generalization, you are in danger of having your reader puncture your argument by pointing out evidence to the contrary which you have not considered. If you do consider the negative evidence, you must, of course, then show why it does not affect your generalization: it is an eccentric minority opinion, the author himself repudiated the opinion at a later time (or it was shown to be invalid by another source), and so forth.

Hasty generalization. The most common varieties of this fallacy are (1) claiming more for the generalization than the evidence proves, and (2) generalizing from an unrepresentative sample. The first fallacy is best illustrated (in its most exaggerated form) in a statement like "All Indians walk in single file; the one I knew up in Maine did." This is the fallacy underlying the stereotypes of race prejudice. Some Negroes may be ignorant, some Jews may be avaricious, and some Mexicans may be lazy, but it does not follow that most or all are. Nor are all college professors absent-minded (though some may be) or "eggheads" (many are not).

The second fallacy is the result of our being unable to examine all the possible instances and, therefore, being forced to generalize from a sample of the population. Suppose you wanted to know what percentage of students believed in subsidizing athletes. You would first need to be sure that the people you polled were drawn from many and varied groups on campus. To interview only members of the athletic teams and then announce that all students favor subsidy (because everyone you talked to urged subsidization enthusiastically) would be to generalize from an unrepresentative sample.

To summarize, then, the inductive process is the process of forming generalizations from the evidence of facts and opinions. In doing so, certain checks must be applied:

1. Is the language clear to both you and your audience?
2. Is your authority competent in the subject?
3. Is your authority unbiased?
4. Have you taken negative authorities into consideration?
5. Does the generalization assert only what the evidence shows?
6. Is the generalization based upon a representative sample?

If you can give an affirmative answer to these questions, you may be reasonably sure that you have formed generalizations that will stand the test of probability. You have provided the basis for establishing the material truth of your assertions.

DEDUCTIVE REASONING

Whereas inductive reasoning combines like items to generalize about them, deductive reasoning reverses the process: it uses generalizations as a means of learning about specific cases. While both induction and deduction are concerned with the material truth of general ideas, the significantly different problem in deduction is that of *formal validity*. If you have avoided the pitfalls of fallacious induction, your problem in deduction is to put your ideas together in such a way as to reach a valid conclusion.

Conan Doyle's famous detective, Sherlock Holmes, provides a familiar example of the way the inductive and deductive processes work together. Holmes, you will recall, is constantly startling his colleague, Dr. Watson, by announcing the most amazingly accurate predictions based, apparently, on almost no evidence whatsoever. It cannot be denied that, strictly speaking, Holmes is luckier than he is logical; however, he reconstructs the inductive-deductive relationship very clearly when he explains to Watson how he solved any particular mystery. For example, Holmes knows that left-handed British soldiers who have served in India *always* hold their cheroots in such a way that the ashes fall in such and such a way. How does he know this? On the basis of having examined a sufficient number of examples: his generalization is based on induction. Therefore, whenever he sees ashes piled in such and such a way, he immediately deduces that they *must* have been dropped there by a left-handed veteran of the Indian campaign.

In a somewhat less gaudy fashion, we combine induction and deduction every day of our lives in order to reach conclusions. For example, the Smiths are watching television one night in their living room. Mrs. Smith plugs in the electric coffee-maker in the kitchen, Smith Jr. turns on his radio in his room, the electric heater goes on automatically in the bathroom—and suddenly the whole house is plunged into darkness. Automatically, Mr. Smith goes out to replace a fuse. Now, it may very well have been a failure at the power station that is the source of the trouble, but Mr. Smith has reasoned without actually reconstructing his ideas in logical fashion, or verbalizing them, that his family has probably overloaded the electric circuits—*as it has done in the past.* The specific conclusion is drawn from a generalization which itself is based on a number of previous instances.

Let us examine two passages in which the deductive process appears:

There is nothing revolutionary in the concept that renewable resources are the property of all the people and, therefore, that land use must be coordinated into an overall plan. . . . In effect, private ownership of the country's resources is countenanced only if the use of such resources is directed towards the interests of the people as a whole.

—FAIRFIELD OSBORN[2]

Americans have drawn from this [Coke's dictum, "Reason is the life of the law; nay, the Common Law itself is nothing but reason"] the obvious inference that if it isn't reasonable, it can't be good law.

. . . .

But such laws [the Fugitive Slave Laws] did not seem either reasonable or right to the people of the Free States; hence, these people could

---

[2] *Our Plundered Planet.* Copyright 1948 by Fairfield Osborn. Reprinted by permission of Little, Brown and Company, Inc.

never be convinced that such statutes had the force and effect of real law.—GERALD JOHNSON[3]

Both writers proceed from a general idea to a specific application. In the first passage, Osborn begins with a general principle that renewable resources are considered to be the property of the people, and he arrives at the conclusion that the use of these resources must be for the benefit of the people as a whole. Johnson states that if the American people believe an act to be unreasonable, it isn't good law. The people believed that the Fugitive Slave Laws were not reasonable, and therefore these laws could not be good (real) law.

Each writer asks his readers to accept a conclusion about a specific case on the basis of a generalization about such cases in general. But there is an interesting thing to note: each writer has left something out. Osborn can be considered logical only if we accept something he leaves unsaid: the reader must believe without being told that what is the property of the people must be used for their benefit. Johnson gives us everything we need in order to see the deduction involved, but bases his argument on a general statement about "the people" which might not always be true of all people. Both passages exemplify informal argument in what is known as the *enthymeme*. This is the form that most of our argument takes; it is a form of deduction which leaves it to the reader to supply some of the ideas essential to following the reasoning.

Another form of deduction is known as the *syllogism,* which is the primary tool of formal logic. This form consists of a major premise which states an absolute general rule, makes a specific application in the minor premise, and draws a conclusion about the specific case on the basis of the general rule.

MAJOR PREMISE: Everything that is the property of the people must always be used for their benefit.

MINOR PREMISE: All the renewable resources are always the property of the people.

---

[3] *Our English Heritage.* Copyright, 1949, by J. B. Lippincott Company.

CONCLUSION: The renewable resources must always be used for the benefit of the people.

. . . .

MAJOR PREMISE: All unreasonable acts are not good law.
MINOR PREMISE: The Fugitive Slave Laws were not reasonable.
CONCLUSION: The Fugitive Slave Laws were not good law.

Testing the deductive argument. The principal problem in deduction is that of drawing valid conclusions from the initial generalization, a problem which applies to both the enthymeme and the syllogism. Logic has given us a method of testing the deductive argument; for the sake of simplicity let us present these arguments in syllogistic form (incidentally pointing out some typical syllogisms) and then examine the procedures for testing them.

The most common syllogism is the categorical (or "all") form. The examples given above are categorical. Here is another:

MAJOR PREMISE: All English professors are sadists.
MINOR PREMISE: Mr. Blakeslee is an English professor.
CONCLUSION: Mr. Blakeslee is a sadist.

The "if" form of deduction indicates what will happen if a given event occurs. It hypothesizes that one act will be produced if another act is initiated, shows a specific instance of this first event, and concludes that therefore the second act will occur.

MAJOR PREMISE: If Professor Morgan calls on me today, I will be embarrassed.
MINOR PREMISE: Professor Morgan will call on me today.
CONCLUSION: I will be embarrassed.

The "either-or" form of deduction is one which gives two alternatives and then removes one.

MAJOR PREMISE: Either a student passes the final examination or he fails the course.
MINOR PREMISE: You did not pass the final examination.
CONCLUSION: You will fail the course.

In each of the deductive forms above, you will note that there are no more and no less than three terms or ideas. In each syllogism, also, you will note that one of these three ideas, called the "middle term," appears in both the major and the minor premise. This middle term is the basic link in the deductive chain, for if two separate ideas are each related to a third, they must in some way be related to each other.

There are a number of principles governing the logical structure of the formal syllogism. Certain of these principles are more obvious than others and are therefore rarely violated in practice, even by people who have never heard of a syllogism. We note them here in order to set the background for those which are more persistent sources of confusion. If the syllogism or the enthymeme meets these criteria, it may be presumed to have formal validity.

The syllogism must contain only three terms.

MAJOR PREMISE: Communist nations have large standing armies.

MINOR PREMISE: The United States is a democratic nation.

CONCLUSION: (Any conclusion would be so ridiculous that you would not need any knowledge of the rules of reasoning to refute it.)

If either of the premises is negative, the conclusion must be negative. In algebra, multiplying a negative and a positive always produces a negative; likewise in deductive reasoning, one negative statement automatically makes the conclusion negative.

MAJOR PREMISE: No students in our class are married.

MINOR PREMISE: Barry Jones is in our class.

CONCLUSION: Barry Jones is married (of course not!).

An interesting variation on this—equally invalid, because it juggles meanings of the terms involved—is the following:

MAJOR PREMISE: No students in our class are married.

MINOR PREMISE: Barry Jones is no student.

CONCLUSION: Barry Jones is married (he still isn't).

The middle term must be distributed; that is, it must be used in a universal sense in at least one of the two places where it appears in the premises.

MAJOR PREMISE: All murderers are criminals.

MINOR PREMISE: Many criminals escape the law.

CONCLUSION: (All murderers escape the law?)

Obviously not. The syllogism proves nothing, because there are many kinds of crime besides murder; it is possible that those who escape the law are arsonists, embezzlers, burglars, and so forth. If the syllogism does not show a necessary conclusion, it shows nothing, and it cannot show a necessary conclusion if the important middle term is not distributed.

No term can be given universal application in the conclusion unless it is used in a universal sense in the premise in which it appears.

MAJOR PREMISE: Many ballplayers go fishing during the winter.

MINOR PREMISE: Men who go fishing are called fishermen.

CONCLUSION: All ballplayers are fishermen.

If a premise makes a statement about some of the members of a class, the conclusion cannot extend to cover all the members. The conclusion does not manufacture truth: it merely points out what is implicit in the premises.

Let us examine the argument in the following advertisement:

Joan Henderson is an American housewife. She lives in a middle-class neighborhood in Newark, N. J., with her husband, a widget maker at the General Products Corporation. Like the other American housewives she knows, she can count as one of her blessings that she has more laborsaving devices than the great majority of the women of the world.

This is good argument by enthymeme. Reconstructed as a syllogism, it would go as follows:

MAJOR PREMISE: American middle-class housewives have more laborsaving devices than any other housewives in the world.

MINOR PREMISE: Joan Henderson is an American middle-class housewife.

CONCLUSION: Joan Henderson has more laborsaving devices than most housewives in the world.

As an example of formal logic, this would never win a prize, but it does illustrate how much of our deductive reasoning is carried on in terms of statements that are probabilities, rather than absolutes. We frequently accept as universally applicable statements that we know are not absolutely true:

All men are created equal.

A college education is beneficial.

What goes up must come down (no longer universally true in the age of man-made satellites orbiting around the sun).

From these statements we deduce conclusions which we accept as true—not partly true or probably true. Regardless of our starting point, however, the tests of deductive method are still to be applied as a measure of determining formal validity.

To summarize: the principal problem in deductive reasoning is that of establishing valid relationships of the ideas from the generalization to the conclusion. It is important to note, however, that we can construct a formally valid argument from even the most nonsensical premise if the rules of deduction are not violated.

MAJOR PREMISE: All Texans are twelve feet tall.

MINOR PREMISE: Jack Davis is a Texan.

CONCLUSION: Jack Davis is twelve feet tall.

Therefore, when we examine an argument for its formal validity, we should not overlook material truth.

SPECIAL FORMS OF REASONING

We rarely find reasoning neatly blocked out in generalizations which are based on organized evidence and followed by syllogisms or easily defined enthymemes. As in the case of Sherlock Holmes, induction and deduction are combined; or certain special forms of reasoning may be taking place. These are, respectively, *reasoning from sign, reasoning from cause and effect,* and *reasoning from analogy.*

Reasoning from sign. This form of reasoning is based on a stated or unstated assumption that two or more things are so related to each other that when one is found, the other item(s) will also be found. Some signs are reciprocal and some are not. A "For Sale" notice on a piece of merchandise is a sign that it is for sale, but not all items which are for sale will have signs on them. On the other hand, seeing fishermen in a boat on a local lake will be a sign (unless they are breaking the law) that the fishing season has begun; and the opening of the fishing season is a sign that there will be fishermen on the lake (barring impossible weather conditions).

In addition to being reciprocal and nonreciprocal, a sign will also be either fallible or infallible. Both signs cited above are fallible; that is, in each case there is a possibility that other factors may invalidate the sign. The merchandise may have been sold, but the seller may have forgotten to remove the notice. The fishermen may be fishing illegally. In each case the probability that the sign is valid is so strong as to make the argument effective, but it is also possible that the sign is wrong. Fallible signs are found most often in social, political, and economic problems. The infallible sign is usually limited to physical phenomena. For example, the presence of gardens, orchards, and vineyards constitutes an infallible sign that there is water in the vicinity. An ice-coated puddle of water is an infallible sign that the temperature has dropped below the freezing point.

The major test of reasoning from sign is to question whether the argument claims more than the degree of fallibility of the particular sign will allow. Is there a claim of infallible sign where other factors may be present? Four tests may be used to check this form of reasoning:

1. Is a reciprocal relationship claimed where none exists?

Because we know that enlightened management provides good working conditions, we cannot therefore assume that good working conditions are a sign of enlightened management (the conditions may be the result of the activity of a strong union).

2. Is there a real relationship?

"That boy will grow up to be a criminal. See how close together his eyes are?" There may be criminals with eyes that are close together, but if there is a relationship between criminal tendencies and the distance between one's eyes it is probably a coincidental one.

3. Have special factors which alter normal relationships been overlooked?

It is a fairly reliable sign to say that school is in session because many people are seen strolling around the campus. But it is possible that business, religious, or farming groups may be holding meetings on the campus during the summer while students and faculty are away on vacation.

4. Where a single sign is not conclusive, do we have other signs to reinforce our conclusion?

The detective often has little to go on but a series of scattered clues. One clue by itself tells him nothing, but each new detail tends to make the signs more and more conclusive. Footprints matching the suspect's shoes. Discovery of a motive. Blood under the suspect's fingernails. A witness who testifies that the suspect was seen loitering near the scene of the crime. Taken together, these signs may be presumed to be conclusive evidence of guilt.

Reasoning from cause and effect. This form of reasoning is both the most difficult to prove and the most vital to argument. It attempts to explain why a given event came to pass or to predict what event will later come to pass as a result of another event. It is difficult to prove because we rarely find single cause-to-effect relationships. Modern science has taught us that we must think in terms of fields of forces exerting their influence to bring about a certain effect. Our historians have also taught us, for example, that the Civil War was not caused solely by argument over the slavery issue. Causal reasoning is the most vital kind of reasoning because we are frequently unable to indicate a solution to a problem until we know its causes. You might take an aspirin for a headache without bothering to determine the exact cause of the pain, but you would hardly kill off all adolescents because of an alarming increase in the juvenile crime rate. In social problems particularly it is necessary first to determine the causes before proceeding to suggest solutions to those problems.

A major problem in causal reasoning is our tendency to confuse it with sign. Even a good sign only indicates what *is* true about a case; it does not indicate *why* it is true. The fishermen on the lake did not cause the season to open. Nor did the opening of the season cause them to go fishing: they may have gone out because of the sport, or the prospect of food, or the desire to get away from their wives. This kind of error is common in causal reasoning, as the following passage shows:

> Moscow is one of the largest cities, with a population in the 5 million bracket, and yet it is reported to have only five gasoline service stations. Add to that the fact that real service is nonexistent. You do-it-yourself— the attendant just collects the rubles. That's what can be expected when the state is owner and boss. No competition. In comparison, there are more than that many stations within a biscuit's throw of the center of Hicksville—and all operated by men anxious to serve you.

The lack of filling stations in Moscow could be a sign of many things—lack of automobiles, Russian emphasis on production of other commodities, the attitude of the government, and so forth— but one would be hard-pressed to say in the light of Russian scientific and technological advances that the lack of filling stations is a necessary consequence of the Soviet form of government.

Another fallacy in causal reasoning is that which assumes a relationship between two events only because one follows close upon another. This error (known to logicians as *post hoc ergo propter hoc,* or *after this, therefore because of this*) is illustrated in the case of a boy who eats parsnips for supper, becomes violently ill in the night, and refuses to eat parsnips the next day because he says they made him sick. When he dies three days later of appendicitis, the fallacy in his reasoning becomes obvious.

Reasoning from analogy. In this form of reasoning, the writer argues that two objects, ideas, or events which are alike in all the recognizable characteristics will also be alike in some other characteristic that is not observable. There are two forms of analogy—the literal and the figurative. In the literal

analogy the writer compares two objects from the same class—
two governments, two cities, two colleges, two movies. The figurative analogy, on the other hand, compares two items from essentially different classes. Although more interesting than the literal
analogy, and sometimes quite helpful in clarifying an idea, the
figurative analogy has no logical basis. It is never logical proof
in itself; it is merely an illumination of the author's original
proposition by means of an imaginative device. Note the analogies
in the following passages:

> Students should be allowed to use their books during examinations.
> Carpenters are allowed to use blueprints and lawyers are allowed to
> use legal briefs.
>
> An income tax form is like a laundry list—you always lose your shirt.
> —FRED ALLEN
>
> Politics in a novel is like a pistol-shot in the middle of a concert,
> something loud and vulgar and yet a thing to which it is not possible
> to refuse one's attention.—STENDHAL

Although interesting and even amusing, they will be recognized
as weak arguments. A less obviously flawed analogy is that contained in a newspaper editorial which pointed out the necessity
of playing a game by the rules and declared that the Constitution
was the rules for the federal government. As one cannot change
the rules of a game every few minutes to suit his mood, so the
administration must not change the rules of the government. It
must play the game. The essential fault here, and one that destroys the effectiveness sought for by the use of analogy, is that
governing a nation is not a game, that the object of governing is
not the same as the object of playing, and that, in consequence,
there may be reasons for changing the "rules" of one which do
not apply to the other.

Two essential tests should be applied to every analogy to
determine whether it is sound. It is necessary to ask if the analogy
is grounded in a sufficient number of specific cases and if the
writer has considered the negative instances. Obviously, finding
things to be alike in a limited number of ways does not mean
that they are alike in all other ways. The fact that two men are

both forty-two years old and Baptists does not necessarily mean that both are Democrats because one is. Likewise, the extensive parallels between the American and Russian constitutions do not mean that each guarantees the civil rights of the individual citizen.

METHODS OF REFUTATION

Our writing is frequently concerned not so much with building a case for an idea of our own as with refuting the case of another. On controversial topics we soon discover that stating our own position is not enough, regardless of eloquence or vehemence; we must refute an opposing argument before building our own. Refutation is of two kinds, the general and the specific.

The general methods of refuting an argument are to take the opponent's generalizations, deductions, signs, causes, and analogies and to point out (if possible) how they fail to meet the tests that have been mentioned earlier. In effect, this results in uncovering hidden assumptions and revealing errors of material truth and formal validity. In addition to the tests already discussed, some common argumentative fallacies are to be noted; these are the fallacies of *begging the question, ignoring the question,* and *equivocation.*

Begging the question is simply reasoning in a circle; the writer states the truth of the proposition he is actually trying to prove. "College traditions are very important. Every student ought to live up to them. Why? Because the traditions mean so much." At the end of this statement one knows no more about college traditions and their importance than he did at the beginning.

"People ought not to eat snails because snails aren't fit for human consumption." Here the second clause merely repeats the first in other words; nothing has been proved about eating snails.

Ignoring the question has been alluded to briefly earlier in this chapter. It is an attempt to shift the argument away from the issues to irrelevancies. One familiar form of ignoring the question is that of attacking the speaker instead—the argument *ad hominem.* "I don't care what his foreign policy is; I don't like the way he treats his wife." Another common tactic, already referred to, is that of sidetracking the argument in favor of a totally new one: "I've already told you, Mr. Thurlby, why you failed the course." "Well, I still don't see why you failed me and passed my roommate. He got about the same grades I did. Do you know that you've got a reputation on campus for being an unfair grader?"

Equivocation (etymologically, "calling equally") is, as the term suggests, saying two things with the same word; that is, shifting the meaning of the term during the course of the argument. A familiar mock syllogism will illustrate this fallacy:

> Some girls have red hair.
> My girl has red hair.
> My girl is some girl!

The most common special methods of refutation are (1) reduction of the argument to an absurdity; (2) dilemma; and (3) turning the tables.

The refutational method of reducing the argument to an absurdity consists of adopting the opposition's line of reasoning and carrying it to its ultimate conclusion, when it is shown to be absurd. Writers and speakers often make probable statements as if they were absolutes; the absolute, taken literally and extended to the utmost, is obviously absurd. A friend tells the story of an experience with his son on a camping trip. The boy had been repeatedly warned not to throw rocks on the trail, because someone might be hit. He was also told not to throw rocks in the water, because they might frighten the fish away. Finally, as the boy continued to throw rocks, the father exclaimed: "Billy, you must never, never, never, NEVER throw rocks!" To which the boy replied, "Even if a bear came after me?" If a writer is prone to use absolute statements, he must suffer the consequences of such refutation.

Using the second method of refutation, the writer detects in the opposition argument only two possibilities and then points out that both have evil consequences. Jacques Barzun uses this

method in attacking the status of science education in college. He
points out that some students study as little science as they can
get away with, and others are forced by curriculum requirements
to take almost nothing else. He then states the dilemma of modern
science education:

> The worst of all this is that neither group of students learns much
> about science but goes on to swell the ranks of the two great classes
> of modern men—the single track expert and the scientific ignoramus.
> Could anything more plainly demonstrate the failure of science to be-
> come a subject fit for college teaching?[4]

The effective refutation by this method must be based on the
realization of two mutually exclusive alternatives. If there are
other good possibilities, your opponent may legitimately reply
that you have ignored these and oversimplified his position.

In turning the tables, the writer takes an argument or a piece
of evidence which is presented as part of the opposition case and
shows how it supports, not the opposition, but his own case. A
good example is found in Stan Freberg's satirical recording,
"Green Chritma," which attacks the commercialization of the
Christmas spirit. In this version of the story, Bob Cratchett says,
at one point: "I know but—wait a minute. Don't you guys make
enough profit the other eleven months? Christmas comes but once
a year." To which Mr. Scrooge, the mercenary advertising executive, replies: "Huh, funny thing you should bring that up. That's
exactly the point I was about to make." And he sings:

> Christmas comes but once a year,
> So you'd better make hay while
> the snow is falling—
> That's opportunity calling you![5]

---

[4] *Teacher in America*. Copyright 1944, 1945 by Jacques Barzun. Reprinted
by permission of Little, Brown and Company and the Atlantic Monthly Press.
[5] Words reprinted by permission of Stan Freberg.

EXERCISES

A.

What faults in sound reasoning occur in the following passages?

1. "These men [economists] can take facts and figures and bring them together, but their predictions are not worth any more than ours. If they were, they would have all the money and we would not have anything."—BERNARD BARUCH

2. "Nature has given to men one tongue but two ears, that we may hear from others twice as much as we speak."—EPICTETUS

3. "Words are but wind, and learning is nothing but words; ergo, learning is nothing but wind."—JONATHAN SWIFT

4. The breakdown of ethical, religious, and cultural traditions has left twentieth-century man without any psychological security.

5. No matter how hot it gets in the daytime, it always cools off in February.

6. There are no typhoid germs in the water of this quarry, so it must be a healthy place to swim.

7. It is dangerous to lean out of windows.

8. The Kinsey Report proved that there is more immorality among people with only grammar school education than among college graduates. I intend to protect my daughter's virtue by sending her to college.

9. The secretary of our farm association assures us that the drought is really a blessing in disguise for the farmers, because, although wheat prices may drop as a result, the price of corn will now go up.

10. If you're so smart, why aren't you rich?

11. Alfred drank a mixture of $\frac{2}{3}$ water and $\frac{1}{3}$ gin; Bernard drank a mixture of $\frac{2}{3}$ water and $\frac{1}{3}$ bourbon; Carl drank a mixture of $\frac{2}{3}$ water and $\frac{1}{3}$ Scotch; David drank a mixture of $\frac{2}{3}$ water and $\frac{1}{3}$ brandy. They all became intoxicated. Therefore, water must be intoxicating.

12. Statistics show that many people every year die while in bathtubs; it is obviously dangerous to take a bath.

13. "All right, so I trumped your ace. You don't have to get angry— we all make mistakes. Last week you got a ticket for speeding."

14. It is a naïve theory to say that Mr. Oppenheimer is an indispensable scientist, or that only a select few scientists are responsible for such things as H-bombs, sputniks, vaccine, and radar. Behind each of these select scientists whose names we happen to know are thousands of humble workers who have gone before, each with a contribution to the whole picture. Where would Dr. Salk have been without the laboratory equipment necessary to achieve his success—where would he have been without Mr. Bunsen's burner?

15. In recent years, dentists have noted an increase in the number of cases of tooth decay among adolescents, this increase dating from the same year in which rock-and-roll music was first introduced. This kind of music is clearly a threat to dental hygiene.

16. This government and its citizens are like one big family; and, like any well-ordered family, we must learn to live within our income. Running up a big debt, either public or private, is ruinous to stability and prosperity.

17. "Had Abraham Lincoln been living today, the Rotary Club would supply him with a set of books; the Lions Club with a good reading lamp; the Cosmopolitan Club with writing equipment; the Kiwanis Club with a wooden floor for the cabin. He would have the protection of the child labor insurance. A kindly philanthropist would send him to college with a scholarship. Incidentally, a case worker would see that his father received a monthly check from the county. He would receive a subsidy for rail splitting; another one for raising a crop he was going to raise anyway; and still another subsidy for not raising a crop he had no intention of raising. Results: There would have been no Abraham Lincoln."—HENRY J. ALLEN, former Governor of Kansas

18. PAT: "I can see the fallacy in the argument that former Governor Allen presented, can't you?"

MIKE: "Yes, I think most people were able to; that's why he's a *former* governor."

19. There must be someone home. Look, there's a light on in the living room.

20. This foolish requirement should be abolished.

21. I haven't read Faulkner's latest novel, but I know it's good because I've enjoyed all his other ones.

22. My home town is the friendliest city in America. I know, because I've traveled around a lot and visited many of them.

23. Of course we were intended to be the leaders in the Pan American Union. Just look at the map. Isn't the United States above South America?

24. My vote goes to William Clark for President of the Board of Supervisors. He doesn't drink or smoke, and he reads a chapter of the Bible every day.

25. Book publishers are in business for only one reason: to make money.

26. I've been having trouble with my backhand, but if I shift to the Western grip my troubles should be over.

27. I don't want to abolish nuclear testing; isn't that exactly what the Communists want?

28. The personnel manager of a large concern: "My test when hiring a man is to see if the back of his shoes is shined as well as the front."

29. A teen-age boy who was severely injured while experimenting with a rocket fuel mixture told police: "Why doesn't the government pass a law so kids like me can't buy that stuff? We only get ourselves in trouble."

30. Newspaper columnist Holmes Alexander:

"Nearly 50 nations have joined with us in a cooperative effort to protect freedom . . . ," said the President of the United States recently. "For every soldier we have under arms our free world allies have five."

"The introduction of the barbarians into the Roman armies," wrote Edward Gibbon in *The Decline and Fall of the Roman Empire,* "became every day more universal, more necessary and more fatal."

The Eisenhower-Gibbon parallel passages, I'm afraid, tell stories that may become parallel reading in times to come.

B.

From your book of readings, a magazine, or a newspaper, select an article, editorial, or column which is clearly argumentative in nature. Test the soundness of the argument by applying the principles of sound reasoning indicated in this chapter. (As a further test, you might select a piece of writing whose argument you agree with.)

C.

In approximately a thousand words, write an argument developing one of the propositions listed below (or another one, with the consent of your instructor). Before writing your essay, decide on the audience you are trying to persuade. Describe this audience briefly in a prefatory note: for example, "A group of college freshmen planning to major in business administration" or "The Chamber of Commerce of Webster Groves, Missouri" or "The budget committee of the Student Council." In planning your paper, be sure to find the issues that will most clearly develop your side of the proposition. Drawing up an outline will help you organize your proofs.

1. The best training for a business executive is a liberal arts education.

2. America's best minds are not in politics.

3. College athletes should be subsidized.

4. Grades are a fair measure of what a student gets out of a course.

5. Power corrupts.

6. Modern art is a pretentious fraud.

7. No work of literature can be considered great unless it contains an important message.

8. The greatest threat to this country today is _____.

9. What this college needs most is _____.

10. _____ is a better _____ than _____ _____.

D.

Analyze the argument that Poor Richard presents in the following passage from the Preface to *Poor Richard's Almanac,* 1734. For the sake of the exercise, assume that you are the rival astrologer and write an essay in reply.

In the Preface to my last Almanack, I foretold the Death of my dear old Friend and Fellow-Student, the learned and ingenious Mr. *Titan Leeds,* which was to be on the 17th of *October,* 1733, 3 h. 29 m. P.M. at the very Instant of the ♂ of ☉ ☿. By his own Calculation he was to survive till the 26th of the same Month, and expire in the Time of the Eclipse, near 11 o'clock A.M. At which of these Times he died, or whether he be really yet dead, I cannot at this present Writing positively assure my Readers; forasmuch as a Disorder in my own Family demanded my Presence, and would not permit me as I had intended, to be with him in his last Moments, to receive his last embrace, to close his Eyes, and do the Duty of a Friend in performing the last Offices to the Departed. Therefore it is that I cannot positively affirm whether he be dead or not; for the Stars only show to the Skilful what will happen in the natural and universal Chain of Causes and Effects; but 'tis well known, that the Events which would otherwise certainly happen at certain Times in the Course of Nature are sometimes set aside or postpon'd for wise and good Reasons by the immediate particular Disposition of Providence; which particular Dispositions the Stars can by no Means discover or foreshow. There is however (and I cannot speak it without Sorrow) there is the strongest Probability that my dear Friend is *no more;* for there appears in his Name, as I am assured, an Almanack for the Year 1734, in which I am treated in a very gross and unhandsome manner; in which I am called *a false Predicter, an Ignorant, a conceited Scribler, a Fool, and a Lyar.* Mr. *Leeds* was too well bred to use any Man so indecently and so scurrilously, and moreover his Esteem and Affection for me was extraordinary: So it is to be feared that Pamphlet may be only a Contrivance of somebody or other, who hopes perhaps to sell two or three Year's Almanacks still, by the sole Force and Virtue of Mr. Leeds' Name; but certainly, to put Words into the Mouth of a Gentleman and a Man of Letters, against his Friend, which the meanest and most scandalous of the People might be asham'd to utter even in a drunken Quarrel, is an unpardonable Injury to his Memory and an Imposition upon the Publick.

E.

Analyze the following two discussions of Boris Pasternak's Nobel Prize-winning novel, *Dr. Zhivago.* Formulate the basic propositions underlying each argument. Are Mr. Stern and Mr. Page conducting a real argument in which the issues are clearly defined?

1. "DOCTOR ZHIVAGO" AS A NOVEL

Last year *By Love Possessed,* this year *Doctor Zhivago.* Their two writers come under the lights with what is probably their worst work; both are celebrated by intelligent critics who looked into mirrors instead

of through windows; both books are defective in conception and materials; both are used as platforms and display cases. And so on.

For seventeen pages, *Doctor Zhivago* looks like an outline for a
Tolstoy novel: three boys, different in character and circumstance, un-
knowingly interconnected, are treated with the sort of care that makes
one anticipate a well-placed unfolding of their careers. End of Chapter
One. Chapter Two takes place about two years later, and its first seventeen pages treat Lara Guishar, the girl who becomes the book's heroine,
her mother, her mother's lover who seduces her (and who, we have been
told in the first chapter, has been partially responsible for the suicide of
the hero's father), a cellist named Tyshkevich who lives next door to the
Guishars, Olga Demina, an apprentice in Madame Guishar's dressmaking
establishment, Faina Silantievna Fetisova, "Madame Guishar's assistant
and senior cutter," the lover's dog, Jack, a strike on the Moscow-Kazan
railroad, the railroad's Divisional Manager, Fulflygin, the Track Over-
seer, Antipov, Tiverzin, Khudoleiev, Yusupka, Gimazetdin, a demonstration march from the Tver Gate to the Kaluga Gate, the uncle of the
hero who "saw the fleeing demonstrators from his window," the—but
this will serve. I have mentioned only some of the characters and some
of the events on those seventeen pages. The "summary" is not less confusing than what it summarizes. Nor is the confusion ever really dispersed, for the characters and scenes are scarcely developed and almost
never exploited—unless they are taken as colorful bits in a confused
panorama. Even this explanation will not do, for many of these characters reappear in the novel, not so that one can distinguish them enough
to compare their present with their past actions, but only because even
this novelist knows that there is a limit to the number of ingredients
which can be crammed into a single dish. The effect of the first two
hundred pages of the Pasternak book might be compared to a thousand-
fold expansion of the Hakagawa–Madame de Tornquist–Fräulein von
Kulp section of "Gerontion."

Pasternak is of course a famous poet, and Edmund Wilson has called
Doctor Zhivago, among other things, including an allegory and a skazka,
the Russian folk tale, a poem. But although even narrative poems can
slight narrative and get away with it, since they have other charms to
rely on, novels cannot. Accretion is not narrative. Pasternak seems to
learn this about a third of the way through this book and begins con-

centrating on his hero, the doctor-poet Yurii Zhivago. Concentration, however, is a comparative term, and it is my view that a very few pages of Tolstoy or Stendhal would give us all of Zhivago that five hundred pages of Pasternak do. The weakness and diffusion of Pasternak's work derive from serious errors in presentation, and these in turn depend in large part on the book's form, or rather the impulses to form, at which, since they are not fulfilled, one may only guess.

Pasternak seems to have had two major formal notions for *Doctor Zhivago:* the first was to write a large, Tolstoyan novel, full of characters and scenes which would render the flavor of society; the second was to write a sort of *The Red and the Black,** an historical chronicle focussing on a hero's life. This two-fold scheme proved to be impossible for Pasternak to execute. In the first place, a Tolstoy novel works not with characters and scenes—despite Tolstoy's famous midnight cry of despair when he was writing *Anna Karenina* that he had forgotten to put in a yacht race—but with situations which pick up characters and scenes as they are needed. Secondly, the Tolstoy situations exist in terms of each other as parallels, contrasts or continuations. In *Zhivago,* there are no real situations, no intrigues which are followed closely, developed suspensefully and in depth. The closest approach to a situation is the love of Zhivago and Lara, but this is so interspersed with other material, so larded with capricious coincidence, that one never has the sense of effort that a serious love story must have. No wonder Wilson and other critics have tended to think of *Zhivago* as an allegory; its narrative materiality is almost everywhere too thin to absorb the reader.

If this thin diet starves the Tolstoy impulse—unfortunately not to death, for we keep meeting characters till the very end—it is fatal to the Stendhalian one. The novel of careers lasts until the death or retirement of the hero; if you begin with the hero as a young boy, and, at the same time, do a kind of Tolstoy and have three boys, you set up an immensely long novel, even if all the careers end as early as does Julian Sorel's. Even with one hero, Stendhal—unlike, say, the author of *Jean-Christophe*—centered the career about two parallel situations, one provincial, one Parisian, and thus brought off his "chronicle" as well as his

---

* Two of the five books Zhivago mentions in the Varykino chapter are *War and Peace* and the Stendhal novel.

career novel. Stendhal's controlling idea—something like, "What would become of a Napoleon in the anti-heroic Restoration?"—looks like the ideal model for Pasternak, whose root idea would seem to have been, "What happens to a good man in the bad times of revolution and collectivism?" Ambition, however, seems to have overlaid and ruined this central notion. Although I do not believe that Pasternak went so far as to attempt what Edmund Wilson suggests, "a phase-by-phase chronicle of Soviet policy, and a discussion of the development of Russian literature which touches on almost all its great figures from Pushkin to the school of modern poetry," or "a historical-political fable—see Larisa's relations with Zhivago, Komarovsky, and Pasha," I do believe that the ambition to present the career of a good man in bad times was fatally jostled by the attempt to present simultaneously the careers of a good many people drawn from many levels of society.

The presentational scheme which Pasternak employs to solve the formal problems into which ambition leads him, is, I think, largely responsible for the qualms which have led Wilson to such literary gymnastics as I have cited, and such equally enraptured critics as Irving Howe, Nicola Chiaromonte, and Stuart Hampshire to the few, soft qualifications in their reviews. The scheme consists in presenting the fictional matter in short, rapidly-shifting scenes, or, to cite Howe's excellent description, in "clipped vignettes . . . apparently meant to suggest a Tolstoyan breadth and luxuriousness of treatment." These scenes, or fragments, are "clipped" by a variety of narrative sins which succeed in blighting almost every breath of life which Pasternak's handsome imagination began to conjure. Here are some of them:

1. Unwarranted, unsignalled transitions:

> Nikolai Nikolaievich refused to believe him and dashed out but was back in a minute. He said bullets whistled down the street knocking chips of bricks and plaster off the corners. There was not a soul outside. All communications had stopped.
> That week Sashenka caught a cold.
> "I've told you a hundred times, he's not to play near the stove," Yurii Andreievich scolded.

2. Displacement of dramatic narrative by curtailed observations:

> For some time they sang the "Marseillaise," the "Varshavianka," and "Victims You Fell." Then a man who had been walking back-

wards at the head of the procession, singing and conducting with
his cap, which he used as a baton, turned around, put his cap on his
head, and listened to what the other leaders around him were saying. The singing broke off in disorder. Now you could hear the
crunch of innumerable footsteps on the frozen pavement.

We see no more of the man walking backwards; we don't know what
"the other leaders were saying." This is the longest of the eight paragraphs which "present" the march from the Tver Gate to the Kaluga
Gate.

3. Coincidence: there is more coincidence in this novel than would
be justified in a farce. The whole of Russia begins to look like the lobby
of a small town hotel. People simply cannot get away from each other
no matter how far they travel (nor is this the point). Coincidence is
Pasternak's way of appearing to continue the Tolstoyan novel when he
has really abandoned it for the novel of Zhivago's career.

4. Inability to relate an anecdote:

> While they were waiting for Dudorov he told the story of Dudo-
> rov's marriage . . . . The improbable gist of this story consisted in
> the following:
> Dudorov had been drafted into the army by mistake. While he
> was serving and his case was being investigated, he was constantly
> punished for absent-mindedly forgetting to salute officers in the
> street. For a long time after his discharge he would raise his arm
> impulsively whenever an officer came into sight, and often he im-
> agined epaulettes where there were none.
> In this latter period his behavior was erratic in other ways as well.
> At one point—so the rumor went—while waiting for a steamer at a
> Volga port, he made the acquaintance of two young women, sisters,
> who were waiting for the same steamer. Confused by the presence
> of a large number of army men and the memories of his misadven-
> ture as a soldier, he fell in love with the younger sister and proposed
> to her on the spot. "Amusing, isn't it," Gordon said. But he had to
> interrupt his story when its hero was heard at the door. Dudorov
> entered the room.

Stories are frequently interrupted or broken off entirely in *Zhivago*,
and for good reason. Or, as in this case, the stories are prefaced by
narrative deprecation: the clause which follows "Dudorov's marriage" in
the cited excerpt is "which he thought was comical." Such deprecation
is allied to the next zhivagary.

5. Narrative deprecation of the philosophical speeches. After Zhivago has made a profound speech about life and death: "What's come over me?" he thought. "I'm becoming a regular quack—muttering incantations, laying on the hands . . . ." Or a comic Tolstoy disciple says after one of the famous ideological speeches in the book, "I haven't understood a word. You should write a book about it!" Or the speaker is said to be drunk. The point here is that the frequent retreats from the speeches begin to sound like the author's apologies for bringing them into the novel, whereas, in reality, they are one of its chief building blocks.

6. Lack of preparation (or proper sequence):

"And now since you've been so frank with me, I'll be frank with you. The Strelnikov you met is my husband, Pasha, Pavel Pavlovich Antipov, whom I went to look for at the front and in whose death I so rightly refused to believe."

This revelation is not only sidestepped into, but around. Zhivago responds to it in this way: "What you say does not come as a surprise. I was prepared for something of the sort."

"One thing I didn't tell her—her brother, who was in the army, I think they've shot him". . . .
Mademoiselle called up Kolia and told him to find Dr. Zhivago a good seat on the train, threatening him with exposure if he did not.

We never learn what it is that can be exposed.

7. I shall end the list with a passage—out of hundreds that could have been chosen—which will indicate one of the novel's stylistic faults which cannot, I think, be blamed on the translators. This is the book's intolerable profusion of simile and metaphor.

Narrow dead-end streets ran off the square, as deep in mud as country lanes and lined with crooked little houses. Fences of plaited willows stuck out of the mud like bow nets in a pond, or lobster pots. You could see the weak glint of open windows. In the small front gardens, sweaty red heads of corn with oily whiskers reached out toward the rooms, and single, pale thin hollyhocks looked out over the fences, like women in night clothes whom the heat had driven out of their stuffy houses for a breath of air.
The moonlit night was extraordinary, like merciful love or the gift of clairvoyance . . . .

Wilson complains* that the translators sometimes lop off fine figures of speech. This is of course an intolerable liberty to take, but such pruning might well help *Zhivago's* luxuriously overweighted prose which helps destroy what little narrative movement there is.

I have gone through a partial list of the narrative flaws in order to hint at the page-to-page difficulty of reading *Zhivago,* if you're reading it as a novel and not as an "historic utterance" (as Howe put it), or as "one of the great events in man's literary and moral history" (as Wilson put it). A fuller account of Pasternak's inexpertness would treat his misuse of detail (the thick glass on p. 152), the abrupt temporal shifts (101, 105, 109), erratic switches in point-of-view (83, 106, 139, 175), and inability to compose a scene (although the meeting with the Mikulit-syns on 270–73 indicates that the inability is not total).

What we have in *Doctor Zhivago* then is a jumbled accretion nerv-ously strewn over a great many pages, its occasional lovely descriptions and speeches floating to the surface like the splintered witnesses of a shipwreck. For paragraphs here and there, the novel sounds like Tolstoy or Dostoevsky; in fact, one might assemble an anthology of passages modelled on the great Russian fiction writers from Gogol through Chek-hov. Here and there, too, there are suggestions that apparently capri-cious events or isolated descriptions are truly and crucially related to each other, not in the artificial fashion of "The Rowan Tree" chapter, but in the subtle one which Stuart Hampshire claims exists between the natural scene and the narrative events. The trouble is that the formal collapse and botched rendering obscure desired connections and indicate undesired ones. The errors of conception and presentation corrode the novelistic ambitions almost beyond recognition.

A melancholy event for a faithful reader of fiction, and if I may, like other reviewers, indulge in the Pasternak affair itself, a melancholy event for the citizen. For two years now, literate readers have been waiting for this novel, their appetites sharpened by the early reports

---

* Wilson is the only critic who seems to have read the original Russian text as well as the Italian and English versions. His demonstration of the in-adequacy of the last is fairly convincing, although he praises, indeed over-praises, its naturalness ("it does not sound translated"), finds that it cuts through some stylistic defects of the original and is a good deal better than the first English versions through which Tolstoy and Turgenev first made their reputations here.

and by its bizarre publication history. That a great poet was treating one of the great themes of modern history, and from the lip of the grave itself, this might well be a great event in "literary and moral history." It is understandable that when the novel did appear, many fine critics saw in this version of their own intellectual history a heroic and beautiful utterance. (Writing in *Dissent,* Lionel Abel confesses as much: "My liking for this book is a personal fact without significance for literary judgment; it is an accident of my own intellectual history; there is no reason why it should influence anybody else.") For those less close to the ideological fires, the misshapen bequest from Soviet Russian literature testifies to what the book itself explicitly mourns, the dissolution of that sense of individual life which the great Western novel celebrates. Who can read Pasternak's letter to Pravda and feel that he has been able to preserve intact his own individuality? That his wounds are noble ones, that they haunt and will haunt the state which inflicted them is, I think, a marvelous fact. That it does not change the other fact, the fact that his famous novel is a bad and weak one, is a melancholy business. It needs no Zhivago, however, to tell us that such a fact should not be concealed.—RICHARD D. STERN[6]

2. "DOCTOR ZHIVAGO" IN THE CLASSROOM

If a book has received the praises that *Doctor Zhivago* by Boris Pasternak has, the teachers of humanities courses may have their day and ask whether it ought to be "enskied" in the usual humanities or world literature course given on the sophomore level. Because my answer will be a tentative "yes," I would like to speak of the problems that this excellent work raises and the high demands it makes upon the reader, and leave the question of its rightful company with Homer, Dante and Shakespeare to another generation.

As everyone by now knows, it is a highly ambitious, complex, "big" novel deserving careful study. Its subject is the fate of people and, equally important, the fate of a man caught in chaos—his tiny part in championing that chaos and his determination to preserve a vestige of life despite it.

The Russian revolution, with its gathering momentum in the First

World War and with its aftermath, holds the center of the stage but is never in full focus. We hear only distant sounds of events at the upper echelons, and yet, as Pasternak says of Zhivago's poetry, "things scarcely named in the lines evoke concrete images."

What we see is the relentless unwinding of raggedy energy and the piecemeal havoc that ensues: people scurrying for food and warmth, forced into strange new roles, slipping into hardships with a gambler's faith in some odds somewhere—one's own resourcefulness, the infinite land.

Pasternak sees the revolution as a titanic happening whose origins "it is petty to explore" and that does not end when it is, officially, over. It has a mystique of its own, perhaps that of an apocalyptic miracle. We see it in expressionistic glimpses: from the enthusiastic but rational support that Zhivago's saintly uncle gives it, from the commitment to something "socially useful" that Zhivago himself makes when he chooses the medical profession, from the belief in violence that propels a railroad worker's son into a masochistic automation.

We see it recasting the loyalties of nearly all; we see distinctions between victim and executioner, Red and White, rich and poor swallowed up in the release of anarchic energies. These we see directed by a new, short-lived type—the born revolutionary, like Strelnikov, "entirely the manifestation of the will," who sets up his own hierarchy of ruthlessness, and when that is shattered must kill himself or be killed. But whether he really directs a patch of the revolution or is directed by a larger force, that is one of the moot issues of the book.

Another new class emerges, those who "adjust" and seem to make out all right, efficient, essentially uncommitted, alert, close-mouthed Samdeviatovs and Komarovskys (and Zhivago's half-brother Evgraf whose strange appearances at crucial points lend him a religious air).

And finally, we see the revolution grow into the furthest reaches of irrationality "when nothing was sacred any more," when dislocation and destruction of people occurs more casually than the mowing of a lawn. "Let us be mad if there is nothing but madness in life"—with this exclamation Zhivago and Lara, his mistress, try to withdraw into isolation only to find that disintegrate too.

And yet one would be mistaken to overlook some of the cleansing effects that Pasternak sees in the revolution. At least a vicious hypocrisy has been sloughed off, and if life has become machinery, there is no longer the ghastly mixture of soot and cosmetics on the faces of wealthy travellers that so nauseated the young Zhivago.

Such a large view of another "time of troubles" demands the form of a chronicle. Pasternak makes it up, or so it appears at first, of bits and pieces: people are there for brief, tortured moments, never to re-appear, or more often to be momentarily reunited by the most unlikely of coincidences. One has the feeling of continuous movement, continuous re-arranging of particles, as though a gigantic new shape were forming itself. Pasternak's control of short scenes is extraordinary (one thinks of his poetry and his translations of plays), but this economy, this con-centration makes for a vast profusion.

The problems that are raised by a novel in the form of a chronicle are, finally, what to exclude and how to maintain drama. Even though Zhivago and Lara gradually emerge as the hero and the heroine, there is altogether so much else, and so many links must necessarily be missing that there is a general diffuseness. One can notice Pasternak's impatience and dissatisfaction with the form as he is led to provide, in effect, four conclusions, if Lara's separation from Zhivago and Strelnikov's death are taken as the logical climax of the action.

A chronicle by its very nature will remain inconclusive. If Zhivago goes to pieces on his return to Moscow, his poetry and his children—especially Tania, who is most like him—must continue from epilogue to appendix, and still leave it unfinished. Content betrays form, or, as Zhivago realizes, "art is a hidden, secret part of content." The formless-ness of the novel is the price paid for its achieved grandeur. One may ask whether a novel can sustain such a succession of overwhelming, terri-fying events. If a discursive description of dullness is dull, can chaos be put on paper with honesty and be anything but chaotic?

The fate of Zhivago himself provides some sort of spine to the story. Even so, it can be studied as mass perpetually overflowing its mold. Zhivago's very strength, which is made up of passivity, of a gift for taking infinite punishment, and of an intuitive understanding that his salvation lies in a highly individual creativity—this strength is also essentially undramatic. He is utterly certain that "nothing can be gained by brute force."

If the point is that he is no match for the engulfing "sea of troubles" and cannot "by opposing end them," if he is a "pygmy before the

monstrous machine of the future," we know this from the very beginning and can only find it stated more and more explicitly and inevitably. On only one occasion is he moved to rebel against rebellion—
when he is on the verge of killing Liberius, the leader of a quasi-
revolutionary band and his abductor, for incessantly intoning slogans
about "the betterment of the people."

Indeed, a seemingly minor but actually a most telling symptom of
the hardening of the terror and of Zhivago's "inward" stand against it is
the breakdown of language—a matter of special interest to English
teachers. (Pasternak, however, does make it plain that a certain corruption of language existed before the revolution—still there was a margin
of play.)

Now an officialese takes over—perhaps by accident, more likely by
crude design—which harasses people, invariably works to their disadvantage, expunges means for rational, imaginative thought, and finally
coerces them into a mouthing of clichés and catchwords. In this debase-
ment Zhivago's writings and his occasional outbreaks into eloquent
speech constitute an island of precarious integrity, an "inward music."
His fits of writing resemble nothing so much as religious ecstasies.

The clarity with which he sees what is happening to language (this
is more generally true: "he saw life as it was") leads him to oppose it in
the only way he knows. Herein lies a tragic grandeur, for his need to
preserve selfhood pushes him to the "outside" as now the forgotten, now
the persecuted man. His poems are his legacy, and so is the quality of
his life as it continues in the memory of a few survivors. In his daughter
Tania's marvellous gift for story-telling we are also led to think his
genius perpetuated. "Life," he said, "is the principle of self-renewal,"
and Pasternak persuades us that his hero has caught—despite the appearance of pointlessness—the soundings of that principle.

Not only his poetry, but his ability to give and accept love ("He was
spared the humiliating, destructive punishment which failure to love is"),
and his Tolstoyan rapture for the land provide stays against the de-
humanizing that life around him has become. He does not succumb
without a struggle, but it is a struggle in the privacy of his being,
and although Pasternak would tell us that that is where the final victory
is won, it is a struggle that like all Christian drama is foreordained
to be undramatic.

If I keep harping on the novel's lack of drama, it is in part to question the validity of that criterion and to seek the secret of Pasternak's success elsewhere. I suspect a study of his more specific devices would be highly rewarding. Just one example—his device of "metaphor by juxta-position"; in a blinding snowstorm in Moscow Zhivago buys a paper, steps into a hallway to read about the Soviet assumption of power, en-counters his mysterious half-brother whom he does not recognize, goes out, and, "without thinking twice," steals some wood.

Another approach that suggests itself is to see the book in relation to its great predecessors. Zhivago is a direct descendant of Dostoyevsky's "meek"—Prince Mishkin, Alyosha, and the reborn Raskolnikov of *Crime and Punishment's* epilogue—and claims even more paternity of the Tolstoyan hero. But these fascinating matters are perhaps outside the usual humanities course.

But very much within it is the novelist's concern with ideas. As a "novel of ideas," *Doctor Zhivago* exceeds the most exorbitant require-ments. I have barely alluded to even the most obvious "themes" that in-fuse the novel. His discussions (direct and indirect) of religion, of death, of history, of love, etc. are of the very substance of the book. What can make the book so vital to young students is to note the striking cor-respondence between ideas and action—the very distinction between them grows spurious. Ideas *mean* action, ideas are made flesh. This is more true of the earlier parts of the book; Zhivago's realization that ideas no longer "count" gives him a clue to his own life and to those of others.

The political storm that the book has raised seems to me to lessen its immediate value somewhat, for the temptation (and clamor) is great "to make capital" of it as a weapon in the cold war. Needless to say, that would be doing it, and literature, a disservice. Even if it has ful-filled what must be the secret wish of all artists and all writers of all time—to ruffle the tempers of men in power—that properly concerns the political scientists or the propaganda officer who may wish to study the strategy by which a fictional commentary upon current events is "rendered into metaphor" of a past event, the revolution. It is a haunt-ing, "rich" novel, which in a course with sufficient leisure could offer ventures and adventures. We need to know it better; it is clearly worth knowing better.—ALEX PAGE[7]

---

[7] *The CEA Critic,* March, 1959. Reprinted by permission of the author.

XI | The Précis

A précis (pronounced *pray-see*) is a summary restatement of the essential thought or thoughts contained in a passage. Its major purpose is to present, as briefly as possible, the important ideas of the original. To make a good précis, the writer must understand the meaning and intent of the original. To do this, he must first distinguish between major and minor ideas, since the finished précis should be free from merely illustrative material but must reproduce faithfully the emphases, proportions, and attitudes of the passage. The writer must also phrase his précis in clear and orderly fashion, using, so far as possible, *his own words*.

Below are two examples of the précis method.

Original Form	Précis
There is a rite much talked about at college commencements and on other solemn occasions, called handing on the torch. It is derived, as you know, from the ancient torch-race, in which the spent runner passes his fire to a fresh athlete, who seizing it in turn, carries it forward for another stage. By a beautiful symbolism, the term is transferred to the transmission of skill and wis-	One function of the true scholar is to transmit significant knowledge to succeeding generations. When, as happens too frequently, this function is usurped by the mere antiquarian, the emphasis is likely to be on facts that, in themselves, have no great significance. From this point of view, the emotional discovery of America —a continuous process—is more

Original Form	Précis
dom and inspiration from one generation to the next. When this business is in the hands of true athletes, I think there can be no doubt that living fire does pass from one generation to the next, and is borne on over new paths. But having studied for many years in academic places what is called the torch-race, or the transmission of the great tradition, I have observed that this semi-priestly function has a certain tendency to fall into the hands of antiquarians; and when this happens, what is transmitted is not the flaming torch but the cold candelabrum, which is rather an impediment than an inspiration to the runner.	important than the fact of its physical discovery. (65 words)

For such students of letters as are interested rather in the torch than in the candelabrum it occurred to me that one might find a more suggestive theme than the landings of the old navigators in the *emotional* discovery of America. Until it is emotionally discovered it remains a barren and rather repugnant land to letters. Certain young men imagine that this process was not even begun till about 1900; but that is a mistake. The special appeal of this theme is

Original Form	Précis
that the emotional discovery of America has been going on for a very long time, that it is still going on, and that it will go on after we are all dead and forgotten, with just as much zest as it had a hundred years ago or thirty years ago, and with just as much room for discovery as it offered thirty years ago or as it offers today.[1] (328 words)	

Original Form	Précis
Few cultures, unless isolated by insuperable barriers and numbed into submission by exceptional rigors of climate, have ever practiced anything like complete self-subsistence, or autarchy. Interregional transport is one of the pillars of urban life: it multiplies contacts, social relations, products; and by the very diversity of the resources it brings together contributes to the specific pattern of the city's life. The clogging of the main routes of transportation, such as the stoppage of oriental trade through the Bosporus after the Turkish conquest of Byzantium, may vitiate the life of a city which, like Venice, lies at the	The social and commercial life of cities depends on their proximity to trade routes. Climate also influences city growth. Although cities generally flourish where growth and storage of the hard grains are possible, each city is uniquely characterized by its own adaptation to climate. (44 words)

[1] Stuart Pratt Sherman, *The Emotional Discovery of America*. Copyright 1932, by Rinehart & Company, publishers.

Original Form

other end of the route. On the other hand, the multiplication of trade routes may pour into a single center a larger population than it can handle competently: witness the uneasy sprawl of Hamburg and London.

No less important is climate. The climatic belt in which cities have flourished is a broad one: it is roughly coincident with the distribution of the hard grains, whose suitability for permanent storage probably contributed greatly to that stability and continuity out of which city life could grow. One may speak of rye cities, wheat cities, maize cities, rice cities. The city is, in effect, a means of overcoming partly the effect of climatic conditioning and direct topographic control: hence their wide range in temperature and height from Angkor to Helsinki, from Rotterdam to Mexico City or Lassa. City life takes one form in the Mediterranean area, where the mild climate decreases the need for protective shelter and increases the opportunity for public life in the open. It takes another form in the North, where the words "chimney" or "roof" are sufficient to indicate

Original Form

a dwelling house. Climate does
not so much limit the existence
of cities as individualize the type
of urban adaptation. Each city
has its characteristic play of
weather, set off against its special
landscape: the fog of London,
the stinging wind of Edinburgh,
the luxuriant warmth of palm-
lined Los Angeles, the dramatic
patches of sunlight in the gloomy
skies of Berlin, set in the midst
of its pine-barrens.[2] (360 words)

It will be observed that both précis above are not only much
shorter than the original passages but differ in other important
respects as well. The extended figure of speech—of the torch and
the candelabrum—used by Stuart Pratt Sherman has been
dropped altogether and with it have disappeared the rhythms
and the diction that constitute his distinctive style. What remains
is a clear but rather matter-of-fact statement of his essential ideas.
The précis made of Lewis Mumford's paragraphs, in compressing
the thought into three sentences, likewise eliminates his telling
examples. The précis should not be thought of as an improvement
upon the original, nor does it in any sense "take the place" of the
original; it is simply a compressed version of the author's main
thoughts which shows that the writer of the précis has understood what he has read and is able to restate those thoughts.

Another point worth considering here is that the précis maker
has a great deal of latitude in choosing the exact words in which
he will express the original author's ideas. Of the passages given
above, for instance, several different précis might be written: the
essential idea will, of course, remain the same, but the phraseology
may vary considerably.

---

[2] Lewis Mumford, *The Culture of Cities.* Copyright, 1938, by Harcourt,
Brace and Company.

THE VALUE OF PRÉCIS MAKING

This preliminary study of the way a précis is made may help to show the potential value of the process. If a person can make a satisfactory précis of a passage, however long the passage may be, he assures himself and he reveals to others that he has comprehended the meaning of the original. He reveals, also, that he has not only understood the details of the passage but has read discriminatingly and has been able to pick out the major ideas of the author.

Précis making, then, can be of great value in aiding one to comprehend what he has read. Consistently practiced, it leads one to pay attention to ideas as well as to words, thereby increasing efficiency in reading; it leads also to adeptness in grasping the important things that a writer has to say. The précis-making habit can be put to a very practical, immediate use in condensing the material of reports, lectures, and other speeches, in taking notes for research papers or other compositions, and in the writing of examination papers, for many an examination question calls for a brief statement of facts that may have been accompanied in the student's reading by a mass of supporting details.

Précis making, also, causes one to strive for an economy of expression in which one word or phrase does the work of a whole series of words and phrases. In this way it helps to teach a sense of word meanings and word values. In attempting to find words that will more concisely express an author's thought, the précis maker is almost sure to add variety and flexibility to his own vocabulary—an accomplishment that will stand him in good stead in any kind of written or oral expression. In order to gain this particular value, the writer of a précis should make every reasonable effort to use his own words. Only by putting the gist of the original passage into his own words does the précis maker show clearly that he has grasped the thought of the original, and made it his own. And only by using his own words can a writer gain from précis making the useful training in economy of expression that the exercise provides.

Finally, a real—and pragmatic—value of précis making is that it is a first-rate study tool in that it can help the student remember what he has read and comprehended.

HOW TO WRITE A PRÉCIS

Through continued practice précis making becomes a simple, natural, and effective process. Once the procedure has been mastered, a writer will probably be able to get good results without paying much attention to its mechanics. Until mastery has been achieved, however, it is advisable to follow a few simple, logical steps in the making of a précis.

1. Read (or listen to) the passage carefully. It is desirable, of course, to read the passage more than once, to make sure that you have a good grasp of the content and have not overlooked any important ideas. Watch out for figures of speech, for paradoxes, for irony; authors do not always intend that their words should be taken literally. Read for *ideas,* for the meanings *behind* as well as *in* the words.

2. Take any necessary notes on what seem to be the important ideas. This step is almost indispensable in making a précis of oral material. In using printed or typewritten material, you may obtain the same results by underlining key words, phrases, and sentences. The notes or underlining will call your attention, later on, to what you have judged to be the important parts of the original passage. A possible test for judging the relative importance of any statement or part of a statement is to ask the question: "If this phrase (clause, sentence) were omitted, would the *basic meaning* of the passage be changed?" If the unit of expression can be omitted without materially changing the essential idea, the chances are that it is not very important—from the point of view of the précis maker.

3. Express the essential ideas, in your own words, in the fewest sentences possible. Try to make sure that you have brought in *all* important ideas, and that you have not sacrificed sense for the sake of brevity. Remember that even among the important

ideas some are more important than others; do not try to reduce all parts equally. Remember, also, that you are, in effect, standing in the author's shoes as you write the précis. Even if you disagree with his ideas, don't introduce your disagreement into the précis, for this is to misrepresent the original passage.

4. Go over the précis to assure yourself that you have avoided awkward or ambiguous sentence structure, repetition of ideas, and wordiness. Check your finished précis with the original to see that you have not misunderstood or misrepresented any of the thoughts of the author. It is well to follow the paragraph divisions of prose material—a paragraph of précis for each paragraph of the original—unless, of course, you are asked to make a single précis of a whole essay.

A WORD ABOUT PRÉCIS LENGTH

It is impossible to give any arbitrary rule for determining the length of a précis. Some passages can be reduced to a third of the original length; others, depending on the amount of merely illustrative material they contain, may be successfully condensed to one tenth. The important principle to keep in mind is that *your précis should state, in your own words and as briefly as possible, all the important ideas of the original passage.*

EXERCISES

A.

A few selections, of varying degrees of difficulty, are given below; it may be interesting to discover how well you can reduce them to précis form. Throughout this book are other passages of quoted matter that can be used for the same purpose. Books, magazines, and newspapers offer a wide variety of material for additional practice.

1. There are today elderly men who can remember a pioneer father's attitude toward work, and the pains he took to inculcate a respect for it in his sons. This devotion to work is exemplified in the custom of early rising. It is said that one father would on Monday morning at four o'clock shout to his sleeping sons: "Get up, boys! Today's Monday, tomorrow's Tuesday, next day's Wednesday—the week's gone and nothing done!" Men everywhere were going to work early and staying late. Others were driven by example or counted worthless. Idleness, even in the name of art, literature, music, or scholarship, was not understood, and he who practiced it enjoyed no prestige. The naturalist Audubon was not able in 1824 to find a single patron who would subscribe to his magnificent work on birds in Philadelphia, and had to go to Europe for publication and support. The devotion to work, which began as a necessity, became a creed and the principal article of economic faith. It brought many rewards, but it ruthlessly crushed out many fine qualities which human beings derive from leisure. The rewards were largely material rather than artistic and spiritual, and so in time it came to be said that America developed a materialistic culture with the dollar mark as its symbol. Other interests than work slowly developed as the culture matured, but they have had to make their way against the vested interests and traditions of useful work.—WALTER PRESCOTT WEBB[3]

2. The sciences of observation and experiment are alike in this, that their aim is to detect the constant or recurring features in all events of a certain kind. A meteorologist studies one cyclone in order to compare it with others; and by studying a number of them he hopes to find out what features in them are constant, that is, to find out what cyclones as such are like. But the historian has no such aim. If you find him on a certain occasion studying the Hundred Years War or the Revolution of 1688, you cannot infer that he is in the preliminary stages of an inquiry whose ultimate aim is to reach conclusions about wars or revolutions as such. If he is in the preliminary stages of any inquiry, it is more likely to be a general study of the Middle Ages or the seventeenth century. This is because the sciences of observation and experiment are organized in one way and history is organized in another. In the organization of meteorology, the ulterior value of what has been

observed about one cyclone is conditioned by its relation to what has been observed about other cyclones. In the organization of history, the ulterior value of what is known about the Hundred Years War is conditioned, not by its relation to what is known about other wars, but by its relation to what is known about other things that people did in the Middle Ages.—R. G. COLLINGWOOD[4]

3. Large-scale production implies regularity of output. The customer must be able to recognize the manufacturer's product by its uniform packaging—hence the various series with their characteristic formats. But a standard label is not enough; the product itself must be uniform and dependable. [Orville J.] Victor's contribution to Beadle's success was the perfection of formulas which could be used by any number of writers, and the inspired alteration of these formulas according to the changing demands of the market. Victor was what would now be called a born "mass" editor; that is, he had an almost seismographic intuition of the nature, degree, and direction of changes in popular tastes.

Writers on Victor's staff composed at great speed and in unbelievable quantity; many of them could turn out a thousand words an hour for twelve hours at a stretch. Prentiss Ingraham, son of the author of *The Prince of the House of David,* produced more than six hundred novels, besides plays and short stories. He is said to have written a thirty-five-thousand-word tale on one occasion in a day and a night. Fiction produced in these circumstances virtually takes on the character of automatic writing. The unabashed and systematic use of formula strips from the writing every vestige of the interest usually sought in works of the imagination; it is entirely subliterary. On the other hand, such work tends to become an objectified mass dream, like the moving pictures, the soap operas, or the comic books that are the present-day equivalents of the Beadle stories. The individual writer abandons his own personality and identifies himself with the reveries of his readers. It is the presumably close fidelity of the Beadle stories to the dream life of a vast inarticulate public that renders them valuable to the social historian and the historian of ideas.—HENRY NASH SMITH[5]

4. The transition from the usual psychological mode of thinking about

---

[4] *The Idea of History*. Copyright, 1946, Oxford University Press.
[5] *Virgin Land*. Copyright © 1950, by Harvard University Press.

the behavior of such an intelligent animal as a dog to a purely objective physiological mode was not an easy matter with Pavlov. He testified several times how painful were his doubts concerning the legitimacy of the purely physiological study and interpretation of animal behavior. The difficulties were manifold. Quite naturally they arose from the novelty of the physiological approach to the study of "psychic" phenomena, an approach of almost revolutionary character. The main difficulty, however, was chiefly seated in Pavlov himself. For a long time he doubted whether the path of objective study of animal behavior was correct. He questioned whether he did not deceive himself when he tried to explain physiologically the psychological phenomena and whether the study of conditioned reflexes would not lead him into a blind alley from which there would be no exit. The old habit of explaining psychologically the behavior of animals still possessed him strongly. I remember well that during the first years of my work in Pavlov's laboratory (1902–5), when the work on conditioned reflexes was already under way, he would often say that if ever he should have some free time, he would write a psychological study of the dog's characteristics and temperament. So many animals passed through his laboratory and he so closely observed many of them that he was convinced that in their psychological aspect they differed from each other as human beings differ. Pavlov attained his desire, though not until much later, in 1927, and he discussed the types of nervous system, i.e., the temperaments of dogs. However, he then discussed this subject not from a psychological but from a purely physiological point of view, which was based on the study of conditioned reflexes in different types of dogs.—B. P. BABKIN[6]

5. Practicing scales is not giving a concert. As an exercise or an experiment, nonrepresentative painting has, I think, unquestionable value. It unbinds the imagination, discloses to the eye of the painter a world of unforeseen possibilities, relationships, correspondences, rhythms, and equilibria, enables him more perfectly to master the prime elements of his means of expression; and over and above all it teaches him himself, in complete freedom, through the release of his own singular inventive resources as a sensitive instrument. All that, nevertheless, has to do with

[6] *Pavlov, A Biography.* The University of Chicago Press. Copyright 1949 by the University of Chicago.

technique, not with poetry, or at best with making technique more supple and tractable to poetry. In this particular order, practice in abstract art has perhaps been made by the very development of modern painting a necessary moment in the individual painter's self education. And with regard to the general evolution of painting, it was also, perhaps, and for the same reasons, an unavoidable moment. Yet in relation to art's real life, and to the progress in creativity and self-awareness achieved in the last hundred years, the irruption of nonrepresentative art can hardly be considered an advance in the process. Of itself it points rather at a period of stagnation or regression.—JACQUES MARITAIN[7]

6. As populations have concentrated in cities, as hungers developed that had not been dreamed of and as the multiplying desires were satisfied out of the growing store collected in all the corners of the world from the never-resting machinery of trade; as one mechanical triumph has followed another and each spectacular project for harnessing natural forces has made way for a greater; as these things have happened, men have been drawn, as if by an accelerating centripetal force, into a stupendous producing-distributing mechanism. It would be useless to argue against this outcome as if we could be persuaded to turn away from it. We cannot be persuaded to turn away from it, because we are part of it, and are conditioned to want what it supplies. And it would not be well for us if we could be persuaded; for although the business mechanism may be misused, it can supply the resources basic to civilized living in a measure not possible before.

We cannot prosper in the fullest and finest sense, I take pains to repeat, if the occupations essential to our very existence are regarded as being inherently devoid of ethical quality, necessarily committed to purely materialistic aims. Those who do the work of feeding, clothing, housing, transporting us, the millions who in one way and another add to the comfort and convenience of living, do more than that. They contribute to life's dignity and beauty. Many of them, although never putting the idea into words, look upon their calling as part of the general effort to make life more livable. Were the inarticulate but practically applied idealism of such merchants, clerks, secretaries, laborers, farmers, to die out, it would be a greater social calamity than if our articulate experts in idealistic theory were reduced to silence.—M. C. OTTO[8]

7. The principle of natural selection seemed a law of the biological world, the mechanism for the transformation or preservation of the species, and no doubt Darwin intended it to be as deterministic in its action as any natural law. But he clearly did not mean by natural selection any conscious choice on the part of nature; he did not intend to give theologians any room for reading design or conscious intelligence into the mechanism of biological events. The economy of nature was to Darwin a flux of life, the appearance and disappearance of biological forms, in which the principle of natural selection seemed to assert itself. This was sufficient clue, however, for the army of theologians and philosophers who wished to convert natural selection into a beneficent principle, to read a cosmic design in the survival of the fittest, and find room for a generous hypothesis of universal progress. In the course of its somewhat singular history, the principle of natural selection served in many disguises as a scientific warrant for the most fantastic speculations, and carried a succeeding generation of thinkers into a wild frenzy of hypothesis. While for Darwin the principle had the status of a hypothesis, of a theory large enough to contain all the facts which his biological studies had uncovered, speculative men were soon erecting cosmic philosophies on it, and a generation of sociologists carried it into the construction of a science of society.—RICHARD D. MOSIER[9]

8. Individuals vary a great deal in their capacity for self-evaluation or insight. Some seem quite completely incapable of it. To be sure, it is always much easier to see the other person's lacks in this respect than it is to see one's own. Traits easily recognized by others as malicious "snoopiness" are rationalized by their possessor as interest in other persons. Rudeness is accepted in one's self as frankness, aggressive dominance as strength, hostile rejection of others as "reserve." Socrates was indeed expressing a fundamental truth when he said, "Know thyself."

---

[8] From *The Human Enterprise,* by M. C. Otto. Copyright, 1940, by F. S. Crofts & Co., Ltd. Reprinted by permission of Appleton-Century-Crofts, Inc.
[9] *The American Temper.* Copyright, 1952, by the University of California Press.

It is a question, however, whether or not Socrates applied this principle very efficiently in evaluating his own personal life. Undoubtedly a great deal of the difficulty which people have in living together harmoniously is due to human inability or unwillingness to view objectively the neurotic elements in their own characters. Perhaps in a less insecure world there would be less need for neurotic defenses. It is a vicious circle. Maladjusted persons make a maladjusted society which in turn favors further individual maladjustment.—BEULAH CHAMBERLAIN BOSSELMAN[10]

9. The development of the power of abstraction is the necessary concomitant of an industrial civilization. The engineer who designs machines or airplanes is not identical with the man in the workshop who makes the machine, or the airplane; for him, his product exists completely in his imagination, materialized only in the form of a blueprint, before it can become concrete reality. The physicist who experiments in his laboratory has before him a maze of wires, glass tubes, and metal bars; but into this maze he sees an order of electric circuits, which makes him control his manual operations in such a way that observations result which reveal general laws of nature. The mathematician, equipped with writing paper and fountain pen, arrives at figures which determine the construction of bridges or airplanes or skyscrapers. Never in the history of mankind has a civilization demanded so intensive an intellectual training from those who work for it.

The philosophy of the nineteenth century is the product of such power of abstraction. It does not offer the persuasive solutions of systems that talk picture language and appeal to aesthetic desires. It presents answers understandable only to a mind trained in abstract thought; it requires that its disciples study every item with the precision of the engineer and the scrutiny of the mathematician. But to those who are willing to submit to these requirements it offers the reward of an intellectual insight of amazing proportions. It answers the questions which the founders of the great philosophical schools could not answer; often, though, it has first to rephrase the question in such a way as to render it capable of an answer. It shows the world in which we live to be of a

---

[10] Beulah Chamberlain Bosselman, *The Troubled Mind.* Copyright 1953 The Ronald Press Company.

much more complicated structure than that which the classical philosopher took for granted. And it has developed methods for dealing with such structures and for making the world comprehensible to human understanding.—HANS REICHENBACH[11]

10. In functional terms, the writer is a craftsman whose medium is the written language; he works with words as a painter works with shapes and colors, a composer with tones, and a cabinetmaker with wood, glass, and metal. Like every good craftsman, he wants to make objects, or artifacts, that will have an independent existence and will play a part in the lives of people he has never seen. Like every good craftsman, he has reasons for believing in the high importance of his own medium; and the writer, so it seems to me, has the best reasons of all. Language is the specifically human gift and the cohesive force that holds each tribe and nation together. One might call it a fifth dimension of human life, for the human community exists in language almost as it does in space and time. From another point of view it is our greatest cooperative undertaking, with millions of persons each year inventing new words or turns of speech, most of which will soon be forgotten. One function of writers is to choose among these innumerable possibilities, fashion a literary medium, and invent new expressions of their own, which in turn may be used by millions of others.

Writers, of course, have other functions too: notably they tell stories that become the myths of the tribe, as well as presenting characters that can serve as tribal heroes and villains. At this point, however, I should like to emphasize their linguistic function, because it is being overlooked by so many theorists. Dr. Bergler—to mention only one— has written a whole book about writers without stopping to think that their words are intended to have a meaning for readers. Words for Dr. Bergler are simply "milk" that the writer produces out of himself; their value is purely subjective. He forgets the most important feature of the "milk." It must be transformed into products with an objective value for others, or else it will be refused and the writer may stop producing it. The words of great writers may set the linguistic patterns of whole nations. Dante—not alone, but vastly more than others—set the pattern

---

[11] *The Rise of Scientific Philosophy*. Copyright, 1951, by the University of California Press.

that would be followed in Italy. If Dante had been born in Venice or Rome or Palermo instead of Tuscany, modern Italian would have been a different language—and one might add that modern Italians, who think mostly in words, like people everywhere, would have had slightly different thoughts.—MALCOLM COWLEY[12]

B.

For your own benefit, the next time you have a fairly lengthy reading assignment in one of your other classes, write a précis of that assigned material. You will be gratified to discover how it will help you see the shape and contour of what otherwise might remain simply a series of paragraphs; you will also be testing your own comprehension of the material by attempting to restate it in your own words.

---

[12] *The Literary Situation.* Copyright, 1954, by Malcolm Cowley. Reprinted by permission of The Viking Press.

XII | The Research Paper

Since in many courses students are required to write term papers or to do other research articles, it has become usual to give students in English some training in the mechanics of research. Research is the investigation of a particular subject in order to ascertain all the available facts and to draw the conclusions that grow out of them; consequently, the writer must know where to look for his facts and how to put his material together. In the course of random searching much time may be lost and much energy uselessly dissipated. We give here, therefore, a brief outline of the various steps in the building of such papers, in the hope that it will show the student how he can obtain the most satisfactory results with the least expenditure of time on merely mechanical matters.

SUBJECT AND POINT OF VIEW

If it is possible, the student should choose for his investigation a subject in which he is interested or one in which he feels that he might become interested. This is not to be taken to mean, however, that he should never leave his own little corner of the pasture; he should, rather, seize every opportunity to venture abroad, to increase his store of general knowledge, and he is offered, in the research paper, an excellent chance to acquaint himself with something new. But it is obvious that if he is interested or can become interested in his chosen subject, he will do his work with more enthusiasm, and is likely to write a more interesting and more forceful paper.

When the student selects a subject, he will find himself confronted by several evident restrictions. The first of these is imposed upon him by the prescribed length of the paper. It is plain that an article of one thousand words and one of five thousand words will not deal with subjects of equal scope. A research paper should be thorough in its investigation; consequently, the student must see that he undertakes a theme that he can treat adequately in the space allotted to him. For instance, five thousand words or more would be necessary for a satisfactory treatment of the influence of Samuel Butler's *Hudibras* on nineteenth-century satiric verse in America, whereas one might treat thoroughly in one thousand words a limitation of that subject, such as Bierce's imitations of *Hudibras* in *The Devil's Dictionary*. Or, in five thousand words one might trace the activities of Black Hawk, chief of the Sauks, in the Black Hawk War, but one thousand might suffice for a consideration of that chief as a prisoner of war.

Two other restrictions are related. The student should not choose an abstruse subject or a technical subject. If he selects an abstruse subject, he is very likely to become involved, entangled, discouraged, and disgusted; it is probable, too, that he will have a hard time getting and retaining the attention of his readers. If he determines upon a technical theme, he is not likely to have, or be able to acquire, sufficient information to justify his undertaking such an investigation. Upper-class students in specialized or technical courses discuss technical subjects as part of their normal work, but in such instances they are writing almost solely for a technical audience. When he has any expectation of readers outside his own strictly professional limits, the writer should take those readers into consideration and avoid the use of involved or technical language and illustration. He should remember that if his paper is to be read it must be interesting; he should not, then, kill the interest of the reader. He should endeavor to work with a definite, concrete subject in such a way that it will hold the attention of his readers to the last word.

The selection of a topic will be limited also by the amount and kinds of reference material available. The writer should consider whether there is likely to be *any* published material on the tentatively chosen topic; he should consider, likewise, the resources of the library or libraries that he has access to.

Having selected a subject that is neither too great nor too slight for thorough treatment in the given allotment of space, having avoided abstruse or technical topics, and having shunned topics on which there is little or no available material, the writer must now determine his point of view. This does not mean that he is to seize upon one attitude toward his subject and hold to it, no matter what evidence he may turn up. The writer should be unbiased in his approach to the investigation. He must note the facts without prejudice, and the conclusion that he forms must grow out of the material he presents. But it is essential that the writer have a point of departure, a governing principle. He must, in other words, have some fairly specific idea upon which he will center his investigation and about which he will gather material.

Let us suppose that he wishes to write on early criticism of the drama in England, and he restricts this to the period from 1570 to 1595. He has now brought his subject within bounds that correspond sufficiently to the space that is allotted him (say five thousand words). But unless he establishes a point of view from which to direct his search, he will spend much time in aimless and uncertain wandering. Since there has been much critical comment upon the extent of romantic influence in the development of Elizabethan drama, he may decide to see how much, if any, classical influence is evident in the dramatic criticism of this particular period. He has now a central idea, about which he can organize his endeavors. He is to look for one thing and one thing only in his survey of dramatic criticism for this period. It is well, before he has gone far in his work, for the writer to formulate, in writing, a tentative *thesis* or *theme sentence,* and to keep this before him throughout his work as a means of maintaining unity. (For example: "Classical elements in Elizabethan dramatic criticism, although less important than romantic influences, are very prominent in some writers and perceptible in almost all.") If, at first, he knows so little about the subject that he is unable to formulate such a statement of his plan of work, he should read some general book or articles on the subject and then proceed as suggested.

SOURCES: THE USE OF THE LIBRARY

There are four principal kinds of material that the research student may use as the nature of his subject dictates: reference works, the general collection of books in the library, periodicals, and miscellaneous other publications.

Reference works. The **general reference works** are commonly to be found in the main reading room of the library, or in a reference room, arranged on open shelves for convenience in use. If the student will look about him in such a room in his own college or university library, he will readily discover for himself all the books of this kind at his disposal. (If he is unable to find reference works, he need only ask the librarian where they are kept.) These general reference works may be divided into five classes: (1) dictionaries and other wordbooks; (2) general encyclopedias and yearbooks; (3) biographical references; (4) other fact books; and (5) references in various special fields.[1] The list below is suggestive of what is generally to be found in a reference or general reading room. In the first four sections, items of special importance are starred (*).

1. DICTIONARIES AND OTHER WORDBOOKS, such as

Century Dictionary and Cyclopedia. New York: The Century Company, 1911. 12 vols.

---

[1] The student should not overlook the possible usefulness of various manuals, handbooks, and guides designed to aid him in the preparation of a bibliography. Among the most valuable of these general bibliographical tools are Isadore G. Mudge, *Guide to Reference Books* (7th ed.; Chicago: American Library Association, 1951); Louis Shores, *Basic Reference Sources* (Chicago: American Library Association, 1954); and Herbert S. Hirshberg, *Subject Guide to Reference Books* (Chicago: American Library Association, 1942). The student will find that many special fields are covered by "bibliographies of bibliographies"; for current topics, he should consult *Bibliographic Index: A Cumulative Bibliography of Bibliographies,* 1938 to date (New York: H. W. Wilson Company, 1938—).

Dictionary of American English on Historical Principles. Ed. by Sir William A. Craigie and James R. Hulbert. Chicago: The University of Chicago Press, 1936–1944. 4 vols.

*_New Standard Dictionary._ New York: Funk & Wagnalls Company, 1952.

*_Oxford English Dictionary._ Ed. by A. H. Murray, and others. Oxford: The Clarendon Press, 1888–1933. 10 vols. and supplement. Corrected reissue, 1933. 12 vols. and supplement. (Also known as the *New English Dictionary.*)

*_Webster's New International Dictionary._ 2nd ed. Springfield, Mass.: G. & C. Merriam Company, 1934.

Crabb, George. *Crabb's English Synonyms.* Revised ed. New York: Harper & Brothers, 1917.

Fowler, Henry W. *Dictionary of Modern English Usage.* Oxford: The Clarendon Press, 1926.

Roget, P. M. *Roget's International Thesaurus of English Words and Phrases.* New ed. New York: Thomas Y. Crowell Company, 1946.

2. ENCYCLOPEDIAS AND YEARBOOKS, such as

*_Columbia Encyclopedia._ Ed. by William Bridgewater and Elizabeth J. Sherwood. New York: Columbia University Press, 1950. Supplement, 1956. (Probably the best single-volume encyclopedia.)

*_Encyclopedia Americana._ New York: Americana Corporation, 1957. 30 vols.

*_Encyclopædia Britannica._ 14th ed. New York: Encyclopædia Britannica, Inc., 1929. 24 vols. Frequent plate revisions.

*_New International Encyclopædia._ 2nd ed. New York: Dodd, Mead and Company, 1914–1916. 24 vols. Plate revision, 1922. Supplements, 1925, 1930.

*_Americana Annual,_ 1923 to date. New York: Americana Corporation, 1923—. (Annually issued supplement to the *Encyclopedia Americana.*)

*_American Year Book,_ 1910–1919, 1925 to date. New York: various publishers, 1911—.

*_Britannica Book of the Year,_ 1938 to date. Chicago: Encyclopædia Britannica, Inc., 1938—. (Annually issued supplement to the *Encyclopædia Britannica.*)

Information Please Almanac, 1948 to date. New York: The Macmillan Company, 1947—.

New International Year Book, 1907 to date. New York: Dodd, Mead and Company, 1908–1931; Funk & Wagnalls Company, 1932—. (Annually issued supplement to the *New International Encyclopædia*.)

Statesman's Year-Book, 1864 to date. London: Macmillan and Co., 1864—.

3. BIOGRAPHICAL REFERENCE WORKS, such as

Bryan, Michael. *Bryan's Dictionary of Painters and Engravers.* Revised ed. London: George Bell & Sons, 1920–1921. 5 vols.

Cattell, Jaques. *American Men of Science.* 9th ed. Lancaster, Pa.: The Science Press; and New York: R. R. Bowker Company, 1955-1956. 3 vols. (The 10th ed., in 5 vols., scheduled for publication, 1959-1963, by the Jaques Cattell Press, Tempe, Ariz.)

Cattell, Jaques. *Directory of American Scholars.* 3rd ed. Lancaster, Pa.: The Science Press, 1957. ("Biographical sketches of scholars in the humanities and social sciences.")

Dictionary of American Biography. Ed. by Allen Johnson and Dumas Malone. New York: Charles Scribner's Sons, 1928–1937. 20 vols. and index. Supplement I, 1944. Supplement II, 1958. (Contains no biographies of *living* Americans; often referred to as the *DAB*.)

Dictionary of Canadian Biography. 2nd ed. Ed. by W. S. Wallace. Toronto: The Macmillan Company of Canada, Ltd., 1945. 2 vols.

Dictionary of National Biography. Ed. by Leslie Stephen and Sidney Lee. London: Smith, Elder and Company; Oxford University Press, 1885–1937. 63 vols. Supplements. (Contains no biographies of *living* Englishmen; often referred to as the *DNB*.)

International Who's Who, 1936 to date. London: Europa Publications, 1936—.

Kunitz, Stanley J., and Howard Haycraft. *American Authors,* 1600–1900. New York: H. W. Wilson Company, 1938. ("A biographical dictionary of American literature"; not uniformly dependable as to facts and interpretations.)

Kunitz, Stanley J., and Howard Haycraft. *British Authors of the Nineteenth Century.* New York: H. W. Wilson Company, 1936.

Kunitz, Stanley J., and Howard Haycraft. *Twentieth Century Authors.* New York: H. W. Wilson Company, 1942. Supplement, 1955.

Millett, Fred B. *Contemporary American Authors.* New York: Har-

court, Brace and Company, 1940. ("A critical survey and 219 bio-bibli-
ographies"; excellent for period covered.)

Millett, Fred B., John M. Manly, and Edith Rickert. *Contemporary
British Literature.* 3rd ed. New York: Harcourt, Brace and Company,
1935. ("A critical survey and 232 author-bibliographies.")

Who Knows—And What. Chicago: A. N. Marquis Company, 1949.
(Biographical directory of American specialists in "subjects likely to
be asked about.")

Who's Who, 1848 to date. London: A. & C. Black, 1849—. (Especially
valuable for sketches of living Englishmen.)

Who's Who in America, 1899–1900 to date. Chicago: A. N. Marquis
Company, 1899—. (Published biennially; especially valuable for
sketches of living Americans.)

4. OTHER FACT BOOKS, such as

*Bartlett, John. *Familiar Quotations.* 13th ed. Boston: Little, Brown &
Company, 1955.

Brewer, E. Cobham. *Dictionary of Phrase and Fable.* New ed. Philadelphia: J. B. Lippincott Company, 1937.

Brewer, E. Cobham. *Reader's Handbook of Famous Names in Fiction,
Allusions, References, Proverbs, Plots, Stories and Poems.* Philadelphia: J. B. Lippincott Company, 1935.

Century Cyclopedia of Names. Revised ed. New York: The Century
Company, 1914. (Out of date, but still useful.)

Chambers, R. *The Book of Days.* London: W. & R. Chambers, [1869].
2 vols. ("A miscellany of popular antiquities in connection with the
calendar.")

Commercial Atlas. Chicago: Rand McNally & Company. (Published
annually.)

De Ford, Miriam Allen. *Who Was When?* 2nd ed. New York: H. W.
Wilson Company, 1950.

Douglas, George W. *American Book of Days.* 2nd ed. Ed. by Helen D.
Compton. New York: H. W. Wilson Company, 1948.

Keller, Helen R. *The Dictionary of Dates.* New York: The Macmillan
Company, 1934. 2 vols. (An older reference work of this sort is *Haydn's
Dictionary of Dates.*)

Webster's Geographical Dictionary. Revised ed. Springfield: G. & C. Merriam Company, 1955.

5. REFERENCES IN VARIOUS SPECIAL FIELDS, such as

AGRICULTURE:

Bailey, Liberty H., ed. *Cyclopedia of American Agriculture.* New York: The Macmillan Company, 1908–1909. 4 vols.

ANTHROPOLOGY:

Frazer, Sir James G. *The Golden Bough.* 3rd ed. London: Macmillan and Co., 1911–1915. 12 vols. Supplement, 1936.

ART:

Larkin, Oliver W. *Art and Life in America.* Revised ed. New York: Rinehart & Company, Inc., 1960.

Reinach, Salomon. *Apollo: An Illustrated Manual of the History of Art throughout the Ages.* Tr. by F. Simmonds. Revised ed. New York: Charles Scribner's Sons, 1935.

BUSINESS:

Coman, Edwin T., Jr. *Sources of Business Information.* Englewood Cliffs, N. J.: Prentice-Hall, Inc., 1949.

Egbert, J. C., E. A. Holbrook, and M. A. Aldrich, eds. *American Business Practice.* New York: The Ronald Press, 1933. 12 vols.

CHEMISTRY:

Thorpe, T. Edward, and M. A. Whiteley. *Dictionary of Applied Chemistry.* 4th ed. London: Longmans, Green and Co., 1937—. (In progress; see also the 3rd ed., 5 vols., 1922–1927.)

Van Nostrand's Chemical Annual, 1907 to date. New York: D. Van Nostrand Company, 1907—.

ECONOMICS:

Palgrave, R. H. Inglis. *Dictionary of Political Economy.* New ed. Ed. by Henry Higgs. London: Macmillan and Co., 1923–1926. 3 vols. (The student should also consult the *Encyclopædia of the Social Sciences,* listed below under Social Sciences.)

HISTORY:

Cambridge Ancient History. Ed. by J. B. Bury, and others. Cambridge: Cambridge University Press, 1923–1939. 12 vols.

Cambridge Medieval History. Ed. by H. M. Gwatkin, and others. Cambridge: Cambridge University Press, 1911–1936. 8 vols.

Cambridge Modern History. Ed. by A. W. Ward, and others. Cambridge: Cambridge University Press, 1902–1926. 13 vols. and atlas.

Dictionary of American History. Ed. by James Truslow Adams. New York: Charles Scribner's Sons, 1940. 5 vols. 6th vol.—index—1941.

Langer, William L. *An Encyclopedia of World History.* Revised ed. Boston: Houghton Mifflin Company, 1952. (A convenient single-volume reference work.)

Schlesinger, Arthur M., and Dixon Ryan Fox, eds. *A History of American Life.* New York: The Macmillan Company, 1927–1948. 13 vols. (Each vol. contains a "Critical Essay on Authorities.")

LITERATURE—AMERICAN:

Cambridge History of American Literature. Ed. by W. P. Trent, and others. New York: G. P. Putnam's Sons, 1917–1922. 4 vols. Reissue, without bibliographies—New York: The Macmillan Company, 1933. 3 vols. (Often referred to as *CHAL.* Parts of this co-operative work are now very much out of date.)

Clark, Harry H., general ed. *American Writers Series.* New York: American Book Company, 1934–1950. 26 vols.

Hart, James D. *Oxford Companion to American Literature.* 3rd ed. New York: Oxford University Press, 1956.

Literary History of the United States. Ed. by R. E. Spiller, and others. New York: The Macmillan Company, 1948. 3 vols. (Vol. III is bibliography.) Revised ed. in one vol., 1953. Bibliography Supplement, 1959. (Often referred to as *LHUS.*)

Parrington, Vernon L. *Main Currents in American Thought.* New York: Harcourt, Brace and Company, 1927–1930. 3 vols. Reissue, in 1 vol., 1939.

LITERATURE—CLASSICAL:

Harvey, Sir Paul. *Oxford Companion to Classical Literature.* 3rd ed. New York: Oxford University Press, 1946.

Peck, Harry T. *Harper's Dictionary of Classical Literature and Antiquities.* New York: Harper & Brothers, 1897.

Sandys, John E. *Companion to Latin Studies.* 3rd ed. Cambridge: Cambridge University Press, 1925.

Whibley, Leonard. *Companion to Greek Studies*. 4th ed. Cambridge: Cambridge University Press, 1931.

LITERATURE—ENGLISH:

Cambridge History of English Literature. Ed. by A. W. Ward and A. R. Waller. Cambridge: Cambridge University Press, 1907–1916. 14 vols. Index vol., 1927. Reissue, without bibliographies—New York: The Macmillan Company, 1933. 15 vols. (Often referred to as *CHEL;* the student should also consult the *Cambridge Bibliography of English Literature*. Ed. by F. W. Bateson. 1941. 4 vols.)

Harvey, Sir Paul. *Oxford Companion to English Literature*. 3rd ed. Oxford: The Clarendon Press, 1946.

MATHEMATICS:

Miller, G. A. *Historical Introduction to Mathematical Literature*. New York: The Macmillan Company, 1916.

MUSIC:

Grove, Sir George. *Grove's Dictionary of Music and Musicians*. 5th ed. Ed. by Eric Blom. New York: St. Martin's Press, Inc., 1954. 9 vols.

Thompson, Oscar. *International Cyclopedia of Music and Musicians*. 7th ed. New York: Dodd, Mead and Company, 1956.

PHILOSOPHY:

Baldwin, James M. *Dictionary of Philosophy and Psychology*. New York: The Macmillan Company, 1918. 3 vols. in 4. (Vol. III [2 vols.] is Benjamin Rand's *Bibliography of Philosophy, Psychology and Cognate Subjects*. This whole work is very much out of date, and should be supplemented by the annual bibliography in the *Journal of Philosophy*, 1934–1937, and the semiannual *International Bibliography of Philosophy*, Paris, 1937—.)

PHYSICS:

Glazebrook, Sir Richard. *Dictionary of Applied Physics*. London: Macmillan and Co., 1922–1923. 5 vols.

International Series of Pure and Applied Physics, 1932 to date. New York: McGraw-Hill Book Company, 1932—.

National Nuclear Energy Series, 1948 to date. New York: McGraw-Hill Book Company, 1948—.

Weld, LeRoy D. *Glossary of Physics*. New York: McGraw-Hill Book Company, 1937.

PSYCHOLOGY:

Harriman, P. L. *Dictionary of Psychology*. New York: Philosophical Library, 1947.

Psychological Abstracts, 1927 to date. Lancaster: American Psychological Association, 1927—.

RELIGION:

Catholic Encyclopedia. New York: R. Appleton, and—later—Catholic Encyclopedia Press, 1907–1914. 16 vols. Supplement, 1922. Revised ed., 1936—.

Hastings, James, ed. *Encyclopædia of Religion and Ethics*. New York: Charles Scribner's Sons, 1908–1927. 12 vols. and index. Reissue, 1928. 7 vols.

Jewish Encyclopedia. New York: Funk & Wagnalls Company, 1901–1906. 12 vols. Reissue, 1925.

Mythology of All Races. Ed. by Louis H. Gray and John A. MacCulloch. Boston: Marshall Jones Company, 1916–1932. 12 vols. and index.

New Schaff-Herzog Encyclopedia of Religious Knowledge. Ed. by S. M. Jackson. New York: Funk & Wagnalls Company, 1908–1912. 12 vols. and index. Supplement, *Twentieth Century Encyclopedia of Religious Knowledge,* 1955, 2 vols.

SCIENCE AND TECHNOLOGY:

Chambers's Technical Dictionary. Revised ed., with supplement. New York: The Macmillan Company, 1948.

Hawkins, R. R. *Scientific, Medical and Technical Books Published in the U. S., 1930–44.* New York: R. R. Bowker, 1946. Supplement for 1945–1948, 1950; supplement for 1949–1952, 1953.

Hough, J. N. *Scientific Terminology*. New York: Rinehart & Company, Inc., 1953.

Hutchinson's Technical and Scientific Encyclopedia. Ed. by C. F. Tweney and I. P. Shirshov. New York: The Macmillan Company, 1936. 4 vols.

Science for All: An Annotated Reading List for the Non-specialist. Cambridge, England: The National Book League, 1958.

Van Nostrand's Scientific Encyclopedia. 3rd ed. Princeton, N. J.: D.
Van Nostrand Company, 1958.

SOCIAL SCIENCES:

Encyclopædia of the Social Sciences. Ed. by Edwin R. A. Seligman and
Alvin Johnson. New York: The Macmillan Company, 1930–1935. 15
vols.

To the student the value of these general works is threefold:
he may obtain a general and condensed view of the subject he
wishes to undertake; second, he may find here factual or basic
information that is as reliable and accurate as it is possible to find,
although reference books vary greatly in this respect; and, third,
he will often find at the end of the articles in the encyclopedias—
and in many of the other works—a list of books or articles on the
subject that it will be to his interest to investigate. There is,
however, one danger to be pointed out in connection with the
use of such reference works: the articles are likely to be condensed
and generalized; the student must not depend upon them entirely
for material. They offer him merely a starting point. He will
find it true also that in the study of many subjects he can get no
especially valuable material from these general reference works.
In such a situation he should go directly to the card catalogue.

General collection: library. The general collection
of books in the library is reached through the **card catalogue.**
This catalogue lists in one alphabetical index all the books in the
library, and the student may look through this index for his
material under the author's name, the title, or the subject heading. If the author's surname is a common one and his initials are
not given, the student will probably find his book more quickly
if he looks for it under the title. If the book is in the library, it
will be listed in the index and all one need do is to note down
the author's name, the title, and the "call number," and the book
will be brought to him.

The student will probably want to examine more books than
are referred to in the bibliography that he has already obtained.

He will then consult likely subject headings in the card catalogue and look into all books having titles that seem to bear upon his subject. For example, if he is doing a paper on English dramatic criticism, he will look under "Criticism," "Drama," "English Literature," "Literature—History and Criticism," "Literature—Comparative," and so forth. A number of titles he will find duplicated under these different heads, but he may also find in one place a book not listed in another. A partial bibliography on this subject, gathered from an examination of the card catalogue, will include *Elizabethan Critical Essays* (in two volumes, with an introduction by George Gregory Smith), J. W. Cunliffe's *The Influence of Seneca upon Elizabethan Tragedy,* C. S. Baldwin's *Renaissance Literary Theory and Practice,* F. E. Schelling's *Foreign Influences on Elizabethan Plays* and *English Literature during the Lifetime of Shakespeare,* R. I. Goldmark's *Studies in the Influence of the Classics on English Literature,* Willard Farnham's *The Medieval Heritage of Elizabethan Tragedy,* and J. E. Spingarn's *Literary Criticism in the Renaissance.*

In using the card catalogue the student has discovered that his library probably uses one of two systems in indexing books: (1) the Library of Congress classification; or (2) the Dewey decimal system. The first of these divides books into the following classes, represented by letters:

A	General Works
B	Philosophy—Religion
C	History—Auxiliary Sciences
D	Foreign History
E-F	American History
G	Geography—Anthropology
H	Social Sciences
J	Political Science
K	Law
L	Education
M	Music
N	Fine Arts
P	Language and Literature

Q   Science
R   Medicine
S   Agriculture—Plant and Animal Industry
T   Technology
U   Military Science
V   Naval Science
Z   Bibliography—Library Science

These sections are subdivided by arrangements of letter and number to indicate the specific classification of a particular book.

The Dewey classification divides books into ten classes, represented by numbers:

000–099	General Works	500–599	Natural Science
100–199	Philosophy	600–699	Useful Arts
200–299	Religion	700–799	Fine Arts
300–399	Sociology	800–899	Literature
400–499	Philology	900–999	History

These main divisions are each split into ten parts, e.g.:

800	General Literature	850	Italian Literature
810	American Literature	860	Spanish Literature
820	English Literature	870	Latin Literature
830	German Literature	880	Greek Literature
840	French Literature	890	Minor Literatures

And each of these parts is also divided, e.g.:

820	English Literature	825	English Oratory
821	English Poetry	826	English Letters
822	English Drama	827	English Satire
823	English Fiction	828	English Miscellany
824	English Essays	829	Anglo-Saxon

Further subdivisions are made by the use of decimals.

The card for a book (which, with the exception of call number, will be the same for whatever system is used) is generally as follows:

843   Whale, *Mrs.* Winifred (Stephens)

W562   French novelists of today, by Winifred Stephens. Second series. London, John Lane; New York, John Lane company, 1915.

xi p., 2 1., 3–301, [1] p. front., ports., double facsim. 19½^{cm}. $1.50.

CONTENTS.—Preface—Introduction: The French novel on the eve of the war.—Marcelle Tinayre.—Romain Rolland.—The novel "Jean Christophe".—Jérôme Tharaud, Jean Tharaud.—René Boysleve.—Pierre Mille.—Jean Aicard.

1. French fiction—19th cent.—Hist. & crit. 2. French fiction—20th cent.—Hist. & crit. I. Title.

15—25109

Library of Congress   PQ656.W5 2d ser.

[30m2]

338.7   Daniels, Mortimer Battey, 1903–

D 228   . . . Corporation financial statements, by Mortimer B. Daniels . . . Ann Arbor, University of Michigan, School of business administration, Bureau of business research, 1934.

vii, 131 p. 22½^{cm}. ([Michigan. University. School of business administration. Bureau of business research] Michigan business studies. vol. VI, no. 1)

Thesis (PH.D.)—University of Michigan, 1933. Without thesis note.

1. Corporations—Finance. 2. Corporations—U. S. I. Title.

34—27529

Library of Congress   HG4028.B2D3
Univ. of Michigan Libr.

————Copy 2.   HF5006.M5 vol. 6, no. 1
Copyright A 69781   [35f5]   (650.82)   658.15

Periodicals. A third class of materials for the research worker is that of **periodicals.** If the student has chosen a topic dealing with recent events, he will be forced to find much or most of his material in periodicals. Current numbers of many periodicals are commonly to be found on open shelves in the main reading room or in a special periodical reading room. The back numbers are kept shelved in the stacks, and any issue dating back six months or more will probably be bound (three, four, six, or twelve months, according to the nature and size of the periodical, constituting one volume). The key to this material is found in a number of indexes or catalogues that are generally placed in the main reading room along with the books of general reference. Among the guides of this type are the following:

Agricultural Index, 1916 to date. New York: H. W. Wilson Company, 1919—.

Annual Magazine Subject Index, 1909–1949. Boston: F. W. Faxon Company, 1909–1950. (A subject index, especially useful for periodicals not indexed in the *International Index* and the *Readers' Guide,* listed below.)

Art Index, 1929 to date. New York: H. W. Wilson Company, 1933—. (An author and subject index.)

Book Review Digest, 1905 to date. New York: H. W. Wilson Company, 1906—. (Monthly and yearly. Quotes from some reviews and gives references to others. Not especially useful for technical or scholarly books and reviews.)

Dramatic Index, 1908–1949. Boston: F. W. Faxon Company, 1909–1950. (A subject index to articles on the drama and the theater. Often bound with *Annual Magazine Subject Index.*)

Engineering Index, 1884 to date. New York: Engineering Magazine, 1892–1919; American Society of Mechanical Engineers, 1920—. (An author and subject index.)

Industrial Arts Index, 1913 to date. New York: H. W. Wilson Company, 1913—. ("Subject index to a selected list of engineering, trade and business periodicals, books and pamphlets.")

International Index to Periodicals, 1907 to date. New York: H. W. Wilson Company, 1916—. ("Devoted chiefly to the humanities and science," covering "scholarly and highly specialized periodicals.")

Poole's Index to Periodical Literature, 1802–1906. Boston: Houghton
Mifflin Company, 1882–1908. 7 vols. (Principally a subject index. For
the period from 1892 to 1906, the *Annual Literary Index* and the
Annual Library Index may be used as author indexes.)

Readers' Guide to Periodical Literature, 1900 to date. New York: H.
W. Wilson Company, 1905—. (Monthly and yearly. An author, title,
and subject index.)

Technical Book Review Index, 1917–1928, 1935 to date. Pittsburgh:
Carnegie Library, 1917–1929; New York: Special Libraries Association,
1935—. (Covers material ordinarily not included in the *Book Review
Digest.*)

Of these, for many students the most valuable index will be the
Readers' Guide to Periodical Literature. In this work the student
may search under author, title, or subject, which are all arranged
in one alphabetical index, just as in the card catalogue of books.
One volume generally covers three or four years, but current
numbers are issued monthly so that the index is kept up to date.

To obtain a bound volume of a periodical, the student must
hand in at the circulation desk the name of the magazine and the
volume number—and perhaps the year of publication. (In some
libraries titles of magazine articles are included in the general
card catalogue.)[2]

Newspapers, bulletins, and pamphlets. In addition
to his other materials, especially when working on current topics,
the student may wish to make use of newspapers, pamphlet
publications, and government bulletins. In most instances, such
sources should be regarded as supplementary, since it is often
very difficult for the student to evaluate them justly. On the other
hand, publications of this sort frequently contain factual material
that is not readily accessible elsewhere, and newspapers, in particular, often give the investigator a sense of immediate contact
with an issue or event—an experience that, wisely used, may help

---

[2] Further suggestions on the use of the library will be found in the various
handbooks and manuals devoted principally to this subject. See, for example,
Margaret G. Cook, *The New Library Key* (New York: H. W. Wilson Company, 1956).

to heighten the interest without destroying the validity of his paper. Several specialized reference works or indexes may be profitably used as guides to material of the kind mentioned in this section.

1. NEWSPAPERS

The New York Times Index, 1913 to date. New York: The New York Times, 1913—. (Quarterly, 1913–1929; monthly and annually, since 1930. Although keyed specifically to *The New York Times,* this index may be used as a guide to events and issues reported in almost all American newspapers.)

2. GOVERNMENT PUBLICATIONS

Boyd, Anne M. *United States Government Publications.* 3rd ed. New York: H. W. Wilson Company, 1949.

Schmeckebier, Laurence F. *Government Publications and Their Use.* 2nd ed. Washington: The Brookings Institution, 1939.

Monthly Checklist of State Publications, 1910 to date. Washington: The Library of Congress, Division of Documents, 1910—.

United States Government Publications: Monthly Catalog, 1895 to date. Washington: Government Printing Office, 1895—.

3. PAMPHLETS

Vertical File Service Catalog: An Annotated Subject Catalog of Pamphlets, 1932–1934. New York: H. W. Wilson Company, 1935. Supplements, 1935—.

Other sources. Other sources of information that may in some cases be useful in the writing of the research paper are **questionnaires** and **interviews.** A questionnaire generally consists of a series of carefully worked out questions to be sent in writing to members of a group of individuals selected because they can speak with authority upon the subject or because they are themselves especially suitable subjects for the investigation concerned. The questionnaire is a particularly useful source of information in psychological, sociological, or economic research. The average class paper, however, does not offer much chance for the use of this method. The interview also is useful in special investigation of the same nature as that for which we suggest the questionnaire. If the writer wishes to interview some authority on a given subject, he should remember that the individual's time is valuable, and consequently he should formulate beforehand the questions that he wishes the authority to answer. It should be repeated, however, that usually the student will get all his material from the books and other publications in the library. Certain subjects may require the use of questionnaires and interviews or of public addresses and radio or TV speeches, but such a topic will be the exception rather than the rule.

READING AND NOTE TAKING

Let us assume that the writer has his subject, has tentatively determined his point of view, and has gathered from one source or another a list of references that he plans to consult for the material of his paper. He must, for one thing, consider the value of his sources. This is difficult, of course, if he does not already have some knowledge of the field that he wishes to investigate. On the authoritativeness of his sources he should consult his instructor or the reference librarian. But there are certain guides that he himself should apply to the matter at hand.

Relative value of sources. Suppose that he is to deal with some phase of party politics in the United States. If the books or articles in question are written by actively interested members of the Democratic party, he can be fairly certain that there will be some prejudice in the point of view expressed; the same will probably be true of books or articles written by ardent Republicans. Such a biased treatment does not mean that the student cannot use this material; he must simply keep in mind its prejudiced nature as he reads and as he uses it for the basis of the conclusions he is to draw.

A second question that the student should ask himself is whether or not the author is in such a position that he can be expected to write competently upon the subject. On this point the student may find, in a periodical, helpful editorial comment on the contributors to any particular issue. The fitness of the writer to handle this subject will also be indicated by the accuracy and reasonableness of his presentation.

A third matter to be considered is the date of the material—especially if the topic is controversial. What may have been held true once may since have been proved unsound. Later criticism, since it can embrace greater experience, is likely to be more trustworthy than earlier. A comparison of the date of publication of the material with the inclusive dates of his subject will also guide the student. In a theme on the presidential campaign of 1956, for instance, the investigator would not attempt to read material dating much before 1955, unless he were especially interested in treating the events that led up to that campaign. The more the student reads on his subject, of course, the better he can tell when the material is satisfactory and when not. He can always drop out references that he has found of doubtful value.

The student will discover in the course of his reading that not all the material in the book or article he examines is for his use. Consequently he must learn to select. The first thing for him to do on drawing a book from the stacks is to examine the table of contents. From this he can usually determine whether the book will be useful. If nothing of value is disclosed by the table of contents, he should turn to the index and look there for subjects that pertain to his work. On looking up the pages referred to, he will find those parts of the book that are of value to him. Occasionally books also bear marginal headings that will aid the student in his hasty search to find those passages that he wants. The student will also discover that most critical books carry at the end a list of the sources consulted in the writing of that particular work. This bibliography may then give him leads to further sources that will aid him. Footnote references likewise may be of aid in suggesting additional sources that may be consulted. In any case the student must remember that he is looking only for one sort of material and that anything else is irrelevant.

Bibliography cards. When he has discovered that a given book or article contains some likely material, the investigator should make out a **bibliography card.** Previously he will have provided himself with cards or slips *of a uniform size* (3″ × 5″ cards, ruled on one side, are frequently used; another convenient size is the 4″ × 6″ card or slip). On these cards he will enter his source references and his notes—in ink, of course, unless he uses a typewriter. He should make out a *bibliography card for each book or article* from which he gathers any material whatsoever. The proper form—or, at least, one proper form—for these cards is illustrated below (the information for a book entry is taken mainly from the title page):

I

```
        Holloway, Emory.  Whitman:
        an Interpretation in
        Narrative.  New York:
        Alfred A. Knopf, 1926.


        Col. Libr.
        B--W615h
```

Card I shows the basic form for a book entry. The essential items of information here are (1) author's name; (2) title of book; (3) facts of publication. The author's name is given in reverse order, and "hanging indention" is also used, to emphasize the alphabetical feature under which most published material is classified or indexed. The title of the book is underlined (for italics) to show that the reference is to a *complete* publication. The facts of publication include (1) the place of publication, followed by a colon; (2) the name of the publisher, followed by a comma; and (3) the year of publication, followed by a period.

The year of publication will usually be found on the back—or *verso*—of the title page, in the copyright entry. The same date may also appear on the title page itself, but one should use title page dates with caution, for they may represent merely the dates of printing—or reprinting—and not the year of publication. If the year of publication is not given or cannot be learned, the abbreviation "n.d." (for "no date") may be used in place, thus:

New York: A. L. Burt, n.d.

The student may find it convenient to enter, in the lower left-hand corner of the card, the location (i.e., name of library) and call number of the book. The abbreviation used on the illustrative card means "College Library"; an even briefer abbreviation may be used, such as UCL for University of Chicago Library, or NYPL for New York Public Library. If such memoranda are accurately entered when a book is first consulted, it will be unnecessary thereafter to look up the call number in the card catalogue.

II

```
     Furness, Clifton J.   "Walt
        Whitman's Politics."
        American Mercury, XVI,
        459-466 (April, 1929).


        Shows that Whitman had a
     real interest in the theory
     of government.
```

Card II shows the basic form for a periodical entry. Here the items of information include (1) author's name, in reverse order, as on the book card; (2) title of the article, in quotation marks, to show that it is part of a larger publication; (3) name of periodical, underlined, to show that, in this case, it is the complete publication; (4) the volume number, in Roman numerals; (5) *inclusive* page numbers of the article, in Arabic numbers; and (6) the date of issue, enclosed in parentheses.

If the article is unsigned (i.e., anonymous), the entry may begin with the title of the article—using the same kind of indention as appears on the illustrative card; or, in place of the author's name, one may write the word Anonymous. If the researcher, making use of other sources of information, *supplies* the author's name for an unsigned article or book, he should enclose the name in square brackets, thus:

A. Unsigned article in periodical; author's name supplied

[Triggs, Oscar L.] "Walt Whitman." <u>Poet-Lore</u>, V, 289-305 (June-July, 1893).

When the periodical is *paged separately for each issue,* instead of throughout the volume, it may be clearer—and slightly more logical—to use a somewhat different form, emphasizing the date of issue rather than the volume number. An illustration of this variant form follows:

B. Article in periodical paged separately for each issue

Jones, Howard Mumford. "The Human Season." <u>Saturday Review of Literature,</u> August 17, 1940, pp. 3-4, 14-15.

For the sake of retaining consistency in form, however, some may prefer to enter such an article thus:

C. Alternative form: article in periodical paged separately for each issue

Jones, Howard Mumford. "The Human Season." <u>Saturday Review of Literature,</u> XXII, 3-4, 14-15 (August 17, 1940).

Note that when an article is "jumped" (i.e., continued on later pages in the periodical), that fact is indicated as in the form above.

The student will observe that Card II contains a brief note by the investigator on the general content of the article in question. This is a useful device that may be used on *any* bibliography card; it will help to remind the researcher of the *general* value or content of the particular article or book. Such a descriptive notation does not, of course, take the place of note cards based on the specific ideas or statements in the source.

III

> Stovall, Floyd, ed. Walt
>   Whitman. New York: Amer-
>   ican Book Company, 1934.
>   (American Writers Series.)
>
>
> Col. Libr.
> 811 W615w

Card III shows the form for a book in series. The series title, it will be seen, is placed in parentheses after the basic items of information. Since this is a volume of selections—accompanied by a critical introduction and bibliography—the author is here designated as "editor," shown by the abbreviation "ed." following his name. If there is more than one editor, the following form should be used:

D. Book: more than one *editor*

> Benét, William Rose, and
>   Norman Holmes Pearson, eds.
>   The Oxford Anthology of
>   American Literature. New
>   York: Oxford University
>   Press, 1938.

When there are *several* editors, the entry may appear thus:

E. Book: *several* editors: more than one volume

> Trent, William Peterfield, and
>   others, eds. The Cambridge
>   History of American Litera-
>   ture. New York: The Mac-
>   millan Company, 1933. 3
>   vols.

Instead of the phrase "and others," one may, if he chooses, use the Latin abbreviation, *et al.,* which means "and others." Whichever form is chosen should be used consistently throughout a given project.

If the investigator makes use of only one volume in a several-volume work, that fact should be indicated. Suppose, for instance, he has used only the second volume of the work referred to immediately above; his entry would then be

F. Book: several editors; more than one volume, but only one volume used	Trent, William Peterfield, and others, eds. <u>The Cambridge History of American Literature.</u> Vol. II. New York: The Macmillan Company, 1933.

When a work has more than one *author,* the same forms as given above may be used, except that, of course, the abbreviation "eds." would not appear. For example:

G. Book: more than one *author*	Lovett, Robert Morss, and Helen Sard Hughes. <u>The History of the Novel in England.</u> Boston: Houghton Mifflin Company, 1932.

IV	Oppenheim, James. "Whitman." <u>American Writers on American Literature.</u> Ed. by John Macy. New York: Horace Liveright, 1931, pp. 258-273. Col. Libr. 810.4 M177

Card **IV** shows the form for an article or a chapter in a book to which several authors have contributed. In this instance, the author is only one of many contributors to a symposium. Note that the volume editor's name is given after the title, and that the inclusive page numbers of Oppenheim's article appear after the year of publication.

If one makes extensive use of the whole volume and not merely of a chapter or two, it is better to enter the book under the editor's name, thus:

H. Anthology or symposium; listed under editor's name

> Macy, John, ed. <u>American Writers on American Literature</u>. New York: Horace Liveright, 1931.

The same general form that appears on Card **IV** may also be used when the student is making reference to only a single essay or poem (and so on) that appears in a collected volume, all the individual items in which—except for possible editorial material —have been written by one author:

I. Book: one item used from collected edition of an author's work; edition and editor shown

> Chaucer, Geoffrey. "Troilus and Criseyde." <u>The Complete Works of Geoffrey Chaucer</u>. Student's Cambridge ed. 2nd ed. Ed. by F. N. Robinson. Boston: Houghton Mifflin Company, 1957.

Note that the edition is identified ("Student's Cambridge ed.") immediately after the title, and that the editor's name is also given.

V

St. Louis <u>Post-Dispatch</u>,
August 19, 1959.

Card V shows the basic form for a newspaper entry. Note that here the essential items of information are (1) the name of the newspaper; and (2) the date of issue. It is customary practice to underline only the distinctive part of the newspaper name, though some bibliographers, in making the entry above, would also underscore (i.e., italicize) *St. Louis,* feeling that the place name is a part of the newspaper's official designation. If more than one issue of the same newspaper is used, all the issues should be included in a single bibliographic entry, thus: St. Louis *Post-Dispatch,* August 19, 1959; March 3, 1960; January 12, 1961. Ordinarily, it is not necessary to give page numbers for newspaper entries, though this is sometimes done when the entry is of material that has appeared in a Sunday supplement or in a newspaper that contains many sections. Under some circumstances, it may be thought desirable to enter a news story under its main headline, or, if it is a signed article, under its author's name. In such circumstances, one of the two variant forms illustrated below may be used:

J.   Newspaper:
news story listed
under main head-
line

"Big Four Discuss Berlin."
New York <u>Herald Tribune,</u>
July 25, 1959.

K. Newspaper:
signed article listed
under author's
name

> Scali, John. "Khrushchev and
>   Nixon Trade Gibes." Wash-
>   ington Post, July 25, 1959.

VI

> Turner, H. A. A Graphic Sum-
>   mary of Farm Tenure. U. S.
>   Department of Agriculture
>   Miscellaneous Publications
>   No. 261. Washington:
>   Government Printing Office,
>   1936.

Card VI shows the basic form for a bulletin, pamphlet, or
government publication. The title is underlined because this is a
separate publication. Additional information, distinguishing this
item from other government publications, follows the title. Published material of this sort takes a great many different forms—
so many that it is impossible to illustrate them all here. One
rather common variant is shown below:

L. Government
publication: issued
under agency's
name

> Social Security Board. Old
>   Age and Survivors Insurance
>   Statistics, Employment and
>   Wages of Covered Workers,
>   1938. Washington: Govern-
>   ment Printing Office, 1940.

Unpublished material. Monographs and theses
that remain unpublished but are available in manuscript or
typescript may be entered thus:

M. Unpublished
thesis

> Daughrity, Kenneth L. The
> Life and Work of Nathaniel
> Parker Willis, 1806-1836.
> Unpublished Doctoral Dis-
> sertation. Charlottes-
> ville: University of Vir-
> ginia, 1935.

On a bibliographical card for oral material, the student should give such identifying data as these: person; kind of material (lecture, radio speech, interview, and so on); title (if the material has a title); place (whenever this seems significant); and date. A card for a lecture, for instance, might appear thus:

N. Lecture

> Loomis, Charles T. Lecture:
> "Adult Education: A Com-
> munity Project." Clinton
> Public Forum, March 14,
> 1960.

With these basic bibliographical forms—and their chief variants—clearly in mind, the investigator should be able to make out a precise, unambiguous card for practically any source he encounters.

Preliminary organization. Before the student takes any large number of notes, he should have a fairly definite idea of what he is looking for. The selection of a specific, limited subject will be of help here, as will the formulation of a tentative thesis or theme sentence (see section O 1A). But if the student's note taking is to be efficient, or even relatively so, he should also have some main topics or "points" for which he can gather potentially useful material.

From his preliminary reading, from his examination of sources in the preparation of his bibliography, and from *thinking about the subject,* he should be able to work out a preliminary outline

—a possible plan of attack. Such an outline is, of course, subject to considerable change as the student does more reading, takes notes, and gets generally better acquainted with his subject. He may, in fact, decide that his subject needs further limitation and that an almost complete reorganization of topics is desirable. But, as a preliminary step toward formal note taking, he should at least decide upon some of the principal divisions of his chosen subject. These divisions may be arranged in *chronological* order or under *topical* headings, depending upon the kind of subject one is dealing with; in some cases a combination of chronological and topical arrangement may be possible. In any event, the student should make out—in writing—a brief tabulation (in I, II, III order) of possible topics that he thinks might logically be discussed in his paper. From an analysis of these topics he may determine which are important and which are subsidiary or irrelevant. If he goes through this process of preliminary organization, he will reduce *useless* note taking to a minimum, and he will have a much better chance to acquire a final set of notes that will be directly applicable to the discussion of his subject.

Note taking.   Note taking implies some discretion on the part of the investigator. Whatever is perfectly obvious and widely accepted he will not need to put down on his note cards, but he will want to enter in his notes all facts that are new to him, that are unusually stated, or for which he wishes to establish authority.

He will wish to quote, occasionally, to give the particular expression of an opinion, to lend authority to his discussion of a given topic—especially a controversial one—to illustrate an author's technique or his own generalizations, or to give the flavor of an author's style. If the direct quotations in a research paper are too lengthy or too numerous, however, its original quality will be lost.

More frequently, then, a note should be in the form of a summary or a précis of the original author's statement. The researcher should not forget that he is dealing with ideas as well as with facts, and that a part of his duty is to comprehend, to digest, the ideas he finds in his sources. By setting down an accurate, condensed restatement of these ideas, the note taker not only saves much time and space, but he also assures himself that he has understood what he has read and that he has a clear conception of the way in which the borrowed material will fit into the projected scheme of his paper.

Regardless of the form in which they are taken, the student's notes should include **everything** *that he has borrowed from any of his sources, with a clear and unmistakable distinction made between direct quotation and material that has been restated in the student's own words.*

It is advisable that the student observe the following suggestions in the make-up of his notes, subject, of course, to the requirements of his local English department or of his instructor:

1. Cards or slips of the same size should be used for all notes. These cards may be of the same size as the bibliography cards (either 3″ × 5″ or 4″ × 6″), although some research workers—and some instructors—prefer the use of 3″ × 5″ cards for bibliographical entries and 4″ × 6″ cards for notes. The latter procedure makes the two kinds of cards readily distinguishable.

2. On the top line of the card the student will find it very useful to place a caption—that is, a key word or phrase. This should be as brief a statement as possible of the content of the note. Obviously a number of notes will be about the same division of the subject (as suggested above, in the discussion of preliminary organization) and will all bear the same or nearly the same caption.

3. One note only should appear on a card. Since the cards are used, in part, to facilitate organization of the material, the student will find himself most successful if he puts only one idea on a card, no matter how short that note may be. There is, of course, no objection to the student's jotting down on a note card his own comment on the quotation or the summary that comprises the note, but he should be careful that there is no confusion between what is the note and what is his notation or comment.

4. The note taker should be careful in quoting (1) *to give the exact words, spelling, and punctuation of the author; and* (2) *to indicate on his card that it is a quotation by the use of quotation marks.*

5. In taking notes, the student may, of course, omit material that is not pertinent, so long as this omission does not distort or change the author's intended meaning. Such omissions from quoted material are shown by the use of the customary three dots (. . .), or four—*including* the period—at the end of a sentence.

6. The student should make sure that his summary or précis notes do not in any way misrepresent the statements of the original author. For a discussion of the details of the précis method, see Chapter XI.

7. Explanatory or other material inserted by the student into a quotation should be enclosed in square brackets—*not* parentheses. *Examples*: "He [Emerson] loved rhyme and return, period and musical reflection." "The Lancastrian system of instruction, coming at the time it did [1806 to 1830], exerted a very important influence in awakening a public interest in and a sentiment for free schools."

8. The student should record the source of each note (either quotation or summary), since he will need this information for the proper annotating of his paper. The last name of the author, the brief title of the work, and the page or pages from which the note was taken are necessary for such later identification.[3]

Note Card I illustrates the note composed of a simple direct quotation. The student will notice the caption at the head of the card. This identifies the content of the note and will be useful in fitting the note into the student's discussion of one of his main topics or subtopics—i.e., wherever it logically belongs. The whole quotation is enclosed in quotation marks; quoted words within

---

[3] For short pieces of research it may be feasible to use a *symbol system* of cross references between bibliography cards and note cards. In using this system, the student places—preferably in the upper right-hand corner—the symbol ① on one of his bibliography cards, the symbol ② on another, the symbol ③ on another, and so on. Then, *every* note card taken from the source identified as ① on the bibliography card is given the same symbol, that is, a ①; every note card based on source ② carries a ②; and so on. The symbol on the note card, of course, takes the place of only the author's last name and the short title; *it will still be necessary to give an exact page reference for each note.* Most research workers prefer the greater accuracy afforded by author-title identification on each note card, as described above in the text.

Note Card I

Whitman: Effect of his "conversion"

"*Whitman, a sensitive young artist, was a bit of a dandy in his twenties, with a boutonnière, smart clothes, a walking stick; but when at thirty-six, a carpenter, he was 'converted,' that is, when he had.his lonely experience of introversion and what he called 'revelation' on Long Island beside the sea, . . . a sensitive man became a primitive and so was the first truly to express what the inarticulate and hard-boiled pioneer could not.*"

Oppenheim, "Whitman," p. 262.

---

the quotation ("converted" and "revelation") are placed within *single* quotation marks. Some omitted words are indicated by the three dots after the phrase "beside the sea." The note is identified, at the lower left-hand corner, by the author's last name, the title of the article, and the exact page reference. This identification might be placed before the note, toward the upper right-hand corner; the position is not so important as the fact that the note *is* identified.

Observe that note cards are not numbered, since the student probably will not use them in the order in which he takes them. If he chooses, the student may identify each note with respect to the topic or subtopic it falls under in his working outline, labeling it—preferably in the upper right-hand corner—I, A; II, B; III, B, or whatever its proper designation may be. The disadvantage of this system is that one may decide to change the order of parts in his outline, and then the symbols must also be changed.

Note Card II illustrates the précis form of note taking. The same mechanical make-up that is used in Note Card I appears here: the student indicates the content of the note by the use of a

Note Card II

Whitman: Later attitude toward party politics.

As he grew older, Whitman came to believe that party politics could do little to ameliorate evil social conditions. He thought that parties were selfish, that they often chose weak or vicious men as candidates for public office. At the same time, he thought that some of the evils of practical politics could be lessened by an extension of the suffrage, whereby greater good might come to the whole mass of the people.

Stovall, Intro., Whitman, pp. xlv-xlvi.

---

caption, and he identifies the source of the note by an author-title-page reference. (Observe that the page reference here is in *small* Roman numerals; the material is taken from an introduction by the editor of the text used.)

The body of the note, instead of being a direct quotation, is a condensed restatement of Stovall's remarks on this particular topic. *The restatement is in the student's own words. If any of the original author's sentences or phrases had been included, they would be enclosed in quotation marks.* This is a very important principle, involving the whole question of the ethics of research. The student should *never* use another's words without benefit of quotation marks; to do so may mean that he has—wittingly or unwittingly—been guilty of plagiarism. *Webster's New Collegiate Dictionary* defines the verb *plagiarize* thus: "To steal or purloin and pass off as one's own (the ideas, words, writings, etc., of another)."

Note Card III illustrates a combination form of note—one that includes both direct quotation and summary, as well as a brief comment (or, in this case, a memorandum) by the student.

Note Card III

Joyce's Ulysses: Symbolism in

"... *Ulysses is elaborately symbolic, and the symbolism
is dual. In the first place, the structure of the book
parallels the Homeric epic from which it takes its name
[the Odyssey]. Stephen Dedalus is Telemachus, Leopold Bloom
is Ulysses, and Bloom's wife . . . is Penelope."*

*The authors point out that minor characters and in-
cidents also parallel those in the Odyssey and that a
"secondary symbolism lies in the representation by each
section of the book of a human organ and some art or science."
They refer, also, to an essay on Joyce's symbolism in Edmund
Wilson's Axel's Castle. (Investigate this.)*

Lovett and Hughes, History of the Novel, pp. 459-460.

Notice that the main direct quotation is given first, enclosed in
quotation marks. The quotation begins in the middle of a sentence, so the first word is preceded by the usual marks of ellipsis
(. . .). Another ellipsis occurs toward the end of the quotation.
The student has supplied an explanatory phrase ("the *Odyssey*"),
which is enclosed in square brackets.

In the second, or summary, part of the note another direct
quotation is used, and the quoted matter is also enclosed in
quotation marks.

This combination form may also be used for a *critical note,* in
which the student gives first a direct quotation or a summary,
and then puts down his own opinion of the source material.

ORGANIZING THE MATERIAL

If the student has worked with a properly limited subject, if
he has had a definite point of view (expressed in a thesis or
theme sentence), if he has used a preliminary outline or working

plan, and if he has gathered his notes systematically, his later problems of organization will be *relatively* simple.

The revised outline. Throughout his work, of course, he should be thinking about ways in which the plan of his paper can be improved. He will probably find that his preliminary outline will need revision from time to time, as he becomes better acquainted with his material and sees more clearly the relative importance of the ideas he is working with, as well as their possible relationships with each other. He may, indeed, find that some topics have no real place in his treatment of the chosen subject, and that other topics, previously overlooked, need to be added. Such reorganizations of his material will probably call for the dropping of some of the notes he has taken and the examination of new sources for additional evidence.

At any rate, having taken all or nearly all his notes, the student should prepare a revised outline, in either topic or sentence form, although the latter will probably be more useful as a guide to the actual writing of his paper. (For a discussion of the principles and the forms of the outline, see Chapter VIII, "Organization," section O 4.) He should check his notes against his outline and his outline against his notes, thereby making sure (1) that he has enough material for each of the topics in his outline, and (2) that he has not omitted from his outline any of the important topics on which he has gathered material.

The first draft. He should now be ready to write the first draft of his paper. In doing so, he should keep in mind that a properly constructed article usually contains an introduction, a body, and a conclusion, but that these three parts are by no means equal in importance or extent. For a paper of three thousand words, the introduction should not generally be more than one paragraph of one hundred to one hundred and fifty words. The opening should not be too formal; the writer need only state the purpose of the paper, so that the reader, knowing in advance what the writer is attempting to do, may follow the argument more intelligently.

The body of the theme is obviously the most important part. It is here that the writer presents all the material that he has been at pains to gather. It is here that he presents his discussion of that material. If he wishes to make his paper at all original or valuable, he should avoid serving up to his reader a mere cold hash of the opinions of others or choking him with an endless string of quotations. He must learn to *use* material, not merely to present it. He should digest it in the sense of *understanding* and *absorbing* it, not of merely *summarizing* it. The material he has brought together is valuable only insofar as he draws conclusions from it.

The conclusion, in turn, should be a brief, compact restatement of the principal ideas of the paper and a clear expression of the decision to which those ideas have led the writer. It, like the introduction, should not be phrased too formally.

The student should, of course, write his first draft with his notes properly arranged (under their respective topics) and immediately before him. He will discover that, in the long run, it is most economical of time and effort to make his first draft as legible, as clearly expressed, and as complete as possible. Many instructors wish to see the first draft of a student's research paper; for this reason, as well as for his own satisfaction, the individual student should make his first draft presentable—with ample margins, the text double-spaced (if the first draft is typewritten), the extended quotations set off as described below, all other quotations properly enclosed in quotation marks, the footnotes set down on their respective pages, and so on. It is well, also, to make an experimental title page, and to draw up the bibliographical list in approximately final form. If, in preparing his first draft, the student pays sufficient attention to these mechanical matters, he can then devote most of his later efforts to the more important task of revising his composition for clarity, unity, and style.

THE FORM OF THE RESEARCH PAPER

General considerations. Many specific points of form are exemplified in the illustrative research paper that concludes this chapter. The student should examine that paper carefully, as well as the comments accompanying it. Particular requirements in the form of the research paper vary considerably throughout American colleges and universities; the student, naturally, should consult the style sheet of his local English department and the wishes of his instructor.

It may be said in general, however, that the completed manuscript should be as neat, as legible, as free from errors as the student can possibly make it. He will ordinarily be asked to hand the paper in flat, enclosed in a folder. Obviously, when a folder is used, there should be enough margin at the left-hand side of the page so that none of the writing is obscured and a fair amount of white space is visible (a margin of an inch and a half to two inches will usually be enough).

Pagination. The various parts of the research paper should be arranged in the following order: (1) title page; (2) prefatory matter—if any (including the outline, if this is a required part of the paper); (3) the theme proper; and (4) the bibliography.

When an outline or other prefatory matter (such as a preface or a foreword) is included as part of the research paper project, such preliminary pages should be numbered with small Roman numerals, *counting but not numbering* the title page as page i, and then proceeding with ii, iii, iv, v, and so on. It is usual to center such numbers at the bottom of the page.

The theme proper should be paginated consecutively, beginning with the first page as 1, and continuing with Arabic numerals throughout the paper. After page 1 the Arabic numeral is at the top of the page. (See the illustrative research paper.)

The bibliography is usually considered to be end matter, and is paged in sequence after the theme proper. That is, if the last page of the theme proper is 12, the first page of the bibliography will be 13.

Quotations. In quotations the exact words, form, and punctuation of the original author must be used. If, for instance, Lewis Carroll chooses to write "ca'n't," any person quoting a passage in which that word appears must write it with the two apostrophes. If, in quoted matter, a word is obviously misspelled or a sentence is obviously ungrammatical, the writer who quotes it may show that the error is not his own by placing the Latin word *sic* (meaning "thus") in square brackets immediately after the word or phrase to which he is calling attention. In manuscript or typescript, *sic* should always be underlined. Ellipsis, as we have said previously, is indicated by the use of three dots.

When a fragment of a line of verse or prose is quoted, it can be written as a part of the sentence in connection with which it appears—in quotation marks, of course. But when a prose quotation runs to four or more lines, it should ordinarily be set off from the text in the following manner:

Nor did the performances on the New York stage

always please him. He once advised a young

actor, who had essayed the part of Hamlet,

> . . . to relinquish the stage; or, if he is
> determined to persist, either to "reform his
> acting altogether," or give his next per-
> formance to the Creek Indians, who will,
> without a doubt, raise the war-whoop for his
> reception.[17]

On another occasion, he deplored the liberties

taken with the text of Sheridan's play, The

School for Scandal. In speaking of . . . .

The footnote-reference number is given at the end of such extended quotations. Passages of verse, if a full line or more, should always be quoted in the original form, centered on the page:

Probably the oldest known version of this

poem is the one that begins:

> Lord Thomas and Fair Annet
>   Sate a' day on a hill;
> Whan night was cum, and sun was sett,
>   They had not talkt their fill.[43]

The essential parts of the ballad, in almost

every variant, remain . . .

Note that when quotations are so set on the page no quotation marks are used; the special form makes sufficiently clear that the passage is a quotation. (For a full discussion of the use of quotation marks, see section P 7.)

        Footnotes. In the body of the paper the writer makes use of the facts or opinions gained through reading; for the use of this material he must make proper acknowledgment. Those facts that are commonly known are public property, and anyone is free to use them. *But any other fact, or any special expression of a fact, or any idea that is not original with the student must be credited to the original author, with the title of his work, and with the specific pages (or other exact reference) in which the borrowed fact or idea appeared.*

This acknowledgment is most conveniently made in the form of footnotes.[4] The student will place a raised figure 1—thus [1]— at the end of the first quotation or otherwise borrowed passage on the page, a raised figure 2—thus [2]—after the second, and so on. He will repeat these numbers at the bottom of the page and give with each the necessary identification of source. The following examples show some of the common variations in the form of *first* references to a source:

1) **Book: first edition, one author:**

[1]Emory Holloway, Whitman: an Interpretation in Narrative (New York, 1926), p. 117.

---

    [4] The authors of this text realize that there are many "systems" of footnoting in more or less general use. The method exemplified here has been selected because it is clear, relatively simple, free from ambiguities, and convenient for the reader as well as the writer. It is, with minor variations, the method followed by the University of Chicago *Manual of Style* and the quarterly periodical *American Literature*. The student will do well to consult his local style sheet on matters of footnote form.

2) Book: later edition:

[2]Sir Paul Harvey, <u>The Oxford Companion to English Literature</u> (3rd ed.; Oxford, 1946), pp. 257-258.

3) Book: more than one author:

[3]Robert Morss Lovett and Helen Sard Hughes, <u>The History of the Novel in England</u> (Boston, 1932), p. 363.

4) Book: more than one volume:

[4]Frank Moss, <u>The American Metropolis</u> (New York, 1897), II, 121.

5) Book: cited under editor:

[5]John Macy, ed., <u>American Writers on American Literature</u> (New York, 1931), p. xix.

6) Book: article by one of several contributors:

[6]James Oppenheim, "Whitman," <u>American Writers on American Literature</u>, ed. John Macy (New York, 1931), pp. 260-261.

7) Book: author quotes another writer:

[7]James Fenimore Cooper, quoted by Carl Van Doren, <u>The American Novel</u> (revised ed.; New York, 1940), p. 41.

8) Article: periodical paginated by volume:

[8] Clyde Kluckhohn, "Frontiers of Anthropological Research," <u>Colorado Quarterly,</u> VII, 271-286 (Winter, 1959).

9) Article: periodical paged separately for each issue:

[9]Daniel P. Moynihan, "A Second Look at the School Panic," <u>Reporter</u>, June 11, 1959, pp. 14-19.

10) **Article: alternative form for same citation as the preceding:**

[10]Daniel P. Moynihan, "A Second Look at the School Panic," Reporter, XX, 14-19 (June 11, 1959).

11) **Encyclopedia article:**

[11]"Dredging," Encylopaedia Britannica (14th ed., 1929), VII, 641.

12) **Newspaper: editorial:**

[12]Editorial, St. Louis Post-Dispatch, August 19, 1959.

13) **Newspaper: news story without by-line:**

[13]"Big Four Discuss Berlin," New York Herald Tribune, July 25, 1959.

14) **Newspaper: signed article:**

[14]John Scali, "Khrushchev and Nixon Trade Gibes," Washington Post, July 25, 1959.

15) **Pamphlets, bulletins, government publications:**

[15]H. A. Turner, A Graphic Summary of Farm Tenure, U.S. Department of Agriculture Miscellaneous Publications No. 261 (Washington, 1936), p. 17.

16) **Pamphlets, bulletins, government publications: no specific author given:**

[16]Social Security Board, Old Age and Survivors Insurance Statistics, Employment and Wages of Covered Workers, 1938 (Washington, 1940), pp. 16-18.

17) Unpublished thesis or other document:

[17]Kenneth L. Daughrity, <u>The Life and Work of Nathaniel Parker Willis, 1806-1836</u> (Unpublished University of Virginia Doctoral Dissertation, 1935), p. 76.

18) Lecture:

[18]Charles T. Loomis, Lecture: "Adult Education: A Community Project," Clinton Public Forum, March 14, 1960.

Footnotes should be placed at the bottom of the page *on which the reference occurs,* and should be numbered consecutively throughout the paper.[5] It is customary to draw a heavy line across the page between text and footnotes, and, if the manuscript is typewritten, the footnotes should be single-spaced (distinct from the double-spacing of the text), with a double space between footnotes.

In general, footnotes should be as brief as possible. The writer may therefore use abbreviations and symbols that he would not ordinarily use in his text. The following abbreviations are common:

c. or *ca.*	*circa,* about (used with dates when the precise date is unknown or when the writer wishes to indicate that the date is approximate)
cf.	*confer,* compare
ch. or chap. (pl.: chaps.)	chapter
col. (pl.: cols.)	column
ed. (pl.: eds.)	editor, or edition

---

[5] An alternative form for the arrangement of footnotes is to place each one immediately below the line of text in which its corresponding reference number is given. When so placed, a footnote should be ruled off from the text by a line above and a line below.

Some writers prefer to number footnotes serially on each page, rather than consecutively throughout the paper.

The student should, again, be guided by his local style sheet if it varies from the practice recommended in this text.

f. or ff.	and the following page, or pages (used after a page number: pp. 241 ff.)
fig. (pl.: figs.)	figure
ibid.	*ibidem,* in the same place (see the illustrative research paper for examples of the use of *ibid.*)
l. (pl.: ll.)	line
loc. cit.	*loco citato,* in the place cited
no. (pl.: nos.)	number
op. cit.	*opere citato,* in the work cited (see the illustrative research paper for an example, and comment)
p. (pl.: pp.)	page
passim	here and there (used when the material cited is scattered throughout a work; when the acknowledgment is general rather than specific)
trans.	translator, translation, or translated by
vol. (pl.: vols.)	volume

For later footnote references to a source already cited, various short forms may be used. The most commonly used of these short forms are exemplified in the illustrative research paper. One of the most convenient forms of this kind is *ibid.,* which is used for successive references to the same source and needs to be followed only by notation of specific page or pages. It must be remembered, however, that it cannot be used after an intervening reference from another source.

It is possible, and frequently advisable, to make part of the acknowledgment in the text. For the sake of clearness, coherence, and honesty in the discussion, the writer will often wish to mention the name of the author of quoted or otherwise borrowed material. All that is necessary then is to add in the footnote that part of the information that has not been expressed in the body of the paper (unless, of course, one wants to repeat the full information in the footnote). It is almost always awkward to introduce into the text the complete information regarding the source.

Footnotes may also be used to give further information about a particular point that does not belong in the body of the paper but that is of sufficient interest to be worthy of mention; such notes may give explanation, definition of terms, and editorial comment. (See, for example, the footnotes used in the present chapter.)

The alert reader will have discovered that many writers use a variety of abbreviations of Latin terms (in addition to those previously listed) in footnotes of this last type. Some of the most common are: *infra* (below), *supra* (above), *ante* (before), *post* (after)—these four, of course, referring to other passages in the paper being written—*v.* or *vide* (see), *viz.* (namely), *et al.* (and others). The use of these abbreviations may give an air of erudition to a paper, but since the English equivalent expresses the idea as well in each instance, it will be simpler, and usually more desirable, to use the English form.

The bibliography. The student will ordinarily be asked to submit a bibliographical list with his research paper. This list—as indicated previously—should follow the theme proper, and should be arranged in an orderly fashion.

If a bibliography does not accompany the research paper, it is advisable to give full bibliographical information—including the name of the publisher—about each source the first time it appears in a footnote. When this type of footnote is used, the publisher's name follows the place of publication, thus:

[1]Henry A. Atkinson, The Church and the People's Play (Boston: The Pilgrim Press, 1915), p. 138.

Illustrative Research Paper with Critical Comment

COMMENT ON ILLUSTRATIVE
RESEARCH PAPER

General. The portion of an actual student research paper which follows is intended as an example for the student. It is not a model in the sense that it is a "perfect" paper. Attention will be called to its strength and weaknesses, and comment will be made on it as it exemplifies research paper form.

Title page

The chief features of this title page are those that mark all good title pages: simplicity and balance. Note that the title is centered from the side margins and that the author's name is centered on the title. The course number and date balance each other at the bottom of the page. All parts of the title page are laid out without crowding, with plenty of white space to make for a neat, balanced display. If there were a subtitle it would be centered beneath the main title.

The title is clear, precise, and informative. "The Haymarket Riot" would make a more attention-compelling one but would lose precision, since the subject of the whole paper is the riot and its aftermath, the trial.

Some instructors may call for additional endorsement, and the style in any given course should be followed.

THE HAYMARKET AFFAIR

Florence L. Jenson

English 102-G   May 14, 1947

COMMENT ON ILLUSTRATIVE
RESEARCH PAPER

Prefatory pages

Such prefatory matter as the outline (or a foreword, if there is one)
is placed between the title page and the first page of the paper proper.
Pagination of all prefatory material is by lower-case Roman numerals
placed at the bottom of the page.

The analytical sentence outline gives not only a plan for the writer
but a brief synopsis for the reader. Most people who read books do not
realize that when they look at the table of contents, they are reading the
author's outline in another form. The table of contents will carry at
least the main headings of the outline, and often the first subheadings
(see page xiii of this book). For a thirteen-page paper such as this, of
course, there is no need for a table of contents.

The theme statement here is not the kind of thesis a researcher can
afford to start out with before he has made his investigation. Over sixty
years after the Haymarket riot, the relatives and friends of police killed
there gather at the square to commemorate that day. The accused, too,
still have their relatives and friends in Chicago. This paper probably
started with Miss Jenson's asking, "What happened at Haymarket, and
in the courtroom afterward?" The theme statement here, a generalization
of her detailed account, is her considered answer.

The outline shows that the writer has put the material in a carefully
organized, well-expressed form. There is nothing mechanical about the
outlines; where only two ranks are needed, two are used; where small
details become important (as in IV, B, 2 and 3) the outline goes to four
ranks. The sentence outline gives a fully developed scheme for the expansion of the material, but it is not a rigid mold in which a paragraph
represents a division. Some sentences in the outline (such as II; II, B;
II, C) appear in the same form in the paper; others (such as IV, A, 1
and 3) are substantially the same.

The sentences of the outline are in general well expressed and balanced to show relation of ideas (note especially IV, B, 2 and 3 and
their subdivisions). There is some awkwardness of expression in IV, C;
this is perhaps more noticeable because of the general smoothness of
the rest.

THE HAYMARKET AFFAIR

Theme statement: There was no concrete evidence to prove that the eight anarchists had in any way participated in the throwing of the Haymarket bomb, but prejudice against them was so strong that they were nevertheless convicted of the crime.

I. When the police attempted to disperse a peaceable labor meeting in Haymarket Square, a bomb was thrown in the midst of the police.

   A. The meeting had been called to denounce the shooting of several strikers by the police during a disturbance at the McCormick plant.

   B. The meeting was orderly and was nearly over when the police appeared.

   C. Immediately after the police gave the order to disperse, a bomb was thrown, and one policeman was killed and several were wounded.

   D. The police opened fire at the crowd, which rapidly dispersed.

II. The Haymarket riot climaxed a period of labor unrest.

   A. Strikes to secure an eight-hour working day were numerous.

   B. Police methods of breaking strikes and dispersing labor meetings were very brutal.

   C. The eight-hour movement received active support from the anarchistic International Working People's Association.

III. The newspapers, which had always opposed the eight-hour movement and its anarchist leaders, accused the anarchists of throwing the bomb.

   A. The press induced general prejudice against the anarchists by hysterical tirades about the peril of an organized anarchist rebellion.

   B. Newspapers throughout the entire nation demanded the death of the anarchists.

IV. Eight anarchists were indicted and tried for the murder of Police Officer Degan, who was killed by the explosion of the bomb.

A. Securing an impartial jury proved impossible.

    1. A great majority of the men examined for jury duty stated that they were prejudiced against anarchists and held an opinion as to their guilt.

    2. Judge Gary did not consider such prejudice as sufficient cause for challenging a prospective juror.

    3. The twelve jurors finally accepted had all formed opinions as to the guilt of the defendants, and most of them were prejudiced against anarchists.

B. None of the evidence presented against the defendants was very substantial.

    1. The evidence that the anarchists planned the bomb throwing the night before the riot was refuted.

    2. The defense completely disproved the state's evidence that:

        a. The bomb was lighted by Spies and thrown by Schnaubelt from Crane's alley;

        b. On the night of the riot Spies and Schwab held a conversation in which the words "police" and "pistols" were mentioned;

        c. Fielden had threatened the police and fired on them when they attempted to disperse the Haymarket meeting.

    3. Evidence against the other anarchists was incontrovertible but not very relevant.

        a. Parsons had made inflammatory speeches.

        b. Engel and Fischer had attended the "Monday night conspiracy," and Fischer issued the call for the Haymarket meeting.

        c. Lingg had manufactured bombs.

        d. Neebe had a small investment in one of the anarchist papers and owned some weapons and a "red flag."

    4. Evidence was introduced to show that the anarchists had written inflammatory articles and had given incendi-

ary speeches which, the prosecution maintained, incited someone to throw the bomb.

C. In the closing arguments, the prosecution urged the jury to convict the defendants because they were anarchists: by making examples of them the jury would save society.

D. Judge Gary gave a new interpretation to the law of conspiracy in which he stated that if anyone acting under the encouragement of conspirators committed murder, then all such conspirators were guilty of murder, whether the person who actually committed the murder was identified or not.

V. The jury declared the anarchists guilty.

A. Neebe was sentenced to fifteen years' imprisonment; the other seven were sentenced to hang.

1. The sentences of Fielden and Schwab were later commuted to life imprisonment.

2. Lingg committed suicide.

3. The other four anarchists were hanged.

B. In 1893 Governor Altgeld pardoned Fielden, Schwab, and Neebe.

COMMENT ON ILLUSTRATIVE
RESEARCH PAPER

First page

The opening of this paper is a refutation of the commonly held misconception that all research writing must be dull. The opening of a research paper usually should be simple and direct, and often it is more formal. Here the approach is simple, but it is more like the opening of a story in which setting is established, characters are introduced, and the plot is put in motion. In this light, one wonders why Miss Jenson fails to clear her setting; her outline (I) mentions Haymarket Square; her notes indicate that the meeting was held in Desplaines Street, just off the Square. Her paper is silent on the exact location. The explanation of all but the immediate circumstances preceding the riot is withheld until the next page. Not all subjects will allow of this type of opening, and certainly no strained effort should be made to startle or excite the reader. But if a writer has a riot or the equivalent on his hands, he should take advantage of it, and this Miss Jenson does.

The footnote-reference figures (in the text) are Arabic numerals (without following periods), raised slightly above the line of the text in which they occur. The figures in the footnotes are also so raised.

The documentation here is a little peculiar. Two thirds of the page seems to carry none. This is partially justifiable, partially not. Reference to Miss Jenson's notes shows that she has used five sources for the description of the riot, and on many points these all say the same thing: the information is common knowledge, peculiar to no one source. Only one source, however, speaks of Parsons as being more moderate than usual, and this should be credited. Only one source testifies to Fielden's moderation, and Miss Jenson's "two or three hundred" in the final audience is given variously as less than six hundred and as a few hundred. Similarly the direct quotations are given in only one source, and thus should be credited. Miss Jenson oddly omits a light shower that thinned out the crowd greatly before the threatening storm began to disperse it.

The last sentence in paragraph 1, a generalizing sentence, comes not so much from notes as from reading that did not get into the notes, and is rightly not documented.

Notice the line separating the footnotes from the text—a useful mark of distinction. This line should be made far enough below the last line of text to prevent its being mistaken for an underlining of the final line.

The footnotes on this page are for a newspaper, a government document, and a book. They are all in the form used for first references.

THE HAYMARKET AFFAIR

"This meeting is called to discuss the general situation, not for the purpose of raising a row or disturbance," stated the first speaker, August Spies.[1] The reporter from the Chicago Tribune was surprised at the mildness of Spies' remarks.[2] The circular announcing the meeting had stated that the speakers would "denounce the latest atrocious act of the police," the shooting of several strikers during a fracas at the McCormick plant. Spies had been extremely infuriated by this occurrence.[3] Albert Parsons and Samuel Fielden, the succeeding speakers, were also more moderate than usual, and the thousand or so working men and women standing in the street listened quietly to their comments about the strike situation. The meeting seemed destined to be just another of the many labor gatherings of 1886.

Toward the end of the meeting, an abrupt change in weather turned the mild May evening into a cold windy night. The people glanced anxiously at the dark, threatening clouds gathered overhead, and many of them departed. Only two or three hundred remained to hear Samuel Fielden's concluding remarks. Suddenly murmers of "police" were heard. The audience turned and saw a large contingent of police, marching in columns the width of the street, approaching them. The police halted at the speakers' stand.

"I command you in the name of the people of the state of Illinois to immediately and peacefully disperse!" ordered the police captain.

"But we are peaceable!" protested Fielden.

---

[1]Chicago Tribune, May 5, 1886.

[2]Illinois Supreme Court, August Spies et al. vs. The People of State of Illinois, Abstract of Record (Chicago, 1887), II, 133.

[3]Samuel Yellen, American Labor Struggles (New York, 1936), pp. 52-53.

-1-

COMMENT ON ILLUSTRATIVE
RESEARCH PAPER

Second page

Documentation for all the material after the middle of the first paragraph on the preceding page is finally made at the end of the first paragraph here. Note that an attempt is made to indicate that more than one source has been used. The criticisms of documentation on the preceding page are still valid, however. There is also some confusion in regard to the Riot Scrapbook; since the title is not underlined, one gathers it is not a printed book; the place and date in parentheses after the title are as for a printed book. As a matter of fact, the source is not a printed book; it is a scrapbook compiled in the year of the riot by the Desplaines Street Police Station, and is now in the Gilpin Library of the Chicago Historical Society. Such unusual sources, which are unique, need precise description and location. Since the material used from the scrapbook consists of three accounts of the riot by other Chicago newspapers, this fact might well have been made clear, too.

Reference number 6 in the text carefully locates the source for the quotation it follows, since it is inserted in material later documented by footnote 7.

The footnotes on this page are of three kinds. The first part of footnote 4 is the short form for a book. (Here *ibid.* could have been used.) The rest of the note gives corroborative source material (note the objections to the incomplete description above). Footnotes 6 and 7 are in the form for first reference to a book. Of footnote 7, it may be noted that "Springfield, Ill.," might be preferable as a place description; where there is no doubt—Chicago, New York, Boston, London—the city name is enough.

Footnote 5 uses *ibid.*, the abbreviation for *ibidem*, "in the same place." Here it is used incorrectly, for it can be used only when a note refers to a single immediately preceding source. Footnote 4 contains three sources; the reader must guess as to the reference for *ibid.*

Note that footnotes are single-spaced, with a double space between the dividing line and between footnotes.

-2-

Suddenly a bomb, its fuse spluttering, hurtled through the air and fell in the midst of the police. The explosion was devastating. One policeman was killed instantly; some sixty others lay wounded in the street. A stunned, horrified silence momentarily gripped the people. Then the police, recovering from the shock, fired round after round of bullets directly into the crowd. The terrified people fled for safety from the enraged police. A few minutes later the street was empty except for the wounded. Chicago's Haymarket riot was over.[4]

The Haymarket riot climaxed an era of labor unrest. The increased use of machinery and the large wave of immigration during the 1880's contributed to a widespread unemployment. As the competition for jobs became intensely keen, wages decreased, working hours increased, and the unemployment problem became ever more acute. Many workingmen believed that the solution to this situation lay in the eight-hour day: the shortening of the work day would necessitate the employment of additional laborers. Thousands of workers joined labor unions, and strikes to obtain the eight-hour day were numerous.[5]

Management, believing that "a mob of strikers is entitled to no more leniency than a mob of lynchers,"[6] enlisted the aid of the police in its bitter fight against the unions. Police methods of breaking strikes were notoriously brutal. Policemen used their clubs freely and at times seriously injured even innocent bystanders. Unwarranted arrests of laborers were frequent.[7]

---

[4]Yellen, American Labor Struggles, pp. 54-55. Also see Chicago Tribune, May 5, 1886, and Chicago Haymarket Square Riot Scrapbook (Chicago, 1886), pp. 1-6.

[5]Ibid., pp. 40-42.

[6]Henry David, The History of the Haymarket Affair (New York, 1936), p. 41.

[7]John P. Altgeld, Reasons for Pardoning Fielden, Neebe, and Schwab (Springfield, 1893), pp. 38-49.

COMMENT ON ILLUSTRATIVE
RESEARCH PAPER

Third page

Three methods of handling quotations are exemplified on this page:
(1) a prose quotation of over four lines is blocked in and single-spaced
without quotation marks; (2) phrases are taken from a full quotation
and worked into a sentence; and (3) at the bottom of the page a single-
sentence quotation is begun which is handled regularly with quotation
marks in the double-spaced text.

In the first paragraph Miss Jenson gets into a difficulty that she does
not quite get out of unscathed. Moving from "social revolutionaries"
to "anarchists" to "socialists and communists," she implies that the
I.W.P.A. had all three in its membership (true), that the general term
"anarchists" applied to all the members was a misnomer in some cases
(true). Although she does not specifically identify Parsons, Spies,
Fielden, and Schwab as anarchists, she refers to them and their organization as "anarchist" (they believed in a mixture of anarchism and
syndicalism). A glance at the most elementary reference books of
political science will show that the definition of "social revolutionaries"
here hardly fits the principles of anarchism. The problem, and Miss
Jenson is hardly to be severely censured, is analogous to the use of the
term "Red" in the United States in the 1950's. This difficulty is likely
to arise in any paper on a highly controversial, complex subject, and
many a more experienced writer than Miss Jenson has emerged from
the attempt to solve it with something less than complete satisfactoriness.

Note that footnote 10 removes the objection made to footnote 4. It
is not clear why the Chicago *Evening Journal* should be cited here, and
the Chicago *Herald, Times,* and *Inter-Ocean* should not have been cited
earlier. Notice also that here Miss Jenson indicates that she has fully
decided the Scrapbook is a published book, which it is not, by italicizing
the title.

-3-

The eight-hour movement received active support from the International Working People's Association. The I.W.P.A. was composed of social revolutionaries who believed that complete extinction of capitalism by armed force was necessary in order to stop the exploitation of the working class and attain a free society. Members of the group were invariably referred to as anarchists, although several of them were actually socialists and communists. I.W.P.A. leaders such as Albert Parsons, August Spies, Samuel Fielden, and Michael Schwab were among the most active promoters in Chicago of the eight-hour movement.[8]

The newspapers had always violently opposed the eight-hour movement and had bitterly condemned its anarchist leaders.[9] But these attacks were mild compared to the vicious tirades against the anarchists that filled the papers after the Haymarket riot. The identity of the person who threw the bomb and the reason for so doing were unknown, but the day following the riot the Chicago *Evening Journal* warned its readers:

> The community is menaced by a peril the magnitude of which it were folly to underestimate. The worst elements of the population are in open and organized rebellion against the law. The insurgents are formidable in numbers, desperate in temper, under full control of the lawless characters [the anarchists] who preach assassination, murder and arson.[10]

The Chicago *Tribune* urged that the "bloody minded anarchists" should be punished "to the full limit without mercy or regret."[11]

And the newspaper attack was not confined to Chicago. "The Anarchists," inveighed the Detroit *Tribune*, "are a loathsome and

---

[8]Yellen, *American Labor Struggles*, pp. 46-50.

[9]Edgar Lee Masters, *The Tale of Chicago* (New York, 1933). pp. 211-12.

[10]Chicago *Evening Journal*, May 5, 1886, included in *Chicago Haymarket Riot Scrapbook*, p. 13.

[11]Chicago *Tribune*, May 7, 1886.

COMMENT ON ILLUSTRATIVE
RESEARCH PAPER

Fourth page

Documentation on this page is very careful and precise through footnote 17.

The last part of the first sentence in the last paragraph illustrates an undesirable practice in research writing. The judge is characterized as "biased." Later Miss Jenson shows this clearly enough. It is better to show the reader first, and then characterize, if the characterization is needed, or the writer wishes to be emphatic.

The note card reproduced below is that from which the part of the paragraph preceding reference number 15 was written:

Police round-up of anarchists, etc.   15

The police staged "raids" in the working class districts and arrested all the known anarchists, socialists and others of the "red brotherhood." Also rounded up men and women who had no radical connections but who "looked like communists." "Make the raids first and look up the law afterward!" State's Attorney Grinnell told the police when asked about search warrants.

 p. 108

Notice the precise caption. It will be seen that Miss Jenson has used the symbol system in recording the source of the note, the bibliography cards having been numbered. The numeral in the upper right-hand corner is the footnote numeral added after the cards have been put in order for writing.

Footnotes 12, 13, 14 show commendable care in noting the sources and the fact that they are being reprinted. Because of the possibility of changed meaning or emphasis when quotations are taken out of context, the student should be meticulous in citing his source exactly where he found it, as well as indicating the ultimate origin.

Footnote 17 illustrates the form for a periodical article, where the periodical is paginated by volume.

-4-

hideous set of lawbreakers."[12] The Denver _Tribune_ suggested that "the citizens of Chicago would be almost excusable if they were to form vigilance committees and hang every man who was known to have advocated the throwing of dynamite bombs and the overturning of the law."[13] The Atlanta _Constitution_ felt that "these Anarchists deserve no mercy and their skulls should be cracked like egg shells."[14]

The police, spurred on by the newspapers, arrested every anarchist, socialist, and communist that could be found. Even people who had no connection with the radical movement but who "looked like communists" were held by the police.[15] Eventually eight men were indicted for having murdered Mathias Degan (the policeman who was killed at the Haymarket) by throwing or having encouraged someone to throw the bomb.[16] All of these men--Spies, Parsons, Fielden, Fischer, Engel, Schwab, Lingg, and Neebe--were members of the anarchistic I.W.P.A.[17]

Nurtured by the vilification of the press, public opinion was such that securing an impartial jury for the anarchists' trial was bound to be difficult, and with an obviously biased judge it was impossible. Nearly a thousand men were examined as to their competence for jury duty. Time after time these veniremen admitted that they were prejudiced against anarchists, that they held a definite opinion as to the guilt of the accused, and that they believed what they had read in the newspapers about the affair. In each such case the de-

---

[12]Detroit _Tribune_, quoted in Chicago _Tribune_, May 7, 1886.

[13]Denver _Tribune_, quoted in Chicago _Tribune_, May 9, 1886.

[14]Atlanta _Constitution_, quoted in Chicago _Tribune_, May 9, 1886.

[15]Harry Barnard, _Eagle Forgotten: The Life of John Peter Altgeld_ (Indianapolis and New York, 1938), p. 108.

[16]Illinois Supreme Court, _August Spies et al. vs. The People of the State of Illinois, Brief and Arguments for Plaintiffs_ (Chicago, 1887), p. 1.

[17]Judge Joseph E. Gary, "The Chicago Anarchists of 1886: The Crime, the Trial, and the Punishment," _The Century Magazine_, XLV, 830 (April, 1893).

COMMENT ON ILLUSTRATIVE
RESEARCH PAPER

Fifth page

Footnote 18 is an example of the kind noted on page 567, which gives information on a matter that would be intrusive if handled in the text. This paper, written not for lawyers or law students but for general readers, cannot assume that such readers will understand the nature of challenge for cause and peremptory challenge. The distinction must be made, and it is clearly made in the footnote.

The material in the text documented by footnote 19 extends from the preceding page. A glance at the page numbers given in the footnote at first causes raised eyebrows. Certain instructors are all too familiar with that kind of student research paper in which the subject is hopelessly large and general (say "The Depression in the Nineteen Thirties"), and in the writing of which a note card appears bearing the words "Life was hard during the depression," with the pages that the note covers being given as "101–230." It is well to realize what has caused such a wide range here as "37–156." Going back to the preceding page, note Miss Jenson's phrase in the fifth line from the bottom. "Nearly a thousand men," and in the fourth line from the bottom, "Time after time." Her page references are to the part of the abstract of the case covering the examination of veniremen.

Note that reference number 20 in the text comes in the middle of a sentence, the last half of the sentence being a matter of common legal knowledge, on which the reader has been enlightened by footnote 18. Note also that *ibid.* is correctly used here.

Miss Jenson's interpolated phrases with the question and answer are indicated by brackets: the first is in a quotation in her notes; the second phrase "By exhausted witness" is not, and is a kind of editorializing from which no research paper profits.

-5-

fendants challenged for cause.[18] Thereupon the prosecution, aided by
the judge, would so manipulate the questioning as to draw from the
prospective juror a statement that, in spite of his prejudice and
opinion, he believed he could render an impartial verdict based solely
on the evidence presented. Judge Gary, who presided in the case,
would then declare the person a competent juror. The defendants, in
order to prevent this admittedly prejudiced person from taking his
seat on the jury, were compelled to resort to peremptory challenge.[19]
Eventually their peremptory challenges were exhausted,[20] and they
could exercise only challenges for cause, which were subject to the
rulings of Judge Gary.

A typical example of the examination of veniremen is the case of
James Walker. Walker stated that he was prejudiced against anarchists
and that he held an opinion as to the guilt of the defendants. If the
testimony were equally balanced, he felt he would be justified in
convicting them. The defense challenged for cause. The court then
questioned Walker at considerable length and finally asked:

> Question[By Judge Gary.] Do you believe that you can
> sit here and fairly and impartially make up your mind,
> from the evidence, whether that evidence proves that
> they are guilty beyond a reasonable doubt or not?

> Answer [By exhausted witness.] I think I could, but I
> should believe that I was a little handicapped in my
> judgment, sir.

---

[18]In criminal cases there are two types of challenges that may
be exercised against a person being examined for jury duty: (1) a
challenge for cause which requires a statement of the reason for
challenging, the trial judge determines whether the cause is sufficient to render the person incompetent for jury duty, or (2) a
peremptory challenge which does not require the assigning of any
reason, and the judge must immediately dismiss any prospective juror
so challenged. The number of peremptory challenges allowed during a
trial is limited by law.

[19]Illinois Supreme Court, _August Spies_ . . . _Abstract of_
Record, I, 37-156.

[20]_Ibid._, p. 140.

COMMENT ON ILLUSTRATIVE
RESEARCH PAPER

Sixth page

Judge Gary's quoted remark, at the top of this page, being less than four lines, might well have been double-spaced and incorporated into the text of the paper.

It is a little puzzling that Miss Jenson did not give in her second paragraph the fact that the defense had 166 peremptory challenges, a fact that is in her notes. It is even more puzzling that the fact that Flavin was dismissed after peremptory challenge should appear in the text but not in her note, it merely being stated there that challenge for cause was overruled.

The use of bracketed material for clarity in the fifth line from the bottom is good.

Footnote 24 makes use of an abbreviation that is used to shorten a footnote when a second note on the same page but not immediately following is from the same source. The Latin abbreviation, meaning "in the work cited," takes the place of the title. Notice that if there had been reference on this same page in a note to either of the other two sources by the Illinois Supreme Court, this abbreviation could not have been used. To avoid possible confusion, in instances of this sort, it is better to use a short-title reference.

Another similar footnote abbreviation, *loc. cit.*, meaning "in the place cited" can be used when both the title and the page referred to are the same.

-6-

Judge Gary then remarked:

"Well, that is a sufficient qualification for a juror
in the case--of course, the more a man feels he is
handicapped, the more he will be guarded against it."

And the challenge for cause was overruled.[21]

Judge Gary even considered M. D. Flavin competent to serve as a
juror although Flavin had stated that he held a "very strong" opinion
as to the guilt of the accused and that he was related to Police
Officer Flavin, who had been fatally wounded in the Haymarket riot.
The defendants, fortunately, had not yet exhausted their peremptory·
challenges and were able to have Flavin dismissed.[22]

All twelve jurors who were finally accepted had formed opinions
as to the guilt of the defendants; at least nine of them held varying
degrees of prejudice against anarchists. An affidavit was filed
asserting that one of the jurors, G. W. Adams, had remarked on the day
following the riot that "if I was on the jury I would hang all the
damned buggars."[23] Another juror, J. B. Greiner, stated in court that
he had formed an opinion as to the guilt of the accused, for "it is
evident that the defendants are connected with it [the bomb-throwing],
from their being here."[24] The eight anarchists were virtually convicted the day their jury was impaneled.

Twenty-one days were consumed in the selection of the jury, and
on July 15th the trial proper began. The defense immediately peti-
tioned the court to hold separate trials for the eight indicted.

---

[21]Illinois Supreme Court, August Spies . . . Abstract of
Record, I, 17-18.

[22]Ibid., p. 85

[23]David, History of the Haymarket Affair, pp. 247-49.

[24]Illinois Supreme Court, op. cit., pp. 121-22.

COMMENT ON ILLUSTRATIVE RESEARCH PAPER

Bibliography page

Most frequently, the bibliography that accompanies a research paper is a listing of the sources cited in the paper. A student may sometimes wish to add a list of sources consulted, but not referred to in the paper. Such a list is usually placed after the main bibliography, and headed "Supplementary Bibliography." *Any source from which the student has taken either quotations or ideas will, of course, be cited in the paper, and will appear in the main bibliography.*

Miss Jenson's bibliographical list is excellent in form and arrangement. The information given here was taken directly from the bibliography cards.

Notice that each book or article is listed alphabetically, under its author's last name, except where there is no author. In that case, as with Chicago Haymarket Square Riot Scrapbook and Chicago *Tribune*, the alphabetizing is by the first main word of the title. (When titles are used as the basis for bibliographical listing, such introductory words as "a," "an," and "the" are not considered.)

When two or more works have the same author, that fact may be indicated for the second and any following works by a series of dashes, equal in length to the author's name in the first listed source. This device could have been used here for the second and third works by the Illinois Supreme Court.

The order of entry, where there is more than one work by the same author, is determined by the first letter of the first main word in each title. In this case, the three Illinois Supreme Court Sources are identical through the first twelve words, and "Abstract," "Brief and Arguments," and "Brief on Facts" are the determining words.

If there is more than one edition of a book, the student should indicate (in both bibliography and footnotes) which edition is used. Straight entries, such as Miss Jenson has used, imply that the first regular edition has been used.

A bibliographical list may be classified under such headings as "Books," "Articles," and so on, with an alphabetical listing under each heading. For short pieces of research, however, a single alphabetical list is ordinarily adequate. As in other matters, the student should consult his local style sheet.

BIBLIOGRAPHY

Altgeld, John P. Reasons for Pardoning Fielden, Neebe, and Schwab.
    Springfield: Privately printed, 1893.

Barnard, Harry. Eagle Forgotten: The Life of John Peter Altgeld.
    Indianapolis and New York: The Bobbs-Merrill Company, 1938.

Chicago Haymarket Square Riot Scrapbook. Scrapbook compiled in the
    Desplaines Street Police Station. Chicago: 1886. In the Gilpin
    Library of the Chicago Historical Society.

Chicago Tribune. April 25 to May 10, 1886.

David, Henry. The History of the Haymarket Affair. New York:
    Rinehart & Company, 1936.

Gary, Judge Joseph E. "The Chicago Anarchists of 1886: The Crime, the
    Trial, and the Punishment," The Century Magazine, XLV, 803-837
    (April, 1893).

Illinois Supreme Court. August Spies et al. vs. The People of the
    State of Illinois. Abstract of Record. Chicago: Barnard &
    Gunthorp, 1887. 2 vols.

Illinois Supreme Court. August Spies et al. vs. The People of the
    State of Illinois. Brief and Arguments for Plaintiffs. Chicago:
    Barnard & Gunthorp, 1887.

Illinois Supreme Court. August Spies et al. vs. The People of the
    State of Illinois. Brief on the Facts for Defendants in Error.
    Chicago: Barnard & Gunthorp, 1887.

Masters, Edgar Lee. The Tale of Chicago. New York: G. P. Putnam's
    Sons, 1933.

Spies, August, and others. The Chicago Martyrs. (Final speeches of
    the eight anarchists.) San Francisco: Free Society Publishing
    Co., 1899.

Stephenson, George M. American History Since 1865. New York: Harper
    & Brothers, 1939.

Yellen, Samuel. American Labor Struggles. New York: Harcourt, Brace
    and Company, 1936.

-14-

XIII | Examinations and Book Reports

Communication, as we have said before, is a two-way process, involving sending a message from one point and receiving it at another. Oddly enough, this commonplace is often lost sight of in the one writing assignment that you are sure to get while in college—the examination. Your examination papers, if they call for any writing, and are not of the multiple-choice, true-false, machine-scored variety (the so-called objective examination), will be read by a human being; your composition does not simply disappear into a great, misty void. As a matter of fact, how you communicate on these occasions may spell the difference between success and failure in your college career, as well as in any particular course.

A student complaint heard frequently is, "But I don't know how to prepare for Professor Blank's examinations!" The implication is that no two instructors expect the same things on their examinations, and that students have to study their instructors as well as the content of their courses. To a certain extent, this is true: one instructor may stress the simple recall of a large amount of factual information, another may stress intensive analysis of a limited amount of data, still another may stress the synthesis of data drawn from various sources, and so forth. The difference between what they want, however, is not the result of whim, eccentricity, or dyspepsia, but is due to their differences in objectives and emphasis. There is no denying that instructors, being all too human, differ from each other, but in the long run what they all want on examinations and reports is fundamentally the same thing—clear, compact, and coherent communication.

What each might want in particular is usually specified rather clearly in the examination itself. If the instructions say, "Compare and contrast the structure of Shakespeare's *Antony and Cleopatra* and Dryden's *All for Love*," that is obviously a different kind of writing assignment from one that reads, "Summarize the plot of *Light in August*," or "Define the various attitudes toward art held by the principal characters in *Portrait of a Lady*," or "Analyze the sound patterns in Poe's 'The Bells.' "

Likewise, the types of book reports you are asked to write will also be specified fairly precisely. If you are asked to characterize the principal figures in a novel, don't summarize the action; if you are asked to discuss the author's use of autobiographical materials in his fiction, don't go into raptures about how much you enjoyed reading the novel. Regardless of stylistic excellencies, you will not be writing to the point. A newspaper reporter sent out to cover a waterfront fire who returned with an account of how a cat got stuck in a tree would soon find himself unemployed.

If your instructor doesn't make the assignment clear enough, ask him what he wants. Are you being directed to write an analysis, an outline, a definition, a précis, a documented report of research, a personal impression? He will be glad to sharpen the point of the assignment. And if his reply is, "Oh, write anything you want to," then he has nobody but himself to blame for what he receives.

Besides being an assignment, of course, every examination and every book report is a piece of written communication. Therefore, try to interest your reader in what you write, or at least try to avoid making him suffer. He will probably be reading twenty or thirty papers on the same assignment, and will greet with expressions of gratitude a well-executed assignment. In his joy, he may even give your work a grade of "A."

THE EXAMINATION

Although the machine-scored examination is widely used today, we will discuss here only the essay examination, in which you may write anything from one sentence to an essay of several hundred words in response to a single question. Needless to say, the preparation for either type of examination is the same: review, recollection, and rereading. Sometimes students find it helpful to put themselves in the position of the instructor: "If I wanted to cover this material in three or four questions, what would I ask my class?" This is not the same as the popular but generally futile game known as "outguessing the instructor." It is, instead, a useful study aid, particularly if you take the time to construct some thoughtful questions and then attempt to answer them. Thorough preparation should enable you to handle any examination confidently and competently.

One variety of examination, designed to measure the ability to use knowledge relevantly and with originality, rather than the ability to supply that knowledge on demand, is the "open-book" examination. Here you are allowed to bring to class your notes, textbooks, and whatever else you need to answer the questions. Don't be deceived into thinking that the open-book examination is easier than the "closed-book" kind. In many ways, it is more difficult. It assumes that you are already thoroughly familiar with the material, and that you will refer to your books and notes only to confirm a particular fact, to cite a passage, or to quote the exact phraseology. Your books should be used to provide documentation for the answers, rather than the answers themselves. Some instructors, who dislike the inevitable pressures that build up during any examination period, carry the open-book principle even further and permit students to take the examination questions home. Needless to say, fuller and better written essays are expected under these circumstances. An instructor may be satisfied with a general summary answer on a closed-book examination; but he will certainly expect documentation and quotation on the open-book, take-home essays.

Except in the take-home essay examination, time is the enemy. It is therefore best to organize and use wisely the time at your disposal. First read the entire examination through quickly to discover its organization.

1. Are the questions weighted? An instructor may indicate his emphasis by weighting question 1 as 40 per cent, questions 2 and 3 as 20 per cent each, and questions 4 through 7 as 5 per cent each. In such a case, it is suicidal to slight the first question and concentrate on the last four.

2. Are the questions timed? Instead of giving weights to each question, the instructor may indicate the relative importance of the questions by suggesting a certain amount of time to be spent on each question.

3. Is length indicated? If the directions read, "Write an essay of about 500–600 words," the instructor has helped you by indicating the scope of your discussion. Likewise, if the directions read, "Explain the significance of the following topics in a single sentence for each," don't write an essay on each topic (and don't write fragments, either)—write sentences.

4. Are alternative questions indicated? If the directions read, "Answer question 1 and either 2 or 3," don't ignore the option— and don't forget to answer question 1.

The preceding suggestions may be summed up in a single rule: *follow the directions carefully.* Not only will you save time, but you will have a better organized examination as a result.

A very effective way of organizing your discussions is to draw up a rough outline before starting to write. Instead of pouring out what you know about a given topic in any order in which the facts and ideas come to mind, regardless of order or emphasis, first decide what your main topics are and the order in which they should be discussed. This procedure will give you a framework for your answer, and it will also keep you from including irrelevant information. Grouping related ideas under topics and subtopics will organize your essay for you. Even if you know your material, a random outpouring may suggest otherwise to your reader.

Avoid "buckshot" answers. Save time and effort by focusing

on the specific question; don't try to impress your instructor by telling him a lot of things he hasn't asked you about. He may suspect either that you haven't understood the question or that, having understood it, you can't answer it and are evading the issue by discussing irrelevant matters. Following an outline will keep you from committing this error.

Even if your answer is organized, however, remember that it should also have substance. Support every generalization with instances and examples. Specific details are not padding but the fleshing-out of the bare bones of your outline. Get into the habit of using those important transitional words "for example." The student who finds that his answers are too short may have dealt only in large, sweeping assertions. Developing general statements by means of specific details will not only give you more substantial essays, but will also keep you from falling into another grievous error—that of desperately trying to pad a short answer by tacking on more and more generalizations. An instructor looks with less favor on a statement like "American fiction is full of heroes who reject the values of civilized society" than on one which goes: "American fiction is full of heroes like Natty Bumppo, Huck Finn, Ike McCaslin, and Holden Caulfield, who reject the values of civilized society."

It goes without saying that an examination paper should be well written. Like every other piece of writing you do, it should have sentences, not fragments; the sentences should hang together to form a coherent paragraph; the relationships between the sentences should be marked by logical transitions to reveal the thrust of the entire paragraph; and the relationships between the paragraphs should reveal the shape and trend of your ideas.

If you use your time wisely—that is, if you first read the directions with understanding, if you organize your answers by outlining your material, and if you develop your topic ideas with relevant supporting illustrations—you will probably also have time to do what many students forget: namely, to proofread and revise what they have written. It is clearly better to catch your errors yourself than to leave that job to your instructor. You wouldn't think of handing in a first draft of a theme, without going over it to detect accidental errors or to polish the rough spots. Yet this crucial phase in the writing process is often overlooked on examinations. Leaving time during the examination period to reread and revise your composition is as important as any of the other suggestions made in the preceding paragraphs.

The passages below are two answers to the same question, asked in an examination in a course in English history. Whereas the first answer is organized, specific, and factual, the second is rambling, vague, and full of irrelevant and ambiguous statements. The question was: "Discuss the role played by Simon de Montfort in the development of the British constitutional system as we know it today."

I

Simon de Montfort, leader in the baronial revolt of 1263–65, was the first to have the idea of bringing together representatives of the middle class from both the towns and the rural areas at meetings of the king's "great council." Like other barons who objected to the misrule of Henry III, he wanted to eliminate the oppressive practices of the king, but unlike some others, he also wanted an increase in popular liberties. He first protested against the king's rule by signing the Provisions of Oxford, which required all royal officials to be responsible to the great council. After Henry repudiated the Oxford Provisions, by 1263 Simon was the acknowledged leader of the reformers, and during the "Barons' War" he was also their military leader. He captured the king at the Battle of Lewes in 1264, and was able to institute certain reforms. The great council of 1265 for the first time included representatives from every city and borough, who now shared legislative power with the barons. Simon's radicalism was resented by the reactionary barons, who went over to the royal side under the leadership of Prince Edward. In the Battle of Evesham, 1265, Simon was killed, and the parliamentary experiment was over. Although the council was dissolved and Henry III resumed full authority, Simon's long-range influence was important. When Edward I came to the throne, he put into practice Simon's ideas about a representative parliament. During his rule he instituted constitutional changes resulting in more widespread participation in government by members of the middle class.

II

Simon de Montfort played an important role in the development of the British constitutional system as we know it today. He was in power for two years. He was originally a Frenchman who married one of the king's younger sisters. At that time Henry III had many foreigners in his court, which made many people dissatisfied with him. In spite of this, Simon led the barons against the king. He was captured in the Battle of Lewes, and the barons took over the government. They appointed their own officials and made many reforms while they were in power. Some of the barons who disagreed with Simon de Montfort's ideas about reform then organized a revolt under Henry's son, Prince Edward I, and killed Simon at the Battle of Evesham. King Edward later was not as oppressive as King Henry, so you can say that Simon de Montfort's ideas had some result after all. His main idea was that parliament should have some other people in it from the towns and boroughs beside the barons. The parliament at that time was called the great council, and Simon de Montfort wanted to reform it.

The two brief paragraphs below represent examination answers in reply to the question: "Briefly define *simile* and *metaphor* by comparing and contrasting the terms. Give an example of each." The first answer is directly and clearly put; the second is both inaccurate and padded.

I

A simile makes a comparison by describing a word in terms of another and uses the words "as" or "like." "His eyes were as keen as an eagle's" is an example of a simile. A metaphor compares one word to another by actually making the word become the comparison; the descriptive word substitutes for the extended comparison. "He looked at the horizon with eagle eyes" is an example of a metaphor.

II

Similes and metaphors are both very definitely similar to each other. In their context you will find the difference. A simile is a group of words with more or less the same meaning as one word, and a metaphor is a word or words with the same meaning but expressed differently. "As cool as a cucumber" is a simile, but "the cool cucumber" is a metaphor.

BOOK REPORTS

One of the most common writing assignments is the report on a book, either fiction or nonfiction. Differences in goal, however, will determine what kind of book report you should write. Alan Paton's novel, *Cry, the Beloved Country,* may be read in a sociology course for its dramatic insights into South African racial problems and in a literature course for its artistic values. J. D. Salinger's *Catcher in the Rye* may be read in a course in the American novel, and it may be read in a course in adolescent psychology. A work of art has many facets, and instructors in various courses may use the same work to illuminate aspects of their own disciplines. The experience of one student may be cited here. While taking concurrent courses in fiction, American colonial history, and abnormal psychology, he remarked: "This semester I'm reading *The Scarlet Letter* three different ways!"

Sometimes the purpose of the more general book report is merely that of providing information: it is designed to give the reader an idea of the scope and style of the work. Although expository, it is also argumentative in the sense that the reviewer may want his audience to read the work under discussion.

There is no set formula or pattern for the book report. As in other kinds of writing, a clear and coherent expression of facts and ideas will serve better than rigid adherence to a mechanical outline. Depending on the book in question, you might choose to emphasize in your discussion the plot, the dialogue, the characterizations, the ideas, the author himself, the relationship between this book and others by the same writer, the importance of the book, and so forth, or any combination of these in any combination. The range and variety of the book review may be seen by examining, for example, the articles in the weekly book sections of *The New York Times,* the New York *Herald-Tribune,* and the Chicago *Tribune,* as well as those appearing in general magazines like the *Saturday Review, Harper's, The Atlantic Monthly,* and in scholarly quarterlies like *American Literature, The Kenyon Review, The Virginia Quarterly Review,* and *The Yale Review.*

We reprint below two kinds of book reviews. The first pair consists of two student reports on Voltaire's tale, *Candide* (1759); the second pair, of a student report and a professional review of a recent nonfiction work, *Dreamers of the American Dream,* by Stewart H. Holbrook (1957). The particular assignment in the reports on *Candide* was to treat the ideas of optimism and pessimism as found in the book. In the second pair of reports, no such restriction limits the focus of the discussion.

The first paper below received an "A" grade; the second was failed. As you read these two reports, try to determine the basis for these judgments.

I

OPTIMISM AND PESSIMISM IN CANDIDE

"This is the best of all possible worlds," says Pangloss, the philosopher, throughout Voltaire's *Candide.* And the more he keeps saying it, the more we know he is an utter fool. This is the essence of the satiric method through which Voltaire gets across to his readers his belief that unthinking optimism concerning human affairs is the height of stupidity.

Voltaire was disgusted with the eighteenth-century philosophers who tried to explain away evil as being part of some mysterious divine plan, and that all was truly for the best. In his mind, evil is a real fact of life that cannot be rationalized away. He shows us, in one episode after another, the cruelty and selfishness of human beings, and the lunacy in believing that mankind is necessarily safe and happy in this world.

On the surface, *Candide* is a novel of rapid adventure. It has three major figures—the hero, Candide; the girl, Cunegonde; and the philosopher, Pangloss. It moves violently from one episode to another, sustaining interest on the level of narrative alone. The characters go from one horrifying and shocking event to another. Candide is beaten and enslaved, and has many narrow escapes from death. Cunegonde sees her parents killed, is raped, and suffers every kind of physical torture. In piling up these actual physical horrors, Voltaire is emphasizing the dangers of human existence. But his real point is made when Pangloss keeps announcing, after each event, that in his opinion this is the best of all possible worlds, and proves it by some far-fetched philosophical reasoning. Voltaire achieves his effects by mixing shock and irony with devastating effect.

Is Voltaire a pessimist? I don't think so. As I have said, he is attacking *unthinking* optimism. This is the kind of optimism that still exists today among people who believe that because we have more automobiles and refrigerators than Russia we are therefore a stronger country and are sure to win in any possible conflict. It is also the kind of optimism that believes that because Russia is a "materialistic" country, it is inferior to America. (I wonder what Voltaire would do with the logic of people who pride themselves on having bigger, better, and more material possessions and then denounce somebody else for being materialistic?)

Voltaire, I think, is a satirist who does not deny the existence of evil, but who believes that it is possible to alleviate it. It is impossible to alleviate it, however, if you don't believe that it exists in the first place. At the end of the novel, Candide retires "to cultivate his garden." Given the foolishness of the philosophers and the horrors of the world, this is sometimes the best thing to do. But the need for change and humanity's instinct for doing something is well expressed at the end:

"I should like to know which is the worst, to be ravished a hundred times by negro pirates, to have one buttock cut off, to run the gauntlet of a Bulgar regiment, to be whipped and hanged at an auto-da-fé, to be dissected, to row in the galleys—in fact, to experience all the miseries through which we have passed—or just to stay here with nothing to do?"

II

OPTIMISM AND PESSIMISM IN *CANDIDE*

Optimism to the fullest degree is expressed by Voltaire in the opening chapter of *Candide* as illustrated by the following passage:

". . . those who have asserted that all is well talk nonsense; they ought to have said that all is for the best."

As pointed out in the edition we read, Voltaire was satirically using Pope's belief of universal good.

The description of the castle where Candide was brought up is made by using excessive superlatives. For instance on page 3, "noblest and most agreeable of all possible castles."

Also the way the author describes Doctor Pangloss, "the greatest philosher [sic] of the province and therefore of the whole world."

Pessimism enters the story in the second chapter, when Candide is forced into military service. Because he took the liberty of walking where he pleased, he had the free choice of whether he wanted twelve bullets through his head or to be trashed [sic] thirty-six times by the whole regiment. What free will he had, to make such a choice! But lucky enough, he was healed from his ordeal in time to go to war under the King of the Bulgarians.

The brilliant armies were drawn up so smartly. The trumpets and cannons formed such a harmony "as never been heard even in hell," as Voltaire sarcasticly [sic] puts it. The guns were getting rid of a lot of men that just infested the world's surface.

And as some people believed everything is put on the earth for a good purpose, Voltaire suggests the ones who had been raped were put there to satisfy the desires of heroes.

Candide's experience with the man preaching charity did not offer him any aid. It shows the difference between the doing and the preaching about doing good deeds.

Voltaire expressed optimism through Doctor Pangloss who always looked on everything in a good light. Even when he was diseased with pox, he said about it, "It has something indispensable in this best of worlds, a necessary ingredient."

Also, he answered Candide by saying, "A private misfortune makes public good, so that the more private misfortunes there are, the more everything is well."

Voltaire, incidentally, is not supporting the philosophy of optimism but rather making fun of it.

Throughout the book Voltaire writes about sufficient reason for any happening or event. For instance, the earthquake at Lisbon took place because the volcano was there and no where else. As simple as that, to quote his way of putting it, "for it is impossible that things should be where they are; for all is well."

So to end on a note of optimism!

The first of the following two book reports is a student paper, written in an American literature course. Holbrook's book was one in a list of suggested supplementary readings.

THE AMERICAN DREAMERS

What is the difference between an idealist and a crackpot? This question came to mind after I had finished Stewart H. Holbrook's fascinating account of some native American visionaries, *Dreamers of the American Dream*. Is an idealist a visionary whose ideas you agree with, and a crackpot one you disagree with? Or is an idealist a crackpot who succeeds? Regardless of definition, however, the story of the various reformers who have passed through American history is both amusing and instructive. The story is amusing because some of the more extreme reformers, together with some of their reforms, strike us as being quaint or ridiculous. It is instructive because, as Mr. Holbrook says in the book's concluding words, they were "a sort of national conscience."

Most of the book is devoted to treating the various reform movements which sprang up during the nineteenth century—from the Oneida Community "Perfectionists" who planned a death-defying Utopia here on earth through communal marriages, to the rise of organized labor. Also included in the survey are the temperance workers, the agrarian reformers, the feminists, and the prison and hospital (social welfare) reformers. Minor reference is made to the minor groups, such as the outfit that believed that eating Graham bread was the answer to all of mankind's ills. There seems to have been no shortage of faddists and reformers. As Mr. Holbrook writes: "The competition was savage. These were stalwart fellows. The moment a man revealed a vision, he was set upon by a dozen other seers, to beat him down as a false prophet. The survivors were certain to know they had been in a fight, and often bore the scars of sore battle." Mr. Holbrook quotes from Ralph Waldo Emerson's report of a meeting of various reformers held in Boston in 1840, sponsored by the Friends of Universal Reform: "Madman, madwomen, men with beards, Dunkers, Muggletonians, Groaners, Agrarians, Seventh-Day Baptists, Quakers, Abolitionists, Calvinists, Unitarians, and Philosophers—all came successively to the top, and seized their moment, if not their hour, wherein to chide, or pray, or protest."

Mr. Holbrook's treatment of the various reform movements is quite objective, I feel, although he cannot help making fun of some of the more "way-out" sects. His deepest sympathies are evident in Chapter 6,

"Thy Brothers' Keepers," which deals with the improvements made in the handling of lunatics, prisoners, and the deaf and dumb.

Personally, as a member of the female sex, I found most interesting the chapter called "The Rights of Woman" which describes the activities of such women (some of whom I had never heard of before) as Lucy Stone, Fanny Wright, Julia Ward Howe, Susan B. Anthony, Mrs. Frank Leslie, and Mrs. Amelia Bloomer. These women, who braved public scorn in order to secure equal rights for women, must have been super-women! They must also have been hard to live with. Like the other reformers described in the book, they had the "mad, earnest, humorless idealism of the period." But they knew what they wanted, which was more than just the right to vote. It was the recognition that women were not inferior creatures. Of course, the first thing they did with their vote, as Mr. Holbrook gleefully points out, was to elect Harding, which shows that they weren't any smarter, either. I recently heard Mort Sahl, the comedian, say: "Women claim that they can do any job as well as a man. What kind of criterion is that?"

I would agree with Mr. Holbrook when he says that, in spite of the eccentricities of some reformers, their final effect was to make our present society a "more perfect union" than it was when originally conceived, and that much of this improvement was brought about by the constant striving of the "assorted dreamers and visionaries who were basically seeking perfection." The point seems to be that we should never laugh away or stifle attempts at reform, as crazy as they may seem. Nonconformists are good for the health of the country.

Another question that occurred to me during the reading of this book is in connection with our class discussion of Emerson's essay on "Self-Reliance," in which Emerson says that there is too much conformity in American life. If Mr. Holbrook's picture of the nineteenth century is accurate, then Emerson must have had a pretty high standard for non-conformity! The people described in *Dreamers of the American Dream* hardly seem like conformists to me. Mr. Holbrook's work is a valuable source of information and insight for students of American literature and history.—STUDENT THEME

The review reprinted below, written by a history professor, appeared in *The Saturday Review,* a magazine aimed at the average literate American. Note that although the article deals with some of the same aspects of Holbrook's book referred to in the student theme, the work itself is placed in the larger context of the author's literary career and is assessed in terms of both its scholarly and popular merits.

CREATORS AND CRANKS

Over the past twenty years, Stewart H. Holbrook has made a considerable reputation as a popularizer of American social and economic history. He has chronicled the lumbering, the railroad, and the iron and steel industries; he has traced the westward migration of New England culture and written biographies of Ethan Allen and James J. Hill. Most recently, in "The Age of the Moguls," he has told the story of the "robber barons." Now, in "Dreamers of the American Dream," he deals with a galaxy of American reform movements and with the cranks, crackpots, geniuses, saints, and fools of both sexes who took part in them.

In his many books, Mr. Holbrook does not pretend to make what scholars call "a contribution." Indeed, his very unpretentiousness is his greatest asset. This new book is typical in that it is written in deceptively simple prose and liberally (but not excessively) interlarded with jaunty colloquial expressions. A group of reformed drunkards are referred to as "six admitted old soaks," an orator becomes "a speaker of tremendous horsepower," a Wichita bartender is said to have "lammed through the rear doorway" at the approach of the formidable Carry Nation, an agrarian radical is reported as having "scared all hell" out of conventional conservatives. Such phrases are obviously intended to make the material more palatable to the reader. If they do so, they are to be commended; in any case they do no serious harm. In the same way, Mr. Holbrook does not try to overpower either himself or his readers with deep investigations of every aspect of his subjects. In this book he deals principally with various utopian movements, with land reformers, Prohibitionists, crusaders for the rights of women, prison reformers, educators of the deaf and the blind, and with radical labor movements. He tells a lively story and avoids detailed analyses of cause and effect. When he offers interpretations they are usually the interpretations of others (and admittedly so, for Mr. Holbrook is scrupulous in giving credit wherever it is due). His account is unfailingly interesting, partly because of his gift for narration, partly because he emphasizes the unusual, the exotic, and the ridiculous aspects of the reform movements wherever possible.

The reader is sure to find something to make him chuckle in Mr. Holbrook's pages. Perhaps it will be Samuel Thomson, the "Botanic Man," who will catch the eye, or Orson Fowler, inventor of the octagonal house, or perhaps Dr. Dioclesian Lewis, author of "New Gymnastics," "Chastity," and "Our Digestion," or Dr. Mary Walker, who wore men's clothes and won a medal for her brave work during the Civil War, or Abigail Scott Duniway, who said: "One half of American women are dolls, the rest are drudges, and we are all fools." Indeed, sometimes the author seems more interested in poking fun than in writing a well-balanced history.

But Mr. Holbrook does not ignore the serious and commendable aspects of the reforms he discusses. He loves to expose frauds and to deflate narrow-minded, intolerant reformers. He is unsparing of most of the Prohibitionists, for example, and almost unfair in his ridicule of some of the utopians. But for reasonable and honest reformers, however zealous, he has ample praise. He is kind to Dorothea Dix, to Margaret Sanger, to Eugene V. Debs, and even to the often-absurd John Humphrey Noyes, founder of the Oneida community and exponent of "Perfectionism," "complex marriage," and "male continence." The men and women who devoted themselves selflessly to aiding the deaf, the dumb, and the blind receive his special praise. Neither glib joviality nor slick "cleverness" can be found in the pages devoted to Thomas Gallaudet, Alexander Graham Bell, Samuel Gridley Howe, Helen Keller, and others prominent in these movements, yet this section is among the most interesting and attractive in the volume.

Mr. Holbrook's methodology and his basic point of view do not make for great history. He is a sort of poor man's Thucydides, a proletarian Gibbon. His works are neither deeply researched nor deeply thought out. But his eminent good sense and honesty, his straightforward prose, and his gift for humor and the pungent phrase make "Dreamers of the American Dream" a good, simple introduction to his subject matter.— JOHN A. GARRATY[1]

----

[1] *The Saturday Review,* October 26, 1957. Reprinted by permission of the author and the publisher.

XIV | Letters

The exchange of correspondence between Thomas Jefferson and John Adams in the eighteenth century and that between Thomas Carlyle and Ralph Waldo Emerson in the nineteenth are landmarks in our literature. Scholars read these letters as important documents in the history of American thought. The letters of Pope, Keats, Thoreau, and Emily Dickinson are likewise preserved and studied as helps toward a fuller understanding of these writers. In the hands of men like Horace Walpole and Lord Chesterfield in the eighteenth century, the letter was a virtual work of art. Today, however, we don't generally regard the letter as a literary form, except, perhaps, those we write for the "Letters to the Editor" column in our newspapers; nor do many of us write letters (as was once the custom) with one eye on posterity. For the most part, our letters are fairly utilitarian.

The letter is certainly the commonest form of written communication, and for some it may well be the most important. The single most important piece of writing you will ever do in your life, for example, may be the letter you write applying for a job after you have graduated from college. For this reason, we will discuss the letter of application in some detail later in this chapter. Because the letter is such an important form of composition, all the principles of good writing dealt with in the earlier portions of this book should be applied to it. A muddled or sloppy business letter may cost your company a contract; a badly written personal letter may convey an idea you didn't mean and may cost you a friend.

In general, letters are classified as belonging to one of the following groups: (1) business letters; (2) friendly or social (or personal) letters; and (3) formal notes and letters. Certain well-established practices used in writing letters of various types have been adopted either for their clarity or for the reason that they have been sanctioned by custom. In the sections that follow will be found examples of correct modern usage.

GENERAL DIRECTIONS

Business letters are ordinarily written on paper of good quality and standard size, 8½ by 11 inches. White paper is preferable, and only one side of the sheet should be written on. If a second sheet is required, blank paper, that is, without a printed or engraved letterhead, should be used. It is desirable to number the second (or later) sheet, and to identify it in some way—usually by a repetition of the recipient's name—at the top of the page.

Personal letters are sometimes written on white paper folded to form a book of four pages. If the letter is no more than two pages in length, pages 1 and 3 should be used. If the letter is more than two pages in length, book order (1, 2, 3, 4) should be followed. The envelope should match the letter paper. The letter should be so folded and placed in the envelope that the recipient will remove it and unfold it in a position convenient for reading. Book-style paper should be folded once horizontally. Commercial stationery (8½ by 11 inches) should be folded once horizontally, and twice vertically, if it is to be placed in a small envelope (3½ by 6½ inches). If it is to be placed in a large envelope (about 4 by 9½ inches), it should be folded horizontally into three equal sections so that the top section is folded down over the bottom section.

Letters should always be written neatly and legibly. Business correspondence should always be typed, in either blue or black ink.

THE FORM OF THE LETTER

The business letter. There are many specific types of business letters, each having its own purpose: inquiry, order, acknowledgment, claim, adjustment, credit, collection, sales, trans-mittal, reference, and application. (For a fuller discussion of these various forms, consult a manual of Business English.) All letters, whatever their purpose, should be clear, to the point, and as con-cise as possible.

The routine nature of most business correspondence dictates the conventional requirements of form. The business letter has the following parts: the heading, the inside address, the greet-ing, the body, the close, and the signature. The heading includes the sender's address and the date; the inside address includes the name and address of the person or company one is writing to; the greeting is the complimentary opening of the letter; the body of the letter reveals the purpose and sets forth the subject of cor-respondence; the close is the complimentary ending of the letter; and the signature is the full name of the sender (often followed by the sender's name typed). These essential parts are illustrated in the model reproduced below.

Heading

```
                    946 Center Street
                    Lincoln, Indiana
                    December 12, 1960
```

Inside
address

```
Republic Life Insurance Company
220 South Michigan Avenue
Chicago 3, Illinois
```

Greeting

```
Gentlemen:
```

Body
of
letter

```
        Please send me details of your In-
come Assurance Plan, advertised recently
in the Chicago Daily News.  It is under-
stood that I incur no obligation by
making this request.
```

Close

```
                    Yours very truly,
```

Signature

George L. Patton

```
                    George L. Patton
```

The social letter. The personal letter has substantially the same form as the business letter with the permissible exception of the omission of the inside address.

Heading

946 Center Street
Lincoln, Indiana
December 15, 1959

Greeting

Dear Carl,

I am glad to hear that you have been promoted, and that your work will bring you to our part of the state. We used to see each other often in "the good old days." But do you realize that it has been nearly two years now since we've been together?

Body
of
letter

You say that you will be coming this way in a few days. Why don't you bring Jeanne and spend Christmas with Alice and me? If you can stay longer than one day, so much the better. It would be like old times for the four of us to be together again.

Alice joins me in best wishes to both of you. So try to come.

Close

Cordially yours,

Signature

Bill

THE PARTS OF THE LETTER

THE HEADING

The heading, placed in the upper right-hand corner of the first page, always gives the address of the sender and the date of the letter. If a business letterhead is used, it is necessary for the writer to supply only the date. Also, if the address is self evident or superfluous (as in intraorganization correspondence), it should naturally be omitted. Two styles of heading are widely used: indented and block. Both are correct, although modern usage gives preference to block style.

Indented heading with end punctuation	1136 East 57th Street, Chicago 37, Illinois, January 7, 1961
Block heading without end punctuation	1136 East 57th Street Chicago 37, Illinois January 7, 1961

Either type of punctuation is correct, although, again, modern usage tends toward the omission of end punctuation. The important principle to be observed is that of consistency; if end punctuation is used for the first line of the heading, it should also be used for the others, and, if it is used in the heading, it should also be used in the inside and outside addresses.

Attention is called to the fact that no abbreviations are used in either heading. For the most part, the use of abbreviations should be avoided, since their use, in a sense, is discourteous, and may lead to confusion. (Certain well-known abbreviations are, of course, used almost universally in commercial correspondence.) Should the writer feel that his use of abbreviations will not be misunderstood, he should see to it that each abbreviated form is followed by a period, and by any additional punctuation that the position of the word requires. The use of such blanket abbreviations as 1/7/61 for January 7, 1961, is highly objectionable because it may lead to confusion.

THE INSIDE ADDRESS

The inside address, which establishes the left-hand margin of the business letter, is begun on a line a space or more below the last line of the heading. In formal personal letters, and in business letters of a professional nature, the inside address is usually placed at the end of the letter at the left-hand side of the page. In friendly letters, the inside address is ordinarily omitted. The style of the inside address, which may be either indented or block, should be the same as that used in the heading.

Indented inside address with end punctuation	Munson Steamship Lines, 67 Wall Street, New York 4, N. Y.
Block inside address without end punctuation	Munson Steamship Lines 67 Wall Street New York 4, N. Y.

THE GREETING

The greeting, or salutation, is placed below the inside address and flush with the left-hand margin of the letter. For most friendly letters, the greeting establishes the left-hand margin. The first word of the greeting and all nouns are capitalized.

Correct greetings for business letters

Gentlemen:	Ladies:
Dear Sir:	Dear Madam:
My dear Mr. Brown:	My dear Madam:
Dear Mr. Brown:	My dear Mrs. Trent:
	Dear Mrs. Trent:

Correct greetings for friendly letters

Dear John,	Dear Father,
Dear Alice,	Dear Uncle David,
Dear Mr. Holman,	Dearest Mother,
My dear Miss Cannon,	

It should be noted that (1) the friendly greeting is followed by a comma, rather than by a colon; (2) "Dear Miss Cannon" is usually thought to be a more intimate greeting than "My dear Miss Cannon"; (3) the same greeting may be equally correct for a business letter and for a friendly letter—correctness is determined by the degree of intimacy that exists between correspondents; (4) such greetings as "Friend John" and "Dear Friend" are not in reputable use; (5) the only abbreviations permitted in greetings are *Mr., Mrs.,* and *Dr.*

My dear Professor Lowry: (NOT: My dear Prof. Lowry:)
Dear Colonel Rogers, (NOT: Dear Col. Rogers,)

THE BODY OF THE LETTER

The body of the letter begins on the line below the greeting, and should be indented about one inch. The first line of each paragraph should be indented the same distance. The body of a typewritten letter begins two spaces below the greeting; its indention is approximately the same as that of a pen-written letter. If the body of a typewritten letter is single-spaced, with double spacing between paragraphs, it is permissible to use block style, without indention. When block style is used in the body of the letter, it should also be used in the heading and in the inside address. Many business organizations, of course, have "house rules" or style sheets that govern all specific matters of form in correspondence.

In general, the same standards of correctness and literary style that apply to other forms of composition apply to the writing of letters. The following paragraphs summarize a few of the common errors made in letter writing.

Faulty paragraphing. A friendly letter should be paragraphed logically rather than in a hit-or-miss fashion. If the content of the letter calls for only one paragraph, write no more. On the other hand, if the subject matter is varied, treat each topic in a separate paragraph. The paragraphing in business letters written for a firm should follow the "house rules" mentioned above.

Telegraphic style. The sentences in a letter should be grammatically and logically complete. Do not omit function group words and pronouns. Avoid "telegraphic style" in all its forms. Do not hesitate to use the pronoun "I" if it is the word demanded by the sentence structure.

We have received your letter of October 8. Your order will be filled as promptly as possible. (NOT: Received yours of the 8th inst., and beg to advise will handle matter quickly as possible.)

Hackneyed formulas. Use simple, straightforward language. Avoid the time-worn formulas that were the chief stock in trade of an earlier generation of letter writers. Some of the formulas are roundabout ways of expressing simple ideas; others are ambiguous short cuts.

Avoid:	*Write:*
your kind favor	your letter
yours of the 2nd	your letter of June 2
yours of the 3rd inst.	your letter of July 3
your letter of 2/4/60	your letter of February 4, 1960
beg to advise	(avoid this phrase)
I beg to enclose	I enclose
please find enclosed	I enclose . . . for which please send me . . . .
in reply would say	(avoid this phrase)
will send same	we will send it (*or* them)
Hoping to hear from you	We (*or* I) hope to hear from you
Thanking you again	I wish to thank you again (*or* Thank you again)

and oblige

I enclose ($5) dollars

I enclose five ($5) dollars

(avoid this phrase)

I enclose five (5) dollars

I enclose five (5) dollars

or

I enclose five dollars ($5)

THE CLOSE

The close is placed near the middle of a separate line below the body of the letter. In typewritten letters a double space should be left between the last line of the body of the letter and the close.

The following are correct closes for business letters:

Yours very truly,   Respectfully yours,

Yours truly,   Yours respectfully,

Very truly yours,

and for friendly letters:

Yours very truly,   Cordially yours,

Yours sincerely,   Faithfully yours,

Very sincerely yours,

Note that (1) the close is always followed by a comma, and only the first word is capitalized; (2) the use of "Respectfully yours" and "Yours respectfully" is confined almost exclusively to official letters—such as those to officers of a government, of a school, or of a church; (3) the same close may be equally correct for a business letter and for a friendly letter. As in the greeting, correctness is determined by the degree of intimacy that exists between correspondents.

THE SIGNATURE

The signature, which should always be handwritten, is placed below the close, and is aligned with the beginning of the close, or slightly to its right. With the exception of personal letters, unless the name of the sender appears on the letterhead, it should also be typed. In business letters, the full name of the writer should be given; it should ordinarily be followed by the typed name, and, when necessary, by a title or by some other indication of authority.

Correct signatures

Yours very truly,

For an individual writing to a firm

George L. Patton

George L. Patton

Yours very truly,
RINEHART & COMPANY, INC.
By

For a firm writing to an individual or to another firm

Frederick R. Rinehart

Frederick R. Rinehart

Yours very truly,

For a company official

Horace Cantwell

Horace Cantwell
President

Yours very truly,

For a married woman writing to a firm

Grace Harper Jones

(Mrs. Harry T. Jones)

A married woman's business signature is composed of (1) her full name, which includes her maiden name; (2) her husband's name, preceded by *Mrs.* She should be addressed by her husband's name; in this case, as *Mrs. Harry T. Jones.*

For an unmarried woman writing to a firm

Yours very truly,

(Miss) Dorothy Brant

Dorothy Brant

For a woman writing an informal social letter (the titles "Mrs." and "Miss" are not used)

Sincerely yours,

Horace Harper Jones

In business correspondence, the stenographer's inscription and notations of enclosures or copies are often added below the signature, at the left-hand margin of the letter. The exact form for such notations varies (depending upon the practice of the individual firm); the general form given below is in fairly wide use.

Signature, with stenographer's inscription and notation of copy to be sent:

Yours very truly,

Horace Cantwell

Horace Cantwell
President

HC:MTS
Copy to Mr. Logan

THE ENVELOPE

Either of the following forms, consistent in style with that of the letter, is correct for the outside address, or superscription. End punctuation may be used, if it has been used in the letter. Notice that a return address is given in the upper left-hand corner.

Block outside address, without end punctuation

```
George L. Patton
946 Center Street
Lincoln, Indiana




          Republic Life Insurance Company
          220 South Michigan Avenue
          Chicago 3
          Illinois
```

Indented outside address, with end punctuation

```
REPUBLIC LIFE INSURANCE COMPANY,
   220 SOUTH MICHIGAN AVENUE,
      CHICAGO 3, ILLINOIS.




     Mr. George L. Patton,
         946 Center Street,
             Lincoln, Indiana.
```

LETTERS OF APPLICATION

The *New Yorker* occasionally runs a feature called "Letters We Never Finished Reading." An employment manager might also make a collection of letters of application falling into this category: illegible letters, ungrammatical letters, long-winded and wordy letters, vague and aimless letters, stiff and pompous letters, and boastful letters ("I'm just the man you're looking for!").

The successful letter of application is neat, clear, and to the point. It is factual, but its intention is persuasive, aiming to bring about a specific response on the part of the reader. The purpose of the letter is not to get a job but to get an interview. It suggests, therefore, that the writer, both by experience and character, is the kind of person the employment manager would want to consider for the job. The model below represents a letter that would probably be successful in achieving its end.

46 East 65th Street
New York 19, N. Y.
September 16, 1959

Telephone: RH4-1366

Mr. Joel E. Harrison
Personnel Manager
Vacuum Products Corporation
138 Madison Avenue
New York 16, N. Y.

Dear Mr. Harrison:

   Through the courtesy of Mr. Leonard Steele of your auditing department I have learned of a vacancy in your secretarial staff. Please consider me an applicant for this position.

   After graduating from Eastview High School (1950) and the Holton-Grey Secretarial School (1952), I was employed as a secretary for two years by the Lockwell Building Corporation.

Since the fall of 1954 I have been private secretary to Mr. Lance Howell, general manager of
the Croton Packing Company, 411 Fifth Avenue,
New York City.

I feel that my work with the Croton Packing Company as Mr. Howell's secretary has given
me a broad knowledge of the canning industry, in
which the Vacuum Products Corporation plays
such a large part. I consider my familiarity
with this field a qualification that might
interest your company.

A personal data sheet, outlining my training and experience in greater detail, together
with a list of references to whom you may write
for statements about my personal and professional qualifications, is enclosed.

I shall be pleased to call for an interview with you at a time that suits your convenience.

Very truly yours,

(Miss) Margaret L. Ryan

Margaret L. Ryan

FORMAL INVITATIONS AND REPLIES

Formal invitations and replies should be written in the third
person, and should follow the general form suggested in the
models given below:

Mr. and Mrs. Harry Anderson request the pleasure of Mr. John
Randall's company at dinner on Thursday, May the eighteenth, at
seven o'clock.

452 Compton Avenue,
    May the ninth.

Mr. John Randall accepts with pleasure Mr. and Mrs. Harry Anderson's invitation to dinner on Thursday, May the eighteenth, at seven o'clock.

2938 Devon Road,
   May the tenth.

Mr. John Randall regrets that he is unable to accept Mr. and Mrs. Harry Anderson's invitation to dinner on Thursday, May the eighteenth, at seven o'clock.

2938 Devon Road,
   May the tenth.

It should be noted that (1) formal invitations and replies omit heading, inside address, greeting, and signature, but the writer gives his street address and the date in the lower left-hand corner; (2) the pronouns *I, me, my, you,* and *your* are not used; (3) formal notes are written in the present tense; (4) the date of the month and the hour of the day are spelled out; (5) if a reason is to be given for declining an invitation, a note should be sent, rather than a formal reply; (6) answers to formal invitations should be written in longhand.

EXERCISES

A.

Assume that an organization you belong to has just elected you to be its representative, with all expenses paid, at a forthcoming state convention. Supplying appropriate details and using the appropriate tone (diction, level of usage, form, and so on) in each letter, write the following:

1. A letter of thanks to be sent to the local secretary and to be read by him at the next meeting.
2. A letter to the state chairman inquiring about accommodations in the convention city.

3. A letter to a good friend telling him the news and your plans for the trip.

4. A letter to Professor Smathers, whose class you will be forced to miss because of your trip.

5. A letter to the local secretary explaining why you cannot accept the appointment.

B.

1. Assuming that he has asked you to do so, write your high school principal or adviser an informative letter evaluating your preparation for college. Be objective and factual.

2. Write a letter to your younger brother or sister, who is still in high school and who is planning to attend your college, advising him (or her) how to prepare for college work.

C.

Write a letter applying for a summer job.

D.

Write a letter applying for the kind of job you would like to have upon graduation.

Index

A

A, an, 246

Abbreviations
  correct use of, 188–189
  exercises, 194
  in letters, 609–610
  punctuation of, 126–127

Accept, except, 246

Acknowledgment, of borrowed material, 166–169

Active voice, 64

Adjective(s), 21, 68–73
  absolute, 70–71
  degrees of, 69–71, 243–244
    comparative, 69–71, 243
    normal, 69
    superlative, 69–71, 243
  endings of comparison, 69–71
  exercises, 114
  formal features of, 69–72
  nouns as (*see* Noun adjuncts)
  as objective complement, 18
  predicate, 18, 76
  prepositional phrase as, 21
  as subject of sentence, 14
  suffixes of, 71–72
    exercises, 112
  word order of, 21–22, 69

Adjective clause (*see* Clause)

Adjective phrase (*see* Phrases)

Adverb(s), 21, 73–77
  comparison of, 74
  degrees of, 74
    comparative, 74
    normal, 74
    superlative, 74
  exercises, 114
  as predicate complement, 18
  as subject of sentence, 14
  with two forms, 76
  word order of, 22–23, 74, 76

Adverbial clause (*see* Clauses)

Adverbial clause-markers, 81, 87, 88

Adverbial phrase (*see* Phrases)

Affect, effect, 246

Agreement
  of pronouns and antecedents, 101–103
    exercises, 120–121
  of subjects and verbs, 104–107
    exercises, 121–122

Agriculture, reference works in field of, 530

Ain't, 247

Alliteration, 293

Allusions, literary, avoidance of, 225

Ambiguous constructions, 98–100

An, a, 246

Analogy
  figurative, 486–487
  literal, 486–487
  reasoning from, 486–488

Analysis
  of concept, 431
  exercises, 462–463
  exposition by, 428–440
  of method, 430–431
  of qualities, 431

Analyzing, 19

Antecedents
  agreement of pronouns with, 101–103
    exercises, 121–122
  collective nouns, 103
  which are both masculine and feminine, 102–103

Anthropology, reference works in field of, 530

Anticlimax, 294

Antithesis, 294

Antonyms, dictionary as source of, 204

Any, as an antecedent, 102

Apostrophe, conventional uses, 151–153

Appeals
  bandwagon, 212